France

Vintage	Red Bordeaux				
	Médoc/Graves	Pom/St-...			
2013	4–7	4–7			
2012	6–8	6–8			
2011	7–9	6–9			
2010	7–10	6–10			
2009	7–10	7–10			
2008	6–9	6–9			7–8
2007	5–7	6–7		8–9	6–8
2006	7–8	7–9	8–9	8–9	6–8
2005	9–10	8–9	8–10	8–10	8–9
2004	7–8	7–9	5–7	6–7	6–8
2003	5–9	5–8	7–8	6–7	6–7
2002	6–8	5–8	7–8	7–8	7–8
2001	6–8	7–8	8–10	7–9	6–8
2000	8–10	7–9	6–8	6–8	8–10
1999	5–7	5–8	6–9	7–10	6–8
1998	5–8	6–9	5–8	5–9	7–9
1997	5–7	4–7	7–9	4–7	7–9
1996	6–8	5–7	7–9	7–10	8–10
1995	7–9	6–9	6–8	5–9	6–9

France continued

Vintage	Burgundy			Rhône	
	Côte d'Or red	Côte d'Or white	Chablis	Rhône (N)	Rhône (S)
2013	5–7	7–8	6–8	7–9	7–8
2012	8–9	7–8	7–8	7–9	7–9
2011	7–8	7–8	7–8	7–8	6–8
2010	8–10	8–10	8–10	8–10	8–9
2009	7–10	7–8	7–8	7–9	7–8
2008	7–9	7–9	7–9	6–7	5–7
2007	7–8	8–9	8–9	6–8	7–8
2006	7–8	8–10	8–9	7–8	7–9
2005	7–9	7–9	7–9	7–8	6–8
2004	6–7	7–8	7–8	6–7	6–7
2003	6–7	6–7	6–7	5–7	6–8
2002	7–8	7–8	7–8	4–6	5–5
2001	6–8	7–9	6–8	7–8	7–9
2000	7–8	6–9	7–9	6–8	7–9

Beaujolais 2011, 10, 09. Crus will keep. **Mâcon-Villages** (white). Drink 12, 10.
Loire (Sweet Anjou and Touraine) best recent vintages: 10, 09, 07, 05, 02, 97, 96, 93, 90, 89; Bourgueil, Chinon, Saumur–Champigny: 10, 09, 06, 05, 04, 02, 00. **Upper Loire** (Sancerre, Pouilly–Fumé): 12, 10. **Muscadet**: DYA.

Hugh Johnson's Pocket Wine Book 2015

Edited and designed by Mitchell Beazley,
an imprint of Octopus Publishing Group Limited,
Endeavour House, 189 Shaftesbury Avenue,
London WC2H 8JY

An Hachette UK Company
www.hachette.co.uk

Distributed in the USA and Canada by Octopus Books USA:
c/o Hachette Book Group USA,
237 Park Avenue, New York, NY 10017

www.octopusbooksusa.com

General Editor **Margaret Rand**
Editoral Director **Tracey Smith**
Commissioning Editor **Hilary Lumsden**
Project Editor **Pauline Bache**
Proofreader **Jamie Ambrose**
Deputy Art Director **Yasia Williams-Leedham**
Designer **Jeremy Tilston**
Assistant Production Manager **Caroline Alberti**

Printed and bound in China

Mitchell Beazley would like to acknowledge and thank the following
for supplying photographs for use in this book:

Alamy Gianni Dagli Orti/The Art Archive 323; **Cephas** Andy Christodolo
11; courtesy **Champagne Aubry** 327; **Getty Images** AM-C 334; Cesar Manso/
AFP 329; Don Bayley 333; Franek Strzeszewski 7; Hendrik Holler 6;
Mauro Grigollo 328; Milton Wordley 16; **Octopus Publishing Group** Adrian
Pope 8; **Shutterstock** PhotostockAR 336 right; Richard Semik 336 centre;
Thinkstock Aneb 331; Gaz Taechin 324; Giovanni Marino 336 left; rogit 1;
Stockbyte 8, 321; Sydney Mills 14

HUGH JOHNSON'S
POCKET WINE BOOK
POCKET WINE BOOK

GENERAL EDITOR
MARGARET RAND

2015

Acknowledgements

This store of detailed recommendations comes partly from my own notes and mainly from those of a great number of kind friends. Without the generous help and cooperation of innumerable winemakers, merchants and critics, I could not attempt it. I particularly want to thank the following for help with research or in the areas of their special knowledge:

Sarah Ahmed, Helena Baker, Nicolas Belfrage MW, Jim Budd, Michael Cooper, Terry Copeland, Cole Danehower, Michael Edwards, Sarah Jane Evans MW, Rosemary George MW, Caroline Gilby MW, Anthony Gismondi, Annie Kay, James Lawther MW, Konstantinos Lazarakis MW, John Livingstone-Learmonth, Wes Marshall, Campbell Mattinson, Adam Montefiore, Jasper Morris MW, Fabricio Portelli, Margaret Rand, Ulrich Sautter, Eleonora Scholes, Stephen Skelton MW, Paul Strang, Marguerite Thomas, Larry Walker, Philip van Zyl

Contents

How to use this book

The top line of most entries consists of the following information:

1. Aglianico del Vulture Bas

2. r dr (s/sw sp)

3. ★★★

4. 05 06' **07** 08 09' 10 (11)

1. Aglianico del Vulture Bas

Wine name and the region the wine comes from, abbreviations of regions are listed in each section.

2. r dr (s/sw sp)

Whether it is red, rosé or white (or brown/amber), dry, sweet or sparkling, or several of these (and which is most important):

r	red
p	rosé
w	white
br	brown
dr	dry*
sw	sweet
s/sw	semi-sweet
sp	sparkling

( ) brackets here denote a less important wine
* assume wine is dry when dr or sw are not indicated

3. ★★★

Its general standing as to quality: a necessarily rough-and-ready guide based on its current reputation as reflected in its prices:

★	plain, everyday quality
★★	above average
★★★	well known, highly reputed
★★★★	grand, prestigious, expensive

So much is more or less objective. Additionally there is a subjective rating:

★ etc. Stars are coloured for any wine which in my experience is usually especially good within its price range. There are good everyday wines as well as good luxury wines. This system helps you find them.

4. 05 06' **07** 08 09' 10 (11)

Vintage information: those recent vintages that can be recommended, and of these, which are ready to drink this year, and which will probably improve with keeping. Your choice for current drinking should be one of the vintage years printed in **bold** type. Buy light-type years for further maturing.

05 etc.   recommended years that may be currently available
06' etc.   vintage regarded as particularly successful for the property in question
07 etc.   years in bold should be ready for drinking (those not in bold will benefit from keeping)
08 etc.   vintages in colour are those recommended as first choice for drinking in 2013. (*See also* Bordeaux introduction, p.96.)
(11) etc. provisional rating

The German vintages work on a different principle again: *see* p.156.

Other abbreviations & styles

DYA   Drink the youngest available.
NV   Vintage not normally shown on label;
                 in Champagne this means a blend of several
                 vintages for continuity.
CHABLIS   Properties, areas or terms cross-referred within
                 the section; all grapes cross-ref to Grape
                 Varieties chapter on pp.16–26.
Aiguilloux   Entries styled this way indicate wine (mid-2013–
                 2014) especially enjoyed by Hugh Johnson.

There are no accurate figures available to measure the size of the world of wine today. Vineyards are easy: there are eight million hectares, or 20 million acres – so the world's vines would cover the whole of, say, Austria, the Alps included. Production is easy too. In 2010 there were 260 million hectolitres, or 34 billion bottles, made. That's nearly five bottles each for everyone on earth.

Not so easy is the economic impact of an industry this size. Making wine is only the start of it; it reaches into half the world's high streets. Its logistics, from bottling and shipping to stacking the shelves to pulling the corks, involve the livelihoods of an unknown number. What is sure is that the number is growing fast – and every addition increases the physical and mental energy of the whole. In other words more intelligence, taste, opinions and ideas are piling up around wine. What used to be a relatively tidy affair with clear assumptions, conventions and indeed, rules has been hit by a following wind. Where will it take us?

In last year's edition I wrote that we are at a tipping point when the old models are no longer sacrosanct. Price, which for centuries was the accepted measure of quality, now only measures rarity and fame. If pleasure, rather than reputation and price, is the new measure, then the wine world will take on a completely new shape. Pleasure, quality and character are abundant, and wine-drinkers are tired of being told what they should prefer. For investors it may be a different matter. But that market, like the market in "fine" art, is easily led by the nose.

Age of divergence

All the indications are that orthodoxy in wine has had its day. We are in the Age of Divergence – of regions, grape varieties, winemaking methods and philosophies – and of course tastes. The small minority of drinkers who can recognize, let alone judge, the long-established classics is not about to disappear, but it is being swamped. Look at the length of this book. Remember when it would go in your pocket? Most (I can't promise all) of the wines it describes are worth tasting, and may give you an enjoyable meal.

In newfound confidence (or occasionally perhaps despair) wine producers are doing radical things – most obviously those who claim that their wine is "natural". Winemaking depends on the controlling of a natural process. *Naturwein* was the old German word for wine made without added sugar. At least that gave it a definite meaning. More convincing, and more interesting, are the mystics who use biodynamic methods (and uncounted hours of sweat, worry and possibly prayer) to make wines that are often of lovely purity and vitality. And thoroughly intriguing are the champions of fermentation in buried clay jars in the manner of ancient Georgia, or in vats in the form of an egg made of concrete – or even, with some difficulty, made of oak. What all these things prove is that wine drives its devotees to extravagant lengths in pursuit of their ideals. Drinkers won't necessarily share your interest in a strange orange-coloured fluid, but there will always be the curious....

Age of the ampelographer

We are certainly in the Age of the Ampelographer: the grape-botanist who, now aided by DNA, dissects the ancient legacy of the vine. At what other time could you sell many hundred copies of a book describing 1,400 different grape varieties – as my colleague Jancis Robinson and her collaborators have just done? Growers in the past have chosen their vines first out of tradition or precedence, second by their track record for ripening in a given climate and soil, third by their health and resistance to disease and hard weather, fourth by their productivity (taking number three into account) and fifth by their flavour (as discussed in this year's supplement; *see p.321*).

The world's new vineyards are reversing this order. Different tastes come first, then the economic factors of health and yield, third track record (often non-existent) and last (or nowhere) what previous generations have seen as normal. We, the drinkers, gain an infinitely wider choice. We lose, on the other hand, the assurance of habit and familiarity. The familiar and the new are constantly in conflict.

Why is Bordeaux, with all its vicissitudes, still the most successful producer of what the world calls "fine" wine? Can it be the convenience of a system that at least appears to be easy to understand? The word "château" is the key to its fortune; it extends a level playing field over the whole vast *département* of the Gironde. In reality few customers can navigate, or even deeply care about, the championship games of *grands crus* and *premiers crus* and crus bourgeois. Familiar names and high prices take care of one end of the market; the rest picks its way through scores and recommendations, happy that the château is a unit it can grasp.

That is until now. If I am right we are reaching the limit of such reassurance: of relying on conventions. Why a new divergence now? Because the newer regions have got over their first-night nerves. The applause has been long enough and loud enough; with a solid box office they feel free to ad lib. And more important still, we the audience have more experience. We are ready to make up our own minds. And ready to ask whether the wine world needs so much bureaucratic apparatus.

The choice is yours, between California's dense, sweet tastes and New Zealand's (NZ) intense fruit flavours, between the edginess of Italy and the harmonies of France or the savours of Spain. The game used to be to compare New World and Old; then we learned to follow the fortunes of particular grape varieties grown in different hemispheres. We have grown so used to comparison and competition that we forget plain one-on-one appreciation. I sometimes envy the inhabitants of wine regions who deeply appreciate (but know only) their native wines. So chauvinistic are the French that a Burgundian scarcely admits there is such a place as Bordeaux. The British like to boast that all the world's wines meet in London. We are spoilt for choice – but is a wide choice the route to real appreciation? I only ask.

Ask yourself

Ask yourself some fundamental questions. How emphatic do you really like your wine to be? It's easier to attract attention with a loud voice. But strength (of flavour, but especially of alcohol) is on the agenda now as never before. Plenty of traditional drinkers, probably still the majority, are in the "more is more" camp. Why not more flavour, more colour, more alcohol – surely that's the point of wine? And *grands crus* have more taste than little ones, don't they?

The view that's gaining ground, though, is aligned with diet-consciousness and new fads about food. While I am still at the stage where a chicken is a chicken, a glorious gift to be chosen with care, cooked with skill and eaten with joy, I know plenty of people (no, too many) who count its calories, analyse its fat(s), avoid the sumptuous skin and reject the "carbs" (roast potatoes to you and me) that complete the feast.

I am always surprised when the same friends tuck gaily into wines heady with alcohol and thick with flavour. They are not applying the same standards to wine as to food.

Each year as I read and edit the extraordinary compilation of fact and opinion that goes into this book (this the 38th year and I have 29 collaborators), I marvel at what it reveals. If you are looking for trends and fashions they are all here; personalities, technologies, discoveries are all on record in the rather abrupt and jerky style I adopt to get them all in. I can browse for hours. But if you want an idea for what to drink with your dinner, then that's here too.

The story of 2013 in France was hail. It sliced through leaves and developing grapes, reducing growers' livelihoods to pulp in minutes. It's hard to overestimate the damage that can be done by hailstones the size of golf balls. It's local, sudden and destructive, damaging the wood of the vine as well as the grapes and leaves so that the next year's crop is also affected.

It started in June in the **Loire**, with hailstones the size of eggs in Vouvray, and in Germany's Mosel. In July **Burgundy**'s Côte de Beaune was hit, and some estates lost the majority of their crop. It hailed for 17 minutes, and wines from Pommard, Volnay and Beaune will be in short supply. Gevrey-Chambertin was hailed on in August. **Provence** too was hit, especially around Ste Victoire; the south of **Alsace** as well, especially on the plains around Turckheim and Colmar, though *grands crus* were less badly affected; and **Champagne**, where 300 hectares had severe damage, especially on the Côte des Blancs. **Cognac** suffered slight damage, and in **Bordeaux** winds of 102 miles per hour felled trees and damaged roofs in Pauillac, and there was hail the other side of the river, around Libourne and in Fronsac and Lalande-de-Pomerol. Entre-Deux-Mers was worst hit by hail, however, with about 5,000 hectares wiped out. Gavin Quinney of Château Bauduc in Entre-Deux-Mers said that the next day there wasn't "a leaf or a grape in sight".

It's easy for the rest of us to say, "But they should have insurance." Hail insurance, if you want good cover, is hugely expensive, and unaffordable for any region (like much of Entre-Deux-Mers) already living on the edge. Burgundy has said it will look again at measures like seeding clouds with dry ice or silver iodide, which is supposed to weaken storms and make them fall as rain rather than hail. But it's not that effective, and it's not clear how much it affects rainfall in adjacent areas, or indeed longer-term weather patterns. Weather can put growers out of business. If the hail doesn't get you the frost might, or the cold, or the rain. High prices for the top wines disguise the fact that much of Bordeaux is barely profitable. As for the quality, it's too soon to say, but don't write the '13s off yet.

Austria had hail as well, especially in May in Mittelburgenland, but also in Lower Austria and Styria; and Austria had already had a difficult flowering, when the weather suddenly changed from warm to cold and wet. *Coulure*, or poor fruit set, was the result; but even so the 2013 crop is slightly bigger than in 2012, when frost cut quantities. But 2013 also provided a warm summer, which after a shiveringly cold and late spring did allow the vines

Vintage report 2013

to recover. In April in **Italy**'s Veneto growers were shaking their heads over vines that were a month behind; so were they in **Germany** (poor weather during flowering, and then floods), in **Spain** and in **England**. A late start means a late finish; but since harvests have been getting earlier the late spring of 2013 simply put the harvest back to where it would have been 20 years ago. It wasn't so much a late harvest as an old-fashioned one.

In **Australia** the summer had been the hottest on record, and among the driest. It was also rather calm: no floods, not much disease and enough water in the dams. In **New Zealand** they're upbeat as well: in Gimblett Gravels, source of superb reds, the weather was perfect all the way through. At Craggy Range, indeed, the winemaker recorded finding just ten berries affected by rot, and he must have had to look pretty hard to find them. Elsewhere in NZ it was good too: a bit of frost in Central Otago, but a good vintage in the end; excellent in Marlborough and very good in Martinborough. **South Africa** had a late, cool spring, but a warm December speeded things up and the wines have structure and freshness. **California** too had a good result, with intense, balanced wines – and an early harvest, with picking in Napa Valley beginning on 1 August. In **Chile**, 2013 was good in both quality and quantity, but the 2014 harvest will probably be cut by September frosts – the worst in 84 years.

A closer look at 2012

By the time this book appears the 2012 Bordeaux will be in bottle and on the shelves, and it seems likely that there will be no shortage of them. Should you buy them? Yes, because some are lovely: wines of finesse and balance, sleek and elegant. No, because they're too expensive.

The latter is the reason they may well be in generous supply. This was the vintage when the Bordelais were supposed to get the message and cut their prices. The first growths did, by about a third; other *grands crus* cut by rather less. The négociants, who are the merchants who buy from the châteaux and sell to retailers, found themselves carrying not only substantial stocks of 2012 but also unsold 2011s and even some unsold 2010s. Winemaking and viticulture in **Bordeaux** get more precise every year, which was why such a wet spring and early summer turned, in the end, into a rather delicious vintage; but their reading of the market seems less perspicacious. Or perhaps they just feared that cutting their price for the 2012 would undermine the value of earlier, more expensive vintages, in particular the 2011. Nobody wants to be the one to prick the bubble – or point out that the emperor is underdressed.

It's not a great vintage, but it has some very nice wines. The Right Bank did best, with its earlier-ripening Merlot; Cabernet-based Médocs sometimes show a touch of greenness, though this was less evident in Pessac-Léognan. It's essentially an uneven year for reds. Sweet whites also showed unevenness, with some top Sauternes châteaux announcing they would not release a *grand vin*. Dry whites were the winners, with balance, freshness and good concentration. Put your money here.

The year was no easier in **Burgundy**, but here the pressure on prices is upwards. It was another small vintage, and the Côte de Beaune suffered the most from hail, after a dreadful flowering on both côtes. There was mildew, oidium (though no botrytis); quality in reds and whites is uneven. Yet the wines are delicious: concentrated, balanced, aromatic. Some will be very slow to come round; others are positively drink-me-now, even at *grand cru* level. As is usual in uneven years, the differences between terroirs, and between good and less good terroirs, is very marked, and the Côte Chalonnaise did very well indeed.

In **Italy**, Tuscan reds are looking rich and powerful. It was a dry year, flowering wasn't great and the summer was hot, but rain in September balanced things out a bit, so that the acidity and the structure are both good. In Piedmont, the Barolos are still in their tight-fisted infancy but are looking extremely promising, but the Dolcettos are emerging as wonderfully sweet and delicate. Dolcetto seems to have got over its flirtation with weight and power – who needs it here? – and wines made with a lighter touch are widespread in 2012. And for something that is a cross between Barolo and Dolcetto, with the grape of one and the freshness of the other, Langhe Nebbiolo looks terrific in 2012. As indeed do the whites: lovely crisp, fresh, balanced wines.

Austria's small 2012 vintage, with quantities cut by May frost, is looking good; reds are compact and promise well, and Rieslings are structured and balanced. Grüner Veltliner was hit worst by the frost, but its quality leaves nothing to complain about. In **Germany**, Ernie Loosen on the Mosel reports that his 2012s have developed grip and concentration with a year's age and are not looking all that different to the excellent 2011s now: "just half a gram of extra acidity", he says. In the **Douro Valley**, however, the 2012 Ports are not serious challengers to the 2011s. That was a classic year; 2012 will be a good single-quinta year. If you feel like tasting the lush delights of baby Vintage Port, opened a year or two after bottling, 2012 could be a good place to start.

If you like this, try this

This book is not just about discovering new wines; sometimes old wines get forgotten and need to be rediscovered. That's when it's fun to find new connections, new resemblances, that put them into a different context. Perspective changes everything.

If you like Grüner Veltliner, try top Muscadet

Muscadet disappeared from most people's tables when Australian Chardonnay came in: nobody wanted lean minerality any more. But now it's exactly what everybody wants, and top *sur lie* Muscadet can deliver ripe "wineyness" plus acidity and subtlety. Was it Grüner Veltliner that brought the world back to the delights of minerality in whites? All that white pepper and bay-leaf fruit? Muscadet is more salt than pepper, and *sur lie* versions have an extra sparkiness that makes them worth seeking out. And they'll age in bottle for a couple of years quite happily.

If you like Albariño, try Petit Manseng

Albariño has glorious apricot fruit streaked with lime – quite irresistible. Petit Manseng, and its near relative Gros Manseng, are less easy to find, but offer a still more intense apricot-and-lime experience, with that same acidity that makes Albariño so refreshing. The Mansengs are to be found in Southwest France, in the appellations of Béarn and Jurançon; but Virginia in the USA has some too, so there's just a chance they might start to become fashionable. Albariño managed it, after all.

If you like Meursault, try Alsace Pinot Blanc

Meursault, alone among white burgundies, offers a fascinating smoke-and-cabbage-leaves fruit that may not sound appealing but is completely seductive. Other white burgundies are complex and mineral: Meursault offers a fatness and an extraordinarily sexy come-on. Alsace Pinot Blanc is less brazen and has a different kind of vegetal smokiness – more earth and mushrooms, more undergrowth, less decay – but if woodsmoke and sour cream are what you seek, Alsace is certainly worth a look.

If you like Sancerre, try Graves Blanc

This is another rediscovery. Graves Blanc has been so hopelessly unfashionable for so long that it's easy to forget that it's made principally from Sauvignon Blanc, and usually in a ripe, mineral style that is the antithesis of NZ green beans and gooseberries. You can get tired of unripe fruit flavours; and when you do, it's time to look again at Bordeaux. Instead of gooseberries, think of blackcurrant leaves: crunchy ripeness and freshness and lightness. But the quality is there, and the drinkability. There's a lot to be said for ripe grapes.

If you like Dolcetto, try Chilean Syrah

Dolcetto should be beloved of anyone who likes fresh reds that taste of cherries dipped in tea: it's usually described as the lightest of the Piedmontese trio, Barolo and Barbaresco being its big brothers. But Dolcetto can pack plenty of flavour. Chilean Syrah? Well, from the northern regions of Elqui and Limarí there are wines aromatic with black olives and violets – not an exact match for the cherries and Darjeeling of Dolcetto, but an interesting comparison. And their structures – powerful, with acidity and silky tannins – help to make the link.

If you like Pauillac, try Boğazkere and Öküzgözö

You probably would, you're saying, if you could pronounce either or had the faintest idea where they came from. The latter is easy: they're grapes native to Turkey. The former is often not necessary because they're often blended together and will probably only appear on the back label, where nobody will make you read them out loud. Boğazkere, full of grippy tannins, spice, bright fruit and acidity, is reminiscent of Cabernet, the mainstay of tobacco-scented, mineral, grippy, spicy Pauillac; Öküzgözö has softer, broader fruit that acts, in a blend of the two, just as Merlot does with Cabernet Sauvignon. Turkish wines might not be up there with Château Latour just yet, but they're worth a try.

If you like Hermitage, try Nero d'Avola

Okay, another Syrah: but great Syrah can lead its lovers in many different directions across the world. This time it's to the south of Italy, where Nero d'Avola, a local grape, has all the black olive and herb flavours that we associate with the rocks and *garrigue* of the northern Rhône. It's an uncompromising style, not for the faint-hearted; it needs strong-flavoured food and probably a winter's evening. Nero d'Avola may not have the finesse of top northern Rhône, but then the world only discovered it relatively recently. Its chewiness and wild aromas are balanced by acidity; and what's more, it should be balanced. It's not an unworthy link to one of the world's greatest reds.

If you like Argentine Malbec, try Mencía

The best new-style Argentine Malbecs are all about aroma, acidity and altitude – a triple A that puts them head-and-shoulders above the more pedestrian efforts that suffer from overoaking and often overpricing. Malbec should feel concentrated, chewy but elegant, with redcurrant and spice fruit. Mencía, the red grape of Spain's Bierzo region, has acidity aplenty, and savoury, redcurrant fruit and spice... it's also currently one of Spain's most fashionable wines, particularly when it comes from rediscovered patches of ancient vines high on inaccessible hills. It's funny how often winemakers produce the best wines when they make life difficult for themselves.

Grape varieties

I n the past two decades a radical change has come about in all except the most long-established wine countries: the names of a handful of grape varieties have become the ready-reference to wine. In senior wine countries, above all France and Italy, more complex traditions prevail. All wine of old prestige is known by its origin, more or less narrowly defined – not just by the particular fruit juice that fermented. For the present the two notions are in rivalry. Eventually the primacy of place over fruit will become obvious, at least for wines of quality. But for now, for most people, grape tastes are the easy reference point – despite the fact that they are often confused by the added taste of oak. If grape flavours were really all that mattered, this would be a very short book. But of course they *do* matter, and a knowledge of them both guides you to flavours you enjoy and helps comparisons between regions. Hence the originally Californian term "varietal wine", meaning, in principle, made from one grape variety. At least seven varieties – Cabernet Sauvignon, Pinot Noir, Riesling, Sauvignon Blanc, Chardonnay, Gewurztraminer and Muscat – taste and smell distinct and memorable enough to form international wine categories. To these add Merlot, Malbec, Syrah, Sémillon, Chenin Blanc, Pinots Blanc and Gris, Sylvaner, Viognier, Nebbiolo, Sangiovese, Tempranillo. The following are the best and/or most popular wine grapes.

All grapes and synonyms listed in this section are cross-referenced through every section in the book.

Grapes for red wine

Aghiorgitiko (Agiorgitiko) Greek; the grape of Nemea, now planted almost everywhere. Versatile and delicious, from soft and charming to dense and age-worthy. A must-try.

Agiorghitiko *See* AGHIORGITIKO.

Aglianico Southern Italian, dark, deep and fashionable.

Aragonez *See* TEMPRANILLO.

Auxerrois *See* MALBEC, if red. White Auxerrois has its own entry in White Grapes.

Băbească Neagră Traditional "black grandmother grape" of Moldova; light body and ruby-red colour.

Babić Dark grape from Dalmatia, grown in stony seaside v'yds round Šibenik. Exceptional quality potential.

Baga Portugal. Bairrada grape. Dark and tannic. Great potential but hard to grow.

Barbera Widely grown in Italy, at its best in Piedmont: high acidity, low tannin, cherry fruit. Ranges from barriqued and serious to semisweet and frothy. Fashionable in California and Australia; promising in Argentina.

Blauburger Austrian cross between BLAUER PORTUGIESER/BLAUFRÄNKISCH. Simple wines.

Blauburgunder *See* PINOT N.

Blauer Portugieser Central European, esp Germany (Rheinhessen, Pfalz, mostly for rosé), Austria, Hungary. Light, fruity reds to drink slightly chilled when young. Not for laying down.

Blauer Zweigelt *See* ZWEIGELT.

Blaufränkisch (Kékfrankos, Lemberger, Modra Frankinja) Widely planted in Austria's Mittelburgenland: medium-body, peppery acidity, characteristic salty note, berries, eucalyptus. Often blended with CAB SAUV or ZWEIGELT. Lemberger in Germany (speciality of Württemberg), Kékfrankos in Hungary, Modra Frankinja in Slovenia.

Boğazkere Tannic and Turkish. Produces full-bodied wines.

Bonarda Several different grapes sail under this flag. In Italy's Oltrepò Pavese, an alias for Croatina, soft fresh *frizzante* and still red; Piedmont's Bonarda is different. Bonarda in Lombardy and Emilia-Romagna is an alias for Uva Rara. Argentina's Bonarda can be any of these, or something else.

Bouchet *See* CAB FR.

Brunello Alias for SANGIOVESE, splendid at Montalcino.

Cabernet Franc [Cab Fr] The lesser of two sorts of Cab grown in Bordeaux but dominant in St-Émilion. Outperforms CAB SAUV in the Loire (Chinon, Saumur-Champigny, rosé), in Hungary (depth and complexity in Villány and Szekszárd) and often in Italy. Much of northeast Italy's Cab Fr turned out to be CARMENÈRE. Used in Bordeaux blends of Cab Sauv/MERLOT across the world.

Cabernet Sauvignon [Cab Sauv] Grape of great character: spicy, herby, tannic, with characteristic blackcurrant aroma. Main grape of the Médoc; also makes some of the best California, South American, East European reds. Vies with Shiraz in Australia. Grown almost everywhere, and led vinous renaissance in eg. Italy. Top wines need ageing; usually benefits from blending with eg. MERLOT, CAB FR, SYRAH, TEMPRANILLO, SANGIOVESE, etc. Makes aromatic rosé.

Cannonau GRENACHE in its Sardinian manifestation; can be v. fine, potent.

Carignan (Carignano, Cariñena) Low-yielding old vines now very fashionable everywhere from south of France to Chile; best: Corbières. Lots of depth and vibrancy. Overcropped Carignan is wine-lake fodder. Common in North Africa, Spain (as Cariñena) and California.

Carignano *See* CARIGNAN.

Cariñena *See* CARIGNAN.

Carmenère An old Bordeaux variety that is now a star, rich and deep, in Chile (where it's pronounced *carmeneary*). Bordeaux is looking at it again.

Castelão *See* PERIQUITA.

Cencibel *See* TEMPRANILLO.

Chiavennasca *See* NEBBIOLO.

Cinsault (Cinsaut) A staple of southern France, very good if low-yielding, wine-lake stuff if not. Makes gd rosé. One of the parents of PINOTAGE.

Cornalin du Valais Swiss speciality, esp in Valais.

Corvina Dark and spicy; one of the best grapes in the Valpolicella blend. Corvinone, even darker, is a separate variety.

Côt *See* MALBEC.

Dolcetto Source of soft, seductive dry red in Piedmont. Now high fashion.

Dornfelder Gives deliciously light reds, straightforward, often rustic and well-coloured, in Germany, parts of the USA and England. German plantings have doubled since 2000.

Fer Servadou Exclusive to Southwest France, particularly important in Marcillac, Gaillac and St-Mont. Redolent of soft fruits and spice.

Fetească Neagră Romania: "black maiden grape" with potential as showpiece variety and being more widely planted. Needs care and low yields in v'yd, but can give deep, full-bodied wines with character.

Frühburgunder An ancient mutation of PINOT N, found mostly in Germany's Ahr but also in Franken and Württemberg, where it is confusingly known as Clevner. Lower acidity and thus more approachable than Pinot N.

Gamay The Beaujolais grape: light, very fragrant wines, at their best young, except in Beaujolais *crus* (*see* France) where quality can be superb, wines for 2–10 yrs. Makes even lighter wine in the Loire Valley, in central France, in Switzerland and Savoie. California's Napa Gamay is Valdiguié.

Gamza *See* KADARKA.

Garnacha (Cannonau, Garnatxa, Grenache) Becoming ultra-fashionable with *terroiristes*, who admire the way it expresses its site. Also gd for rosé and *vin doux naturel* – esp in the south of France, Spain and California – but also the mainstay of beefy Priorat. Old-vine versions are prized in South Australia. Usually blended with other varieties. Cannonau in Sardinia, Grenache in France.

Garnatxa *See* GARNACHA.

Graciano Spanish; part of Rioja blend. Aroma of violets, tannic, lean structure, reminiscent of PETIT VERDOT. Difficult to grow but fashionable, planted more now.

Grenache *See* GARNACHA.

Grignolino Italy: gd everyday table wine in Piedmont.

Kadarka (Gamza) Spicy, light reds in East Europe. Hungary, revived esp for Bikavér.

Kékfrankos Hungarian BLAUFRÄNKISCH.

Lagrein Northern Italian, deep colour, bitter finish, rich, plummy fruit. DOC in Alto Adige (*see* Italy).

Lambrusco Productive grape of the lower Po Valley; quintessentially Italian, cheerful, sweet and fizzy red.

Lefkada Rediscovered Cypriot variety, higher quality than Mavro. Usually blended as tannins can be aggressive.

Lemberger *See* BLAUFRÄNKISCH.

Malbec (Auxerrois, Côt) Minor in Bordeaux, major in Cahors (alias Auxerrois) and the star in Argentina. Dark, dense, tannic but fleshy wine capable of real quality. High-altitude versions in Argentina are the bee's knees.

Maratheftiko Deep-coloured Cypriot grape with quality potential. Tricky to grow well, but getting better as winemakers learn to manage it.

Mataro *See* MOURVÈDRE.

Mavro The most planted black grape of Cyprus. Easier to cultivate than MARATHEFTIKO, but only moderate quality. Best for rosé.

Mavrodaphne Greek; the name means "black laurel". Used for sweet fortifieds; speciality of Patras, but also found in Cephalonia. Dry versions on the increase and show great promise.

Mavrotragano Greek, almost extinct but now revived; found on Santorini. Top quality.

Mavrud Probably Bulgaria's best. Spicy, dark, plummy late-ripener native to Thrace. Ages well.

Melnik Bulgarian grape originating in the region of the same name. Dark colour and a nice dense, tart-cherry character. Ages well.

Mencía Making waves in Bierzo, Spain. Aromatic with steely tannins, and lots of acidity. Excellent with a gd producer.

Merlot The grape behind the great fragrant and plummy wines of Pomerol and (with CAB FR) St-Émilion, an important element in Médoc reds, soft and strong (and *à la mode*) in California, Washington, Chile, Australia. Lighter but often gd in north Italy (can be world-class in Tuscany), Italian Switzerland, Slovenia, Argentina, South Africa, NZ, etc. Perhaps too adaptable for its own gd: can be very dull; less than ripe it tastes green. Much planted in East Europe; Romania's most planted red.

Modra Frankinja *See* BLAUFRÄNKISCH.

Modri Pinot *See* PINOT N.

Monastrell *See* MOURVÈDRE.

Mondeuse Found in Savoie; deep-coloured; gd acidity. Related to SYRAH.

Montepulciano Deep-coloured grape dominant in Italy's Abruzzo and important along Adriatic coast from Marche to southern Puglia. Also the name of a famous Tuscan town, unrelated.

Morellino Alias for SANGIOVESE in Scansano, southern Tuscany.

Mourvèdre (Mataro, Monastrell) A star of southern France and Australia (sometimes as Mataro) and, as Monastrell, Spain. Excellent dark, aromatic, tannic grape, gd for blending. Enjoying new interest in eg. South Australia and California.

Napa Gamay Identical to Valdiguié (south of France). Nothing to get excited about.

Nebbiolo (Chiavennasca, Spanna) One of Italy's best red grapes; makes Barolo, Barbaresco, Gattinara and Valtellina. Intense, nobly fruity, perfumed wine but v. tannic: improves for yrs.

Negroamaro Puglian "black bitter" red grape with potential for both high quality or high volume.

Nerello Mascalese Medium-coloured, characterful Sicilian red grape capable of making wines of considerable elegance.

Nero d'Avola Dark-red grape of Sicily, quality levels from sublime to industrial.

Nielluccio Corsican; plenty of acidity and tannin. Gd for rosé.

Öküzgözü Soft, fruity Turkish grape, usually blended with BOĞAZKERE, rather like MERLOT in Bordeaux is blended with CAB SAUV.

Pamid Bulgarian: light, soft, everyday red.

Periquita (Castelão) Planted throughout south Portugal, esp in Península de Setúbal. Originally nicknamed Periquita after Fonseca's popular (trademarked) brand. Firm-flavoured, raspberryish reds develop a figgy, tar-like quality.

Petite Sirah Nothing to do with SYRAH; gives rustic, tannic, dark wine. Brilliant blended with ZIN in California; also found in South America, Mexico, Australia.

Petit Verdot Excellent but awkward Médoc grape, now increasingly planted in CAB areas worldwide for extra fragrance. Mostly blended, some gd varietals, esp in Virginia.

Pinotage Singular South African grape (PINOT N x CINSAULT). Has had a rocky ride, but is emerging engaging, satisfying, even profound, from best producers. Gd rosé too. Fashionable "coffee Pinotage" is expresso-toned, sweetish and aimed at youth market.

Pinot Crni *See* PINOT N.

Pinot Meunier (Schwarzriesling) Third grape of Champagne, scorned by some, used by most. Softer, earlier drinking than PINOT N so useful for blending. Found in many places, either vinified as a white for fizz, or occasionally (eg. Germany's Württemberg, as Schwarzriesling) as still red. Samtrot is a local variant in Württemberg.

Pinot Noir (Blauburgunder, Modri Pinot, Pinot Crni, Spätburgunder) [Pinot N] The glory of Burgundy's Côte d'Or, with scent, flavour and texture that are unmatched anywhere. Recent German efforts have been excellent. V.gd. in Austria, esp in Kamptal, Burgenland, Thermenregion. Light wines in Hungary; light to weightier in Switzerland, where it is the main red variety and also known as Clevner. Splendid results in California's Sonoma, Carneros, Central Coast, as well as Oregon, Ontario, Yarra Valley, Adelaide Hills, Tasmania, NZ's South Island (Central Otago) and South Africa's Walker Bay. Some v. pretty Chileans. New French clones promise improvement in Romania. Modri P in Slovenia; probably country's best red. In Italy, best in northeast and gets worse as you go south. PINOTS BL and GR are mutations of Pinot N.

Plavac Mali (Crljenak) Croatian, and related to ZIN, like so much round there. Lots of quality potential, can age well, though can also be alcoholic and dull.

Primitivo Southern Italian grape, originally from Croatia, making big, dark, rustic wines, now fashionable because genetically identical to ZIN. Early ripening, The original name for both seems to be Tribidrag.

Refosco (Refošk) Various DOCs in Italy, esp Colli Orientali. Deep, flavoursome and age-worthy wines, particularly in warmer climates. Dark, high acidity. Refošk in Slovenia and points east, genetically different, tastes similar.

Refošk *See* REFOSCO.

Rubin Bulgarian cross, NEBBIOLO x SYRAH. Peppery, full-bodied. Gd in blends, but increasingly used on its own.

Sagrantino Italian grape found in Umbria for powerful, cherry-flavoured wines.

St-Laurent Dark, smooth, full-flavoured Austrian speciality. Can be light and juicy or deep and structured, fashion for overextraction is over. Also in the Pfalz.

Sangiovese (Brunello, Morellino, Sangioveto) Principal red grape of west-central Italy with a reputation of being difficult to get right, but sublime, long-lasting when it is. Research produced great improvements. Dominant in Chianti, Vino Nobile, Brunello di Montalcino, Morellino di Scansano, various fine IGT offerings. Also in Umbria generally (eg. Montefalco, Torgiano), across the Apennines in Romagna, the Marches. Not so clever in warmer, lower-altitude v'yds of Tuscan coast, nor in other parts of Italy despite its nr ubiquity. Interesting in Australia.

Sangioveto *See* SANGIOVESE.

Saperavi Gd, balanced, v. long-lived wine in Georgia, Ukraine, etc. Blends v. well with CAB SAUV (eg. in Moldova). Huge potential, seldom gd winemaking.

Schiava *See* TROLLINGER.

Schwarzriesling PINOT MEUNIER in Württemberg.

Sciacarello Corsican, herby and peppery. Not v. tannic.

Shiraz *See* SYRAH.

Spanna *See* NEBBIOLO.

Spätburgunder German for PINOT N.

Syrah (Shiraz) The great Rhône red grape: tannic, purple, peppery wine that matures superbly. Important as Shiraz in Australia, increasingly gd under either name in Chile, South Africa, terrific in NZ (esp Hawke's Bay). Widely grown.

Tannat Raspberry-perfumed, highly tannic force behind Madiran, Tursan and other firm reds from Southwest France. Also rosé. Now the star of Uruguay.

Tempranillo (Aragonez, Cecibel, Tinto Fino, Tinta del País, Tinta Roriz, Ull de Llebre) Aromatic, fine Rioja grape, called Ull de Llebre in Catalonia, Cencibel in La Mancha, Tinto Fino in Ribera del Duero, Tinta Roriz in Douro, Tinta del País in Castile, Aragonez in southern Portugal. Now Australia too. V. fashionable; elegant in cool climates, beefy in warm. Early ripening, long maturing.

Teran (Terrano) Close cousin of REFOSCO, same dark colour, high acidity, appetizing, esp on limestone (karst). Slovenia and thereabouts.

Teroldego Rotaliano Italian: Trentino's best indigenous variety makes serious, full-flavoured wine, esp on the flat Campo Rotaliano.

Tinta Amarela See TRINCADEIRA.

Tinta del País See TEMPRANILLO.

Tinta Negra (Negramoll) Until recently called Tinta Negra Mole. Easily Madeira's most planted grape and the mainstay of cheaper Madeira. Now coming into its own in Colheita wines (see Port, Sherry & Madeira chapter).

Tinta Roriz See TEMPRANILLO.

Tinto Fino See TEMPRANILLO.

Touriga Nacional Top Port grape in the Douro Valley, now widely used for floral, stylish table wines. Australian Touriga is usually this; California's Touriga can be either this or Touriga Franca.

Trincadeira (Tinta Amarela) Portuguese; v.gd in Alentejo for spicy wines. Tinta Amarela in the Douro.

Trollinger (Schiava, Vernatsch) Popular pale red in Germany's Württemberg; aka Vernatsch, Schiava. Covers group of vines, not necessarily related. Snappy in Italy.

Vernatsch See TROLLINGER.

Xinomavro Greece's answer to NEBBIOLO. "Sharp-black"; the basis for Naoussa, Rapsani, Goumenissa, Amindeo. Some rosé, still or sparkling. Top quality, can age for decades. Being tried in China.

Zinfandel (Zin) Fruity, adaptable grape of California with blackberry-like, and sometimes metallic, flavour. Can be structured and gloriously lush, ageing for decades, but also makes "blush" pink, usually sweet, jammy. Genetically the same as southern Italian PRIMITIVO.

Zweigelt (Blauer Zweigelt) BLAUFRÄNKISCH X ST-LAURENT, popular in Austria for aromatic, dark, supple, velvety wines. Also found in Hungary, Germany.

Grapes for white wine

Airén Bland workhorse of La Mancha, Spain: fresh if made well.

Albariño (Alvarinho) Fashionable, expensive in Spain: apricot-scented, gd acidity. Superb in Rías Baixas; shaping up elsewhere; not all live up to hype. Alvarinho in Portugal just as gd: aromatic Vinho Verde, esp in Monção and Melgaço.

Aligoté Burgundy's second-rank white grape. Sharp wine for young drinking, perfect for mixing with cassis (blackcurrant liqueur) to make kir. Widely planted in East Europe, esp Russia.

Alvarinho See ALBARIÑO.

Amigne One of Switzerland's speciality grapes, traditional in Valais, esp Vétroz. Total planted: 43 ha. Full-bodied, tasty, often sweet but also bone-dry.

Ansonica See INSOLIA.

Arinto Portuguese; the mainstay of aromatic, citrus wines in Bucelas; also adds welcome zip to blends, esp in Alentejo.

Arneis Northwest Italian. Fine, aromatic, appley-peachy, high-priced grape, DOCG in Roero, DOC in Langhe, Piedmont.

Arvine Rare Swiss spécialité, from Valais. Also Petite Arvine. Dry and sweet, elegant, long-lasting wines with salty finish.

Assyrtiko Greek; one of the best grapes of the Mediterranean, balancing power, minerality, extract and high acid. Built to age. Could conquer the world....

Auxerrois Red Auxerrois is a synonym for MALBEC, but white Auxerrois is like a fatter, spicier version of PINOT BL. Found in Alsace, used in Crémant; also Germany.

Beli Pinot *See* PINOT BL.

Blanc Fumé *See* SAUV BL.

Boal *See* BUAL.

Bourboulenc This and the rare Rolle make some of the Midi's best wines.

Bouvier Indigenous aromatic Austrian grape, esp gd for Beerenauslese and Trockenbeerenauslese, rarely for dry wines.

Bual (Boal) Makes top-quality sweet Madeira wines, not quite so rich as Malmsey.

Carricante Italian. Principal grape of Etna Bianco, regaining ground.

Catarratto Prolific white grape found all over Sicily, esp in west in DOC Alcamo.

Cerceal *See* SERCIAL.

Chardonnay (Morillon) [Chard] White grape of Burgundy and Champagne, now ubiquitous worldwide, partly because it is one of the easiest to grow and vinify. Also the name of a Mâcon-Villages commune. The fashion for overoaked butterscotch versions now thankfully over. Morillon in Styria, Austria.

Chasselas (Fendant, Gutedel) Swiss (originated in Vaud). Neutral flavour, takes on local character: elegant (Geneva); refined, full (Vaud); exotic, racy (Valais). Fendant in Valais. Makes almost a third of Swiss wines but giving way, esp to red. Gutedel in Germany; grown esp in southern Baden. Elsewhere usually a table grape.

Chenin Blanc [Chenin Bl] Wonderful white grape of the middle Loire (Vouvray, Layon, etc). Wine can be dry or sweet (or v. sweet), but with plenty of acidity. Bulk wine in California. Taken v. seriously (alias Steen) in South Africa; still finding its way there, but huge potential.

Cirfandli *See* ZIERFANDLER.

Clairette A low-acid grape, part of many southern French blends. Improved winemaking helps.

Colombard Slightly fruity, nicely sharp grape, makes everyday wine in South Africa, California and Southwest France. Often blended.

Dimiat Perfumed Bulgarian grape, made dry or off-dry, or distilled. Far more synonyms than any grape needs.

Ermitage *See* MARSANNE.

Ezerjó Hungarian, with sharp acidity. Name means "thousand blessings".

Falanghina Ancient grape of Italy's Campanian hills. Top dense, aromatic dry whites.

Fendant *See* CHASSELAS.

Fernão Pires *See* MARIA GOMES.

Feteascǎ Albǎ / Regalǎ Romania has two Feteascǎ grapes, both with slight MUSCAT aroma. F. Regalǎ is a cross of F. Albǎ and GRASǍ; more finesse, gd for late-harvest wines. F. Neagrǎ is dark-skinned.

Fiano High-quality grape giving peachy, spicy wine in Campania, south Italy.

Folle Blanche (Gros Plant) High acid/little flavour make this ideal for brandy. Gros Plant in Brittany, Picpoul in Armagnac, but unrelated to true PICPOUL. Also respectable in California.

Friulano (Sauvignonasse, Sauvignon Vert) North Italian: fresh, pungent, subtly floral. Used to be called Tocai Friulano. Best in Collio, Isonzo, Colli Orientali. Found in nearby Slovenia as Sauvignonasse; also in Chile, where it was long confused with SAUV BL. Ex-Tocai in Veneto now known as Tai.

Fumé Blanc *See* SAUV BL.

Furmint (Šipon) Superb, characterful. The trademark of Hungary, both as the principal grape in Tokaji and as vivid, vigorous table wine, sometimes mineral, sometimes apricot-flavoured, sometimes both. Šipon in Slovenia. Some grown in Rust, Austria for sweet and dry.

Garganega Best grape in Soave blend; also in Gambellara. Top, esp sweet, age well.

Garnacha Blanca (Grenache Blanc) White version of GARNACHA/Grenache, used in Spain and southern France. Low acidity. Can be innocuous, or surprisingly gd.

Gewurztraminer (Traminac, Traminec, Traminer, Tramini) [Gewurz] One of the most pungent grapes, spicy with aromas of rose petals, face cream, lychees, grapefruit. Wines are often rich and soft, even when fully dry. Best in Alsace; also gd in Germany (Baden, Pfalz, Sachsen), Eastern Europe, Australia, California, Pacific Northwest and NZ. Can be relatively unaromatic if just labelled Traminer (or variants). Italy uses the name Traminer Aromatico for its (dry) "Gewürz" versions. (The name takes an Umlaut in German.) Identical to SAVAGNIN.

Glera Uncharismatic new name for the Prosecco vine: Prosecco is now only a wine, no longer a grape.

Godello Top quality (intense, mineral) in northwest Spain. Called Verdelho in Dão, Portugal, but unrelated to true VERDELHO.

Grasă (Kövérszölö) Romanian; name means "fat". Prone to botrytis; v. important grape in Cotnari, potentially superb sweet wines. Kövérszölö in Hungary's Tokaj region.

Graševina *See* WELSCHRIESLING.

Grauburgunder *See* PINOT GR.

Grechetto Ancient grape of central and south Italy noted for the vitality and stylishness of its wine. Blended, or used solo in Orvieto.

Greco Southern Italian: there are various Grecos, probably unrelated, perhaps of Greek origin. Brisk, peachy flavour, most famous as Greco di Tufo. Greco di Bianco is from semi-dried grapes. Greco Nero is a black version.

Grenache Blanc *See* GARNACHA BLANCA.

Grignolino Italy: gd everyday table wine in Piedmont.

Gros Plant *See* FOLLE BLANCHE.

Grüner Veltliner [Grüner V] Austria's flagship white grape. Remarkably diverse: from simple, peppery everyday wines to others of great complexity and ageing potential. Found elsewhere in Central Europe to some extent, and now showing potential in NZ. The height of fashion.

Gutedel *See* CHASSELAS.

Hárslevelű Other main grape of Tokaji, but softer, peachier than FURMINT. Name means "linden-leaved". Gd in Somló, Eger as well.

Heida *See* SAVAGNIN.

Humagne Swiss speciality, older than CHASSELAS. Fresh, plump, not v. aromatic. Humagne Rouge (HR), also common in Valais, is not related but increasingly popular. HR is the same as Cornalin du Aosta; Cornalin du Valais is different. (Keep up at the back, there.)

Insolia (Ansonica, Inzolia) Sicilian; Ansonica on Tuscan coast. Fresh, racy wine at best. May be semi-dried for sweet wine.

Irsai Olivér Hungarian cross of two table varieties, makes aromatic, MUSCAT-like wine for drinking young.

Johannisberg *See* SILVANER.

Kéknyelű Low-yielding, flavourful grape giving one of Hungary's best whites. Has the potential for fieriness and spice. To be watched.

Kerner Quite successful German crossing. Early ripening, flowery (but often too blatant) wine with gd acidity.

Királyleanyka Hungarian; gentle, fresh wines.

Kövérszölö *See* GRASĂ.

Laski Rizling *See* WELSCHRIESLING.

Leányka Hungarian. Soft, floral wines.

Listán *See* PALOMINO.

Loureiro Best Vinho Verde grape after ALVARINHO: delicate floral whites. Also Spain.

Macabeo *See* VIURA.

Malagousia Rediscovered Greek grape for gloriously perfumed wines.

Malmsey *See* MALVASIA. Sweetest style of Madeira, made from grape of same name.

Malvasia (Malmsey, Malvazija, Malvoisie, Marastina) Italy, France and Iberia. Not a single variety but a whole collection of them, not necessarily related or even alike. Can be white or red, sparkling or still, strong or mild, sweet or dry, aromatic or neutral. Slovenia's and Croatia's version is Malvazija Istarka, crisp and light, or rich, oak-aged. Sometimes called Marastina in Croatia. "Malmsey" (as in the sweetest style of Madeira) is a corruption of Malvasia.

Malvoisie *See* MALVASIA. A name used for several varieties in France, incl BOURBOULENC, Torbato, VERMENTINO. Also PINOT GR in Switzerland's Valais.

Manseng, Gros / Petit Gloriously spicy, floral whites from Southwest France. The key to Jurançon. Superb late-harvest and sweet wines too.

Maria Gomes (Fernão Pires) Portuguese; aromatic, ripe-flavoured, slightly spicy whites in Barraida and Tejo.

Marsanne (Ermitage) Principal white grape (with ROUSSANNE) of the northern Rhône (Hermitage, St-Joseph, St-Péray). Also gd in Australia, California and (as Ermitage Blanc) the Valais. Soft, full wines that age v. well.

Melon de Bourgogne *See* MUSCADET.

Misket Bulgarian. Mildly aromatic; the basis of most country whites.

Morillon CHARD in parts of Austria.

Moscatel *See* MUSCAT.

Moscato *See* MUSCAT.

Moschofilero Pink-skinned, rose-scented, high-quality, high-acid, low-alcohol Greek grape. Makes white, some pink, some sparkling.

Müller-Thurgau [Müller-T] Aromatic wines to drink young. Makes gd sweet wines but usually dull, often coarse, dry ones. In Germany, most common in Pfalz, Rheinhessen, Nahe, Baden, Franken. Has some merit in Italy's Trentino-Alto Adige, Friuli. Sometimes called RIES X SYLVANER (incorrectly) in Switzerland.

Muscadelle Adds aroma to white Bordeaux, esp Sauternes. In Victoria used (with MUSCAT, to which it is unrelated) for Rutherglen Muscat.

Muscadet (Melon de Bourgogne) Makes light, refreshing, v, dry wines with a seaside tang around Nantes in Brittany. Also found (as Melon) in parts of Burgundy.

Muscat (Moscatel, Moscato, Muskateller) Many varieties; the best is Muscat Blanc à Petits Grains (alias Gelber Muskateller, Rumeni Muškat, Sarga Muskotály, Yellow Muscat). Widely grown, easily recognized, pungent grapes, mostly made into perfumed sweet wines, often fortified, as in France's *vin doux naturel*. Superb, dark and sweet in Australia. Sweet, sometimes v.gd in Spain. Most Hungarian Muskotály is Muscat Ottonel except in Tokaj where Sarga Muskotály rules, adding perfume (in small amounts) to blends. Occasionally (eg. Alsace, Austria, parts of south Germany) made dry. Sweet Cap Corse Muscats often superb. Light Moscato fizz in Italy.

Muskateller *See* MUSCAT.

Narince Turkish; fresh and fruity wines.

Neuburger Austrian, rather neglected; mainly in the Wachau (elegant, flowery), Thermenregion (mellow, ample-bodied) and north Burgenland (strong, full).

Olaszrizling / Olasz Riesling *See* WELSCHRIESLING.

Païen *See* SAVAGNIN.

Palomino (Listán) The great grape of Sherry; with little intrinsic character, it gains all from production method. Of local appeal (on a hot day) for table wine. As Listán, makes dry white in Canaries.

Pansa Blanca *See* XAREL-LO.

Pecorino Italian: not a cheese but alluring dry white from a recently nr-extinct variety. IGT in Colli Pescaresi.

Pedro Ximénez [PX] Makes sweet Sherry under its own name; used in Montilla, Málaga. Also grown in Argentina, Canaries, Australia, California, South Africa.

Picpoul (Piquepoul) Southern French, best known in Picpoul de Pinet. High acidity. Picpoul Noir is black-skinned.

Pinela Local to Slovenia. Subtle, lowish acidity; drink young.

Pinot Bianco *See* PINOT BL.

Pinot Blanc (Beli Pinot, Pinot Bianco, Weissburgunder) [Pinot Bl] A cousin of PINOT N, similar to but milder than CHARD. Light, fresh, fruity, not aromatic, to drink young. Good for Italian *spumante*, and potentially excellent in the northeast, esp high sites in Alto Adige. Widely grown. Weissburgunder in Germany and best in south: often racier than Chard.

Pinot Gris (Pinot Grigio, Grauburgunder, Ruländer, Sivi Pinot, Szürkebarát) (Pinot Gr) Light and fashionable as Pinot Grigio in northern Italy, even for rosé, but top, characterful versions can be excellent (from Alto Adige, Friuli). Cheap versions are just that. Terrific in Alsace for full-bodied, spicy whites. Once important in Champagne. In Germany can be alias Ruländer (sweet) or Grauburgunder (dry): best in Baden (esp Kaiserstuhl) and southern Pfalz. Szürkebarát in Hungary, Sivi Pinot in Slovenia (characterful, aromatic).

Pošip Croatian; mostly on island of Korčula. Quite characterful, citrus; high yielding.

Prosecco *See* GLERA.

Renski Rizling *See* RIES.

Ribolla Gialla / Rebula Acidic but characterful. In Italy, best in Collio. In Slovenia, traditional in Brda. V. high quality potential, in macerated and classical vinifications.

Rieslaner German cross (SILVANER X RIES); low yields, difficult ripening, now a rarity (less than 50 ha). Makes fine Auslesen in Franken and Pfalz.

Riesling Italico *See* WELSCHRIESLING.

Riesling (Renski Rizling, Rhine Riesling) [Ries] As gd as CHARD if not better, though diametrically opposite in style. Offers a range from steely to voluptuous, always positively perfumed and with more ageing potential than Chard. Great in all styles in Germany; forceful and steely in Austria; lime-cordial and toast fruit in South Australia; rich and spicy in Alsace; Germanic and promising in NZ, New York State, Pacific Northwest; has potential in Ontario, South Africa.

Rkatsiteli Found widely in Eastern Europe, Russia, Georgia. Can stand cold winters and has high acidity, which protects it to some degree from poor winemaking. Also grown in northeastern USA.

Robola In Greece (Cephalonia) a top-quality, floral grape, unrelated to Ribolla Gialla.

Roditis Pink grape grown all over Greece, usually whites. Gd when yields low.

Roter Veltliner Austrian; unrelated to GRÜNER V. There is also a Frühroter and an (unrelated) Brauner Veltliner.

Rotgipfler Austrian; indigenous to Thermenregion. With ZIERFANDLER, makes lively, lush, aromatic blend.

Roussanne Rhône grape of finesse, now popping up in California and Australia. Can age many yrs.

Ruländer *See* PINOT GR.

Sauvignonasse *See* FRIULANO.

Sauvignon Blanc [Sauv Bl] Distinctive aromatic, grassy-to-tropical wines, pungent in NZ, often minerally in Sancerre, riper in Australia. V.gd in Rueda, Austria, north Italy (Isonzo, Piedmont, Alto Adige), Chile's Casablanca Valley, South Africa. Blended with SÉM in Bordeaux. Can be austere or buxom (or indeed nauseating). Sauv Gris is pink-skinned, less aromatic version with untapped potential.

Sauvignon Vert *See* FRIULANO.

Savagnin (Heida, Païen) Grape of Vin Jaune from Savoie: aromatic form is GEWURZ. In Switzerland known as Heida, Païen or Traminer. Full-bodied, high acidity.

Scheurebe (Sämling) Grapefruit-scented German RIES X SILVANER (possibly), v. successful in Pfalz, esp for Auslese and up. Can be weedy: must be v. ripe to be gd.

Sémillon [Sém] Contributes lusciousness to Sauternes; decreasingly important for Graves and other dry white Bordeaux. Grassy if not fully ripe; can make soft dry wine of great ageing potential. Superb in Australia; NZ, South Africa promising.

Sercial (Cerceal) Portuguese: makes the driest Madeira. Cerceal, also Portuguese, seems to be this plus any of several others.

Seyval Blanc [Seyval Bl] French-made hybrid of French and American vines. V. hardy and attractively fruity. Popular and reasonably successful in eastern US states and England but dogmatically banned by EU from "quality" wines.

Silvaner (Johannisberg, Sylvaner) Germany's former workhorse grape, can be excellent in Rheinhessen, Pfalz, esp Franken, where its plant/earth flavours and mineral notes reach their apogee. V.gd (and powerful) as Johannisberg in the Valais, Switzerland. The lightest of the Alsace grapes.

Šipon See FURMINT.

Spätrot See ZIERFANDLER.

Sylvaner See SILVANER.

Tămâioasă Românească Romanian: "frankincense" grape, with exotic aroma and taste. Belongs to MUSCAT family.

Torrontés Name given to a number of grapes, mostly with an aromatic, floral character, sometimes soapy. A speciality of Argentina; also in Spain. DYA.

Traminac Or Traminec. See GEWURZ.

Traminer Or Tramini (Hungary). See GEWURZ.

Trebbiano (Ugni Blanc) Principal white grape of Tuscany, found all over Italy in many different guises. Rarely rises above the plebeian except in Tuscany's Vin Santo. Some gd dry whites under DOCs Romagna or Abruzzo. Trebbiano di Soave or di Lugana, aka VERDICCHIO, is only distantly related. Grown in southern France as Ugni Blanc, and Cognac as St-Émilion. Mostly thin, bland wine; needs blending (and more careful growing).

Ugni Blanc (Ugni Bl) See TREBBIANO.

Ull de Llebre See TEMPRANILLO.

Verdejo The grape of Rueda in Castile, potentially fine and long-lived.

Verdelho Great quality in Australia (pungent, full-bodied); rare but gd (and medium-sweet) in Madeira.

Verdicchio Potentially gd, muscular, dry in central-eastern Italy. Wine has same name.

Vermentino Italian, sprightly with satisfying texture and ageing capacity. Potential here.

Vernaccia Name given to many unrelated grapes in Italy. Vernaccia di San Gimignano is crisp, lively; Vernaccia di Oristano is Sherry-like.

Vidal French hybrid much grown in Canada for Icewine.

Viognier Ultra-fashionable Rhône grape, finest in Condrieu, less fine but still aromatic in the Midi. Gd examples from California, Virginia, Uruguay, Australia.

Viura (Macabeo, Maccabéo, Maccabeu) Workhorse white grape of northern Spain, widespread in Rioja and Catalan Cava country. Also found over border in Southwest France. Gd quality potential.

Weißburgunder PINOT BL in Germany.

Welschriesling (Graševina, Laski Rizling, Olaszrizling, Olasz Riesling, Riesling Italico) Not related to RIES. Light and fresh to sweet and rich in Austria; ubiquitous in Central Europe, where it can be remarkably gd for dry and sweet wines.

Xarel-lo (Pansa Blanca) Traditional Catalan grape, for Cava, along with Paréllada, MACABEO. Neutral but clean. More character (lime cordial) in Alella, as Pansa Blanca.

Xynisteri Cyprus's most planted white grape. Can be simple and is usually DYA, but when grown at altitude makes appealing, minerally whites.

Zéta Hungarian; BOUVIER X FURMINT used by some in Tokaji Aszú production.

Zierfandler (Spätrot, Cirfandl) Found in Austria's Thermenregion; often blended with ROTGIPFLER for aromatic, orange-peel-scented, weighty wines.

Wine & food

Which comes first, food or wine? The usual answer is food, which is why this chapter is a list of dishes and wines we have liked with them. On page 38 is a wine-first list for very special bottles. Are there rules? Make up your own if you like, but don't choose either food or wine you don't know you'll enjoy. If you like both separately, whatever they are, you'll probably like them together. You quickly find out what to avoid: oily fish doesn't go with tannic wine, but most things do, in these days of silky tannins. Vinegary salad dressing ruins everything – even the salad. And go from light to dark, dry to sweet. Now for the suggestions....

Before the meal – apéritifs

The conventional apéritif wines are either sparkling (epitomized by Champagne) or fortified (epitomized by Sherry in Britain, Port in France, vermouth in Italy, etc.). A glass of a light table wine before eating is the easy choice.

Warning Avoid peanuts; they destroy wine flavours. Olives are too piquant for many wines, esp. Champagne; they need Sherry or a Martini. With Champagne eat almonds, pistachios, cashews, or walnuts, plain crisps or cheese straws instead.

First courses

Aïoli A thirst-quencher is needed for its garlic heat. Young Rhône white, Provence rosé, VERDICCHIO, SAUV BL. And marc or grappa too, for courage.

Antipasti Dry or medium white: Italian (ARNEIS, Soave, PINOT GRIGIO, VERMENTINO, GRECHETTO); light but gutsy red, eg. Valpolicella. Or Fino Sherry.

Artichoke vinaigrette Not great for wine. An incisive dry white: NZ SAUV BL; Côtes de Gascogne or a modern Greek (precisely, 4-yr-old Malagousia, but easy on the vinaigrette); young red: Bordeaux, Côtes du Rhône.

    with hollandaise Full-bodied crisp dry white: Pouilly-Fuissé, German *Erstes Gewächs*.

Asparagus A difficult flavour for wine, being slightly bitter, so the wine needs plenty of its own. Rheingau RIES is a classic, but RIES generally gd to try. SAUV BL echoes the flavour. SÉM beats CHARD, esp Australian, but Chard works well with melted butter or hollandaise. Alsace PINOT GR, even dry MUSCAT is gd or Jurançon Sec.

Aubergine purée (*Melitzanosalata*) Crisp New World SAUV BL, eg. from South Africa or NZ; or modern Greek or Sicilian dry white. Baked aubergine dishes need sturdy reds: SHIRAZ, ZIN. Or indeed Turkish.

Avocado and tiger prawns Dry to medium slightly sharp white: Rheingau or Pfalz Kabinett, GRÜNER V, Wachau RIES, Sancerre, PINOT GR; Australian CHARD (unoaked), or a dry rosé. Or *premier cru* Chablis.

    with mozzarella and tomato Crisp but ripe white: Soave, Sancerre, Greek white.

Carpaccio, beef Works well with most wines, incl reds. Tuscan is appropriate, but fine CHARDS are gd. So are vintage and pink Champagnes.

    salmon Chard or Champagne.

    tuna VIOGNIER, California Chard or NZ SAUV BL.

Caviar Iced vodka (and) full-bodied Champagne (eg. Bollinger, Krug). Cuvée Anna-Maria Clementi from Ca' del Bosco. Don't add raw onion.

Ceviche Australian RIES or VERDELHO, Chilean SAUV BL, TORRONTÉS.

Charcuterie / salami Young Beaujolais-Villages, Loire reds (ie. Saumur), NZ or Oregon PINOT N. LAMBRUSCO or young ZIN. Young Argentine or Italian reds. Bordeaux Blanc and light CHARD (eg. Côte Chalonnaise) can work well too.

Chorizo Fino is best; or Austrian RIES, GRÜNER V, but not a wine-friendly taste... either on its own or in sauces.

Crostini Dry Italian white works best such as VERDICCHIO or Orvieto, or standard-grade (not Riserva) Morellino di Scansano, MONTEPULCIANO d'Abruzzo, Valpolicella, Manzanilla.

Crudités Light red or rosé: Côtes du Rhône, Minervois, Chianti, PINOT N; or Fino Sherry. Alsace SYLVANER or PINOT BL.

Dim sum Classically, China tea. For fun: PINOT GR or RIES; light PINOT N. For reds, soft tannins are key; mature reds go surprisingly well. Bardolino, Rioja, light southern Rhône also contenders. Also NV Champagne or gd New World fizz.

Eggs See also SOUFFLÉS. Not easy; they clash with most wines and can ruin gd ones. VIOGNIER, esp Australian, is remarkably gd. As a last resort I can bring myself to drink Champagne with scrambled eggs – easily at weekends.

    quail eggs Blanc de blancs Champagne; Viognier.

    seagull (or gull) eggs Mature white burgundy or vintage Champagne.

    oeufs en meurette Burgundian genius: eggs in red wine with glass of the same.

Escargots (or frogs legs) A comfort dish calling for Rhône reds (Gigondas, Vacqueyras). In Burgundy white: St-Véran or Rully. In the Midi *petits-gris* go with local white, rosé or red. In Alsace, PINOT BL or dry MUSCAT. On the Loire, frogs legs and semi-dry CHENIN BL.

Fish terrine or fish salad (including crab) Calls for something fine. Pfalz RIES Spätlese Trocken, GRÜNER V, *premier cru* Chablis, Clare Valley RIES, Sonoma CHARD; or Manzanilla.

Foie gras Sweet white. In Bordeaux, Sauternes. Others prefer a late-harvest PINOT GR or RIES, Vouvray, Montlouis, Jurançon *moelleux* or GEWURZ. Tokaji Aszú 5 Puttonyos is a Lucullan choice. Old dry Amontillado can be sublime. With hot foie gras, mature vintage Champagne. But not on any account CHARD or SAUV BL. Or any red.

Goats cheese, cooked (eg. in a salad) The classic: Sancerre, Pouilly-Fumé, or New World SAUV BL.

    chilled Chinon, Saumur-Champigny, or Provence rosé. Or strong red: Château Musar, Greek, Turkish, Australian sparkling SHIRAZ.

Guacamole Mexican beer. Or California CHARD, NZ SAUV BL, dry MUSCAT or Sherry.

Haddock, smoked, mousse, soufflé or brandade Wonderful for showing off any stylish, full-bodied white, incl *grand cru* Chablis, or Sonoma, South African, or NZ CHARD.

Ham, raw or cured See *also* PROSCIUTTO. Alsace Grand Cru PINOT GR or gd, crisp Italian Collio white. With Spanish *pata negra* or *jamón*, Fino Sherry or Tawny Port. *See also* HAM, COOKED (MEAT, POULTRY, GAME).

Herrings, raw or pickled Dutch gin (young, not aged) or Scandinavian akvavit, and cold beer. If wine essential, try MUSCADET.

Mackerel, smoked An oily wine-destroyer. Manzanilla, proper dry Vinho Verde or Schnapps, peppered or bison-grass vodka. Or lager. Or black tea.

Mayonnaise Adds richness that calls for a contrasting bite in the wine. Côte Chalonnaise whites (eg. Rully) are gd. Try NZ SAUV BL, VERDICCHIO or a Spätlese Trocken. Or Provence rosé.

    with lobster: Pfalz RIES Erstes Gewächs, Chablis Premier Cru.

Mezze A selection of hot and cold vegetable dishes. Fino Sherry is in its element.

Mozzarella with tomatoes, basil Fresh Italian white, eg. Soave, Alto Adige. VERMENTINO from Liguria or Rolle from the Midi. *See also* AVOCADO.

Oysters, raw NV Champagne, Chablis, MUSCADET, white Graves, Sancerre, or Guinness. Manzanilla is excellent.

    cooked Puligny-Montrachet or gd New World CHARD. Champagne gd with either.

Pasta Red or white according to the sauce:

    cream sauce (eg. carbonara) Orvieto, Frascati, GRECO di Tufo. Young SANGIOVESE.

    meat sauce MONTEPULCIANO d'Abruzzo, Salice Salentino, MALBEC.

    pesto (basil) sauce BARBERA, Ligurian VERMENTINO, NZ SAUV BL, Hungarian FURMINT.

    seafood sauce (eg. vongole) VERDICCHIO, Soave, white Rioja, Cirò, unoaked CHARD.

    tomato sauce Chianti, Barbera, Sicilian red, ZIN, South Australian GRENACHE.

Pastrami Alsace RIES, young SANGIOVESE or St-Émilion.

Pâté, chicken liver Calls for pungent white (Alsace PINOT GR or MARSANNE), a smooth red eg. light Pomerol, Volnay or NZ PINOT N, even Amontillado Sherry. More strongly flavoured pâté (duck, etc.) needs Châteauneuf-du-Pape, Cornas, Chianti Classico or gd white Graves.

Pipérade Navarra rosado, Provence or Midi rosé. Or dry Australian RIES. For a red: Corbières.

Prawns, shrimps or langoustines MUSCADET is okay, but better a fine dry white: burgundy, Graves, NZ CHARD, Washington RIES, Pfalz Ries, Australian Ries – even fine mature Champagne. ("Cocktail sauce" kills wine and, in time, people.)

Prosciutto (also with melon, pears or figs) Full, dry or medium white: Orvieto, GRECHETTO, GRÜNER V, Tokaji FURMINT, Australian SEM or Jurançon Sec.

Risotto Follow the flavour: **with vegetables** (eg. Primavera) PINOT GR from Friuli, Gavi, youngish SÉM, DOLCETTO or BARBERA d'Alba.

    with fungi porcini Finest mature Barolo or Barbaresco.

    nero A rich dry white: VIOGNIER or even Corton-Charlemagne.

Salads Any dry and appetizing white or rosé wine.

    NB Vinegar in salad dressings *destroys* the flavour of wine. Why don't the French know this? If you want salad at a meal with fine wine, dress it with wine or lemon juice instead of vinegar.

Salmon, smoked Dry but pungent white: Fino (esp Manzanilla) Sherry, Condrieu, Alsace PINOT GR, *grand cru* Chablis, Pouilly-Fumé, Pfalz RIES Spätlese, vintage Champagne. Vodka, Schnapps or akvavit.

Soufflés As show dishes these deserve ★★★ wines.

    cheese Mature red burgundy or Bordeaux, CAB SAUV (not Chilean or Australian), etc. Or fine white burgundy.

    fish Dry white: ★★★ Burgundy, Bordeaux, Alsace, CHARD, etc.

    spinach (tougher on wine) Mâcon-Villages, St-Véran or Valpolicella. Champagne (esp vintage) can also be gd with the texture of a soufflé.

Tapas Perfect with cold fresh Fino Sherry, which can cope with the wide range of flavours in both hot and cold dishes. Or sake.

Tapenade Manzanilla or Fino Sherry, or any sharpish dry white or rosé.

Taramasalata A rustic southern white with personality; even possibly retsina. Fino Sherry works well. Try a Rhône MARSANNE. A bland supermarket tarama submits to fine, delicate whites or Champagne.

Tempura The Japanese favour oaked CHARD with acidity. I prefer Champagne.

Tortilla Rioja Crianza, Fino Sherry or white Mâcon-Villages.

Trout, smoked Sancerre; California or South African SAUV BL. Rully or Bourgogne ALIGOTÉ, Chablis or Champagne. German RIES Kabinett.

Vegetable terrine Not a great help to fine wine, but Chilean CHARD makes a fashionable marriage, CHENIN BL such as Vouvray a lasting one.

Whitebait Crisp dry whites, eg. FURMINT, Greek, Touraine SAUV BL, VERDICCHIO, or Fino Sherry.

Fish

Abalone Dry or medium white: SAUV BL, Meursault, PINOT GR, GRÜNER V. Chinese-style: vintage Champagne (at least) or Alsace RIES.

Anchovies, marinated Skip the marinade; it will clash with pretty well everything. In, eg. salade niçoise: Provence rosé.

Bass, sea WEISSBURGUNDER from Baden or Pfalz. V.gd for any fine/delicate white, eg. Clare dry RIES, Chablis, white Châteauneuf-du-Pape. But rev the wine up for more seasoning, eg. ginger, spring onions; more powerful Ries, not necessarily dry.

Beurre blanc, fish with A top-notch MUSCADET *sur lie*, a SAUV BL/SÉM blend, *premier cru* Chablis, Vouvray, ALBARINO, or Rheingau RIES.

Brandade *Premier cru* Chablis, Sancerre Rouge or NZ PINOT N.

Brill V. delicate: hence a top fish for fine old Puligny and the like.

Cod, roast Gd neutral background for fine dry/medium whites: Chablis, Meursault, Corton-Charlemagne, *cru classé* Graves, GRÜNER V, German Kabinett or *Grosses Gewächs*, or gd lightish PINOT N.

    black cod with miso sauce NZ or Oregon Pinot N, Meursault Premier Cru or Rheingau RIES Spätlese.

Crab Crab and RIES together are part of the Creator's Plan.

    Chinese, with ginger and onion German Ries Kabinett or Spätlese Halbtrocken. Tokaji FURMINT, GEWURZ.

    cioppino SAUV BL; but West Coast friends say ZIN. Also California sparkling.

    cold, dressed Top Mosel Ries, dry Alsace or Australian Ries or Condrieu.

    softshell Unoaked CHARD, ALBARIÑO or top-quality German Ries Spätlese.

    Thai crabcakes Pungent Sauv Bl (Loire, South Africa, Australia, NZ) or Ries (German Spätlese or Australian).

    with black bean sauce A big Barossa SHIRAZ or SYRAH. Even Cognac.

    with chilli and garlic Quite powerful Ries, perhaps German *Grosses Gewächs* or Wachau Austrian.

Curry A generic term for a multitude of flavours. Chilli emphasizes tannin, so reds need supple, evolved tannins. Any fruity, non-arid rosé can be gd bet. Hot-and-sour flavours (with tamarind, tomato, eg.) need acidity (perhaps SAUV BL); mild, creamy dishes need richness of texture (dry Alsace RIES). But best of all is Sherry: Fino with fish, Palo Cortado or dry Amontillado with meat. And a glass of water. It's revelatory.

Eel, smoked RIES, Alsace, or Austrian or dry Tokaji FURMINT. Vintage Champagne or Fino Sherry. Schnapps.

Fish and chips, *fritto misto*, tempura Chablis, white Bordeaux, SAUV BL, PINOT BL, Gavi, Fino Sherry, Montilla, Koshu, sake, tea; or NV Champagne or Cava.

Fish pie (with creamy sauce) ALBARIÑO, Soave Classico, RIES *Erstes Gewächs* or Spanish GODELLO.

Gravadlax SERCIAL Madeira (eg. 10-yr-old Henriques), Amontillado, Tokaji FURMINT.

Haddock Rich, dry whites: Meursault, California CHARD, MARSANNE or GRÜNER V.

Hake SAUV BL or any fresh fruity white: Pacherenc, Tursan, white Navarra. Cold with mayonnaise; fine CHARD.

Halibut As for TURBOT.

Herrings, fried / grilled Need a sharp white to cut their richness. Rully, Chablis, MUSCADET, Bourgogne ALIGOTÉ, Greek, dry SAUV BL. Or cider.

Kedgeree Full white, still or sparkling such as Mâcon-Villages, South African CHARD, GRÜNER V, German *Grosses Gewächs* or (at breakfast) Champagne.

Kippers A gd cup of tea, preferably Ceylon (milk, no sugar). Scotch? Dry Oloroso Sherry is surprisingly gd.

Lamproie à la Bordelaise Glorious with 5-yr-old St-Émilion or Fronsac. Or Douro reds with Portuguese lampreys.

Lobster, richly sauced Vintage Champagne, fine white burgundy, *cru classé* Graves, even Sauternes, *Grosses Gewächs*, Pfalz Spätlese.

    cold with mayonnaise NV Champagne, Alsace RIES, *premier cru* Chablis, Condrieu, Mosel Spätlese or a local fizz.

Mackerel, grilled Hard or sharp white to cut the oil: SAUV BL from Touraine, Gaillac, Vinho Verde, white Rioja or English white. Or Guinness.

Monkfish A succulent but neutral dish; depends on the sauce. Full-flavoured white or red, depending.

Mullet, grey VERDICCHIO, Rully or unoaked CHARD.

Mullet, red A chameleon, adaptable to gd white or red, esp PINOT N.

Mussels marinières MUSCADET *sur lie*, *premier cru* Chablis, unoaked CHARD.

    curried something half-sweet; Alsace RIES.

    with garlic / parsley *see* ESCARGOTS.

Paella, shellfish Full-bodied white or rosé, unoaked CHARD. Or the local Spanish red.

Perch, sandre Exquisite fish for finest wines: top white burgundy, *grand cru* Alsace RIES or noble Mosels. Or try top Swiss CHASSELAS (eg. Dézaley, St-Saphorin).

Prawns with mayonnaise Menetou-Salon

    with garlic keep the wine light, white or rosé, and dry.

    with spices up to and incl chilli, go for a bit more body, but not oak: dry RIES gd.

Salmon, seared or grilled PINOT N is the fashionable option, but CHARD is better. MERLOT or light claret not bad. Best is fine white burgundy: Puligny- or Chassagne-Montrachet, Meursault, Corton-Charlemagne, *grand cru* Chablis; GRÜNER V, Condrieu, California, Idaho or NZ CHARD, Rheingau Kabinett/ Spätlese, Australian RIES.

    fishcakes Call for similar, but less grand, wines.

Sardines, fresh grilled Very dry white: Vinho Verde, MUSCADET or modern Greek.

Sashimi The Japanese preference is for white wine with body (Chablis Premier Cru, Alsace RIES) with white fish, PINOT N with red. Both need acidity: low-acidity wines don't work. Simple Chablis can be a bit thin. If soy is involved, then a low-tannin red (again, Pinot). Remember sake (or Fino). And as though you'd forget Champagne.

Scallops An inherently slightly sweet dish, best with medium-dry whites.

    in cream sauces German Spätlese, -Montrachets or top Australian CHARD.

    grilled or seared Hermitage Blanc, GRÜNER V, Pessac-Léognan Blanc, vintage Champagne or PINOT N.

    with Asian seasoning NZ Chard, CHENIN BL, VERDELHO, GODELLO, GEWURZ.

Shellfish Dry white with plain boiled shellfish, richer wines with richer sauces. RIES is the grape.

    with *plateaux de fruits de mer* Chablis, MUSCADET, PICPOUL de Pinet, Alto Adige, or PINOT BL.

Skate / raie with brown butter White with some pungency (eg. PINOT GR d'Alsace or ROUSSANNE) or a clean, straightforward wine ie. MUSCADET or VERDICCHIO.

Snapper SAUV BL if cooked with oriental flavours; white Rhône or Provence Rosé with Mediterranean flavours.

Sole, plaice, etc., plain, grilled or fried Perfect with fine wines: white burgundy or its equivalent.

    with sauce According to the ingredients: sharp, dry wine for tomato sauce, fairly rich for creamy preparations.

Sushi Hot wasabi is usually hidden in every piece. German QbA Trocken wines, simple Chablis, or NV Brut Champagne. Obvious fruit doesn't work. Or, of course, sake or beer.

Swordfish Full-bodied, dry white (or why not red?) of the country. Nothing grand.

Tagine, with couscous North African flavours need substantial whites to balance –

Austrian, Rhône – or crisp, neutral whites that won't compete. Go easy on the oak. VIOGNIER or ALBARIÑO can work well.

Trout, grilled or fried Delicate white wine, eg. Mosel (esp Saar or Ruwer), Alsace PINOT BL, FENDANT.

Tuna, grilled or seared Best served rare (or raw) with light red wine: Loire CAB FR or PINOT N. Young Rioja is a possibility.

Turbot The king of fishes. Serve with your best rich, dry white: Meursault or Chassagne-Montrachet, Corton-Charlemagne, mature Chablis or its California, Australian or NZ equivalent. Condrieu. Mature Rheingau, Mosel or Nahe Spätlese or Auslese (not Trocken).

Meat, poultry, game

Barbecues The local wine: Australian, South African, Chilean, Argentina are right in spirit. Reds need tannin and vigour.

    Asian flavours (lime, coriander, etc.) Rosé, PINOT GR, RIES.

    chilli SHIRAZ, ZIN, PINOTAGE, MALBEC, Chilean SYRAH.

    Middle Eastern (cumin, mint) Crisp dry whites, rosé.

    Fish with oil, lemon, herbs SAUV BL.

    tomato sauces Zin, SANGIOVESE.

Beef, boiled Red: Bordeaux (Bourgogne or Fronsac), Roussillon, Gevrey-Chambertin or Côte-Rôtie. Medium-ranking white burgundy is gd, eg. Auxey-Duresses. Mustard softens tannic reds, horseradish kills your taste – but can be worth the sacrifice.

    roast An ideal partner for your fine red wine of any kind. Amarone perhaps? See above for mustard.

    stew, daube Sturdy red: Pomerol or St-Émilion, Hermitage, Cornas, BARBERA, SHIRAZ, Napa CAB SAUV, Ribera del Duero or Douro red.

Beef stroganoff Dramatic red: Barolo, Valpolicella Amarone, Priorat, Hermitage, late-harvest ZIN – even Georgian SAPERAVI or Moldovan Negru de Purkar.

Boudin blanc **(white pork sausage)** Loire CHENIN BL, esp when served with apples: dry Vouvray, Saumur, Savennières; mature red Côte de Beaune if without.

Boudin noir **(blood sausage)** Local SAUV BL or CHENIN BL – especially in the Loire. Or Beaujolais cru, esp Morgon. Or light TEMPRANILLO. Or Fino.

Cabbage, stuffed Hungarian CAB FR/KADARKA; village Rhône; Salice Salentino, PRIMITIVO and other spicy southern Italian reds. Or Argentine MALBEC.

Cajun food Fleurie, Brouilly or New World SAUV BL. **With gumbo** Amontillado.

Cassoulet Red from Southwest France (Gaillac, Minervois, Corbières, St-Chinian or Fitou) or SHIRAZ. But best of all Fronton, Beaujolais cru or young TEMPRANILLO.

Chicken Kiev Alsace RIES, Collio, CHARD, Bergerac rouge.

Chicken / turkey / guinea fowl, roast Virtually any wine, incl v. best bottles of dry to medium white and finest old reds (esp burgundy). The meat of fowl can be adapted with sauces to match almost any fine wine (eg. coq au vin with red or white burgundy).

Chilli con carne A young red eg. Beaujolais, TEMPRANILLO, ZIN, Argentine MALBEC, Chilean CARMENÈRE.

Chinese food, Cantonese Rosé or dry to dryish white – Mosel RIES Kabinett or Spätlese Trocken – can be gd throughout a Chinese banquet. Ries should not be too dry; GEWURZ is often suggested but rarely works; Cantonese food needs acidity in wine. Dry sparkling (esp Cava) works with the textures. Reds can work, but you need the complexity of maturity, and a silky richness. Young tannins are disastrous, as are overoaked, overextracted monsters. PINOT N is first choice; try also St-Émilion ★★ or Châteauneuf-du-Pape. I often serve both whites and reds concurrently during Chinese meals; Peking duck is pretty forgiving. Champagne becomes a thirst-quencher.

Shanghai Richer, oilier than Cantonese, not great for wine. Shanghai tends to be low on chilli but high on vinegar of various sorts. German and Alsace whites can be a bit sweeter than for Cantonese. For reds, mature Pinot N is again best.

Szechuan style VERDICCHIO, Alsace PINOT BL or v. cold beer. Mature Pinot N can also work; but make sure the tannins are silky.

Choucroute garni Alsace PINOT BL, PINOT GR, RIES or lager.

Cold roast meat Generally better with full-flavoured white than red. Mosel Spätlese or Hochheimer and Côte Chalonnaise are v.gd, as is Beaujolais. Leftover cold beef with leftover vintage Champagne is bliss.

Confit d'oie / de canard Young, tannic red Bordeaux, California CAB SAUV and MERLOT, Priorat cut richness. Alsace PINOT GR or GEWURZ match it.

Coq au vin Red burgundy. Ideal: one bottle Chambertin in dish, two on the table.

Duck or goose Rather rich white: Pfalz Spätlese or off-dry *grand cru* Alsace. Or mature, gamey red: Morey-St-Denis, Côte-Rôtie, Pauillac. With oranges or peaches, the Sauternais propose drinking Sauternes, others Monbazillac or RIES Auslese. Mature, weighty vintage Champagne is gd too, and handles red cabbage surprisingly well.

Peking *See* CHINESE FOOD.

wild duck Big-scale red: Hermitage, Bandol, California or South African CAB SAUV, Australian SHIRAZ – Grange if you can afford it.

with olives Top-notch Chianti or other Tuscans.

roast breast & confit leg with Puy lentils Madiran, St-Émilion, Fronsac.

Frankfurters German/New York RIES, Beaujolais, light PINOT N. Or Budweiser Budvar.

Game birds, young, plain-roasted Best red wine you can afford, but not too heavy.

older birds in casseroles Red (Gevrey-Chambertin, Pommard, Châteauneuf-du-Pape, or *grand cru classé* St-Émilion, Rhône).

well-hung game Vega Sicilia, great red Rhône, Château Musar.

cold game Mature vintage Champagne.

Game pie, hot Red: Oregon PINOT N.

cold Gd-quality white burgundy, cru Beaujolais or Champagne.

Goulash Flavoursome young red: Hungarian Kékoportó, ZIN, Uruguayan TANNAT, MORELLINO di Scansano, MENCÍA, young Australian SHIRAZ. Or dry Tokaj white.

Grouse See GAME BIRDS – but push the boat right out.

Haggis Fruity red, eg. young claret, young Portuguese red, New World CAB SAUV or MALBEC or Châteauneuf-du-Pape. Or, of course, malt whisky.

Ham, cooked Softer red burgundies: Volnay, Savigny, Beaune; Chinon or Bourgueil; sweetish German white (RIES Spätlese); Tokaji FURMINT or Czech Frankovka; lightish CAB SAUV (eg. Chilean), or New World PINOT N. And don't forget the heaven-made match of ham and Sherry. See HAM, RAW OR CURED.

Hamburger Young red: Australian CAB SAUV, Chianti, ZIN, Argentine MALBEC, Chilean CARMENÈRE or SYRAH, TEMPRANILLO. Or full-strength cola (not diet).

Hare Jugged hare calls for flavourful red: not-too-old burgundy or Bordeaux, Rhône (eg. Gigondas), Bandol, Barbaresco, Ribera del Duero, Rioja Res. The same for saddle or for hare sauce with pappardelle.

Indian dishes Various options, though a new discovery has been how well dry Sherry goes with Indian food. Choose a fairly weighty Fino with fish, and Palo Cortado, Amontillado or Oloroso with meat, according to the weight of the dish; heat's not a problem. The texture works too. Otherwise, medium-sweet white, v. cold: Orvieto *abboccato*, South African CHENIN BL, Alsace PINOT BL, TORRONTÉS, Indian sparkling, Cava or NV Champagne. Rosé can be a safe all-rounder. Tannin – Barolo or Barbaresco, or deep-flavoured reds, ie. Châteauneuf-du-

Pape, Cornas, Australian GRENACHE or MOURVÈDRE, or Valpolicella Amarone – will emphasize the heat. Hot-and-sour flavours need acidity.

Japanese dishes Texture and balance are key; flavours are subtle. Gd mature fizz works well, as does mature dry RIES; you need acidity, a bit of body, and complexity. Umami-filled meat dishes favour light, supple, bright reds: Beaujolais perhaps, or mature PINOT N. Full-flavoured *yakitori* needs lively, fruity, younger versions of the same reds. *See also* SUSHI, SASHIMI.

Kebabs Vigorous red: modern Greek, Corbières, Chilean CAB SAUV, ZIN or Barossa SHIRAZ. SAUV BL, if lots of garlic.

Kidneys Red: St-Émilion or Fronsac, Castillon, Nuits-St-Georges, Cornas, Barbaresco, Rioja, Spanish or Australian CAB SAUV, Douro red.

Korean dishes Fruit-forward wines seem to work best with strong, pungent Korean flavours. PINOT N, Beaujolais, Valpolicella can all work: acidity is needed. Non-aromatic whites: GRÜNER V, SILVANER, VERNACCIA. But I drink beer.

Lamb, roast One of the traditional and best partners for v.gd red Bordeaux, or its CAB SAUV equivalents from the New World. In Spain, finest old Rioja and Ribera del Duero Res or Priorat, in Italy ditto SANGIOVESE.

cutlets or chops As for roast lamb, but a little less grand.

slow-cooked roast Flatters top reds, but needs less tannin than pink lamb.

shanks Young red burgundy eg. Santenay. Crozes-Hermitage. Montefalco SAGRANTINO.

Liver Young red: Beaujolais-Villages, St-Joseph, Médoc, Italian MERLOT, Breganze CAB SAUV, ZIN, Priorat, Bairrada.

calf's Red Rioja Crianza, Fleurie. Or a big Pfalz RIES Spätlese.

Meatballs Tangy, medium-bodied red: Mercurey, Crozes-Hermitage, Madiran, MORELLINO di Scansano, Langhe NEBBIOLO, ZIN, CAB SAUV.

Keftedes or spicy Middle-Eastern style Simple, rustic red.

Moussaka Red or rosé: Naoussa, SANGIOVESE, Corbières, Côtes de Provence, Ajaccio, young ZIN, TEMPRANILLO.

Mutton A stronger flavour than lamb, and not served pink. Robust red; top-notch, mature CAB SAUV, SYRAH. Some sweetness of fruit (eg. Barossa) suits it.

Osso bucco Low-tannin, supple red such as DOLCETTO d'Alba or PINOT N. Or dry Italian white such as Soave.

Ox cheek, braised Superbly tender and flavoursome, this flatters the best reds: Vega Sicilia, St-Émilion. Best with substantial wines.

Oxtail Rather rich red: St-Émilion, Pomerol, Pommard, Nuits-St-Georges, Barolo, or Rioja Res, Priorat or Ribera del Duero, California or Coonawarra CAB SAUV, Châteauneuf-du-Pape, mid-weight SHIRAZ, Amarone.

Paella Young Spanish wines: red, dry white or rosé: Penedès, Somontano, Navarra, or Rioja.

Pigeon PINOT N is perfect; young Rhône, Argentine MALBEC, young SANGIOVESE. Or try Franken SILVANER Spätlese.

Pork, roast A gd, rich, neutral background to a fairly light red or rich white. It deserves ★★ treatment: Médoc is fine. Portugal's suckling pig is eaten with Bairrada Garrafeira; Chinese is gd with PINOT N.

pork belly Slow-cooked and meltingly tender, this needs a red with some tannin or acidity. Italian would be gd: Barolo, DOLCETTO or BARBERA. Or Loire red, or lightish Argentine MALBEC.

Pot au feu, bollito misto, cocido Rustic reds from region of origin; SANGIOVESE di Romagna, Chusclan, Lirac, Rasteau, Portuguese Alentejo or Yecla, Jumilla (Spain).

Quail Carmignano, Rioja Res, mature claret, PINOT N. Or a mellow white: Vouvray or St-Péray.

Rabbit Lively, medium-bodied young Italian red, eg. AGLIANICO del Vulture; Chiroubles, Chinon, Saumur-Champigny or Rhône rosé.

with prunes Bigger, richer, fruitier red. **with mustard** Cahors.

as ragu Medium-bodied red with acidity.

Satay Australia's McLaren Vale SHIRAZ or Alsace or NZ GEWURZ. Peanut sauce is a problem with wine.

Sauerkraut (German) Franken SILVANER, lager or pils. (But *see also* CHOUCROUTE GARNI.)

Sausages *See also* CHARCUTERIE, FRANKFURTERS. The British banger requires a young MALBEC from Argentina (a red wine, anyway) or London Pride (ale).

Singaporean dishes Part Indian, part Malay and part Chinese, Singaporean food has big, bold flavours that don't match easily with wine. Off-dry RIES is as gd as anything. With meat dishes, ripe, supple reds: Valpolicella, PINOT N, DORNFELDER, unoaked MERLOT or CARMENÈRE.

Steak

au poivre A fairly young Rhône red or CAB SAUV.

filet, ribeye or tournedos Any gd red, esp burgundy (but not old wines with Béarnaise sauce: top New World PINOT N is better).

Fiorentina (bistecca) Chianti Classico Riserva or BRUNELLO. The rarer the meat, the more classic the wine; the more well-done, the more you need New World, sweet/ strong wines. Argentine MALBEC is the perfect partner for steak Argentine style, ie. cooked to death.

Korean *yuk whe* (world's best steak tartare) Sake.

tartare Vodka or light young red: Beaujolais, Bergerac, Valpolicella.

T-bone Reds of similar bone structure: Barolo, Hermitage, Australian CAB SAUV or SHIRAZ, Chilean SYRAH.

Steak-and-kidney pie or pudding Red Rioja Res or mature Bordeaux.

Stews and casseroles Burgundy such as Nuits-St-Georges or Pommard if fairly simple; otherwise lusty, full-flavoured red: young Côtes du Rhône, Toro, Corbières, BARBERA, SHIRAZ, ZIN, etc.

Sweetbreads A rich dish, so grand white wine: Rheingau RIES or Franken SILVANER Spätlese, *grand cru* Alsace PINOT GR or Condrieu, depending on sauce.

Tafelspitz Best-known of a series of typical Viennese boiled beef and veal dishes. A glass of GRÜNER V is mandatory.

Tagines These vary enormously, but fruity young reds are a gd bet: Beaujolais, TEMPRANILLO, SANGIOVESE, MERLOT, Morrocan SHIRAZ.

Chicken with preserved lemon, olives VIOGNIER.

Tandoori chicken RIES or SAUV BL, young red Bordeaux or light north Italian red served cool. Also Cava and NV Champagne and dry Palo Cortado or Amontillado Sherry.

Thai dishes Ginger and lemongrass call for pungent SAUV BL (Loire, Australia, NZ, South Africa) or RIES (Spätlese or Australian). Most curries suit aromatic whites with a touch of sweetness: GEWURZ is also gd.

Tongue Gd for any red or white of abundant character, esp Italian. Also Beaujolais, Loire reds, TEMPRANILLO and full, dry rosés.

Veal, roast Gd for any fine old red that may have faded with age (eg. a Rioja Res) or a German or Austrian RIES, Vouvray, Alsace PINOT GR.

Venison Big-scale reds, incl MOURVÈDRE, solo as in Bandol or in blends. Rhône, Bordeaux, NZ Gimblett Gravels or California CAB SAUV of a mature vintage; or rather rich white (Pfalz Spätlese or Alsace PINOT GR). With a sweet and sharp berry sauce, try a German *Grosses Gewächs* RIES, or a Chilean CARMENÈRE or SYRAH.

Vitello tonnato Full-bodied whites: CHARD; light reds (eg. Valpolicella) served cool.

Wild boar Serious red: top Tuscan or Priorat. NZ SYRAH.

Vegetarian dishes

(*See also* FIRST COURSES)

Baked pasta dishes *Pasticcio*, lasagne and cannelloni with elaborate vegetarian fillings and sauces: an occasion to show off a grand wine, especially finest Tuscan red, but also claret and burgundy.

Beetroot Mimics a flavour found in red burgundy. You could return the compliment. **and goats cheese gratin** Sancerre, Bordeaux SAUV BL.

Cauliflower cheese Crisp, aromatic white: Sancerre, RIES Spätlese, MUSCAT, ALBARIÑO, GODELLO. Beaujolais-Villages.

Couscous with vegetables Young red with a bite: SHIRAZ, Corbières, Minervois; or well-chilled rosé from Navarra or Somontano; or a robust Moroccan red.

Fennel-based dishes SAUV BL: Pouilly-Fumé or NZ SYLVANER or English SEYVAL BL; or young TEMPRANILLO.

Grilled Mediterranean vegetables Brouilly, BARBERA, TEMPRANILLO or SHIRAZ.

Lentil dishes Sturdy reds such as Corbières, ZIN or SHIRAZ.
 dhal, with spinach Tricky. Soft light red or rosé is best, and not top-flight.

Macaroni cheese As for CAULIFLOWER CHEESE.

Mushrooms (in most contexts) A boon to many reds. Pomerol, California MERLOT, Rioja Res, top burgundy or Vega Sicilia. On toast, best claret. Ceps/porcini, Ribera del Duero, Barolo, Chianti Rufina, Pauillac or St-Estèphe, or NZ Gimblett Gravels.

Onion / leek tart Fruity, off-dry or dry white: Alsace PINOT GR or GEWURZ; Canadian, Australian or NZ RIES; Jurançon. Or Loire CAB FR.

Peppers or aubergines (eggplant), stuffed Vigorous red wine: Nemea, Chianti, DOLCETTO, ZIN, Bandol, Vacqueyras.

Pumpkin / squash ravioli or risotto Full-bodied, fruity dry or off-dry white: VIOGNIER or MARSANNE, demi-sec Vouvray, Gavi or South African CHENIN.

Ratatouille Vigorous young red: Chianti, NZ CAB SAUV, MERLOT, MALBEC, TEMPRANILLO; young red Bordeaux, Gigondas or Coteaux du Languedoc.

Spanacopitta (spinach and feta pie) Young Greek or Italian red or white.

Spiced vegetarian dishes *See* INDIAN DISHES, THAI DISHES (MEAT, POULTRY, GAME).

Watercress, raw Makes every wine on earth taste revolting. Soup is slightly easier, but doesn't need wine.

Wild garlic leaves, wilted Tricky: a fairly neutral white with acidity will cope best.

Desserts

Apple pie, strudel or tarts Sweet German, Austrian or Loire white, Tokaji Aszú or Canadian Icewine.

Apples, Cox's Orange Pippins Vintage Port (and sweetmeal biscuits) is the Saintsbury [wine] Club plan.

Bread-and-butter pudding Fine 10-yr-old Barsac, Tokaji Aszú, or Australian botrytized SEM.

Cakes and gâteaux *See also* CHOCOLATE, COFFEE, GINGER, RUM. BUAL or MALMSEY Madeira, Oloroso or Cream Sherry.

Cheesecake Sweet white: Vouvray, Anjou or Vin Santo – nothing too special.

Chocolate A talking point. Generally only powerful flavours can compete. Texture matters. Bual, California Orange MUSCAT, Tokaji Aszú, Australian Liqueur Muscat, 10-yr-old Tawny or even young Vintage Port; Asti for light, fluffy mousses. Experiment with rich, ripe reds: SYRAH, ZIN, even sparkling SHIRAZ. Banyuls for a weightier partnership. Médoc can match bitter black chocolate, though Amarone is more fun. Armagnac, or a tot of gd rum.
 and olive oil mousse 10-yr-old Tawny Port or as for black chocolate, above.

Christmas pudding, mince pies Tawny Port, Cream Sherry or liquid Christmas pudding itself, PEDRO XIMÉNEZ Sherry. Tokaji Aszú. Asti or Banyuls.

Coffee desserts Sweet MUSCAT, Australia Liqueur Muscats or Tokaji Aszú.

Creams, custards, fools, syllabubs *See also* CHOCOLATE, COFFEE, GINGER, RUM. Sauternes, Loupiac, Ste-Croix-du-Mont or Monbazillac.

Crème brûlée Sauternes or Rhine Beerenauslese, best Madeira or Tokaji Aszú. (With concealed fruit, a more modest sweet wine.)

Crêpes Suzette Sweet Champagne, Orange MUSCAT or Asti.

Ice cream and sorbets Fortified wine (Australian Liqueur MUSCAT or Banyuls). PEDRO XIMÉNEZ.

Lemon flavours For dishes like tarte au citron, try sweet RIES from Germany or Austria or Tokaji Aszú; v. sweet if lemon is v. tart.

Meringues Recioto di Soave, Asti or top vintage Champagne, well-aged.

Mille-feuille Delicate sweet sparkling, eg. MOSCATO d'Asti, demi-sec Champagne.

Nuts (including praliné) Finest Oloroso Sherry, Madeira, Vintage or Tawny Port (nature's match for walnuts), Tokaji Aszú, Vin Santo or Setúbal MOSCATEL. **salted nut parfait** Tokaji Aszú, Vin Santo.

Orange flavours Experiment with old Sauternes, Tokaji Aszú, or California Orange MUSCAT.

Panettone Jurançon *moelleux*, late-harvest RIES, Barsac, Tokaji Aszú.

Pears in red wine Pause before the Port. Or try Rivesaltes, Banyuls or RIES Beerenauslese.

Pecan pie Orange MUSCAT or Liqueur Muscat.

Raspberries (no cream, little sugar) Excellent with fine reds which themselves taste of raspberries: young Juliénas, Regnié.

Rum flavours (baba, mousses, ice cream) MUSCAT – from Asti to Australian Liqueur, according to weight of dish.

Salted caramel mousse / parfait Late-harvest RIES, Tokaji Aszú.

Strawberries, wild (no cream) Serve with red Bordeaux (most exquisitely Margaux) poured over.

Strawberries and cream Sauternes or similar sweet Bordeaux, Vouvray *moelleux* or *vendange tardive* Jurançon.

Summer pudding Fairly young Sauternes of a gd vintage.

Sweet soufflés Sauternes or Vouvray *moelleux*. Sweet (or rich) Champagne.

Tiramisú Vin Santo, young Tawny Port, MUSCAT de Beaumes-de-Venise, Sauternes or Australian Liqueur Muscat.

Trifle Should be sufficiently vibrant with its internal Sherry.

Zabaglione Light-gold Marsala or Australian botrytized SEM or Asti.

WINE & CHEESE

The notion that wine and cheese were married in heaven is not borne out by experience. Fine red wines are slaughtered by strong cheeses; only sharp or sweet white wines survive. Principles to remember (despite exceptions): first, the harder the cheese, the more tannin the wine can have; second, the creamier the cheese, the more acidity is needed in the wine – and don't be shy of sweetness. Cheese is classified by its texture and the nature of its rind, so its appearance is a guide to the type of wine to match it. Below are examples. I always try to keep a glass of white wine for my cheese.

Bloomy rind soft cheeses, pure-white rind if pasteurized, or dotted with red: Brie, Camembert, Chaource, Bougon (goats milk "Camembert") Full, dry white burgundy or Rhône if the cheese is white and immature; powerful, fruity St-Émilion, young Australian (or Rhône) SHIRAZ/SYRAH or GRENACHE if it's mature.

Blue cheeses It is the sweetness of Sauternes (or Tokaji), especially old, that complements the extreme saltiness of Roquefort. Stilton and Port, (youngish) Vintage or Tawny, is a classic. Intensely flavoured old Oloroso, Amontillado, Madeira, Marsala and other fortifieds go with most blues.

Fresh, no rind – cream cheese, crème fraîche, mozzarella Light crisp white: Chablis, Bergerac, Entre-Deux-Mers; rosé: Anjou, Rhône; v. light, young, fresh red: Bordeaux, Bardolino, Beaujolais.

Hard cheeses, waxed or oiled, often showing marks from cheesecloth – Gruyère family, Manchego and other Spanish cheeses, Parmesan, Cantal, Comté, old Gouda, Cheddar and most "traditional" English cheeses Hard to generalize; Gouda, Gruyère, some Spanish, and a few English cheeses complement fine claret or CAB SAUV and great SHIRAZ/SYRAH. But strong cheeses need less refined wines, preferably local ones. Sugary, granular old Dutch red Mimolette or Beaufort are gd for finest mature Bordeaux. Also for Tokaji Aszú. But try whites too.

Natural rind (mostly goats cheese) with bluish-grey mould (the rind becomes wrinkled when mature), sometimes dusted with ash – St-Marcellin Sancerre, Valençay, light SAUV BL, Jurançon, Savoie, Soave, Italian CHARD.

Semi-soft cheeses, thickish grey-pink rind – Livarot, Pont l'Evêque, Reblochon, Tomme de Savoie, St-Nectaire Powerful white Bordeaux, CHARD, Alsace PINOT GR, dryish RIES, southern Italian and Sicilian whites, aged white Rioja, dry Oloroso Sherry. The strongest of these cheeses kill almost any wines. Try marc or Calvados.

Washed-rind soft cheeses, with rather sticky, orange-red rind – Langres, mature Epoisses, Maroilles, Carré de l'Est, Milleens, Munster Local reds, esp for Burgundy cheeses; vigorous Languedoc, Cahors, Côtes du Frontonnais, Corsican, southern Italian, Sicilian, Bairrada. Also powerful whites, esp Alsace GEWURZ, MUSCAT.

FOOD & FINEST WINES

With very special bottles, the wine guides the choice of food rather than vice versa. The following suggestions are based largely on gastronomic conventions and newer experiments, plus much diligent research. They should help bring out the best in your best wines.

Red wines

Amarone Classically, in Verona, *risotto all'Amarone* or *pastissada*. But if your butcher doesn't run to horse, then shin of beef, slow-cooked in more Amarone.

Barolo, Barbaresco Risotto with white truffles; pasta with game sauce (eg. *pappardelle alla lepre*); porcini mushrooms; Parmesan.

Great Syrahs: Hermitage, Côte-Rôtie, Grange; Vega Sicilia Beef (such as the super-rich, super-tender, super-slow-cooked ox cheek I had at Vega Sicilia), venison, well-hung game; bone marrow on toast; English cheese (esp best farm Cheddar) but also hard goats milk and ewes milk cheeses such as England's Berkswell or Ticklemore.

Great Vintage Port or Madeira Walnuts or pecans. A Cox's Orange Pippin and a digestive biscuit is a classic English accompaniment.

Red Bordeaux V. old, light, delicate wines, (eg. pre-59) Leg or rack of young lamb, roast with a hint of herbs (not garlic); *entrecôte*; simply roasted partridge or grouse; sweetbreads.

fully mature great vintages (eg. 59 61 82 85) Shoulder or saddle of lamb, roast with a touch of garlic; roast ribs or grilled rump of beef.

mature but still vigorous (eg. 89 90) Shoulder or saddle of lamb (incl kidneys) with rich sauce. Fillet of beef *marchand de vin* (with wine and bone marrow). Avoid beef Wellington: pastry dulls the palate.

Merlot-based Beef as above (fillet is richest) or well-hung venison. In St-Émilion, lampreys.

Red burgundy Consider the weight and texture, which grow lighter/more velvety with age. Also the character of the wine: Nuits is earthy, Musigny flowery, great Romanées can be exotic, Pommard renowned for its four-squareness. Roast chicken or capon is a safe standard with red burgundy; guinea fowl for slightly stronger wines, then partridge, grouse or woodcock for those progressively more rich and pungent. Hare and venison (*chevreuil*) are alternatives.

   great old burgundy The Burgundian formula is cheese: Époisses (unfermented); a fine cheese but a terrible waste of fine old wines.

   vigorous younger burgundy Duck or goose roasted to minimize fat. Or *faisinjan* (pheasant cooked in pomegranate juice). Or lightly smoked gammon.

Rioja Gran Reserva, Pesquera... Richly flavoured roasts: wild boar, mutton, saddle of hare, whole suckling pig.

White wines

Beerenauslese / Trockenbeerenauslese Biscuits, peaches, or greengages. Desserts made from rhubarb, gooseberries, quince, apples.

Condrieu, Château-Grillet, Hermitage Blanc V. light pasta scented with herbs and tiny peas or broad beans. Or v. mild tender ham.

Grand cru **Alsace: Riesling** *Truite au bleu*, smoked salmon or *choucroute garni*.

   Pinot Gr Roast or grilled veal. Or truffle sandwich (slice a whole truffle, make a sandwich with salted butter and gd country bread – not sourdough or rye – wrap and refrigerate overnight. Then toast it in the oven).

   Gewurztraminer Cheese soufflé (Münster cheese).

   vendange tardive Foie gras or tarte tatin.

Old vintage Champagne (not Blanc de Blancs) As an apéritif, or with cold partridge, grouse, woodcock. The evolved flavours of old Champagne make it far easier to match with food than the tightness of young wine. Hot foie gras can be sensational. Don't be afraid of garlic or even Indian spices, but omit the chilli.

Late-disgorged old wines have extra freshness plus tertiary flavours. Try with truffles, lobster, scallops, crab, sweetbreads, pork belly, roast veal, chicken.

Sauternes Simple crisp buttery biscuits (eg. *langues de chat*), white peaches, nectarines, strawberries (without cream). Not tropical fruit. Pan-seared foie gras. Lobster or chicken with Sauternes sauce. Château d'Yquem recommends oysters (and indeed lobster). Experiment with blue cheeses. Rocquefort is classic, but needs a powerful wine.

Tokaji Aszú (5–6 puttonyos) Foie gras recommended. Fruit desserts, cream desserts, even chocolate can be wonderful. It even works with some Chinese, though not with chilli – the spice has to be adjusted to meet the sweetness. Szechuan pepper is gd. Havana cigars are splendid. So is the naked sip.

Very good Chablis, white burgundy, other top-quality Chards White fish simply grilled or *meunière*. Dover sole, turbot, halibut are best; brill, drenched in butter, can be excellent. (Sea bass is too delicate; salmon passes but does little for the finest wine.)

Vouvray *moelleux*, **etc.** Buttery biscuits, apples, apple tart.

White burgundy (ie. Montrachet, Corton-Charlemagne) or equivalent Graves Roast veal, farm chicken stuffed with truffles or herbs under the skin, or sweetbreads; richly sauced white fish (turbot for choice) or scallops as above. Or lobster or poached wild salmon.

France

More heavily shaded areas are
the wine-growing regions.

Abbreviations used in the text:

Al	Alsace
Beauj	Beaujolais
Burg	Burgundy
B'x	Bordeaux
Champ	Champagne
Cors	Corsica
C d'O	Côte d'Or
L'doc	Languedoc
Lo	Loire
Mass C	Massif Central
Prov	Provence
Pyr	Pyrénées
N/S Rhô	Northern/Southern Rhône
Rouss	Roussillon
Sav	Savoie
SW Fr	Southwest
AC	appellation contrôlée
ch, chx	château(x)
dom, doms	domaine(s)

Le Havre

Caen

Brest

LOIRE

Loire

Nantes
Muscadet
Anjou-Saumur

La Rochelle

BORDEAUX

Médoc
Bordeaux
Pomerol
St-Emilion
Graves
Entre-Deux-
Sauternes
Côtes du
Marmanda
Buzet
Tursan
Côtes du
St-Mon
Biarritz
Madira
Jurançon

Since we're looking particularly at grapes in this year's book, it's worth pointing out that France has always been at the centre of the international versus indigenous debate. First, nearly all the grapes that have become known as international varieties – Cabernet Sauvignon, Merlot, Chardonnay, Sauvignon Blanc, and now Syrah and Pinot Noir – have their origins in France, and are responsible for some of the country's greatest wines. But second, France's appellation laws have prevented winemakers in less lucky regions from taking advantage of the popularity of Cabernet, Chardonnay and the rest of them.

At least, that was how we might have put it back in the 1980s, when it seemed blinkered to forbid growers in, say, Pacherenc du Vic-Bihl from uprooting their barely saleable Courbu and Petit Manseng and planting Chardonnay. Now we applaud them for their

foresight and tenacity in making growers hold on to a precious heritage. Chardonnay!. Huh! We're over Chardonnay. But Petit Manseng, now....

France's vineyards are, thankfully, still full of such vines – some of them becoming familiar, some still hardly known. The Southwest has many; so does the Midi, even though international varieties made great headway there by ducking the AC rules and selling themselves as Vins de Pays. You'll find many mentioned in the pages that follow. And even if many of them never get a single mention on a back label, far less get bandied about over the dinner table, they're still important: they remind us where we've come from, and of the vast complexity of that wonderful plant, the grapevine.

France entries also cross-reference to Châteaux of Bordeaux

Recent vintages of the French classics

Red Bordeaux

Médoc / Red Graves For some wines, bottle age is optional: for these it is indispensable. Minor châteaux from light vintages need only 2 or 3 years, but even modest wines of great years can improve for 15 or so, and the great châteaux of these years can profit from double that time.

2013 Worst vintage since 1992. Disastrous spring, rain and rot. Patchy success at classed-growth level; some good wines are emerging.

2012 Erratic weather. Small crop. Difficulties ripening Cab Sauv. Forward, fruit-driven style. Be choosy.

2011 Complicated year: spring drought, cool July, rain, heat, rot. Indian summer saved the day. Mixed quality. Classic freshness with moderate alcohol levels. Modest crus ready to drink.

2010 Outstanding. Magnificent Cab Sauv, deep-coloured, concentrated, firmly structured. At a price. To keep for years.

2009 Outstanding year, touted as "The Greatest". Structured wines with an exuberance of fruit. Don't miss this. Start simple wines for a treat.

2008 Much better than expected; fresh, classic flavours. Cab Sauv ripened in late-season sun. Ageing potential.

2007 Miserable summer, a difficult year. Not many will age. Be selective.

2006 Cab Sauv difficulty ripening; best fine, tasty, nervous, long-ageing. Good colour, acidity. Starting to drink.

2005 Rich, balanced, long-ageing; outstanding vintage. Keep all major wines.

2004 Mixed bag; top wines good in a classic mould. Drinking now.

2003 Hottest summer on record. Cab Sauv can be great (St-Estèphe, Pauillac). Atypical but rich, powerful at best (keep), unbalanced at worst (drink up). Be warned. Soon, for most.

2002 Some good wines if selective. Drink now–2018.

2001 Some excellent fresh wines. Drinking well now.

Older fine vintages: 00 98 96 95 90 89 88 86 85 82 75 70 66 62 61 59 55 53 49 48 47 45 29 28.

St-Émilion / Pomerol

2013 Difficult flowering (so tiny crop) and rot in Merlot. Modest to poor year.

2012 Conditions as Médoc. Earlier harvested Merlot marginally more successful.

2011 Complicated, as in the Médoc. Lower alcohol than 2010 and 2009. Good Cab Fr. Pomerol perhaps best overall. Don't shun it.

2010 Outstanding. Powerful wines again with high alcohol. Small berries so a lot of concentration.

2009 Again, outstanding. Powerful wines (high alcohol) but seemingly balanced. Hail in St-Émilion cut production at certain estates.

2008 Similar conditions to the Médoc. Tiny yields helped quality, which is surprisingly good. Starting to drink but best will age.

2007 Same pattern as the Médoc. Huge disparity in picking dates (up to five weeks). Extremely variable, but nothing to keep for long.

2006 Rain and rot at harvest. Earlier-ripening Pomerol a success but St-Émilion and satellites variable.

2005 Same conditions as the Médoc. An overall success. Start to drink.

2004 Merlot often better than 2003 (Pomerol). Good Cab Fr.

2003 Merlot suffered in the heat, but exceptional Cab Fr. Very mixed. Top St-Émilion on the plateau good. Most need drinking.

2002 Problems with rot and ripeness. Modest to good. Drink.

2001 Some powerful Merlot, sometimes better than 2000. Drinking well now. Older fine vintages: 00 98 95 90 89 88 85 82 71 70 67 66 64 61 59 53 52 49 47 45.

Red burgundy

Côte d'Or Côte de Beaune reds generally mature sooner than grander wines of Côte de Nuits. Earliest drinking dates are for lighter commune wines – eg. Volnay, Beaune; latest for *grands crus*, eg. Chambertin, Musigny. Even the best burgundies are more attractive young than equivalent red Bordeaux.

2013 Another hailstorm horror for red Côte de Beaune: looks tricky for Volnay, Pommard, Beaune, Savigny. Small crop for Nuits, unlikely to be as fine as 2012.

2012 Very small crop of fine wines in Côte de Nuits after disastrous flowering. Côte de Beaune even worse affected after multiple hailstorms. Exuberant yet classy wines.

2011 Some parallels with 2007, an early harvest but indifferent summer. But thicker skins in 2011 mean more structured wine. Small crop again.

2010 Much better than expected. Fresh and classic red, gaining in reputation all the time. Fine-boned classics. Now to 2030?

2009 Beautiful, ripe, plump reds; will be accessible before the 2005s. Slightly clumsy adolescents now. Beware overripe examples. Now to 2030?

2008 Fine, fresh, structured wines from those who avoided fungal diseases, disaster for others. Pick carefully. Start drinking. Best wines show Pinot purity. Now to 2025.

2007 Small crop of attractive, perfumed wines. Many now ready to drink. Rather good in Côte de Beaune. Now to 2020.

2006 An attractive year in Côte de Nuits (less rain) with power to develop in medium term. Côte de Beaune reds good now. Best to 2025.

2005 Best for more than a generation, outstanding everywhere. Top wines must be kept, however tempting. Enjoy generics and lesser village wines now. Otherwise 2018–2040.

2004 Lighter wines, some pretty, others spoiled by herbaceous flavours. Drink up.

2003 Reds coped with the heat better than the whites. Muscular, rich. Best outstanding, others short and hot. No hurry for top wines.

2002 Mid-weight wines of great class with an attractive point of freshness. Now showing their paces. No hurry. Now to 2027.

2001 Just needed a touch more sun for excellence. Good to drink now.

Older fine vintages: 99 96 (keep) 95 93 90 88 85 78 71 69 66 64 62 61 59 (mature).

White burgundy

Côte de Beaune White wines now rarely made for ageing as long as they used to. Top wines should still improve for up to ten years.

2013 The July hail spared the white vineyards. It won't be uniform, but some whites are looking good already.

2012 Tiny production after calamitous flowering and subsequent hail. Decent weather later; very intense, sometimes fine but some are clumsy.

2011 Large harvest; fine potential for conscientious producers, some flesh and good balance, but was easy to overcrop. Attractive early and drinking well.

2010 Exciting wines with good fruit-acid balance, some damaged by September storms. Meursault and Corton-Charlemagne are first class. Now to 2020.

2009 Full crop, healthy grapes, definite charm, but enough acidity to age? Yes if picked early, otherwise start drinking.

2008 Small crop, ripe flavours yet high acidity. Very fine; keep best. Now to 2020.

2007 Big crop – those who picked late did very well. Drink soon.

2006 Plentiful crop of charming, aromatic wines. Drink up.

2005 Small, outstanding crop; dense, concentrated wines. Some currently lack charm so give them time. Some showing at least superficial oxidation.

2004 Aromatic, sometimes herbaceous whites. Drink soon.

Mâconnais (Pouilly-Fuissé, St-Véran, Mâcon-Villages) follow a similar pattern, but do not last as long: appreciated more for their freshness than their richness.

Chablis *Grand cru* Chablis of vintages with both strength and acidity can age superbly for 10 years or more; *premiers crus* proportionately less, but give them 3 years at least.

2013 Small crop, late harvest, some rot issues. Expect a mixed bag at best.

2012 Crop not quite as tiny as the Côte d'Or, but too small nonetheless. Early pickers ultra-concentrated and classically austere; late pickers soft and low-acid, after rain.

2011 Early season with large crop of attractive wines. Similar to 2002. 2015–2025.

2010 Harvested at same time as Côte d'Or; excellent results. Fine vintage: body, powerful mineral acidity. A great year for classical Chablis. 2015–2030.

2009 Rich, accessible wines, less mineral than 2007 or 2008. 2012–2016.

2008 Excellent; small crop of powerful, juicy wines; ageing potential. 2012–2020.

2007 Brilliant *grands crus* and *premiers crus* where not damaged by hail. Basic Chablis not so good, drink up. 2012–2017.

Beaujolais 13 Late vintage with mixed results. 12 Tiny crop, economic misery, vineyards abandoned. 11 Third smasher in a row! The best of all? 10 Compact and concentrated, maturing now. 09 Wonderful, the best for years, reigniting interest in Beaujolais. 08 Tough going with widespread hail. 05 Concentrated wines, best still worth keeping.

Southwest France

2013 As for 2012, but more so. Appalling hail, storms and rot drastically reduced yields. Good harvest conditions, ironically.

2012 Hail, frost and cold weather until mid-June reduced the crop, but what was made shows promise.

2011 Good, but Cahors and Madiran tend to be overblown. Excellent whites.

2010 Indian summer ensured good crop overall. Good year for current drinking.

2009 Reliable. For current drinking.

2008 Moderate. Late sunshine just about saved the day.

2007 Late rain spoiled all but Madiran and sweet whites.

The Midi

2013 Very wet spring. Tricky flowering, some areas better than others. Late harvest (until mid-October). Good results: no water stress; ripe, healthy grapes.

2012 Quantity was down, but quality is good; wines developing well.

2011 Coolish summer, so fresher wines, nicely balanced. Quality, quantity good.

2010 Fine quality; yields lower than usual thanks to a summer drought.

2009 Cool spring; hot, dry summer. Excellent quality, drinking beautifully.

2008 Similar to 2007, some elegant wines are drinking well. Severe hail damage in Faugères.

Northern Rhône

2013 Tricky summer, late, reduced harvest. Syrah has good body, tannins fit in well. 15 years for top wines. Good, sustained whites, especially Condrieu.

2012 Good to very good; slow evolution reds with strong structure. Best will go at least 15 years. Whites have style, freshness, especially Condrieu.

2011 Mid-weight year. Sound, fun fruit at Crozes-Hermitage, gd at Hermitage, Cornas. Côte-Rôtie needs time. Better than 2008. Whites fresh, satisfactory.

2010 Wonderful. Reds: marvellous fruit, balance, freshness, flair. Long-lived. Côte-Rôtie as good as 1978. Very good Condrieu, rich whites elsewhere.

2009 Excellent, sun-packed wines. Some deep, rich Hermitage, very full Côte-Rôtie. Best Crozes, St-Joseph ageing well. Rather big whites: can live.

2008 Rain; wines gaining depth bit by bit. Top names best. Good, clear whites: will live (Condrieu). Reds: 8–12 years.

2007 Shapely, attractive depth, ageing well. Best Hermitage, Côte-Rôtie, Cornas, St-Joseph for 18 years+. Good whites, still doing well.

2006 Rich, satisfying wines, now excellent, especially Côte-Rôtie. Good acidity in robust whites, heady Condrieu.

2005 Mostly excellent, be patient with tannins. Long ageing potential for Hermitage, Cornas, fullest Côte-Rôtie. Full whites drinking well now.

2004 Mid-weight, supple but fine wines, especially Côte-Rôtie. Superb whites really singing now in complex maturity.

2003 Intense sun gave cooked "southern" flavours. Best reds show genuine richness but still need time. 25 years+ for best.

Southern Rhône

2013 Tiny Grenache yields, so blends will reflect that. Fair quality, lower alcohol than usual. Laudun, Lirac, Tavel fared okay. Good whites.

2012 Very good. Full, dark reds. Well-filled, food-friendly whites. Good rosés (Tavel).

2011 Immediate, supple fruit; tannins very mild: drink quite early. Grenache top at Châteauneuf. Côtes du Rhône reds very good value.

2010 Excellent, full-bodied, well-balanced reds. Top year at Châteauneuf. Clear-fruited, well-packed tannins. Interesting, full, food-friendly whites.

2009 Full reds. Drought: some baked features, grainy tannins. Châteauneuf reds very ripe; Côtes du Rhône/Villages reds good now. Sound whites.

2008 Dodgy, but best now drink well, ideal in restaurants; life 12–15 years or so. Stay with top names. Very good, lively whites.

2007 Very good: Grenache-only wines big, but drink with gusto. Exceptional Châteauneuf from top names. Drink up Côtes du Rhônes, whites.

2006 Underrated; fruity, flavoursome Châteauneufs, Gigondas: more open than 2005, less sweet, potent than 2007. Good full whites, ideal for food.

2005 Very good, slow to evolve. Tight-knit, serious, concentrated. Will age well: 20 years+ for top Châteauneufs. Whites developed well, have real body.

2004 Good, but variable. Mineral, intricate flavours in Châteauneuf. Gigondas best: grainy, profound. Drinking well now. Gd, complex whites ageing well.

2003 Chunky, high-octane wines (Châteauneuf, Gigondas) coming together. Go for best names, areas.

Champagne

2013 Cold spring, uneven flowering, but sun smiled on latest Marne harvest for 20 years. Reverse of 2012, Chard year of great vintage promise: Pinot N more mixed, Aÿ the glorious exception. Aube hit by hail, rain.

2012 Sunny August and warm September saved day. Small crop of outstanding Pinot N and Meunier, best since 1952. Chards less brilliant.

2011 Dubious vintage quality.

2009 Ripeness, charm and refined aromas will give great pleasure earlier than the 2008s. Sumptuous Pinot N from Aube.

2008 One of the three best vintages since 2000. Classic balance of acidity, ripeness; real keeper, though more austere than lovely 2002.

2006 Ripe, expressive wines. Supple, fine, drink soon while you wait for best 2002s. Deutz, Roederer Cristal, Armand Margaine stand out.

Older fine vintages: 04 02 00 96 95 92 90 89 88 82 76.

The Loire

2013 Very difficult, challenging, late vintage. Widespread rot forced producers' hands. Low sugar levels, high acidity. Some attractive wines for early drinking. A little sweet in Anjou. Small crop, not as small as 2012.

2012 Very difficult and small vintage: frost, widespread mildew. Melon de Bourgogne, Sauv Bl high quality, little sweet wine made.

2011 Topsy-turvy year needed skill, timing. Rot in Muscadet. Quality very variable. Some fine sweet Anjou.

2010 Beautifully balanced dry whites, great Anjou sweet. Some reds better than 2009. Long ageing potential.

2009 Generally very good. High alcohol a problem in some Sauv Bl.

2008 Very healthy grapes, high acidity. Good age-worthy reds, excellent dry whites (Chenin Bl), sweets hit by wet November.

2007 Producer's name crucial. Austere dry whites, exceptional Anjou sweets. Drink up reds.

Alsace

2013 Fine, crisp and mineral wines with elegant acidity. Ries year.

2012 Small crop of concentrated wines, in style of 2010.

2011 Wines of charm and aroma for early drinking.

2010 Very small crop, excellent wines for long keeping, most naturally dry.

2009 Great Pinot Gr, Gewurz; some fine late-harvest wines.

2008 Dry, crisp wines: Ries a great delight, especially Weinbach, Trimbach.

2007 Hot spring; cold, wet summer; sunny autumn: ripe grapes. Drink up.

2006 Hottest recorded July, coolest August. Top names made subtle, fine Ries.

Abymes Sav w ★ DYA. Hilly area nr Chambéry; light, mild VIN DE SAV AC from Jacquère grape has Alpine charm. Sav has many such crus.

Ackerman Lo r p w (dr) (sw) (sp) ★→★★ Major négociant. First SAUMUR sparkling wine house. Alliance Loire (eight CAVE-co-ops) a shareholder. Ackerman group, incl Rémy-Pannier and Monmousseau (bought 2010), wines throughout Loire, many from its own wineries. Only large pan-Loire négociant still in local hands.

Agenais SW Fr r p w ★ DYA IGP of Lot-et-Garonne. Gd-value DOMS du Boiron, Lou Gaillot, Campet head competition with usually dull co-ops.

Alliet, Philippe Lo r w ★★→★★★ 02 04 05' 06 08 09' 10 11 12 Top CHINON producer; CUVÉES to age. Best: oak-aged Coteau Noire (steep slope east of Chinon) Tradition, VIEILLES VIGNES from flat gravel; hill v'yd L'Huisserie. Believes in wood ageing.

Aloxe-Corton Burg r w ★★ →★★★ 99' 02' 03 05' 06 07 08 09' 10' 11 12' 13 Northern end of the CÔTE DE BEAUNE, famous for its GRANDS CRUS (CORTON, CORTON-CHARLEMAGNE), but less interesting at village or PREMIER CRU level. Reds attractive if not overextracted. Best producers: Follin-Arbelet, PIERRE ANDRÉ, Senard, TOLLOT-BEAUT.

Alquier, Jean-Michel L'doc r w Leading FAUGÈRES producer. White MARSANNE/GRENACHE BLANC. Also SAUV Les Pierres Blanches IGP, red CUVÉES Les Premières (younger vines), Maison Jaune, outstanding age-worthy old-vine SYRAH, Les Bastides. Do not confuse with brother, Frédéric.

Alsace (r) w (sw) (sp) ★★ →★★★★ 04 05 06' 08' 09 10' 11 12 13' Sheltered eastern slope of Vosges Mts makes France's Rhine wines: aromatic, fruity, full-strength,

> **AOP and IGP: what's happening in France**
> The Europe-wide introduction of AOP (*Appellation d'Origine Protegée*) and
> IGP (*Indication Géographique Protegée*) means that these terms may now
> appear on labels. AC will continue to be used, but for simplicity and
> brevity this book now uses IGP for all former VDP.

mostly dry and expressive of variety. Sugar levels vary widely: dry wines now
mainstream again. Much sold by variety (PINOT BL, RIES, GEWURZ). Matures well
(except Pinot Bl, MUSCAT) 5–10 yrs; GRAND CRU even longer. Gd-quality and
-value CRÉMANT. Formerly fragile PINOT N improving fast (esp 10) now looking v.
drinkable. *See* VENDANGE TARDIVE, SÉLECTION DES GRAINS NOBLES.

Alsace Grand Cru w ★★★→★★★★★ 90' 9702 05 06 07 08' 09 10' 11 12 13' AC restricted
to 51 (KAEFFERKOPF added in 2006) of the best-named v'yds (approx 1,600 ha, 800
in production) and four noble grapes (RIES, PINOT GR, GEWURZ, MUSCAT), mainly dry,
some sweet. New, much-needed production rules incl higher min ripeness, ban
on *chaptalization*.

Amiel, Mas Rouss r w sw ★★★ Leading and innovative MAURY DOM, with others
following. Serious CÔTES DU ROUSS *Carérades* (r), Altaïr (w), *vin de liqueur* Plénitude
from MACCABEU. Vintage wines and cask-aged VDN. Prestige 15 yrs the star.
STÉPHANE DERENONCOURT (B'X) consults.

Amirault, Yannick Lo r ★★→★★★★ 03 04 05' 06 08' 09' 10' 11 Standout producer of
BOURGUEIL, ST-NICOLAS-DE-BOURGUEIL. Organic. Top CUVÉES: La Petite Cave, Les
Quartiers (BOURGUEIL); Malagnes, La Mine (St-Nicolas). Son Benoît fully involved.

André, Pierre C d'O r w ★★ Sound producer, mainly négociant but also grower at CH
Corton-André, ALOXE-CORTON; 5 ha v'yds in and around CORTON.

Alsace Pinot Noir improving enormously; being chased by Baden Spätburgunder.

Anjou Lo r p w (dr) (sw) (sp) ★→★★★★ Both region and umbrella AC covering ANJOU,
SAUMUR. Many styles: CHENIN BL dry whites, light quaffers to potent agers; juicy
reds, incl GAMAY; fruity CAB FR-based Anjou Rouge; age-worthy but tannic ANJOU-
VILLAGES, incl CAB SAUV. Strong, mainly dry SAVENNIÈRES; lightly sweet to luscious
COTEAUX DU LAYON CHENIN BL; dry and semi-sweet rosé, sparkling. AC Anjou v.
variable (can be excellent, v.gd value). Little sweet made 2012 or 13; buy 10 11.

Anjou-Coteaux de la Loire Lo w sw s/sw ★★→★★★ 02 03 05' 07' 09 10' 11 Small
westernmost ANJOU AC for sweet whites from CHENIN BL; less rich but nervier than
COTEAUX DU LAYON. Esp Delaunay, Fresche, Musset-Roullier, CH de Putille. Little
made in 2012 or 13.

Anjou-Villages Lo r ★→★★★ 03 05' 06 08 09' 10' 11 12 (13) Superior central ANJOU
AC for reds (CAB FR/CAB SAUV, but a few pure Cab Sauv often top wines). Tannins
can be fierce but top wines are gd-value esp, Bergerie, Branchereau, Brizé, CADY,
CLOS de Coulaine, Delesvaux, Ogereau, CH Pierre-Bise, Sauveroy. Sub-AC Anjou-
Villages-Brissac covers same zone as COTEAUX DE L'AUBANCE; esp Bablut, DOM de
Haute Perche, Montigilet, Princé, Richou, Rochelles, Ch de Varière.

Appellation Contrôlée (AC or AOC) / AOP Government control of origin and
production (but not quality) of most top French wines; around 45% of total. Now
being converted to AOP (*Appellation d'Origine Protegée*).

Aprémont Sav w ★★ DYA One of the best villages of SAV for pale, delicate whites,
mainly from Jacquère grapes, but recently gd CHARD.

Arbin Sav r ★★ Deep-coloured, lively red from MONDEUSE grapes, rather like a Loire
CAB SAUV. Ideal après-ski. Drink at 1–2 yrs.

Arbois Jura r p w (sp) ★★→★★★ Various gd original wines, real sense of terroir;
speciality is VIN JAUNE. Best producers: Stephane Tissot, Jacques Puffeney. Gd
CRÉMANT sparkling from local co-op.

Ariège SW Fr r p w ★ 10 11 (12') (13) Tiny cult IGP south of Toulouse, headed by ★★ DOM des Coteaux d'Engravies. Also ★ Doms Sabarthès, Lastronques.

Arlaud C d'O r ★★★ Fine MOREY-ST-DENIS estate: CHARMES-CHAMBERTIN, CLOS DE LA ROCHE, etc; energized by new generation. Ploughing by horse. Fine BOURGOGNE Roncevie.

Arlot, Domaine de l' C d'O r w ★★→★★★ Formerly famous exponent of whole-bunch fermentation (to 2010), but style modified under new management. AXA taking closer control. NUITS-ST-GEORGES CLOS des Forêts St Georges offers haunting fragrance, also VOSNE-ROMANÉE Suchots, ROMANÉE-ST-VIVANT. Rare whites v.gd too.

Armand, Comte C d'O r ★★★ Sole owner of exceptional CLOS des Epeneaux in POMMARD and other v'yds in AUXEY, VOLNAY. On top form since 1999. Bio.

Aube Champ Southern v'yds of CHAMP, aka Côte de Bar. V.gd PINOT N 09 10.

Auxey-Duresses C d'O r w ★★ 99' 02' 03 05' 06 07 08 09' 10' 11 12 CÔTE DE BEAUNE village tucked away out of sight behind MEURSAULT. Reds more fragrant, less rustic than before; attractive mineral whites. Best: (r) COMTE ARMAND, COCHE-DURY, Gras, MAISON LEROY (Les Boutonniers), Prunier; (w) Lafouge, ROULOT.

Aveyron proverb: "Wine should be drunk neat in the morning, without water at midday and in the evening just as the good Lord gave it us."

Aveyron SW Fr r p (w) ★ IGP DYA. Upland *département*, incl MARCILLAC ENTRAYGUES. Cult NATURAL winemakers ★★ Nicolas Carmarans, Patrick Rols revive obscure local grapes (eg. Négret de Banhars). DOMS Bertau, Pleyjean more orthodox.

Avize Champ Fine Côte des Blancs CHARD village. Excellent growers' wines, Selosses (incl Agrapart) on top form.

Aÿ Champ Revered PINOT N village, home of BOLLINGER; powerful wines. Mix of merchants and growers', wines often made in barrel: eg. Claude Giraud, master of Argonne oak and seminal influence.

Ayala Champ sp Revitalized AŸ-based house, owned by BOLLINGER. Fine BRUT Nature zéro *Dosage*, v.gd Rosé. Excellent Prestige Perle d'Ayala 05 06 08' 09 12'. New winemaker. Value.

Bachelet Burg r w ★★→★★★ Widespread family name in Burg. Excellent whites from B-Monnot (MARANGES), Jean-Claude B (ST-AUBIN), B-Ramonet (CHASSAGNE) while at other end of C D'O Denis Bachelet makes heady GEVREY-CHAMBERTIN.

Bandol Prov r p (w) ★★★ 96 97 98 99 00 01 02 03 04 05 06 07 08 09 10 11 12 13 Compact coastal AC; PROV's best. Superb barrel-aged reds; ageing potential enormous. MOURVÈDRE the key, with GRENACHE, CINSAULT; stylish rosé from young vines, and a drop of white from CLAIRETTE, UGNI BLANC, occasionally SAUV BL. Stars incl: DOMS de la Laidière, Lafran Veyrolles, La Suffrène, TEMPIER, Pibarnon, Mas de la Rouvière, La Bégude, La Bastide Blanche, Terrebrune, Vannières, Gros'Noré.

Banyuls Rouss br sw ★★ →★★★ Characterful VDN, mainly GRENACHE (GRAND CRU, aged 2 yrs+). Newer vintage style resembles Ruby Port; more satisfying are traditional RANCIOS, aged for yrs. Think fine old Tawny Port or even Madeira. Best: DOMS du Mas Blanc (★★★), de la Rectorie (★★★), Vial Magnères, Courne del Mas (★★), la Tour Vieille (★★★). CLOS de Paulilles, Madeloc. *See also* MAURY.

Barrique The B'X (and Cognac) term for an oak barrel holding 225 litres. Used globally, but the global mania for excessive new oak is now mercifully fading. Oak dominating fruit now looks dated.

Barsac Saut w sw ★★→★★★★ 88' 89' 90' 95 96 97' 98 99' 01' 02 03' 05' 07' 09' 10' 11' 12 (13) Neighbour of SAUTERNES with similar superb botrytized wines from lower-lying limestone soil; fresher, less powerful. Some success in 2012, contrary to Sauternes. Top: CLIMENS, COUTET, DOISY-DAËNE, DOISY-VÉDRINES, NAIRAC.

Barthod, Ghislaine C d'O r ★★★→★★★★ Wines of perfume, delicacy, yet depth, concentration. Impressive range of nine PREMIER CRUS in CHAMBOLLE-MUSIGNY incl Les Baudes, Charmes, Cras, Fuées.

Bâtard-Montrachet C d'O w ★★★★ 99' 00 02' 04' 05' 06 07' 08' 09' 10 11 12 13 12 ha GRAND CRU downslope from LE MONTRACHET itself. Grand, hefty whites that should need time. Neighbours Bienvenues-B-M and Criots B-M usually a touch lighter. Seek out: BACHELET-Monnot, BOILLOT, CARILLON, GAGNARD, FAIVELEY, LATOUR, DOM LEFLAIVE, MOREY, Pernot, Ramonet, SAUZET, VOUGERAIE.

Baudry, Domaine Bernard Lo r p w ★★ →★★★ 03 05 06 08 09' 10' 11 12 (13) 30 ha; gravel plain and limestone slopes. Top CHINON across the range, from CHENIN BL whites to CAB FR (r p); from delicious Les Granges to structured Les Grézeaux, CLOS Guillot, Croix Boissées. Organic; hand-harvested. Son Matthieu now in charge.

Baudry-Dutour Lo r p w (sp) ★★ →★★★ 03 05' 06 08 09' 10' 11 (13) CHINON's largest producer, incl CHX de St Louand and La Grille (bought 2009; new visitor centre 2013). Reliable quality from light, early drinking to age-worthy reds. Modern wineries at Panzoult, la Grille. Screwcapped Chinon Blanc.

Baumard, Domaine des Lo r p w sw sp ★★→★★★ 03 05 06 07' (sw) 08 09 10 11 Controversial producer of ANJOU wine, esp CHENIN BL whites, incl SAVENNIÈRES (CLOS St Yves, Clos du Papillon), QUARTS DE CHAUME, Clos Ste Catherine. Proponent of high yielding *vignes larges* and cryoextraction (freezing grapes to concentrate sugars). Big declaration of 2012 Quarts de Chaume. 2013 looks more credible.

Baux-en-Provence, Les Prov r p w ★★ →★★★ 06 07 08 09 10 11 12 13 V'yds on dramatic bauxite outcrop of the Alpilles round tourist village of Les Baux. White from CLAIRETTE, GRENACHE, Rolle, ROUSSANNE. Reds CAB SAUV, SYRAH, Grenache. Most v'yds organic. Best estate by far is TRÉVALLON: Cab Sauv/Syrah blend (IGP for lack of Grenache). Tourism can breed complacency. Also Estoublon, Mas de la Dame, DOM Hauvette, Ste Berthe, CH Romanin, Terres Blanches.

Béarn SW Fr r p w ★→★★ (r) 10 11 (12) (13) (p w) DYA. AOP rosés best here, esp from co-op at Bellocq. ★★ DOM Lapeyre/Guilhémas best for reds and rare whites from Ruffiat de Moncade grape.

Beaujolais r (p) (w) ★ DYA. The most basic appellation of the huge Beauj region. Light wines; dire straits. Can now be rebranded as COTEAUX BOURGUIGNONS. Beauj from hills can be excellent.

Beaujolais Primeur / Nouveau More of an event than a drink.The BEAUJ of the new vintage, hurriedly made for release at midnight on the third Wednesday in Nov. Should be headily fruity and tempting; may be sharp or alcoholic.

Beaujolais-Villages r ★★ 09' 10' 11' 12 13 The middle category between straight BEAUJOLAIS and the ten named crus, ie. MOULIN-À-VENT. Pay the extra. Best, around Beaujeu, Lantigné, worth waiting for.

Beaumes-de-Venise S Rhô r (p) (w) br ★★ (r) 07' 08 09' 10' 11 12' (MUSCAT) DYA. CÔTES DU RHÔ village south of GIGONDAS, known for VDN Muscat apéritif. Serve v. cold: grapey, honeyed, can be fine, eg. DOMS Beaumalric, Bernardins (musky, traditional), Durban (rich), Fenouillet, JABOULET, Pigeade (fresh, v.gd), VIDAL-FLEURY, co-op. Also punchy, grainy reds, best in warm yrs. (CH Redortier, Doms Cassan, de Fenouillet, Durban, St-Amant, la Ferme St-Martin.) Leave for 2–3 yrs. Simple whites (some dry Muscat, VIOGNIER), lively rosés are Côtes du Rhô.

Beaumont des Crayères Champ sp Côte d'Epernay co-op making model PINOT MEUNIER-based Grande Rés NV. Vintage Fleur de Prestige top value 04 06 08' 09 11 12. Great CHARD-led CUVÉE Nostalgie 02' 06 08. Fleur de Rosé 05 06 09.

Beaune C d'O r (w) ★★★ 02' 03 05' 07 08 09'10' 11 12 Historic walled wine capital of Burg, home of HOSPICES DE BEAUNE and classic merchants: BOUCHARD, CHAMPY, CHANSON, DROUHIN, JADOT, LATOUR, Remoissenet as well as young pretenders Gambal, Lemoine, Leroux, Roche de Bellene. No GRANDS CRUS v'yds but some graceful, perfumed reds from PREMIER CRU, eg. Bressandes, Cras, Teurons, Vignes Franches; more power from Grèves, and an increasing amount of white: Drouhin's CLOS DES MOUCHES best.

Becker, Caves J Al r w ★→★★ Organic estate, progressively bio. Stylish wines, incl exceptional GRAND CRU Froehn in GEWURZ, RIES 06 08' 10 13.

Bellet Prov r p w ★★ Miniscule AC; 32 ha within city of Nice, but scarcely seen there. White from Rolle grape is best, can age surprisingly. Braquet, Folle Noire for light red (DYA). A handful of valiant producers: CH de Bellet is oldest; also Les Coteaux de Bellet, CLOS St Vincent, DOM de la Source, Collet de Bovis, Toasc.

Bellivière, Domaine de Lo r w sw ★★★ 03 05' 07 08 09' 10' 11 Spread-out 13-ha bio DOM of Christine and Eric Nicolas: precise CHENIN BL in JASNIÈRES and COTEAUX DU LOIR, peppery red Pineau d'Aunis.

Bergerac SW Fr r p w dr sw ★→★★★ 05' 07' (sw) 08 09 10 11 12 (13) B'X style wines (same grapes) but without the price tag. Note esp dry crisp whites (mostly SÉM), recently more hefty reds. See recommended growers in MONBAZILLAC, MONTRAVEL, PÉCHARMANT, ROSETTE, SAUSSIGNAC, all sub-AOPs. Also: ★★★ CLOS des Verdots, *Tour des Gendres*, ★★ DOMS Jaubertie, Jonc Blanc, Les Marnières, CHX Fontenelles, Grinou.

Bertrand, Gérard L'doc r p w ★★ Ambitious ex-rugger player now one of biggest growers in the MIDI; Villemajou in CORBIÈRES cru Boutenac, Laville-Bertou in MINERVOIS-LA LIVINIÈRE, l'Aigle in LIMOUX, IGP PAYS D'OC Cigalus, la Sauvageonne in Terrasses du Larzac. Flagship is l'Hospitalet in LA CLAPE.

Besserat de Bellefon Champ Épernay house specializing in gently sparkling CHAMPAGNES (old CRÉMANT style). Part of LANSON-BCC group. Respectable quality, decent value.

Beyer, Léon Al r w ★★→★★★ V. fine, intense, dry wines often needing 10 yrs+ bottle age. Superb RIES Comtes d'Eguisheim 08' 10 but no mention on label of v'yd (GRAND CRU PFERSIGBERG). Pure, dry wines for great cuisine. Now finer PINOT NS 10' 12.

Bichot, Maison Albert Burg r w ★★→★★★ Major BEAUNE merchant/grower. Steadily more impressive wines in a powerful, somewhat oaky style. Best wines from own DOMS, LONG-DEPAQUIT (CHABLIS), CLOS Frantin (NUITS), du Pavillon (Beaune).

Bienvenues-Bâtard-Montrachet C d'O ★★★→★★★★ 02' 04 05 06 07 08 09 10 11 12 13 Fractionally lighter, earlier-maturing version of BÂTARD, with accessible, creamy texture. Best: BACHELET-Monnot, CARILLON, LEFLAIVE, Pernot, Ramonet.

Billecart-Salmon Champ Family house with beautiful, long-lived wines, vintage CUVÉES fermented in wood. Superb CLOS St-Hilaire BLANC DE NOIRS 96' 99 02, NF Billecart 98 99 00 02' 04 08' 12', top BLANC DE BLANCS 99 00, BRUT 06, Extra Brut ★★★ NV. New oaked CUVÉE Sous Bois. Exquisite *Elizabeth Salmon Rosé* 99' 02 04.

Bize, Simon C d'O r w ★★→★★★ Key producer in SAVIGNY-LÈS-BEAUNE with wide range of PREMIER CRU v'yds, esp Vergelesses; also v.gd-value BOURGOGNE (r w). Top wine: LATRICIÈRES-CHAMBERTIN. Owner Patrick Bize much mourned after untimely death in Oct 2013.

Blagny C d'O r ★★→★★★ 99' 02' 03' 05' 07 08 09' 10' 11 12 13 On hill south of MEURSAULT, above PULIGNY. Austere reds out of fashion as growers replant with CHARD, sold as Meursault-Blagny PREMIER CRU. Best red v'yds: Pièce sous le Bois, Sous le Dos d'Ane, La Jeunelotte. Best growers (r): Matrot, Martelet de Cherisey.

Blanc de Blancs Any white wine made from white grapes only, esp CHAMP. Indication of style, not of quality.

Blanc de Noirs White (or slightly pink or "blush") wine from red grapes, esp CHAMP. Generally rich, even four-square, in style.

Blanck, Paul & Fils Al r w ★★→★★★ Grower at Kientzheim with huge range. Finest from 6 ha GRAND CRU Furstentum (RIES, GEWURZ, PINOT GR), *grand cru* SCHLOSSBERG (great Ries 06 08' 10 12 13). Also gd PINOT BL.

Blanquette de Limoux L'doc w sp ★★ Great-value bubbles from cool hilly area southwest of Carcassonne; older history than CHAMP. Based on Mauzac; much improved by CHARD, CHENIN BL and, more recently, PINOT N. AC CRÉMANT de Limoux is more elegant. Large co-op with Sieur d'Arques label. Also Rives-Blanques, Antech, Laurens, Robert, Delmas.

Blaye B'x r ★→★★ 05' 06 08 09' 10' 11 12 Designation for top, concentrated reds (lower yields, etc.) from what used to be Premières Côtes de Blaye, renamed AC BLAYE-CÔTES DE B'X (2008).

Blaye-Côtes de Bordeaux r w ★→★★ 08 09' 10' 12 Mainly red AC on right bank of Gironde. A little dry white. Formerly Premières Côtes de Blaye, renamed 2008. Much better quality. Best CHX: Bel Air la Royère, Cantinot, Gigault (CUVÉE Viva), Haut-Bertinerie, Haut-Colombier, Haut-Grelot, Jonqueyres, Monconseil-Gazin, Mondésir-Gazin, Montfollet, Roland la Garde, Segonzac, des Tourtes. Also Charron and CAVE des Hauts de Gironde co-op for whites.

Boillot C d'O r w Interconnected Burg growers. Look for Jean-Marc (POMMARD) ★★★, fine oaky reds and whites; Henri (DOM and merchant in MEURSAULT) ★★→★★★★, concentrated whites and modern reds; Louis (Chambolle, married to GHISLAINE BARTHOD) ★★★ and his brother Pierre (GEVREY) ★★→★★★.

Boisset, Jean-Claude Burg r w Ultra-successful group created over last 50 yrs. Boisset label and own v'yds DOM DE LA VOUGERAIE excellent. Latest addition to empire is VINCENT GIRARDIN brand. Also projects in Canada, California, Chile, Uruguay looked after by son Jean-Charles, married to Gina Gallo of eponymous US giant.

Boizel Champ Fine aged BLANC DE BLANCS NV and prestige Joyau de France 02' 04 06 08, Joyau Rosé 02' 04 06 09. Also Grand Vintage BRUT 02' 04 06 08 09, CUVÉE Sous Bois. Fine quality, great value.

Bollinger Champ Great classic house, ace in recent vintages (viz Grande Année 95 97 00 02' 04 06). Now a NV Rosé. Great attention to PINOT N; superb GA Rosé 02. Luxury wines: RD 99' 02' 04', VIEILLES VIGNES Françaises 02, La Côte aux Enfants, AŸ 09' 12' New winemaker. *See also* LANGLOIS-CH.

Bonneau du Martray, Domaine C d'O r w (r) ★★★ (w) ★★★★ Reference producer for CORTON-CHARLEMAGNE, glorious mineral wines once again designed for long ageing. Small amount of fine red CORTON.

Bonnes-Mares C d'O r ★★★→★★★★ 90' 91 93 95 96' 98 99' 00 02' 03 05' 06 07 08 09' 10' 11 12' 13 GRAND CRU between CHAMBOLLE-MUSIGNY and MOREY-ST-DENIS with some of latter's wilder character. Sturdy, long-lived wines, less fragrant than MUSIGNY. Best: BOUCHARD PÈRE, BRUNO CLAIR, Drouhin-Laroze, DUJAC, Groffier, JADOT, MUGNIER, ROUMIER, DE VOGÜÉ, VOUGERAIE.

Bonnezeaux Lo w sw ★★★→★★★★ 89' 90' 95' 96' 97' 03' 05' 07' 09 10' 11 Wonderfully rich, almost everlasting CHENIN BL from top south-facing site in COTEAUX DU LAYON. Now less rigorous than QUARTS DE CHAUME. Esp: CHX de Fesles, de Varière, Grandes Vignes, du Petit Val. V. little 2012; 13 difficult.

Bordeaux r (p) w ★→★★ 09' 10' 12 Catch-all AC for generic B'x (represents nearly half region's production). Mixed quality, but usually recognizable. Most brands (DOURTHE, MOUTON CADET) are in this category. *See also* CHX Bauduc, BONNET, Tour de Mirambeau.

Bordeaux Supérieur r ★→★★ 08 09' 10' 12 Superior denomination to above. Higher min alcohol, lower yield and longer ageing. Mainly bottled at the property. Consistent CHX: de Courteillac, Grand Village, Landereau, PARENCHÈRE, Penin, PEY LA TOUR (Réserve), Pierrail, Reignac, THIEULEY.

Borie-Manoux B'x Admirable B'x shipper, CH-owner. Chx incl BATAILLEY, BEAU-SITE, Croix du Casse, DOM DE L'ÉGLISE, HAUT-BAGES-MONPELOU, TROTTEVIEILLE.

Bouchard Père & Fils Burg r w ★★→★★★★ Largest v'yd owner in C D'O, based in CH de Beaune. Whites esp strong in MEURSAULT and GRANDS CRUS, esp CHEVALIER-MONTRACHET. Flagship reds are BEAUNE Grèves, Vigne de L'Enfant Jésus, VOLNAY

Caillerets Ancienne CUVÉE Carnot. Basic wines okay. Part of HENRIOT Burg interests with WILLIAM FÈVRE (CHABLIS), Villa Ponciago (BEAUJ).

Bouches-du-Rhône Prov r p w ★ IGP from Marseille environs. Simple, hopefully fruity, reds from southern varieties, plus CAB SAUV, SYRAH, MERLOT.

Bourgeois, Henri Lo r w ★★ →★★★ 05 06 07 08 10 11 12 (13) Dynamic, continually investing SANCERRE grower-merchant. High quality incl POUILLY-FUMÉ, MENETOU-SALON, QUINCY, COTEAUX DU GIENNOIS, CHÂTEAUMEILLANT, IGP Petit Bourgeois. Top wines: MD de Bourgeois, La Bourgeoise (r w), Jadis, Sancerre d'Antan. Also CLOS Henri (r w) in Marlborough, NZ.

Bourgogne Burg r (p) w ★★ (r) 05' 09' 10 11 12 13 (w) 10' 11 12 13 Ground-floor AC for Burg, ranging from mass-produced to bargain beauties from fringes of C D'O villages, top tip for value. Sometimes comes with subregion attached, eg. CÔTE CHALONNAISE, Hautes Côtes or local would-be appellation, Chitry, Tonnerre, VÉZELAY, etc. From PINOT N (r) or CHARD (w) but can be declassified BEAUJ crus (sold as Bourgogne GAMAY).

Bourgogne Grand Ordinaire Burg *See* COTEAUX BOURGUIGNONS.

Bourgogne Passe-Tout-Grains Burg r (p) ★ Age 1–2 yrs. Not just any old grape but a Burg mix of PINOT N (more than 30%) and GAMAY. Can be fun from C D'O DOMS eg. CHEVILLON, Clavelier, LAFARGE, ROUGET.

Bourgueil Lo r (p) ★★ →★★★ 96' 02 03 05' 06 08 09' 10' 11 Burly, full TOURAINE reds and big, fragrant rosés based on CAB FR. Gd vintages can age 40 yrs+. Esp AMIRAULT, Audebert, DOMS de la Butte, la Chevalerie, Courant, Druet, Gambier, Herlin, Lamé Delisle Boucard, Minière, Nau Frères. *See* ST-NICOLAS-DE-BOURGUEIL.

Bouvet-Ladubay Lo w sp ★→★★★ Major sparkling SAUMUR house owned by United Breweries. MD is dynamic Patrice Monmousseau. CUVÉE Trésor (p w) best. Still wines mainly from ANJOU-Saumur. Hosts Journées Nationales du Livre et du Vin.

Bouzereau C d'O r w ★★ →★★★ Family in MEURSAULT making gd whites at sensible prices and improving reds. Jean-Baptiste (DOM Michel B), Vincent B are two best but try also B-Gruère & Filles.

Bouzeron Burg w ★★ CÔTE CHALONNAISE AC (since 1998) for ALIGOTÉ, with stricter rules and greater potential than straight BOURGOGNE AC. Briday, FAIVELEY, Jacquesson gd, A & P de Villaine best: BOURGOGNE Rouge La Digoine ★★.

Bouzy Rouge Champ r ★★★ 95 97 99 02 09 12 Still red of famous PINOT N village. Formerly like v. light burg, now more intensity (climate change?). CLOS Colin ★★★.

Brocard, J-M Chab w ★★ →★★★ Father Jean-Marc created dynamic business with ACS in and around CHABLIS. Son Julien has introduced bio principles. Successful alliance of commerce, quality. Try DOM Ste Claire.

Brouilly Beauj r ★★ 09' 10' 11' 12 13 Largest of the ten BEAUJ crus: solid, rounded wines with some depth of fruit, approachable early but can age 3–5 yrs. Top growers: CH de la Chaize, Chermette, Dubost, Lapalu, Michaud, Piron.

Brumont, Alain SW Fr r w ★★★ Still makes wines in beefy MADIRAN style (Le Tyre, CHX Montus, Bouscassé, all need long ageing), though ★ Torus is nodding towards something more modern. ★ IGPS (eg. 100% GROS MANSENG, TANNAT/CAB blends) gd for early drinking.

Brut Champ Term for the dry classic wines of CHAMP. Most houses have reduced *dosage* (adjustment of sweetness) in recent yrs.

Brut Ultra / Zéro Term for bone-dry wines (no *dosage*) in CHAMP (also known as Brut Nature) back in fashion, mixed success. Needs ripeness, old vines, maximum care.

Bugey Sav r p w sp ★→★★ DYA Sub-Alpine VDQS for light sparkling, still, or half-sparkling wines from Roussette (or Altesse), CHARD (gd). Best from Montagnieu; also Rosé de Cerdon, mainly GAMAY.

Burguet, Alain C d'O r ★★ →★★★ Compact VIGNERON for outsize GEVREY-CHAMBERTIN, esp *Mes Favorites*. Sons Eric and Jean-Luc now in charge.

FRANCE

Buxy, Caves de Burg r (p) w ★→★★ Leading co-op for decent CHARD, PINOT N; easily largest supplier of AC MONTAGNY.

Buzet SW Fr r (p) (w) ★★ 10 11 12 (13) Country claret from 60 miles up the Garonne. Quirky, bio, independent ★★★ DOM du Pech, more traditional ★★ CHX du Frandat, de Salles, easily outclass the domineering co-op. Watch for ★★ Ch Mazelières.

Cabardès L'doc r ★→★★ 06 07 08 09 10 11 12 13 MIDI/B'X crossover nr Carcassonne. CAB/MERLOT meet SYRAH/GRENACHE for unusual blends, 60% max B'x grapes, 40% min Midi. Best is DOM de Cabrol with Vin de l'Est, Vin d'Ouest; also Jouclary, Font Juvénal, Cazaban. CH Pennautier is largest.

Cabernet d'Anjou Lo p s/sw ★→★★ Sweetish rosé back in fashion. Age-worthy old vintages (★★★) rare but stunning. Now DYA. CH PIERRE-BISE, Bablut, CADY, Chauvin, Clau de Nell, Grandes Vignes, Montgilet, Ogereau, de Sauveroy, Varière.

Cabrières L'doc (r) p ★★ DYA. Energetic village co-op dominates, for warming reds, full-bodied rosé. Vines on schist hillsides nr Pic de Vissou. New estate Deux Rocs.

Cadillac-Côtes de Bordeaux B'x r ★→★★ 05' 08 09' 10' 12 Long, narrow, hilly zone on right bank of Garonne opposite GRAVES. Formerly Premières Côtes de B'X, renamed from 2008 vintage. Medium-bodied, fresh reds. Quality extremely varied. Best: Alios de Ste-Marie, Biac, Carignan, *Carsin*, CLOS Chaumont, Clos Ste-Anne, Le Doyenné, Grand-Mouëys, Lezongars, Mont-Pérat, Plaisance, Puy Bardens, REYNON, Suau. Chinese interests here.

Cady, Domaine Lo r p sw sp ★★→★★★ 03 04 05' 07' (sw) 09 10' 11' Excellent ANJOU family grower of range from dry whites, off-dry rosés to lusciously sweet COTEAUX DU LAYON, Chaume. Sweet wines best.

Cahors SW Fr r ★★→★★★★ 01' 02 '04 05' 06 08 09 10 (11) (12') Reds only here (70% MALBEC min). Lack of policy in this AOP, so a wide range of styles to explore. Lighter, fruitier from ★★ CHX Latuc, Paillas, Les Ifs, CLOS Coutale. Bigger from ★★ Chx Armandière, La Coustarelle, Croze de Pys, Gaudou, DOMS de la Bérengeraie, du Garinet (bio), Pinéraie, Les Rigalets, Savarines (bio). Traditional, requiring ageing: ★★★ *Clos de Gamot* (Vignes Centenaires, ★★★★ Clos St Jean), Clos Triguedina. Modern: ★★★ Ch DU CÈDRE, Clos d'Un Jour, Les Croisille, Lamartine, La Périé, La Reyne, ★★ La Caminade, Eugénie. Cult ★★★★ Dom Cosse-Maisonneuve straddles the range.

Cailloux, Les S Rhô r (w) ★★★ 78' 79' 81' 85' 89' 90' 95' 96' 98' 99 00' 01 03' 04' 05' 06' 07' 09' 10' 11' 12' 18 ha CHÂTEAUNEUF DOM; stylish, floral GRENACHE, top-value elegant handmade reds. Special wine Centenaire, oldest Grenache 1889 noble, costly. Also Dom André Brunel (esp CÔTES DU RHÔ red Est-Ouest), decent Féraud-Brunel Côtes du Rhô merchant range.

Cairanne S Rhô r p w ★★→★★★ 05' 06' 07' 09' 10' 11 12' Best of CÔTES DU RHÔ-VILLAGES. Range of quality DOMS, wines of character, punchy dark fruits, smoky tannins, esp doms Alary, Ameillaud, Armand, Brusset, Escaravailles, Féraud-Brunel, Grosset, les Hautes Cances (traditional), Oratoire St Martin (classy), Présidente, Rabasse-Charavin, Richaud (great fruit), Famille Perrin. Food-suited, deep whites.

Canard-Duchêne Champ House owned by ALAIN THIÉNOT. BRUT Vintage 06 08' 09 12 13. V. fine CUVÉE Léonie ★★★. Basic wine simple and fruity.

Canon-Fronsac B'x r ★★→★★★ 01 03 05' 06 08 09' 10' 11 12 Small enclave within

---

Natural wine

An undefined, but cultish category: wine made with no chemicals, minimal sulphur (whatever that means) or none; embraces organic and bio, even skin-macerated ("orange") whites. Can be v. fine indeed, but intentionally oxidative wines can be challenging. Has seized the hand-knitted moral high ground, regardless of flavour. Made worldwide, but this entry has to go somewhere.... Best advice: go carefully.

FRONSAC, otherwise same wines. Best are rich, full, finely structured. Try CHX Barrabaque, Canon Pécresse, Cassagne Haut-Canon la Truffière, la Fleur Cailleau, DU GABY, Grand-Renouil, Haut-Mazeris, MOULIN PEY-LABRIE, Pavillon, Vrai Canon Bouché.

Carillon, Louis C d'O w ★★★ Classic PULIGNY producer, now separated between brothers. Jacques carries on old tradition; more ambitious François has added new v'yds. Top sources for PREMIERS CRUS, eg. Combettes, Perrières, Referts. Reds less interesting.

Cassis Prov (r) (p) w ★★ DYA. Fashionable pleasure port east of Marseille known for dry whites based on CLAIRETTE, MARSANNE, eg. DOM de la Ferme Blanche, CLOS Ste Magdeleine, Paternel, Fontcreuse. Growers struggle with property developers, so prices high.

Castillon-Côtes de Bordeaux r ★★ →★★★ 01 02 03 04 05' 08 09' 10' 12 Previously Côtes de Castillon, renamed 2008. Exciting easten neighbour of ST-ÉMILION; similar wines, usually less plump, with ageing potential; much recent investment. Top: DE L'A, D'AIGUILHE, Alcée, Ampélia, Cap de FAUGÈRES, La Clarière-Laithwaite, CLOS l'Eglise, Clos Les Lunelles, Clos Puy Arnaud, Côte Montpezat, Joanin Bécot, Montlandrie, Poupille, Robin, Verniotte, Veyry, Vieux CH Champs de Mars.

Cathiard C d'O r ★★★ Sylvain Cathiard produced brilliant, perfumed VOSNE-ROMANÉE, esp Malconsorts, and NUITS-ST-GEORGES, esp Murgers, from 90s. Since 2011 son Sébastien continues, maybe more precision but less seductive wines.

Cave Cellar, or any wine establishment.

Cave coopérative Wine-growers' co-op winery; over half of all French production. Often well-run, well-equipped and wines gd value for money, but many disappearing in economic crisis.

Cazes, Domaine Rouss r p w sw ★★→★★★ Largest organic producer in ROUSS. IGP pioneer with MERLOT, CAB SAUV. Le Canon du Maréchal now incl SYRAH, and Crédo now CÔTES DU ROUSS-VILLAGES with Ego, Alter. COLLIOURE and sublime aged RIVESALTES CUVÉE Aimé Cazes. CLOS de Paulilles in BANYULS. Now part of Advini, but still family-run. Great value.

Cépage Grape variety. *See* pp.16–26 for all.

Cérons B'x w sw ★★ 03' 05' 07 09' 10' 11 (13) Little-known sweet AC next to SAUTERNES. Less intense wines, eg. CHX de Cérons, CHANTEGRIVE, Grand Enclos.

Chablis w ★★ →★★★ 07' 08' 10' 11 12 13 Lean but lovely northern burg CHARD (except where overcropped or overoaked). My default white when properly made.

Chablis Grand Cru w ★★★ →★★★★ 00' 02' 05' 06 07' 08' 09 10' 11' 12 13 Small block of v'yds on steep slope north of river Serein. The richest CHABLIS, comparable to fine CÔTE DE BEAUNE whites. Needs age for minerality and individual style to develop. V'yds: Blanchots (floral), Bougros (incl Côte Bougerots), CLOS (usually best), Grenouilles (spicy), Preuses, Valmur, Vaudésir (plus brand La Moutonne).

Chablisienne, La Chab r w ★★→★★★ Major player, many own-label CHABLIS are supplied by this dynamic co-op. Sound wines across the whole range; top is GRAND CRU Grenouilles.

Chablis Premier Cru w ★★★ 00' 02' 05' 07' 08' 09 10' 11' 12 13 Well worth premium over straight CHABLIS: better sites on rolling hillsides; more white-flower character on south bank of river Serein (Vaillons, Montmains, Côte de Léchet), yellow fruit on north bank (Fourchaume, Mont de Milieu, Montée de Tonnerre).

Chambertin C d'O r ★★★★ 88 89 90' 93 95 96' 98 99' 01 02' 03 05' 06 07 08 09' 10' 11 12' 13 13 ha (or 28 ha incl CHAMBERTIN-CLOS DE BÈZE) of Burg's most imperious wine; amazingly dense, sumptuous, long-lived, expensive. Not everybody up to standard, but try from BOUCHARD PÈRE & FILS, Charlopin, Damoy, DUGAT-Py, DROUHIN, DOM LEROY, MORTET, PRIEUR, Rémy, ROSSIGNOL-TRAPET, ROUSSEAU, TRAPET.

Chambertin-Clos de Bèze C d'O r ★★★★ 88 89 90' 93 95 96' 98 99' 01 02' 03 05'

FRANCE

06 07 08 09' 10' 11 12' 13 May be sold under name of neighbouring CHAMBERTIN. Similarly splendid wines, velvet texture, possibly more accessible in youth. Best CLAIR, Damoy, DROUHIN, Drouhin-Laroze, FAIVELEY (incl super-CUVÉE Les Ouvrées Rodin), Groffier, JADOT, Prieuré-Roch, ROUSSEAU.

Chablis
There is no better expression of the all-conquering CHARD than the full but tense, limpid but stony wines it makes on the heavy limestone soils of CHABLIS. Best makers use little or no new oak to mask the precise definition of variety and terroir: Barat, Bessin ★, Samuel Billaud ★, Billaud-Simon ★, Boudin ★, J-M BROCARD, J Collet ★, D Dampt, V DAUVISSAT ★, B Defaix, Droin ★, DROUHIN ★, Duplessis, JEAN DURUP, FÈVRE ★, Geoffroy, J-P Grossot ★, LAROCHE, LONG-DEPAQUIT, DOM des Malandes, L Michel ★, Christian MOREAU ★, Picq ★, Pinson ★, Piuze, RAVENEAU ★, G Robin ★, Servin, Temps Perdu, Tribut, Vocoret. Simple, unqualified "Chablis" may be thin; best is PREMIER CRU or GRAND CRU. The co-op, LA CHABLISIENNE, has high standards (esp Grenouille ★) and many different labels. (★ = outstanding)

Chambolle-Musigny C d'O r ★★★ →★★★★ 90' 93 95' 96' 98 99' 02' 03 05' 07 08 09' 10' 11 12' 13 The epitome of elegance in the CÔTE DE NUITS: look for fragrance and silky texture from BONNES-MARES, MUSIGNY, Amoureuses, Charmes, Cras, Fuées. BARTHOD, MUGNIER, ROUMIER, DE VOGÜÉ the superstars but try also Amiot-Servelle, Bertheau, Digioia-Royer, DROUHIN, Felletig, Groffier, RION.

Champagne Sparkling wines of PINOTS N and MEUNIER and/or CHARD, and region (33,000 ha, 150-km east of Paris); made by *méthode traditionnelle*. Bubbles from elsewhere, however gd, cannot be Champ.

Champagne le Mesnil Champ Top-flight co-op in greatest GRAND CRU CHARD village. Exceptional CUVÉE Sublime 04 08' 11' 12 13' from finest sites. Real value.

Champs-Fleuris, Domaine des Lo r p w sw ★★ →★★★ 05' 06 08 09' 10 11 12 (13) Dynamic; v.gd SAUMUR Blanc; SAUMUR-CHAMPIGNY, incl juicy, screwcapped Audace; fine CRÉMANT, incl Prestige Zéro. Succulent COTEAUX DE SAUMUR CUVÉE Sarah.

Champy Père & Cie Burg r w ★★→★★★ Ancient négociant house (1720) revitalized by Meurgey family. Own bio DOM, strong in BEAUNE and around CORTON, incl former Dom Laleure-Piot. Since 2011 also controls former Dom Louis BOILLOT, incl MONOPOLE VOLNAY CLOS de la Chapelle.

Chandon de Briailles, Domaine C d'O r w ★★→★★★ DOM known for fine, lighter style reds, esp PERNAND-VERGELESSES, Île de Vergelesses, CORTON Bressandes. Bio farming, lots of stems, no new oak define style. Some sulphur-free wines.

Chanson Père & Fils Burg r w ★→★★★ An old name in BEAUNE, now one to watch for quality, fair pricing. Try any of its Beaunes (r w) esp CLOS des Fèves (r), Clos des Mouches (w). Also great CORTON-Vergennes (w).

Chapelle-Chambertin C d'O r ★★★ 90' 93 95 96' 98 99' 01 02' 03 05' 07 08 09' 10' 11 12' 13 Neighbour of CHAMBERTIN. Fine-boned wine, less meaty. V.gd in cooler yrs. Top producers: Damoy, Drouhin-Laroze, JADOT, ROSSIGNOL-TRAPET, TRAPET, Tremblay.

Chapoutier N Rhô ★★ →★★★★ Vocal, bio grower-merchant, esp for HERMITAGE. Stylish wines, many low-yield, small plot-specific CUVÉES: thick GRENACHE CHÂTEAUNEUF: Barbe Rac, Croix de Bois (r); CÔTE-RÔTIE La Mordorée; Hermitage: L'Ermite (outstanding), Le Pavillon (r), L'Ermite, Cuvée de l'Orée (w), Le Méal (w). Also ST-JOSEPH Les Granits (r w). Complex, 100% MARSANNE N Rhô whites. Gd-value *Meysonniers Crozes*. V'yds in COTEAUX D'AIX-EN-PROV, CÔTES DU ROUSS-VILLAGES (gd DOM Bila-Haut), RIVESALTES. Michel Chapoutier has AL v'yds and Australian joint ventures, esp Doms Tournon and Terlato & Chapoutier (fragrant; fine); Portuguese: Estremadura.

> **Champagne growers to watch in 2015**
> **Claude Cazals** Exciting EXTRA-BRUT BLANC DE BLANCS 00 02' 04 06, exceptional CLOS Cazals 96 ★★★★ 99 02 04.
> **Fleury Père et Fils** Father of bio farming in Aube (1989), still the best. Lovely 09 Sonate, PINOT N 09, superb ★★★★ vintage rosé 09'. No slouch at Blanc de Blancs, incl extant PINOT BL.
> **Gonet-Médeville** Exciting DOM with fine holdings in Ambonnay and LE MESNIL. Gastronomic CHAMP built to last: superb Chante Alouette Le Mesnil, Ambonnay Grandes Ruelles 04 06 08' 09 12'.
> **Jacques Selosse** Avize's best-known grower in top form with two top releases: Le Mesnil, Les Caresses 99; Ambonnay Le Bout du Clos 02.
> **Jean-Luc Lallement** Exceptional Verzenay grower; muscular yet exquisitely refined BLANC DE NOIRS. Outstanding 12' from 2020. Great rosé too.
> **Lancelot-Pienne** Seriously underrated Cramant producer making top unoaked CHARD CUVÉES. Exquis ★★★★ Marie Pienne 08 09.
> **Lilbert et Fils** Scion of blue-chip Cramant DOM takes his GRAND CRU Chard Champ to higher level: great purity of flavours, great energy. Textbook 04 06 08 Cramant GRAND CRU.
> **Michel Loriot** Top grower on the great hill of Festigny, Marne Valley. Subtle, poised PINOT MEUNIER, expansive Chards.
> **J-M Seleque** Coming young star of Pierry, Cubry Valley, close to Épernay. Brilliant Chard, Pinots N/M cuvées. Vinous rosé, ace Vintage Comedie 08.
> **J-L Vergnon** Fine restored Le Mesnil estate making exquisite all-Chard Extra-Brut cuvées, esp Confidence 06 08' ★★★★ 09 11'.
> **Veuve Fourny** Rising Côte des Blancs star at Vertus: ★★★★★ Extra-Brut 02' 04, superb single-v'yd Clos du Faubourg Notre Dame 00 02 04' 08'.

Charbonnière, Domaine de la S Rhô r (w) ★★★ 95' 98 99' 00 01' 03 04 05' 06' 07' 09' 10' 11' 12' Progressive CHÂTEAUNEUF estate run by sisters. Sound Tradition wine, distinguished, authentic Mourre des Perdrix, also Hautes Brusquières, new L'Envol, VIEILLES VIGNES. Tasty, fresh white. Also genuine VACQUEYRAS red.

Chardonnay As well as a white wine grape, also the name of a MÂCON-VILLAGES commune, hence Mâcon-Chardonnay.

Charmes-Chambertin C d'O r ★★★ 90' 93 95 96' 98 99' 01 02' 03 05' 06 07 08 09' 10' 11 12' 13 31 ha, incl neighbour MAZOYÈRES-CHAMBERTIN, not all worthy of GRAND CRU. Best eg. have explosive deep dark-cherry fruit, sumptuous texture, fragrant finish. Try ARLAUD, BACHELET, DUGAT, DUJAC, Duroché, Jouan, LEROY, Perrot-Minot, Roty, ROUSSEAU, VOUGERAIE.

Chassagne-Montrachet C d'O r w ★★→★★★★ (w) 00 02' 04 05' 06' 07 08' 09' 10 11 12' 13 Large village at south end of CÔTE DE BEAUNE. Great whites from eg. Caillerets, La Romanée, Blanchots, GRANDS CRUS. Best reds from CLOS St Jean, Morgeot, others more rustic. Try from Coffinet, COLIN, GAGNARD, MOREY, Pillot families plus top DOMS MOREAU, Niellon, Ramonet (reds too), CH de Maltroye. But too much indifferent village white grown on land better suited to red.

Château Means an estate, big or small, gd or indifferent, particularly in B'X (see pp.96–121). Means, literally, castle or great house. In Burg, DOM is usual term.

Château-Chalon Jura w ★★★ Not a CH but AC and village. Unique dry, yellow, Sherry-like wine (SAVAGNIN grape). Develops flor (see Sherry) while ageing in barrels for min 6 yrs. Madly expensive compared to often better Sherry. Ready to drink when bottled, but ages almost forever. A curiosity, but great from top growers: Berthet-Bondet, Macle, Mossu.

Château d'Arlay Jura r w sw ★→★★ Major estate; in skilful hands. Wines incl: v.gd VIN JAUNE, VIN DE PAILLE, PINOT N, MACVIN.

Château de Beaucastel S Rhô r w ★★★★ 78′ 81′ 83 85 88 89′ 90′ 94′ 95′ 96′ 97 98′ 99′ 00′ 01′ 03′ 04 05′ 06′ 07′ 08 09′ 10′ 11′ 12′ Long time organic, top CHÂTEAUNEUF estate: old MOURVÈDRE, 100-yr ROUSSANNE. Excellent Famille Perrin S Rhô (some owned, others managed). Gd N Rhô merchant venture, Nicolas Perrin. Smoky, dark, complex, occasionally rustic wines, drink at 2 yrs or from 7–8 yrs. Recent vintages softer. Swell, top-grade 60% Mourvèdre Hommage à Jacques Perrin (r). *Wonderful old-vine Roussanne*: enjoy over 5–25 yrs. Polished CÔTES DU RHÔ Coudoulet de Beaucastel (r), lives 8 yrs+. Famille Perrin CAIRANNE (gd value) GIGONDAS, RASTEAU, VINSOBRES all v.gd, authentic. Gd organic Perrin Nature Côtes du Rhô (r w). (*See also* Tablas Creek, California.)

Château de la Chaize Beauj r ★★★ Showplace of BEAUJ, magnificent CH, seventh-generation ownership, also fine gardens, with 99 ha of BROUILLY all in one block.

Château de Meursault C d'Or r w ★★ 61-ha estate making BEAUNE, MEURSAULT, POMMARD, VOLNAY. CH itself is impressive, cellars open to public. Owned by Patriarche. More tourist attraction than top producer, for the moment.

Château de Villeneuve Lo r w ★★ →★★★★ 96 99 03 05 06 07 08′ 09′ 10′ 11 12 (13) Meticulous producer. Wonderful, age-worthy SAUMUR Blanc (esp Les Cormiers) and SAUMUR-CHAMPIGNY (esp VIEILLES VIGNES, Grand CLOS only made in gd vintages. Converting to organic viticulture. Small 2013.

Château du Cèdre SW Fr r w ★★ →★★★ 01′ 02 04 06 08 09 10 11 (12′) (13) The Verhaeghe brothers make best-known modern CAHORS. ★★ Le Prestige is quicker-maturing than oaky top growths. Delicious VIOGNIER IGP.

Château Fuissé Burg w ★★ →★★★ Substantial producer with some of the best terroirs of POUILLY-FUISSÉ. Esp Les CLOS, Combettes. Also négociant lines.

Château-Grillet N Rhô w ★★ 91′ 95′ 98′ 00′ 01′ 04′ 05 06′ 07′ 08 09′ 10′ 11 12 France's smallest AC. 3.6-ha amphitheatre v'yd at CONDRIEU, loose granite. Bought by F Pinault of CH LATOUR in 2011, prices jumped with updated wine. Smooth, less deep, more neutral take on VIOGNIER now: subtle, big, drink at cellar temp, decanted, with new-wave food (in a smart restaurant).

Château Montus SW Fr r w ★★★ 00 01′ 02 04 05′ 06 08 09 (10′) (11) (12) ALAIN BRUMONT's famous MADIRAN property. All TANNAT, long extractions, huge oaking, needs long ageing. Alternatively there's classy oaked PACHERENC-DU-VIC-BILH (dr sw).

Château la Nerthe S Rhô r w ★★★ 78′ 81′ 89′ 90′ 95′ 96′ 98′ 99′ 00 01 03 04′ 05′ 06′ 07′ 09′ 10′ 11 12 CHÂTEAUNEUF estate. Sleek, oaked, polished-up wines, sadly more hands-off, mainstream lately. Special CUVÉES delicious Cadettes (r), oaked, rich Beauvenir (w). Also runs v. fine TAVEL Prieuré Montézargues, gd-value DOM de la Renjarde CÔTES DU RHÔ, gd CH Signac CHUSCLAN.

Châteaumeillant Lo r p ★ →★★ DYA. New SMALL AC area, promoted 2010, southwest of Bourges in Georges Sand country. GAMAY, PINOT N for light reds (75%), gris and rosés (25%). Foolishly 100% Pinot N not allowed. Look for: BOURGEOIS, Chaillot, Geoffrenet-Morval, Rouzé, Siret-Courtauld.

Châteauneuf-du-Pape S Rhô r (w) ★★★ 78′ 81′ 83 85 88 89′ 90′ 95′ 96 98′ 99′ 00′ 01′ 03′ 04′ 05′ 06′ 07′ 08 09′ 10′ 11 12 Nr Avignon, about 45 gd DOMS for best wines (remaining 85 inconsistent to poor). Up to 13 varieties (r w), headed by GRENACHE, plus SYRAH, MOURVÈDRE, Counoise. Aromatic, textured, long-lived; should be fine, round, pure, but too many sweet, heavy, sip-only wines (Parker taste). Small, traditional names can be gd value (great in 2010), while prestige old-vine wines (worst are late-harvest, new oak) are often too pricey. Whites fresh, fruity, or sturdy, best can age 15 yrs. Top: CHX DE BEAUCASTEL, Fortia, Gardine, Mont-Redon, LA NERTHE, RAYAS (marvellous), Sixtine, Vaudieu; DOMS de Barroche, Beaurenard, Bois de Boursan, Bosquet des Papes, LES CAILLOUX, Chante Cigale, Chante Perdrix, CHARBONNIÈRE, Charvin (terroir), Cristia, Font-de-Michelle, Grand Veneur (oak), Marcoux (fantastic

VIEILLES VIGNES), Pegaü, Roger Sabon, VIEUX TÉLÉGRAPHE, Henri Bonneau, CLOS du Mont-Olivet, CLOS DES PAPES, Clos St-Jean (sip), P Usseglio, Vieux Donjon.

Château Pierre-Bise Lo r p w ★★ →★★★★ 02 03 04 05' 06 07' (sw) 08 09 10' 11 Benchmark family DOM in COTEAUX DU LAYON, incl Chaume, QUARTS DE CHAUME, SAVENNIÈRES (CLOS de Grand Beaupréau, ROCHE-AUX-MOINES). V.gd ANJOU-GAMAY, ANJOU-VILLAGES (both CUVÉE Schist, Spilite), Anjou Blanc Haut de la Garde. New generation taking over from Claude & Joëlle Papin.

Château Rayas S Rhô r w ★★★→★★★★ 78' 79 81' 85 86 88' 89 90' 93 94 95' 96' 98' 99 00 01 03 04' 05' 06' 07' 08 09' 10' 11' 12' Extraordinary, out-of-the-loop, supremely traditional CHÂTEAUNEUF estate. Pale, subtle, aromatic, complex reds (100% GRENACHE) age superbly. White Rayas (GRENACHE BLANC, CLAIRETTE) v.gd over 18 yrs+. Gd-value second label: **Pignan**. Supreme CH Fonsalette CÔTES DU RHÔ, incl SYRAH. Decant all. Gd Ch des Tours VACQUEYRAS, VIN DE PAYS.

Château Simone Prov r p w ★★ →★★★ Historic estate south of Aix-en-PROV, where Winston Churchill painted Mont STE-VICTOIRE. Same family for over two centuries. Virtually synonymous with AC PALETTE. Age-worthy whites worth seeking out; characterful rosé, warming reds. Some rare grape varieties: (r) Castet, Manosquin.

Chave, Domaine Jean-Louis N Rhô r w ★★★★ 85' 88' 89' 90' 91' 94 95' 96 97 98' 99' 00 01' 03' 04 05' 06' 07' 08 09' 10' 11' 12' 13 Excellent family DOM at heart of HERMITAGE. Clever, precise blending from best hillside sites. Classy, supple, long-lived reds, incl expensive, occasional Cathelin. V.gd white (mainly MARSANNE); marvellous, occasional VIN DE PAILLE. Deep, copious ST-JOSEPH red (incl Dom Florentin 2009 and new v'yds), fruity J-L Chave brand St-Joseph Offerus, sound merchant Hermitage (r w).

Chavignol Lo Picturesque SANCERRE village with famous steep v'yds Les Monts Damnés and Cul de Beaujeu. Clay-limestone soil gives full-bodied, mineral whites and reds that age 10 yrs+; esp from Boulay, BOURGEOIS, Cotat, DAGUENEAU, Thomas Laballe, Yves & Pierre Martin, ALPHONSE MELLOT, Paul Thomas. Whites perfect with *crottin de Chavignol*.

Chénas Beauj r ★★★ 09' 10' 11' 12 13 Smallest BEAUJ cru, between MOULIN-À-VENT and JULIÉNAS, less well-known so gd-value for meaty wine. Try: Aufranc, DUBOEUF, LAPIERRE, Pacalet, Piron, Thillardon (rising star), Trichard, co-op.

Chevalier-Montrachet C d'O w ★★★★ 99' 00' 02' 04 05' 06' 07' 08 09' 10 11 12 13 Just above MONTRACHET geographically, just below in quality, though still capable of brilliant crystalline wines. Long-lived but often enjoyable early. Special CUVÉES Les Demoiselles from JADOT and LATOUR and La Cabotte from BOUCHARD, but top example is LEFLAIVE. Try also Dancer, Niellon, SAUZET.

Cheverny Lo r p w ★ →★★ 06 08 09' 10 11 Lo AC nr Chambord. Pungent dry white from SAUV BL, CHARD. Light reds mainly GAMAY, PINOT N (also CAB FR, CÔT). Richer, more age-worthy **Cour-Cheverny**, local Romorantin grape only. Severely hit by frost in April 2012. Esp Cazin, CLOS Tue-Boeuf, Gendrier, Huards, de Montcy Philippe Tessier; DOMS de la Desoucherie, du Moulin, Veilloux, Villemade.

Chevillon, R C d'O r ★★★ Delicious, not-too-tannic NUITS-ST-GEORGES with v'yds in the best sites, esp Les St-Georges, Cailles, Vaucrains, Roncières.

Chidaine, François Lo (r) w dr sw sp ★★★ 05' 08' 09 10' 11 12 Producer of v. precise MONTLOUIS, VOUVRAY. In 2002 took over historic Vouvray CLOS Baudoin. Concentrates on dry, DEMI-SEC. AC TOURAINE at Chissay (Cher Valley). Bio champion. Big new winery but frosted (2012) and hailed on (2013 in Vouvray).

Chignin Sav w ★ DYA. Light, soft white from Jacquère grapes for alpine summers. Chignin-Bergeron (with ROUSSANNE grapes) is best and liveliest.

Chinon Lo r p (w) ★★→★★★ 96' 97 02 03 05' 06 08 09' 10' 11 12 (13) Home of Rabelais. Big range: light to rich TOURAINE CAB FR, 10% rosé. Top wines age 20 yrs+. A little steely, dry CHENIN BL. ALLIET, BAUDRY, BAUDRY-DUTOUR, Couly-Dutheil,

Couly (Pierre & Bertrand), Grosbois, Pain, J M Raffault; CHX de la Bonnelière, de Coulaine, DOM de la Noblaie. Easy-drinking 2012s. Seven communes west of Chinon to be incl in AC from 2015.

Chiroubles Beauj r 11′ 12 13 Rarely seen BEAUJ cru in the hills above FLEURIE: fresh, fruity, silky wine for early drinking (1–3 yrs). Growers: Cheysson, Coquelet, DUBOEUF, Fourneau, Métrat, Passot, Raousset, Trenel.

Chorey-lès-Beaune C d'O r (w) ★★ 05′ 06 07 08 09′ 10′ 11 12 Pleasurable, affordable burg adjoining BEAUNE. TOLLOT-BEAUT is leader. Try Arnoux, DROUHIN, JADOT, Loichet.

Chusclan S Rhô r p w ★→★★ 09′ 10′ 11′ 12′ 13 CÔTES DU RHÔ-VILLAGES with above-average Laudun-Chusclan co-op, incl gd, fresh whites. Easy reds, crisp rosés. Best co-op labels (r) Chusclan DOM de l'Olivettte, CÔTES DU RHÔ Femme de Gicon, LIRAC. Also full CH Signac (can age), Dom La Romance, special CUVÉES from *André Roux*. Drink most young.

Clair, Bruno C d'O r p w ★★★→★★★★ Terrific MARSANNAY estate; major holdings in GEVREY-CHAMBERTIN (esp CLOS de Bèze, CLOS ST JACQUES, Cazetiers), FIXIN, MOREY-ST-DENIS. Note also old-vine SAVIGNY La Dominode, whites incl CORTON-CHARLEMAGNE.

Clairet B'x Between rosé/red. B'x Clairet is AC. Try CHX Fontenille, Penin, Turcaud.

Clairette de Bellegarde S Rhô w ★ DYA. S Rhô AC nr Nîmes: attractive crisp dry white from CLAIRETTE, esp stylish, top-value Mas Carlot.

Clairette de Die N Rhô w dr s/sw sp ★★ NV Alpine bubbles: flinty or (better) semi-sweet MUSCAT sparkling wine from low Alps. Underrated, muskily fruited; or dry CLAIRETTE, can age 3–4 yrs. NB: Achard-Vincent, Carod, Poulet et Fils, J-C Raspail.

Clairette du Languedoc L'doc w ★ DYA. Old but neglected small white AC, nr Pézenas, from the traditional CLAIRETTE grape. Soft, dry whites, more characterful late-harvest *moelleux*, RANCIO. Try DOM La Croix Chaptal.

Clape, Auguste, Pierre, Olivier N Rhô r (w) ★★★→★★★★ 90′ 95′ 97 98′ 99′ 00 01′ 02 03′ 04′ 05′ 06′ 07′ 08 09′ 10′ 11′ 12′ 13 *The kings of Cornas*. Network of supreme SYRAH central v'yds at CORNAS, many old vines. Profound, v. consistent reds, vivid reminder of an unhurried era, need 6 yrs+. Well-fruited youngish-vines Renaissance. Gd CÔTES DU RHÔ, VIN DE FRANCE (r), ST-PÉRAY.

Clape, la L'doc r p w ★★→★★★ Compact area of limestone hills, once an island outside Narbonne. Warming, spicy reds. Original *tangy, salty whites* benefit from maritime influence and age surprisingly well. Appellation status imminent, as well as Cru du L'doc; *see* COTEAUX DU L'DOC. Gd: CHX *l'Hospitalet*, Moyau, La Négly, Pech-Céléyran, Pech-Redon, *Rouquette-sur-Mer*, Ricardelle, Anglès, Mas du Soleila, Camplazens, Mire l'Etang.

Climat Burg Burg word for individually named v'yd, eg. MEURSAULT Tesson.

Clos A term carrying some prestige, reserved for distinct (walled) v'yds, often in one ownership (esp Burg, CHAMP, AL).

Clos de Gamot SW Fr r ★★★ 00 01′ 02′ 04 05′ 06 08 09 10′ (11) (12) Pure taste of MALBEC as made by Jouffreau family since before we were all born. ★★★ CUVÉE Vignes Centenaires (best yrs only) and hilltop ★★★★ CLOS St Jean miraculously survive modern fashions, deer and wild boar.

Clos de la Roche C d'O r ★★★ 90′ 93′ 95 96′ 98 99′ 01 02′ 03 05′ 06 07 08 09′ 10′ 11 12′ 13 Maybe the finest GRAND CRU of MOREY-ST-DENIS, with as much grace as power, more savoury than sumptuous. Needs time. PONSOT, DUJAC are references but try Amiot, ARLAUD, Castagnier, LEROY, LIGNIER, ROUSSEAU.

Clos des Lambrays C d'O r ★★★ 99′ 02 03 05′ 06 07 09′ 10′ 11 12′ 13 GRAND CRU v'yd at MOREY-ST-DENIS. A virtual monopoly of the DOM du CLOS des Lambrays, invigorating wine in an early picked, spicy, stemmy style, in total contrast to neighbour CLOS DE TART.

Clos des Mouches C d'O r w ★★★ 02 05′ 09′ 10′ 11 13 Splendid PREMIER CRU BEAUNE v'yd, made famous by DROUHIN. Whites and reds, spicy, memorable and consistent.

BICHOT, CHANSON gd too. Little-known v'yds of the same name also found in SANTENAY (Clair, Moreau, Muzard), MEURSAULT (Germain).

Clos des Papes S Rhô r w ★★★★ 90' 95 98' 99' 00 01' 03' 04' 05' 06' 07' 08 09' 10' 11 12' Always classy CHÂTEAUNEUF DOM of Avril family, tiny yields. Rich, complex red, more obviously succulent recently (mainly GRENACHE, MOURVÈDRE, drink in 2–3 yrs or from 8 yrs); *great white* (6 varieties, classy, allow time, deserves fine cuisine; 5–18 yrs).

Clos des Papes (S Rhône) lost the equivalent of two vintages in last six: tiny crops.

Clos de Tart C d'O r ★★★★ 90' 96' 99' 01' 02' 03 05' 06 07 08' 09 10 11 12' 13 MOREY-ST-DENIS GRAND CRU, upgraded substantially in quality and price on the watch of director Sylvain Pitiot. Often most exciting in less ripe yrs.

Clos de Vougeot C d'O r ★★★→★★★★ 90' 93' 96' 98 99' 01 02' 03' 05' 06 07 08 09' 10' 11 12' 13 Celebrated CÔTE DE NUITS GRAND CRU, with many owners. Occasionally sublime. Maturity depends on grower's philosophy, technique, position. Top growers: CH de la Tour, DROUHIN, EUGÉNIE, FAIVELEY, GRIVOT, GROS, HUDELOT-Noellat, JADOT, LEROY, LIGER-BELAIR, MÉO-CAMUZET, MONTILLE, MUGNERET, *Vougeraie*.

Clos du Mesnil Champ CHAMP KRUG's famous walled v'yd in GRAND CRU Le Mesnil. Esp long-lived, pure CHARD vintage CUVÉES, great yrs like 92 95 perfect now and to 2020+. Current 00 a delight.

Clos du Roi C d'O r ★★→★★★ Best v'yd in GRAND CRU CORTON, top PREMIER CRU v'yd in MERCUREY, less so in BEAUNE, special site in MARSANNAY. The king usually chose well.

Clos Rougeard Lo r w (sw) ★★★★ 03 04 05' 06 07 08 09' 10' 11 Small, iconic DOM for wonderful SAUMUR-CHAMPIGNY, great SAUMUR Blanc, luscious COTEAUX DE SAUMUR. Made "natural" wine before it was fashionable.

Clos St-Denis C d'O r ★★★ 90' 93' 95 96' 98 99' 01 02' 03 05' 06 07 08 09' 10' 11 12' 13 GRAND CRU at MOREY-ST-DENIS. Sumptuous wine in youth, growing silky with age. Try from ARLAUD, Bertagna, Castagnier, DUJAC, Jouan, Leroux, PONSOT.

Clos Ste-Hune Al w ★★★★ Top TRIMBACH bottling from GRAND CRU ROSACKER. Greatest RIES in ALSACE (00' 04 06 08' 10' 12 13'). V. fine, initially austere; needs 5–10 yrs+ ageing. For great fish, esp turbot.

Clos St-Jacques C d'O r ★★★★ 90' 93 95' 96' 98 99' 01 02' 03 05' 06 07 08 09' 10' 11 12' 13 Hillside PREMIER CRU in GEVREY-CHAMBERTIN, with perfect southeast exposure. Excellent producers: CLAIR, ESMONIN, FOURRIER, JADOT, ROUSSEAU; powerful, velvety reds often ranked above many GRANDS CRUS.

Coche-Dury C d'O r w ★★★★ Superb MEURSAULT DOM led by Jean-François Coche and son Raphaël. Exceptional whites from ALIGOTÉ to CORTON-CHARLEMAGNE and v. pretty reds too. Hard to find.

Colin C d'O r w ★★★ Leading CHASSAGNE-MONTRACHET and ST-AUBIN family; new generation making waves, esp Pierre-Yves C-Morey (outstanding whites) and DOM Marc C. Try also Bruno or Philippe C (sons of Michel C-Deleger).

Collines Rhodaniennes N Rhô r w ★★ Quality N Rhô IGP, clear-fruited hillside reds v.gd value. Can contain young-vine CÔTE-RÔTIE, also recent v'yds at Seyssuel (deep, flinty, expensive). Mostly SYRAH (best), also MERLOT, GAMAY, mini-CONDRIEU VIOGNIER (best), CHARD. Reds: Bonnefond, L Cheze, J-M Gérin, Jamet (v.gd), Jasmin, Monier, M&S Ogier, S Pichat. Whites: Alexandrins, Barou, Y Cuilleron, F Merlin, Perret (v.gd), *G Vernay (v.gd)*.

Collioure Rouss r p w ★★ Table-wine twin of BANYULS, Most producers making both. Gutsy reds, mainly GRENACHE, from dramatic terraces above picturesque town, Also rosé, GRENACHE BLANC white since 2002. Top: Les CLOS de Paulilles, DOMS du Mas Blanc, de la Rectorie, La Tour Vieille, Vial-Magnères, Madeloc, Coume del Mas. Co-op Cellier des Templiers.

Comté Tolosan SW Fr r p w ★→★★ Mostly DYA IGP found all over Southwest. The luscious sweet PETIT MANSENG from ★★★ CH de Cabidos, ★★ DOM de Moncaut (JURANÇON in all but name) and groundbreaking ★★ Dom DE RIBONNET are miles ahead of most, for whom this appellation is an umbrella for mediocrity.

Condrieu N Rhô w ★★★ 05 08′ 09 10′ 11′ 12′ 13 Floral, mineral to musky aromas of apricot/pear bounce out from white from granite hills; home of VIOGNIER. Best: cool, pure, precise. Rare white to match asparagus, smoked salmon. 75 growers, so quality varies (v.gd 08, lovely 10); danger of excess oak, sweetness, alcohol. Best: CHAPOUTIER, Y Cuilleron, DELAS, Gangloff (great style), GUIGAL, F Merlin, Niéro, A Perret, C Pichon, ROSTAING, G Vernay (esp Coteau de Vernon), F Villard.

Corbières L'doc r (p) (w) ★★→★★★ 06 07 08 **09 10** 11 12 13 Largest AC of the L'DOC, with cru of Boutenac. Wines as wild as the scenery: sun-soaked, rugged. Best: CHX Aiguilloux, de Cabriac, la Baronne, Borde-Rouge, Les CLOS Perdus, Lastours, Ollieux Romanis, Les Palais, Pech-Latt, la Voulte Gasparets, DOMS du Grand Crès, de Fontsainte, Trillol, du Vieux Parc, de Villemajou, Villerouge. Clos de l'Anhel, Grand Arc, Serres-Mazard, Co-ops: Camplong, Castelmaure.

Cornas N Rhô r ★★★ 78′ 83′ 85′ 88′ 89′ 90′ 91′ 94′ 95′ 96 97′ 98′ **99′** 00′ 01′ 02 03′ 04 05′ 06′ 07′ 08 09′ 10′ **11′** 12′ 13 High-quality N Rhô SYRAH. Deep, plentifully fruited, mineral-tinted. Can drink some on vibrant early fruit, mostly needs to age 5–15 yrs. Stunning 2010. Top: Allemand (top 2), Balthazar (traditional), M Barret, *Clape* (benchmark), Colombo (new oak), Courbis (modern), *Delas*, J & E Durand (racy fruit), G Gilles, JABOULET (St-Pierre CUVÉE), Lemencier, V Paris, Tardieu-Laurent (oak), DOM *du Tunnel*, Voge (oak).

Corsica / Corse r p w ★→★★ From France's wild island. ACS Ajaccio, PATRIMONIO; better crus Coteaux du Cap Corse, Sartène, Calvi. IGP: Île de Beauté. Light, spicy reds from SCIACARELLO, more tannic wines from Nielluccio; gd rosés; *tangy, herbal Vermentino whites*. Also sweet MUSCATS. Top growers: Abbatucci, Antoine Arena, CLOS d'Alzeto, Clos Capitoro, Gentile, Yves Leccia, Montemagni, *Peraldi*, Vaccelli, Saperale, Fiumicicoli, *Torraccia*, Canarelli, Pieretti, Nicrosi, Alzipratu, Clos Poggiale. Original wines that rarely travel.

Corton C d'O r (w) ★★★ 90′ 95 96′ 98 99′ 01 02′ 03′ 05′ 06 07 08 09′ 10′ 11 12′ 13 The 160 ha classified as GRAND CRU is much too much: only top Corton v'yds CLOS DU ROI, Bressandes, Le Rognet deserve it with weight and structure; others make fair, softer reds. Look for d'Ardhuy, BONNEAU DU MARTRAY, CHANDON DE BRIAILLES, DOM des Croix, DRC (since 2009), Dubreuil-Fontaine, FAIVELEY, Camille Giroud, MÉO-CAMUZET, Senard, TOLLOT-BEAUT. Occasional whites, eg. HOSPICES DE BEAUNE less interesting than CORTON-CHARLEMAGNE.

Corton-Charlemagne C d'O w ★★★ →★★★★★ 99′ 00′ 02′ 03 04 05′ 06 07′ 08 09′ 10′ 11 12′ 13 One-off white burg, unlike the others. Southwest- and west-facing limestone on hill of Corton, plus easterly band round the top. Intense minerality, great ageing potential often insufficiently realized. Top growers: BONNEAU DU MARTRAY, BOUCHARD, COCHE-DURY, FAIVELEY, HOSPICES DE BEAUNE, JADOT, P Javillier, LATOUR, Rapet, Rollin, VOUGERAIE.

Costières de Nîmes S Rhô r p w ★→★★ 07′ 09′ 10′ 11 12′ Strong quality S Rhô region, southwest of CHÂTEAUNEUF, similar stony soils. Red (GRENACHE, SYRAH) ages 5–8 yrs, gd value. Best: CHX de Grande Cassagne, Mas des Bressades, Mas Carlot, Mas Neuf, Mourgues-du-Grès, Nages, d'Or et des Gueules, Roubaud; DOMS Petit Romain, Tardieu-Laurent, du Vieux Relais. Lively rosés, stylish whites (ROUSSANNE).

Côte Chalonnaise Burg r w sp ★★ Region immediately south of C D'O; lower prices. BOUZERON for ALIGOTÉ, *Mercurey* and GIVRY for structured reds and interesting whites; *Rully* for lighter wines in both colours; MONTAGNY for its leaner CHARD. The region lacks a real champion, though.

Côte de Beaune C d'O r w ★★→★★★★ The southern half of the C D'O. Also a little-seen AC in its own right applying to top of the hill above BEAUNE itself.

Côte de Beaune-Villages C d'O r ★★ 09' 10' 11 12 Red wines from the lesser villages of the southern half of the C D'O. Rarely exciting, now rarely seen.

Côte de Brouilly Beauj r ★★ 09' 10' 11' 12 13 Flanks of the hillside above BROUILLY provide one of the richest BEAUJ cru. Deserves to be much better known. Try J-P Brun, L Martray, CH Thivin.

Côte de Nuits C d'O r (w) ★★ →★★★★ Northern half of C D'O. Mostly red wine from MARSANNAY, FIXIN, GEVREY-CHAMBERTIN, MOREY-ST DENIS, CHAMBOLLE-MUSIGNY, VOUGEOT, VOSNE-ROMANÉE, NUITS-ST GEORGES.

Côte de Nuits-Villages C d'O r (w) ★★ 05' 06 08 09' 10' 11 12' 13 Junior AC for extreme north and south ends of CÔTE DE NUITS; well worth investigating for bargains. Single-v'yd versions beginning to appear. Try Ardhuy, BACHELET, Chopin, Gachot-Monot, Jourdan, Loichet.

Côte d'Or Burg *Département* name applied to the central and principal Burg v'yd slopes: CÔTE DE BEAUNE and CÔTE DE NUITS. Not used on labels except for proposed BOURGOGNE C d'O AC, expected imminently.

Cote d'Or vineyards: France's next candidate for Unesco World Heritage site status.

Côte Roannaise Lo r p ★★ 10 11 12 13 Quality AC on lower slopes of high granite hills west of Roanne; cousin of BEAUJ. Excellent juicy GAMAY. Producers: Désormière, Fontenay, Giraudon, Paroisse, Plasse, Pothiers, Sérol, Vial. Also white IGP Urfé from CHARD and increasingly VIOGNIER.

Côte-Rôtie N Rhô r ★★★ →★★★★ 78' 85' 88' 89' 90' 91' 95' 98' 99' 00 01' 03' 04 05' 06' 07' 08 09' 10' 11 12' 13 Finest Rhô red, mainly SYRAH, touch of VIOGNIER, style connects to Burg. Violet scents, pure, complex, v. fine with age (5–10 yrs+). Glorious 2010. Top: *Barge* (traditional), Bernard, Bonnefond (oak), Bonserine (GUIGAL-owned), Burgaud, CHAPOUTIER, Clusel-Roch (organic), DELAS, Duclaux, Gaillard (oak), Garon, J-M Gérin (oak), GUIGAL (long oaking), *Jamet* (wonderful), Jasmin, M&S Ogier (oak), ROSTAING (fine), J-M Stéphan (organic), VIDAL-FLEURY (La Chatillonne).

Coteaux Bourguignons Burg ★ DYA. New AC from 2011 replacing BOURGOGNE GRAND ORDINAIRE. Mostly reds, GAMAY, PINOT N. Main take-up is hard-to-sell basic BEAUJ (neither from Coteaux, nor Bourguignon) that may be reclassified under this sexier name. Rare whites ALIGOTÉ, CHARD, MELON, PINOTS BL & GR.

Coteaux Champenois Champ r (p) w ★★★ (w) DYA. AC for still wines of CHAMP, eg. BOUZY. Vintages as for Champ. Better reds with climate change and better viticulture (esp 09 12').

Coteaux d'Aix-en-Provence Prov r p w ★★ Sprawling AC without a real identity, from hills north of Aix and nearby plain north of Etang de Berre. Fruit-salad of varieties, both B'X and MIDI. Reds are best, esp CHX Beaupré, Calissanne, Revelette, les Bastides, la Realtière, les Béates, Bas. Vignelaure. *See also* LES BAUX-EN-PROV.

Coteaux d'Ancenis Lo r p w (sw) ★ →★★ Generally DYA. AOP (transition between Nantais and ANJOU). Chiefly for dry, DEMI-SEC, sweet CHENIN BL whites, plus age-worthy *Malvoisie*; also light reds and rosés mainly GAMAY, plus CABS FR, SAUV. Esp Athimon et ses Enfants, Guindon, Quarteron.

Coteaux de Chalosse SW Fr r p w ★ DYA. Modest IGP from local grapes, popular in local restaurants, rarely found elsewhere. Co-op (now merged with TURSAN) dominates.

Coteaux de Glanes SW Fr r p ★★ DYA. A must if you are in the upper Dordogne. The local eight-member co-op uses Ségalin grape to spike up its MERLOT, GAMAY.

Coteaux de l'Ardèche S Rhô r p w ★→★★ Hilly area west of Rhô, wide selection, gd value. New DOMS; fresh reds, some oaked; VIOGNIER (eg. Mas de Libian, CHAPOUTIER), MARSANNE. Best from SYRAH, also GAMAY (often old vines), CAB SAUV (Serret). Burg-style Ardèche CHARD by LOUIS LATOUR. DOMS du Colombier, J & E Durand, Favette, Flacher, Grangeon, Mazel, Vigier, CH de la Selve.

Coteaux de l'Aubance Lo w sw ★★ →★★★★ 89' 90' 95' 96' 97' 02 03 05' 07' 09 10'
11' (13) Small AC for sweet whites from CHENIN BL. Nervier, less rich than COTEAUX
DU LAYON except SÉLECTION DES GRAINS NOBLES. South of Lo nr Angers, slopes more
gentle than in Layon. Often gd value. Esp Bablut, Haute-Perche, Montgilet, CH
Princé, Richou, Rochelles, Ch la Varière.

Coteaux de Saumur Lo w sw ★★ →★★★ 03, 05, 07' 09 10' 11 Sweet, hand-picked CHENIN
BL. Resembles COTEAUX DU LAYON but less rich, more delicate, citric. Esp CHAMPS
FLEURIS, CLOS ROUGEARD, Régis Neau, St Just, Targe, Vatan. Little 2012/13 made.

Coteaux des Baronnies S Rhô r p w ★ DYA. Late-ripening Rhô IGP in pasturelands,
high hills east of VINSOBRES. SYRAH (best), CAB SAUV, MERLOT, CHARD (gd, cheap), plus
GRENACHE, CINSAULT, etc. Improving, simple reds, also fresh VIOGNIER. NB: DOMS du
Rieu-Frais, Rosière, Le Mas Sylvia.

Coteaux du Giennois Lo r p w ★ →★★ DYA. Small appellation north of Pouilly.
Scattered v'yds from Cosne to Gien. SAUV BL like a junior SANCERRE or POUILLY-
FUMÉ. Light reds hampered by unconvincing statutory blend of GAMAY/PINOT N.
Best: Emile Balland, Jean Marie Berthier (esp L'Inédit), BOURGEOIS, Catherine &
Michel Langlois, Paulat, Treuillet, Villargeau.

Coteaux du Languedoc r p w ★★ →★★★ 06 06 07 08 09 10 11 12 13 AC from Narbonne
to Nîmes, with various sub-divisions. An enormous quality range. Destined to
disappear in 2017, in favour of even larger AC L'DOC (created in 2007). Potential
hierarchy of crus, incl newer GRÈS DE MONTPELLIER, TERRASSES DU LARZAC, PÉZENAS, also
est ST-CHINIAN, FAUGÈRES. New estates galore to explore, with exciting potential.

Coteaux du Layon Lo w sw ★★ →★★★★ 89 90 95 96 97 02 03 05' 07' 09 10' 11 Heart
of ANJOU: sweet CHENIN BL varying considerably in sweetness with admirable
acidity, best nearly immortal. Seven villages can add name to AC with Chaume
as a PREMIER CRU. Top ACs: BONNEZEAUX, QUARTS DE CHAUME. Growers: Baudouin,
BAUMARD, Delesvaux, des Forges, DOM des Grands Vignes, Guegniard, Dom de
Juchepie, Ogereau, CH PIERRE-BISE, Pithon-Paillé.

Coteaux du Loir Lo r p w dr sw ★ →★★★ 05' 07 08 09' 10' 11 (13) Northern tributary
of the Loire, Le Loir is a marginal but dynamic region with Coteaux du Loir,
JASNIÈRES. *Steely, fine, apple-scented Chenin Bl*, GAMAY, peppery Pineau d'Aunis
occasionally sparkling, plus Grolleau (rosé), CAB, CÔT. Top growers: Ange Vin,
DOM DE BELLIVIERE, Breton, Le Briseau, Fresneau, Gigou, Janvier, Les Maisons
Rouges, de Rycke. 2012 hit by frost, mildew. 2013 small but gd.

Coteaux du Lyonnais Beauj r p (w) ★ DYA Junior BEAUJ. Best *en primeur*.

Coteaux du Quercy SW Fr r p ★ 06 08 09' 10 11) (12) AOP south of CAHORS. Based
on CAB FR; led by ★ co-op's gd-value Bessey de Boissy, but independents ★★ DOM
du Merchien (IGP), ★ Doms d'Ariès, de Guyot, de Lafage, Lagarde have more
character. They cut the local cuisine well.

Coteaux du Vendômois Lo r p w ★ →★★ DYA. AC, 28 communes: Vendôme,
Montoire in Le Loir Valley. Most characteristic wines are VIN GRIS from Pineau
d'Aunis grape, which also gives peppery notes to red blends alongside CAB FR,
PINOT N, GAMAY. Whites are CHENIN BL, CHARD. Producers: Brazilier, Patrice Colin,
Four à Chaux, J Martellière, Montrieux, CAVE du Vendôme-Villiers.

Coteaux et Terrasses de Montauban SW Fr r p w ★ →★★ DYA IGP. Highly successful
DOM de Montels with huge range of gd-value wines doesn't quite have things all
its own way. Try ★ DOM Biarnès, Mas des Anges.

Coteaux Varois-en-Provence Prov r p w ★ →★★ 07 08 09 10 11 12 13 Overlooked AC
sandwiched between bigger COTEAUX D'AIX and CÔTES DE PROV. Warming reds, fresh
rosés from usual southern varieties. Potential being realized, esp SYRAH. Try CHX
la Calisse, Miraval (Brangelina's), DOM des Alysses, *des Aspras*, du Deffends, du
Loou, des Chaberts, *Routas*, Trians.

Côtes Catalanes Rouss r p w ★★ →★★★ A mere IGP, covering much of ROUSS, but quality easily exceeds ACS. Exciting source of innovation, investment. Old vines galore, mainly GRENACHE, CARIGNAN, provide rewarding drinking. Best: DOMS Casenove, *Dom of the Bee*, GAUBY, L'Horizon, *Jones*, Matassa, La Préceptorie de Centernach, Olivier Pithon, Padié, Soulanes, le Soula, Treloar, Vaquer.

Côtes d'Auvergne Mass C r p (w) ★→★★ Generally DYA. Small AC. GAMAY, though some PINOT N (idiotically 100% banned), CHARD. Best reds improve 2–3 yrs. Top villages: Boudes, Chanturgue, Châteaugay, Madargues (r), Corent (p). Producers: CAVE St-Verny, Maupertuis, Sauvat.

Côtes de Bordeaux B'x ★ Unnecessarily complex AC launched in 2008 for reds. Embraces and permits cross-blending between CASTILLON, FRANCS, BLAYE, CADILLAC (formerly Premières Côtes de B'x). Growers who want to maintain the identity of a single terroir have stiffer controls but can put Castillon, Cadillac, etc. before Côtes de B'x. BLAYE-CÔTES DE B'X, FRANCS-CÔTES DE B'X also produce a little dry white. CÔTES DE BOURG is not part of new system.

Côtes de Bourg B'x r w ★→★★ 04 05' 08 09' 10' 12 Solid, savoury reds, a little white from east bank of Gironde. Independent of CÔTES DE B'X AC. China the top export market. Top CHX: Brûlesécaille, Bujan, Civrac, *Falfas*, Fougas-Maldoror, Grand-Maison, Grave (Nectar VIEILLES VIGNES), Haut-Guiraud, Haut-Maco, Haut Mondésir, Macay, Mercier, Nodoz, *Roc de Cambes*, Rousset, Sociondo.

Côtes de Duras SW Fr r p w (sw) ★→★★★ 10 11' 12 (13) AOP between B'X and BERGERAC. Growth led by organic independents such as ★★★ DOMS Mouthes-les-Bihan, Petit Malromé, Dom Mont Ramé and Nadine Lussau ahead of ★★ Les Hauts de Riquet, Le Petit CLOS des Vents, Les Cours. CH Condom Perceval's sweet ★★★ still top of the stickies. Older growers ★★ Doms des Allegrets and Laulan still good, and even the dull old ★ Berticot co-op.

Côtes de Gascogne SW Fr (r) (p) w ★★ DYA IGP. Plausible thirst-quencher whites for theatre intervals, dominated by giant exporters ★★ PRODUCTEURS PLAIMONT, Tariquet. Smaller independents incl ★★ DOMS d'Arton, Chiroulet, Haut-Campagnau, Ménard, Millet, Pellehaut, de San Guilhem. Or ★ CH des Cassagnoles, de Jöy, de Laballe, de Lauroux, de Magnaut, Papolle, St Lannes, Sédouprat (esp red CUVÉE Sanglier), Uby. *See also* BRUMONT.

Côtes de Millau SW Fr r p w IGP ★ DYA. Foster's great Tarn viaduct may have spurred enthusiastic co-op and six serious independents (incl ★ DOM du Vieux Noyer) to put new life into this once enormous vineyard. Gd-value ordinary drinking.

Côtes de Montravel SW Fr w sw ★★ 09 10 11' 12 (13) Sub-AOP of BERGERAC; for lovers of old-fashioned *moelleux* styles, sadly out of fashion. Not as sweet as HAUT-MONTRAVEL, but more than off-dry. Delicious apéritif.

Côtes de Provence Prov r p w ★→★★★ 06 07 08 09 10 11 12 13 (p w) DYA. Large AC. Mainly rosé, with research improving quality. (Nowhere else takes rosé as seriously.) Satisfying reds, with CAB as well as southern varieties. Herbal whites. STE-VICTOIRE, Fréjus, La Londe and most recently, Pierrefeu are subzones. Leaders incl: Castel Roubine, Commanderie de Peyrassol, none Bernarde, de la Courtade, Léoube, *Gavoty* (superb), CHX d'Esclans, de Selle and CLOS Mireille, des Planes, Rabiéga, *Richeaume*, Rimauresq, Ste Rosaline. *See* COTEAUX D'AIX, BANDOL, COTEAUX VAROIS.

Côtes de Thongue L'doc r p w ★★ (p w) DYA. Most dynamic IGP of HÉRAULT, in Thongue Valley. Experimental blends in preference to single varietals. Reds will age. DOMS Arjolle, les Chemins de Bassac, la Croix Belle, Monplézy, des Henrys.

Côtes de Toul Al r p w ★ DYA. V. light wines from Lorraine; mainly VIN GRIS.

Côtes du Brulhois SW Fr r p (w) ★→★★ 09 10 11 12 Expanding AOP nr Agen; "black" wines, calling for local cooking; must incl some TANNAT. ★ Co-op really does cooperate with independents ★★ DOM des Thermes, le Bois de Simon, ★ CH la Bastide, DOMS du Pountet, Coujétou-Peyret.

FRANCE

Côtes du Couchois Burg ★ ⊳★★ 09' 10' 11 12 13 Subdistrict of BOURGOGNE Rouge at southern end of C D'O v'yds. Powerful reds on tannic side. Hasn't kicked on since best grower Alain Hasard left for RULLY.

Côtes du Forez Lo r p (sp) ★ ⊳★★ DYA. Exciting, southernmost Lo AC. GAMAY (r p). Les Vignerons Foréziens, Bonnfoy, Gaumon, Guillot, Mondon & Demeure, Real, Verdier/Logel. IGP: CHARD, PINOT GR, ROUSSANNE, VIOGNIER.

Côtes du Jura r p w (sp) ★★ ⊳★★★ 99' 00 03' 05' 06 09 10 11 12 Revitalized region for CHARD, SAVAGNIN (w), many different styles, from fresh and fruity to deliberately oxidative, incl VIN JAUNE. Light bright reds from PINOT N, Poulsard, Trousseau. Look for Berthet-Bondet, Bourdy, CH D'ARLAY, GANEVAT, GRAND, Mossu, PIGNIER.

Côtes du Rhône S Rhô r p w ★ ⊳★★ 09' 10' 11' 12' The engine room of S Rhô, across 170 communes. Split between interesting, rising handmade quality and mass-produced. Fruit emphasis a winner in best (esp 11 12). Mainly GRENACHE, also SYRAH, CARIGNAN. Best drunk young. Vaucluse top, then Gard (Syrah).

Côtes du Rhône-Villages S Rhô r p w ★ ⊳★★ 07' 09' 10' 11' 12' Punchy, bold reds from 7,700 ha, incl 18 named S Rhô villages. Best hold generous, spiced dark fruit, gd value. Red core is GRENACHE, with SYRAH, MOURVÈDRE. Improving whites, often incl VIOGNIER, ROUSSANNE added to CLAIRETTE, GRENACHE BLANC – gd with food. *See* CHUSCLAN, LAUDUN, ST-GERVAIS, SABLET, SÉGURET, VISAN (improving). New villages from 2005: MASSIF D'UCHAUX (gd), PLAN DE DIEU (robust), PUYMÉRAS, SIGNARGUES, Gadagne (12, nr Avignon). NB: CHX Fontségune, Signac, DOMS Aphillantes, Aure, Cabotte, Coulange, Coste Chaude, Grand Moulas, Grand Veneur, Jérome, Montbayon, Mourchon, Pique-Basse, Rabasse-Charavin, Renjarde, Romarins, Ste-Anne, St-Siffrein, Saladin, Valériane, Viret (cosmopolitan), Mas de Libian, CAVE Estézargues, Cave RASTEAU.

Côtes du Roussillon r p w ★ ⊳★★ 06 07' 08 09 10 11 12 13 East Pyrénées AC, behind Perpignan. Dominated by co-ops, notably VIGNERONS Catalans. Warming reds are best, particularly from old-vine CARIGNAN, GRENACHE.

Côtes du Roussillon-Villages r ★★ ⊳★★★ 06 07 08 09 10 11 12 13 28 Villages in best part of ROUSS. Dominated by co-ops and VIGNERONS Catalans; also gd independent estates: des Chênes, CAZES, *la Cazenove*, GAUBY (also characterful white IGP), Piquemal, CH de Jau, Mas Crémat, CLOS des Fées, Clot de l'Oum, Bila Haut, Roc des Anges, Thunevin-Calvet, Modat, Rancy. *See* CÔTES CATALANES.

Côtes du Tarn SW Fr r p w ★ DYA. IGP that overlaps but is slightly larger than GAILLAC. ★★ DOMS d'en Ségur (esp off-dry SAUV BL), VIGNES de Garbasses (Lou Bio range) surprisingly gd. Used by Gaillac growers who don't want to obey Gaillac rules.

Côtes du Vivarais S Rhô r p w ★ 10' 12 Mostly DYA. Across hilly Ardèche country west of Montélimar. Definite improvement: quaffable wines based on GRENACHE, SYRAH; some more sturdy, oak-aged reds. NB: Gallety (best), Mas de Bagnols, VIGNERONS de Ruoms (value).

Coulée de Serrant Lo w dr sw ★★★ 95 96 97 98 99 02 03 04 05 07 08 10' 11 (12) Historic, steep CHENIN BL v'yd at SAVENNIÈRES. Nicolas Joly is high priest of bio,

---

Top Côtes du Rhône producers

La Courançonne, Fonsalette (beauty), Grand Moulas, Haut-Musiel, Hugues, Montfaucon (w also), St-Estève, Trignon (incl VIOGNIER); co-ops CAIRANNE, RASTEAU; CAVE Estézargues, DOMS Bramadou, André Brunel, Charvin (terroir, v.gd), Chaume-Arnaud, Combebelle, Coudoulet de BEAUCASTEL (classy r), Cros de la Mûre (great-value), M Dumarcher, Espigouette, Ferrand (full), Gourget, Gramenon (bio), Janasse (old GRENACHE), Jaume, Famille Perrin, Manarine, Réméjeanne (w also), Romarins, Rouge-Bleu (organic, clear), Soumade, Vieille Julienne (classy); Mas Poupéras; DUBOEUF, GUIGAL (great value).

but wines were below par, better now daughter Virginie in charge. Don't chill; decant well in advance. Old vintages can be v. fine.

Courcel, Domaine de C d'O r ★★★ Leading POMMARD estate, fine floral wines with whole-bunch vinification. Top PREMIERS CRUS Rugiens and Epenots, plus interesting Croix Noires. Wines age well.

Crémant In CHAMP, meant "creaming" (half-sparkling): now called *demi-mousse/ perle*. Since 1975, AC for quality classic-method sparkling from AL, B'X, BOURGOGNE, Die, Jura, LIMOUX, Lo and Luxembourg.

Crépy Sav w ★★ DYA. Light, soft, Swiss-style white from south shore of Lake Geneva. *Crépitant* has been coined for its faint fizz.

Criots-Bâtard-Montrachet C d'O ★★★ 02' 04 05 06 07 08 09 10 11 12 13 Tiniest of the MONTRACHET family, just 1.57 ha. Not quite the concentration of full-blown BÂTARD, but pure, sensual at best: try Belland, Blain-GAGNARD, Fontaine G.

Crozes-Hermitage N Rhô r w ★★ 05' 06 07 09' 10' 11' 12' 13 SYRAH from flat v'yds nr river Isère, also granite hills next to HERMITAGE; lively, dark-berry fruit, liquorice, tar; mostly early drinking (2–5 yrs). Best (simple CUVÉES) versatile for grills, parties. Some oaked, older-vine wines cost more. Top: Belle, Y Chave, CH Curson, Darnaud, DOMS Les Bruyères, du Colombier, Combier, Dumaine (organic), des Entrefaux (oak), *A Graillot*, Hauts-Chassis, Lises (fine), Mucyn, de Thalabert of JABOULET, *Chapoutier, Delas* (Tour d'Albon, Le CLOS v.gd). Drink white (MARSANNE) early, v.gd 10 11 12.

Cuve close Short-cut method of making sparkling wine in a tank. Sparkle dies away in glass much quicker than with *méthode traditionnelle* wine.

Cuvée Wine contained in a *cuve* or vat. A word of many uses, incl synonym for "blend" and first-press wines (as in CHAMP). Often just refers to a "lot" of wine.

Dagueneau, Didier Lo w ★★★ →★★★★ 02 03 04 05' 07 08' 09' 10 11 12 (13) Best producer of POUILLY-FUMÉ, reference for brilliantly precise SAUV BL, was killed in 2008. Meticulous son Louis-Benjamin now in charge. Top CUVÉES: Pur Sang, Silex and ungrafted, astronomically priced Asteroide. Also SANCERRE, small v'yds in CHAVIGNOL; JURANÇON. Gd but tiny 2013.

d'Angerville, Marquis C d'O r w ★★★★ Bio superstar in VOLNAY, esp legendary CLOS des Ducs (MONOPOLE), but Champans, Taillepieds also first rate. New interests in Jura (Dom du PÉLICAN) to watch out for.

Dauvissat, Vincent Chab w ★★★★ Imperturbable bio producer of great classic CHABLIS from old barrels, esp local 132-litre *feuillettes*. Age-worthy wines similar to his RAVENEAU cousins. Best: Les CLOS, Les Forêts, Séchet, Preuses.

Degré alcoolique Degrees of alcohol, ie. % by volume.

d'Eguisheim, Cave Vinicole Al r w ★★ V.gd AL co-op for its size. Excellent value: fine GRANDS CRUS Hatschbourg, HENGST, Ollwiller, Spiegel. Owns Willm. Top label: WOLFBERGER. Best: Grande Rés 08 10, Sigillé, Armorié. Gd CRÉMANT, PINOT N (esp 09 10' 11 12).

Deiss, Domaine Marcel Al r w ★★★ Bio grower at Bergheim. Favours blended wines from individual v'yds, often different varieties co-planted, mixed success. Best wine RIES Schoenenbourg 08 10.

Delamotte Champ BRUT; *Blanc de Blancs* 97 02 04 06 08; CUVÉE Nicholas Delamotte. Fine small CHARD-dominated CHAMP house at LE MESNIL. V.gd *saignée* rosé. Managed with SALON by LAURENT-PERRIER. Called "the poor man's Salon" but sometimes surpasses it, as in 85 97.

Delas Frères N Rhô r p w ★ →★★★ Consistent, v. reliable, N Rhô merchant; CONDRIEU, CROZES-HERMITAGE, CÔTE-RÔTIE, HERMITAGE v'yds. Best: Condrieu (CLOS Boucher), *Côte-Rôtie Landonne*, Hermitage DOM des Tourettes (r), M de la Tourette (w), Les Bessards (red, v. fine, smoky, long life). Whites lighter recently. ROEDERER-owned.

Demi-sec Half-dry: in practice more like half-sweet (eg. of CHAMP).

Deutz Champ BRUT Classic NV; Rosé NV; Brut 00 02 04 06. Top-flight CHARD CUVÉE Amour de Deutz 04 08. One of top small CHAMP houses, ROEDERER-owned. V. dry, classic wines. *Superb Cuvée William Deutz* 02' 04 08 13'. Careful buyers in top sites.

Domaine Bouscassé SW Fr r w ★★★ 04 05' 06 08 09 10 (11) (12) BRUMONT's nerve-centre in MADIRAN. The wines are beefy like his CH MONTUS, perhaps more so. Lovely unoaked dry PACHERENC.

Domaine (Dom) Property, particularly in Burg and rural France. *See* under name, eg. TEMPIER, DOM.

Dom Pérignon Champ Superb 02', gd 03 (a surprise) 04 06 08'; rosé 02 04 06 08' 12. Luxury CUVÉE of MOËT & CHANDON. Ultra-*consistent quality*, creamy character, esp with 10–15 yrs bottle age; v. tight in youth. Late-disgorged *Oenothèque* releases 95' 88, magical Rosé 02'. More evident PINOT N recently.

Champagne in clear glass bottles + shop lights = off flavours. Beware.

Dopff & Irion Al w ★ →★★ 17th-century firm at Riquewihr, now part of PFAFFENHEIM. MUSCAT Les Amandiers, GEWURZ Les Sorcières. Fair quality.

Dopff au Moulin Al w ★★★ Ancient, top-class family producer at Riquewihr. Best: GEWURZ GRANDS CRUS Brand, Sporen 09 10' 11 12 13; RIES SCHOENENBOURG 08' 10' 12 13'; *Sylvaner de Riquewihr*. Pioneers of Alsace CRÉMANT; gd CUVÉES: Bartholdi, Julien. All wines esp gd in vintages favouring dry wines, now sought again.

Dourthe, Vins & Vignobles B'x Merchant/grower; wide range, quality emphasis: gd, notably CHX BELGRAVE, LE BOSCQ, LA GARDE. Grand Barrail Lamarzelle Figeac improving ST-ÉMILION. PEY LA TOUR, *Dourthe No 1* are well-made generic B'x, reliable quality.

Drappier, André Champ Great family-run AUBE CHAMP house. *Pinot-led NV*, BRUT ZÉRO, Brut *sans souffre* (no sulphur) ★★, Millésime d'Exception 04 06, superb Prestige CUVÉE Grande Sendrée 04' 05 09'. Cuvée Quatuor (four *cépages*). Superb older vintages 95 85 82 (magnums).

DRC C d'O The wine geek's shorthand for DOM DE LA ROMANÉE-CONTI.

Drouhin, J & Cie Burg r w ★★★ →★★★★ Deservedly prestigious grower and merchant in BEAUNE; v'yds (all bio) incl (w) Beaune *Clos des Mouches*, LAGUICHE MONTRACHET. Notably fragrant reds from pretty CHOREY-LÈS-BEAUNE to majestic *Musigny*, GRANDS-ECHÉZEAUX, etc. Also DDO (Dom Drouhin Oregon), *see* North America.

Duboeuf, Georges Beauj r w ★★ →★★★ Most famous name of BEAUJ, proponent of Nouveau. Huge range of CUVÉES and crus, consistent over many yrs.

Dugat C d'O r ★★★ Cousins Claude & Bernard (Dugat-Py) make excellent, deep-coloured GEVREY-CHAMBERTIN, respective labels. Tiny volumes, esp GRANDS CRUS, huge prices; esp Dugat-Py.

Dujac, Domaine C d'O r w ★★★ →★★★★ MOREY-ST-DENIS grower; exceptional range of seven GRANDS CRUS, esp CLOS ST DENIS, CLOS DE LA ROCHE, ÉCHÉZEAUX. Lighter colours but intense fruit, smoky, strawberry character from use of stems. Slightly deeper, denser wines in recent years. Also DOM Triennes in COTEAUX VAROIS.

Dureuil-Janthial Burg r w ★★ Top DOM in RULLY in capable hands of Vincent D-J, with *fresh, punchy whites* and cheerful, juicy reds. Try Maizières (r w) or PREMIER CRU Meix Cadot (w).

Durup, Jean Chab w ★★ Volume CHABLIS producer as DOM de l'Eglantière and CH de Maligny, now allied by marriage to Dom Colinot in IRANCY.

Duval-Leroy Champ Dynamic Côte des Blancs CHAMP house. Family-owned v'yds; source of gd, crowd-pleasing Fleur de Champagne NV, fine Blanc de CHARD 04, excellent Prestige *Femme* 96' 00' 04. New single-village/-v'yd bottlings, esp Authentis Cumières 04 06 09.

Échézeaux C d'O r ★★★ 90' 93 96' 99' 02' 03 05' 06 07 08 09' 10' 11 12' 13 GRAND CRU next to CLOS DE VOUGEOT. Middling weight, but can have exceptionally intricate flavours and startling persistence. Best: Arnoux, DRC, DUJAC, EUGÉNIE, GRIVOT, GROS, Lamarche, LIGER-BELAIR, Mongeard-MUGNERET, MUGNERET-Gibourg, ROUGET, Tremblay.

Ecu, Domaine de l' Lo (r) w dr (sp) ★★★ 05 06 09' 10' 11 12 (13) Fine bio MUSCADET-SÈVRE-ET-MAINE (esp CUVÉE Granite), GROS PLANT, sparkling Gros Plant, plus excellent CAB FR. Guy Bossard/Frédéric Niger Van Herck partnership.

Edelzwicker Al w ★ DYA. Blended light white. Delicious CH d'Ittenwiller II; HUGEL Gentil is tops.

Entraygues et du Fel and Estaing SW Fr r p w ★→★★ DYA. Miniature twin AOPS in remote Ardèche. Ice-cool whites (zinging CHENIN) best. ★★ DOM Méjanassère (w), Laurent Mousset (w; also La Pauca r, will keep). Richer white (Selves) from ★★ Nicolas Carmarans. Alaux (r) and Fages (w) best Estaing growers.

Entre-Deux-Mers (E-2-M) B'x w ★→★★ DYA. Often gd-value, dry white B'X from between the rivers Garonne and Dordogne. Best CHX BONNET, Castenet Greffier, Fontenille, Landereau, Lestrille, Marjosse, La Mothe du Barry French Kiss, Nardique-la-Gravière, Ste-Marie, *Tour de Mirambeau*, Toutigeac, Turcaud.

Esmonin, Domaine Sylvie C d'O r ★★★ Rich, dark wines from fully ripe grapes, esp since 2000. Lots of oak and lots of stems. Notable GEVREY-CHAMBERTIN VIEILLES VIGNES, CLOS ST-JACQUES. Cousin Frédéric has Estournelles St-Jacques.

Eugénie, Domaine C d'O r (w) ★★★ →★★★★ Formerly DOM Engel, bought by François Pinault of CH LATOUR (2006). Now more concentrated wines at higher prices. Hitting its stride from 2008. CLOS VOUGEOT, GRANDS-ÉCHÉZEAUX best.

Faiveley, J Burg r w ★★ →★★★★ More grower now than merchant, making succulent and richly fruity wines since sea change in 2007. Gd value from big holdings in CÔTE CHALONNAISE, but save up for top wines from CHAMBERTIN-CLOS DE BÈZE, CHAMBOLLE-MUSIGNY, CORTON, NUITS. Ambitious acquisitions in MEURSAULT, PULIGNY plus DOM Dupont-Tisserandot in GEVREY.

Food tip: dishes that go with Grenache are also likely to be good with Viognier.

Faller, Théo / Domaine Weinbach Al w ★★★ →★★★★ Founded by Capuchin monks in 1612, now run by Catherine Faller and son Théo. Outstanding wines, great complexity, now often drier, esp GRANDS CRUS SCHLOSSBERG (RIES, esp 06' 08 10'), Furstentum (GEWURZ VT 09). Wines of great *character and elegance*. Esp CUVÉE Ste Catherine SÉLECTION DES GRAINS NOBLE Gewurz 06' 09 10.

Faugères L'doc r (p) (w) ★→★★★ 07 08 09' 10 11 12 13 Leading L'DOC AC, in line for cru status, and developing category Terroir de Schiste, focusing on individuality of schist soil. Warm, spicy reds from SYRAH, GRENACHE, CARIGNAN, plus MOURVÈDRE, CINSAULT, grown only on schist hillsides; whites from MARSANNE, ROUSSANNE, Rolle. Much outside investment. Drink DOMS JEAN-MICHEL ALQUIER, Léon Barral, des Trinités, St Antonin, Ollier-Taillefer, Cébène, Mas d'Alezon, Chenaie, Chaberts, Sarabande.

Fèvre, William Chab w ★★★ Star turn in CHABLIS since HENRIOT purchase in 1998. Biggest owner of GRANDS CRUS. Les CLOS outstanding. No expense spared, priced accordingly, once again a consistent source after wobbles in early 2000s.

Fiefs Vendéens Lo r p w ★ →★★★ Mainly DYA AC. Wines from the Vendée nr Sables d'Olonne, from tourist wines to serious and age-worthy. CHARD, CHENIN BL, SAUV BL, MELON (whites), Grolleau Gris, CAB FR, CAB SAUV, GAMAY, Negrette, PINOT N (r p). Producers: Coirier, Mourat, Prieure-la-Chaume, DOM St-Nicolas. Tricky 2013.

Fitou L'doc r ★★ 07' 08 09 10 11 12 13 Powerful red from hills south of Narbonne as well as coastal v'yds. The MIDI's oldest AC for table wine, created in 1948, 11 mths barrel-ageing, benefits from bottle-age. Seek out CH de Nouvelles, DOM Bergé-Bertrand, Jones, Lérys, Maria Fita, Rolland.

Fixin C d'O r (w) ★★★ 99' 02' 03 05' 06 07 08 09' 10' 11 12' 13 Worthy and undervalued northern neighbour of GEVREY-CHAMBERTIN. Sometimes splendid

FRANCE

reds. Best v'yds: CLOS de la Perrière, Clos du Chapitre, Clos Napoléon. Growers: Bart, CLAIR, FAIVELEY, Gelin, Guyard, MORTET and revitalized Manoir de la Perrière.

Fleurie Beauj r ★★★ 09' 10' 11' 12 13 Top BEAUJ cru for perfumed, strawberry fruit, silky texture. Racier from La Madone hillside, richer below. Look for Chapelle des Bois, Chignard, CLOS de la Roilette, Depardon, Desprès, DUBOEUF, CH de Fleurie, Métrat, Sunier, Villa Ponciago, co-op.

Fourrier, Jean-Claude C d'O r ★★★★ In the hands of Jean-Marie Fourrier this GEVREY-CHAMBERTIN DOM has reached cult status, prices to match. Profound yet succulent reds, esp Combe aux Moines, CLOS ST-JACQUES, GRIOTTE-CHAMBERTIN.

Francs-Côtes de Bordeaux B'x r w ★★ 05' 08 09' 10' 12 Tiny B'x AC next to CASTILLON. Previously Côtes de Francs; new name from 2008. Mainly red but some gd white: can be tasty, attractive. Reds can age a little. Top CHX: Charmes-Godard, Francs, Laclaverie, Marsau, Pelan, La Prade, *Puygueraud*.

Fronsac B'x r ★★ →★★★ 01 03 05' 06 08 09' 10' 11 12 Underrated hilly AC west of ST-ÉMILION; some of best-value reds in B'x. Top CHX: DALEM, *la Dauphine*, Fontenil, la Grave, Haut-Ballet, Haut-Carles, Mayne-Vieil, *Moulin-Haut-Laroque*, Richelieu, la Rivière, la Rousselle, Tour du Moulin, LES TROIS CROIX, LA VIEILLE CURE, Villars. *See also* CANON-FRONSAC.

Fronton SW Fr r p ★★ 10 11 12' (13) AOP north of Toulouse. Speciality Négrette grape (sometimes as varietal) makes ideal fat-cutting partner for cassoulet: violets, cherries, liquorice. Try ★★ CHX Baudare, *Bellevue-la-Forêt*, *Bouissel*, Boujac, Caze, du Roc, Flotis, Plaisance (esp Alabets), DOM Viguerie de Belaygues.

Gagnard C d'O r w ★★★ →★★★★ A well-known clan in CHASSAGNE-MONTRACHET. Long-lasting wines, esp Caillerets, BÂTARD from Jean-Noël G; while Blain-G, Fontaine G have full range incl rare CRIOTS-BÂTARD, MONTRACHET itself. Gd value offered by all Gagnards.

Gaillac SW Fr r p w dr sw sp ★ →★★ (r) 09 10 11 12 (w sw) 05' 07' 09 10 11' 12 (p w dr) DYA. Big, complex AOP around the river Tarn. Exclusively local grape varieties (Duras, Braucol, Len de l'El, Mauzac) yield ecletic range of wines. ★★★ *Plageoles*, Causse-Marines, de la Ramaye, Peyres-Roses (all bio), newcomer Stéphane Lucas, ★★ L'Enclos des Roses, DOMS Brin, d'Escausses, Laubarel, Mayragues (bio), Rotier, Sarrabelle, CHX Bourguet (w sw), Lecusse, Larroque, Palvié (r). Gd all-rounders ★★ Mas Pignou, Mas d'Aurel, DOMS la Chanade, Duffau, Lamothe.

Gauby, Domaine Rouss r w ★★★ Leading ROUSS producer, bio. White IGP CÔTES CATALANES, eg. Les Calcinaires; red CÔTES DU ROUSSILLON-VILLAGES Muntada; Les Calcinaires VIEILLES VIGNES. Associated with DOM Le Soula. Dessert wine Le Pain du Sucre. Son Lionel developing new CUVÉES. Inspiration to other newcomers.

Gers SW Fr r p w ★ DYA IGP usually sold as CÔTES DE GASCOGNE, and indistinguishable.

Gevrey-Chambertin C d'O r ★★★ 90' 96' 98' 99' 01 02' 03 05' 06 07 08 09' 10' 11 12' 13 Village containing the great CHAMBERTIN, its GRAND CRU cousins and many other noble v'yds eg. PREMIERS CRUS Cazetiers, Combe aux Moines, Combottes, CLOS ST-JACQUES. More consistent quality these days. Top growers: BACHELET, L BOILLOT, BURGUET, Damoy, DROUHIN, Drouhin-Laroze, DUGAT, Dugat-Py, Duroché, ESMONIN, FAIVELEY, FOURRIER, Géantet-Pansiot, Harmand-Geoffroy, JADOT, LEROY, MORTET, ROSSIGNOL-TRAPET, Roty, ROUSSEAU, SÉRAFIN, TRAPET.

Gigondas S Rhô r p ★★ →★★★ 78' 89' 90' 95' 98' 99' 00' 01' 03' 04' 05' 06' 07' 08 09' 10' 11 12' V'yds on Alpine, limestone hills and stony clay-sand plain in east S Rhô Valley; GRENACHE, plus SYRAH, MOURVEDRE. Robust, smoky, often cool wines, best offer fine, clear, red fruit. Ace 2010s. More oak now, esp for US market, higher prices, but genuine local feel in many. Top: CH de Montmirail, St-Cosme (swish), CLOS du Joncuas (trad), P Amadieu, DOM Boisson, Bouïssière, Brusset, Cayron, Espiers, Goubert, Gour de Chaulé (fine), Grapillon d'Or, *les Pallières*, Pesquier, *Raspail-Ay*, Roubine, St-Gayan (long lived), Santa Duc, *Famille Perrin*. Heady rosés.

Girardin, Vincent C d'O r w ★★ ⋯★★★ Vincent has left, but the business continues as before under BOISSET ownership, with same winemaking. Sound, polished whites; competent reds.

Givry Burg r (w) ★★ 09' 10' 11 12 13 Top tip in CÔTE CHALONNAISE for tasty reds that can age. Pretty whites too. Best: JOBLOT, CLOS Salomon, *Faiveley*, F Lumpp, Masse, THÉNARD.

Gosset Champ Old house founded in the 16th century, for complex CHAMP in vinous style. Now in new premises in Épernay. V.gd CUVÉE Elegance NV. Traditional Grand Millésime 02 04 06 08' 12'. Gosset Celebris 02 04 06 08' is finest cuvée. Remarkable Celebris Rosé 05 09.

Gouges, Henri C d'O r w ★★★ Grégory Gouges continues family success with rich, meaty, long-lasting NUITS-ST-GEORGES from several PREMIER CRU v'yds. Try Vaucrains, Les St-Georges or Chaignots. Interesting white too.

Grand Cru Official term neaning different things in different areas. One of top Burg v'yds with its own AC. In ALSACE, one of 51 top v'yds. In ST-ÉMILION, 60% of production is St-Émilion Grand Cru, often run-of-the-mill. In MÉDOC there are five tiers of GRANDS CRUS CLASSÉS. In CHAMP top villages are *grand cru*. Now a new designation in Lo for QUARTS DE CHAUME, and an emerging system in L'DOC. Take with pinch of salt in PROVENCE.

Grande Champagne SW Fr AC of the best area of Cognac. Nothing fizzy about it.

Grande Rue, La C d'O r ★★★ 90' 95 96' 98 00 02' 03 05' 06 07 08 09' 10' 11 12' 13 Narrow strip of GRAND CRU between LA TÂCHE, ROMANÉE-CONTI; if not quite in same league or price. MONOPOLE of DOM Lamarche, new generation making strides.

Grands-Échézeaux C d'O r ★★★★ 90' 93 95 96' 99' 00 02' 03 05' 06 07 08 09' 10' 11 12' 13 Superlative GRAND CRU next to CLOS DE VOUGEOT, may be more akin to MUSIGNY. Wines not weighty but aromatic. Viz BICHOT (CLOS Frantin), DRC, DROUHIN, EUGÉNIE, GROS, Lamarche, Mongeard-MUGNERET.

Grange des Pères, Domaine de la L'doc r w ★★★ IGP Pays l'HÉRAULT. Cult estate neighbouring MAS DE DAUMAS GASSAC, created by Laurent Vaillé for first vintage (1992). Red from SYRAH, MOURVÈDRE, CAB SAUV; white 80% ROUSSANNE, plus MARSANNE, CHARD. Stylish wines with ageing potential; well worth seeking out.

Gratien, Alfred and Gratien & Meyer Champ ★★ ⋯★★★ BRUT 83' 98 02 04 06 08'; Brut NV. Superb Prestige CUVÉE Paradis Brut, Rosé (blend of fine yrs). Excellent quirky CHAMP house, now German-owned. Fine, v. dry, lasting, barrel-fermented wine, incl *The Wine Society's house Champagne*. Gratien & Meyer is counterpart at SAUMUR. (Cuvée Flamme and CRÉMANT.)

Graves B'x r w ★ ⋯★★ 04 05' 06 08 09' 10' 11 12 Region south of B'X city. Improving, appetizing reds, delightful SAUV/SÉM dry whites. Gd value. Top CHX: ARCHAMBEAU, Brondelle, CHANTEGRIVE, *Clos Floridene*, CRABITEY, Ferrande, Fougères, Haura, l'Hospital, Léhoul, Magneau, Rahoul, Respide, *Respide-Médeville*, St-Robert CUVÉE Poncet Deville, Venus, Vieux Ch Gaubert, Villa Bel Air.

Graves de Vayres B'x r w ★ DYA. Tiny AC within E-2-M zone. Mainly red, drunk locally.

Grès de Montpellier L'doc r p w Newish subzone of AC L'DOC with aspirations to cru status, from hills behind Montpellier, incl longer-established areas, St-Georges d'Orques, La Méjanelle, St-Christol, St-Drézery. Growers: Clavel, Terre Megère, Prose, Grès St Paul, CH de Flaugergues, L'Engarran, Haut-Blanville.

Grignan-les-Adhémar S Rhô r (p) w ★ ⋯★★ 09' 10' 11 12' Mid-Rhô AC; limited quality spread: best reds hearty, tangy, herbal. Leaders: DOMS de Bonetto-Fabrol, Grangeneuve best (esp VIEILLES VIGNES), de Montine (gd white), St-Luc, CH La Décelle (incl white CÔTES DU RHÔ).

Griotte-Chambertin C d'O r ★★★★ 90' 95 96' 99' 00 02' 03 05' 06 07 08 09' 10' 11 12' 13 Small GRAND CRU next to CHAMBERTIN. Less weight but brisk red fruit and ageing potential, at least from DUGAT, DROUHIN, FOURRIER, *Ponsot*.

Grivot, Jean C d'O r w ★★★ ⋯★★★★ Huge improvements at this VOSNE-ROMANÉE DOM in the past decade, reflected in higher prices. Superb range topped by GRANDS CRUS CLOS DE VOUGEOT, ÉCHÉZEAUX, RICHEBOURG.

Gros, Domaines C d'O r w ★★★ →★★★★ Fine family of VIGNERONS in VOSNE-ROMANÉE; stylish wines from Anne (sumptuous RICHEBOURG), succulent reds from Michel (CLOS de Réas), much-improved Anne-Françoise (now in BEAUNE) and Gros Frère & Soeur. Most offer value HAUTES-CÔTES DE NUITS; Anne has a stake in CORBIÈRES.

Gros Plant du Pays Nantais Lo w (sp) ★ →★★ DYA. AC from GROS PLANT, best (only) crisply citric: gd with oysters and other shellfish. Try: Basse Ville, Bossard, Luneau-Papin, Preuille, Poiron-Dabin. Also sparkling.

Guigal, Ets E N Rhô r w ★★ →★★★★ Global fame grower-merchant: CÔTE-RÔTIE at heart, plus CONDRIEU, CROZES-HERMITAGE, HERMITAGE, ST-JOSEPH v'yds. Merchant: Condrieu, Côte-Rôtie, Crozes-Hermitage, Hermitage, S Rhô. Owns DOM de Bonserine, VIDAL-FLEURY (fruit, quality rising). Top, v. expensive Côte-Rôties La Mouline, La Landonne, La Turque (profound, rich, new oak for 42 mths, so atypical); all reds dense. Standard wines: v. consistent, esp led by great-value CÔTES DU RHÔ (r p w). Top whites: Condrieu, Condrieu La Doriane (oaky), Hermitage.

Hautes-Côtes de Beaune / Nuits C d'O r w ★★ (r) 09' 10 11 12 13 (w) 10' 11 12' 13 ACS for the villages in the hills behind the CÔTE DE BEAUNE/NUITS. Attractive lighter reds, whites for early drinking. Best whites: Devevey, Montchovet, Naudin-Ferrand, Thevenot-le-Brun. Top reds: Carré, Cornu, Duband, Féry, GROS, Jacob, Jouan, Mazilly, Naudin-Ferrand, Verdet. Also useful large co-op nr BEAUNE.

The dodo is joined on extinction list by concept of affordable *grand cru* burgundy.

Haut-Médoc B'x r ★★ →★★★ 01 02 03 04 05' 06 08 09' 10' 11 12 Prime source of minerally, digestible CAB/MERLOT reds. Some variation in soils and wines: sand and gravel in south; heavier clay and gravel in north; sturdier. Need age. Five classed growths (BELGRAVE, CAMENSAC, CANTEMERLE, LA LAGUNE, LA TOUR-CARNET). Other top CHX: D'AGASSAC, BELLE-VUE, CAMBON LA PELOUSE, Charmail, CISSAC, Gironville, LANESSAN, Larose Perganson, Paloumey, SÉNÉJAC, SOCIANDO-MALLET. Six top communes (eg. PAUILLAC) have own ACS.

Haut-Montravel SW Fr w sw ★★ 05' 07' 08 09 10 11' 12 (13) Sweetest of the three Montravel sub-AOPS of BERGERAC, overshadowed by MONBAZILLAC and SAUSSIGNAC. Ages well. ★★ CH Puy-Servain-Terrement, DOMS Moulin Caresse and gd-value Libarde. Undervalued.

Haut-Poitou Lo r p w sp ★ →★★ Top age 3–4 yrs. AC from CAB SAUV, CAB FR, GAMAY, CHARD, PINOT N, SAUV BL. Cave du Haut-Poitou was largest producer but now bust. Dynamic Ampelidae (Frédéric Brochet) IGP wines from 107 ha; 93 ha ex-co-op under contract.

Heidsieck, Charles Champ Legendary CHAMP house, now fine under enlightened new owners. Smaller than it used to be, even better; BRUT Rés has ever more rigorous selection; Vintage 00 02' 04 08' 12' 13'. Outstanding *Blanc des Millénaires* 95' perfect now. *See* also PIPER-HEIDSIECK.

Heidsieck Monopole Champ Once illustrious CHAMP house. Fair quality. Silver Top 02 04 06 08 09 12 best wine.

Hengst Al AL GRAND CRU. Gives powerful wines. Excels with top GEWURZ from ZIND-HUMBRECHT, JOSMEYER; also AUXERROIS, CHASSELAS, PINOT N (latter not *grand cru*).

Henriot Champ BRUT Souverain NV improved by new winemaker; ★★★ BLANCS DE BLANCS de CHARD NV (base 2006); Brut 04 06 08'; Brut Rosé 05 06 09. Fine family CHAMP house. Elegant, fresh, creamy style. Outstanding long-lived Prestige CUVÉE Les Enchanteleurs 88' 95' 02 04 08'. Also owns BOUCHARD PÈRE & FILS, FÈVRE, Villa Ponciago (BEAUJ).

Hérault L'doc Largest v'yd *départment*: 84,540 ha (2010), incl FAUGÈRES, ST-CHINIAN, PIC ST-LOUP, PICPOUL DE PINET, GRÈS DE MONTPELLIER, PÉZENAS, TERRASSES DU LARZAC,

L'DOC. Source of IGP Pays l'Hérault encompassing full quality spectrum, from pioneering and innovative quality to v. basic. SYRAH, CARIGNAN, MERLOT largest plantings. Also VDT.

Hermitage N Rhô r w ★★★ →★★★★ 61' 66' 78' 83' 85' 88 89' 90' 91' 95' 96 97' 98' 99' 00 01' 03' 04 05' 06' 07' 09' 10' 11' 12' 13 Robust, "manly" SYRAH from striking granite hill on east bank of Rhô. Red, white both develop well over 20 yrs+. Complex, nutty/white-fruited, fascinating white (MARSANNE, some ROUSSANNE) best left for 6–7 yrs+. Best: Belle, *Chapoutier*, *J-L Chave* (elegant), Colombier, DELAS, Faurie (pure wines), GUIGAL, Habrard (w), JABOULET, M Sorrel, Tardieu-Laurent (oak). TAIN co-op gd (esp Epsilon, Gambert de Loche).

Hortus, Domaine de l' L'doc r w ★★★ A top L'DOC DOM. Jean Orliac was a pioneering producer of PIC ST-LOUP. Sons taking over. Stylish white IGP Val de Montferrand; elegant reds Bergerie and oak-aged Grande Rés. Also red CLOS du Prieur in TERRASSES DU LARZAC.

Hospices de Beaune C d'O Spectacular medieval foundation with grand charity auction on third Sunday in Nov, revitalized since 2005 by Christie's. Individuals can now buy as well as trade. Standards more consistent under stewardship of Roland Masse; look out for gd-value BEAUNE CUVÉES, VOLNAYS or expensive GRANDS CRUS, eg. (r) CORTON, ÉCHÉZEAUX (new in 2013), (w) BÂTARD-MONTRACHET.

Hudelot C d'O r w ★★★ VIGNERON family in CÔTE DE NUITS. New life breathed into H-Noellat (VOUGEOT), while H-Baillet (CHAMBOLLE) challenging hard. Former more stylish, latter more punchy.

Huet Lo w ★★★★ 88 89' 90' 95' 96' 97' 02' 03' 05' 06 07 08' 09' 10' 11 VOUVRAY bio estate. Anthony Hwang (owner) also has Királyudvar in Tokaji (*see* Central & SE Europe). Three single-v'yds: Le Haut Lieu, Le Mont, Clos du Bourg. Great agers: look for vintages such as 1919, 21, 24, 47, 59, 89, 90. Also *pétillant*. CHENIN BL benchmark. Noël Pinguet left 2011; tricky 2012–13 for new team.

Hugel & Fils Al r w sw ★★ ·★★★ Top AL house at Riquewihr. Entry-level Gentil (EDELSWICKER) is a delicious bargain. Late-harvest wines are often superb, esp GEWURZ VENDANGE TARDIVE 09, RIES SÉLECTION DE GRAINS NOBLES 05 06 09.

Indication Géographique Protegée / IGP The successor to VDP. No difference in status, only in unhelpful name.

Irancy Burg r (p) ★★ 05' 09' 10 11 12 13 Light red, made nr CHABLIS from PINOT N and local César. Best v'yds: Palotte, Mazelots. Best growers: *Colinot*, DAUVISSAT, Goisot, Renaud, Richoux.

Climate change, smarter viticulture make burgundy from Epineuil, Irancy, Coulanges-la-Vineuse more interesting.

Irouléguy SW Fr r p (w) ★ ·★★★ 08 09 10 11' 12 (13) Basque AOP. Brilliant rosé for picnics and barbecues masks seriousness of TANNAT/CAB FR reds and rarer (Petit Courbu) whites. ★★★ Arretxea, Mourguy and ★★ Ameztia, Brana, Etchegaraya, Ilarria; ★ Abotia, Bordathio, Gutizia. Excellent co-op (esp ★★★ Xuri d'Ansa white).

Jaboulet Ainé, Paul N Rhô r w Celebrated 19th-century owner-merchant at Tain, sold to Swiss investor 2006, prices shot up, wines now sleek, international. Once leading producer of HERMITAGE (esp La Chapelle ★★★★, quality varies 90s on), CORNAS St-Pierre, CROZES Thalabert, Roure (sound); merchant of other Rhô, notably CÔTES DU RHÔ *Parallèle 45*, CONDRIEU, VENTOUX, VACQUEYRAS. Whites lack Rhô body, drink most young. Luxury-gds emphasis, incl new v. expensive La Chapelle white.

Jacquart Champ Simplified range from co-op-turned-brand, concentrating on what it does best: PREMIERS CRUS Côte des Blancs CHARD from its member growers. Fine range of Vintage BLANC DE BLANCS 10 08 07 06 05 02 targeted at restaurants. V.gd Vintage Rosé 99 02 04 06. Globetrotting new winemaker.

Jacquesson Champ Bijou Dizy CHAMP house for lovely precise wines. Outstanding single-v'yd Avize Champ Caïn 02 04 05 08'; *saignée* Rosé Terre Rouge 04 05 – buy now, to be discontinued. Corne Bautray, Dizy 02 04 08', excellent *numbered* NV *cuvées* 728 730' 731 732 733 734 735 736 (the best yet).

Jadot, Louis Burg r p w ★★ ›★★★★ High-performance merchant house across the board with significant v'yd holdings in C D'O, MÂCON, BEAUJ; esp POUILLY-FUISSÉ (DOM Ferret), MOULIN-À-VENT (CH des Jacques, *Clos du Grand Carquelin*). Mineral whites as gd as structured reds. New winemaker expected to continue in same style but expect some refinement.

Jasnières Lo w dr (sw) ★★ ›★★★ 02 03 05' 07 08' 09' 10' 11 (13) VOUVRAY-like wine (CHENIN BL), both dry and off-dry dynamic AC, south-facing slopes in Loire Valley, Growers: L'Ange Vin, Aubert la Chapelle, DE BELLIVIÈRE, Breton, le Briseau, Gigou, Janvier, les Maisons Rouges, Ryke. 2012 minimal, 13 better but small.

Jobard C D'O r w ★★★ VIGNERON family in MEURSAULT. Top DOMS are Antoine J, esp long-lived Poruzots, Genevrières, Charmes; and Rémi Jobard for immediately classy Meursaults plus reds from MONTHÉLIE, VOLNAY.

Joblot Burg r w ★★★ Outstanding GIVRY DOM with v. high viticultural standards. Try PREMIER CRU La Servoisine in both colours.

Joseph Perrier Champ Excellent smaller CHAMP house at Châlons with fine PINOTS N, MEUNIER v'yds at sunny DOM Cumières. Supple, fruity style. Top Prestige CUVÉE Joséphine 02 ★★★★ 04 08' 12; Cuvée Royale BRUT NV; Cuvée Royale distinctive BLANC DE BLANCS 02 04 06 08.

Josmeyer Al w ★★ ›★★★ Fine, elegant, long-lived, organic dry wines. Superb RIES *grand cru* Hengst 06' 08 10 12 13'. Also v.gd lesser varieties, esp 10 AUXERROIS. Smart bio, rigorous but realistic.

Juliénas Beauj r ★★★ 09' 10' 11' 12 13 Rich, hearty BEAUJ, from surprisingly unfashionable cru. Worth discovering, eg. Aufranc, Santé, Michel Tête, Trenel.

Jurançon SW Fr w dr sw ★→★★★ (sw) 97' 03 04' 05' 07' 10 11' (12') (dr) 04' 05' 07 08 09 10' 11' (12') Geographically isolated, thus neglected, pair of AOPs for sweet and dry whites. Balance of acidity/richness key to quality. Fabulous boutique ★★★★ Jardins de Babylon (DAGUENEAU) does not overshadow ★★★ DOMS *Cauhapé*, Lapeyre, Larrédya, de Souch, Thou, ★★ CH Jolys, Doms Bellauc, Bellegarde, Bordenave, Capdevielle, Castéra, Guirardel, Nigri, Uroulat, CLOS Benguères. ★ Gd-value dry whites from Gan co-op.

Kaefferkopf Al w dr (sw) ★★★ The 51st GRAND CRU of AL at Ammerschwihr. Permitted to make blends as well as varietal wines, possibly not top-drawer.

Kientzler, Andre Al w sw ★★ ›★★★ Small, v. fine grower at Ribeauvillé. V.gd RIES from GRANDS CRUS Osterberg, Geisberg 06 08 09 10 11 12 13, lush GEWURZ from *grand cru* Kirchberg 05 09. Rich, aromatic sweet wines.

Kreydenweiss, Marc Al w sw ★★ ›★★★ Fine bio grower, esp for PINOT GR (v.gd GRAND CRU Moenchberg), PINOT BL, RIES. Top wine: *grand cru* Kastelberg, ages 20 yrs 06 08 10 11 12 13; also fine AUXERROIS Kritt Klevner, gd VENDANGE TARDIVE. Use of oak now more subtle. Gd Ries/PINOT GR blend CLOS du Val d'Eléon. Also in Rhô Valley.

Krug Champ Grande CUVÉE esp mature Grande Cuvée ("Equilibre" 2002 base) ★★★; Vintage 96 98' 00 02 03; Rosé; CLOS du Mesnil (BLANC DE BLANCS) 92 95' 00' 02'; Krug Collection 69' 76' 81 85. Supremely prestigious CHAMP house. Rich, nutty wines, oak-fermented: highest quality, ditto price. Vintage BRUT great in 98', a challenging yr. Vintage 03, still more challenging, v. successful. ££££ Clos d'Ambonnay 95' 96 98 00. Shame, no straight vintage in 2012, small but v. great for PINOT N.

Kuentz-Bas Al w sw ★★ ›★★★ Grower-merchant at Husseren-les CHX, esp PINOT GR, GEWURZ. Gd VENDANGES TARDIVES (esp 05 09). Fine, classic drier RIES 08 10.

Ladoix C d'O r w ★★ 02' 03 05' 07 08 09' 10' 11 12 13 Village at north end of CÔTE DE BEAUNE, incl some CORTON, CORTON-CHARLEMAGNE. Juicy reds and whites both exuberant and mineral, esp les Joyeuses (r), Gréchons (w). DOMS Chevalier, Loichet, Mallard, Ravaut leading revival.

Ladoucette, de Lo (r) (p) w ★★★ 08 09 10 11 12 (13) Largest individual producer of POUILLY-FUMÉ at CH du Nozet. Expensive deluxe brand Baron de L. SANCERRE Comte Lafond, La Poussie (v. serious v'yd erosion now under repair); VOUVRAY Marc Brédif, CHABLIS Albert Pic.

Lafarge, Michel C d'O r ★★★★ Classic VOLNAY bio estate run by Frédéric L, son of ever-present Michel. Outstanding, long-lived PREMIERS CRUS *Clos des Chênes*, Caillerets, CLOS du CH des Ducs. Also fine BEAUNE, POMMARD.

Lafon, Domaine des Comtes Burg r w ★★★→★★★★ Iconic DOM for great MEURSAULT, MONTRACHET, with red VOLNAY (esp *Santenots*) equally outstanding. Try separate Mâconnais DOM for value, with Dominique L also has own label in MEURSAULT.

Laguiche, Marquis de C d'O r w ★★★★ Largest owner of Le MONTRACHET and a fine PREMIER CRU CHASSAGNE, both excellently made by DROUHIN.

Lalande de Pomerol B'x r ★★ 00' 01' 04 05' 06 08 09' 10' 11 12 Emergent satellite neighbour of POMEROL. Similar style but less opulent. Variations with soils and winemaking. Top CHX: Belles-Graves, BERTINEAU ST-VINCENT, Chambrun, Les Cruzelles, La Fleur de Boüard, Garraud, Grand Ormeau, Jean de Gué, Haut-Chaigneau, *Les Hauts Conseillants*, Laborderie-Mondésir, Perron (La Fleur), Sabines, La Sergue, Siaurac, TOURNEFEUILLE.

Landron (Domaines) Lo w dr sp ★★→★★★ 05 09 10 11 12 Bio MUSCADET-SÈVRE-ET-MAINE: Amphibolite, age-worthy Fief du Breil. Gd sparkling GROS PLANT/PINOT N.

Langlois-Château Lo ★★→★★★ Fine SAUMUR sparkling (CRÉMANT de Lo only) house, BOLLINGER-owned. Still wines, esp v.gd age-worthy Saumur Blanc VIEILLES VIGNES.

Languedoc r p w General term for the MIDI, and often linked with ROUSS. Now AC enlarging COTEAUX DU L'DOC to incl MINERVOIS, CORBIÈRES and also Rouss. Rules same as for COTEAUX DU L'DOC, with period for name-changing extended to May 2017. Bottom of pyramid of Midi ACs. Hierachy of crus in pipeline.

Lanson Champ Black Label NV; Rosé NV; ace BRUT 02' ★★★, 04 06 08' 12 13. Improving CHAMP house, part of Lanson-BCC group. Long-lived luxury brand: Noble CUVÉE as BLANC DE BLANCS, rosé and vintage; pricey but no better than Brut vintage. Single-vyd CLOS Lanson 07 08 09. Blanc de B esp gd. Change of cellar guard as J-P Gandron retires.

Lapierre, Marcel Beauj r ★★★ Cult MORGON DOM run by Mathieu Lapierre, in succession to his late father, pioneer of sulphur-free winemaking in BEAUJ. Try also idiosyncratic Raisins Gaulois.

Laroche Chab w ★★ Large-scale CHABLIS grower and merchant with interests in south of France, Chile, South Africa. Majority owner now Groupe Jeanjean. Try GRAND CRU *Réserve de l'Obédiencerie*.

Latour, Louis Burg r w ★★→★★★ Famous traditional family merchant making fine

---

Champagne: ideal for a date

At last, extra figures to look at on labels. It may sound unenticing, but more producers are starting to put disgorgement dates on CHAMP labels, and this is A Good Thing. BRUNO PAILLARD was first, and is now joined by PHILIPPONNAT, JACQUESSON, CHARLES HEIDSIECK, Moutard, BEAUMONT DES CRAYÈRES, KRUG, LANSON; RUINART, MOËT and VEUVE CLICQUOT plan to do the same. It's usually only stated for vintage wines, but is useful information: the wine ages differently after disgorgement, and needs time to round out. So it helps us judge if the wine is at its peak, and thus prevents expensive infanticide.

to sound whites from C D'O V'YDS (esp CORTON-CHARLEMAGNE), Mâconnais, Ardèche (all CHARD) and less exciting reds (all PINOT) from C d'Or, Coteaux du Verdon. Now also owns Henry Fessy in BEAUJ.

Latricières-Chambertin C d'O r ★★★★ 90′ 93 95 96′ 99′ 02′ 03 05′ 06 07 08 09′ 10′ 11 12′ 13 GRAND CRU next to CHAMBERTIN, rich if not quite as intense. Best from BIZE, Drouhin-Laroze, Duband, FAIVELEY, LEROY, ROSSIGNOL-TRAPET, TRAPET.

Laudun S Rhô r p w ★→★★ 09′ 10′ 11′ 12′ 13 Front-rank CÔTES DU RHÔ-VILLAGE, west bank, top whites. Early, peppery reds (SYRAH), go-go rosés. Immediate flavours from CHUSCLAN-Laudun co-op. *Dom Pelaquié* best (esp white). Also CHX de Bord, Courac, Juliette, Marjolet, St-Maurice, DOM Duseigneur (bio), Prieuré St-Pierre.

Laurent-Perrier Champ V.gd BRUT NV; Rosé NV; Brut 02 04 06 08′ 09 12 13. Dynamic family-owned CHAMP house at Tours-sur-Marne. Fine mineral NV; excellent luxury brands: Grand Siècle la CUVÉE Lumière du Millésime (extra-special version of Grand Siècle: 02) Grand Siècle Alexandra Brut Rosé 02. But Ultra Brut still fails to impress.

Limoux: only place in France where AC white must by law be fermented in barrel.

Leflaive, Domaine Burg r w ★★★★ Top bio white burg producer at PULIGNY-MONTRACHET with a clutch of GRANDS CRUS, incl Le MONTRACHET, CHEVALIER. *Fabulous premiers crus*: Pucelles, Combettes, Folatières, etc. Try MÂCON Verzé for value.

Leflaive, Olivier C d'O r w ★★ →★★★ Négociant at PULIGNY-MONTRACHET, cousin of above. Reliable wines, mostly white, but drink young. Olivier's share from family DOM now incorporated as Récolte du Domaine. Also La Maison d'Olivier, hotel, restaurant and tasting room.

Leroy, Domaine C d'O r w ★★★★ DOM built around purchase of Noëllat in VOSNE-ROMANÉE in 1988 by Lalou Bize Leroy. Extraordinary quality (and prices) from tiny bio yields. Also original Leroy family holding, Dom d'Auvenay. *See* next entry.

Leroy, Maison C d'O r w ★★★★ Burgundy's ultimate NÉGOCIANT-ÉLEVEUR at AUXEY-DURESSES. Small parcels of grand old wines at prices to make you rub your eyes.

L'Etoile Jura w dr (sw) sp ★★ Subregion of the Jura known for stylish whites, incl VIN JAUNE, similar to CH-CHALON; gd sparkling. Top grower Philippe Vandelle.

Liger-Belair C d'O r ★★★ →★★★★ Two recently re-established DOMS of high quality. Comte Louis-Michel L-B makes brilliantly ethereal wines in VOSNE-ROMANÉE, while cousin Thibault makes plump reds in NUITS-ST-GEORGES. The former now also in Chile, the latter in MOULIN-À-VENT.

Lignier C d'O r w ★★ →★★★ Family in MOREY-ST-DENIS. Best is Hubert (eg. CLOS DE LA ROCHE), now managed by son Laurent. Class also from Virgile Lignier-Michelot, but still awaiting return to form at DOM Georges L.

Limoux Rouss r w ★★ Table wine AC to complement sparkling BLANQUETTE, CRÉMANT de Limoux. Obligatory oak-ageing for white, from CHARD, CHENIN, Mauzac. White may become a Cru du L'DOC. Red AC since 2003 based on MERLOT, plus SYRAH, GRENACHE, CABS, CARIGNAN. PINOT N illogically for a cool climate, only in CRÉMANT and for IGP. Growers: DOMS de Fourn, Martinolles, Mouscaillo, Rives-Blanques, Baron d'Arques, *Jean-Louis Denois*.

Lirac S Rhô r p w ★★ 07′ 09′ 10′ 11 12′ 13 Four villages nr TAVEL, stony soils. Medium depth, spiced red (can age 5 yrs+), recent momentum from new CHÂTEAUNEUF owners obtaining improved fruit, more flair. Reds best, esp DOMS Beaumont, Famille Brechet, Duseigneur, Giraud, Joncier, Lafond Roc-Epine, Lorentine, Maby (Fermade), André Méjan, *de la Mordorée* (best), Rocalière, Rocca Maura, R Sabon, CHX Bouchassy, Manissy, Mont-Redon, St-Roch, Ségriès, Mas Isabelle. Whites combine freshness, body (5 yrs).

Listrac-Médoc H-Méd r ★★ →★★★ 01 03 05′ 06 08 09′ 10′ 11 12 Neighbour of MOULIS in southern MÉDOC. Much improved AC for Médoc-lovers with shallow(er) pockets; now more fruit, depth. A little white AC B'X. Best CHX: Cap Léon Veyrin, CLARKE, DUCLUZEAU, l'Ermitage, FONRÉAUD, Fourcas-Borie, FOURCAS-DUPRÉ, FOURCAS-HOSTEN, Mayne-Lalande, Reverdi, SARANSOT-DUPRÉ.

Long-Depaquit Chab w ★★★ BICHOT-owned CHABLIS DOM, incl flagship GRAND CRU brand La Moutonne.

Lorentz, Gustave Al w ★★ ·★★★ Grower and merchant at Bergheim. Esp GEWURZ, RIES from GRANDS CRUS Altenberg de Bergheim, Kanzlerberg 06 09. As fine for aged as young, volume wines.

Lot SW Fr ★ ·★★ DYA. Increasingly important IGP for wines that stray beyond AOP rules (eg. whites from CAHORS growers). Ambitious ★★ DOMS Belmont, Sully, Tour de Belfort, do not eclipse ★ CLOS d'Auxonne.

Loupiac B'x w sw ★★ 02 03' 05' 07 09' 10' 11 (13) Opposite SAUTERNES across river Garonne. Lighter, fresher in style. Top CHX: CLOS-Jean, Dauphiné-Rondillon, LOUPIAC-GAUDIET, Noble, DE RICAUD, Les Roques.

Lubéron S Rhô r p w ★ ·★★ 10' 11 12' Hilly, touristy, new-money area, annex to S Rhô. Terroir okay, not top-notch. Too many technical wines, low on soul. SYRAH lead role; many wannabes. Bright star: CH de la Canorgue. Also gd: DOM de la Citadelle, chx Clapier, Edem, Fontvert, O Ravoire, St-Estève de Neri (improving), Tardieu-Laurent (rich, oak), Cellier de Marrenon, Val-Joanis, *La Vieille Ferme*.

Lussac-St-Emilion B'x r ★★ 03 05' 08 09' 10' 12 Lightest of ST-ÉMILION satellites; co-op main producer. Top CHX: Barbe Blanche, Bel Air, Bellevue, Courlat, la Grenière, DE LUSSAC, DU LYONNAT, Mayne-Blanc, Le Rival, La Rose-Perrière.

Macération carbonique Traditional fermentation technique: whole bunches of unbroken grapes in a closed vat. Fermentation inside each grape eventually bursts it, giving vivid, fruity, mild wine, not for ageing. Esp in BEAUJ, though not for best wines; now much used in the MIDI and elsewhere, even CHÂTEAUNEUF.

Mâcon Burg r (p) w DYA. Simple, juicy GAMAY reds and most basic rendition of Mâconnais whites from CHARD.

Mâcon-Villages Burg w ★★·★★★ 10' 11 12' 13 Chief appellation for Mâconnais whites. Individual villages may also use own names eg. Mâcon-Lugny. Gd choice of quality individual growers now. Try: Guillot, Guillot-Broux, LAFON, Maillet, Merlin, Rijckaert, VERGET, or for value co-ops at Lugny, Prissé, Viré.

Macvin Jura w sw ★★ AC for "traditional" MARC, grape-juice apéritif. Popular in Jura.

Madiran SW Fr r ★★ ·★★★ 05' 06 07 08 09 10' 11 12 (13) Gascon AOP; tough old styles are partly giving way to newer, fruitier wines, sometimes from same growers. ★★★ DOMS Berthoumieu, Capmartin, CLOS Basté, Damiens, Labranche-Laffont, Laffitte-Teston and *Laplace* yapping at heels of CHX *Montus* and Bouscassé. Also gd: ★★ Barréjat, Crampilh, Dou Bernés. For whites *see* PACHERENC-DU-VIC-BILH.

Mähler-Besse B'x First-class Dutch négociant in B'X. Loads of old vintages. Has share in CH PALMER.

Mailly-Champagne ★★★ Top CHAMP co-op, all GRAND CRU grapes. Prestige CUVÉE des *Echansons* 02' 04 08' 12' great for long ageing. V. refined L'Intemporelle 99 02 04.

Maire, Henri Jura r w sw ★ ·★★ Largest Jura grower-merchant, with half of entire AC. Some top wines, but many cheerfully commercial. Fun to visit, though.

Malepère L'doc r ★ DYA. AC, nr LIMOUX, for reds that combine B'X, MIDI: fresh, with touch of rusticity. Original drinking, esp CH Guilhem, de Cointes, DOM le Fort.

Mann, Albert Al r w ★ ·★★★ Top grower at Wettolsheim: rich, elegant wines. V.gd PINOT BL, AUXERROIS, PINOT N; gd range of GRAND CRU wines from SCHLOSSBERG, HENGST, Furstentum, Steingrubler. Esp fine 08 10. Immaculate bio v'yds.

Maranges C d'O r (w) ★★ 05' 07 08 09' 10' 11 12 13 Southernmost AC of CÔTE DE BEAUNE with relatively tannic reds. Gd value from PREMIER CRU. Best growers: BACHELET-Monnot, Chevrot, Contat-Grangé, Moreau.

Marc Grape skins after pressing; the strong-smelling brandy made from them.

Marcillac SW Fr r p ★★ Characterful AOP from Aveyron: light, blue-tinged, spicy, curranty wine from Mansois grape (aka FER SERVADOU). Versatile (eg. sausages or strawberries). Co-op sometimes rivals independents ★★ DOMS du Cros, Costes, Vieux Porche and ★ de l'Albinie, Carles-Gervas, la Carolie. Best at 3 yrs old.

Margaux H-Méd r ★★ ▸★★★★ 98 00′ 01 02 04 05′ 06 08 09′ 10′ 11 12 Large communal AC in southern MÉDOC famous for elegant, fragrant wines. Reality is diversity of style. Latterly much improved. Top CHX: BOYD-CANTENAC, BRANE-CANTENAC, DAUZAC, FERRIÈRE, GISCOURS, ISSAN, KIRWAN, LASCOMBES, MALESCOT-ST-EXUPÉRY, MARGAUX, PALMER, RAUZAN-SÉGLA, SIRAN, DU TERTRE.

Marionnet, Henry Lo r w ★★ ▸★★★ 09′ 10 11 12 Henry and Jean-Sébastien in TOURAINE, fascinated by grape varieties: SAUV BL (M de Marionnet, gd vintages), *Gamay* (esp Première VENDANGE), Provignage (ungrafted Romorantin vines planted 1850). Ungrafted wines, incl juicy *Côt*, mineral CHENIN BL. Small but gd 2012.

Marmande SW Fr r p (w) ★ ▸★★★ (r) 05′ 06 08 09 10 11′ (12′) Ambitious AOP on threshold of Gascony, where newly merged co-ops are improving. Rare Abouriou grape favoured esp by ★★★ cult-grower DOM Elian da Ros. Try ★★ *Ch de Beaulieu*, Doms Beyssac, Bonnet, Cavenac and CH Lassolle.

Marque déposée Trademark.

Marsannay C d'O r p (w) ★★ ▸★★★ (r) 09′ 10′ 11 12′ 13 Far north of CÔTE DE NUITS. Easy-to-drink wines of all three colours. Reds best from eg. Audoin, Bouvier, Charlopin, CLAIR, Fournier, *Pataille*, TRAPET. No PREMIERS CRUS yet, but plans afoot. Top v'yds CLOS du Roy, Longeroies; rosé gd with 1–2 yrs age.

Mas, Domaines Paul L'doc r p w ★★ Big player in south; 478 ha of own estates, controls 1,285 ha nr Pézenas as well as LIMOUX. Mainly IGP. Innovative marketing. Known for Arrogant Frog IGP range; La Forge, Les Tannes, Les Vignes de Nicole. Recent purchase of DOM Crès Ricards in TERRASSES DU LARZAC, Martinolles in LIMOUX. Côté Mas Pézenas a new project.

Mas de Daumas Gassac L'doc r p w ★★(★) 02 03 04 05 06 07 08 09 10 11 12 Once-pioneering estate that set new standards in MIDI, with CAB-based reds from apparently unique soil. Quality now surpassed by others, eg. neighbouring GRANGE DES PÈRES. Also perfumed white from CHARD, PETIT MANSENG, VIOGNIER; super-CUVÉE Émile Peynaud (r); rosé Frizant. Delicious sweet wine Vin de Laurence (MUSCAT, SERCIAL).

Massif d'Uchaux S Rhô r ★★ 10′ 11 12′ Cool, pine tree-fringed v'yds of Rhô village with talented growers, clearly fruited wines, not easy to sell. NB: CH St Estève, DOMS La Cabotte, Chapoton, *Cros de la Mûre* (v.gd, gd value), de la Guicharde, Renjarde (sleek fruit).

Maury Rouss r sw ★★ ▸★★★ NV VDN from ROUSS. GRENACHE Noir, Blanc, Gris grown on island of schist in midst of limestone hills. Much recent improvement, esp at *Mas Amiel*. Several new estates, eg. *Dom of the Bee*; sound co-op. RANCIOS age beautifully. Red table wines now also AC Maury, but SEC to distinguish from *doux*.

Mazis- (or Mazy-) Chambertin C d'O r ★★★★ 90′ 93 95 96′ 99′ 02′ 03 05′ 06 07 08 09′ 10′ 11 12′ 13 Northernmost GRAND CRU of GEVREY-CHAMBERTIN, top-class in upper part; *heavenly wines*. Best: Bernstein, DUGAT-PY, FAIVELEY, HOSPICES DE BEAUNE, LEROY, Maume, ROUSSEAU.

Mazoyères-Chambertin C d'O *See* CHARMES-CHAMBERTIN.

Médoc B'x r ★★ ▸★★★ 00′ 03 04 05′ 06 08 09′ 10′ 11 AC for reds in the flatter, northern part of the Médoc peninsula. Need to be selective, can be gd value. Top CHX: CLOS Manou, Fontis, *Goulée*, Les Grands Chênes, GREYSAC, LOUDENNE, Lousteauneuf, LES ORMES-SORBET, PATACHE D'AUX, POITEVIN, *Potensac*, PREUILLAC, Rollan de By (HAUT-CONDISSAS), *La Tour-de-By*, TOUR HAUT-CAUSSAN, Vieux Robin.

Meffre, Gabriel S Rhô r w ★★ Large Rhô merchant under BOISSET/Eric Brousse control since 2009. Owns gd GIGONDAS DOM Longue-Toque. Recent progress: less obvious oak. Also bottles, sells small CHÂTEAUNEUF doms. Reliable N Rhô Laurus (new oak) range, esp CROZES-HERMITAGE, ST-JOSEPH.

Mellot, Alphonse Lo r p w ★★→★★★★ 05 06 07 08' 09' 10' 11 12' (13) V.gd range of SANCERRE (w, esp r) small yields, bio, La Moussière (r w), CUVÉE Edmond, Génération XIX (r w), single-v'yds: Les Demoiselles, En Grands Champs (r), Romains, *Satellite* (w). Les Pénitents (Côtes de La Charité IGP) CHARD, PINOT N.

Menetou-Salon Lo r p w ★★→★★★ 05 06 07 08 10 11 12 13 Growing AOP adjacent to SANCERRE; similar if lighter whites (SAUV BL) from v'yds on gentler hills. Some gd reds (PINOT N). Best: BOURGEOIS, *Clément* (Chatenoy), Gilbert (bio), Jacolin, *Henry Pellé*, Jean-Max Roger, Teiller, Tour St-Martin.

Méo-Camuzet C d'O r w ★★★★ V. fine DOM in VOSNE-ROMANÉE (NB: Brûlées, Cros Parantoux), plus GRANDS CRUS CORTON, CLOS DE VOUGEOT, RICHEBOURG. Also less expensive négociant CUVÉES.

Mercier & Cie Champ BRUT NV, Brut Rosé NV, DEMI-SEC Brut. One of biggest CHAMP houses at Épernay. Controlled by MOËT & CHANDON. Sold mainly in France. Quality not remarkable but Demi-Sec gd. Full-bodied, PINOT N-led CUVÉE Eugene Mercier.

Mercurey Burg r (w) ★★→★★★ 03 05' 09' 10' 11 12 13 Leading red wine village of CÔTE CHALONNAISE. Gd middle-rank burg, incl improving whites. Try CH de Chamirey, FAIVELEY, M Juillot, Lorenzon, Raquillet, de Suremain.

Mesnil-sur-Oger, Le Champ ★★★★ One of top Côte des Blancs villages. Structured mineral CHARD for long life.

Méthode champenoise Champ Traditional method of putting bubbles into CHAMP by refermenting wine in its bottle. Outside Champ region, makers must use terms "classic method" or *méthode traditionnelle*.

Grapes: raising the (nearly) dead

Before 1900 there were 150+ grape varieties grown in the MIDI; most disappeared in the face of oidium, phylloxera and industrialization of the v'yds. Now some are reviving. Look for Oeillade (related to CINSAULT) from Mas des Chimères; Ribeyrenc from Thierry Navarre. CLOS Centeilles grows Piquepoul Noir, Morastel, Oeillade, Ribeyrenc Gris and Blanc and Araignan Blanc. Carignan Blanc and Terret Blanc are now appreciated for their natural acidity: try CLOS des Papillons from Mas Gabriel. There is even a revival of interest in formerly shunned Aramon and Alicante Bouschet.

Meursault C d'O (r) w ★★★→★★★★ 00' 02' 04 05' 06' 07' 08 09' 10' 11 12 13 CÔTE DE BEAUNE village with some of world's greatest whites: savoury, dry, nutty, mellow. Best v'yds: Charmes, Genevrières, Perrières. Also: Goutte d'Or, Meursault-Blagny, Poruzots, Narvaux, Tesson, Tillets. Producers: Boisson-Vadot, M BOUZEREAU, *V Bouzereau*, Boyer-Martenot, CH DE MEURSAULT, COCHE-DURY, Ente, Fichet, *Javillier*, JOBARD, *Lafon*, Latour-Labille, Martelet de Cherisey, Matrot, Mikulski, *P Morey*, PRIEUR, *Roulot*. *See also* BLAGNY.

Midi South of France. Broad term covering L'DOC, ROUSS, even PROV. Extremes of quality, improvements with every vintage. Great promise, but of course no guarantee.

Minervois L'doc r (p) (w) br sw ★★ 06 07' 08 09 10 11 12 13 Hilly AC region, with cru La Livinière; lively characterful reds, esp CHX Bonhomme, Coupe-Roses, la Grave, Oupia, St Jacques d'Albas, La Tour Boisée, Villerembert-Julien, CLOS Centeilles, Borie-de-Maurel, *Ste Eulalie*, Faiteau, co-ops Peyriac, Pouzols. *See* MUSCAT DE ST-JEAN DE MINERVOIS. New wines from Burg couple GROS and Tollot raising the bar.

Minervois-La Livinière L'doc r ★★→★★★ Quality village and Cru du L'DOC. Stricter selection and longer ageing than MINERVOIS. Best growers: Abbaye de Tholomies,

Borie de Maurel, Combe Blanche, *Ch de Gourgazaud*, CLOS Centeilles, Laville-Bertrou, *Ste-Eulalie*, DOM l'Ostal Cazes.

Mis en bouteille au château / domaine Bottled at CH, property, or estate. NB: *dans nos caves* (in our cellars) or *dans la région de production* (in the area of production) often used but mean little.

Moët & Chandon Champ By far largest CHAMP house and enlightened leader of v'yd research, development. Now owns 1,500 ha, often in best sites. Greatly improved BRUT NV, fresher, with less sugared *dosage*. Recent fine run of Grand Vintages, some 40 years+ age esp 59 76 90 93. Excellent 06 current vintage. Impressive DOM PÉRIGNON. Branches across Europe and New World.

Monbazillac SW Fr w sw ★★→★★★★ 95′ 01′ 03′ 05′ 07′ 09 10 11′ 12 (13) BERGERAC AOP: World-class sticky ★★★★ *Tirecul-la-Gravière* leads challenge to SAUTERNES from ★★★ L'Ancienne Cure, CLOS des Verdots, La Grande Maison and Les Hauts de Caillavel, ★★ CHX de Belingard-Chayne, Ladesvignes, la Rayre, Pécoula, Theulet and the co-op's *Ch de Monbazillac*.

Mondeuse Sav r ★★ DYA. SAVOIE red grape and wine. Potentially gd, deep-coloured wine. Don't miss a chance, eg. *G Berlioz*.

Monopole A v'yd that is under single ownership.

Montagne-St-Émilion B'x r ★★ 03 05′ 08 09′ 10′ 12 Largest, possibly best satellite of ST-ÉMILION. Similar style of wine. Top CHX: Beauséjour, Calon, La Couronne, Croix Beauséjour, Faizeau, La Fleur-Carrère, Haut Bonneau, Maison Blanche, Roudier, Teyssier, *Vieux Ch St-André*.

Montagny Burg w ★★ 10′ 11 12 13 CÔTE CHALONNAISE village with crisp whites, mostly in hands of CAVE de BUXY and négociants. More growers needed; Aladame is best.

Monthélie C d'O r (w) ★★→★★★ 99′ 02′ 03′ 05′ 08 09′ 10′ 11 12 Up the hill from VOLNAY but a touch more rustic. Best v'yds: Champs Fulliot, Duresses. Best from BOUCHARD PÈRE & FILS, COCHE-DURY, Darviot-Perrin, Florent Garaudet, LAFON, *Ch de Monthélie* (Suremain).

Montille, de C d'O r w ★★★ Etienne de M has expanded DOM with purchases in BEAUNE, NUITS-ST-GEORGES and outstanding VOSNE-ROMANÉE Malconsorts. Top whites incl PULIGNY-MONTRACHET Caillerets. Other interests are mini-négociant Deux Montille (white wines), CH de Puligny, both with sister Alix.

Montlouis Lo w dr sw sp ★★→★★★★ 89′ 90′ 95′ 96′ 97′ 02′ 03′ 05′ 07 08′ 09 10′ 11 Sister AC to VOUVRAY on south side of Lo, CHENIN BL; 55% sparkling. *One of Loire's most exciting ACs.* Tiny vintages 2012, 13. Top: Berger, CHANSON, CHIDAINE, Delecheneau, Jousset, Les Loges de la Folie, Moyer, Saumon, TAILLE-AUX-LOUPS, Weisskopf.

Montpeyroux L'doc ★★→★★★ Village within TERRASSES DU LARZAC with a growing number of talented growers. Aspring to cru status. Try Aupilhac, Chabanon, Villa Dondona, other newcomers. Gd co-op.

Montrachet C d'O w ★★★★ 92′ 93 95 96′ 99 00′ 01 02′ 04 05′ 06 07 08 09′ 10 11 12 13 GRAND CRU v'yd in both PULIGNY- and CHASSAGNE-MONTRACHET. Potentially greatest white burg: strong, perfumed, intense, dry yet luscious. Top wines: LAFON, LAGUICHE (DROUHIN), LEFLAIVE, Ramonet, ROMANÉE-CONTI. DOM THÉNARD improving?

Montravel SW Fr p w dr ★★ (r) 05′ 06 08 09 10 11 12 (13) (p w) DYA. Sub-AOP of BERGERAC. Oak-ageing compulsory. Hefty reds incl ★★ DOMS de Bloy, de Krevel, CHX Jonc Blanc, Laulerie, Masburel, Masmontet, Moulin-Caresse. SAUV BL-based dry whites and rosés ★★ from same and other growers. Sweet white from CÔTES DE MONTRAVEL, HAUT-MONTRAVEL, in limited sub-areas.

Moreau Burg r w ★★→★★★ Top-class CHABLIS from *Dom Christian M* (try CLOS des Hospices) and DOM M-Naudet. Separate Moreau families in CHASSAGNE and SANTENAY also v.gd.

Morey, Domaines C d'O r w ★★★ VIGNERON family in CHASSAGNE-MONTRACHET, esp Jean-Marc (Chenevottes), Marc (Virondot), Thomas (fine, mineral Baudines),

Vincent (Embrazées, plumper style), Michel M-Coffinet (La Romanée). Also Pierre Morey in MEURSAULT, best-known for Perrières and BÂTARD-MONTRACHET.

Morey-St-Denis C d'O r (w) ★★★ 90' 93 96' 98 99' 02' 03 05' 06 07 08 09' 10' 11 12' 13 Small village with four GRANDS CRUS between GEVREY-CHAMBERTIN and CHAMBOLLE-MUSIGNY. Glorious wine often overlooked. Amiot, ARLAUD, Castagnier, CLOS DE TART, CLOS DES LAMBRAYS, DUJAC, Jeanniard, H LIGNIER, LIGNIER-Michelot, Perrot-Minot, PONSOT, ROUMIER, Taupenot-Merme.

Morgon Beauj r ★★★ 09' 10' 11' 12 13 Firm, tannic BEAUJ cru, esp from Côte du Py. Becomes meaty with age. Les Charmes softer for earlier drinking. Try Burgaud, Desvignes, Foillard, Gaget, Lafont, LAPIERRE, **Ch des Lumières** (JADOT), CH de Pizay.

Mortet, Denis C d'O r ★★★ ›★★★★ Arnaud Mortet has refined late father's dark, powerful wines from BOURGOGNE Rouge to GRAND CRU CHAMBERTIN. Key wines GEVREY-CHAMBERTIN En Champs, PREMIERS CRUS Lavaut St-Jacques and Champeaux.

Moueix, J-P et Cie B'x Libourne-based négociant and proprietor named after legendary founder. Son Christian runs company, his son Edouard increasingly prominent. CHX incl: LA FLEUR-PÉTRUS, HOSANNA, Providence, TROTANOY, BELAIR-MONANGE (now incorporating MAGDELAINE since 2012). Distributes PETRUS. Also in California (see Dominus Estate).

Moulin-à-Vent Beauj r ★★★ 99 03 05' 09' 10' 11' 12 13 Potentially finest BEAUJ cru, transcending the GAMAY grape. Weight, richness of Rhô but can mature towards gamey PINOT flavours. Increasing interest in single-v'yd bottlings from eg. CH du Moulin-à-Vent, JADOT's Ch *des Jacques*, Janin (CLOS Tremblay), Janodet, LIGER-BELAIR (Les Rouchaux), Merlin (La Rochelle).

Moulis H-Méd r ★★›★★★ 01 02 03 04 05' 06 08 09' 10' 11 12 Tiny inland AC adjacent to LISTRAC-MÉDOC, with some honest, gd-value wines. Top CHX: Anthonic, Biston-Brillette, BRANAS GRAND POUJEAUX, BRILLETTE, CHASSE-SPLEEN, Duplessis, Dutruch Grand Poujeaux, GRESSIER-GRAND-POUJEAUX, MAUCAILLOU, POUJEAUX.

Moutard Champ Quirky Aubois house attached to old CHAMP grape varieties incl PINOT BL and esp boudoirish Arban(n)e. Quality greatly improved by François Moutard, son of Lucien, a character. FINE CUVÉE des Six CÉPAGES 00 02 04 06 09.

Mouton Cadet B'x Biggest-selling red B'x brand (12 million bottles). Same owner as MOUTON ROTHSCHILD. Also white, rosé and Rés GRAVES, MÉDOC, ST-ÉMILION, SAUTERNES.

Mugneret C d'O r w ★★★ VIGNERON family in VOSNE-ROMANÉE. Dr. Georges M-Gibourg best (esp ÉCHÉZEAUX), also Gérard M, Dominique M and returning to form DOM Mongeard-M.

Mugnier, J-F C d'O r w ★★★ ›★★★★ Outstanding grower of CHAMBOLLE-MUSIGNY *les Amoureuses* and MUSIGNY at CH de Chambolle. Expect finesse not blockbusters. Style works well with NUITS-ST-GEORGES CLOS de la Maréchale (reclaimed 2004).

Mumm, G H & Cie Champ Cordon Rouge NV; Mumm de Cramant now renamed BLANC de BLANCS NV (just as gd); Cordon Rouge 98 00 (★★★★) 02' 04 06'; Rosé NV. Major grower-merchant, owned by Pernod-Ricard. Marked rise in quality recently, esp CUVÉE R Lalou 99 02, GRAND CRU Verzenay.

Muré, Clos St-Landelin Al r w ★★ ›★★★ One of AL's great names; esp fine, full-bodied GRAND CRU **Vorbourg Ries** and PINOT GR. The PINOT N CUVÉE "V" 05 09 10 11 12 13, ripe and vinous, is region's best. Exceptional 09s across range.

Muscadet Lo w ★ ›★★★ DYA. (But see also below.) Popular, often delicious bone-dry wine from nr Nantes. Should never be acidic, but always refreshing. Perfect with fish, seafood. Choose a SUR LIE. Best from zonal ACS: MUSCADET-COTEAUX DE LA LOIRE, MUSCADET CÔTES DE GRAND LIEU, MUSCADET-SÈVRE-ET-MAINE. Often v.gd value but many growers struggling financially, made worse by small crops in 2012, 13.

Muscadet-Coteaux de la Loire Lo w ★ ›★★ 10 12 (13) Small, least-known MUSCADET zone east of Nantes (best SUR LIE). Esp Guindon, CH du Ponceau, Quarteron, Les VIGNERONS de la Noëlle.

Muscadet Côtes de Grand Lieu Lo ★ `·`★★★ 10 11 12 (13) MUSCADET's zonal AOP closest to Atlantic. Best SUR LIE from eg. Eric Chevalier, Choblet (DOM des Herbauges), Malidain. 2012 bad frost; 13 also small vintage.

Muscadet-Sèvre-et-Maine Lo ★ `·`★★★ 02 03 05' 06 09' 10 12 (13) Largest and best of MUSCADET's delimited zones. Top: Brégeon, Bonnet-Huteau, Caillé, Chereau Carré, Cormerais, Delhommeau, Douillard, DOM DE L'ECU, Gadais, Gunther-Chereau, Dom de la Haute Fevrie, Landron, Luneau-Papin, Métaireau, Olivier, Sauvion. Great value and ages brilliantly. *NB:* New Crus Communaux: extra lees ageing adds extra dimension. Three so far.

Muscat de Frontignan L'doc sw ★★ NV Small AC outside Sète for MUSCAT VDN. Also with late-harvest, unfortified, oak-aged IGP wines. Quality improving. Leaders: CHX la Peyrade, de Stony, DOM du Mas Rouge. Delicious with blue cheese.

Muscat de Lunel L'doc sw ★★ NV Tiny AC based on MUSCAT VDN, luscious, sweet. Some experimental late-harvest IGP wines.

Muscat de Mireval L'doc sw ★★ NV Tiny but delicious MUSCAT VDN AC nr Montpellier. A handful of small producers, plus co-op. Try new DOM de la Rencontre.

Muscat de Rivesaltes Rouss sw ★★ NV Sweet, fortified MUSCAT VDN AC wine nr Perpignan. Now preference for Muscat SEC IGP, but best worth seeking out: DOM CAZES, CH de Jau, Corneilla, Treloar, Baixas co-op.

Muscat de St-Jean de Minervois L'doc w sw ★★ Fine honeyed VDN MUSCAT. Much recent improvement, esp from DOM de Barroubio, Michel Sigé, CLOS du Gravillas, Clos Bagatelle, village co-op.

Iron Age French wine was flavoured with rosemary and basil, according to remains from near Montpellier.

Musigny C d'O r (w) ★★★★(★) 85' 88' 89' 90' 91 93 95 96' 98 99' 01 02' 03 05' 06 07 08 09' 10' 11 12' 13 GRAND CRU in CHAMBOLLE-MUSIGNY. Can be most beautiful, if not most powerful, of all red burg. Best growers: DROUHIN, JADOT, LEROY, MUGNIER, PRIEUR, ROUMIER, DE VOGÜE, VOUGERAIE.

Nature Unsweetened, esp for CHAMP – no *dosage*. Fine if v. ripe grapes, raw otherwise.

Négociant-éleveur Merchant who "brings up" (ie. matures) the wine.

Nuits-St-Georges C d'O r ★★ `·`★★★★ 90' 93 96' 98 99' 02' 03 05' 06' 07 08 09' 10' 11 12' 13 Important wine town: underrated wines, typically sturdy, tannic, need time. Best v'yds: Cailles, Vaucrains, Les St-Georges in centre; Boudots, Cras, Murgers nearer VOSNE; various CLOS – des Corvées, des Forêts, de la Maréchale, St-Marc in Prémeaux. Many merchants and growers: Ambroise, L'ARLOT, J Chauvenet, R CHEVILLON, Confuron, *Faiveley*, Gavignet, GOUGES, GRIVOT, Lechéneaut, LEROY, *Liger-Belair*, Machard de Gramont, Michelot, *Mugnier*, *Rion*.

Orléans Lo r p w ★ DYA. Scattered AC (in 2009) for white (chiefly CHARD), VIN GRIS, rosé, reds (PINOTS N, esp MEUNIER); 13 communes around Orléans; esp CLOS St Fiacre.

Orléans-Clery Lo r ★ DYA. Separate AC for simple CAB FR (difficult to ripen in poor yrs) reds from same zone as AC ORLÉANS. Try Deneufbourg.

Pacherenc du Vic-Bilh SW Fr w dr sw ★★ `·`★★★ AOP for whites of MADIRAN. Drink dry within 4 yrs; keep sweet esp if oaked; ★★★ CHX MONTUS, BOUSCASSÉ, DOMS Damiens, Berthoumieu, Capmartin, ★★ Chx Laffitte-Teston, Mascaaras, DOMS Crampilh, Labranche-Laffont, Poujo.

Paillard, Bruno Champ BRUT Première CUVÉE NV; Rosé Première Cuvée; CHARD Rés Privée, Brut 02 04 06 08 New vintage BLANC DE BLANCS 95 02 04. Superb Prestige Cuvée Nec-Plus-Ultra 95' 02. Youngest major CHAMP house. Refined, v.-dry style esp in long-aged Blanc de Blancs Rés Privée, Nec-Plus-Ultra. Bruno P heads LANSON-BCC and owns CH de Sarrin, PROV.

Palette Prov r p w ★★★ Tiny AC nr Aix-en-PROV. Full reds, fragrant rosés, intriguing whites. Traditional, serious *Ch Simone*; more innovative CH Henri Bonnaud.

Patriarche Burg r w sp ★→★★ One of larger BEAUNE-based Burg merchants, purchased by Castel (2011). Owns CH de MEURSAULT. Main brand: sparkling Kriter.

Patrimonio Cors r p w ★★ →★★★ AC Some of island's finest, from dramatic limestone hills in northern CORS. Characterful reds from NIELLUCCIO, intriguing whites, even late-harvest, from VERMENTINO. Top growers: Antoine Arena, CLOS de Bernardi, Gentile, Yves Leccia at E Croce, Pastricciola, Montemagni.

Pauillac H-Méd r ★★★→★★★★ 90' 94 95' 96' 98 00' 01 02 03' 04' 05' 06 08' 09' 10' 11 12 Communal AC in MÉDOC with three First Growths (LAFITE, LATOUR, MOUTON). Famous for its powerful, long-lived wines, stressing CAB SAUV. Other top CHX: D'ARMAILHAC, CLERC MILON, DUHART-MILON, GRAND-PUY-LACOSTE, LYNCH-BAGES, PICHON-LONGUEVILLE, PICHON-LALANDE, PONTET-CANET.

Pays d'Oc, IGP L'doc r p w ★→★★ Largest IGP, formerly VDP d'Oc, covering the whole of L'DOC-ROUSS with focus on varietal wines. 56 different varieties. Technical advances continue apace. Main producers: Jeanjean, VAL D'ORBIEU, DOMS PAUL MAS, GÉRARD BERTRAND; village co-ops, plus many individual growers. Extremes of quality; best innovative, exciting.

Pécharmant SW Fr r ★★→★★★ 05' 06 08 09 10 11 (12) (13) Inner AOP of BERGERAC noted for structure-giving iron and manganese in soil. Ageing required. Best: ★★★ *Ch de Tiregand*, Les Chemins d'Orient, CLOS des Côtes, DOM du Haut-Pécharmant, ★★ La Métairie, CHX de Biran, Champarel, d'Elle, Terre Vieille; doms des Bertranoux, de Costes.

Pélican, Domaine du Jura New property started by Burg's MARQUIS D'ANGERVILLE: 2012 first vintage. Wants to be tops in Jura.

Pernand-Vergelesses C d'O r w ★★★ (r) 99' 02' 03' 05' 06 07 08 09' 10' 11 12 13 Village next to ALOXE-CORTON containing part of great CORTON-CHARLEMAGNE, CORTON v'yds. Île des Vergelesses also first rate for reds. Growers: CHANDON DE BRIAILLES, CHANSON, Delarche, Dubreuil-Fontaine, JADOT, LATOUR, Rapet, Rollin.

Perrier-Jouët Champ BRUT NV; Blason de France NV; Blason de France Rosé NV; Brut 02 04 06 08. Fine new BLANC DE BLANCS (09 base). One of first to make dry CHAMP; strong in GRAND CRU CHARD and best for gd vintage wines and de luxe Belle Epoque 95 02' 04 06 08' (Rosé 04 06) in a painted bottle.

Pessac-Léognan B'x r w ★★★→★★★★ 95 96 98 00' 01 02 04 05' 06 08 09' 10' 11 12 AC created in 1987 for best part of north GRAVES, incl all GRANDS CRUS: HAUT-BAILLY, HAUT-BRION, LA MISSION-HAUT-BRION, PAPE-CLÉMENT, DOM DE CHEVALIER, etc. Plump, minerally reds; B'X's finest barrel-fermented dry whites.

Petit Chablis Chab w ★ DYA. Fresh and easy would-be CHABLIS from outlying v'yds not on kimmeridgian clay. LA CHABLISIENNE co-op is gd.

Pézenas L'doc r p w ★★→★★★ L'DOC subregion from v'yds around Molière's town, and aspiring Cru du L'DOC. Try: Prieuré de St-Jean-de-Bébian, DOMS du Conte des Floris, des Aurelles, Magellan, Stella Nova, Monplézy, Trinités.

Pfaffenheim Al ★→★★ Respectable AL co-op. Ripe, balanced, reflecting warm sites.

Pfersigberg Al GRAND CRU in two parcels; v. aromatic wines. GEWURZ does v. well. RIES, esp in 08 from Paul Ginglinger, BRUNO SORG, LÉON BEYER (Comtes d'Eguisheim). Top grower: KUENTZ-BAS.

Philipponnat Champ NV; Rosé NV; BRUT 99 02; CUVÉE 1522 02; CLOS des Goisses 85' 92 95 96 02 04 08 12' Small house known for winey CHAMP, now owned by LANSON-BCC group. Remarkable single-v'yd *Clos des Goisses* on a roll.

Picpoul de Pinet L'doc w ★→★★ DYA. MUSCADET of the MIDI. New AC, and Grand Vin du L'DOC, from old variety PICPOUL. Best growers: Félines-Jourdan, co-ops Pomerols, Pinet. Perfect *with an oyster* but less characteristic since it became fashionable.

Pic St-Loup L'doc r (p) ★★→★★★ 06 07 08 09 10 11 12 13 One of northernmost L'DOC v'yds, based on SYRAH. Potential AC and possibly Cru du L'doc. Growers: Cazeneuve, CLOS Marie, de Lancyre, Lascaux, Mas Bruguière, DOM DE L'HORTUS,

Valflaunès and many new. Great potential, some of MIDI's best: stylish, long-lasting. Whites are IGP, COTEAUX DU L'DOC or L'DOC.

Pierrevert Prov r p w ★ Cool high area for easy-drinking wines nr Manosque. Off the beaten track. DOM la Blaque, CHX Régusse, Rousset. AC since 1998.

Pignier Jura r w sw sp ★★→★★★★ Two bio brothers, at hilltop village Montaigu. Eclectic range, incl Poulsard, Trousseau, PINOT N, SAVAGNIN. Excellent CRÉMANT de Jura, great VIN JAUNE 99', *vin de liqueur* François Pignier.

Pineau des Charentes SW Fr Strong, sweet apéritif: white grape juice and Cognac.

Pinon, François Lo w sw sp ★★★ 89 90 95 96 97 02 03 04 05 08 09 10' 11 Excellent organic producer of v. pure VOUVRAY. Sadly hit by frost (2012) and hail (13).

Piper-Heidsieck Champ CHAMP house on up again with gd new owner. Much-improved BRUT NV and fruit-driven Brut Rosé Sauvage 04; Brut 02 04 06 09. V.gd CUVÉE Sublime DEMI-SEC, rich yet balanced. Piper-Heidsieck Rare (esp 04 06 08') is one of Champ's best-kept secrets.

Plageoles, Robert & Bernard SW Fr r w sp *Enfants terribles* and also ultra-traditional GAILLAC producers promoting many lost grape varieties: Ondenc makes fantastic sweet ★★★★ *Vin d'Autan*, ★★★ Prunelard a deep, fruity red, Verdanel (dry white of unusual personality), Duras a spicy red, Mauzac a sparkling Nature.

Plan de Dieu S Rhô r ★→★★ 10' 11 12' Vast, stony, windy plain for Rhô village nr CAIRANNE. Heady, full-bodied, authentic, mainly GRENACHE wines, drink with game. Best: CH la Courançonne, DOMS Aphillantes, Amesque, Durieu, Espigouette, Martin, Pasquiers, St-Pierre (gd trad).

Pol Roger Champ BRUT White Foil renamed Brut Rés NV; Brut 96 98' 99 00 02' 04 06 08'; Rosé 02 04 06; Blanc de CHARD 04 06 08'. Family-owned Épernay house now with vines in AVIZE joining family v'yds. V. fine, floral NV, new *Pure Brut* (zero dosage) great with seafood. Sumptuous CUVÉE Sir Winston Churchill 96' 02 04 08'. Always a blue-chip choice.

Pomerol B'x r ★★★ →★★★★ 95 96 98' 00' 01 04 05' 06' 08 09' 10' 11 12 Tiny AC bordering ST-ÉMILION but no limestone; only clay, gravel, sand. Famed MERLOT-dominated, rich, supple style. Top estates: CLINET, LA CONSEILLANTE, L'ÉGLISE-CLINET, L'ÉVANGILE, LA FLEUR-PÉTRUS, HOSANNA, LAFLEUR, PETRUS, LE PIN, TROTANOY, VIEUX-CH-CERTAN. Lack of a classification doesn't inhibit prices.

Pommard C d'Or ★★★ 90' 96' 98 99' 02' 03 05' 06 07 08 09' 10' 11 12 V. different neighbour of VOLNAY; potent, tannic wines to age 10 yrs+. Best v'yds: Rugiens for power, Epenots for grace. Talk of promotion to GRAND CRU for these two. Growers: COMTE ARMAND, J-M BOILLOT, COURCEL, HOSPICES DE BEAUNE, Huber-Vedereau, Lejeune, DE MONTILLE, Parent, CH de Pommard, Pothier-Rieusset.

Pommery Champ BRUT NV always reliable; Rosé NV; Brut 00 02 04 06 08. Historic house; brand now owned by VRANKEN. Outstanding *Cuvée Louise* 90' 02 04 08', supple Wintertime BLANC DE NOIRS.

Ponsot C d'O r w ★★ →★★★★ Idiosyncratic, top-quality MOREY-ST-DENIS DOM now with 12 GRANDS CRUS, from CORTON to CHAMBERTIN, but esp *Clos de la Roche*, CLOS ST-DENIS. Laurent-P also at forefront of fight against fraud.

Potel, Nicolas C d'O r w ★★ →★★★ Brand owned by Cottin Frères but since 2009 without its founder, Nicolas, who now owns DOM de Bellene and Maison Roche de Bellene in BEAUNE.

Pouilly-Fuissé Burg w ★★ →★★★ 05' 06 07 08 09' 10' 11 12 13 Top AC of MÂCON; potent whites; classification of terroirs pending. Wines from Chaintré softest, Fuissé most powerful, Vergisson for minerality. Top names: Barraud, de Beauregard, Cornin, Ferret, Forest, CH de FUISSE, Merlin, Ch des Rontets, Saumaize, VERGET.

Pouilly-Fumé Lo w ★ →★★★ 05' 07 08 09' 10 12 13 Across-river neighbour of SANCERRE, similar wines; best round, full, can improve 7–8yrs+. Growers: Bain, BOURGEOIS, Cailbourdin, Chatelain, DIDIER DAGUENEAU, Serge Daguenau & Filles,

CH de Favray, Edmond and André Figeat, Masson-Blondelet, Jean Pabiot, Jonathan Pabiot, Redde, Tabordet, Ch de Tracy, Ch du Nozet, Treuillet.

Pouilly-Loché Burg w ★★ 10' 11 12 13 Usually sold as POUILLY-VINZELLES. CLOS des Rocs, Tripoz, Bret Bros gd, co-op dominant for volume.

Pouilly-sur-Loire Lo w ★ DYA. Historic but now marginal, CHASSELAS wine from same v'yds as POUILLY-FUMÉ. Only 30 ha in production. Best: Serge Dagueneau & Filles, Landrat-Guyollot, Masson-Blondelet, Jonathan Pabiot, Redde.

Pouilly-Vinzelles Burg w ★★ 10' 11 12 13 Superior neighbour to POUILLY-LOCHÉ. Best v'yd: Les Quarts. Best producers: Bret Bros, Valette. Volume from CAVE des GRANDS CRUS Blancs.

Premier Cru First growth in B'x; second rank of v'yds (after GRAND CRU) in Burg. New second rank in Lo: one so far, COTEAUX DU LAYON Chaume; expect legal challenges.

Premières Côtes de Bordeaux B'x w sw ★ ·★★ 07 09' 10' 11 (13) Same zone as CADILLAC-CÔTES DE B'X but for sweet white wines only. Gently sweet rather than full-blown, noble-rotted *liquoreux*. Quality varies. Best CHX: Crabitan-Bellevue, Fayau, du Juge, Suau.

Prieur, Domaine Jacques C d'O ★★★ MEURSAULT estate with exceptional range of GRANDS CRUS from MONTRACHET to MUSIGNY. Style aims at weight from late picking and oak more than finesse, but signs of livelier approach now.

Primeur "Early" wine for refreshment and uplift; esp from BEAUJ; VDP too. Wine sold *en primeur* is still in barrel, for delivery when bottled. Caution: fingers can get burned.

Producteurs Plaimont SW Fr Brilliant co-op specializing in *oeno-tourisme*, straddles three appellations: MADIRAN, ST-MONT, CÔTES DE GASCOGNE. Phasing out all but authentic Gascon grapes. Huge range, all colours, styles, mostly ★★, all tastes, purses.

Propriétaire récoltant Champ Owner-operator, literally "owner-harvester".

Fancy a signed barrel of Brangelina's Ch Miraval? Yours for €10,000 (2013 charity auction price).

Provence *See* CÔTES DE PROV, CASSIS, BANDOL, PALETTE, LES BAUX-EN-PROV, BOUCHES-DU-RHÔ, PIERREVERT, COTEAUX D'AIX-EN-PROV, COTEAUX VAROIS-EN-PROV.

Puisseguin St-Emilion B'x r ★★ 03 05' 08 09' 10' 12 Satellite neighbour of ST-ÉMILION; wines firm, solid. Top CHX: Bel Air, Branda, Clarisse, Durand-Laplagne, Fongaban, Guibot la Fourvieille, DES LAURETS, La Mauriane, Soleil. Also Roc de Puisseguin from co-op.

Puligny-Montrachet C d'O (r) w ★★★ ·★★★★ 02' 04 05' 06 07 08 09' 10' 11 12 13 Smaller neighbour of CHASSAGNE-MONTRACHET: potentially even finer, more vital, floral, complex wine (though apparent finesse can signal overproduction). V'yds: BÂTARD-MONTRACHET, BIENVENUES-BÂTARD-MONTRACHET, Caillerets, CHEVALIER-MONTRACHET, Combettes, Folatières, MONTRACHET, Pucelles. Producers: *J-M Boillot, Bouchard Père & Fils*, CARILLON, Chartron, DROUHIN, JADOT, LATOUR, CH de Puligny, *Dom Leflaive*, O LEFLAIVE, Pernot, *Sauzet*.

Puyméras S Rhô r w ★ 10' 11' 12' Respectable, low-profile S Rhô village, high, breezy v'yds, straightforward, supple reds based on Grenache, fair whites, decent co-op. Try CAVE la Comtadine, DOM du Faucon Doré, Puy du Maupas.

Pyrénées-Atlantiques SW Fr DYA. IGP for wines not qualifying for local AOPs in far Southwest. Esp ★★★ CH Cabidos (superb PETIT MANSENG, w sw), ★★ DOM Moncaut (nr Pau), ★ BRUMONT varietals. Otherwise pot luck.

Quarts de Chaume Lo w sw ★★★ ·★★★★ 89' 90' 95' 96' 97' 02 03 04 05' 07' 09 10' 11' Tiny, exposed slopes close to Layon devoted to CHENIN BL. Loire's first GRAND CRU: v. strict rules. Best is richly textured. Esp Baudouin, *Baumard*, Bellerive, FL, Yves Guegniard, *Ch Pierre-Bise*, Pithon-Paillé, Suronde.

Quatourze L'doc r (p) w ★★ DYA. Tiny potential Grand Vin du L'DOC by Narbonne.

CH Notre Dame du Quatourze courageously maintains reputation virtually single-handedly.

Quincy Lo w ★ ·★★ Drink within 3 yrs. Small AOP on gravel west of Bourges in Cher Valley. Citric, quite SANCERRE-style SAUV BL. Hail-prone. Growers: Mardon, Portier, Rouzé, Siret-Courtaud, Tatin-Wilk (DOMS Ballandors, Tremblay).

Rancio Rouss The most original, lingering, delicious style of VDN, reminiscent of Tawny Port, in BANYULS, MAURY, RIVESALTES, RASTEAU, wood-aged and exposed to oxygen and heat. Same flavour (pungent, tangy) is a fault in table wine.

Rangen Al Most southerly GRAND CRU of AL at Thann. Extremely steep (average 90%) slopes, volcanic soils. Top wines: powerful RIES, PINOT GR from ZIND-HUMBRECHT (CLOS St-Urbain 00' 05 09' 10 12) and SCHOFFIT (St-Theobald). With climate change, cooler vintages may show more finesse.

Rasteau S Rhô r (p) (w) br (dr) sw ★★ 07' 09' 10' 11 12' Punchy reds from clay soils, carry local identity, mainly GRENACHE. NB: Beaurenard, *Cave Ortas* (gd), CH du Trignon, DOMS Beau Mistral, Didier Charavin, Collière, Coteaux des Travers, Escaravailles, Girasols, Gourt de Mautens (talented, IGP wines from 2010), Grand Nicolet, Rabasse-Charavin, Soumade, St Gayan, Famille Perrin. Grenache dessert VDN quality rising (Doms Banquettes, Coteaux des Travers, Escaravailles, Trapadis).

Ratafia de Champagne Champ Sweet apéritif made in CHAMP of 67% grape juice and 33% brandy. Not unlike PINEAU DES CHARENTES.

Raveneau Chab w ★★★★ Great CHABLIS producer using old methods for *extraordinary long-lived wines*. Cousin of DAUVISSAT. Look for Vaillons, Blanchots, Les CLOS.

Regnié Beauj r ★★ 11' 12 13 Most recently promoted, often lightest of BEAUJ crus. Sandy soil gives easy, fruity wines; try Burgaud, Dupré, de la Plaigne, Rochette, Sunier.

Reuilly Lo r p w ★ ·★★★ 05' 08 09' 10 11 12 13 Small improving AC west of Bourges for SAUV BL whites, plus rosés and *Vin Gris* from PINOT N and/or PINOT GR, and Pinot N. Best: Jamain, Claude Lafond, Mardon, Rouze, Sorbe. 2012 frosted.

Ribonnet, Domaine de SW Fr r p w ★★ South of Toulouse, Christian Gerber (godfather to the IGP ARIÈGE) uses grape varieties from all over Europe to make fascinating varietals and blends in all colours.

Riceys, Rosé des Champ p ★★★ DYA. Minute AC in AUBE for a notable PINOT N rosé. Principal producers: *A Bonnet*, Jacques Defrance, Morize. Great 09.

Richebourg C d'O r ★★★★ 90' 93' 95 96' 98 99' 00 02' 03 05' 06 07 08 09' 10' 11 12' 13 VOSNE-ROMANÉE GRAND CRU. Magical burg, great depth of flavour, vastly expensive. Growers: DRC, GRIVOT, GROS, HUDELOT-Noellat, LEROY, LIGER-BELAIR, MÉO-CAMUZET.

Rimage Rouss Increasingly fashionable trend for a vintage VDN. Super-fruity for drinking young. Think gd Ruby Port.

Rion, Patrice C d'O r ★★★ Prémeaux-based DOM with excellent NUITS-ST-GEORGES holdings, esp CLOS des Argillières, Clos St-Marc, CHAMBOLLE. NB: also Dom Daniel R in Prémeaux, B & A Rion in VOSNE-ROMANÉE.

Rivesaltes Rouss r w br dr sw ★★ Often NV or solera. Fortified wine, nr Perpignan. A struggling but worthwhile tradition. Top producers: DOM CAZES, de Rancy (des Chênes), CH de Jau,, Sarda-Malet, des Schistes, Vaquer. Best are delicious, original, esp old RANCIOS of extraordinary longevity. *See* MUSCAT DE RIVESALTES.

Roche-aux-Moines, La Lo w sw ·★★★ 89' 90' 96' 99 02 03 05' 06 07 08' 09 10' 11 12 (13) Cru of SAVENNIÈRES, ANJOU. New strict rules. Powerful, intensely mineral, age-worthy wine. Growers: Le CLOS de la Bergerie (Joly), DOM des Forges, FL, Dom M Laroche, Damien Laureau, CH PIERRE-BISE.

Roederer, Louis Champ BRUT Premier NV; Rich NV; Brut 00 02' 04 06; BLANC DE BLANCS 99 00 02 04 07 08' 10 13; Brut Rosé 06 07 08. Top family-owned house; enviable estate of top v'yds, many now bio. Flavoury NV, magnificent *Cristal* (can be greatest of all prestige CUVÉES, viz 88' 90' 96 02' 04), Cristal Rosé 96'

02' 05 06. New late-release Cristal 95 due 2015. Brut Nature project shelved for moment. Also owns DEUTZ, DELAS, CHX DE PEZ, PICHON-LALANDE. *See also* California.

Rolland, Michel B'x Ubiquitous and fashionable consultant winemaker and MERLOT specialist working in B'X and worldwide. Recently sold family properties (BERTINEAU ST-VINCENT, BON PASTEUR) to a Chinese concern.

Rolly Gassmann Al w sw ★★ Revered grower at Rorschwihr, esp from Moenchreben. Off-dry style culminates in great rich GEWURZ CUVÉE Yves 05 06 08 09 10 12. Bio methods bring more finesse here.

Romanée, La C d'O r ★★★★ 96' 99' 00 01 02' 03 05' 06 07 08 09' 10' 11 12' 13 Tiniest GRAND CRU in VOSNE-ROMANÉE, MONOPOLE of Comte LIGER-BELAIR. Exceptionally fine, perfumed, intense and understandably expensive.

Romanée-Conti, Dom de la / DRC C d'O r w ★★★★ Grandest estate in Burgundy. Incl the whole of ROMANÉE-CONTI and LA TÂCHE, major parts of ÉCHÉZEAUX, GRANDS-ÉCHÉZEAUX, RICHEBOURG, ROMANÉE-ST-VIVANT and a tiny part of MONTRACHET. CORTON is new from 2009. Crown-jewel prices (if you can buy them at all). Keep top vintages for decades.

Romanée-Conti, La C d'O r ★★★★ 78' 85' 88' 89' 90' 93' 95 96' 97 98 99' 00 01 02' 03 05' 06 07 09' 10' 11 12' 13 MONOPOLE GRAND CRU in VOSNE-ROMANÉE; 450 cases/annum. Most celebrated and expensive red wine in world, at best with reserves of flavour beyond imagination. Cellar 15 yrs+ for best results.

Romanée-St-Vivant C d'O r ★★★★ 90' 93 95 96' 99' 02' 03 05' 06 07 08 09' 10' 11 12' 13 GRAND CRU in VOSNE-ROMANÉE. Downslope from LA ROMANÉE-CONTI, hauntingly perfumed, with intensity more than weight. Ready a little earlier than its famous neighbours. Growers: if you can't afford DRC or LEROY, try ARLOT, CATHIARD, J J Confuron, Follin-Arbelet, HUDELOT-Noellat, LATOUR.

Rosacker Al GRAND CRU at Hunawihr. Some of best AL RIES (CLOS STE-HUNE, SIPP-MACK).

Rosé d'Anjou Lo p ★→★★ DYA. Slightly sweet rosé (Grolleau grape dominates). Often price-sensitive. Some gd, esp: Mark Angeli, Clau de Nell, DOMS de la Bergerie, les Grandes Vignes, des Sablonnettes.

Rosé de Loire Lo p ★→★★ DYA. Driest of ANJOU's rosés: six varieties, esp GAMAY, Grolleau. AC technically covers SAUMUR, TOURAINE. Best: Bablut, CAVE de Saumur, Ogereau, CH PIERRE-BISE, Richou, Soucherie. Refreshing summer wine.

Rosette SW Fr w s/sw ★★ DYA BERGERAC's Cinderella AOP makes flowery off-dry apéritif wines, perfect with foie gras or mushrooms. Try ★★ CLOS Romain, CHX Puypezat-Rosette, Combrillac, Spingulèbre, DOMS de la Cardinolle, de Coutancie, du Grand-Jaure.

Rossignol-Trapet Burg r ★★★ Equally bio cousins of DOM TRAPET, with healthy holdings of GRAND CRU v'yds esp CHAMBERTIN. Gd-value across range from GEVREY VIEILLES VIGNES up. Also some BEAUNE v'yds from Rossignol side.

Rostaing, René N Rhô r w ★★★ 95' 99' 01' 05' 06' 07' 09' 10' 11 12' 13 CÔTE-RÔTIE DOM: old, central v'yds; three tight-knit wines, all v. fine, silky fruit, careful oak, wait 5–6 yrs. Enticing, top-class Côte Blonde (5% VIOGNIER), also La Landonne (dark fruits, 15–20 yrs). Decant. Intricate, unshowy CONDRIEU, also L'DOC Dom Puech Noble (r w).

Rouget, Emmanuel C d'O r ★★★★ Inheritor of the legendary estate of Henri Jayer in ÉCHÉZEAUX, NUITS-ST-GEORGES, VOSNE-ROMANÉE. Top wine Vosne-Romanée Cros Parantoux (alarming price).

Roulot, Domaine C d'O w ★★★→★★★★ Outstanding MEURSAULT producer; great PREMIERS CRUS eg. CLOS des Bouchères (from 2011), Charmes, Perrières, but try also top village sites Luchets, esp Tesson Clos de Mon Plaisir.

Roumier, Georges C d'O r ★★★★ Reference DOM for BONNES-MARES and other *brilliant Chambolle* wines in capable hands of Christophe R. Long-lived wines but still attractive early. Has become expensive thanks to secondary market.

Rousseau, Domaine Armand C d'O r ★★★★ Unmatchable GEVREY-CHAMBERTIN DOM with thrilling CLOS ST-JACQUES and GRANDS CRUS. Fragrance, balance, persistence throughout range, now inceased with CH de Gevrey-Chambertin v'yds.

Roussette de Savoie Sav w ★★ DYA. Tastiest fresh white from south of Lake Geneva.

Roussillon Leading region for traditional VDN (eg. MAURY, RIVESALTES, BANYULS). Younger vintage RIMAGE wines are competing with aged RANCIO wines. Also fine table wines. *See* CÔTES DU ROUSS (and CÔTES DU ROUSS-VILLAGES), COLLIOURE, new AC MAURY and IGP CÔTES CATALANES. Region incl under AC L'DOC.

Ruchottes-Chambertin C d'O r ★★★★ 90' 93' 95 96' 98 99' 00 02' 03 05' 06 07 08 09' 10' 11 12' 13 Tiny GRAND CRU neighbour of CHAMBERTIN. Less weighty but ethereal, intricate, lasting wine of great finesse. Top growers: MUGNERET-Gibourg, ROUMIER, ROUSSEAU.

Ruinart Champ "R" de Ruinart BRUT NV; Ruinart Rosé NV; "R" de Ruinart Brut 02' 04 06 08. Oldest house, owned by Moët-Hennessy. Already high standards going higher still. Rich, elegant wines. Prestige CUVÉE *Dom Ruinart* is one of two best vintage BLANC DE BLANCS in CHAMP (viz 88' 95' 02' 04). DR Rosé also v. special 88 96 02'. NV Blanc de Blancs improving; could be better still.

Rully Burg r w ★★ (r) 09' 10' 12 13 (w) 09' 10' 12 13 CÔTE CHALONNAISE village. *Whites are light, fresh, tasty*, gd value. Reds also fruit-forward. Try Devevey, DROUHIN, DUREUIL-JANTHIAL, FAIVELEY, Jacqueson, Claudie Jobard, Ninot, Rodet.

Sable de Camargue L'doc r p w ★ DYA. Used to be called Sables du Golfe du Lion. IGP from Mediterranean coastal sand-dunes: esp pink Gris de Gris from CARIGNAN, CINSAULT. Giant Listel dominates, but small growers developing.

Pity the vignerons of Savigny-lès-Beaune, heavily hailed on in 2012 and in 2013.

Sablet S Rhô r (p) w ★★ 10' 11' 12' Fun but also serious wines from improving CÔTES DU RHÔ-VILLAGE. Sandy soils, red-berry reds, esp CAVE co-op Gravillas, DOMS de Boisson, Espiers, Les Goubert, Pasquiers, Piaugier. Gd full whites for apéritifs, food.

St-Amour Beauj r ★★ 11' 12 13 Northernmost cru of BEAUJ: light, fruity, somewhat anonymous. Tediously recommended on 14 Feb. Try: Janin, *Patissier*, Revillon.

St-Aubin C d'O r w ★★★ (r) 05' 08 09' 10' 11 12 13 (w) 07 08 09' 10' 11 12 13 Fine source for *lively, refreshing whites*, adjacent to PULIGNY and CHASSAGNE, also pretty reds. Best v'yds: En Remilly, Murgers Dents de Chien. Best growers: J C Bachelet, COLIN, COLIN-MOREY, Lamy, Prudhon.

St-Bris Burg w ★ DYA. Neighbour to CHABLIS. Unique AC for SAUV BL in Burg. Fresh, lively, worth keeping from J-H Goisot. Try also Bersan, de Moor, Simonnet-Febvre.

St-Chinian L'doc r ★→★★★ 06 07' 08 09' 10 11 12 13 Hilly area of growing reputation in L'DOC. AC for red (since 1982) and white (since 2005). Incl crus of Berlou, Roquebrun. Warm, spicy southern reds, based on SYRAH, GRENACHE, CARIGNAN. Gd co-op Roquebrun; CH de Viranel, Coujan. DOMS Madura, Rimbaud, Navarre, Borie la Vitarèle, la Dournie, des Jougla, CLOS Bagatelle, Mas Champart and many others, new and old. Well worth exploring.

Ste-Croix-du-Mont B'x w sw ★★ 03' 05' 07 09' 10' 11 (13) Sweet white AC facing SAUTERNES across the river Garonne. Worth trying the best, ie. CHX Crabitan-Bellevue, *Loubens*, du Mont, Pavillon, la Rame.

St-Émilion B'x r ★★ →★★★★ 96 98' 00' 01 03 04 05' 08 09' 10' 11 12 Large MERLOT-dominated district on B'x's Right Bank. CAB FR also important. St-Émilion PREMIER GRAND CRU CLASSÉ the top designation. Warm, full, rounded style (can drink early); best firm, v. long-lived. Also modern and traditional styles. Quality can vary. Top CHX: ANGÉLUS, AUSONE, CANON, CHEVAL BLANC, CLOS FOURTET, FIGEAC, PAVIE.

St-Estèphe H-Méd r ★★ →★★★★ 95' 96' 98 00' 01 02 03 04 05' 06 08 09' 10' 11 12 Most northerly communal AC in the MÉDOC. Solid, structured wines of increasingly reliable quality. Top CHX: COS D'ESTOURNEL, MONTROSE, CALON-SÉGUR have had enormous investment. Also many top unclassified estates eg. CLAUZET, LE CROCK, HAUT-MARBUZET, MEYNEY, ORMES-DE-PEZ, DE PEZ, PHÉLAN-SÉGUR.

Ste-Victoire Prov r p ★★ Subzone of CÔTES DE PROV from southern slopes of Montagne Ste-Victoire. Dramatic scenery goes with gd wine. Try Mas de Cadenet, Mauvan.

St-Gall Champ BRUT NV; Extra Brut NV; Brut BLANC DE BLANCS NV; Brut Rosé NV; Brut Blanc de Blancs **02 04 06** 08'; CUVÉE Orpale Blanc de Blancs **95 02 04 06** 08' 09 10. Brand used by Union-CHAMP: top growers' co-op at AVIZE. Fine-value Pinot-led *Pierre Vaudon NV.*

St Georges d'Orques L'doc r p ★★ ·★★★ More individual part of sprawling GRÈS DE MONTPELLIER, aspiring to individual cru status. Try l'Engarran, la Prose.

St-Georges-St-Emilion B'x r ★★ **03 05' 08 09' 10'** 12 Miniscule ST-ÉMILION satellite. Usually gd quality. Best CHX: Calon, MACQUIN-ST-GEORGES, ST-GEORGES, TOUR DU PAS-ST-GEORGES, Vieux Montaiguillon.

St-Germain, Dom Sav Organic DOM of two young brothers in the Combe de SAVOIE. Try their MONDEUSE Le Pied de la Barme, a red keeper.

St-Gervais S Rhô r (p) (w) ★ **09' 10' 11 12'** 13 West bank Rhô village; gd soils but limited choice. Co-op trying to improve, but best is top-grade, long-lived (10 yrs+) DOM Ste-Anne red (firm, strong MOURVÈDRE liquorice flavours); gd VIOGNIER.

Whole-bunch fermentation

Some talk of stems, others of whole-bunch fermentation, or *vendanges entières* in French. It's becoming trendy again in Burg, having previously been the preserve of a few celebrated exponents such as DRC, DOMS DUJAC, DE L'ARLOT. The late Henri Jayer didn't approve of it at all, but he is no longer with us, and with riper grapes and browner stems in recent yrs, the idea is gaining in appeal. If you ferment your grapes with the stems still part of the bunches, it changes the texture and enhances the aromatic profile, adding peppery or crushed-strawberry notes. You may love it or hate it, but if you are in either camp, it's worth finding out who does what.

St-Joseph N Rhô r w ★★ **99' 01' 05' 06' 07' 09' 10' 11' 12'** 13 65 km granite v'yds along west bank of N Rhô. SYRAH reds. Oldest, best zone nr Tournon: stylish, red-fruited wines; further north darker, peppery, oak. More complete, structured wines than CROZES-HERMITAGE, esp CHAPOUTIER (Les Granits), J-L CHAVE, Gonon (top class), *B Gripa*, GUIGAL (*lieu-dit* St-Joseph); also Chèze, Courbis, Coursodon (racy, modern), Cuilleron, *Delas*, J & E Durand, B Faurie (delicate), Faury, Gaillard, P Marthouret, Monier-Perréol (organic), A Perret, Nicolas Perrin, Vallet, P-J Villa, F Villard. Gd food-friendly *white (mainly Marsanne)*, esp Barge, CHAPOUTIER (Les Granits), Cuilleron, Gonon (fab), Gouye, B Gripa, Faury, A Perret, J Pilon.

St-Julien H-Méd r ★★★ ·★★★★ **95' 96' 98 00' 01 02 03 04 05' 06 08 09' 10' 11** 12 Small mid-MÉDOC communal AC. 11 classified (1855) estates own 80% of the v'yds. Includes three LÉOVILLES, BEYCHEVELLE, DUCRU-BEAUCAILLOU, GRUAUD-LAROSE. The epitome of harmonious, fragrant, savoury red wine.

Saint Mont SW Fr r p w ★★ (r) **09 10 11** 12' (p w) DYA. AOP in Gers, sandwiched between Armagnac, MADIRAN. Virtual *monopole* of PRODUCTEURS PLAIMONT. Or from ★ DOM des Maouries, saxophonist J-L Garoussia (Dom de Turet), CH la Bergalasse.

St-Nicolas-de-Bourgueil Lo r p ★ ·★★★ **89' 90' 96' 02' 03 05' 06 08 09 10' 11** 12 (13) Companion AC to BOURGUEIL: identical but pricier wines from CAB FR. Mostly gravel soils. Ranges from light (sand/gravel) to age-worthy (limestone slopes). Try: YANNICK AMIRAULT, Cognard, David, Delanoue, Lorieux, Frédéric Mabileau, Laurent Mabileau, Mabileau-Rezé, Taluau-Foltzenlogel, Vallée.

St-Péray N Rhô w sp ★★ 09' 10' 11' 12' 13' Underrated white Rhô (MARSANNE plus ROUSSANNE) from hilly granite, lime v'yds opposite Valence. *Méthode Champenoise, worth trying* (J-L Thiers). Still white should have grip, be smoky. Avoid fat wines from v. ripe fruit plus oak. Best: S Chaboud, CHAPOUTIER, *Clape* (pure), Colombo (stylish), Cuilleron, B Gripa (v.gd), J-L Thiers, TAIN co-op, du Tunnel, Voge (oak).

St-Pourçain Mass C r p w ★→★★ DYA. AC (19 communes. Light red, rosé from GAMAY, PINOT N (AOP rules stupidly forbid pure PINOT N), white from local Tressalier and/or CHARD or SAUV BL. Growers: Berioles, DOM de Bellevue, Grosbot-Barbara, Laurent, Nebout, Pétillat, Ray, gd co-op (VIGNERONS de St-Pourçain) with range of styles, incl drink-me-up CUVÉE Ficelle.

St-Romain C d'O r w ★★ (w) 09' 10' 11 12 13 *Crisp, mineral whites*, clean-cut reds from vines tucked away in back of CÔTE DE BEAUNE. PREMIER CRU v'yds under discussion for eg. Sous le CH. Alain Gras best. Also Bellene, Buisson, De Chassorney.

St-Véran Burg w ★★ 10' 11 12 13 AC outside POUILLY-FUISSÉ with variable results, depending on soil and producer. Best are exciting. DUBOEUF, Deux Roches, Poncetys for value, Cordier, Corsin, Merlin for top quality.

Salon Champ ★★★★ Original BLANC DE BLANCS, from LE MESNIL in Côte des Blancs. Tiny quantities. Awesome reputation for long-lived wines: in truth, sometimes inconsistent but on song recently, viz 88' 96' 97', but 99 disappoints. Occasional releases of old wines from cellars, but not to the likes of you or me.

Sancerre Lo (r) (p) w ★→★★★ 05' 08' 10 11 12 13 Benchmark SAUV BL, often more aromatic and vibrant than POUILLY-FUMÉ. Best wines age 10 yrs+. Increasingly fine reds (PINOT N). Rosé rarely worth money. Best: Boulay, BOURGEOIS, Cotat, François Crochet, Lucien Crochet, Dezat, Dionysia, Fouassier, Thomas Laballe, ALPHONSE MELLOT, Pierre Martin, Mollet, Pinard, Pascal & Nicolas Reverdy, *Raimbault, Claude Riffault*, Jean-Max Roger, Roblin, Vacheron, André Vatan, Michel Vattan. 2013 smallish crop.

Santenay C d'O r (w) ★★★ 99' 02' 03 05' 06 07 08 09' 11 12 13 Sturdy reds from spa village south of CHASSAGNE-MONTRACHET. Best v'yds more succulent: La Comme, Les Gravières, CLOS Rousseau, Clos de Tavannes. Increasing interest in whites. Top growers: Belland, GIRARDIN, Lequin-Colin, Jessiaume, MOREAU, V MOREY, Muzard, Vincent.

Saumur Lo r p w sp ★→★★★ 05' 06 07 08 09' 10' 11 12 (13) Umbrella AC for whites from light to serious, mainly easy reds except SAUMUR-CHAMPIGNY zone, pleasant rosés, big sparkling production: CRÉMANT, Saumur Mousseux. Saumur-Le-Puy-Notre-Dame AOP for CAB FR reds covering 17 communes: misleadingly wide. Producers: *Bouvet-Ladubay*, CHAMPS FLEURIS, *Antoine Foucault*, René-Hugues Gay, Guiberteau, CLOS Mélaric, Paleine, St-Just, Clos ROUGEARD, CHX DE VILLENEUVE, Parnay, Yvonne; CAVE des VIGNERONS de Saumur. Difficult 2012, 13.

Saumur-Champigny Lo r ★★ →★★★ 96' 02' 03 05' 06 08' 09' 10 11 12 (13) Popular nine-commune AC for CAB FR, ages 15–20 yrs in gd vintages. Look for Bruno Dubois, CHX de Targé, DE VILLENEUVE; CLOS Cristal, CLOS ROUGEARD, CHAMPS FLEURIS, de la Cune, Filliatreau, Hureau, Legrand, Nerleux, Roches Neuves, St-Just, Antoine Sanzay, Saumur Co-op, Vadé, Val Brun, Yvonne.

Saussignac SW Fr w sw ★★ →★★★ 07' 09 10 11 12' BERGERAC AOP adjoining MONBAZILLAC, fully sweet but with a touch more acidity. Best: ★★★ DOMS de Richard, La Maurigne, Les Miaudoux, *Clos d'Yvigne*, Lestevénie, ★★ CHX Le Chabrier, Court-des-Mûts, Le Payral, Le Tap.

Sauternes B'x w sw ★★ →★★★★ 88' 89' 90' 95 96 97' 98 99' 01' 02 03' 05' 07' 09' 10' 11' (13) District of five villages (incl BARSAC) that make France's best sweet wine. Strong, luscious, golden. Spate of great yrs recently (except 2012). Top CHX: D'YQUEM, CLOS HAUT-PEYRAGUEY, FARGUES, GUIRAUD, LAFAURIE-PEYRAGUEY, RIEUSSEC, SUDUIRAUT, LA TOUR-BLANCHE, etc. Dry wines cannot be sold as Sauternes.

Sauzet, Etienne C d'O w ★★★ Leading PULIGNY DOM with superb PREMIERS CRUS (Combettes, Folatières) and GRANDS CRUS (BÂTARD, etc). Fresh, lively wines, once again capable of ageing.

Savennières Lo w dr sw ★★★→★★★★ 89' 96' 97' 99 02' 03 05' 06 07 08' 09 10' 11 12 (13) A small ANJOU district for fine, stylistically varied, long-lived whites (CHENIN BL). Baudouin, BAUMARD, Boudignon, Closel, *Clos de Coulaine (see* CH PIERRE-BISE), CH d'Epiré, FL, Guigniard, Laureau, Mahé, Mathieu-Tijou, Morgat, Ogereau, Pithon-Paillé, *Ch Soucherie*. Top sites: COULÉE DE SERRANT, ROCHE-AUX-MOINES, CLOS du Papillon.

Savigny-lès-Beaune C d'O r (w) ★★★ 99' 02' 03 05' 07 08 09' 10' 11 12 Important village next to BEAUNE; similar mid-weight wines, should be delicious and lively; can be rustic. Top v'yds: Dominode, Guettes, Lavières, Marconnets, Vergelesses. Growers: *Bize*, Camus, *Chandon de Briailles*, CLAIR, Ecard, Girard, Guyon, LEROY, Pavelot, TOLLOT-BEAUT.

Savoie Sav r w sp ★★ DYA. Alpine area with light, dry wines like some Swiss or minor Loires. APRÉMONT, CRÉPY, SEYSSEL best-known whites; Roussette more interesting. *Also gd Mondeuse red.*

Schlossberg Al GRAND CRU at Kientzheim famed since the 15th century. Glorious compelling RIES from FALLER. Outstanding 2010.

Schlumberger, Domaines Al w sw ★ →★★★ Vast, top-quality AL DOM at Guebwiller owning approx 1% of all AL v'yds. Holdings in GRANDS CRUS Kitterlé, Kessler, Saering (08' ★★★ 09 10' 12 13), Spiegel. Rich wines. Rare RIES, signature CUVÉE Ernest and now PINOT GR Grand Cru Kessler 09' 10' 12 13.

Schoenenbourg Al V. rich, successful Riquewihr GRAND CRU: PINOT GR, RIES, v. fine VENDANGE TARDIVE, SÉLECTION DES GRAINS NOBLES, esp DOPFF AU MOULIN. Also v.gd MUSCAT.

Schoenheitz Al Coming estate in Munster Valley. Esp gd dry entry-level RLES 09 10 11. Lovely floral RIES Linnenberg 08 10 12.

Schoffit, Domaine Al w ★★★ Exceptional Colmar grower Bernard Schoffit makes superb late-harvest GEWURZ and PINOT GR VENDANGE TARDIVE GRAND CRU RANGEN CLOS St Theobald 00' 05 08 09' 10' 12 on volcanic soil. Contrast with RIES Grand Cru Sonnenberg 08' 10' on limestone. Delicious CHASSELAS.

Sec Literally means dry, though CHAMP so called is medium-sweet (and better at breakfast, teatime, weddings than BRUT).

Séguret S Rhô r p w ★★ 09' 10' 11 12' Classic PROV hillside village nr GIGONDAS. V'yds a mix of plain and heights. One of leading 18 CÔTES DU RHÔ-VILLAGES. Mainly GRENACHE, peppery, direct reds, some full-on; clear-fruited whites. Esp CH la Courançonne, DOMS *de l'Amauve* (fine), de Cabasse (elegant), J David (bold, organic), Garancière, *Mourchon* (robust), Pourra (big), Soleil Romain.

Sélection des Grains Nobles Al Term coined by HUGEL for AL equivalent to German Beerenauslese, and subject to ever stricter regulations (since 1984). *Grains nobles* are individual grapes with "noble rot".

Sérafin C d'O r ★★★ Christian S's intense GEVREY-CHAMBERTIN VIEILLES VIGNES, CHARMES-CHAMBERTIN. Plenty of new wood but refinement now niece is making the wines.

Seyssel Sav w sp ★★ NV Delicate white, pleasant sparkling. eg. Corbonod.

Sichel & Co B'x r w One of B'x's most respected merchant houses (Sirius a top brand): interests in CHX D'ANGLUDET, PALMER and in CORBIÈRES.

Signargues S Rhô ★ →★★ 10' 11 12' 13 Low-profile CÔTES DU RHÔ village in four areas between Avignon and Nîmes (west bank). Fruity, slightly spiced reds to drink inside 4 yrs. NB: CAVE Estézargues (punchy), La Font du Vent (best, deepest), Haut-Musiel, DOM Valériane.

Sipp, Louis Al w sw ★★ →★★★ Grower/négociant in Ribeauvillé. V.gd RIES GRAND CRU Kirchberg, superb *grand cru* Osterberg GEWURZ VENDANGE TARDIVE (esp 05' 09'). Fine in classic drier yrs 08 10.

Sipp-Mack Al w sw ★★ →★★★ Excellent DOM at Hunawihr. Great RIES from GRANDS CRUS ROSACKER 02 07 08 10' 11, Osterberg; also v.gd PINOT GR.

Sorg, Bruno Al w ★★ →★★★ First-class small grower at Eguisheim for GRANDS CRUS Florimont (RIES 08 09 10' 11 12 13) and PFERSIGBERG (MUSCAT). Immaculate eco-friendly v'yds. Winemaking with feeling.

Sur lie "On the lees". MUSCADET is often bottled straight from the vat, for max zest, body, character.

Tâche, La C d'O r ★★★★ 90' 93' 95 96' 98 99' 00 01 02' 03 05' 06 07 09' 10' 11 12' 13 GRAND CRU of VOSNE-ROMANÉE, MONOPOLE of DRC. One of best v'yds on earth: full, perfumed, luxurious wine, tight in youth.

Taille-aux-Loups, Domaine de la Lo w sw sp ★★★ 02' 03' 05' 07' 08' 09 10' 11 Jacky Blot is one of the Lo's most dynamic producers: barrel-fermented MONTLOUIS, VOUVRAY, majority dry, esp single-v'yds, a few sweet; Triple Zéro MONTLOUIS *pétillant*, and fine reds from DOM de la Butte BOURGUEIL. Acquired CLOS Mosny (Montlouis) late 2010. Small crops 2012, 13.

Tain, Cave de N Rhô ★★ Top N Rhô co-op, 290 members, often mature v'yds, incl a full 25% of HERMITAGE. Sound red Hermitage, esp Epsilon, Gambert de Loche, full white Hermitage Au Coeur des Siècles. Gd St-Joseph (r w), others modern, mainstream. Promising new CROZES from hill and plain v'yds. MARSANNE whites gd value, accomplished VIN DE PAILLE.

Taittinger Champ BRUT NV; Rosé NV; Brut 90 95' 02' 04 06; Collection Brut 90 95 96. Once-fashionable Reims grower and merchant back under family control. Distinctive silky, flowery touch, on a roll and less dosed. Excellent luxury brand *Comtes de Champagne* BLANC DE BLANCS 95' 99 02' 04 05 and Rosé 96 02 06, also gd, rich Pinot Prestige Rosé NV. New CUVÉES Nocturne, Prélude. Also excellent single-v'yd La Marqueterie. (*See also* DOM Carneros, California.)

Tavel S Rhô p ★★ DYA. GRENACHE rosé, once red-tinted, robust, suited to Mediterranean food. Now many slighter PROV-style wines, often for apéritif, a pity. Best: DOM Corne-Loup, GUIGAL, Lafond Roc-Epine, Maby, Dom de la Mordorée (full), Prieuré de Montézargues (fine), Moulin-la-Viguerie, Rocalière (fine), CH Corrençon, de Manissy, Trinquevedel (fine), VIDAL-FLEURY.

Hill of Hermitage is now an official historic monument. So is the co-op in Tavel.

Tempier, Domaine Prov r p w ★★★★ Pioneering estate of BANDOL. Wines of elegance, longevity. Excellent quality now challenged by several others.

Terrasses du Larzac L'doc r p w ★★ →★★★ Northernmost part of AC L'DOC. Wild, hilly region from the Lac du Salagou to Aniane, incl MONTPEYROUX, St-Saturnin. Cooler temperatures make fresher wines, but identity less homogenous than some areas, so elevation to cru status depends on whim of INAO. Several est and many rising stars, incl: Mas de l'Ecriture, CLOS des Serres, Cal Demoura, Montcalmès, Pas de l'Escalette, *Mas Jullien*. Definitely to watch.

Thénard, Dom Burg r w Major grower of GIVRY AC, excellent reds. Whites improving, incl large holding of Le MONTRACHET, mostly sold on to merchants eg. JADOT.

Thévenet, Jean Burg r w sw ★★★ MÂCONNAIS purveyor of rich, some semi-botrytized CHARD, eg. CUVÉE Levroutée at DOM de la Bongran. Also Dom Emilian Gillet.

Thézac-Perricard SW Fr r p ★★ 10 11 12 (13) MALBEC-based IGP adjoining CAHORS, for earlier drinking. ★★ Sandrine Annibal's DOM de Lancement keeps on improving. Also small ★ co-op worth a try.

Thiénot, Alain Champ New generation takes this house forward. Ever-improving quality: impressive, fairly priced BRUT NV. Rosé NV Brut. Vintage Stanislas 02 04 06 08' 09 12, voluminous Vigne aux Gamins (single-v'yd Avize 02 04). Top Grande CUVÉE 96' 98 02'. Also owns Marie Stuart, CANARD-DUCHÊNE in CHAM, CH Ricaud in LOUPIAC.

Thomas, André & fils Al w ★★★ V. fine grower at Ammerschwihr, rigorously organic. An artist-craftsman in the cellar: v.gd RIES Kaefferkopf 08 10', magnificent GEWURZ VIEILLES VIGNES 05 09' 10' 12.

Tollot-Beaut C d'O r ★★★ Consistent CÔTE DE BEAUNE grower with 20 ha in BEAUNE (Grèves, CLOS du Roi), CORTON (Bressandes), SAVIGNY and at CHOREY-LÈS-BEAUNE base (NB: Pièce du Chapitre). Oaky style but it works.

Touraine Lo r p w dr sw sp ★→★★★★ 08 09' 10 11 12 13 Huge region with many ACS (eg. VOUVRAY, CHINON, BOURGUEIL) as well as umbrella AC of variable quality: zesty reds (CAB FR, CÔT, GAMAY, PINOT N), whites (SAUV BL), rosés, sparkling. Often value. Producers: Bois-Vaudons, Corbillières, Joël Delaunay, de la Garrelière, Gosseaume, CLOS Roche Blanche, Mandard, Jacky Marteau, *Marionnet*, Morantin, *Oisly & Thesée*, Presle, Puzelat, Petit Thouars, Ricard, Roussely, Tue-Boeuf. Large village ACs Touraine-Oisly and esp Touraine-Chenonceaux (27 communes). Over-concentration on Sauv Bl.

Touraine: far too much Sauvignon Blanc, far too little Arbois, Meslier St-François, Sauvignon Gris.

Touraine-Amboise Lo r p w ★→★★ TOURAINE sub-AC. Mixed quality, 60% red. François 1er is entry-level local blend (GAMAY/CÔT/CAB FR) or CHENIN BL. Best: Closerie de Chanteloup, Delecheneau (Grange Tiphaine), des Bessons, Dutertre, Frissant, de la Gabillière. Wants to be a cru.

Touraine-Azay-le-Rideau Lo p w ★→★★ Small TOURAINE sub-appellation for CHENIN BL-based dry, off-dry white, rosé (Grolleau 60% min). Producers: CH de l'Aulée, Nicolas Paget, Pibaleau, de la Roche.

Touraine-Mesland Lo r p w ★→★★ Small TOURAINE sub-appellation for red blends (GAMAY/CÔT/CAB FR), 70% of production. No better than straight Touraine. Whites mainly CHENIN. CH Gaillard, CLOS de la Briderie (bio).

Touraine-Noble Joué Lo p ★→★★ DYA. Historic rosé revived, from three PINOTS (N, GR, MEUNIER). AC (2001), now 28 ha just south of Tours. Esp Cosson, Rousseau, Sard.

Trapet C d'O r ★★→★★★ Long-est GEVREY-CHAMBERTIN DOM enjoying new life: sensual bio wines. CHAMBERTIN flagship, PREMIER CRUS also v.gd. *See also* ROSSIGNOL-TRAPET.

Trévallon, Domaine de Prov r w ★★★★ 97 98 99 00' 01 03 04 05 06' 07 08 09 10 11 12 13 Pioneer estate in LES BAUX, but IGP BOUCHES-DU-RHÔ as no GRENACHE grapes. Deserves its huge reputation. Intense CAB SAUV/SYRAH to age. *Barrique-aged white* from MARSANNE, ROUSSANNE, drop of CHARD and now GRENACHE BL. Worth seeking out.

Trimbach, F E Al w ★★★→★★★★ Matchless grower of AL RIES on limestone soils at Ribeauvillé, esp CLOS STE-HUNE 06 08 09 10' 12; almost-as-gd (and much cheaper) *Frédéric Emile* 06 08 10 12. Dry, elegant wines for great cuisine.

Tursan SW Fr r p w ★★ (Mostly DYA.) AOP in the Landes. ★★ DOM de Perchade the most authentic independent; chef Michel Guérard's atypical wines ★★ are chic but not cheap. ★ co-op worthy source of everyday quaffers.

Vacqueyras S Rhô r (p) w ★★→★★★ 01' 05' 06' 07' 09' 10' 11 12' Hearty, peppery, GRENACHE-led neighbour of GIGONDAS with earlier, hotter v'yds, so can be wine for game, big flavours. Lives 10 yrs+. NB: Arnoux Vieux Clocher, JABOULET, CHX de Montmirail, *des Tours* (v. fine); CLOS des Cazaux (gd value), DOMS Amouriers, Archimbaud-Vache, Charbonnière, Couroulu (v.gd, traditional), Font de Papier, Fourmone (gd form), Garrigue (traditional), Grapillon d'Or, Monardière (v.gd), Montirius (organic), Montvac, Famille Perrin, Roucas Toumba (organic), Sang des Cailloux (v.gd). Full whites (Clos des Cazaux, Sang des Cailloux).

Val de Loire Lo r p w DYA. One of France's four regional IGPS, was Jardin de la France.

Valençay Lo r p w ★→★★ AOP in east TOURAINE; easy wines from esp SAUV BL, (CHARD) reds CÔT, GAMAY, PINOT N. CLOS Delorme, Lafond, Jacky Preys, Sinson, Sébastien Vaillant, VIGNERONS de Valençay.

Valréas S Rhô r (p) (w) ★★ 09' 10' 11' 12' Gradual progress at previously humdrum, late-ripening CÔTES DU RHÔ-VILLAGE in north Vaucluse black truffle area; large co-op. Grainy, peppery, can be heady, red (mainly GRENACHE), improving white. Esp Emmanuel Bouchard (character), CH la Décelle, CLOS Bellane (gd white), DOMS des Grands Devers, du Séminaire, du Mas de Ste-Croix.

VDQS *Vins délimite de qualité supérieure.* Now phased out.

Vendange Harvest. **Vendange tardive:** late-harvest; AL equivalent to German Auslese but usually higher alcohol.

Venoge, de Champ Venerable house revitalized under LANSON-BCC ownership. Gd niche blends: Cordon Bleu Extra-Brut, Vintage BLANC DE BLANCS 00 04 06 08, CUVÉE 20 ans, Prestige CUVÉE Louis XV 10-yr-old BLANC DE NOIRS.

Ventoux S Rhô r p w ★★ 10' 11' 12' Rambling AC all around Mont Ventoux between Rhô and PROV. Juicy, tangy red (GRENACHE/SYRAH), café-style to deeper, improving quality), rosé, gd white (more oak). Some high v'yds supply cool flavours. Best: CLOS des Patris, Ferme St-Pierre (p w), Gonnet, *La Vieille Ferme* (r) owned by BEAUCASTEL, CHX Unang, Valcombe, co-op Bédoin, Goult, St-Didier, DOMS Anges, Berane, Brusset, Cascavel, Champ-Long, Croix de Pins, Fondrèche (v.gd), Grand Jacquet, JABOULET, Martinelle, Murmurium, *Pesquié* (excellent), Pigeade, St-Jean du Barroux, Terres de Solence, Verrière, VIDAL-FLEURY.

Verget Burg w ★★→★★★ Jean-Marie Guffens' MÂCONNAIS-based white wine merchant venture, nearly as idiosyncratic as his own DOM. Fine quality, plans for reds too.

Veuve Clicquot Champ Yellow Label NV; White Label Demi-Sec NV; Vintage Rés 02 04 06 08 12'; Rosé Rés 04 06 08' 12 Historic house of highest standing. Full-bodied, rich, fine: one of CHAMP's sure things. Luxury brands: La Grande Dame 98' 04'★★★ 08' set to be BLANC DE NOIRS in future, Rich Rés 02 06, La Grande Dame Rosé 95 04. Part-oak-fermented vintages from 08. New Cave Privée re-release of older vintages in fine condition (esp 90). New project to increase serious rosé production from lower yields.

Veuve Devaux Champ Premium brand of powerful Union Auboise co-op. Excellent aged Grande Rés NV, Œil de Perdrix Rosé, Prestige CUVÉE D 02' 04, BRUT Vintage 04 06 09'.

Vézelay Burg r w ★→★★ Age 1–2 yrs. Rising northern subdistrict of generic BOURGOGNE for reds. Tasty whites from CHARD or resurrected MELON sold as COTEAUX BOURGUIGNONS. Try DOM de la Cadette, La Croix Montjoye, des Faverelles, Elise Villiers.

Vidal-Fleury, J N Rhô r w sw ★★→★★★ Swish new cellars, pursuit of fresher wines at GUIGAL-owned Rhô merchant and grower of CÔTE-RÔTIE. Top-notch, v. elegant *La Chatillonne* (12% VIOGNIER; wait min 5 yrs). Range making progress. Gd CAIRANNE, CÔTES DU RHÔ (r p w), TAVEL, VENTOUX, MUSCAT DE BEAUMES-DE-VENISE.

Vieille Ferme, La S Rhô r w ★→★★ Lighter in last 2 yrs; otherwise extremely reliable gd-value brand. VENTOUX (r), LUBÉRON (w) from Famille Perrin (CH DE BEAUCASTEL).

Vieilles Vignes Old vines, which should make the best wine. Eg. DE VOGÜÉ, MUSIGNY, Vieilles Vignes. But no rules about age and can be a tourist trap.

Price of vineyard land in Champagne? Around €2 million/ha.

Vieux Télégraphe, Domaine du S Rhô r w ★★★ 78' 81' 85 88 89' 90 94' 95' 96' 97 98' 99' 00 01' 03' 04' 05' 06' 07' 09' 10' 12' Top-rank large estate, maker of smoky, complex, slow-to-develop red CHÂTEAUNEUF, top two wines La Crau and since 2011 Pied Long, also rich whites La Crau, CLOS La Roquète (great with food, gd in lesser yrs eg. 02 08 11). Owns fine, slow-to-evolve, quietly complex *Gigondas Dom Les Pallières* with US importer Kermit Lynch.

Vigne or vignoble Vineyard (v'yd), vineyards (v'yds).

Vigneron Vine-grower.

Vin de France Replaces VDT. Allows mention of grape variety and vintage. Often blends of regions with brand name. Can be source of unexpected delights if talented winemaker uses this category to avoid bureaucratic hassle. Eg. Yves Cuilleron VIOGNIER (N Rhô).

Vin de paille Wine from grapes dried on straw mats, so v. sweet, like Italian passito. Esp in the Jura. *See also* CHAVE, VIN PAILLÉ DE CORRÈZE.

Vin de Pays (VDP) Potentially most dynamic category in France (with over 150 regions), allowing scope for experimentation. Renamed IGP (*Indication Géographique Protegée*) from 2009 vintage, but position unchanged and new terminology still not accepted by every area. Zonal names are most individual: eg. CÔTES DE GASCOGNE, CÔTES DE THONGUE, Haute Vallée de l'Orb, Duché d'Uzès, among others. Enormous variety in taste, quality but never ceases to surprise.

Vin de Pays du Gard L'doc ★ The Gard *département* west of Rhô estuary gives sound IGP reds, incl Cévennes, du Pont du Gard. Duché d'Uzès AOP from 2013.

Vin de table (VDT) Category of standard table wine now replaced by VIN DE FRANCE.

Vin doux naturel (VDN) Rouss Sweet wine fortified with wine alcohol, so sweetness is natural, not strength. The speciality of ROUSS based on GRENACHE Noir, Blanc or Gris, or MUSCAT. Top wines, esp aged RANCIOS, can provide fabulous drinking.

Vin gris "Grey" wine is v. pale pink, made of red grapes pressed before fermentation begins, unlike rosé that ferments briefly before pressing. Or from eg. PINOT GR, not-quite-white grapes. "Œil de Perdrix" means much the same; so does "blush".

Vin jaune Jura w ★★★ Speciality of ARBOIS: odd yellow wine like Fino Sherry. Normally ready when bottled (after at least 6 yrs). Best: CH-CHALON. A halfway-house oxidized white is sold locally as *vin typé*.

Vin paillé de Corrèze SW Fr r w Old tradition now revived with modern makeover. 25 growers and small co-op nr Beaulieu-sur-Dordogne make a wine that is an acquired taste, historically recommended for breast-feeding mothers. Will keep as long as you like. Try ★ Christian Tronche.

Vinsobres S Rhô r (p) (w) ★★ 09' 10' 11 12' AC notable for SYRAH, older hill v'yds, younger windy plateau v'yds, nr Nyons. Best reds offer direct red fruit, punchy body, drink with red meats. Leaders: CAVE la Vinsobraise, DOMS les Aussellons, Bicarelle, Chaume-Arnaud, Constant-Duquesnoy, Coriançon, Deurre (traditional), Jaume (modern), Moulin (traditional), Famille Perrin (value), Péquélette (bio), CH Rouanne.

Viré-Clessé Burg w ★★ 09' 10' 11 12 13 AC based around two of best white villages of MÂCON. Known for exuberant, rich style, sometimes late-harvest. Try Bonhomme, Bret Bros, Chaland, LAFON, Michel, Rijckaert, THÉVENET, co-op.

Visan S Rhô r (p) (w) ★★ 10' 11' 12' Later-ripening Rhô village, medium-full reds with clear fruit, pepper, some more suave. Fair whites. Young growers driving quality. Best: DOMS Coste Chaude (gd fruit), Florane, Fourmente (esp Nature), des Grands Devers, Montmartel, Roche-Audran.

Vogüé, Comte Georges de C d'O r w ★★★★ Iconic CHAMBOLLE estate, incl lion's share of MUSIGNY. Heralded vintages from 1990s taking time to come round.

Volnay C d'O r ★★★ →★★★★ 90' 95 96' 98 99' 02' 03 05' 06 07 09' 10' 11 12 Best source for CÔTE DE BEAUNE reds except when it hails. Can be structured, should be silky. Best v'yds: Caillerets, Champans, CLOS des Chênes, Clos des Ducs, Santenots, Taillepieds, etc. Best growers: D'ANGERVILLE, H BOILLOT, HOSPICES DE BEAUNE, LAFARGE, LAFON, DE MONTILLE, Pousse d'Or, N Rossignol.

Volnay-Santenots C d'O r ★★★ Best red wine v'yds of MEURSAULT use this name. Indistinguishable from other PREMIER CRU VOLNAY, unless more body, less delicacy. Best growers: AMPEAU, HOSPICES DE BEAUNE, LAFON, LEROY, PRIEUR.

Vosne-Romanée C d'O r ★★★ →★★★★ 90' 93' 95 96' 98 99' 02' 03 05' 06 07 08 09' 10' 11 12 13. Village with Burg's grandest crus (eg. ROMANÉE-CONTI, LA TÂCHE) and outstanding PREMIERS CRUS Malconsorts, Suchots, Brûlées, etc. There are (or

Southwest growers to watch in 2015

Domaine Arretxea (Irouléguy) Michel Rieuspeyrous has planted Petit Gros and PETIT MANSENG on only known terroir in France based on ophites.

Château Bellauc (Jurançon) Boutique DOM, exquisite sweet wines.

Châteaux Boissel & Boujac (Fronton) New-generation rival cousins are upping the standards at these properties, winning local acclaim. Ventures incl GEWURZ.

Clos des Rocaillous (Gaillac) English newcomers showing promise esp with whites.

Domaine Mourguy (Irouléguy) Reaching for the top, with much improved wines: brother-and-sister partnership have est own style.

Laurent Mousset (Entraygues) Est red winemaker proving that white CHENIN BL can grow as well on schist as on clay.

Château Lecusse (Gaillac) Rose-breeder to the Danish royal family, by appointment. Wines (esp medal-winning red) are distinguished.

Domaine Pichard (Madiran) Signs of returning to former greatness. Spring-cleaning the *chai* and restructuring the v'yd have produced rapid improvement.

Stéphane Lucas (Gaillac) Has gone straight to the top with two all-Braucol reds, one oaked the other not. Tiny DOM nr GAILLAC, great wines.

should be) no common wines in Vosne. Many gd if increasingly pricey growers. Try Arnoux-lachaux, CATHIARD, Clavelier, DRC, EUGÉNIE, GRIVOT, GROS, Lamarche, LEROY, LIGER-BELAIR, MÉO-CAMUZET, MUGNERET, ROUGET, Tardy, Vigot.

Vougeot C d'O r w ★★★ 90' 96' 99' 02' 03 05' 06 07 08 09' 10' 11 12 13 Mostly GRAND CRU as CLOS DE VOUGEOT but also village and PREMIER CRU, incl outstanding white MONOPOLE, *Clos Blanc de V.* HUDELOT-Noellat, VOUGERAIE best.

Vougeraie, Domaine de la C d'O r w ★★★→★★★★ DOM uniting all BOISSET's v'yd holdings (since 1999). BOURGOGNE Rouge up to fine GRANDS CRUS eg. CHARMES-CHAMBERTIN, BONNES-MARES, MUSIGNY and unique white CLOS Blanc de VOUGEOT. Various top whites being added, esp BÂTARD-MONTRACHET.

Vouvray Lo w dr sw sp ★★→★★★★ (dr) 89 90 96' 02' 03 05' 07 08' 09 10 11 12 (13) (sw) 89' 90' 95' 96' 97' 03' 05' 08 09' AC east of Tours famous for sweet wines and fizz: still wines from top producers gd and reliable. DEMI-SEC is classic style, but in gd yrs *moelleux* can be intensely sweet, virtually immortal. Fizz variable (60% of production): look for *pétillant*. Producers: Bonneau, Brunet, Carême, *Champalou*, CLOS Baudoin, Cosme, Dhoye-Deruet, Foreau, Fouquet (DOM des Aubuisières), CH Gaudrelle, *Huet*, de la Meslerie, Pinon, *Dom de la Taille-aux-Loups*, Vigneau-Chevreau. June 2013: 40% of AC badly hit by hail. Old vintages, ie. 21 24 47 59 70 71 a must-try.

Vranken Champ Ever more powerful CHAMP group. Sound quality. Leading brand: Demoiselle. Owns HEIDSIECK MONOPOLE, POMMERY.

Wolfberger Al ★★ Principal label of Eguisheim co-op. V.gd quality for such a large-scale producer. Important for CRÉMANT.

"Y" B'x (pronounced "ygrec") 85 86 88 94 96 00 02 04 05 06 07 08 09 10 11 12 Intense dry white wine produced at CH D'YQUEM, now every vintage. Enticing young but interesting with age. Dry style in 2004, otherwise in classic off-dry mould. Vintages since 05 purer, fresher than in past.

Zind Humbrecht, Domaine Al w sw ★★★★ Leading bio DOM sensitively run by Olivier Humbrecht, great winemaker and thinker: rich, balanced wines, drier, more elegant than before, v. low yields. Top wines from single-v'yds *Clos St-Urbain*, ace 00' 05 08' 09 10' 12; Jebsal, superb PINOT GR 02 08 09 10' 12), Windsbuhl, esp GEWURZ 05 08 09 10 12, plus GRANDS CRUS RANGEN, HENGST, Brand, Goldert.

Châteaux of Bordeaux

Abbreviations used in the text:

B'x	Bordeaux
Bar	Barsac
E-2-M	Entre-Deux-Mers
Grav	Graves
H-Méd	Haut-Médoc
L de P	Lalande de Pomerol
List	Listrac
Marg	Margaux
Méd	Médoc
Mou	Moulis
Pau	Pauillac
Pe-Lé	Pessac-Léognan
Pom	Pomerol
St-Ém	St-Émilion
St-Est	St-Estèphe
St-Jul	St-Julien
Saut	Sauternes
AC	appellation contrôlée
ch(x)	château(x)
dom(s)	domaine(s)

Just as the successful years in Bordeaux seem to come in threes (1988, 1989, 1990 or 2008, 2009, 2010) so the more challenging do as well. 1991, 1992 and 1993 were blighted by frost and rain, and more recently 2011, 2012 and 2013 fell foul of the climate. Greater care in the vineyard and meticulous sorting helped produce acceptable but strict 2011s and light but charming 2012s. However, 2013 was another story. A disastrous flowering, rain, grey rot and a devastating hailstorm in Entre-Deux-Mers

Châteaux of Bordeaux entries also cross-reference to France

mean that rosé, dry whites and Sauternes were the only real success stories. Luckily, there is a reserve of good red vintages already in the bank. If the 2010s and 2008s are mainly for ageing, the luscious fruit of the 2009s is already tempting at *petit château* level, where prices remain stable. Likewise, the 2005s are drinking well in appellations like Castillon, Fronsac, Haut-Médoc and Graves.

Among the *grands crus* the mature vintages to look for are 1998 (particularly Right Bank), 2000, 2001 and 2004, with the very best 2007s also worthy of consideration. Dry white Bordeaux remains consistent in quality and value (though volumes were down in 2013) so don't hesitate here. And Sauternes was back with a winning ticket in 2013, with the coveted noble rot making an appearance. The problem is one of being spoilt for choice as 2011, 2010, 2009, 2007, 2005, 2003 and 2001 are as good as it gets in this sweet wine appellation.

L'A, Domaine de C de B'x r ★★ 02 03 04 05' 06 07 08 09' 10' 11 12 Owned by winemaking consultant STÉPHANE DERENONCOURT and one of the best in CASTILLON. Bio run. More finesse than usual for the AC.

d'Agassac H-Méd r ★★ 03 04 05 06 07 08 09' 10' 11 12 Southern H-MÉD with turreted Renaissance CH. Visitors welcome. Modern, accessible wine.

d'Aiguilhe C de B'x r ★★ 05 06 07 08 09 10 11 12 Leading player in CASTILLON-CÔTES DE BORDEAUX on high plateau. Same ownership as CANON LA GAFFELIÈRE and LA MONDOTTE. Wine with *power and finesse*.

Andron-Blanquet St-Est r ★★ 98 00' 01 03 04 05' 06 08 09' 10' 11 Sister CH to COS-LABORY since 1971. Same rigour. Usually gd value.

Angélus St-Ém r ★★★★ 90' 95 96 98' 99 00' 01 02 03' 04 05 06 07 08 09' 10' 11 12 13 Promotion to PREMIER GRAND CRU CLASSÉ (A) in 2012 so prices up. Pioneer of modern ST-ÉM; dark, rich, sumptuous. New bell tower and winery in 2013. Second label: Le Carillon de L'Angélus. Fleur de Boüard in L DE P and Bellevue in St-Ém same ownership.

d'Angludet Marg r ★★★ 96' 98' 00 02 04 05 06 08 09' 10' 11 12 Owned and run by négociant SICHEL. Lively, fragrant, stylish, popular in the UK. Gd value. Also CH Argadens (B'X SUPERIEUR, r and *w*).

Archambeau Grav r w d (sw) ★★ (r) 05 06 08 09 10 11 (w) 07 08 09 10 11 12 (13) Consistent property owned by branch of Dubourdieu family. Gd *fruity dry white*; fragrant barrel-aged reds. Improving BAR classed-growth CH Suau in same stable.

d'Arche Saut w sw ★★ 96 97' 98 99 00 01' 02 03' 05 07 09' 10' 11' Consistent Second Growth on edge of SAUT. Perle d'Arche is lighter-weight second label. B&B in 17th-century chapter house.

d'Armailhac Pau r ★★★ 96' 98 99 00 01 02 03 04 05' 06 07 08 09' 10' 11 12 13 Substantial Fifth Growth under (MOUTON) ROTHSCHILD ownership. Top quality, and more finesse than sister CLERC MILON; 15–20% CAB FR. On top form and well-priced.

l'Arrosée St-Ém r ★★★ 00 01 02 03 04 05' 06' 07 08 09' 10' 11 12 RIP from 2013, now sold and integrated into neigbouring QUINTUS. Until then on top form since 2003. Mellow, harmonious wines with plenty of CAB FR and CAB SAUV (40%).

Aurelius St-Ém r ★★ 05 06 08 09 10 11 12 Top CUVÉE from the go-ahead ST-ÉM co-op. Low yields. Modern, concentrated, oaky style.

Ausone St-Ém r ★★★★ 88 89' 90 95 96' 97 98' 99 00' 01' 02 03' 04 05' 06' 07 08 09' 10' 11 12 13 Tiny but illustrious ST-ÉM First Growth (around 1,500 cases); best position on the côtes. Lots of CAB FR (55%) – oldest plot dated 1906. Long-lived wines with volume, texture and finesse. Second label: Chapelle d'Ausone (500 cases) also excellent. MOULIN-ST-GEORGES, Simard, DE FONBEL in same Vauthier-family ownership.

> **St-Émilion classification – 2013 version**
> A total of 82 CHX were classified in 2012: 18 as PREMIER GRAND CRU
> CLASSÉ and 64 as GRAND CRU CLASSÉ. The new classification, now legally
> considered an exam rather than a competition, was conducted by a
> commission of seven wine professionals nominated by INAO, none
> from B'X. Chx ANGÉLUS and PAVIE were upgraded to PREMIER GRAND CRU
> CLASSÉ (A) while added to the rank of PREMIER GRAND CRU CLASSÉ (B) were
> CANON LA GAFFELIÈRE, LARCIS DUCASSE, LA MONDOTTE and VALANDRAUD. New to
> the status of GRAND CRU CLASSÉ were Chx BARDE-HAUT, Le Chatelet, CLOS
> de Sarpe, La Commanderie, Côte de Baleau, FAUGÈRES, DE FERRAND, La
> Fleur Morange, FOMBRAUGE, JEAN FAURE, Clos la Madeleine, Péby Faugères,
> DE PRESSAC, QUINAULT L'ENCLOS, Rochebelle and SANSONNET. Although a
> motivating force for the producers, the classification (which is reviewed
> every 10 yrs) remains an unwieldy guide for consumers. Three
> disappointed candidates are challenging the classification in court.
> If successful the hierarchy could be sunk for ever.

Balestard la Tonnelle St-Ém r ★★ 00' 01 03 04 05 06 08 09 10 11 12 Historic DOM
with 15th-century watchtower. Now rich, modern style but limestone terroir
lurks behind.

Barde-Haut St-Ém r ★★ 98 00 01 02 03 05' 06 07 08 09 10 11 12 Elevated to
GRAND CRU CLASSÉ in 2012. Sister property of CLOS L'ÉGLISE and HAUT-BERGEY. Rich,
modern and opulent.

Bastor-Lamontagne Saut w SW ★★ 96' 97' 98 99 01' 02 03' 05 07 09' 10 11 Large
unclassified Preignac sister to BEAUREGARD. Gd value; pure, harmonious. Second
label: Les Remparts de Bastor. New, fruity "So" for early drinking. Also CH St-
Robert at Pujols: GRAV (r w).

Batailley Pau r ★★★ 96 00' 02 03 04 05' 06 08 09' 10' 11' 12 Fifth Growth property
owned by BORIE-MANOUX connections. *On steady form* in the last decade. At this
level gd value.

Beaumont H-Méd r ★★ 00' 02 04 05' 06 08 09 10' One of the largest estates in
the MÉD peninsula (around 42,000 cases); early maturing, *easily enjoyable wines.*
Second label: CH Moulin d'Arvigny.

Beauregard Pom r ★★★ 00' 01 02 03 04 05' 06 08 09' 10' 12 Consistent mid-
weight POM, converting to organics. Pavillon Beauregard sister estate in L DE P.
Second label: Benjamin de Beauregard.

Beau-Séjour-Bécot St-Ém r ★★★ 90' 95' 96 98' 99 00' 01 02 03 04 05' 06 07
08 09' 10' 11 12 Distinguished PREMIER GRAND CRU CLASSÉ on the limestone
plateau. Combines elegance with depth of fruit. Can age. Former GARAGE wine la
Gomerie integrated from 2012.

Beauséjour-Duffau St-Ém r ★★★ 96 98 99 00 01 02 03 04 05' 06 08 09' 10' 11 12
Tiny PREMIER GRAND CRU CLASSÉ estate on the côtes owned by Duffau-Lagarrosse
family. Has had the critics purring since 2009: STÉPHANE DERENONCOURT consults.

Beau-Site St-Est r ★★ 00 03 04 05 06 08 09 10 11 CRU BOURGEOIS (2011) property in
same hands as BATAILLEY, etc. 70% CAB SAUV. Supple, fresh and accessible.

Belair-Monange St-Ém r ★★★ 90' 94 95' 96 98 99 00' 01 02 03 04 05' 06 08
09' 10' 11 12 13 Classed-growth neighbour of AUSONE owned by négociant J-P
MOUEIX. Absorbed MAGDELAINE in 2012 so now double the size. Big replanting
programme. Fine, fragrant, elegant style; riper, broader since 2008.

Belgrave H-Méd r ★★ 00' 02' 03 04' 05' 06 07 08 09' 10' 11 12 Sizeable Fifth
Growth, well-managed by CVBG-DOURTHE (*see* LA GARDE, REYSSON). Modern-classic
in style. Now consistent quality. Second label: Diane de Belgrave.

Bellefont-Belcier St-Ém r ★★ 00 01 02 03 04 05' 06 07 08' 09' 10' 11 12 ST-ÉM GRAND CRU CLASSÉ now owned by Chinese businessman (2012). Neighbour of LARCIS DUCASSE. 19th-century circular cellar. Suave, fresh, refined. Ageing potential.

Belle-Vue H-Méd r ★★ 04 05 06 07 08 09 10 11 12 Consistent, gd-value southern H-MÉD. Lots of PETIT VERDOT (21%). Dark and dense but firm, fresh and refined. CH Gironville same stable.

Bel-Orme-Tronquoy-de-Lalande H-Méd r ★★ Northern H-MÉD CRU BOURGEOIS (2011). Clay-limestone soils, so MERLOT (60%) dominates. Firm, muscular style. Same owner as CROIZET-BAGES, RAUZAN-GASSIES.

Berliquet St-Ém r ★★ 00' 01 02 04 05' 06 08 09 10 12 A tiny GRAND CRU CLASSÉ situated on the côtes. Managed by Nicolas Thienpont. DERENONCOURT consults. Fresh and elegant style.

Bernadotte H-Méd r ★★ →★★★ 00' 01 02 03 04 05' 06 07 08 09' 10' 11 CRU BOURGEOIS (2011) close to PAU. Owned by a Hong Kong-based group since 2012. Savoury H-MÉD style. Recent vintages have more finesse.

Bertineau St-Vincent B'x r ★★ 00' 01 04 05 06 08 09 10 12 Tiny L DE P estate now owned (2013) by Chinese businessman. Previous owner, MICHEL ROLLAND, manages the property. Fairly consistent quality.

Beychevelle St-Jul r ★★★ 99 00' 01 02 03 04 05' 06 07 08 09' 10' 11 12 Fourth Growth with eye-catching boat label (helps sales in Asia). Castel (since 2011) and Suntory (LAGRANGE) owners. Wines of consistent elegance rather than power. On gd form. Second label: Amiral de Beychevelle.

Biston-Brillette Mou r ★★ 01 02 03 04 05' 06 08 09 10' 11 12 Family-owned MOU estate. Attractive, fruit-bound wines. Consistent quality and value.

Bonalgue Pom r ★★ 00 01 04 05 06 08 09 10 11 12 Dark, rich, meaty. As gd value as it gets. Sister estate CLOS du Clocher. CHX du Courlat in LUSSAC ST-ÉM and Les Hauts Conseillants in L DE P same stable.

Bonnet B'x r w ★★ (r) 06 08 09 10 11 (w) DYA. Owned by octogenarian André Lurton. Big producer of some of the best E-2-M and red (Rés) B'x. Devastated by hail in 2013. LA LOUVIÈRE, COUHINS-LURTON, ROCHEMORIN same stable.

Bon Pasteur, le Pom r ★★★ 98' 99 00 01 02 03 04 05' 06 08 09' 10' 11 12 Excellent property on ST-ÉM border now owned (2013) by Chinese concern. Former owner, MICHEL ROLLAND, manages. Ripe, opulent, seductive wines guaranteed.

Boscq, le St-Est r ★★ 03 04 05' 06 08 09' 10 11 12 Quality-driven CRU BOURGEOIS (2011) owned by CVBG-DOURTHE. Consistently gd value.

Bourgneuf Pom r ★★ 00 01' 03 04 05' 06 08 09 10 11 12 Dropped the "-Vayron" in 2010. Subtle and savoury wines. Recently more depth and precision. Offers gd value for POM.

Bouscaut Pe-Lé r w ★★ (r) 00 01 02 04 05' 06 07 08 09 10' 11 12 (w) 02 03 04 05' 06 07 08 09 10' 11 12 13 Classed growth owned by branch (Sophie) of the Lurton family. MERLOT-based reds. Sappy, age-worthy whites.

Boyd-Cantenac Marg r ★★★ 00 02 03 04 05' 06 07 08 09' 10' 11 12 Little-known MARG Third Growth on top form these days. CAB SAUV-dominated with a little peppery PETIT VERDOT. Second label: Jacques Boyd. *See also* POUGET.

Branaire-Ducru St-Jul r ★★★ 96 98 00' 01 02 03 04 05' 06 08 09' 10' 11 12 13 Fourth Growth with CAB SAUV-dominated v'yd scattered around AC. Consistent since the mid-1990s and relatively gd value. Ageing potential. Second label: Duluc.

Branas Grand Poujeaux r ★★ 05 06 08 09 10 11 12 The tiny neighbouring estate of CHASSE-SPLEEN and POUJEAUX. Quality assured since 2005. Ripe and fine with supple tannins. DERENONCOURT consults. Owner has PRIEURÉ-LICHINE and Villemaurine in ST-ÉM connections.

Brane-Cantenac Marg r ★★★ 96 98 99 00' 01 02 03 04 05' 06 07 08 09' 10' 11 12 Large Second Growth on the Cantenac plateau. Owner Henri Lurton manages with aplomb. Dense, fragrant MARG. Laser-optical sorting since 2010. Second label: Baron de Brane.

Brillette Mou r ★★ 02 03 04 05 06 08 09 10 11 12 CRU BOURGEOIS (2011) with v'yd on gravelly soils. Wines of gd depth and fruit. Second label: Les Hauts de Brillette.

Cabanne, La Pom r ★★ 00 04 05 06' 08 09 10 11 12 V'yd west of the POM plateau. Cellar fire in 2010; new cellar since. Looks to be improving. Second label: DOM de Compostelle.

Caillou Saut w sw ★★ 95 96 97 98 99 01' 02 03' 05' 07 09' 10' 11' (13) Well-run Second Growth BAR for firm, fruity wine. 2010 and 2011 cracking. CUVÉE Reine is a top selection, Prestige Cuvée another.

Calon-Ségur St-Est r ★★★ 90' 95 96' 98 99 00' 01 02 03' 04 05' 06 07 08' 09' 10' 11 12 Third Growth with great historic reputation. Sold to a French insurance company in 2012. Prices on the secondary market have risen since. Estate really flying since 2008. Second label: Marquis de Calon.

Cambon la Pelouse H-Méd r ★★ 03 04 05' 06 07 08 09 10' 11 12 Big, supple, accessible southern H-MÉD cru. L'Aura, a micro-CUVÉE from MAR.

Camensac H-Méd r ★★ 98 01 02 03 05 06 08 09 10' 11 12 Fifth Growth in northern H-MÉD. Same owner as CHASSE-SPLEEN; change for the better from 2006; riper CAB SAUV expression. Second label: La Closerie de Camensac.

Canon St-Ém r ★★★ 98' 99 00 01 02 03 04 05' 06 07 08' 09' 10' 11 12 13 Famous PREMIER GRAND CRU CLASSÉ with walled-in v'yd on plateau. Same owners as RAUZAN-SÉGLA. Now on flying form; elegant, long-lived wines. Neigbouring CH Matras integrated in 2012. Renovated Chapelle de Mazerat new cellar for second label: CLOS Canon.

Canon la Gaffelière St-Ém r ★★★ 96 98' 99 00' 01 02 03 04 05' 06 08 09' 10' 11 12 13 Just promotion to PREMIER GRAND CRU CLASSÉ in 2012. Same ownership as CLOS DE L'ORATOIRE, LA MONDOTTE and AIGUILHE in Castillon. Stylish, upfront, impressive wines with 40% CAB FR and 5% CAB SAUV.

Cantemerle H-Méd r ★★★ 00 01 02 03 04 05' 06' 07 08 09' 10' 11 12 13 Large property in southern H-MÉD. Merits its Fifth Growth status – more consistency lately. Sandy/gravel soils give finer style. Second label: Les Allées de Cantemerle.

Cantenac-Brown Marg r ★★→★★★ 96 98 99 00 01 02 03 04 05' 06 08 09' 10' 11 12 Third Growth with mock-Tudor CH. Owned by British businessman since 2005. Previously robust style; now more voluptous and refined. Dry white Alto from 2012. Second label: Brio de Cantenac Brown.

Capbern-Gasqueton St-Est r ★★ 00 04 05 06 08' 09' 10' 11 12 Benefits from same new investor and winemaker as sister CALON-SÉGUR. New cellars in 2010. Raised its game since 2008 – solid but polished wines.

Cap de Mourlin St-Ém r ★★→★★★ 00 01 03 04 05 06 08 09 10 11 12 16th-century property owned by Capdemourlin family, as are CH BALESTARD LA TONNELLE and Ch Roudier. Riper and more concentrated than in the past.

Carbonnieux Pe-Lé r w ★★★ 98 99 00 02 04 05' 06 07 08 09' 10 11 12 Large historic estate at Léognan for sterling red and white; large volumes of both. *The whites*, 65% SAUV BL eg. 02 03 04 05 06 07 08 09 10 11 12 (13), can age 10 yrs or more. Red can age as well. CHX Haut-Vigneau, Lafont Menaut and Le Sartre are also in the family.

Carles, de B'x r ★★★ 03 04 05' 06' 07 08 09 10 11 12 13 FRONSAC. Haut Carles (★★★) is the principal selection here with its own modern, gravity-fed cellars. Can rival top ST-ÉM.

Carmes Haut-Brion, les Pe-Lé r ★★★ 00 01 02 03 04 05' 06 07 08 09' 10' 11 12' Tiny walled-in neighbour of HAUT-BRION; considerably expanded under new (2010) ownership. Plenty of investment; new cellars in 2014. DERENONCOURT consults. Second label: Le CLOS des Carmes.

BORDEAUX

Caronne-Ste-Gemme H-Méd r ★★ 01 02 03 04 05 06 08 09' 10' 11 12 Northern H-MÉD estate. Olivier Dauga consults. Recent vintages show more depth, class.

Carruades de Château Lafite Pau The second label of CH LAFITE is a relatively easy-drinker (40% MERLOT). Prices down 45% on 2011 peak (less Chinese demand).

Carteau Côtes-Daugay St-Ém r ★★ 02 03 04 05 08 09 10 Gd-value ST-ÉM GRAND CRU; full-flavoured wines with freshness and elegance as well. Mainly MERLOT.

Certan-de-May Pom r ★★★ 96 98 00' 01' 04 05' 06 08 09' 10' 11 12 Tiny property on the POM plateau opposite VIEUX-CH-CERTAN. Solid wines with ageing potential.

Certan-Marzelle Pom Little J-P MOUEIX estate for *fragrant, light, juicy Pomerol.*

Chantegrive Grav r w ★★ →★★★ 02 03 04 05' 06 07 08 09' 10' 11 12 The largest estate in the GRAV; modern and v.gd quality. Reds rich and finely oaked. CUVÉE Caroline is top, *fragrant white* 04 05' 06 07 08 09 10 11 12 13.

Chasse-Spleen Mou r (w) ★★★ 00 01 02 03 04 05' 06 07 08 09' 10' 11 Big MOU estate producing consistently gd, often outstanding, long-maturing wine. Second label: L'Heritage de Chasse-Spleen. One of the surest things in B'X. Makes a little white. *See also* CAMENSAC and GRESSIER-GRAND-POUJEAUX.

Chauvin St-Ém r ★★ 03 04 05 06 08 09 10' 11 12 Family-owned GRAND CRU CLASSÉ in northwest ST-ÉM. Steady performer; increasingly serious.

Cheval Blanc St-Ém r ★★★★ 89 90' 93 94 95 96' 97 98' 99 00' 01' 02 03 04 05' 06 07 08 09' 10' 11 12 13 PREMIER GRAND CRU CLASSÉ (A) of ST-ÉM. High percentage of CAB FR (60%). Firm, fragrant, vigorous wines with some of the voluptuousness of neighbouring POM. Delicious young; lasts a generation, or two. Same ownership and management as YQUEM, LA TOUR DU PIN, QUINAULT L'ENCLOS. New eco-friendly winery won Chicago Athenaeum's International Architecture Award 2013. Second label: Le Petit Cheval.

The number of wine-growers in Bordeaux has dwindled from 25,000 in 1980 to 7,900 today

Chevalier, Domaine de Pe-Lé r w ★★★★ 95 96' 98' 99' 00' 01' 02 03 04' 05' 06 07 08 09' 10' 11 12 13 Superb estate in Léognan. Bernard family celebrated 30 yrs of ownership in 2013. Pure, dense, finely textured red. Impressive. Complex, long-ageing white has remarkable consistency; wait for rich flavours 95 96' 97 98' 99 00 01 02 03 04 05' 06 07' 08' 09' 10' 11 12 13. Second label: Esprit de Chevalier. New dry white B'X, CLOS des Lunes, launched by same owners in 2012.

Cissac H-Méd r ★★ 98 00 02 03 04 05 08 09 10 11 CRU BOURGEOIS (2011) west of PAU. Firm, tannic wines that need time. Recent vintages less rustic. Second label: Reflets du CH Cissac.

Citran H-Méd r ★★ 00 02 03 04 05' 06 08 09 10' Large southern H-MÉD estate with CHASSE-SPLEEN, CAMENSAC connections. Modern, ripe and oaky through the 2000s. 2011 and 2012 disappointing. Second label: Moulins de Citran.

Clarence de Haut-Brion, Le Pe-Lé r ★★★ 89' 90 95 96' 98 99 00 01 02 03 04 05' 06 07 08 09' 10' 11 12 The second label of CH HAUT-BRION, known as Bahans Haut-Brion until 2007. Blend changes considerably with each vintage but same suave texture and elegance as the *grand vin*.

Clarke List r (p) (w) ★★ 01 02 03 04 05' 06 08 09' 10' 11 12 Large estate, massive (Edmond) Rothschild investment. Now v.gd MERLOT-based red; possibly best in LIST. Dark fruit and fine tannins. Also a dry white: Le Merle Blanc du CH Clarke. Ch Malmaison in MOU same connection. Foreign ventures too, incl gd new Rimapere, NZ.

Clauzet St-Est r ★★ 05 06 08 09 10 11 12 CRU BOURGEOIS (2011) estate owned by Baron Velge since 1997. Steady investment and improvement. Now consistent quality and value. Also sister CH de Côme.

Clerc Milon Pau r ★★★ 89' 90' 95 96' 98' 99 00 01 02 03 04 05' 06 07 08 09' 10' 11 12 13

V'yd tripled in size since (MOUTON) Rothschilds purchased in 1970 (now 40 ha). Broader and weightier than sister D'ARMAILHAC. New winemaking team in 2009 and eco-friendly cellar in 2011.

Climens Saut w sw ★★★★ 88' 89 90' 95 96 97' 98 99' 00 01' 02 03' 04 05' 06 07 09' 10' 11' 12' BAR classed growth making *some of the world's most stylish wine*. Wines are concentrated with vibrant acidity giving balance; ageing potential guaranteed. Bio conversion from 2009. Exceptional 2012 for the yr. Second label: Les Cyprès.

Clinet Pom r ★★★★ 96 98' 99 00 01 02 03 05' 06 07 08' 09' 10 11 12 Made a name for intense, sumptuous wines in the 1980s (89 and 90 legendary). Back on same form with 08 and 09. Now greater consistency. Second label: Fleur de Clinet introduced in 1997, but now a négociant brand.

Michel Reybier (Cos d'Estournel) is said to have refused €600 million for it from a Chinese investor.

Clos de l'Oratoire St-Ém r ★★ 00' 01 03 04 05' 06 07 08 09 10' 11 12 Serious performer on the northeastern slopes of ST-ÉM. Same stable as CANON-LA-GAFFELIÈRE and LA MONDOTTE, polished and fair value.

Clos des Jacobins St-Ém r ★★ ›★★★ 98 00 01 02 03 04 05' 06 07 08 09' 10' 11 12 Côtes classed growth with greater stature since 2000. New ownership from 2004; new creamy style. ANGÉLUS owner consults. Same family owns GRAND CRU CLASSÉ (2012) CH La Commanderie.

Clos du Marquis St-Jul r ★★→★★★ 98 99 00 01 02 03 04 05' 06 07 08 09' 10' 11 12 13 More typically ST-JUL than stablemate LÉOVILLE-LAS-CASES. Until 2007 considered the latter's second label but always a separate v'yd. As gd as many classed growths.

Clos Floridène Grav r w ★★ (r) 04 05 06 08 09' 10' 11 12 (w) 01' 04' 05' 07 08' 09 10 11' 12 (13) *A sure thing* from one of B'x's most famous white winemakers, Denis Dubourdieu. SAUV BL/SÉM from limestone allows the wine to age well; much improved red. CHX CANTEGRIL, DOISY-DAËNE and REYNON same owner.

Clos Fourtet St-Ém r ★★★ 98 99 00 01 02 03 04 05' 06 07 08 09' 10' 11 12 13 First Growth on the limestone plateau. Classic, stylish ST-ÉM. Consistently gd form. POUJEAUX in MOU same owner. As are GRAND CRU CLASSÉ CHX CLOS St-Martin, Côte de Baleau and Les Grandes Murailles from 2013. Second label: DOM de Martialis.

Clos Haut-Peyraguey Saut w sw ★★★ 90' 95' 96 97' 98 99 00 01' 02 03' 04 05' 06 07 09' 10' 11' 12 Magnate Bernard Magrez made this his fourth Classed Growth in 2012 (*see* PAPE-CLÉMENT, LA TOUR-CARNET, FOMBRAUGE). Elegant, harmonious wines with ageing potential. Haut-Bommes same stable.

Clos l'Église Pom r ★★★ 00' 01 02 03 04 05' 06 07 08 09' 10 11 12 13 Well-sited plateau v'yd. Opulent, elegant wine. Same family owns HAUT-BERGEY, Branon and BARDE-HAUT. Second label: Esprit de l'Église.

Clos Puy Arnaud B'x r ★★ 02 03 04 05' 06 08 09' 10 11 12 Bio estate. A leading light in CASTILLON-CÔTES DE BORDEAUX. Wines of depth and distinction. Owner formerly connected to PAVIE.

Clos René Pom r ★★ 98' 00' 01 04 05' 06 08 09 10 11 MERLOT-dominated wine with a little spicy MALBEC from sandy/gravel soils. Less sensuous and celebrated than top POM but gd value.

Clotte, la St-Ém r ★★ 00' 01 02 03 04 05 06 08 09' 10' 11 12 Tiny côtes GRAND CRU CLASSÉ: fine, perfumed, supple wines. Confidential but gd value.

Conseillante, la Pom r ★★★★ 89 90' 95' 96' 98' 99 00' 01 02 03 04 05' 06' 07 08 09' 10' 11 12 13 POM neighbour of L'EVANGILE. Same family ownership for 140 yrs. Some of the noblest and most fragrant POM; almost Médocain in style; long-ageing. New circular *cuvier* inaugurated in 2012. Second label: Duo de Conseillante.

Corbin St-Ém r ★★ 00' 01 02 04 05 07 08 09' 10' 11 12 A much-improved GRAND

CRU CLASSÉ nr POM. Elegant and rich. Consistent and gd-value wines. Second label: Divin de Corbin.

Cos d'Estournel St-Est r ★★★★ 90' 94 95 96' 98' 00 01 02 03 04 05' 06 07 08 09' 10' 11 12 13 Large and fashionable Second Growth with eccentric pagoda *chai*. Most refined ST-EST. State-of-the-art cellars with lift system for gravity pumping-over. Pricey white from 2005. Second label: Les Pagodes de Cos (and CH MARBUZET for some markets). Super-modern Goulée (MÉD) same stable. As is CHAMPAGNE producer Pressoirs de France (2013).

Cos-Labory St-Est r ★★ 95 96' 98' 99 00 02 03 04 05' 06 07 08 09' 10' 11 12 Gd-value Fifth Growth neighbour of COS D'ESTOURNEL. Recent vintages have more depth and structure. ANDRON-BLANQUET is sister CH.

Coufran H-Méd r ★★ 00 01 02 03 04 05 06 08 09 10' 11 12 Coufran and VERDIGNAN, in extreme north of the H-MÉD, are co-owned. Coufran is mainly MERLOT (85%) for supple wine. SOUDARS is another, smaller sister.

Couhins-Lurton Pe-Lé r w ★★→★★★ (r) 03 04 05 06 08' 09 10' 11 12 (w) 00 01 02 03 04 05 06 07 08' 09 10' 11 12 (13) *Fine*, minerally, long-lived, classed-growth *white* made from SAUV BL. Supple, MERLOT-based red. Same family as LA LOUVIÈRE and BONNET.

Couspaude, la St-Ém r ★★★ 00' 01 02 03 04 05 06 07 08 09' 10' 11 12 Classed growth located on the plateau close to the town of ST-ÉM. Modern style; rich and creamy with lashings of spicy oak.

Coutet Saut w sw ★★★ 89' 90' 95 96 97' 98' 99 01' 02 03' 04 05 07 09' 10' 11' 12 Traditional rival to CLIMENS, but zestier style. Consistently v. fine. Long ageing. CUVÉE Madame is a v. rich selection 89 90 95 97 01. Dry white, barrel-fermented Opalie from 2010.

Couvent des Jacobins St-Ém r ★★ 98' 00' 01 03 04 05 06 08 09' 10' 11 12 GRAND CRU CLASSÉ vinified within the walls of the town. Splendid cellars. Lighter style but can age. Denis Dubourdieu consults. Second label: Le Menut des Jacobins.

Crabitey Grav rw ★★ (r) 05 06 08 09 10 11 12 (w) 09 10 11 12 (13) Former orphanage run by religious order. V'yd was replanted in the 80s and 90s. Owner Arnaud de Butler now making harmonious red wines and small volume of lively SÉM/SAUV BL white.

Losing out

It has been estimated that the cost of producing a *tonneau* (900 litres) of B'x these days is €1,078. Unfortunately the average price in bulk is around €1,000/*tonneau*. Production costs for those who bottle their wine runs to €2.88/bottle before a margin (and tax) has been added. Bear that in mind the next time you buy a bottle of generic B'x.

Crock, le St-Est r ★★ 00' 01 02 03 04 05 06 07 08 09' 10 11 12 Gd-value CRU BOURGEOIS (2011) in same family (Cuvelier) as LÉOVILLE-POYFERRÉ. Solid, fruit-packed.

Croix, la Pom r ★★ 00 01 04 05 06 07 08 09 10 11 12 Owned by négociant Janoueix. Organically run. Appealing, rich, plummy. La Croix-St-Georges and HAUT-SARPE in the same stable.

Croix-de-Gay, la Pom r ★★★ 98 99 00' 01' 02 04 05 06 09' 10' 11 12 On the POM plateau. Round, elegant style. Some parcels sold to L'EVANGILE in 2011. LA FLEUR-DE-GAY is the special CUVÉE. Same ownership as Faizeau (MONTAGNE ST-ÉM).

Croix du Casse, la Pom r ★★ 00' 01' 04 05 06 08 09 10 11 12 On sandy/gravel soils in the south of POM. Owned by BORIE-MANOUX; investment and improvement from 2008. Medium-bodied; value for the AC.

Croizet-Bages Pau r ★★ ·★★★ 96' 98 00' 02 03 04 05 06 07 08 09 10' 11 12 Much-improved Fifth Growth. Lately, more depth, power and consistency. Value for AC. Same owners as RAUZAN-GASSIES.

Cru Bourgeois Now a certificate awarded annually. 256 CH'X in 2011. Quality variable.

Cruzeau, de Pe-Lé r sw sw ★★ (r) 04 05 06 08 09 10 12 (w) 05 06 07 08 09 10 11 12 (13) Large (two-thirds red) v'yd developed by André Lurton of LA LOUVIÈRE and COUHINS-LURTON. Gd-value wines. SAUV BL-dominated white.

Dalem B'x r ★★ 03 04 05' 06 08 09' 10' 11 12 Old (17th-century) FRONSAC property. Family-owned, MERLOT-dominated. More finesse and charm in new millennium.

Dassault St-Ém r ★★ 00 01 02 03 04 05' 06 08 09' 10 11 12 Consistent, modern, juicy GRAND CRU CLASSÉ. Owning family of Dassault aviation (since 1955). Also La Fleur in ST-ÉM and Eventures in Chile and Argentina.

Dauphine, de la B'x r ★★→★★★ 00 01 03 04 05 06' 08 09' 10' 11 12' Substantial FRONSAC estate. Wholesale change in last 15 yrs. Renovation of CH and v'yds plus new winery. Stablemate Canon-de-Brem integrated in 2006. More land acquired in 2012. Organic certification in 2015. MICHEL ROLLAND consults. Second label: Delphis.

Dauzac Marg r ★★→★★★ 95 96 98' 99 00' 01 02 04 05 06 08' 09' 10' 11 12 Fifth Growth at Labarde; now dense, rich, dark wines. Owned by an insurance company; managed by Christine Lurton, daughter of André, of LA LOUVIÈRE. Second label: La Bastide Dauzac.

Derenoncourt, Stéphane B'x Leading international consultant; self-taught, focused on terroir, fruit, balance. Own property, *Dom de L'A* in CASTILLON.

Desmirail Marg r ★★→★★★ 02 03 04 05 06 07 08 09' 10' 11 12 Third Growth owned by Denis Lurton, brother of Henri (BRANE-CANTENAC). Fine, delicate style.

Destieux St-Ém r ★★ 98 99 00' 01 03' 04 05' 06 07 08 09' 10' 11 12 Compact GRAND CRU CLASSÉ located on the second-highest spot in ST-ÉM at St-Hippolyte. Bold, powerful style; consistent. MICHEL ROLLAND consults.

Doisy-Daëne Bar (r) w dr sw ★★★ 89' 90' 95 96 97' 98' 99 01' 02 03 04 05' 07 09 10' 11' 12 Family-owned (Dubourdieu) estate producing an age-worthy, dry white and *fine, sweet Barsac*. CHX Cantegril, CLOS FLORIDÈNE and REYNON same stable. L'Extravagant 96 97 01 02 03 04 05 06 07 09 10 11 12 is an intensely rich and expensive CUVÉE.

Doisy-Védrines Saut w sw ★★★ 89' 90 95 96 97' 98 99 01' 03' 04 05 07 09 10' 11' 12 BAR Second Growth owned by Castéja family (Joanne négociant). Delicious, sturdy, rich: ages well. A sure thing for many yrs.

Dôme, le St-Ém r ★★★ 04 05 06 08 09 10' 11 12 13 Microwine; used to be super-oaky, from 2004 more elegant and related to terroir. Two-thirds old-vine CAB FR. Owned by Jonathan Maltus, who has a string of other ST-ÉMS (eg. CH Teyssier, Le Carré, Les Astéries, Vieux-Ch-Mazerat) and wines from California's Napa Valley (World's End).

Dominique, la St-Ém r ★★★ 95 96 98 99 00' 01 04 05' 06 08 09' 10' 11 12 Classed growth adjacent to CHEVAL BLANC. Solid value until 1996, then went off the boil. Back on form since 06. New €11m winery with restaurant on the roof in 2013 (architect Jean Nouvel). Second label: St Paul de Dominique.

Ducluzeau List r ★★ 01 03 04 05 06 08 09 10 Tiny sister property of DUCRU-BEAUCAILLOU. 50/50 MERLOT/CAB SAUV. Round, well-balanced wines.

Ducru-Beaucaillou St-Jul r ★★★★ 95' 96' 98 99 00' 01 02 03 04 05' 06 07 08 09' 10' 11 12 13 Outstanding Second Growth, excellent form except for a patch in the late 1980s. Added impetus from owner Bruno Borie from 2003. Classic cedar-scented claret, suited to long ageing. Croix de Beaucaillou (Jade Jagger designed label in 2010) and LALANDE-BORIE sister estates.

Duhart-Milon Rothschild Pau r ★★★ 95 96' 98 00' 01 02 03 04' 05' 06 07 08 09' 10' 11 12 13 Fourth Growth stablemate of LAFITE. Greater precision in last 10 yrs;

increasingly fine quality. Price surge with Chinese demand for Rothschild brand now abated. Second label: Moulin de Duhart.

Durfort-Vivens Marg r ★★★ 90 95 96 98 99 00 02 03 04 05' 06 08 09' 10' 11 12 Much improved MARG Second Growth owned by Gonzague Lurton. CAB SAUV-dominated and bio. Also co-owner of CH Domeyne in ST-EST. Second label: Vivens.

l'Eglise, Domaine de Pom r ★★ 98 99 00 01 02 03 04 05' 06 07 08 09 10' 11 12 Small property on the clay-gravel plateau: on gd form since 2006. Denis Dubourdieu consults. Same stable as TROTTEVIEILLE and CROIX DU CASSE.

l'Eglise-Clinet Pom r ★★★ →★★★★ 89' 90' 93' 94 95 96 98' 99 00' 01' 02 03 04 05' 06 07 08 09' 10' 11' 12 13 Tiny but top-flight estate with great consistency; full, concentrated, fleshy wine. V'yd close to POM church. Expensive and limited quantity. Second label: La Petite Eglise.

L'Evangile Pom r ★★★★ 88' 89' 90 95 96 98' 99 00' 01 02 03 04 05' 06 07 08 09' 10' 11 12 13 Neighbour of CH LA CONSEILLANTE. Rich, opulent style. Investment by owners (LAFITE) Rothschild greatly improved quality; 6 ha purchased from LA CROIX-DE-GAY in 2011. Second label: Blason de L'Evangile.

By 2018, all Pomerol will have to be vinified within the boundary of the AC.

Fargues, de Saut w sw ★★★ 89 90 95 96 97 98 99' 01 02 03' 04 05' 06 07 09' 10' 11' V'yd attached to ruined castle owned by Lur-Saluces, ex-owner of YQUEM. Techniques same. Rich, unctuous wines, but balanced. Long ageing potential.

Faugères St-Ém r ★★→★★★★ 98 00' 02 03 04 05 06 07 08 09' 10' 11 12 Powerful, rich, modern. Promoted to GRAND CRU CLASSÉ in 2012 as was sister CH Péby Faugères (100% MERLOT). Imposing Mario Botta-designed state-of-the-art winery. Sister to *Cap de Faugères* in CASTILLON and Chambrun in L DE P.

Faurie-de-Souchard St-Ém r ★★ 98' 00 03 04 05 06 07 08 09 10' 11 12 Previously underperforming GRAND CRU CLASSÉ. North-facing côtes v'yd. Recent investment and greater effort from new generation. STÉPHANE DERENONCOURT consults.

de Ferrand St-Ém r ★★ 00 01 03 04 05 06 08 09' 10' 12 Big St-Hippolyte estate owned by Pauline Bich (Bic pens) and husband Philippe Chandon-Moët. Upgraded to GRAND CRU CLASSÉ in 2012.

Ferrande Grav r (w) ★★ 04 05 06 08 09 10 11 12 Substantial estate at Castres owned by négociant Castel. Greater consistency. Easy, enjoyable red; clean, fresh white.

Ferrière Marg r ★★→★★★ 96' 98 99 00' 02 03 04 05 06 08 09' 10' 12 Tiny Third Growth with a CH in MARG village. LA GURGUE and HAUT-BAGES-LIBÉRAL same stable. Dark, firm, perfumed wines need time.

Feytit-Clinet Pom r ★★ 98 99 00 01 03 04 05' 06 07 08 09' 10' 11 12 13 Tiny family-owned and -run property. 90% MERLOT on clay-gravel soils. On great form since 2000. Rich, full POM with ageing potential. A sure-fire bet.

Fieuzal Pe-Lé r (w) ★★★ (r) 00 01 06 07 08 09' 10' 11 12 (w) 03 05 06 07 08 09' 10' 11 12 13 Classified PE-LÉ estate with Irish owner. White consistent; red best from 2006. New gravity-fed winery (2011). Seven of the 63 vats carry names of the owner's grandchildren. ANGÉLUS owner consults for reds.

Figeac St-Ém r ★★★★ 95' 96 98' 99 00' 01' 02 03 04 05' 06 07 08 09' 10' 11 12 13 First Growth; gravelly v'yd with unusual 70% CAB FR and CAB SAUV. Rich but always elegant wines, which are deceptively long ageing. Management upheaval in 2013: new business manager, winemaker and general manager; MICHEL ROLLAND consults. I hope elegance doesn't give way to power. Second label: Grange Neuve de Figeac.

Filhot Saut w dr sw ★★ 96' 97' 98 99 01' 02 03' 04 05 07 09' 10' 11' SAUT Second Growth with splendid CH, extensive v'yd. Difficult young, more complex with age. Richer and purer from 2009.

Fleur Cardinale St-Ém r ★★ 00 01 02 03 04 05' 06 07 08 09' 10' 11 12 Classified property in St-Etienne-de-Lisse. In overdrive for the last 15 yrs. Always one of the last to harvest. Ripe, unctuous, modern style.

Fleur-de-Gay, la Pom r ★★★ Tiny super-CUVÉE of CH LA CROIX-DE-GAY. 100% MERLOT.

Fleur-Pétrus, la Pom r ★★★★ 90' 95 96 98' 99 00' 01 02 03 04 05' 06 08 09' 10' 11 12 13 J-P MOUEIX property; v'yd opposite LAFLEUR. More parcels (4.7 ha) added with purchase of CH Guillot in 2012. Finer style than PETRUS or TROTANOY. Needs time.

Fombrauge St-Ém r ★★→★★★ 98 99 00' 01 02 03 04 05 06 08 09' 10' 11 12 Large Bernard Magrez estate (*see* PAPE-CLÉMENT, LA TOUR-CARNET, CLOS HAUT-PEYRAGUEY) promoted to GRAND CRU CLASSÉ in 2012. Rich, dark, chocolatey, modern. A little white B'x as well. Magrez-Fombrauge is the special CUVÉE.

Fonbadet Pau r ★★ 00' 01 02 03 04 05' 06 08 09' 10' 12 Family-owned CRU BOURGEOIS (2011). Eric Boissenot consults. Reliable, gd-value and typically PAU.

de Fonbel St-Ém r ★★ 05 06 07 08 09 10 11 12 Regular source of juicy, fresh, gd-value ST-ÉM. Same owner as AUSONE and MOULIN-ST-GEORGES.

Fonplégade St-Ém r ★★ 98 00' 01 03 04 05 06' 07 08 09' 10 12 GRAND CRU CLASSÉ owned by American Stephen Adams. Investment and progression; concentrated, modern style. MICHEL ROLLAND consults. CH L'Enclos in POM same owner.

Fonréaud List r ★★ 98 00' 01 02 03 04 05 06 08 09' 10' 11 12 One of the bigger and better LISTS making savoury, mouthfilling wines. Small volume of dry white: Le Cygne, barrel-fermented. *See* LESTAGE. Gd value.

Fonroque St-Ém r ★★★ 96 98 01 03 04 05 06 08 09' 10' 11 12 GRAND CRU CLASSÉ on the plateau n of ST-ÉM. Bio paying off; more character and elegance. Managed by Alain Moueix (*see* MAZEYRES). MOULIN DU CADET sister estate.

Fontenil B'x r ★★ 03 04 05 06 08 09' 10' 11 12 Leading FRONSAC, owned by MICHEL ROLLAND. Ripe, opulent and balanced wines. Défi de Fontenil is the 100% MERLOT special CUVÉE.

A ha of generic Bordeaux vineyard costs approximately €15,000. For Pauillac, €2 million.

Forts de Latour, les Pau r ★★★ →★★★★ 89' 90' 95' 96' 98 99 00' 01 02 03 04' 05' 06 07 08 09' 10' 11 12 13 The (worthy) second label of CH LATOUR; authentic flavour in slightly lighter format at Second Growth price. No more *en primeur* sales; only released when deemed ready to drink – the 2005 in 2013 (barely ready in fact).

Fourcas-Dupré List r ★★ 98' 00' 01 02 03 04 05 06 08 09 10' 11 12 Well-run property making fairly consistent wine in tight LIST style. Yields have been lowered, chemical weedkillers banned. Better with bottle age. Second label: CH Bellevue-Laffont.

Fourcas-Hosten List r ★★→★★★ 01 02 03 05 06 08 09 10' 11 12 Large LIST estate. Considerable investment and steady improvement over last 10 yrs. Owners have Hermès fashion connection. More precision and finesse.

France, de Pe-Lé r w ★★ (r) 00 02 03 04 05 06 08 09 10' 11 12 (w) 03 04 05 06 07 08 09 10 11 12 (13) Neighbour of FIEUZAL making consistent wines in a ripe, modern style. Owner (since 1971) Berrnard Thomassin died in 2013; son Arnaud now holds the reins.

Franc-Mayne St-Ém r ★★ 98' 00' 01 03 04 05 06 08 09 10' 12 Small GRAND CRU CLASSÉ on the côtes. Same ownership as CH DE LUSSAC and Vieux Maillet in POM. Investment and renovation. Luxury accommodation as well. Fresh, fruity, round but structured style.

Gaby, du B'x r ★★ 00' 01' 03 04 05 06 07 08 09 10 12 Splendid south-facing slopes in CANON-FRONSAC. Serious wines age well. Sister CH Moya in CASTILLON-CÔTES DE BORDEAUX same Canadian ownership.

Gaffelière, la St-Ém r ★★★ 89' 90' 95 96 98' 99 00' 01 02 03 04 05' 06 07 08 09' 10' 11 12 13 First Growth at foot of the côtes. Owning Malet Roquefort family oldest in ST-ÉM (400 yrs). Elegant, long-ageing wines. Greater precision lately. STÉPHANE DERENONCOURT consults.

Garde, la Pe-Lé r w ★★ (r) 01' 02 04 05 06 07 08 09' 10' 11 12 (w) 04 05 06 07 08 09 10' 11 12 (13) Substantial property owned by négociant CVBG-DOURTHE; reliable, supple reds. Tiny production of SAUV BL/Sauv Gris white.

Gay, le Pom r ★★★ 98 99 00 01 03 04 05' 06 07 08 09' 10' 11 12 Fine v'yd on northern edge of POM. Major investment, with MICHEL ROLLAND consulting. Now v. ripe and plummy in style. Owner Catherine Péré-Vergé died in 2013; son now manages. CH Montviel and La Violette same stable plus v'yds in Argentina.

Gazin Pom r ★★★ 90' 95 96 98' 99 00' 01 02 03 04 05' 06 07 08 09' 10' 11 12 13 Large (for POM), family-owned neighbour of PETRUS. Well-distributed and on v.gd form since mid-1990s. Second label: L'Hospitalet de Gazin.

Gilette Saut w sw ★★★ 53 55 59 61 67 70 71 75 76 78 79 81 82 83 85 86 88 89 90 Extraordinary small Preignac CH stores its sumptuous wines in concrete vats for 16–20 yrs. Only around 5,000 bottles of each. Some bottle age still advisable. Ch Les Justices is its sister 99 01 02 03' 05 07 09 10' 11.

Giscours Marg r ★★★ 96' 98 99 00' 01 02 03 04 05' 06 07 08' 09' 10' 11 12 Substantial Third Growth south of Cantenac. V.gd vigorous wine in 1970s and now. 1980s were wobbly; steady improvement over last 20 yrs with change of ownership. Second label: La Sirène de Giscours. CH DU TERTRE stablemate. As are Ch Duthil and Le HAUT-MÉDOC de Giscours.

Glana, du St-Jul r ★★ 00 02 03 04 05 06 08 09 10' 12 Large estate, expanded through acquisition of land from CH LAGRANGE. Undemanding; undramatic; value. Same owner as Bellegrave in PAU. Second label: Pavillon du Glana.

Gloria St-Jul r ★★ •★★★ 98 99 00' 01 02 03 04 05' 06 07 08 09' 10' 11 12 A widely dispersed estate with v'yds among the classed growths. Same ownership as ST-PIERRE. Regularly overperforms. Second label: Peymartin.

Grand-Corbin-Despagne St-Ém r ★★ •★★★ 95 96 98 99 00' 01 03 04 05 06 08 09' 10' 11 12 13 Gd-value GRAND CRU CLASSÉ on top form. Family-owned (Despagne) since 1812: 2012 the 200th vintage. Aromatic wines now with a riper, fuller edge. Organic cultivation. Also CH Maison Blanche, MONTAGNE ST-ÉM and Ch Ampélia, CASTILLON. Second label: Petit Corbin-Despagne.

Grand Cru Classé See ST-ÉM classification box, p.98.

Grand-Mayne St-Ém r ★★★ 90' 94 95 96 98 99 00' 01 02 03 04 05' 06 07 08 09' 10' 11 12 Leading family-owned (Nony since 1934) GRAND CRU CLASSÉ on west côtes. Consistent, firm, full, structured wines.

Grand-Pontet St-Ém r ★★★ 00' 01 02 03 04 05 06 08 09 10 11 12 GRAND CRU CLASSÉ on the côtes. Powerful and concentrated style. A family connection to BEAU-SÉJOUR-BÉCOT.

Grand-Puy-Ducasse Pau r ★★★ 95 96' 98' 99 00 01 02 03 04 05' 06 07 08 09' 10' 11 12 Fifth Growth owned by a bank (RAYNE VIGNEAU, MEYNEY same stable); stop-start quality. Lately more consistent. New winemaker 2010. ANGÉLUS owner consults from 2013. Second label: Prélude à Grand-Puy-Ducasse.

Grand-Puy-Lacoste Pau r ★★★ 89' 90' 94 95' 96' 98 99 00' 01 02 03 04 05' 06 07 08' 09' 10' 11 12 13 Fifth Growth famous for gd-value CAB SAUV-driven PAU to lay down. Same ownership as HAUT-BATAILLEY. Recent investment. Second label: Lacoste-Borie.

Grave à Pomerol, la Pom r ★★★ 98' 00 01 02 04 05 06 08 09' 10 11 12 Small property facing L DE P. Owned by Christian MOUEIX. Accessible, medium richness. Formerly known as La Grave Trigant de Boisset.

Gressier-Grand-Poujeaux Mou r ★★ 98 00 01 04 05 09 10' 11 CRU BOURGEOIS (2011) estate. Same owner as CHASSE-SPLEEN. 50/50 CAB SAUV/MERLOT. Fresh and fruit-driven. Some ageing potential.

Greysac Méd r ★★ 03 04 05' 06 08 09 10' 11 12 Large, elegant estate acquired by owner of CH Rollan-de-By and HAUT-CONDISSAS in 2012. Fine, consistent quality.

Gruaud-Larose St-Jul r ★★★★ 89' 90' 95' 96' 98 99 00' 01 02 03 04 05' 06 07 08 09' 10' 11 12 One of the biggest, best-loved Second Growths. Smooth, rich, vigorous claret; ages 20 yrs+. More finesse from 2007. Second label: Sarget de Gruaud-Larose.

Guadet St-Ém ★★ 01 04 05 06 08 09 10 11 12 Classed growth with quarried cellars in the rue Guadet, ST-ÉM. Form wobbly pre-2000. Improvement since. Organic certification from 2010.

Guiraud Saut (r) w (dr) sw ★★★ 89' 90' 95 96' 97' 98 99 01' 02 03 04 05' 06 07 09' 10' 11' Large, organically certified (2011) classed growth. Owning consortium incl long-time manager, Xavier Planty and Peugeot (cars) family. Top quality – more SAUV BL than most. Dry white G de Guiraud. Second label: Petit Guiraud.

Gurgue, la Marg r ★★ 02 03 04 05' 06 08 09' 10 11 12 Neighbour of CH MAR. Same management as FERRIÈRE and HAUT-BAGES-LIBÉRAL. Fine. Gd value.

> **Bordeaux dries up?**
> With annual sales of B'x running at around 5.5 million hectolitres and the 2013 crop estimated at 3.9 million hectolitres, there could be a dearth of B'x. The gd news for some growers is that the bulk price has risen to €1,200/*tonneau* (900 litres). The bad news: buyers might look elsewhere.

Hanteillan H-Méd Cissac r ★★ 00' 02 03 04 05' 06 09' 10 12 Large, northern H-MÉD estate. Round, balanced, early-drinking. Second label: CH Laborde.

Haut-Bages-Libéral Pau r ★★★ 96' 98 99 00 01 02 03 04 05' 06 08 09' 10' 11 12 Lesser-known Fifth Growth (next to LATOUR) in same stable as FERRIÈRE and LA GURGUE. Results are excellent, full of PAU vitality. Usually gd value.

Haut-Bages-Monpelou Pau r ★★ 98 00 03 04 05 06 08 09 10 11 Stablemate of BATAILLEY on former DUHART-MILON land. Full-bodied PAU style.

Haut-Bailly Pe-Lé r ★★★★ 89' 90' 95 96' 98' 99 00' 01 02 03 04 05' 06 07 08' 09' 10' 11' 12 Top-rank PE-LÉ classed growth owned by American banker, run by Véronique Sanders. Continued progress over last 17 yrs. Only red wine – refined, elegant style (parcel of very old vines). CH Le Pape (Léognan) new acquisition in 2012. Second label: La Parde de Haut-Bailly.

Haut-Batailley Pau r ★★★ 95 96' 98 99 00 02 03 04 05' 06 07 08 09' 10' 11 12 Smaller part of divided Fifth Growth BATAILLEY. Gentler than sister GRAND-PUY-LACOSTE. More precision in last 10 yrs. Second label: La Tour-l'Aspic.

Haut-Beauséjour St-Est r ★★ 00 01 03 04 05 08 09 10 11 Property revitalized by owner CHAMPAGNE ROEDERER. Round but structured. Sister of DE PEZ.

Haut-Bergeron Saut w sw ★★ 01 02 03 04 05 06 07 09 10 11 Fifth-generation family estate. One of the most consistent non-classified SAUT. 60 parcels of old vines. Mainly SÉM (90%). Rich, opulent, gd value.

Haut-Bergey Pe-Lé r (w) ★★ (r) 00 01 02 04 05 06 07 08 09 10 11 12 (w) 06 07 08 09 10 11 12 (13) Property of sister of owner of SMITH-HAUT-LAFITTE. Completely renovated in the 1990s. Rich, modern GRAV with oak overlay. Also a little dry white. BARDE-HAUT, CLOS L'ÉGLISE and CH Branon same stable.

Haut-Brion Pe-Lé r ★★★★ (r) 83' 85' 86' 88' 89' 90' 93 94 95' 96' 97 98' 99 00' 01 02 03 04 05' 06 08 09' 10' 11' 12 13 Est in the 16th century. Only non-MÉD First Growth of 1855, owned by American Dillon family since 1935. Deeply harmonious, wonderful texture. Consistently great since 1975. Neighbouring DOM Allary Haut-Brion v'yd integrated in 2012. A little dry, sumptuous *white*:

95 96 98 99 00' 01 02 03 04' 05' 06 07 08' 09 10' 11' 12 13. *See* LE CLARENCE DE HAUT-BRION, LA MISSION-HAUT-BRION, LAVILLE-HAUT-BRION.

Haut Condissas Méd r ★★★ 03 04 05 06 07 08 09' 10' 11 12 MÉD with an international flavour. Sister to CH Rollan-de-By and GREYSAC. Rich, concentrated and oaky. MERLOT (60%) and PETIT VERDOT (20%) the essential components.

Haut-Marbuzet St-Est r ★★ →★★★ 98 99 00' 01 02 03 04 05' 06 07 08 09' 10' 11 12 Only 7 ha when started in 1952; now 70 ha. Fourth-Growth quality, but unclassified. Two-thirds of the production sold directly by the CH. Rich, unctuous MERLOT-based (60%) wines that age well. Chambert-Marbuzet, Tour de Marbuzet and Layauga-Duboscq same stable. Second label: MacCarthy.

Haut-Sarpe St-Ém r ★★ 98 00' 01 04 05 06 08 09 10 11 12 GRAND CRU CLASSÉ with elegant CH and park, 70% MERLOT. Same owner (Janoueix) as CH La Confession and LA CROIX. Rich, dark, modern style.

Hosanna Pom r ★★★★ 99 00 01 03 04 05' 06 07 08 09' 10' 11' 12 Formerly Certan-Guiraud until purchased and renamed by J-P MOUEIX in 1999. Only best part retained. Wines have power, complexity and class. New cellar in 2008, shared with Providence. Stablemate of TROTANOY.

d'Issan Marg r ★★★ 98 00' 01 02 03 04' 05' 06 07 08 09' 10' 11 12 Third Growth v'yd with moated CH. Fragrant wines; with more substance since late 1990s. 50% owned by owner of LILIAN LADOUYS and PEDESCLAUX as of 2013. Second label: Blason d'Issan.

Jean Faure St-Ém r ★★ 05 06 08 09 10 11 12 Neighbour of LA DOMINIQUE promoted to GRAND CRU CLASSÉ in 2012. Organic cultivation. 50% CAB FR helps produce a fresh, elegant style. Dynamic owner (2004) also the proprietor of Mas Amiel in MAURY.

Kirwan Marg r ★★★ 95 96 98 99 00' 01 02 03 04 05' 06 07 08 09 10' 11' 12 Third Growth owned by négociant Schröder & Schÿler. Dense and fleshy in the 90s; more finesse from 2007. Former PALMER winemaker at the helm. Second label: Les Charmes de Kirwan.

Labégorce Marg r ★★→★★★ 01 02 03 04 05' 07 08 09 10' 11 12 Substantial unclassified MAR. Considerable investment since 2006. Neighbouring LABÉGORCE-ZÉDÉ absorbed in 2009. Fine, modern style. CH MARQUIS-D'ALESME same stable.

Lafaurie-Peyraguey Saut w sw ★★★ 83' 85 86' 88' 89' 90' 95 96' 97 98 99 01' 02 03' 04 05' 06 07 09' 10' 11' Leading classed growth at Bommes, changed hands early 2014. Expect investment, and a new focus on dry white as well as rich, concentrated, harmonious sw. 90% SÉM. Part of CH dates from 13th century. Consistent and relatively gd-value since remarkable 83. Second label: La Chapelle de Lafaurie.

Lafite-Rothschild Pau r ★★★★ 85 86' 88' 89' 90' 93 94 95 96' 97 98' 99 00' 01' 02 03' 04' 05' 06 07 08' 09' 10' 11' 12 13 First Growth of famous elusive perfume and style, but never great weight, although more dense and sleek these days. Great vintages need keeping for decades. Lost most of its celebrated weeping willows to a gale in 2013. Joint ventures in Chile (1988), California (1989), Portugal (1992), Argentina (1999), now the MIDI, Italy, even China. Second label: CARRUADES DE LAFITE. Also owns CHX DUHART-MILON, L'EVANGILE, RIEUSSEC.

Lafleur Pom r ★★★★ 85' 86 88' 89' 90' 93 94 95 96 98' 99' 00' 01' 02 03 04' 05' 06' 07 08 09' 10' 11' 12 13 Superb but tiny family-owned and -managed property cultivated like a garden. Elegant, intense wine for maturing. 50% CAB FR. Expensive. B'X CH Grand Village same stable. Second label: *Pensées de Lafleur*.

La Fleur de Boüard B'X r ★★ →★★★ 04 05 06 07 08 09 10 11 12 13 Leading estate in L DE P. Rich, dark, dense, modern. Same owner as ANGÉLUS, Bellevue in ST-ÉM. Special CUVÉE, Le Plus, more extreme: 100% MERLOT aged 3 yrs in new-oak barrels.

Lafleur-Gazin Pom r ★★ 00 01 04 05 06 08 09 10 11 12 Small J-P MOUEIX estate located between LAFLEUR and GAZIN. Lighter, supple style.

Lafon-Rochet St-Est r ★★★ 90' 95 96' 98 99 00' 01 02 03' 04 05' 06 08 09' 10' 11 12 13 Fourth-Growth neighbour of COS D'ESTOURNEL. Distinctive yellow cellars (and label). A high percentage of MERLOT (40%) adds opulence and texture but the CAB SAUV provides structure to age. Former PETRUS winemaker (J-C Berrouet) consulting since 2012. Second label: Les Pèlerins de Lafon-Rochet.

Google Streetview is available for St-Émilion and Ch Lafon-Rochet, among others.

Lagrange St-Jul r ★★★ 89' 90' 94 95 96 98 99 00' 01 02 03 04 05' 06 08 09' 10' 11 12 13 Substantial (115 ha) Third Growth owned by Suntory (since 1983). Now in tip-top condition. Much investment in v'yd and cellars. Dry white Les Arums de Lagrange (since 1997). Second label: Les Fiefs de Lagrange (gd value). Third label: HAUT-MÉDOC de Lagrange (from 2012).

Lagrange Pom r ★★ 96 98 00 01 04 05 06 09 10 Tiny POM v'yd owned by the ubiquitous house of J-P MOUEIX since 1953. 95% MERLOT. Gd value but not in the same league as HOSANNA, LA FLEUR-PÉTRUS, etc.

Lagune, la H-Méd r ★★★ 90' 95 96' 98 00' 02 03 04 05' 07 08 09' 10' 11 12 Third Growth with sandy/gravel soils. Dipped in 1990s; now on form. Fine-edged with added structure and depth. Bought neighbour CH D'ARCHE in 2013. Owned by J-J Frey; *see also* JABOULET AÎNÉ. Daughter Caroline is winemaker. Also CUVÉE Mademoiselle L from v'yd in Cussac-Fort-MÉDOC.

Lalande-Borie St-Jul r ★★ 01 02 03 04 05 06 07 08 09' 10' 11 12 A baby brother of the great DUCRU-BEAUCAILLOU with v'yd on the western plateau of ST-JUL. Merlot 53%. Gracious, easy-drinking wine.

Lamarque, de H-Méd r ★★ 00' 02 03 04 05' 06 08 09' 10' 11 12 Central H-MÉD v'yd with splendid medieval fortress. Competent, mid-term wines. Second label: D de Lamarque.

Lamothe Bergeron H-Méd r ★★ 00 02 03 04 05 09' 10' 11 12 Large estate in Cussac-Fort-MÉDOC. Owned by Cognac houses Hardy and Mounier (since 2009). Attractive early drinking.

Lanessan H-Méd r ★★ 00' 02 03 04 05 08 09 10' 11 12 Distinguished property just south of ST-JUL. Former Calvet and Cordier-Mestrezat winemaker, Paz Espejo, now in charge – improvements since 2010. Horse museum and tours.

Langoa-Barton St-Jul r ★★★ 95' 96' 98 99 00' 01 02 03 04' 05' 06 07 08 09' 10' 11 12 13 Third Growth sister CH to LÉOVILLE-BARTON. 18th-century CH; impeccable standards, consistent value. Second label: Rés de Léoville-Barton.

Larcis Ducasse St-Ém r ★★★ 89' 90' 95 96 98 00 02 03 04 05' 06 07 08 09' 10' 11 12 13 Well-sited, family-owned estate on the côtes at St-Laurent. Great in the 50s and 60s. Spectacular form since 2004. Promotion to PREMIER GRAND CRU CLASSÉ (2012) as recompense. Top vintages can age 40+ yrs.

Larmande St-Ém r ★★ 00' 01 03 04 05 06 07 08 09' 10 12 Substantial property owned by Le Mondiale insurance (as is SOUTARD). Replanted, re-equipped; now consistently solid if vapid wines. Second label: le Cadet de Larmande.

Laroque St-Ém r ★★ →★★★ 98 99 00' 01 03 04 05 06 08 09' 10' 11 12 Large GRAND CRU CLASSÉ at St-Christophe-des-Bardes; 17th-century CH; fresh, terroir-driven wines.

Larose-Trintaudon H-Méd r ★★ 04 05 06 07 08 09' 10 11 12 The largest v'yd in the MÉD (190 ha). Sustainable viticulture. Previously light and easy-drinking but improved quality from 2007. Second label: Larose St-Laurent. Special CUVÉE, Larose Perganson, from separate parcels; denser and more polished.

Laroze St-Ém r ★★ 98' 99 00 01 05 06 07 08 09' 10' 12 Family-owned (since 1610) estate. Large v'yd w of ST-ÉM. Lighter-framed wines from sandy soils; more depth in last 15 yrs; ANGÉLUS owner consults. Second label: La Fleur Laroze.

Larrivet-Haut-Brion Pe-Lé r w ★★★ (r) 00 01 02 03 04 05' 06 07 08 09 10' 11 12 PE-LÉ property owned by Bonne Maman jam connection. Rich, modern red. Also creamy SAUV BL/SÉM barrel-fermented white 05 06 07 08 09 10' 11 12 (13). Former MONTROSE manager in charge since 2007. MICHEL ROLLAND consults. Second label: Les Demoiselles de Larrivet-Haut-Brion.

Lascombes Marg r (p) ★★★ 90' 96' 98' 99 00 01 02 03 04 05' 06 07 08 09' 10' 11 12 Second Growth owned by French insurance group (2011). Wines were wobbly; now rich, dark and concentrated. Winemaker previously with L'EVANGILE. Modern style. Second label: Chevalier de Lascombes.

Latour Pau r ★★★★(★) 82' 85 86 88' 89 90' 91 94 95' 96' 97 98 99 00' 01 02 03' 04' 05' 06 07 08 09' 10' 11' 12 13 First Growth considered the grandest statement of the MÉDOC. Profound, intense, almost immortal wines in great yrs; even weaker vintages have the unique taste and run for many yrs. Latour always needs 10 yrs to show its hand. Part of v'yd bio cultivated (incl horses for ploughing). Set cat among pigeons when it ceased *en primeur* sales in 2012; wines now only released when considered ready to drink (the 1995 in 2013). New cellars for greater storage capacity. Second label: LES FORTS DE LATOUR; **third label: Pauillac**.

> **Square-shouldered *bordelaise***
> The B'X bottle as we know it took shape in 17th-century England. The advent of coal-fired glass-furnaces and the realization that wine shipped in 900-litre *tonneaux* was easier to sell and keep in bottles were the motivating forces. Thicker brown globular bottles with a high, tapered neck, reinforced collar (for cork stoppers) and punt were already being manufactured in the 1630s. In B'x, the industrial production of bottles *à la méthode anglaise* began in the early 18th century, driven by demand from merchants. The bottle in its present square-shouldered form appears to have been in place by the beginning of the 19th century. It was first called the *frontignan*, then the *bordelaise*.

Latour-à-Pomerol Pom r ★★★ 89' 90' 95 96 98' 99 00' 01 02 04 05' 06 07 08 09' 10' 11 12 Top growth on plateau nr POM church. Managed by J-P MOUEIX. Rich, well-structured wines that age. Rarely disappoints.

Latour-Martillac Pe-Lé r w ★★ (r) 98 00 01 02 03 04 05' 06 08 09' 10' 11 12 Classed-growth property owned by Kressmann family (since 1929). Regular quality (r w); gd value at this level. White can age as well 02 03 04 05 06 07 08 09 10' 11 12 13.

Laurets, des St-Ém r ★★ 04 05 06 08 09 10 12 Major property in PUISSEGUIN-ST-ÉM and MONTAGNE-ST-ÉM, with v'yd evenly split (40,000 cases). Late 19th-century CH. Owned by Benjamin de Rothschild of Ch CLARKE (2003).

Laville Saut w sw ★★ 01 03 04 06 07 09 10 11 Family-owned Preignac estate nr BASTOR-LAMONTAGNE. Winemaker also lectures at B'x University's Faculty of Oenology. SÉM-dominated (85%), rich, lush, botrytized wine. Gd-value, non-classified SAUT.

Laville-Haut-Brion Pe-Lé w ★★★★ 94 95' 96' 98 00' 01 02 03 04' 05' 06 07 08' Former name for LA MISSION HAUT-BRION BLANC (renamed in 2009). Only 8,000 bottles/yr of v. best white GRAV for long, succulent maturing. Great consistency. Mainly SÉM. Second label: La Clarté de Haut-Brion (formerly Les Plantiers); also incl wine from HAUT-BRION.

Léoville-Barton St-Jul r ★★★★ 88' 89' 90' 94' 95' 96' 98 99 00' 01 02 03' 04 05' 06 07 08' 09' 10' 11 12 13 Second Growth with the longest-standing family ownership; in Anglo-Irish hands of the Bartons for over 180 yrs (Anthony Barton is present incumbent, assisted by daughter Lilian). Smallest of the three Léovilles; harmonious, classic claret. Generally traditional methods but optical-laser sorter from 2011. Shares cellars with LANGOA-BARTON.

Léoville-las-Cases St-Jul r ★★★★ 85' 86' 88 89' 90' 93 94 95' 96' 97 98 99 00' 01 02 03' 04' 05' 06 07 08 09' 10' 11' 12 13 The largest Léoville and original "Super Second"; *grand vin* from Grand Enclos v'yd. Elegant, complex, powerful wines, for immortality. Sometimes more PAU than ST-JUL. Second label: Le Petit Lion (2007); previously CLOS DU MARQUIS but latter now considered a separate wine.

Léoville-Poyferré St-Jul r ★★★★ 86' 88 89' 90' 94 95 96' 98 99 00' 01 02 03 04 05' 06 07 08 09' 10' 11' 12 13 The third part of the great Léoville estate; its best vines lie opposite the Grand Enclos of LÉOVILLE-LAS-CASES. Now at "Super Second" level with dark, rich, spicy, long-ageing wines. Second label: *Ch Moulin-Riche*. LE CROCK same stable.

Les Cruzelles B'x r ★★ 05 06 08 09 10 11 12 Rich, generous wine from L DE P. Ageing potential in top yrs. Denis Durantou of L'EGLISE-CLINET the owner and winemaker.

Lestage List r ★★ 00 02 03 04 05 06 08 09 10 11 12 LIST estate in same hands as CH FONRÉAUD. More MERLOT (56%). Firm, slightly austere claret. Second label: La Dame de Coeur de Ch Lestage.

Les Trois Croix B'x r ★★ 05 06 07 08 09 10 11 12 13 Fine, balanced wines from this consistent producer in FRONSAC. Owned by former MOUTON-ROTHSCHILD winemaker. Son and daughter manage estate.

Lilian Ladouys St-Est r ★★ 98 00 02 03 04 05 06 07 08 09' 10' 11 12 Created in the 80s, the v'yd has 100 parcels of vines. Firm, sometimes robust wines; recent vintages more finesse. New owner 2008 (owns rugby club Racing Métro 92 and PÉDESCLAUX; also 50% share in D'ISSAN.) Same management as Belle-Vue in H-MÉD.

Liversan H-Méd r ★★ 98 00 02 03 04 05 07 08 09 10 12 Situated in northern H-MÉD. Same owner as PATACHE D'AUX. Round but structured. Second label: Les Charmes de Liversan.

Loudenne Méd r ★★ 00' 01 02 03 04 05 06 09' 10' 11 An 18th-century pink-washed *chartreuse* by the river made famous by Gilbey's. Sold to Chinese in 2013. €5m investment planned. Ripe, round reds. Also an oak-scented SAUV BL 06 07 08 09 10 11 12. And, of course, a rosé, Pink de Loudenne.

Loupiac-Gaudiet B'x w sw ★★ 01 02 03' 05 07 09 10 11 A reliable source of gd-value "almost-SAUT", just across river Garonne in LOUPIAC AC.

Louvière, la Pe-Lé r w ★★★ (r) 00' 01 02 04 05' 06 07 08 09' 10' 11 12 (w) 01 02 03 04' 05' 06 07 08 09' 10' 11 12 13 André Lurton's pride and joy. Excellent *white* and red of classed-growth standard. *See also* BONNET, COUHINS-LURTON, DE CRUZEAU, DE ROCHEMORIN.

Lussac, de St-Ém r ★★ 00 03 04 05 06 07 08 09 10 11 12 One of the best estates in LUSSAC-ST-ÉM. Same stable as FRANC-MAYNE and Vieux Maillet in POM. Second label: Le Libertin de Lussac.

Lynch-Bages Pau r (w) ★★★★ 86' 88' 89' 90' 94 95' 96' 98 99 00' 01 02 03 04' 05' 06 07 08 09' 10' 11 12 13 Always popular, now a regular star, far higher than its Fifth Growth rank. Rich, robust wine. Second label: Echo de Lynch-Bages. Third label from 2009. Gd white, *Blanc de Lynch-Bages*, now fresher style. Same owners (Cazes family; new generation – Jean-Charles – now in charge) as LES ORMES-DE-PEZ, Villa Bel-Air and l'Ostal Cazes in MINERVOIS-LA LIVINIÈRE.

Hail and farewell

Hail has taken over from frost as the major climatic hazard in B'X. The last spring frost of any consequence was in 1997, but hail struck in 1999, 2003, 2008, 2009, 2011 and 2013. The storm in August 2013 hit 22,000 ha, mainly in E-2-M; 5,000 ha suffered 80–100% crop loss – all in a matter of minutes. Few growers are covered by insurance, as the premiums are too high.

Lynch-Moussas Pau r ★★ 98 00′ 01 02 03 04 05′ 07 08 09 10′ 11 12 Fifth Growth owned by BORIE-MANOUX. Improvement in the new millennium; more depth. A PAU second-stringer but gd value.

Lyonnat St-Ém r ★★ 01 03 04 05 06 08 09 10 12 Property in LUSSAC-ST-ÉM. Reliable wine. 100% MERLOT. ANGÉLUS owner consults.

Macquin-St-Georges St-Ém r ★★ 00 01 03 04 05 06 08 09 10 11 Producer of delicious, not weighty, satellite ST-ÉM at ST-GEORGES. Consistent quality.

Magdelaine St-Ém r ★★★ 89′ 90′ 95 96 98′ 99 00 01 03 04 05 06 07 08 09′ 10′ 11 RIP from 2012, now integrated into BELAIR-MONANGE. Delicate, fine, deceptively long-lived. Denser weight from 2008.

Malartic-Lagravière Pe-Lé r (w) ★★★ (r) 98 99 00′ 01 02 03 04′ 05′ 06 08 09′ 10′ 11 12 (w) 00 01′ 02 03 04′ 05′ 06 07 08 09′ 10′ 11 12 13 Léognan classed growth. Rich, modern red wine since late 1990s; a little lush SAUV BL white. Belgian owner has revolutionized the property and tripled the size. MICHEL ROLLAND advises. CH Gazin Rocquencourt (PE-LÉ) acquired in 2006.

Malescasse H-Méd r ★★ 01 02 03 04 05 06 08 09 10 11 12 CRU BOURGEOIS (2011) nr MOU. New ownership in 2012. Supple, value wines, accessible early. Second label: La Closerie de Malescasse.

The 1855 Classification is seeking UNESCO World Heritage status.

Malescot-St-Exupéry Marg r ★★★ 95 96 98 99 00′ 01 02 03 04 05′ 06 07 08′ 09′ 10′ 11 12 Third Growth returned to fine form in the 1990s. Now ripe, fragrant and finely structured. Ages well. Second label: La Dame de Malescot.

Malle, de Saut r w dr sw ★★★ (w sw) 89′ 90′ 94 95 96′ 97′ 98 99 00 01′ 02 03′ 05 06 07 09 10′ 11′ Beautiful 17th-century Preignac CH making v. fine, medium-bodied SAUT; also M de Malle dry white and GRAV Ch du Cardaillan.

Margaux, Château Marg r (w) ★★★★ 85′ 86′ 88′ 89′ 90′ 93 94 95′ 96′ 97 98′ 99 00′ 01′ 02 03′ 04′ 05′ 06′ 07 08 09′ 10′ 11′ 12 13 MARG First Growth; most seductive, fabulously perfumed and consistent wines. Owned and run by Corinne Mentzelopoulos. New Norman Foster-designed cellars in 2014. Pavillon Rouge 00′ 01 02 03 04′ 05′ 06 08 09′ 10′ 11 12 is second label; third label M de Margaux; first vintage 2009. *Pavillon Blanc* (100% SAUV BL) is best white of MÉDOC, at First Growth price 04′ 05 06 07 08 09′ 10′ 11′ 12.

Marojallia Marg r ★★★ 99 00′ 01 02 03 04 05′ 06 07 08 09′ 10 11 12 Micro-CH looking for big prices for big, rich, un-MARG-like wines. 2011 and 12 less full throttle. Also upmarket B&B. Second label: CLOS Margalaine.

Marquis-d'Alesme Marg r ★★ 98 00 01 04 05 07 08 09′ 10′ 11 12 Third Growth purchased by LABÉGORCE in 2006. Dropped "Becker" from name in 2009. Disappointing in recent yrs; steady progress from 2009.

Marquis-de-Terme Marg r ★★→★★★ 90′ 95 96 98 99 00′ 01 02 03 04 05′ 06 07 08 09′ 10′ 11 12 Fourth Growth with v'yd dispersed around MARG. On better form since 2000. New manager in 2009 and richer style. Previously solid rather than elegant.

Maucaillou Mou r ★★ 01 02 03 04 05 06 08 09 10 11 12 Visitor-friendly (museum, shop, film, tasting) MOU property. Clean, fresh, value wines. Second label: No 2 de Maucaillou.

Mayne Lalande List r ★★ 05 08 09 10 11 12 Launched by Bernard Lartigue in 1982. Now a leader in LIST. Full and finely textured. CH Myon de l'Enclos in MOU same stable.

Mazeyres Pom r ★★ 98′ 99 00 01 04 05′ 06 08 09 10 12 Lighter but consistent POM. Substantial v'yd for AC. Alain Moueix, cousin of Christian (J-P MOUEIX), manages. Bio from 2012. *See* FONROQUE.

Meyney St-Est r ★★ →★★★ 98 00 01 02 03 04 05′ 06 08 09′ 10′ 11′ 12 Large riverside-slope property next to MONTROSE. Rich, robust, well-structured wines. Same stable as GRAND-PUY-DUCASSE and RAYNE VIGNEAU (CA GRANDS CRUS). Hubert de Boüard of ANGÉLUS consultant from 2013. Second label: Prieur de Meyney.

Mission Haut-Brion, La Pe-Lé r ★★★★ 85' 86 88 89' 90' 93 94 95 96' 98' 99 00'
01 02 03 04 05' 06 07 08 09' 10' 11' 12 13 Thirtieth anniversary of ownership by the Dillon family of HAUT-BRION in 2013. Average age of the v'yd also 30 yrs. Consistently grand-scale, full-blooded, long-maturing wine; more flamboyant than HAUT-BRION. Now considered the unofficial sixth First Growth (1855). Second label: La Chapelle de la Mission. White: previously LAVILLE-HAUT-BRION; renamed (2009) La Mission-Haut-Brion Blanc 09' **10' 11' 12'** 13.

There are 20 estates in the Médoc producing white wine from a total of 100 ha.

Monbousquet St-Ém r (w) ★★★ 00' 01 02 03 04 05' 06 07 08 09' 10' 11 12 Substantial GRAND CRU CLASSÉ on sand and gravel plain revolutionized by owner Gerard Pérse since 1994. Now concentrated, oaky, voluptuous wines. Rare *v.gd white* (AC B'X) from 1998. Same ownership as PAVIE and PAVIE-DECESSE.

Monbrison Marg r ★★ →★★★ 90 95 96' 98 99 00 01 02 04 05' 06 08 09' 10' 11 12 Small, family-owned property at Arsac (6,500 cases). Delicate, fragrant MARG.

Mondotte, la St-Ém r (★★★) ★ 96' 97 98' 99 00' 01 02 03 04' 05' 06 07 08 09' 10' 11 12 13 Tiny estate on the limestone plateau promoted to PREMIER GRAND CRU CLASSÉ in 2012. Intense, always firm, virile wines. Same owner as CANON-LA-GAFFELIÈRE, CLOS DE L'ORATOIRE.

Montrose St-Est r ★★★ 88 89' 90' 93 94 95 96' 98 99 00' 01 02 03' 04' 05' 06 07 08 09' 10' 11 12 Second Growth with v'yd overlooking Gironde estuary. Famed for deep-coloured, forceful, long-ageing claret. Vintages 1979–85 (except 82) were lighter. After 110 yrs in same family, new owners in 2006. Huge investment since. New cellar for 800 barrels. Second label: La Dame de Montrose.

Moulin du Cadet St-Ém r p ★★ 96 98 00 01 03 05 08 09 10' 12 Tiny GRAND CRU CLASSÉ on the limestone plateau, managed by Alain Moueix (*see also* MAZEYRES). Certified bio. Robust wines, more depth and finesse since 2009.

Moulinet Pom r ★★ 00 01 04 05 06 08 09 10 11 12 One of POM's bigger CH'X. DERENONCOURT consultant from 2009. Lighter style. Value.

Moulin-Haut-Laroque B'x r ★★ 04 05' 06 08 09' 10' 11 12 Leading FRONSAC CH. Consistent quality. Structured wines that can age from MERLOT, CAB FR and 80-yr-old MALBEC. Value.

Moulin Pey-Labrie B'x r ★★ 00' 01 02 03 04 05' 06 08 09' 10' 11 12 Leading CH in CANON-FRONSAC. Stylish wines, MERLOT-dominated, with elegance and structure.

Moulin-St-Georges St-Ém r ★★★ 00' 01 02 03 04 05' 06 08 09' 10' 11 12 13 Sits facing AUSONE across valley; same family ownership. Dense, stylish wines.

Mouton Rothschild Pau r (w) ★★★★ 82' 83' 85' 86' 88' 89' 90' 93' 94 95' 96 97 98' 99 00' 01' 02 03 04' 05' 06' 07 08' 09' 10' 11' 12 13 The most exotic and voluptuous of the PAU First Growths. Attains new heights from 2004. New cellar from 2012. Artwork for the artists' labels (Picasso, Dalí, Miró, etc. 2011: Guy de Rougemont) now on show at the CH. White Aile d'Argent from 1991. Second label: Le Petit Mouton from 1997. *See also* Opus One (California) and Almaviva (Chile).

Nairac Saut sw sw ★★ 95' 96 97' 98 99 01' 02 03' 04 05' 06 07 09' 10 11 Rich style of BAR; on top form since 2003. Second label: Esquisse de Nairac, equally rich but fresher in style.

Nénin Pom r ★★★ 95 96 98 99 00' 01 02 03 04 05 06 07 08 09' 10' 11 12 13 LÉOVILLE-LAS-CASES ownership since 1997. Massive investment. New cellars. V'yd expanded. A less opulent and generous POM but built to age. Recent vintages show the work has paid off. Gd-value second label: Fugue de Nénin.

Olivier Pe-Lé r w ★★★ (r) 95 96 00 01 02 04' 05' 06 08 09' 10' 11 12 13 (w) 01 02

03 04' 05' 06 07' 08 09 10' 11 12 13 Classified PE-LÉ property with moated castle. New investment and greater purity, expression and quality from 2002. Once coasting, now one to follow.

Ormes-de-Pez, les St-Est r ★★ →★★★ 96 98 99 00' 01 02 03 04 05 06 07 08 09' 10' 11 12 Outstanding ST-EST owned by LYNCH-BAGES. Dense, fleshy wines need 6–7 yrs.

Ormes-Sorbet, les Méd r ★★ 00' 01 02 03' 04 05 06 08 09' 10' 11 12 Reliably consistent CRU BOURGEOIS (2011) in AC MÉDOC. Elegant, gently oaked wines that age. CH Fontis same stable. Second label: Ch de Conques.

Palmer Marg r ★★★★ 83' 85 86' 88' 89 90 93 94 95 96' 98' 99 00 01' 02 03 04 05' 06' 07 08' 09' 10' 11' 12 13 Third Growth on a par with "Super Seconds" (occasionally Firsts). Wine of power, delicacy and much MERLOT (40%). Dutch (MÄHLER-BESSE) and British (SICHEL family) owners. Recent investment in new cellars and buildings. Unique white made from Lauzet and MUSCADELLE. Second label: *Alter Ego de Palmer.*

Pape-Clément Pe-Lé r (w) ★★★ →★★★★ (r) 90' 94 95 96 98' 99 00' 01 02 03 04 05 06 07 08 09' 10' 11 12 13 (w) 02 03 04 05' 07 08 09 10' 11 12 13 Owned by Pope Clément V (of Avignon), by Bernard Magrez since 1985 (*see* FOMBRAUGE, LA TOUR-CARNET); potent, oak-scented, long-ageing if not typical reds. Tiny production of rich, exotic white. Fastidious winemaking. Oxen do ploughing; beehives in v'yd.

Parenchère, de B'x r (w) ★★ 05 06 07 08 09' 10' 11 12 Useful AC Ste-Foy B'x and AC BORDEAUX SUPÉRIEUR from large estate with handsome CH. CUVÉE Raphael best.

Patache d'Aux Méd r ★★ 03 04 05' 06 07 09 10 11 12 CRU BOURGEOIS (2011) often-seen MÉD property at Bégadan. Value, reliable largely CAB SAUV wine. *See also* LIVERSAN.

Pavie St-Ém r ★★★★ 90' 94 95 96 98 99 00' 01 02 03' 04 05' 06 07 08 09' 10' 11 12 13 Promoted to PREMIER GRAND CRU CLASSÉ (A) in 2012. Splendidly sited on the plateau and southern côtes. Owner Gérard Persse of MONBOUSQUET (1998) and adjacent PAVIE-DECESSE. New-wave ST-ÉM: intense, oaky, strong. €14m winery unveiled in 2013: cellars, boutique, reception.

Rover, sit!

Now, Rover, go and cut the grass.... It could happen. A ST-ÉM-based company has developed a Vitirover, a mini-robot that mows the grass between rows of vines. It weighs 11 kg (not a big dog, then) and is powered by solar energy. It can even be retrieved from a plot of vines by pressing a button on a phone and ordering it to "heel".

Pavie-Decesse St-Ém r ★★ 98' 99 00' 01 02 03 04 05' 06 07 08 09' 10' 11 12 Tiny classed growth (only 1,000 cases). As powerful and muscular as sister PAVIE.

Pavie-Macquin St-Ém r ★★★ 89' 90' 94 95 96' 98' 99 00' 01 02 03 04 05' 06 07 08 09' 10' 11 12 13 PREMIER GRAND CRU CLASSÉ with v'yd on limestone plateau next to TROPLONG-MONDOT. Astute management, winemaking by Nicolas Thienpont of PUYGUERAUD; DERENONCOURT consults. Powerful, structured wines that need time.

Pédesclaux Pau r ★★ 98' 99 00 02 03 04 05 06 09 10' 11 12 Underachieving Fifth Growth being revived and reorganized. New owner in 2009 (*see* LILIAN LADOUYS) and improvement. New v'yds added, incl 14 prime ha between LAFITE and MOUTON. Recent vintages gd value.

Petit-Village Pom r ★★★ 98' 99 00' 01 03 04 05 06 07 08 09' 10' 11 12 13 Top POM opposite VIEUX-CH-CERTAN. Lagged until 2005. DERENONCOURT consults. New boutique/reception in 2013. Same owner (AXA Insurance) as PICHON-LONGUEVILLE. Suave, dense, increasingly finer tannins. Second label: Le Jardin de Petit-Village.

Petrus Pom r ★★★★ 78 79' 81 82' 83 85' 86 88' 89' 90 93' 94 95' 96 97 98' 99 00' 01 02 03 04' 05' 06 07 08 09' 10' 11' 12 13 The (unofficial) First Growth of

POM: MERLOT solo *in excelsis*. V'yd on gravelly clay gives 2,500 cases of massively rich, concentrated wine, on allocation to millionaires. Each vintage adds lustre. Olivier Berrouet (son of Jean-Claude) winemaker since 2007. Jean-François MOUEIX owner. New cellar complex in 2012.

Pey La Tour B'x r ★★ 08 09 10 11 12 Value, quality-driven generic BORDEAUX SUPÉRIEUR produced on a vast scale (200 ha). Owned by DOURTHE. Rés du CH is top selection.

Peyrabon H-Méd r ★★ 01 02 03 04 05 06 09' 10 11 12 Consistent northern H-MÉD owned by négociant (Millésima). Also La Fleur-Peyrabon in PAU.

Pez, de St-Est r ★★★ 98' 00 01 02 03 04 05' 06 07 08 09' 10' 11 12 13 Ancient ST-EST estate revamped by owner ROEDERER. Same winemaking team as PICHON-LALANDE. Generous and reliable in style.

Phélan-Ségur St-Est r ★★★ 95 96' 98 99 00' 0 1 02 03 04 05' 06 07 08 09' 10' 11 12 Top ST-EST; reputation solid since 1988 but unclassified; long, supple style. Owning family has luxury restaurants: Les Crayères (Reims), Taillevent (Paris).

Pibran Pau r ★★ 96 99 00' 01 03 04 05' 06 07 08 09' 10' 11 12 Small property allied to PICHON-LONGUEVILLE. Classy wine with PAU drive.

Pichon-Longueville Pau (Pichon Baron) r ★★★★ 88' 89' 90' 93 94' 95 96 98 99 00' 01 02 03' 04 05' 06 07 08 09' 10' 11' 12 13 Revitalized Second Growth with powerful consistent PAU for long ageing. Owners AXA Insurance (1987). Now a front-running "Super Second". Second label: Les Tourelles de Longueville (approachable: more MERLOT).

Pichon-Longueville Comtesse de Lalande (Pichon Lalande) Pau r ★★★★ 85' 86' 88' 89' 90' 94 95 96 98 99 00 01 02 03' 04 05' 06 07 08 09' 10' 11 12 13 ROEDERER-owned (2007) Second Growth, beside LATOUR. Always among top performers; long-lived, MERLOT-marked wine of fabulous breed. More CAB SAUV in recent yrs as v'yd is replanted. 2013 vinified in new cellar. New guest reception in 2014. Second label: Rés de la Comtesse. DE PEZ same stable.

Pin, Le Pom r ★★★★ 85 86' 88 89 90' 94 95 96 97 98' 99 00 01' 02 04' 05' 06' 07 08 09' 10' 11 12 The original of the B'x cult mini-crus (first vintage: 1979) made in a cellar the size of a garage. Now a new (2011) winery. A mere 500 cases of 100% MERLOT. Almost as rich as its drinkers, but prices are scary. L'If is new (2011) ST-ÉM stablemate.

Plince Pom r ★★ 00' 01 04 05 06 08 09 10 11 12 V'yd nr NÉNIN and LA POINTE. Supple, fruit-driven style. Relatively gd value.

Pointe, La Pom r ★★ 98' 99 00' 01 04 05 06 07 08 09' 10' 11 12 Large (for POM) estate. New owner and investment (2007). ANGÉLUS owner consults. Distinct improvement from 2009. Value.

Poitevin Méd r ★★ 08 09 10 11 Supple, elegant CRU BOURGEOIS (2011) from the northern MÉDOC. Consistent quality in recent yrs.

Pontac-Monplaisir Pe-Lé r (w) ★★ 00 02 04 05' 06 07 08 09 10 12 Mainly red estate in Villenave d'Ornon. Attractive white; supple, decent red. Value.

Pontet-Canet Pau r ★★★★ 88 89' 90 94' 95 96' 98 99 00' 01 02' 03 04' 05' 06' 07 08 09' 10' 11 12 13 Bio certified (2011), family-owned PAU Fifth Growth. Radical improvement has seen prices soar. One-third now aged in concrete amphorae. Second label: Les Hauts de Pontet-Canet.

Potensac Méd r ★★ 98 00' 01 02 03 04' 05' 07 08 09' 10' 11 12 Well-known property of northern MÉDOC. Delon family of LÉOVILLE-LAS-CASES; class shows. Firm, vigorous wines for long ageing. Second label: Chapelle de Potensac.

Pouget Marg r ★★ 00' 01 02 03 04 05' 06 07 08 09' 10' 11 12 Obscure Fourth Growth attached to BOYD-CANTENAC. Old vines. Solid rather than elegant.

Poujeaux Mou r ★★ 95' 96' 98 00' 01 03 04 05 06 08 09' 10' 11 12 Same owner as CLOS FOURTET. With CHASSE-SPLEEN the high point of MOU. DERENONCOURT consults. Full, robust wines that age. Second label: La Salle de Poujeaux.

Premier Grand Cru Classé St-Ém *See* ST-ÉM classification box (p.98).

de Pressac St-Ém r ★★ 05 06 08 09 10 11 12 Restored estate in St-Etienne-de-Lisse rewarded with classification in 2012. Quality now assured. Elegance and power combined.

Preuillac Méd r ★★ 05 06 08 09 10 11 12 Savoury, structured wine from AC MÉDOC. Owning Mau family have invested for quality. CH Brown in PE-LÉ same stable.

Prieuré-Lichine Marg r ★★★ 89' 90' 95 96 98' 99 00' 01 02 03 04 05 06 07 08 09' 10' 11 12 13 Fourth Growth owned by a négociant; put on the map by Alexis Lichine. V'yds v. dispersed. DERENONCOURT consults. Fragrant MARG currently on gd form. Open to the public. Second label: Confidences du Prieuré-Lichine. A gd white B'X too.

Puygueraud B'x r ★★ 00' 01' 02 03' 05' 06 08 09 10 11 12 Leading CH of this tiny FRANCS-CÔTES DE BORDEAUX AC. Oak-aged wines of surprising class. Value Les Charmes-Godard white, same owner. Special CUVÉE George with MALBEC (35%+) in blend. Same winemaker as PAVIE-MACQUIN and LARCIS-DUCASSE.

Quinault L'Enclos St-Ém r ★★→★★★ 09 10 11 12 GRAND CRU CLASSÉ (2012) located in Libourne. New owner CHEVAL BLANC in 2008 and change of style. Now more freshness and finesse. Organic cultivation.

Quintus St-Ém r ★★★ 11 12 Formerly the well-respected TERTRE DAUGAY. Now owned by the Dillons of HAUT-BRION, and great improvement on the way. Neighbouring L'ARROSÉE acquired and merged in 2013 making this a 28-ha estate. Price has soared. Second label: Le Dragon de Quintus.

Bordeaux plantings are 88% red, 12% white. Fifty years ago it was closer to 50/50.

Rabaud-Promis Saut w sw ★★→★★★ 96 97' 98 99 01' 02 03' 04 05' 06 07 09' 10 11 12 Family-owned First Growth at Bommes. Discreet but generally v.gd.

Rahoul Grav r w ★★ (r) 02 04 05 06 08 09' 10 11 12 V'yd at Portets; Supple, SÉM-dominated white (05 07 08 09 10 11 12 13). Considerable progress under DOURTHE management (since 2007).

Ramage-la-Batisse H-Méd r ★★ 03 04 05' 07 08 09 10 11 12 Reasonably consistent, widely distributed, northern H-MÉD. Owned by insurance company. Second label: L'Enclos de Ramage.

Rauzan-Gassies Marg r ★★★ 98 99 00 01' 02 03 04 05' 06 07 08 09' 10' 11 12 Second-Growth neighbour of RAUZAN-SÉGLA that has long lagged behind it; now catching up. New generation making strides. Greater consistency since 2008.

Rauzan-Ségla Marg r ★★★★ 88' 89' 90' 94' 95 96 98 99 00' 01 02 03 04' 05 06 07 08 09' 10' 11 12 13 MARG Second Growth long famous for its fragrance; owned by owners of Chanel (*see* CANON). 35 ha added since the Chanel purchase in 1994. On fine form. Second label: Ségla (value).

Raymond-Lafon Saut w sw ★★★ 88 89' 90' 95 96' 97 98 99' 01' 02 03' 04 05' 06 07' 09' 10' 11' saut estate acquired by former YQUEM manager (1972); now run by his children. Rich, complex wines that age. No 2012 made.

Rayne Vigneau Saut w sw ★★★ 89 90' 95 96 97 98 99 01' 02 03 05' 07 09' 10' 11' Large First Growth at Bommes. Same owner as GRAND-PUY-DUCASSE and MEYNEY. Investment and improvement. Second label: Madame de Rayne.

Respide Médeville Grav r w ★★ (r) 04 05' 06 08 09 10 11 12 (w) 04' 05' 07 08 09 10 11 12 One of the better GRAV properties for both red and white. CH GILETTE, CHAMPAGNE Gonet-Medeville same stable. Drink reds at 4–6 yrs.

Reynon B'x r w ★★ Leading CADILLAC-CÔTES DE BORDEAUX estate. Serious red (05' 06 07 09' 10 11 12). Fragrant B'X white from SAUV BL 09 10' 11' 12 (13). *See also* CLOS FLORIDÈNE. Owned by Dubourdieu family.

Reysson H-Méd r ★★ 04 05 06 08 09' 10' 11 12 Renovated estate; mainly MERLOT; managed by négociant CVBG-DOURTHE (*see* BELGRAVE, LA GARDE). Rich, modern style.

Ricaud, de B'x (r) w (dr) sw ★★ 01' 02 03' 05 07 09 10 11 Substantial LOUPIAC estate; producer of SAUT-like, age-worthy wine just across the river. Red B'x too.

Rieussec Saut w sw ★★★★ 83' 85 86' 88' 89' 90' 95 96' 97' 98 99 01' 02 03' 04 05' 06 07 09' 10' 11' Worthy neighbour of YQUEM with v'yd in Fargues, owned by the (LAFITE) Rothschilds. Fabulously powerful, opulent wine. As in 1993 no Rieussec produced in 2012, only Carmes de Rieussec, the second label. Dry wine is "R", now made in modern style – with less character.

Rivière, de la B'x r ★★ 00' 01 02 03 04 05' 06 08 09' 10 12 Largest (60 ha) and most impressive FRONSAC property, with a Wagnerian castle and cellars. Formerly big, tannic wines; now more refined. Special CUVÉE, Aria, made from the best parcels; sometimes 100% MERLOT. Tragic accident 2014 killed both old and new owners.

Roc de Cambes B'x r ★★★ 04 05 06 07 08 09 10 11 12 Undisputed leader in CÔTES DE BOURG; wines as gd as top ST-ÉM. Depth, intensity, opulence. But pricey. Sister of TERTRE-RÔTEBOEUF.

Rochemorin, de Pe-Lé r w ★★ →★★★ (r) 01 02 04 05 06 08 09' 10' 11 12 (13) An important restoration at Martillac by André Lurton of LA LOUVIÈRE: vast estate (three-quarters red). SAUV BL-dominated white. Modern winery. Fairly consistent quality and widely distributed. (w) 05 06 07 08 09 10 11 12 (13)

Rol Valentin St-Ém r ★★★ 00' 01' 02 03 04 05' 06 07 08 09' 10' 11 12 13 Launched in 1994; now new owner (2010) and bigger v'yd. Wines rich, modern but balanced. DERENONCOURT consults.

Rouget Pom r ★★ 96 98' 99 00' 01' 03 04 05' 06 07 08 09' 10' 11 12 13 Much-improved estate on the north edge of POM. Same owner as DOM JACQUES PRIEUR in Burgundy. Now excellent; rich, unctuous wines. Gd value.

St-André-Corbin St-Ém r ★★ 00' 01 03 04 05 08 09 10 12 Family-owned ST-GEORGES-ST-ÉM v'yd. Supple, MERLOT-dominated wine. Value.

St-Georges St-Ém r ★★ 00' 01 03 04 05' 06 08 09 10 11 Family-owned property overlooking ST-ÉM from the north. Gallo-Roman origins. V'yd represents 25% of ST-GEORGES AC, unchanged since 1891. Gd wine sold direct to the public. Second label: Puy St-Georges.

St-Pierre St-Jul r ★★★ 89 90' 95' 96' 98 99 00' 01' 02 03 04 05' 06 07 08 09' 10' 11 12 13 Once-understated Fourth Growth owned by the president of B'x football club. Stylish, consistent, classic ST-JUL. Only 17 ha. *See* GLORIA.

Sales, de Pom r ★★ 00' 01' 04 05 06 08 09 10 12 Biggest v'yd of POM on sandy/gravel soils, attached to 16th-century CH. Lightish wine; never quite poetry. Try top vintages. Second label: Ch Chantalouette.

Sansonnet St-Ém r ★★ 00' 01 02 03 04 05' 06 08 09' 10' 11 12 13 Promoted to GRAND CRU CLASSÉ in 2012. Plateau estate adjacent to TROTTEVIEILLE. Ambitiously run in modern style (rich, dark, concentrated).

Want fizz? Bordeaux makes 1.7 million bottles of Crémant de Bordeaux each year.

Saransot-Dupré List r (w) ★★ 00' 01 02 03 04 05 06 09' 10' 11 12 Small property with firm, fleshy wines. Lots of MERLOT but PETIT VERDOT significant. Also one of LIST's little band of whites (60% SÉM).

Sénéjac H-Méd r (w) ★★ 00 01 02 03 04 05' 06 08 09' 10' 11 12 Situated in southern H-MÉD (Pian). Consistent, well-balanced wines. Bio run v'yd by PONTET-CANET team (since 2009).

Serre, la St-Ém r ★★ 98' 00' 01 02 03 04 05 06 08 09' 10 11 12 Small GRAND CRU CLASSÉ on the limestone plateau. Fresh, stylish wines with plenty of fruit.

Sigalas-Rabaud Saut w sw ★★★ 88 89' 90' 95' 96' 97' 98 99 01' 02 03 04 05' 07' 09' 10' 11 12 First Growth; the smaller part of the former Rabaud estate in Bommes. Eric Boissenot consults. V. fragrant and lovely. Top-ranking now. Second label: Le Lieutenant de Sigalas.

Siran Marg r ★★→★★★ 96 98 00' 01 02 03 04 05 06 07 08 09' 10' 11 12 Owned by the Miailhe family since 1859; Edouard runs the show today. Neighbour of DAUZAC. The wines age well and have masses of flavour. Second label: S de Siran.

Smith-Haut-Lafitte Pe-Lé r (p) (w) ★★★ (r) 95 96 98 99 00' 01 02 03 04' 05' 06 07 08 09' 10' 11 12 13 (w) 01 02 03 04 05 06 07' 08' 09 10' 11 12 13 Celebrated classed growth with spa hotel, regularly one of the stars of PE-LÉ. White is full, ripe, sappy; red oaky/generous but fine. New carbon-neutral cellar for second label (2013): Les Hauts de Smith. Also CAB SAUV-based Le Petit Haut Lafitte from 2007. Neighbouring Le Thil Comte Clary same stable since 2012.

Sociando-Mallet H-Méd r ★★★ 89' 90' 94 95 96' 98' 99 00' 01' 02 03 04 05' 06 07 09' 10' 11 12 Splendid, widely followed estate just north of ST-EST. Built from scratch by independently minded owner (1969); now 85 ha. Conservative, big-boned wines to lay down for yrs. Second label: Demoiselle de Sociando. Also special CUVÉE Jean Gautreau.

Sours, de B'x r p w ★★ Valid reputation for B'x rosé (DYA). 300,000 bottles annually. Gd white plus improving B'x red. CLOS Cantenac in ST-ÉM same owner.

Premature oxidation and how to avoid it

Growers who pick later for riper grapes, increase their percentage of new oak barrels and use lower doses of sulphur dioxide run the risk of premature oxidation in their red wines. At least that is what researchers at B'x University's Faculty of Oenology are investigating. It could be that these practices, coupled with ripe, low-acid years like 2003 and 2009, encourage the development of oxidized, stewed-fruit aromas and a rapid evolution in colour. Even with the best of intentions it seems producers can sometimes go too far.

Soutard St-Ém r ★★★ 95 96 98' 99 00' 01 03 04 05 06 07 08 09 10 11 12 *Potentially excellent* classed growth on the limestone plateau. Owned by same insurance group as LARMANDE. Cadet-Piola integrated in 2012. Massive investment; new cellars, visitor centre 2010. Finer style since 2007. Second label: Jardins de Soutard.

Suduiraut Saut w sw ★★★★ 86 88' 89' 90' 95 96 97' 98 99' 01' 02 03' 04 05' 06 07' 09' 10' 11' 13 One of the best classed-growth SAUT. Owner AXA Insurance has achieved greater consistency and luscious quality. *See* PICHON-LONGUEVILLE. Dry wine "S" v. promising. New fresher, fruitier Sauternes Les Lions de Suduiraut from 2009. No CH Suduiraut produced in 2012.

Tailhas, du Pom r ★★ 98' 00 01 04 05' 08 09' 10 12 Modest property in same family hands since 1932. Sandy-gravel soils. Agreeable, earlier drinking.

Taillefer Pom r ★★ 98' 00' 01' 02 03 04 05' 06 08 09' 10 11 12 V'yd on the edge of POM. Denis Dubourdieu consults. Less power than top estates but suave and refined. Gd value.

Talbot St-Jul r (w) ★★★ 90 94 95 96' 98' 99 00' 01 02 03 04 05' 08' 09' 10' 11 12 Substantial Fourth Growth in the heart of AC ST-JUL. Wine rich, *consummately charming, reliable* (though wobbly in 2006–7). DERENONCOURT consults (from 2008). Second label: Connétable de Talbot. Excellent white to age 5–6 yrs: Caillou Blanc. SÉNÉJAC in same family ownership. New barrel cellar 2012.

Tertre, du Marg r ★★★ 96' 98' 99 00' 01 03 04' 05' 06 08 09' 10' 11 12 Fifth Growth isolated south of MARG. History of undervalued fragrant (20% CAB FR) and fruity wines. Since 1997, same owner as CH GISCOURS. Former LATOUR winemaker. New techniques; massive investment. Now a concentrated, structured wine. On top form in new millennium.

Tertre Daugay St-Ém r ★★★ 96 98 99 00' 01 04 05 06 07 09' 10 Former name for what has now been baptized CH QUINTUS (2011). Classified (GRAND CRU CLASS) until 2012. Wobbly in the 1990s but improvement from 2000.

Tertre-Rôteboeuf St-Ém r ★★★★ 89' 90' 93 94 95 96 97 98' 99 00' 01 02 03' 04 05' 06' 07 08 09' 10' 11 12 13 Tiny cult star making concentrated, dramatic, largely MERLOT wine since 1979. Frightening prices. Also CÔTES DE BOURG property, ROC DE CAMBES of ST-ÉM classed-growth quality.

Thieuley B'x r p w ★★ E-2-M supplier of consistent quality AC B'x (r w); fruity CLAIRET; oak-aged CUVÉE Francis Courselle (r w). Also owns CLOS Ste-Anne in CADILLAC-CÔTES DE BORDEAUX.

Tour-Blanche, la Saut (r) w sw ★★★ 86 88' 89' 90' 95 96 97' 98 99 01' 02 03' 04 05' 06 07 09' 10' 11' 12 First Growth SAUT. Also a winemaking school. Rich, powerful wines. One of the rare successes in the difficult 2012 vintage. Second label: Les Charmilles de Tour-Blanche.

Tour-Carnet, La H-Méd r ★★ 98 99 00' 01 02 03 04 05' 06 08 09' 10' 11 12 Fourth Growth with medieval moated fortress, owned by Bernard Magrez (*see* FOMBRAUGE, PAPE-CLÉMENT). Rich, dark, concentrated wines in modern style. Second label: Les Douves de CH La Tour Carnet. Also special CUVÉE Servitude Volontaire du Tour Carnet.

Tour-de-By, La Méd r ★★ 00 01 02 03 04 05' 06 08 09 10 11 12 Large (109 ha) family-run estate in n MÉDOC. 500,000 bottles yearly of sturdy, reliable wines with a fruity note. Also rosé and special CUVÉE Héritage Marc Pagès.

Tour de Mons, la Marg r ★★ 98' 00 01 02 04 05' 06 08 09' 10 12 MARG CRU BOURGEOIS (2011). A long dull patch, then investment and improvement in the new millennium. 2009, 2010 v.gd.

Tour-du-Haut-Moulin H-Méd r ★★ 98 00' 02 03 04 05' 06 08 09 10 11 CRU BOURGEOIS (2011) estate in Cussac; intense, consistent wines to mature.

Tour-du-Pas-St-Georges St-Ém r ★★ 00' 01 03 04 05' 06 08 09' 10 11 12 ST-GEORGES-ST-ÉM estate owned by Pascal Delbeck (ex-BELAIR-MONANGE). Consistent quality.

Tour du Pin, La St-Ém r ★★ 98 00' 01 04 05 06 08 09' 10' 11 Formerly La Tour du Pin Figeac-Moueix but bought and renamed by CHEVAL BLANC in 2006. Same winemaking team. Previously classified but classification not requested in 2012. Steady improvement from 2007 but limited volume now.

Tour Figeac, La St-Ém r ★★ 98' 00' 01' 02 04 05' 06 07 08 09' 10' 11 12 GRAND CRU CLASSÉ between FIGEAC and POM. Bio methods (DERENONCOURT and his wife consult). Full, fleshy, harmonious.

Tour Haut-Brion, La Pe-Lé r ★★★ 95 96' 98' 99 00' 01 02 03 04' 05' RIP from 2005 for this classed growth. Now *see* LA MISSION-HAUT-BRION.

Tour Haut-Caussan Méd r ★★ 02 03 04 05' 06 08 09' 10' 11 12 Consistent CRU BOURGEOIS (2011) at Blaignan. Value. Interests in CORBIÈRES too.

Tournefeuille B'x r ★★ 00' 01' 02 03 04 05' 06 07 08 09 10' 11 12 Reliable L DE P property. 30% CAB FR adds spice. CHX Lécouyer (POM), La Révérance (ST-ÉM) same stable.

Tour-St-Bonnet Méd r ★★ 02 03 04 05 06 08 09' 10 11 12 CRU BOURGEOIS (2011) in the northern MÉD at St-Christoly. Reliable. Value.

Tronquoy-Lalande St-Est r ★★ 00' 02 03 04 05 06 07 08 09' 10' 11 12 Same owners as MONTROSE from 2006; progress since. Lots of MERLOT and PETIT VERDOT. Second label: Tronquoy de Ste-Anne.

Troplong-Mondot St-Ém r ★★★ 89' 90' 94' 95 96' 98' 99 00' 01' 02 03 04 05'

Why Bordeaux?
People ask whether B'X still justifies its own separate section of this international guide. The answer: it remains the motor of the fine-wine world, by far its biggest producer, stimulating debate, investment and collectors worldwide. Besides, there are few better drinks.

> **Where to stay? Where to eat?**
> Tourism is booming in B'X, and with it, new projects. Why not try
> the Philippe Starck-decorated Mama Shelter hotel (2013); 270-seater
> brasserie Le Grand Comptoir at the St-Jean railway station (2013);
> Coup 2 Foudres accommodation in two Seguin Moreau-built *foudres*
> (2013); Bernard Magrez boutique hotel and restaurant in partnership
> with multi-Michelin starred chef Joël Robuchon (2014) and the €63m
> wine cultural centre, the *Cité des Civilisations du Vin*, which opens its
> doors in 2016.

06 07 08 09' 10 11 12 First Growth on a high point of the limestone plateau nr a water tower. *Wines of power and depth* with increasing elegance. On-site restaurant (Les Belles Perdrix). Second label: Mondot.

Trotanoy Pom r ★★★★ 89' 90' 93 94 95 96 98' 00' 01 02 03 04' 05' 06 07 08 09' 10' 11 12 13 Part of the J-P MOUEIX stable since 1953. Top site on the plateau with clay and gravel soils. On flying form since 89. Second label: L'Espérance de Trotanoy (from 2009; not every yr).

Trottevieille St-Ém r ★★★ 89' 90 94 95 96 98 99 00' 01 03' 04 05' 06 07 08 09' 10' 11 12 First Growth on the limestone plateau. BORIE-MANOUX connection. Much improved in new millennium. Limited bottling of old, ungrafted CAB FR. Former GRAND CRU CLASSÉ CH Bergat integrated in 2012. Second label: La Vieille Dame de Trottevieille.

Valandraud St-Ém r ★★★★ 93 94 95' 96 98 99 00' 01' 02 03 04 05' 06 07 08 09' 10' 11 12 13 The wine that launched the GARAGE movement. Now a PREMIER GRAND CRU CLASSÉ. Officially 8 ha located at St-Etienne-de-Lisse. Originally super-concentrated; since 1998 greater complexity. Virginie de Valandraud another selection. White Blanc de Valandraud from 2003.

Verdignan H-Méd r ★★ 00' 01 02 03 04 05 06 08 09 10 11 12 Substantial northern H-MÉD. Sister to COUFRAN and SOUDARS. More CAB SAUV than Coufran. Value and ageing potential.

Vieille Cure, La B'x r ★★ 00' 01' 02 03 04 05' 06 08 09' 10' 11 12 13 Leading FRONSAC estate; US-owned. VALANDRAUD owner consults since 2013. Value.

Vieux-Château-Certan Pom r ★★★★ 83' 85 86' 88' 89 90' 94 95' 96' 98' 99 00' 01 02 04' 05' 06 07 08 09' 10' 11' 12 13 Traditionally rated close to PETRUS in quality, but totally different in style (30% CAB FR and 10% CAB SAUV); elegance, harmony, even beauty. Old vines (average 40–50 yrs). 2010 utterly superb.

Vieux Château St-André St-Ém r ★★ 03 04 05 06 08 09' 10 11 12 Small v'yd in MONTAGNE-ST-ÉM owned by former PETRUS winemaker. Regular quality. Value.

Villegeorge, de H-Méd r ★★ 98' 00' 02 03 04 05 06 08 09' 10 12 Southern H-MÉD owned by Marie-Laure Lurton. Classic MÉD style. CHX Duplessis in MOU and La Tour de Bessan in MARG same stable.

Vray Croix de Gay Pom r ★★ 95 96 98' 00' 04 05' 06 08 09' 10' 11 12 Tiny v'yd in the best part of POM. Greater consistency since 2005. Sister CHX Siaurac in L DE P and Le Prieuré in ST-ÉM, and all now in same stable as LATOUR.

Yon-Figeac St-Ém r ★★ 00' 02 03 04 05 06 09 10' 11 12 MERLOT-based GRAND CRU CLASSÉ at foot of slope; lighter, supple style. Dubourdieu consults. Better since 2005.

Yquem Saut w sw (dr) ★★★★ 79 80' 81' 83' 85 86' 88' 89' 90' 93 94 95' 96' 97' 98 99' 00 01' 02 03' 04 05' 06' 07' 08 09' 10' 11' The king of sweet wines. Strong, intense, luscious; kept 3 yrs in barrel. Most vintages improve for 15 yrs+, some live 100 yrs+ in transcendent splendour. Subtle changes since 2000 under LVMH ownership: more freshness, less time in barrel. As in 52, 72, 92 no Yquem made in 2012. From 2011 mention of SAUT relegated to back label. Also makes dry "Y" (pronounced *ygrec*).

Italy

VALLE
D'AOSTA

L Como

L Maggiore

Milan

Turin ○
PIEDMONT

LOMBARDY

Genoa ○

Po

LIGURIA

Ligurian Sea

More heavily shaded areas are
the wine-growing regions.

Abbreviations used in the text:

Ab	Abruzzo	Mol	Molise
Bas	Basilicata	Pie	Piedmont
Cal	Calabria	Pug	Puglia
Cam	Campania	Sar	Sardinia
E-R	Emilia-Romagna	Si	Sicily
F-VG	Friuli-Venezia Giulia	T-AA	Trentino-Alto Adige
Lat	Latium	Tus	Tuscany
Lig	Liguria	Umb	Umbria
Lom	Lombardy	VdA	Valle d'Aosta
Mar	Marches	Ven	Veneto

Eurocrats love to tinker with the rules governing the sale of wine.
Tinker is what they do. Italy is a prime target. Much more important
is Italy's soaring ambition, and achievement. And versatility. You need
never get bored. As for the tinkering, here goes:

The biggest change currently happening is in the ever-accelerating
switch from Italy's DOC (*Denominazione di Origine Controllata*) and IGT
(*Indicazione Geografica Tipica*) to the EU's DOP and IGP (P = *protetta* =
protected). There is some sense to this in that the EU bloc is better
placed than any individual state to "protect" a denomination from
non-European imitation – a good recent example being Prosecco. But
it can be confusing for label decipherers. And the individual
governments are better able to "control" a wine's production. The
change from "controlled" to "protected" will in any case be completed
sooner rather than later – by *force majeure*.

There is another significant, if regional, denomination change
affecting Italian wines. From the 2012 vintage IGT Sicilia disappears

and DOC Sicilia is born, the old IGT Sicilia being replaced by IGP Terre Siciliane (quite a mouthful). Not the least important of considerations is that IGT is allowed approximately double the production per hectare and may, unlike DOC, be bottled outside the zone of production.

In Tuscany another major change is mooted: the removal of the name "Chianti" from any wine other than Chianti Classico. This may take years to effect and the battle will be fierce. But all it would really do, while protecting an Italian classic from erosion by association, is return the situation to what it was less than a century ago.

Recent vintages

Amarone, Veneto & Friuli

2013 Good weather in September for whites. Reds, especially passito wines, suffered from sporadic rain and hail in October/November.

2012 Prolonged heat and drought hit quantity and quality. Amarone should be good.

2011 "Best year ever" for Amarone. Whites balanced and concentrated. Some reds very tannic, with high alcohol.

2010 Cool year, good for lighter wines. Start drinking soon.

2009 Ideal drying conditions for passito: classic wines. Good for Prosecco, Pinot Gr etc. Drink Amarone from 2015.

2008 Classic wines of high quality. Drink from 2016.

2007 Some excellent wines; selection needed.

2006 Outstanding; more Amarone made than ever before. Drink from 2012.

Campania & Basilicata

2013 As elsewhere, whites balanced and perfumed, reds less so, especially late-picked Aglianico, hit by late rains.

2012 September rains saved the whites. Indian summer produced outstanding Aglianicos.

2011 Wines concentrated and rich; high alcohol and tannin in reds. Whites better balanced.

2010 Whites lightish with good aromas; reds good to average.

2009 Ripe, healthy, aromatic whites; reds with substance and concentration. Drink Aglianico/Taurasi from 2014.

2008 Classic year for Aglianico; good too for whites. Drink from 2013.

2007 Good to excellent quality. Drink from 2013.

2006 Rain and rot in lower-lying zones, sun in higher vineyards. Selection needed.

Marches & Abruzzo

2013 A difficult year: hailstorms and rot. Fine September saved whites; reds not as compromised as feared.

2012 Warm days and cool nights at vintage time. Later-picked varieties best.

2011 Some overconcentrated, alcoholic and tannic reds. Best should age well.

2010 A difficult year but some good results. Drinking now.

2009 Good to very good quality, especially whites. Montepulciano d'Abruzzo/ Conero to drink now.

2008 Some excellent wines. Drink from now for 5 years.

2007 Some top-quality reds. Drinking now.

Piedmont

2013 Cool, wet spring delayed picking well into October, which was mixed. Bright, crisp whites and reds good but not great.

2012 Quality good to very good, volume very low.

2011 High alcohol; danger of overconcentration. Good average quality.

2010 Quality patchy, but patient growers made very good wines. Choose with care.

2009 Good to very good, especially Nebbiolo. Drink Barolo/Barbaresco from 2014 for 10 years+.

2008 Some great Barberas; Nebbiolos good, balanced, not spectacular. Drink for 10 years.

2007 Good to excellent Barolo, Barbaresco, Barbera. Some classic wines. Drink now–10 years+.

2006 Excellent Nebbiolo and Barbera. Laying-down vintage of the decade. Drink from 2014 for 20 years.

Older fine vintages: 04 01 00 99 98 97 96 95 90 89 88. Vintages to keep: 01 99 96. Vintages to drink up: 03 00 97 90 88.

Tuscany

2013 Cool spring weather caused uneven ripening. A warm September helped with the catch-up, but patchy October rainfall destabilized things. Not a great year, but some peaks.

2012 Drought and protracted heat, but classic wines saved by early September rains and could turn out very well.

2011 Some charmingly fruity if somewhat alcoholic classic reds. Whites a bit unbalanced.

2010 Patchy. Brunello very successful.

2009 Quality very good at least. Drink Chianti/Brunello from 2014–16.

2008 Mixed results with points of excellence; not necessarily for long keeping. Drink from now for 5 years.

2007 High-quality crop. Drink from 2013–15 for 10 years.

2006 Probably greatest of last 20 vintages. Drink from now for 20 years.

Older fine vintages: 04 01 99 97 95 90. Vintages to keep: 01 99. Vintages to drink up: 03 00 97 95 90.

What do the initials mean?

Denominazione di Origine Controllata (DOC)
Controlled Denomination of Origin, cf. AC in France.
Denominazione di Origine Controllata e Garantita (DOCG)
"G" = "Guaranteed". Italy's highest quality designation.
Indicazione Geografica Tipica (IGT)
Geographic Indication of Type. Broader and more vague than DOC, cf. Vin de Pays in France.
Denominazione di Origine Protetta / IndicazioneGeografica Protetta (DOP / IGP)
"P" = "Protected". *See* Italy's introduction.

Aglianico del Vulture Bas DOC(G) r dr ★→★★★ 06 07 08 10 11 (12) DOC with min 1 yr ageing, DOCG SUPERIORE after 2 yrs, DOCG Superiore RISERVA after 5 yrs. Regulatory confusion surrounds this potentially noble red from the ancient AGLIANICO grape on volcanic Monte Vulture. Best: Alovini, Basilisco, Bisceglia, Cantine del Notaio, Donato d'Angelo, Elena Fucci, Macarico, Madonna delle Grazie, PATERNOSTER, Terre degli Svevi.

Alba Pie Major wine city of PIE, southeast of Turin in LANGHE hills; truffles, hazelnuts and Pie's, if not Italy's, most prestigious wines: BAROLO, BARBARESCO, NEBBIOLO D'ALBA, Langhe, ROERO, BARBERA d'Alba, DOGLIANI (DOLCETTO).

Albana di Romagna E-R DOCG w dr sw s/sw (sp) ★→★★★ DYA. Historically Italy's first white DOCG, justifiably only for sweet PASSITO, dry versions being unremarkable. Bertinoro is commune with best producers: Raffaella Alessandra Bissoni, Celli, Madonia Giovanna, *Fattoria Paradiso*. ZERBINA's Scacco Matto is perhaps best sweet version.

Alberello Bush-trained or head-trained vines, the traditional method of pruning in the south, now increasingly in the centre, notably Tuscany. Most of the best and oldest v'yds of trendy ETNA, for example, are trained to *alberello*.

Allegrini Ven ★★★ World-famous for VALPOLICELLA; outstanding single-v'yd wines (La Grola, Palazzo della Torre, La Poja), AMARONE, RECIOTO. Also owner of POGGIO al Tesoro in BOLGHERI and Poggio San Polo in MONTALCINO, TUS.

Alto Adige T-AA DOC r p w dr sw sp ★★→★★★★ Largely German-speaking province of Bolzano, alias SÜDTIROL. Phenomenal success with mtn-fresh whites; less so with reds, except for the odd outstanding PINOT N or native *Lagrein*. Excellent co-ops; many quality private companies.

Ama, Castello di Tus ★★★ Top CHIANTI CLASSICO estate of Gaiole. RISERVAS worth seeking, also TUS-Bordeaux blend Haiku. MERLOT l'Apparita is v.gd but perhaps not worth the high price.

Amarone della Valpolicella Ven DOCG r ★★→★★★★ 03′ 04 06′ 07 08 09 10 (11′) (12) Intense strong red from air-dried VALPOLICELLA grapes: one of Italy's true classics, now finally recognized as DOCG, with appendage "CLASSICO" if from historic zone. Relatively dry version of the ancient RECIOTO DELLA VALPOLICELLA. (For producers, *see* box, p.151.) Older vintages are rare; beyond 20 yrs they tend to dry out.

Angelini, Tenimenti Tus ★★→★★★ Wealthy proprietor of three estates/wineries in strategic positions in TUS: San Leonino in CHIANTI CLASSICO; Trerose at MONTEPULCIANO; Val di Cava in MONTALCINO – total over 170 ha. Vigna Spuntali BRUNELLO di MONTALCINO is most prestigious wine, but special effort to upgrade Montepulciano in general and Trerose in particular. Also owns Puiatti in F-VG.

Antinori, Marchesi L & P Tus ★★→★★★★ V. influential Florentine house of the Antinori family, led by Piero, one of Italy's wine's heroes, and his three daughters. Famous for CHIANTI CLASSICO (Tenute Marchese Antinori and *Badia a Passignano*), Umb (*Castello della Sala*), PIE (PRUNOTTO) wines. Revolutionary TIGNANELLO and SOLAIA are among the few successful SUPER TUSCANS remaining. Also estates in TUS MAREMMA (Fattoria Aldobrandesca), MONTEPULCIANO (La Braccesca), MONTALCINO (Pian delle Vigne), BOLGHERI (Guado al Tasso), FRANCIACORTA (*Montenisa*), PUG (Tormaresca).

Argiano, Castello di Tus Aka **Sesti**. Astronomer Giuseppe Maria Sesti makes classy bio BRUNELLO and Brunello RISERVA Phenomena. Not to be confused with neighbour called simply Argiano.

Ten top Barberas
Most of the best BARBERAS are from the PIE DOCS of Barbera d'ASTI and Barbera d'ALBA, but there are occasional examples of excellence from elsewhere.
Barbera d'Alba: BOGLIETTI (Vigna dei Romani); CLERICO (Trevigne); PRUNOTTO (Pian Romualdo); Gianni Voerzio (Ciabot della Luna); ROBERTO VOERZIO (Pozzo dell'Annunziata).
Barbera d'Asti: BRAIDA (Bricco dell'Uccellone); COPPO (Pomorosso); Perrone (Mongovone); CS Vinchio Vaglio (Vigne Vecchie).
Langhe: Altare (Larigi).

Argiolas, Antonio Sar ★★→★★★ Top SAR producer using native grapes and making outstanding crus Turriga (★★★), Antonio Argiolas, Iselis Rosso, Iselis Bianco. Well-crafted standards.

Asti Pie DOCG sw sp ★→★★★ NV PIE sparkler from MOSCATO Bianco grapes; known in past as Asti SPUMANTE. Low prices trump high quality; DOCG status questionable. *See* MOSCATO D'ASTI, BARBERA. Rare top producers: BERA, Cascina Fonda, Caudrina, Vignaioli di Santo Stefano.

Azienda agricola / agraria An estate (large or small) making wine from own grapes.

Azienda Monaci Pug r p ★★→★★★ Estate owned by family of Severino Garofano, leading oenologist in SALENTO. Characterful NEGROAMARO red (Eloquenzia, I Censi, late-picked Le Braci) and ROSATO (Girofle), also Uva di Troia (Sine Pari) and AGLIANICO (Sine Die).

Badia a Coltibuono Tus ★★→★★★ Historic CHIANTI CLASSICO estate making comeback after yrs in doldrums. Top wine: 100% SANGIOVESE barrique-aged SUPER TUSCAN Sangioveto.

Banfi (Castello or Villa) Tus ★→★★★ MONTALCINO CANTINA of major US importer of Italian wine. Huge plantings on lower-lying southern slopes of Montalcino, incl in-house-developed clones of SANGIOVESE; also CAB SAUV, MERLOT, SYRAH, PINOT N, CHARD, SAUV BL, PINOT GR. SUPER TUSCAN blends like Cum Laude and *Summus* tend to work better than somewhat overextracted BRUNELLOS.

ITALY

Ten top Barbarescos

Here are ten outstanding examples of BARBARESCO, worth hunting down:
Cantina del Pino (Ovello); Castello di Neive (RISERVA Santo Stefano); Castello di Verduno (Rabajà); GAJA (Barbaresco); BRUNO GIACOSA (Asili RISERVA); Marchesi di Gresy (Camp Gros); Paitin (Vecchie Vigne); PRODUTTORI DEL BARBARESCO (Ovello); Albino Rocca (Brich Ronchi); BRUNO ROCCA (Rabajà).

Barbaresco Pie DOCG r ★★→★★★★ 01 04 06' 07 08 09 10 11 (12) Like its twin, BAROLO, 100% NEBBIOLO. Similar complex aromas and flavour; less power, more elegance. Minimum 2 yrs ageing, 1 yr in wood; at 4 yrs becomes RISERVA. (*See* box, above for best producers.)

Bardolino Ven DOC(G) r p ★→★★ DYA Light summery red from Italy's largest lake, GARDA. Bardolino SUPERIORE DOCG has much lower yield than Bardolino DOC. The pale-pink CHIARETTO is one of Italy's best rosés. Gd producers: Cavalchina, Costadoro, *Guerrieri Rizzardi*, Le Fraghe, ZENATO, Zeni.

Barolo Pie DOCG r ★★★→★★★★ 96' 99' 01' 04' 06' 07' 08 09' (10) (11) (12) Italy's greatest red, 100% NEBBIOLO, from village of the same name south of ALBA or any of 10 others (or parts thereof). The best combine power and elegance, plentiful, sometimes rasping tannins and alluring floral scent with an almost sweet, porty finish. Must be 3 yrs old before release (5 for RISERVA, of which 2 in wood. (For top producers *see* box, p.128.) Divided between traditionalists (long maceration, large oak barrels) and modernists (shorter maceration, often barriques).

Beato Bartolomeo da Breganze Ven ★★ Well-run co-op in hills of Ven with one of the largest plantings of genuine PINOT GRIGIO. Also still, sparkling, sweet (TORCOLATO) wines from native Vespaiolo grape.

Bellavista Lom ★★★ FRANCIACORTA estate with convincing Champagne-style wines (Gran Cuvée Franciacorta is top). Also Extra Brut Vittorio Moretti and Satèn (*Crémant*-style sparkling).

Bera, Walter Pie ★★→★★★ Small estate for top-quality MOSCATO (Moscato d'Asti, ASTI), also fine reds (BARBERA d'Asti, BARBARESCO, LANGHE NEBBIOLO).

Berlucchi, Guido Lom ★★ Italy's largest producer of sparkling METODO CLASSICO with five million+ bottle production. Main wine flies under the Cuvée Imperiale flag, but increasing attention is being paid to FRANCIACORTA DOCG.

Bertani Ven ★★→★★★ Long-est producer of VALPOLICELLA and SOAVE wines, with v'yds in various parts of Verona province. Now upgrading by reverting to abandoned styles of winemaking, eg. white modelled on traditional skin-maceration techniques. Iconic house-wine Valpolicella Valpantena Secco Bertani also revitalized.

Bianco di Custoza or Custoza Ven DOC w (sp) ★→★★ DYA Fresh uncomplicated white from Lake GARDA, made from GARGANEGA, Cortese. Gd: Cavalchina, Le Tende, Le Vigne di San Pietro, Montresor, Zeni.

Biferno Mol DOC r p w ★→★★ (r) 08 10 11 12 Gd to interesting wines from easily forgotten region of Molise, sandwiched between Ab and PUG. Red based on MONTEPULCIANO, white on TREBBIANO. DI MAJO NORANTE (Ramitello), Borgo di Colloredo (Gironia) worthwhile.

Ten top Barolos

"Italy's greatest wine" is too tough for some. Here are a few top crus with which to test both parts of that statement.

BURLOTTO (Monvigliero); Cavallotto (Bricco Boschis Vigna San Giuseppe); CONTERNO FANTINO SORÌ Ginestra); GIACOMO CONTERNO (Monfortino); Giuseppe MASCARELLO (Monprivato); GIUSEPPE RINALDI (Brunate-Le Coste); SANDRONE (Cannubi Boschis); PAOLO SCAVINO (Bric dël Fiasc); VIETTI (Lazzarito); ROBERTO VOERZIO (La Serra).

Biondi-Santi Tus ★★★★ Recently deceased Franco Biondi-Santi maintained the classic traditions of this famous MONTALCINO estate to the end, making BRUNELLOS and esp RISERVAS so uncompromising that, from top vintages, they couldn't be drunk for decades. His son, Jacopo, is tipped to bring more user-friendliness into the wines, possibly at the expense of elegance.

Boca Pie *See* GATTINARA.

Boglietti, Enzo Pie ★★★ Dynamic young producer at La Morra in BAROLO. Top modern-style Barolos (VIGNA Arione, Case Nere); outstanding BARBERA D'ALBA (Vigna dei Romani, Roscaleto).

Bolgheri Tus DOC r p w (sw) ★★→★★★★ Arty walled village on TUS's Tyrrhenian coast giving its name to a stylish and expensive group of SUPER TUSCANS mainly based on French varieties. Big names: SASSICAIA (original inspirer of the cult), ANTINORI (at Guado al Tasso), FRESCOBALDI (at ORNELLAIA), GAJA (at CÀ MARCANDA), ALLEGRINI (at POGGIO al Tesoro), FOLONARI (at Campo al Mare), plus the odd local in LE MACCHIOLE and MICHELE SATTA. Many of the best producers are following Sassicaia's lead and dumping IGT status for BOLGHERI DOC.

Bolla Ven ★★ Historic Verona firm for SOAVE, VALPOLICELLA, AMARONE, RECIOTO DELLA VALPOLICELLA, RECIOTO DI SOAVE. Today owned by powerful GRUPPO ITALIANO VINI.

Borgo del Tiglio F-VG ★★★→★★★★ Nicola Manferrari is one of Italy's top white winemakers. COLLIO FRIULANO RONCO della Chiesa and Studio di Bianco are esp impressive.

Boscarelli, Poderi Tus ★★★ Small estate with v.gd VINO NOBILE DI MONTEPULCIANO Nocio dei Boscarelli and RISERVA.

Botte Large barrel, anything from 6–250 hl, usually between 20–50, traditionally of Slavonian but increasingly of French oak. To traditionalists, the ideal vessel for ageing wines in which an excess of oak aromas is undesirable.

Brachetto d'Acqui / Acqui Pie DOCG r sw (sp) ★★ DYA. Sweet sparkling red with enticing MUSCAT scent. Elevated DOCG status disputed by some.

Braida Pie ★★★ The late Giacomo Bologna's estate, now well run by his children Giuseppe and Raffaella. Top BARBERA D'ASTI (Bricco dell'Uccellone, Bricco della Bigotta, Ai Suma).

Bramaterra Pie *See* GATTINARA.

Breganze Ven DOC r w sp ★→★★★ (w) DYA (r) 06 07 08 09 10 11 13 Major production area for PINOT GR, also gd Vespaiolo (white, still and sparkling, and sticky TORCOLATO); PINOT N, CAB. Main producers MACULAN, BEATO BARTOLOMEO.

Brindisi Pug DOC r p ★★ (r) 06 07 08 09 10 11 (12) (13) (p) DYA. Smooth NEGROAMARO-based red with MONTEPULCIANO, esp from VALLONE, Due Palme, Rubino. ROSATO can be among Italy's best.

Brolio, Castello di Tus ★★→★★★ Historic estate, CHIANTI CLASSICO's largest, now thriving again under RICASOLI family after foreign-managed decline. *V.gd* Chianti Classico and IGT Casalferro.

Brunelli, Gianni Tus ★★★ Small-scale producer of elegant, refined BRUNELLO DI MONTALCINO. Not to be confused with others in MONTALCINO called Brunelli. Now run by Gianni's widow, Laura.

Brunello di Montalcino Tus DOCG r ★★★→★★★★ 90' 95 97 99' 00 01' 04' 05 06' 07 09 (10') (11) (12) (13) Top wine of TUS, dense but elegant with scent and structure, potentially v. long-lived. Min 4 yrs ageing, after 5 yrs RISERVA. Moves to allow small quantities of French grapes in this supposedly 100% varietal (SANGIOVESE) have been fought off, but continual vigilance is needed. *See also* ROSSO DI MONTALCINO.

Bucci Mar ★★★ Quasi-Burgundian VERDICCHIOS, slow to mature but complex with age. Compared with most Verdicchio RISERVA Villa Bucci is on another planet. Red Pongelli is less exciting.

Burlotto, Commendatore G B Pie ★★★ Beautifully crafted and defined wines, esp BAROLO Cannubi and Monvigliero, the latter's grapes being crushed by foot.

Bussola, Tommaso Ven ★★★★ Leading producer of AMARONE, RECIOTO and RIPASSO in VALPOLICELLA. Excellent Amarone Vigneto Alto and Recioto TB.

Ca' dei Frati Lom ★★★ Foremost among quality estates of revitalized DOC LUGANA, I Frati a fine example at entry level and Brolettino a special cru, lightly oaked. A soon-to-be-launched VALPOLICELLA, Pietro dal Cero, is eagerly awaited.

Ca' del Bosco Lom ★★★★ No 1 FRANCIACORTA estate owned by the giant PINOT GR producer Santa Margherita, but still run by founder Maurizio Zanella. **Outstanding Classico-method fizz**, esp Annamaria Clementi (Italy's Dom Pérignon), Dosage Zero; also excellent Bordeaux-style red Maurizio Zanella, burgundy-style PINOT N Pinero and CHARD.

The best of Brunello – top ten and the rest
Any of the below provides a satisfying BRUNELLO DI MONTALCINO, but we have put a star next to the ten we think best:
Pieri Agostina, Altesino, ARGIANO (CASTELLO DI), Baricci, BIONDI-SANTI ★, GIANNI BRUNELLI ★, Camigliano, La Campana, Campogiovanni, CANALICCHIO DI SOPRA, Canalicchio di Sotto, Caparzo, CASANOVA DI NERI, CASE BASSE ★, Castelgiocondo, Ciacci Piccolomini, COL D'ORCIA, Collemattoni, Corte Pavone, Costanti, Eredi FULIGNI, Il Colle, La Fuga, La Gerla, Lambardi, LISINI ★, La Magia, La Mannella, IL PARADISO DI MANFREDI, Le Potazzine, Marroneto, Mastrojanni ★, Oliveto, Salvioni ★, Siro Pacenti, Palazzo, Pertimali, PIEVE DI SANTA RESTITUTA, La Poderina, Pian dell'Orino ★, POGGIO ANTICO, Poggio di Sotto ★, Salvioni-Cerbaiola ★, TENUTA IL POGGIONE ★, Uccelliera, Val di Suga, Valdicava.

Caiarossa Tus ★★★ Dutch owner Eric Jelgersma (Château Giscours; *see* Bordeaux chapter) and Australia-trained French oenologist Dominique Genot run this internationally accented estate, north of BOLGHERI, turning out excellent Caiarossa Bianco and reds: Pergolaia (SANGIOVESE plus CAB, MERLOT).

Caluso / Erbaluce di Caluso Pie DOCG w ★★ DYA. Bright, mineral white from Erbaluce grape in northern PIE. Best: Orsolani, esp La Rustia.

Campania The country playground of the Romans has turned out, in modern as in ancient times, to be one of the most fascinating wine regions. Viticulture is divided between coast, incl islands like ISCHIA and Capri, and inland mtn areas, almost invariably better. Characterful white grapes incl FALANGHINA, FIANO, GRECO, while AGLIANICO rules among reds. Classic DOCS incl FIANO d'Avellino, GRECO DI TUFO, TAURASI, with newer areas emerging eg. Sannio and Benevento. Gd producers: Caggiano, CANTINA del Taburno, Caputo, COLLI di Lapio, D'Ambra, De Angelis, Benito Ferrara, *Feudi di San Gregorio*, GALARDI, LA GUARDIENSE, *Mastroberardino*, Molettieri, MONTEVETRANO, Mustilli, Luigi Tecce, Terredora di Paolo, Trabucco, VILLA MATILDE.

Canalicchio di Sopra Tus ★★★ Dynamic terroir-conscious Ripaccioli family produce from two v'yds, one on Montosolo slopes, beautifully balanced, complex yet drinkable BRUNELLO, ROSSO DI MONTALCINO.

Cantina A cellar, winery or even a wine bar.

Caparra & Siciliani Cal ★→★★ Co-op in Cal's best-known zone, CIRÒ. 200 ha+ of CLASSICO v'yds, 50 yrs experience.

Capezzana, Tenuta di Tus ★★★ Noble TUS family estate west of Florence, until recently headed by Tus wine legend Count Ugo Contini Bonacossi, today run by his children. Gd Barco Reale DOC, excellent CARMIGNANO (Villa di Capezzana, Villa di Trefiano). Also v.gd Bordeaux-style red, Ghiaie della Furba and an exceptional VIN SANTO.

Capichera Sar ★★★ V.gd if pricey producer of VERMENTINO DI GALLURA, esp VENDEMMIA *tardiva*. Excellent red Mantèghja from CARIGNANO grapes.

Cappellano Pie ★★★ The late Teobaldo Cappellano was one of the characters of BAROLO, devoting part of his v'yd in cru Gabutti to ungrafted NEBBIOLO vines (Pie Franco). Excellent Barolos in highly traditional style; also "tonic" Barolo Chinato, invented by an ancestor.

Caprai Umb ★★★→★★★★ Large, v.-high-quality, experimental producer situated in MONTEFALCO. Superb DOCG *Montefalco Sagrantino*, esp 25 Anni, and v.gd DOC ROSSO DI MONTEFALCO.

Carema Pie DOC r ★★→★★★ 04' 06' 07 08 09 10 (11) (13) Obscure, light, intense NEBBIOLO from lower, if precipitous, Alpine slopes nr Aosta. Best: Luigi Ferrando (esp Etichetta Nera), Produttori Nebbiolo di Carema.

Carignano del Sulcis Sar DOC r p ★★→★★★ 06 07 08 09 10 (12) (13) Mellow but intense red from SAR's southwest. Best: *Terre Brune*, Rocca Rubia from CS di SANTADI.

Carmignano Tus DOCG r ★★★ 02 04 06 07 08 09 10 11 (12) (13) Fine TUS SANGIOVESE/ Bordeaux-grape blend invented in 20th century by late Count Bonacossi of CAPEZZANA. Best: Ambra, CAPEZZANA, Farnete, Piaggia, Le Poggiarelle, Pratesi.

Carpenè-Malvolti Ven ★★ Historic and still important brand of PROSECCO and other sparkling wines at CONEGLIANO.

Cartizze Ven ★★ Famous, frequently too expensive and too sweet, DOC PROSECCO of supposedly best subzone of Valdobbiadene.

Casanova di Neri Tus ★★★ Modern BRUNELLO DI MONTALCINO, highly prized Cerretalto and TENUTA Nuova, plus Petradonice CAB SAUV and v.gd ROSSO DI MONTALCINO.

Case Basse Tus ★★★★ Victim of horrific vandalism in Dec 2012, eco-geek Gianfranco Soldera has defiantly declared that he will carry on making bio, long-oak-aged, definitive-quality BRUNELLO as before. Remaining bottles will be more rare and precious than ever. (*See also* Tus, p.129.)

Castel del Monte Pug DOC r p w ★→★★ (r) 06 07 08 09 10 11 (13) (p w) DYA. Dry, fresh, increasingly serious wines of mid-PUG DOC. Gd Pietrabianca and excellent *Bocca di Lupo* from Tormaresca (ANTINORI). V.gd Le More from Santa Lucia. Interesting reds from Cocevola, Giancarlo Ceci. *See also* RIVERA, whose Il Falcone RISERVA is considered iconic cru of zone.

Castellare Tus ★★→★★★ CHIANTI CLASSICO producer. First-rate SANGIOVESE-based IGT I Sodi di San Niccoló and updated CHIANTI, esp RISERVA VIGNA Poggiale. Also POGGIO ai Merli (MERLOT), Coniale (CAB SAUV).

Castell' in Villa Tus ★★★ Individual, traditionalist CHIANTI CLASSICO estate in extreme southwest of zone. Wines of class, excellence made by self-taught Princess Coralia Pignatelli.

Castelluccio E-R ★★→★★★ Quality SANGIOVESE from E-R estate of famed oenologist Vittorio Fiore: IGT Ronco dei Ciliegi, Ronco delle Ginestre. Massicone is excellent Sangiovese/CAB SAUV blend.

Cavallotto Pie ★★★ Leading BAROLO traditionalist of Castiglione Falletto, v'yds in heart of zone. Outstanding Barolo RISERVA Bricco Boschis VIGNA San Giuseppe, Riserva Vignolo, v.gd LANGHE NEBBIOLO.

Cerasuolo Ab DOC p ★ DYA ROSATO version of MONTEPULCIANO D'ABRUZZO, not to be confused with red CERASUOLO DI VITTORIA from SI. Can be brilliant; try CONTESA.

Cerasuolo di Vittoria Si DOCG r ★★ 09 10 11 (13) Medium-bodied red from Frappato, NERO D'AVOLA grapes in southeast SI: try COS, Nicosia, PLANETA, Valle dell'Acate.

Ceretto Pie ★★→★★★ Leading producer of BARBARESCO (Bricco Asili), BAROLO (Bricco Rocche, Brunate, Prapò), plus LANGHE Rosso Monsoro (French-variety blend), Langhe Bianco Blange (ARNEIS).

Cerro, Fattoria del Tus ★★★ Estate owned by insurance giant SAI, making v.gd DOCG VINO NOBILE DI MONTEPULCIANO (esp cru Antica Chiusina). SAI also owns La Poderina (BRUNELLO DI MONTALCINO), Colpetrone (MONTEFALCO SAGRANTINO) and 1,000-ha northern MAREMMA estate of Monterufoli.

Cesanese del Piglio or Piglio Lat DOCG r ★→★★ Medium-bodied red, gd for moderate ageing. Best: Petrucca e Vela, Terre del Cesanese. Cesanese di Olevano Romano, Cesanese di Affile are similar.

Who makes really good Chianti Classico?

CHIANTI CLASSICO is a seriously large zone with hundreds of producers, so picking out the best is tricky. The top ten get a ★: AMA ★, ANTINORI, BADIA A COLTIBUONO ★, Bibbiano, Le Boncie, Il Borghetto, Bossi, BROLIO, Cacchiano, Cafaggio, Capannelle, Capraia, Carobbio, Casaloste, Casa Sola, CASTELLARE, CASTELL' IN VILLA, Le Cinciole, Collelungo, Le Corti, Mannucci Droandi, FELSINA ★, Le Filigare, FONTERUTOLI, FONTODI ★, ISOLE E OLENA ★, Lilliano, Il Molino di Grace, MONSANTO ★, Monte Bernardi, Monteraponi ★, NITTARDI, NOZZOLE, Palazzino, Paneretta, Petroio-Lenzi, Poggerino, POGGIO al Sole, Poggiolino, POGGIOPIANO, QUERCIABELLA ★, RAMPOLLA, Riecine, Rocca di Castagnoli, Rocca di Montegrossi ★, RUFFINO, San Fabiano Calcinaia, SAN FELICE, SAN GIUSTO A RENTENNANO ★, Savignola Paolina, Selvole, Vecchie Terre di Montefili, Verrazzano, Vicchiomaggio, VIGNAMAGGIO, Villa La Rosa ★, Viticcio, VOLPAIA ★.

Chianti Tus DOCG r ★→★★★ Since forever the glugging wine of central TUS, fresh, fruity, astringent, easy to drink, once with a percentage of white grapes. The creation of subzones, unwarranted elevation to DOCG and the banishing of the whites introduced unnecessary complication. 'Twould be better if 'twere a simple DOC (see Italy introduction).

Chianti Classico Tus DOCG r ★★→★★★★ 04 06 07 08 09 10 11 (12) (13) The historic CHIANTI zone was allowed to add CLASSICO to its name when the Chianti area was extended to most of central TUS in the early 20th century. Covering all or part of nine communes, the land is hilly and rocky with altitudes of 250–500 metres.

The "Black Rooster" wine is traditionally blended: the debate now is whether the support grapes should be French or native.

Chiaretto Ven Pale, light-blush-hued rosé (the word means "claret"), produced esp around Lake GARDA. *See* BARDOLINO, Riviera del Garda Bresciano.

Ciabot Berton Pie ★★★ Small La Morra grower, classy BAROLOS at modest prices. Crus incl Roggeri and new Rochettevino.

Ciliegiolo Tus Varietal wine of TUS MAREMMA, made from eponymous grape of which SANGIOVESE is an offspring. Try Rascioni e Cecconello, Sassotondo.

Cinque Terre Lig DOC w dr sw ★★ Dry VERMENTINO-based whites from steepest Riviera coast of LIG. Sweet version is called SCIACCHETRÀ. Seek out Arrigoni, Bisson and Buranco.

Cirò Cal DOC r (p) (w) ★→★★★ Strong red from Cal's main grape, Gaglioppo; or light, fruity white from GRECO (DYA). Best: CAPARRA & SICILIANI, Ippolito, *Librandi* (Duca San Felice ★★★), San Francesco (Donna Madda, RONCO dei Quattroventi), Santa Venere.

Classico Term for wines from a restricted, usually historic and superior-quality area within limits of a commercially expanded DOC. *See* CHIANTI CLASSICO, VALPOLICELLA, SOAVE, numerous others.

Clerico, Domenico Pie ★★★ Est modernist BAROLO producer of Monforte d'ALBA, esp crus Percristina, Ciabot Mentin Ginestra; recently introduced Aeroplan Servaj.

Coffele Ven ★★★ Grower with some of the finest v'yds in SOAVE CLASSICO, making steely, mineral wines of classic style. Try cru Ca' Visco.

Col d'Orcia Tus ★★★ Third-largest and top-quality MONTALCINO estate owned by Francesco Marone Cinzano. Best wine: BRUNELLO RISERVA POGGIO al Vento.

Colli = hills; singular: Colle. **Colline** (singular Collina) = smaller hills. *See also* COLLIO, POGGIO.

Colli Euganei Ven DOC r w dr s/sw (sp) ★→★★ DYA. DOC southwest of Padua. Red, white, sparkling are pleasant, rarely better. Best producers: Ca' Lustra, La Montecchia, Vignalta.

Colline Novaresi Pie *See* GATTINARA.

Collio F-VG DOC r w ★★→★★★★ Hilly zone on border with Slovenia. Esp known for complex, sometimes deliberately oxidized whites, some vinified on skins in earthenware vessels/amphorae in the ground. Some excellent, some shocking blends from various French, German, Slavic grapes. There are numerous gd-to-excellent producers incl BORGO DEL TIGLIO, La Castellada, Castello di Spessa, MARCO FELLUGA, Fiegl, GRAVNER, Renato Keber, Livon, Aldo Polencic, Primosic, Princic, Russiz SUPERIORE, *Schiopetto*, Tercic, Terpin, Venica & Venica, VILLA RUSSIZ and Zuani.

Italy has more varieties of vine cultivated for wine than any other country: 377.

Colli Orientali del Friuli F-VG DOC r w dr sw ★★→★★★★ Hills in eastern F-VG. Zone similar to COLLIO but less experimental, more oriented towards reds and stickies. Top producers: Meroi, Miani, Moschioni, LIVIO FELLUGA, Rosa Bosco, RONCO del Gnemiz. Sweet wines from VERDUZZO grapes (called Ramandolo if from around Nimis: Anna Berra, Giovanni Dri) or PICOLIT grapes (Ronchi di Cialla) can be amazing.

Colli Piacentini E-R DOC r p w ★→★★ DYA Light gulping wines, often fizzy (r or w), from various grapes incl BARBERA, BONARDA (r), MALVASIA, Pignoletto (w), plus various PINOT varieties. Similar to OLTREPÒ PAVESE but tending to serve E-R rather than Lom. Gd producers: Montessisa, Mossi, Romagnoli, Solenghi, La Stoppa, Torre Fornello, La Tosa. *See also* GUTTURNIO DEI COLLI PIACENTINI.

Colognole Tus ★★ Ex-Conti Spalletti estate making increasingly classy CHIANTI RÙFINA, RISERVA del Don from steep south-facing slopes of Monte Giovi.

Colterenzio CS / Schreckbichl T-AA ★★→★★★ Cornaiano-based main player among ALTO ADIGE co-ops. Whites (SAUV Lafoa, CHARD Altkirch, PINOT BIANCO Weisshaus Praedium) tend to be better than reds, despite renown of CAB SAUV Lafoa.

Conegliano Valdobbiadene Ven DOCG w sp ★→★★ DYA. Name for top PROSECCO, daunting to pronounce: may be used separately or together.

Conterno, Aldo Pie ★★★→★★★★ Recently deceased top grower of Monforte d'ALBA, was considered a traditionalist, esp concerning top BAROLOS Granbussia, Cicala, Colonello. His sons moving winery in more modernist direction.

Conterno, Giacomo Pie ★★★★ Iconic grower of super-traditional BAROLO with cellar at Monforte d'ALBA, Giacomo's grandson Roberto now carrying on father Giovanni's work. Two Barolos from Cascina Francia v'yd in Serralunga: Cascina Francia and *Monfortino*, long-macerated to age for yrs.

In 2013 Italy was once again the country making the largest volume of wine in the world.

Conterno Fantino Pie ★★★ Two families joined to produce excellent modern-style BAROLO Sorì Ginestra and VIGNA del Gris at Monforte d'ALBA. Also NEBBIOLO/BARBERA blend Mon Prà.

Conterno Paolo Pie ★★→★★★ A family of NEBBIOLO and BARBERA growers since 1886, current *titolare* Giorgio. continues with textbook cru BAROLOS Ginestra and Riva del Bric, plus particularly fine LANGHE Nebbiolo Bric Ginestra.

Contesa Ab ★★→★★★ Collecorvino, Pescara, v'yd of oenologist Rocco Pasetti makes excellent red MONTEPULCIANO D'ABRUZZO, rosé CERASUOLO and white PECORINO under the Contesa label.

Contini, Attilio Sar ★→★★★ Famous SAR producer of Sherry-like, *flor*-affected VERNACCIA DI ORISTANO. Best is vintage blend Antico Gregori.

Conti Zecca Pug ★★→★★★ Large SALENTO estate with 320-ha v'yd producing almost two million bottles. Donna Marzia line of Salento IGT wines is gd value, as is SALICE SALENTINO Cantalupi. Best-known among many wines is NEGROAMARO/CAB SAUV blend Nero.

Contucci Tus ★★→★★★ Millennial producer of traditional-style VINO NOBILE. An ancient cellar at MONTEPULCIANO *vaut le detour*.

Copertino Pug DOC r (p) ★★★ 08 10 11 (12) Smooth, savoury red of NEGROAMARO from heel of Italy. Gd producers: AZIENDA MONACI, CS Copertino.

Coppo Pie ★★→★★★ Top producers of BARBERA d'ASTI (Pomorosso, RISERVA della Famiglia). Also excellent CHARD Monteriolo, sparkling Riserva del Fondatore.

Cortona Tus Tuscan DOC contiguous to MONTEPULCIANO VINO NOBILE. Various indigenous and international red and white grape varieties, gd wines incl Avignonesi's Desiderio, MERLOT/CAB, first-rate SYRAH from Luigi d'Alessandro, Il Castagno, *La Braccesca*.

CS (Cantina Sociale) Cooperative winery.

Cusumano Si ★★→★★★ Relatively recently arrived; 450-ha v'yd in various parts of SI. Reds from NERO D'AVOLA, CAB SAUV, SYRAH; whites from CHARD, INSOLIA. Gd quality, gd value.

Dal Forno, Romano Ven ★★★★ V.-high-quality VALPOLICELLA, AMARONE, RECIOTO grower whose perfectionism is the more remarkable for the fact that his v'yds are outside the CLASSICO zone.

De Bartoli, Marco Si ★★★ Famous estate for MARSALA Vergine-like Vecchio Samperi. Best is barrel-aged Ventennale, blend of young and v. old vintages. Sons of recently deceased owner Marco de Bartoli make top DOC MARSALAS too and outstanding table wines like *Grillo*. Also excellent PASSITO at their Bukkuram winery on PANTELLERIA.

Dei Pie ★★→★★★ Pianist Caterina Dei runs this elegant aristocratic estate in

MONTEPULCIANO, making VINO NOBILES with artistry and passion. Her *chef d'oeuvre* is Nobile di Montepulciano Bossona.

Di Majo Norante Mol ★★ →★★★ Rare quality producer of Mol with v.gd Biferno Rosso Ramitello, Don Luigi Molise Rosso RISERVA, Mol AGLIANICO Contado, white blend FALANGHINA/GRECO Biblos, MOSCATO PASSITO Apianae.

DOC / DOCG Quality wine designation: *see* box, p.125.

Dogliani Pie DOCG r ★→★★★ 08 09 10 11 12 DOCG DOLCETTO from PIE, though they have dropped the grape from the label to confuse you. Some versions to drink young, others for moderate ageing. Gd producers: Marziano Abbona, Osvaldo Barbaris, Francesco Boschis, Chionetti, Clavesana, Einaudi, Pecchenino.

Donnafugata Si r w ★★ →★★★ Classy range of SI wines incl reds Mille e Una Notte, Sherazade, Tancredi; whites Chiaranda, Ligheia. Also v. fine MOSCATO PASSITO di PANTELLERIA Ben Ryé.

Duca di Salaparuta Si ★★ Once on the list of every trattoria in Christendom with its Corvo brand, now – under the ownership of Ilva (Amaretto) of Saronno – concentrating on more upmarket fare like Kados (w) from Grillo grapes and Passo delle Mule 9Ro, Triskele (NERO D'AVOLA/MERLOT) Lavico (NERELLO MASCALESE), old favourite Duca Enrico (Nero d'Avola).

Elba Tus r w (sp) ★→★★ DYA. The island's white, based on Ansonica and TREBBIANO, can be v. drinkable with fish. Dry reds are based on SANGIOVESE. Gd sweet white (MOSCATO) and red (*Aleatico Passito DOCG*). Gd producers: Acquabona, Sapereta.

Enoteca Wine library; also shop or restaurant with ambitious wine list. There is a national enoteca at the *fortezza* in Siena.

Esino Mar DOC r w ★→★★★ (r) 06 07 08 09 10 11 (12) (13) Alternative DOC of VERDICCHIO country, allowing 50% of other grapes with Verdicchio for Bianco and 40% with SANGIOVESE/MONTEPULCIANO for Rosso. Best reds from MONTE SCHIAVO (Adeodato), Belisario (Colferraio).

Est! Est!! Est!!! Lat DOC w dr s/sw ★ DYA. Unextraordinary white from Montefiascone, north of Rome. Trades on the improbable origin of its name. Best is FALESCO.

Etna Si DOC r p w ★★→★★★ (r) 06 07 08 09 10 11 (12) Wine from volcanic slopes, often high on north side of mtn. Etna's v'yds declined in the 20th century, but new money has brought a flurry of planting and some excellent wines, rather in style of burgundy, though based on NERELLO MASCALESE (r) and CARRICANTE (w). Gd producers: Benanti, Calcagno, Il Cantante, Cottanera, Terre Nere, Nicosia, *Passopisciaro*, Girolamo Russo, *Barone di Villagrande*.

Falchini Tus ★★→★★★ Producer of gd DOCG VERNACCIA DI SAN GIMIGNANO (VIGNA a Solatio and oaked Ab Vinea Doni), plus top Bordeaux blend *Campora*, SANGIOVESE-based Paretaio. Riccardo Falchini was a champion of fine SAN GIMIGNANO, ably succeeded by his half-American children.

Falerno del Massico Cam ★★→★★★ DOC r w ★★ (r) 04 06 07 08 09 10 11 (12) (13) Falernum was the Château d'Yquem of Roman times. Today elegant red from AGLIANICO, fruity dry white from FALANGHINA. Best: VILLA MATILDE, Amore Perrotta, Felicia, Moio, Trabucco.

Fara Pie *See* GATTINARA.

Faro Si DOC r ★★★ 06' 07 08 09 10 11 (12) (13) Intense, harmonious red from NERELLO MASCALESE and Nerello Cappuccio in hills behind Messina. Salvatore Geraci of Palari, the major producer, administered the kiss of life when extinction seemed likely. Also Bonavita.

Felluga, Livio F-VG ★★★ Consistently fine COLLI ORIENTALI DEL FRIULI wines, esp blends Terre Alte and Illivio, also *Pinot Gr*, SAUV BL, FRIULANO, PICOLIT, MERLOT/REFOSCO blend Sossó.

Felluga, Marco F-VG *See* RUSSIZ SUPERIORE.

Felsina Tus ★★★ Giuseppe Mazzocolin has run this CHIANTI CLASSICO estate for over 30 yrs: classic RISERVA Rancia and IGT Fontalloro, both 100% SANGIOVESE. Also gd CHARD, I Sistri. Giuseppe also runs Castello di Farnetella, gd CHIANTI COLLI Senesi.

Ferrari T-AA ★★→★★★ Trento maker of the best METODO CLASSICO wines outside FRANCIACORTA. Giulio Ferrari is top cru; also gd are CHARD-based Brut RISERVA Lunelli, PINOT N-based Extra Brut Perlé Nero.

Feudi di San Gregorio Cam ★★→★★★ Much-hyped CAM producer, with DOCGS TAURASI Piano di Montevergine, FIANO di Avellino Pietracalda, GRECO DI TUFO Cutizzi. Also IGT reds Serpico (AGLIANICO), Patrimo (MERLOT), whites *Falanghina*, Campanaro.

Florio Si Historic quality maker of MARSALA. Specialist in Marsala Vergine Secco. For some reason Terre Arse (= burnt lands), its best wine, doesn't do well in the UK.

Folonari Tus Ambrogio Folonari and son Giovanni, having split from the giant RUFFINO, have quite a quiverful of their own. NB *Cabreo* (CHARD and SANGIOVESE/ CAB SAUV), wines of NOZZOLE (incl top Cab Sauv Pareto), BRUNELLO DI MONTALCINO La Fuga, VINO NOBILE DI MONTEPULCIANO Gracciano Svetoni, plus wines from BOLGHERI, MONTECUCCO, COLLI ORIENTALI DEL FRIULI.

Fontana Candida Lat ★★ Biggest producer of once-fashonable FRASCATI. Single-v'yd Santa Teresa stands out. Part of huge GRUPPO ITALIANO VINI.

Fontanafredda Pie ★★→★★★ Much-improved large producer of PIE wines on former royal estates, incl BAROLO Serralunga and Barolo crus Lazzarito Mirafiore, VIGNA La Rosa. Excellent LANGHE NEBBIOLO *Mirafiore* Plus ALBA DOCS, sparklers dry (Contessa Rosa Pas Dosè) and sweet (ASTI).

Fonterutoli Tus ★★★ Historic CHIANTI CLASSICO estate of Mazzei family at Castellina with castle and space-age CANTINA in wild heart of TUS hills. Notable: Castello di Fonterutoli (dark, oaky CHIANTI), IGT Siepi (SANGIOVESE/MERLOT). The Mazzei also own TENUTA di Belguardo in MAREMMA, gd MORELLINO DI SCANSANO and IGT wines.

Fontodi Tus ★★★→★★★★ Outstanding Manetti family estate at Panzano making one of the absolute best CHIANTI CLASSICOS, RISERVA VIGNA del Sorbo, and outstanding all-SANGIOVESE Flaccianello, an IGT that could and ought to be Chianti Classico. Proper IGTs PINOT N, SYRAH Case Via among best of these varieties in TUS.

Foradori T-AA ★★★ Elizabeth Foradori has been one of the pioneers of Italian viniculture for 30 yrs, mainly via *the great red grape of* Trentino, TEROLDEGO. Now she ferments in *anfora* with reds like Morei, Sgarzon and whites like Nosiola Fontanabianca. Top wine remains Teroldego-based Granato.

Franciacorta Lom DOCG w (p) sp ★★→★★★★ Italy's major zone for top-quality METODO CLASSICO sparkling. Best producers: Barone Pizzini, BELLAVISTA, CA' DEL BOSCO, Castellino, Cavalleri, Gatti, Uberti, Villa. Also v.gd: Contadi Gastaldi, Monte Rossa, Ricci Curbastri.

Frascati Lat DOC w dr sw s/sw (sp) ★→★★ DYA. Best-known wine of Roman hills, under constant threat from urban expansion. From MALVASIA and/or TREBBIANO, most is disappointingly neutral: look for Castel de Paolis, Conte Zandotti, Villa Simone, or Santa Teresa from FONTANA CANDIDA. The sweet version is known as Cannellino.

Freisa d'Asti Pie DOC r dr sw s/sw (sp) ★→★★★ Two distinct styles: frivolous, maybe FRIZZANTE, maybe sweetish; or serious, dry and tannic for ageing (so follow BAROLO vintages). Best: Brezza, Cigliuti, CLERICO, ALDO CONTERNO, COPPO, Franco Martinetti, GIUSEPPE MASCARELLO, Parusso, Pecchenino, Pelissero, Sebaste, Trinchero, VAJRA, VOERZIO.

Frescobaldi Tus ★★→★★★★ Ancient noble family, leading CHIANTI RÚFINA pioneer at NIPOZZANO estate (look for *Montesodi* ★★★), also BRUNELLO from Castelgiocondo estate in MONTALCINO. Sole owners of LUCE estate (MONTALCINO), ORNELLAIA (BOLGHERI). V'yds also in MAREMMA, Montespertoli, COLLIO.

Friulano F-VG ★→★★ Recently changed name of what used to be called Tocai

FRIULANO; the "Tocai" part disappeared due to pressure from Hungary. Fresh, pungent, subtly floral whites, best from COLLIO, ISONZO, COLLI ORIENTALI. Gd producers: BORGO DEL TIGLIO, LIVIO FELLUGA, LIS NERIS, Pierpaolo Pecorari, Ronco del Gelso, Ronco del Gnemiz, Russiz SUPERIORE, SCHIOPETTO, LE VIGNE DI ZAMÒ, VILLA RUSSIZ. The new name for ex-Tocai from Ven, by the way, is "Tai".

Friuli-Venezia Giulia The northeast region. The best part wine-wise is the hills on the Slovenian border rather than on the wide alluvial plains. Quality DOCs are ISONZO, COLLIO, COLLI ORIENTALI. Some gd reds, but considered the home of Italy's most adventurous and accomplished whites.

Frizzante Semi-sparkling, up to 2.5 atmospheres, eg. MOSCATO D'ASTI, much PROSECCO, LAMBRUSCO and the like. The northwest of Italy is home to large numbers of lightly fizzing wines that never seem to make it out into the wide world. It's the world's loss.

Fuligni Tus ★★★→★★★★ Outstanding producer of BRUNELLO, ROSSO DI MONTALCINO.

Gaja Pie ★★★★ Old family firm at BARBARESCO led by Angelo Gaja, highly audible apostle of Italian wine; daughter Gaia G following. High quality, even higher prices. BARBARESCO is the only PIE DOCG Gaja makes, having declassified his crus Sorì Tildìn, Sorì San Lorenzo, Costa Russi as well as BAROLO Sperss to LANGHE DOC (so he can add a little BARBERA to his NEBBIOLO). Splendid CHARD (Gaia e Rey), CAB SAUV Darmagi. Also owner of Pieve di Santa Restituta in MONTALCINO, Ca' Marcanda in BOLGHERI.

Galardi Cam ★★★ Producer of Terra di Lavoro, a highly touted blend of AGLIANICO and Piedirosso, in north CAM.

Garda Ven DOC r p w ★→★★ (r) 08 09 10 11 12 (13) (w p) DYA. Catch-all DOC for early drinking wines of various colours from provinces of Verona in Ven, Brescia and Mantua in Lom. Gd producers: Cavalchina, Zeni.

Garofoli Mar ★★→★★★ Quality leader in the Marches, specialist in VERDICCHIO (Podium, Macrina, Serra Fiorese), ROSSO CONERO (Piancarda, Grosso Agontano).

Gattinara Pie DOCG r ★★→★★★ 04' 06 07 08 09 10 (11) (12) (13) Best-known of a cluster of northern PIE DOC(G)s based on NEBBIOLO, here called Spanna. Best producers: Travaglini, Antoniolo, Bianchi, Nervi, Torraccia del Piantavigna. Similar DOC(G)s of the zone: GHEMME, Boca, Bramaterra, Colline Novaresi, Costa della Sesia, Fara, Lessona, Sizzano. None of them, sadly, measure up to BAROLO/BARBARESCO at their best.

Gavi / Cortese di Gavi Pie DOCG w ★→★★★ DYA. At best, subtle dry white of Cortese grapes, though much is dull. Most comes from commune of Gavi, hence Gavi di Gavi. Best: Castellari Bergaglio, Franco Martinetti, Toledana, Villa Sparina, Broglia, Cascina degli Ulivi, Castello di Tassarolo, Chiarlo, La Giustiniana, Podere Saulino.

Ghemme Pie DOCG. *See* GATTINARA.

Giacosa, Bruno Pie ★★→★★★★ Considered by some Italy's greatest winemaker, this brooding genius suffered a stroke in 2006, but goes on crafting splendid traditional-style BARBARESCOS (Asili, Santo Stefano), BAROLOS (Falletto, Rocche del Falletto). Top wines (ie. RISERVAS) get famous red label. Also makes a range of fine reds (DOLCETTO, NEBBIOLO, BARBERA), whites (ARNEIS), amazing METODO CLASSICO Brut.

Grappa Pungent and potent spirit made from grape pomace (skins, etc., after pressing), can be anything from disgusting to inspirational. What the French call "marc".

Grasso, Elio Pie ★★★→★★★★ Top BAROLO producer (crus Vigna Chiniera, Casa Maté); v.gd BARBERA D'ALBA VIGNA Martina, DOLCETTO d'Alba, CHARD Educato.

Grave del Friuli F-VG DOC r w ★→★★ (r) 08 09 10 11 (12) (13) Largest DOC of F-VG, mostly on plains. Important volumes of underwhelming wines. Exceptions from Borgo Magredo, Di Lenardo, RONCO Cliona, Villa Chiopris, San Simone.

ITALY

Gravner, Josko F-VG ★★★ Controversial COLLIO producer, believes in maceration of reds and whites on skins in buried amphorae, followed by long ageing. Wines either loved for complexity or loathed for oxidation and phenolic flavours. Wines incl: Rosso, white blend Breg, varietal RIBOLLA. The 2006s might appear one day.

Greco di Tufo Cam DOCG w (sp) ★★→★★★ DYA One of the best whites of the south: fruity, slightly wild-tasting, at best age-worthy, from the GRECO grape. V.gd examples from Caggiano, Caputo, Benito Ferrara, FEUDI DI SAN GREGORIO, Macchialupa, *Mastroberardino* (Nova Serra, Vignadangelo), Vesevo, Villa Raiano.

Hunting rarities

Continuing the search for Italian rarities, this yr we challenge readers to seek out the unexpected from the Centre and South – one winery/region – starting with TUS: San Lorenzo (Ciliegiolo) from Sassotondo; LE MARCHE: LACRIMA DI MORRO D'ALBA from MONTE SCHIAVO; Umb: Calcaia (noble rot) from BARBERANI; LAZIO: CESANESE DEL PIGLIO SUPERIORE Romanico from Coletti Conti; Ab: PECORINO from CONTESA; Mol: Tintilia from Angelo d'Uva; CAM: Sannio Fiano Colle di Tilio; Bas: AGLIANICO DEL VULTURE Alvolo from Alovini; PUG: Dunico (PRIMITIVO) from Racemi; Cal: Terre di Gerace Bianco from Barone Macrì; SI: ZIBIBBO from Ottoventi; SAR: VERNACCIA DI ORISTANO from CONTINI. Write to the publisher if you collect labels of the whole set.

Grignolino Pie DOC r ★★ DYA lively light red of ASTI zone. Best: BRAIDA, Marchesi Incisa della Rocchetta. Also, G del Monferrato Casalese DOC (Accornero, Bricco Mondalino, La Tenaglia).

Gruppo Italiano Vini (GIV) Complex of co-ops and wineries, biggest v'yd holders in Italy. Estates incl: Bigi, BOLLA, Ca'Bianca, Conti Serristori, FOLONARI, FONTANA CANDIDA, Lamberti, Macchiavelli, MELINI, Negri, Santi, Vignaioli di San Floriano. Has also expanded into south: SI, Bas.

Guardiense, La Cam ★★ Dynamic co-op, 1,000+ grower-members, 2,000-ha v'yd, for better-than-average whites and reds at lower-than-average prices under technical direction of Riccardo Cotarella. World's largest producer of FALANGHINA.

Guerrieri Rizzardi ★★→★★★ Long-est aristocratic producers of the wines of Verona, esp of Veronese GARDA. Gd BARDOLINO CLASSICO Tacchetto, elegant AMARONE Villa Rizzardi and cru Calcarole, and ROSATO Rosa Rosae. V.gd SOAVE Classico Costeggiola.

Gutturnio dei Colli Piacentini E-R DOC r dr ★→★★ DYA. BARBERA/BONARDA blend from the COLLI PIACENTINI; sometimes frothing. Producers: Castelli del Duca, La Pergola, La Stoppa, La Tosa.

Hofstätter T-AA ★★★ Tramin-based top-quality private producer of ALTO ADIGE; maker of outstanding *Pinot N*, possibly best in Italy. Look for Barthenau VIGNA Sant'Urbano. Also range of typical South Tyrol whites, mainly, of course, GEWURZ.

Il Paradiso di Manfredi Tus ★★★ Hand-crafted BRUNELLO DI MONTALCINO from this tiny property is worth seeking out for a taste of the real thing, not always technically perfect but with bags of soul.

Indicazione Geografica Tipica (IGT) Increasingly known as Indicazione Geografica Protetta (IGP). (*See* box, p.125.)

Ischia Cam DOC (r) w ★→★★ DYA. Island off Naples, with own grape varieties (eg. Forastera, Biancolella); its wines are mainly sold to tourists. Top producer is D'Ambra (Biancolella Frassitelli, Forastera Euposia). Also gd: Il Giardino Mediterraneo, Pietratorcia.

Isole e Olena Tus ★★★→★★★★ Top CHIANTI CLASSICO estate run by astute Paolo de

Marchi, with superb red IGT Cepparello. V.gd VIN SANTO, CAB SAUV, CHARD, SYRAH. Also owns Sperino in Lessona (*see* GATTINARA).

Isonzo F-VG DOC r w ★★★ Gravelly, well-aired plain of Friuli Isonzo, a multi-DOC area with many varietals and blends. The stars are mostly white, scented and structured, such as VIE DI ROMANS' Flors di Uis, LIS NERIS' Fiore di Campo. Also gd: Borgo Conventi, Pierpaolo Pecorari, RONCO del Gelso.

Jermann, Silvio F-VG ★★→★★★ Famous estate with v'yds in COLLIO and ISONZO: top white blend Vintage Tunina, oak-aged blend Capo Martino, CHARD ex-Dreams.

Lacrima di Morro d'Alba Mar DYA. Curiously named MUSCATTY light red from a small commune in the Mar, no connection with ALBA or La Morra (PIE). Gd producers: Mancinelli, MONTE SCHIAVO.

Lacryma (or Lacrima) Christi del Vesuvio Cam r p w dr (sw) (sp) ★→★★ DOC Vesuvio wines based on Coda di Volpe (w), Piedirosso (r). Despite romantic name Vesuvius comes nowhere nr ETNA in quality stakes. Caputo, De Angelis, MASTROBERARDINO make uninspired versions.

Lageder, Alois T-AA ★★→★★★ Top ALTO ADIGE producer. Most exciting wines are single-v'yd varietals: *Sauv Bl Lehenhof*, PINOT GR Benefizium Porer, CHARD Löwengang, GEWURZ Am Sand, PINOT N Krafuss, LAGREIN Lindenberg, CAB SAUV Cor Römigberg. Also owns Cason Hirschprunn for v.gd IGT blends.

Lago di Corbara Umb r ★★ 07' 08 09 10 11 (12) Relatively recent DOC for quality reds of the ORVIETO area. Best comes from Barberani (Villa Monticelli), Decugnano dei Barbi (Il).

Lagrein Alto Adige T-AA DOC r p ★★→★★★ 04 06 07 08 09 (11) (12) *Plummy reds with bitter finish* from LAGREIN grape. Best growing zone: Gries, suburb of Bolzano. Best producers: Colterenzio co-op, Gojer, Gries co-op, HAAS, HOFSTÄTTER, LAGEDER, Laimburg, Josephus Mayr, Thomas Mayr, MURI GRIES, NALS MARGREID, Niedermayr, Niedrist, ST-Magdalena, TERLANO CO-OP, TIEFENBRUNNER.

Lambrusco E-R DOC (or not) r p w dr s/sw ★→★★ DYA. Once v. popular fizzy red from nr Modena, mainly in industrial, semisweet, non-DOC version. The real thing is dry, acidic, fresh, lively and combines magically with fatty E-R fare. DOCs: L Grasparossa di Castelvetro, L Salamino di Santa Croce, L di Sorbara. Best: Albinea Canali, Bellei, Caprari, Casali, CAVICCHIOLI, Graziano, Lini Oreste, Medici Ermete (esp Concerto), Rinaldo Rinaldini, Venturini Baldini.

Langhe Pie The hills of central PIE, home of BAROLO, BARBARESCO, etc. DOC name for several Pie varietals plus blends Bianco and Rosso. Producers wishing to blend other grapes with their NEBBIOLO, such as GAJA, can do so at up to 15% as "Langhe Nebbiolo".

Le Potazzine Tus ★★★ BRUNELLO and ROSSO DI MONTALCINO of Giuseppe and Gigliola Gorelli; high-altitude site just south of MONTALCINO. Wines keep improving; now attract wide admiration. All may be found at the family's restaurant in centre of Montalcino.

Le Pupille Tus ★★★ Elisabetta Geppetti remains the most respected force in MORELLINO DI SCANSANO, with fine versions of the DOCG topped by RISERVA POGGIO Valente. Also excellent IGT blend Saffredi (CAB SAUV/MERLOT/SYRAH/Alicante).

Lessona Pie *See* ISOLE E OLENA.

Librandi Cal ★★★ Top producer pioneering research into Cal varieties. V.gd red CIRÒ (*Riserva Duca San Felice* is ★★★), IGT Gravello (CAB SAUV/Gaglioppo blend), Magno Megonio (r) from Magliocco grape, IGT Efeso (w) from Mantonico. Other local varieties in experimental phase. To follow.

Liguria ★→★★ Steep, rocky Italian riviera: most wines sell to sun-struck tourists at fat profits, so don't travel much. Main grapes: VERMENTINO (w) – best producer is Lambruschi – and DOLCETTO (r), but don't miss CINQUE TERRE'S SCIACCHETRÀ or red Ormeasco di Pornassio.

ITALY

Lisini Tus ★★★→★★★★ Historic estate for some of the finest and longest-lasting BRUNELLO, esp RISERVA Ugolaia.

Lis Neris F-VG ★★★ Top ISONZO estate for whites, esp PINOT GR (Gris), CHARD (Jurosa), SAUV BL (Picol), FRIULANO (Fiore di Campo), plus blends Confini and Lis. Also v.gd Lis Neris Rosso (MERLOT/CAB SAUV), sweet white Tal Luc (VERDUZZO/RIES).

Locorotondo Pug DOC w (sp) ★ DYA Thirst-quencher dry white from Verdeca and Bianco d'Alessano grapes.

Luce Tus ★★★ FRESCOBALDI is sole owner of this exercise in hyperbole and high price, having bought out original partner Mondavi. A SANGIOVESE/MERLOT blend for oligarchs.

Lugana DOC w (sp) ★★→★★★ DYA. The much-improved white wine of southern Lake GARDA, main grape TREBBIANO di Lugana (= VERDICCHIO). Best incl CA' DEI FRATI, ZENATO. Particularly fine crus (Lugana SUPERIORE): Ottella (Molceo), Selva Capuzza (Menasasso).

Lungarotti Umb ★★★ Leading producer of TORGIANO, with cellars, hotel and museum, nr Perugia. Star wines DOC Rubesco, DOCG RISERVA **Villa Monticchio**. Gd IGT Sangiorgio (SANGIOVESE/CAB SAUV), Aurente (CHARD), Giubilante. Gd MONTEFALCO SAGRANTINO.

Italy at auction

Italy's stars are increasingly coming under the hammer, and auction house Gelardini & Romani has revealed the crus most in demand. First: BRUNELLO DI MONTALCINO RISERVA from BIONDI SANTI. 2: Masseto from ORNELLAIA. 3: BAROLO Riserva Monfortino from GIACOMO CONTERNO. 4: AMARONE dal Forno. 5: Barolo Riserva Le Rocche del Falletto from BRUNO GIACOSA. 6: Amarone Riserva from GIUSEPPE QUINTARELLI. 7: SASSICAIA from Tenuta San Guido. 8: MONTEPULCIANO D'ABRUZZO from VALENTINI. 9: BARBARESCO from Giacosa. 10: BRUNELLO DI MONTALCINO Riserva from Gianfranco Soldera. What? No GAJA?

Macchiole, Le Tus ★★★ One of the few native-owned wineries of BOLGHERI. Cinzia Merli, with oenologist Luca d'Attoma, continues late husband's fine work with CAB FR (Paleo Rosso), MERLOT (Messorio), also SYRAH (Scrio).

Maculan Ven ★★★ Quality pioneer of Ven, Fausto Maculan continues to make excellent CAB SAUV (Fratta, Palazzotto). Perhaps best-known for sweet TORCOLATO (esp RISERVA Acininobili).

Malvasia delle Lipari DOC w sw ★★★ Luscious sweet wine, from MALVASIA grape, from fascinating island off SI coast.

Mamete Prevostini Lom ★★→★★★ Relatively new producer of VALTELLINA. Pure varietal (NEBBIOLO) DOCG wines of class mainly from Sassella SUPERIORE but also Inferno, Grumello Superiore. Two fine SFORZATOS.

Manduria (Primitivo di) Pug DOC r s/sw ★★→★★★ Manduria is the spiritual home of PRIMITIVO, alias ZIN, so expect wines that are gutsy, alcoholic, sometimes porty to go with full-flavoured fare. Gd producers, located in Manduria or not: Cantele, de Castris, Polvanera, Racemi, CS Manduria.

Marchesi di Barolo Pie ★★ Historic, perhaps original, BAROLO producer, in commune of Barolo, making crus Cannubi and Sarmassa, plus other ALBA wines.

Maremma Tus Fashionable coastal area of southern TUS, largely recovered from malarial marshland in the early 20th century. DOC(G)s: MONTEREGIO, MORELLINO DI SCANSANO, PARRINA, Pitigliano, SOVANA (Grosseto). Maremma Toscana IGT now Maremma Toscana DOC.

Marsala Si DOC w sw SI's once-famous fortified wine (★→★★★), invented by

Woodhouse Bros from Liverpool in 1773. Deteriorated in the 20th century to cooking wine, which no longer qualifies for DOC status. Several versions from dry to v. sweet; best is bone-dry Marsala Vergine, potentially a useful, if unfashionable, apéritif. *See also* VECCHIO SAMPERI.

Marzemino Trentino T-AA DOC r ★→★★ 09 10 11 12 Pleasant everyday red, fruity and slightly bitter. Esp from Bossi Fedrigotti, CA' VIT, De Tarczal, Gaierhof, Letrari, Longariva, Simoncelli, E Spagnolli, Vallarom.

Mascarello Pie The name of two top producers of BAROLO: the late Bartolo M, of Barolo, whose daughter Maria Teresa continues her father's highly traditional path; and Giuseppe M, of Monchiero, whose son Mauro makes v. fine, traditional-style Barolo from the great Monprivato v'yd in Castiglione Falletto. Beware other Mascarellos.

Traceability

A major issue in TUS'S MONTALCINO zone has turned on whether BRUNELLO and ROSSO DI MONTALCINO are, as they are supposed to be, 100% SANGIOVESE. Today researchers at the Institute of San Michele all'Adige are perfecting a method of verifying the contents by focusing on the profile of vegetable pigments. Meanwhile work goes on to bring DNA analysis – which has hitherto been considered unreliable in the context of alcohol – into the fray. Rita Vignani, of Siena's Serge Genomics, commented: "Today, the genetic footprint allows us to determine whether a wine sold as made from a single grape variety really is so."

Masi Ven ★★→★★★ Exponent/researcher of VALPOLICELLA, AMARONE, RECIOTO, SOAVE, etc., incl fine Rosso Veronese *Campo Fiorin* and Amarone-style wines from F-VG and Argentina. V.gd barrel-aged red IGT Toar, from CORVINA and Oseleta grapes, also Osar (Oseleta). Top Amarones Costasera, Campolongo di Torbe.

Massa, La Tus ★★★ Giampaolo Motta is a Bordeaux-lover making claret-like IGT wines with a TUS accent (La Massa, Giorgio Primo), from CAB SAUV, MERLOT and, decreasingly, SANGIOVESE, at his fine estate in Panzano (CHIANTI CLASSICO), which denomination he has abandoned.

Massolino Vigna Rionda Pie ★★★ One of the finest estates of the BAROLO commune of Serralunga, reputed for typically tannic wines. The excellent B Parafada and B Margheria have firm structure, but fruity drinkability too. Top cru is RISERVA Vigna Rionda, capable of v. long ageing.

Mastroberardino Cam ★★→★★★ Historic producer of mountainous Avellino province in CAM, quality torch-bearer for Italy's south during dark yrs of mid-20th century. Top *Taurasi* (look for Historia Naturalis, Radici), also FIANO di Avellino More Maiorum, GRECO DI TUFO Nova Serra.

Matura, Gruppo Group of agronomists and oenologists headed by Alberto Antonini and Attilio Pagli, helping producers not only throughout TUS but elsewhere in country and indeed world.

Melini Tus ★★ Major producer of CHIANTI CLASSICO at Poggibonsi, part of GIV. Gd quality/price, esp Chianti Classico Selvanella, RISERVAS La Selvanell, Masovecchio.

Metodo classico or tradizionale Italian for "Champagne method", which term is not permitted.

Mezzacorona T-AA ★→★★ Massive TRENTINO co-op in the commune of Mezzocorona (sic) with wide range of gd technical wines, esp TEROLDEGO ROTALIANO Nos and METODO CLASSICO Rotari.

Monferrato Pie DOC r p w sw ★→★★ Hills between river Po and Apennines; mostly wines for everyday drinking rather than of serious intent.

Monica di Sardegna Sar DOC r ★→★★ DYA. Lightish quaffing-wine red grape widely grown in SAR.

Monsanto Tus ★★★ Esteemed CHIANTI CLASSICO estate, esp for Il POGGIO RISERVA (first single-v'yd Chianti Classico), Chianti Classico Riserva, IGTS Fabrizio Bianchi (CHARD) and Nemo (CAB SAUV).

Montalcino Tus Small but exquisite hilltop town in province of Siena, famous for concentrated, expensive BRUNELLO and more approachable, better-value ROSSO DI MONTALCINO.

Montecarlo Tus DOC r w ★★ (w) DYA. White, and increasingly red, wine area nr Lucca. Producers incl Buonamico, Carmignani, La Torre, Montechiari, Fattoria del Teso.

Montecucco Tus SANGIOVESE-based TUS DOC between Monte Amiata and Grosseto, increasingly trendy as MONTALCINO land prices ineluctably rise. As Montecucco Sangiovese it is DOCG. Look out for CASTELLO DI POTENTINO (Sacromonte, Piropo), also Begnardi, Ciacci Piccolomini, Colli Massari, Fattoria di Montecucco and Villa Patrizia.

Montefalco Sagrantino Umb DOCG r dr (sw) ★★★→★★★★ Super-tannic, powerful, long-lasting wines, until recently thought potentially great. Now doubts; difficult to tame the phenolics without denaturing the wine. Traditional bitter-sweet PASSITO version may be better suited to the grape, though harder to sell. Gd: Adanti, Antonelli, Paolo Bea, Benincasa, CAPRAI, Colpetrone, LUNGAROTTI, Scacciadiavoli, Tabarrini, Terre de' Trinci.

Montepulciano d'Abruzzo Ab DOC r p ★★→★★★ (r) 08 09 10 11 12 (13) Gd-value, full-flavoured red and zesty, savoury pink (CERASUOLO) from grapes of this name. Region, east of Rome, dominated by co-ops; gd ones incl Citra, Miglianico, Roxan, Tollo. Some excellent privates: Cornacchia, Contesa, Illuminati, Marramiero, Masciarelli, Contucci Ponno, Pepe, La Valentina, VALENTINI, Zaccagnini. Not to be confused with TUS town where SANGIOVESE-based VINO NOBILE DI MONTEPULCIANO comes from.

Monteregio Tus DOC nr Massa Marittima in MAREMMA, gd SANGIOVESE, CAB SAUV (r) and VERMENTINO (w) wines from eg. MORIS FARMS and TENUTA del Fontino. Big-name investors have been attracted by relatively low land prices, but DOC remains obscure.

Monte Schiavo Mar ★★→★★★ Switched-on, medium-size producer of VERDICCHIO, MONTEPULCIANO-based wines of various qualities, gd to excellent. Owned by world's largest manufacturer of olive-oil processing equipment, Pieralisi.

Montescudaio Tus DOC r w ★★ Modest DOC between Pisa and Livorno; best are SANGIOVESE or Sangiovese/CAB SAUV blends. Try Merlini, POGGIO Gagliardo, La Regola and Sorbaiano.

Montevertine Tus ★★★★ Radda estate. Non-DOCG but classic CHIANTI-style wines. IGT *Le Pergole Torte* a fine, sometimes great example of pure, long-ageing SANGIOVESE.

Montevetrano Cam ★★★ Iconic CAMPANIA azienda, wine supervised by consultant Riccardo Cotarella. Superb IGT Montevetrano (CAB SAUV, MERLOT, AGLIANICO).

Morellino di Scansano Tus DOCG r ★→★★★ 08 09 10 11 (13) SANGIOVESE red from the MAREMMA. Used to be relatively light and simple, now, sometimes regrettably, gaining weight and substance, perhaps to justify its lofty DOCG status. Best: Belguardo, Mantellasi, MORIS FARMS, *Podere 414*, POGGIO Argentiera, LE PUPILLE, Terre di Talamo, Vignaioli del Morellino di Scansano.

Moris Farms Tus ★★★ One of first new-age producers of TUS's MAREMMA, with MONTEREGIO and *Morellino di Scansano* DOCS, plus VERMENTINO IGT. The top cru is the now iconic IGT Avvoltore, a rich SANGIOVESE/CAB SAUV/SYRAH blend. But also try the basic MORELLINO.

Moscato d'Asti Pie DOCG w sw sp ★★→★★★ DYA Similar to DOCG ASTI, but usually better grapes; lower alcohol, sweeter, fruitier, often from small producers. Best DOCG MOSCATO: L'Armangia, BERA, BRAIDA, Ca'd'Gal, Cascina Fonda, Cascina Pian d'Oro, Caudrina, Il Falchetto, Forteto della Luja, *Marchesi di Grésy*, Icardi, Isolabella, Manfredi/Patrizi, Marino, La Morandina, Marco Negri, Elio Perrone, Rivetti, Saracco, Scagliola, VAJRA, Vietti, Vignaioli di Sante Stefano.

Muri Gries T-AA ★★→★★★ This monastery, in the Bolzano suburb of Gries, is a traditional and still top producer of LAGREIN ALTO ADIGE DOC. Esp cru Abtei-Muri.

Nals Margreid T-AA ★★→★★★ Small quality co-op making mtn-fresh whites (esp PINOT BIANCO Sirmian, *voted Italy's best white* wine in 2013) from two separate communes of ALTO ADIGE.

Nebbiolo d'Alba Pie DOC r dr ★★→★★★ 08 09 10 11 12 (13) Sometimes a worthy replacement for BAROLO/BARBARESCO, gd examples: PIO CESARE, GIACOSA, SANDRONE, VAJRA. Sometimes fresh and unoaked, more of a quaffing wine, eg. Boglietti.

Negrar, Cantina Ven ★★→★★★ Aka CS VALPOLICELLA. Major producer of high-quality Valpolicella, RIPASSO, AMARONE; grapes from various parts of the CLASSICO zone. Look for the brand name Domini Veneti.

Nino Franco Ven ★★★→★★★★ The winery of Primo Franco, named after his grandfather. Among the v. finest PROSECCOS are Rive di San Floriano Brut, Primo Franco Dry. Excellent CARTIZZE, *delicious basic Prosecco di Valdobbiadene Brut*.

Nipozzano, Castello di Tus ★★★ FRESCOBALDI estate in RÚFINA, east of Florence, making excellent CHIANTI Rúfina RISERVAS Nipozzano and esp *Montesodi*.

Nittardi Tus ★★→★★★ Reliable source of quality modern CHIANTI CLASSICO. German proprietor helped by oenologist Carlo Ferrini.

Nozzole Tus ★★→★★★ Famous estate in heart of CHIANTI CLASSICO, north of Greve, owned by Ambrogio and Giovanni FOLONARI. V.gd Chianti Classico Nozzole, excellent CAB SAUV Pareto.

Nuragus di Cagliari Sar DOC w ★★ DYA. Lively, uncomplicated SAR wine from Nuragus grape.

Occhio di Pernice Tus "Partridge's eye". A type of VIN SANTO made predominantly from black grapes, mainly SANGIOVESE. *Avignonesi's is definitive*. Also an obscure black variety found in RÚFINA and elsewhere.

Oddero Pie ★★→★★★ Traditionalist La Morra estate for gd to excellent BAROLO (Brunate, Villero) and BARBARESCO (Gallina) crus, plus other serious PIE wines.

Oltrepò Pavese Lom DOC r w dr sw sp ★→★★★ Multi-DOC, incl numerous varietal and blended wines from Pavia province, mostly drunk in Milan. Sometimes v.gd PINOT N and SPUMANTE. Gd growers: Anteo, Barbacarlo, Casa Re, Castello di Cigognola, CS Casteggio, Le Fracce, Frecciarossa, Monsupello, Mazzolino, Ruiz de Cardenas, Travaglino, La Versa co-op.

Ornellaia Tus ★★→★★★★ 04' 06' 08 10 11 (12) Fashionable estate nr BOLGHERI founded by Lodovico ANTINORI, who sold to FRESCOBALDI/Mondavi consortium, now owned solely by Frescobaldi. Top wines are of Bordeaux grapes and method: Bolgheri DOC Ornellaia, IGT Masseto (MERLOT). Bolgheri DOC Le Serre Nuove, IGT Le Volte also gd.

Orvieto Umb DOC w dr sw s/sw ★→★★★ DYA The classic Umbrian white, from ancient Etruscan hilltop city. Wines can be comparable to Vouvray from tufa soil. *Secco* most popular today, *amabile* is more traditional. Sweet versions from noble rot (*muffa nobile*) grapes can be superb, eg. Barberani's Calcaia. Other gd producers: Bigi, Cardeto, CASTELLO DELLA SALA, Decugnano dei Barbi, La Carraia, Palazzone.

Pacenti, Siro Tus ★★★ Modern-style BRUNELLO and ROSSO DI MONTALCINO from a small, caring producer.

Pantelleria Si Windswept, black- (volcanic) earth SI island off the Tunisian coast, famous for superb MOSCATO d'Alessandria stickies. PASSITO versions are particularly dense/intense. Look for: Abraxas, Colosi, DE BARTOLI, DONNAFUGATA and Murana.

Pasqua, Fratelli Ven ★→★★ A massive producer and bottler of Verona wines (VALPOLICELLA, AMARONE, SOAVE, BARDOLINO) and other Italians.

Passito Tus, Ven One of Italy's most ancient and most characteristic wine styles, from grapes hung up, or spread on trays to dry, briefly under the harvest sun (in the south) or over a period of weeks or months in the airy upper parts of the winery – a process called *appassimento*. Best-known versions: VIN SANTO (TUS); VALPOLICELLA/SOAVE, AMARONE/RECIOTO (Ven). *See also* MONTEFALCO, ORVIETO, TORCOLATO, VALLONE.

Pecorino Ab ★★→★★★★ Not cheese but complex and highly drinkable (and age-worthy) dry white from a just-rescued old variety native to Abruzzo. Gd producers: CONTESA, *Farnese*, Franco Pasetti, Illuminati, San Lorenzo, Terre d'Aligi, Tiberio.

Pian dell'Orino ★★★ A couple from ALTO ADIGE run this small MONTALCINO estate. The BRUNELLO is both seductive and technically perfect, and the Rosso is nearly as gd.

Piave Ven DOC r w ★→★★ (r) 08 09 10 11 (12) (w) DYA. Volume DOC on plains of eastern Ven for budget varietals. CAB SAUV, MERLOT, Raboso reds can all age moderately. Above-average examples from Loredan Gasparini, Molon and Villa Sandi.

Picolit F-VG DOCG w sw s/sw ★★→★★★★ 08 09 10 (12). Quasi-mythical sweet white from COLLI ORIENTALI DEL FRIULI, might disappoint those who can a) find it and b) afford it. Gd from LIVIO FELLUGA, Meroi, Perusini, Specogna, VILLA RUSSIZ and Vinae dell'Abbazia.

Piedmont / Piemonte Alpine foothill region; with TUS, Italy's most important for top quality. Turin is the capital, ASTI and ALBA the wine centres. No IGTS allowed; Piedmont DOC is lowest denomination, covering basic reds, whites, SPUMANTES, FRIZZANTES. Grapes incl: NEBBIOLO, BARBERA, BONARDA, Brachetto, Cortese, DOLCETTO, GRIGNOLINO, CHARD, MOSCATO. *See also* BARBARESCO, BAROLO, GATTINARA, ROERO.

Pieropan Ven ★★★ Nino Pieropan is the veteran quality leader of SOAVE, the man who brought a noble wine back to credibility. Cru *La Rocca* is still the ultimate Soave, and Calvarino, indeed the screwcapped CLASSICO, are not far behind.

Pieve di Santa Restituta Pie ★★★ GAJA estate for a PIE interpretation of BRUNELLO DI MONTALCINO under names Sugarille, Rennina.

Pio Cesare Pie ★★→★★★ Veteran ALBA producer, offers BAROLO and BARBARESCO in both modern (barrique) and traditional (large-cask-aged) versions. Also the Alba range, incl whites (eg. GAVI). Particularly gd NEBBIOLO D'ALBA, *a little Barolo at half the price.*

Venetian gondoliers are subject to spot-breathalyzer tests, following complaints.

Planeta Si ★★→★★★ Leading SI estate with six v'yd holdings in various parts of the island incl Vittoria (CERASUOLO), Noto (NERO D'AVOLA Santa Cecilia) and most recently on ETNA. Wines are made from native and imported varieties. La Segreta is brand of gd-value white (Grecanico, CHARD, VIOGNIER, FIANO) and red (NERO D'AVOLA, MERLOT, SYRAH).

Podere Tus Small TUS farm, once part of a big estate.

Poggio Tus Means "hill" in TUS dialect. "**Poggione**" means "big hill".

Poggio Antico Tus ★★★ Admirably consistent, sometimes inspired producer of MONTALCINO. Basic BRUNELLO is aged in traditional BOTTE. Altero is Brunello aged in barriques. RISERVA blends the two.

Poggio di Sotto ★★★★ Small MONTALCINO estate but a quality giant of the illustrious denomination. Outstanding BRUNELLO and Rosso; traditional character with an idiosyncratic twist. New owner Claudio Tipa is pursuing existing lines.

Poggione, Tenuta Il Tus ★★★ Marker for fine BRUNELLO, esp considering large volume; also v.gd ROSSO DI MONTALCINO.

Poggiopiano Tus ★★→★★★ Easy-drinking yet serious CHIANTIS from San Casciano; a blend of old and new techniques. Polished CHIANTI CLASSICO and RISERVA Tradizione. Chiantis are pure SANGIOVESE, but Rosso di Sera incl up to 15% of Colorino grape.

Poggio Scalette Tus ★★★ Oenologist Vittorio Fiore's family estate. Above-average CHIANTI CLASSICO and Bordeaux-blend Capogatto. Pride of place goes to 100% SANGIOVESE Il Carbonaione; needs several yrs bottle age.

Pomino Tus DOC r w ★★★ (r) 08 09 10 11 (12) (13) An appendage of RÚFINA, with fine red and white blends (esp Il Benefizio). Virtually a FRESCOBALDI exclusivity.

Potentino, Castello di Tus ★★ English eccentric Charlotte Horton takes on the might of what she calls "Mort-alcino" at this medieval redoubt on Monte Amiata. V.gd SANGIOVESE *Sacromonte*; better PINOT N Piropo, Lyncurio (blush).

Prà Ven ★★★ Leading SOAVE CLASSICO producer, esp crus Monte Grande, Staforte, the latter six mths in steel tanks on lees with mechanical *bâtonnage*. Now also excellent VALPOLICELLAS under the names Morandina, La Formica.

Produttori del Barbaresco Pie ★★★ One of Italy's earliest co-ops, considered by some the best, if not indeed best in the world. Aldo Vacca and his team make excellent traditional straight BARBARESCO as well as crus Asili, Montefico, Montestefano, Ovello, Pora, Rio Sordo.

> **The best of Prosecco**
>
> PROSECCO continues to boom in the market, helped no doubt by a massive planting programme, recently altered laws categorizing Prosecco as a wine from a specific area and no longer a grape (thus eliminating, or at least reducing, copycat wines from emerging v'yds of the world) and a consequent noticeable rise in the general quality level. Gd producers: Adami, Biancavigna, Bisol, Bortolin, Canevel, CARPENÈ-MALVOLTI, Case Bianche, Col Salice, Le Colture, Col Vetoraz, Nino Franco, Gregoletto, La Riva dei Frati, Ruggeri, Vignarosa, Zardetto.

Prosecco Ven DOC(G) w sp ★→★★ DYA. Italy's favourite fizz. New laws, designed to protect the name, mean "Prosecco" is no longer a grape but only a wine derived from the GLERA grape grown in specified DOC/DOCG zones (IGT no longer permitted) of Ven, F-VG. May be still, SPUMANTE, FRIZZANTE. (*See also* box, above.)

Prunotto, Alfredo Pie ★★★→★★★★ Traditional ALBA company modernized by ANTINORI in 1990s, run by Piero's daughter Albiera. V.gd BARBARESCO (Bric Turot), BAROLO (Bussia), NEBBIOLO (Occhetti), BARBERA D'ALBA (Pian Romualdo), Barbera d'ASTI (Costamiole), MONFERRATO Rosso (Mompertone, Barbera/SYRAH blend).

Puglia / Apulia The 360-km heel of the Italian boot, now in wine context generally known by Italian Puglia rather than Latin Apulia. Generally gd-value, easy-drinking wines (mainly red) from various grapes like NEGROAMARO, PRIMITIVO and Uva di Troia. Most interesting wines are from SALENTO peninsula incl DOCS BRINDISI, COPERTINO, SALICE SALENTINO.

Querciabella Tus ★★★★ Top CHIANTI CLASSICO estate with IGT crus Camartina (CAB SAUV/SANGIOVESE) and barrel-fermented CHARD/PINOT BL Batàr. Purchases in Radda and MAREMMA provide more grapes for Chianti Classico and recent, as yet unconvincing, Turpino (CAB FR, SYRAH, MERLOT), respectively.

Quintarelli, Giuseppe Ven ★★★★ Arch-traditionalist, artisanal producer of sublime VALPOLICELLA, RECIOTO, AMARONE; plus fine Bianco Secco, blend of various grapes. Bepi died 2012; daughter Fiorenza and sons have taken over, altering nothing.

Rampolla, Castello dei Tus ★★★ A CAB SAUV-loving estate in Panzano in CHIANTI CLASSICO. The top wines are IGTS Sammarco and d'Alceo. International-style Chianti Classico.

Ratti, Renato ★★→★★★ Iconic BAROLO estate. Renato's son Pietro now runs the show. Modern-style wines of abbreviated maceration but plenty of substance, esp Barolos Rocche dell'Annunziata and Conca.

Recioto della Valpolicella Ven DOCG r sw (sp) ★★★→★★★★ Finally a DOCG, this most historic of all Italian wines (written testimony from sixth-century AD) is unique and potentially stunning, with sumptuous cherry-chocolate fruitiness.

Recioto di Soave Ven DOCG w sw (sp) ★★★→★★★★ SOAVE from half-dried grapes: sweet, fruity, slightly almondy; sweetness is cut by high acidity. Outstanding from Anselmi, COFFELE, Gini, PIEROPAN, Tamellini, often v.gd from Ca' Rugate, PASQUA, PRÀ, Suavia, Trabuchi. As with RECIOTO DELLA VALPOLICELLA the vintage is less important than the process.

Refosco (dal Peduncolo Rosso) F-VG ★★ 09 10 11 12 (13) Gutsy red of rustic style. Best from: COLLI ORIENTALI DOC, Moschioni, Le Vigne di Zamo, *Volpi Pasini*; gd from LIVIO FELLUGA, Miani and from Dorigo, Ronchi di Manzano, Venica, Ca' Bolani, Denis Montanara in Aquileia DOC.

Regaleali Si *See* TASCA D'ALMERITA.

Ribolla F-VG Colli Orientali del Friuli and Collio DOC w ★→★★ DYA. Characterful acidic white, the best from COLLIO. Top estates: Il Carpino, La Castellada, Damijan, Fliegl, GRAVNER, Primosic, Radikon, Tercic.

Ricasoli Tus Historic Tuscan family. 19th-century Prime Minister Bettino R. devised the classic CHIANTI blend. The main branch occupies the medieval Castello di BROLIO. Related Ricasolis own Castello di Cacchiano, Rocca di Montegrossi.

Rinaldi, Giuseppe Pie ★★★ Beppe Rinaldi is an arch-traditionalist BAROLO personality whose CANTINA on the outskirts of Barolo is not always a model of hygiene. Characterful Barolos incl crus Brunate-Le Coste and Cannubi San Lorenzo – Ravera.

Ripasso Ven *See* VALPOLICELLA RIPASSO.

Riserva Wine aged for a statutory period, usually in casks or barrels.

Rivera Pug ★★ Reliable winemakers at Andria in CASTEL DEL MONTE DOC, best example being RISERVA Il Falcone. V.gd Nero di Troia-based Puer Apuliae.

Rivetti, Giorgio (La Spinetta) Pie ★★★ Fine MOSCATO D'ASTI, excellent BARBERA, interesting IGT Pin and a series of super-concentrated, oaky BARBARESCOS. Now owner of v'yds in BAROLO, CHIANTI COLLI Pisane DOCGS, and of traditional SPUMANTE house Contratto.

Rizzi Pie ★★→★★★ Sub-area of Treiso, commune of BARBARESCO, where the Dellapiana family look after 35 ha of v'yd. Top cru is Barbaresco Pajore. Fondetta and Boito also gd, seem light but go deep.

Rocca, Bruno Pie ★★★ Admirable modern-style BARBARESCO (Rabajà) and other ALBA wines, also v. fine BARBERA D'ASTI.

Rocca Albino ★★★ A foremost producer of elegant, sophisticated BARBARESCO: top crus Vigneto Loreto and Brich Ronchi.

Roero Pie DOCG r ★★→★★★ 06 07 08 09 10 11 (13) Serious, occasionally BAROLO-level NEBBIOLOS from the LANGHE hills across river Tanaro from ALBA. Best: Almondo, Buganza, Ca' Rossa, Cascina Chicco, Correggia, Funtanin, Malvirà, Monchiero-Carbone, Morra, Pace, Pioiero, Taliano, Val di Prete. *See also* ARNEIS.

Ronco Term for a hillside v'yd in northeast Italy, esp F-VG.

Rosato The general Italian name for rosé. Other rosé wine names incl CHIARETTO from Lake GARDA; CERASUOLO from Abruzzo; Kretzer from ALTO ADIGE.

Rosso Conero Mar DOCG r ★★→★★★ 08 09 11 (12) (13) Aka plain "Conero". Some of Italy's best MONTEPULCIANO (the grape, that is). Recommended: GAROFOLI's Grosso

Agontano, Moroder's Dorico, MONTE SCHIAVO's Adeodato, TERRE CORTESI MONCARO's Nerone and Vigneti del Parco, Le Terrazze's Sassi Neri and Visions of J.

Rosso di Montalcino Tus DOC r ★★→★★★ 08 09 10 11 12 (13) DOC for earlier maturing wines from BRUNELLO grapes, usually from younger or lesser v'yd sites. Recently an attempt by a few big producers to allow "international" grapes into the blend was defeated. They'll try again.

Rosso di Montefalco Umb DOC r ★★→★★★ 07 08 09 10 11 (12) (13) SANGIOVESE/ SAGRANTINO blend, often with a splash of softening MERLOT. For producers, *see* MONTEFALCO SAGRANTINO.

Rosso di Montepulciano Tus DOC r ★★ 10 11 12 (13) Junior version of VINO NOBILE DI MONTEPULCIANO, growers similar. Seen much less than ROSSO DI MONTALCINO, probably because of confusion with MONTEPULCIANO D'ABRUZZO, with which it has nothing in common.

Rosso Piceno Mar DOC r ★ 07 08 09 10 11 (13) Gluggable MONTEPULCIANO/SANGIOVESE blend from southern half of Marches; SUPERIORE from classic zone nr Ascoli, much improved in recent yrs and v.gd value. Best: Aurora, Boccadigabbia, BUCCI, Fonte della Luna, Montecappone, MONTE SCHIAVO, Saladini Pilastri, TERRE CORTESI MONCARO, Velenosi Ercole, Villamagna.

Ruchè di Castagnole Monferrato Pie DOCG r ★★ DYA. Intense pale red of quintessentially PIE style: sour-berry fruit, sharp acid, firm tannins. Calls for a bit of practice. Gd: Pierfrancesco Gatto.

Ruffino Tus ★→★★★ The venerable CHIANTI firm of Ruffino, in hands of FOLONARI family for 100 yrs, split apart a few yrs ago. Both branches are busy acquiring new TUS estates. At last count this branch – the one that kept the name Ruffino – was up to seven, of which three are in CHIANTI CLASSICO, incl Santedame (top wine Romitorio), one in MONTALCINO (Greppone Mazzi), one in MONTEPULCIANO (Lodola Nuova). Also owns Borgo Conventi in F-VG.

Rúfina Tus ★★★ Small but important northern subregion of CHIANTI, east of Florence, hilly and cool. Best wines: Basciano, CASTELLO DI NIPOZZANO (FRESCOBALDI), Castello del Trebbio, Colognole, Frascole, Lavacchio, SELVAPIANA, TENUTA Bossi, Travignoli. Villa di Vetrice/Grati does old vintages, sometimes aged 20 yrs+ in barrels or vats.

Sala, Castello della Umb ★★→★★★ ANTINORI estate at ORVIETO. Top wine is splendid *Cervaro della Sala*, oak-aged CHARD/GRECHETTO. Bramito del Cervo is lesser but still v.gd, same grapes. Muffato della Sala was pioneer example of an Italian botrytis dessert wine.

Salento Pug Flat southern peninsula at tip of Italy's heel; seems unlikely for quality grapes, but deep soils, old ALBERELLO vines and constant sea breezes combine to produce remarkable red and rosé wines from NEGROAMARO, PRIMITIVO, with a bit of help from MONTEPULCIANO, MALVASIA Nera, local Sussumaniello. *See also* PUG, SALICE SALENTINO.

Pinot Bianco

PINOT BIANCO (PINOT BL) arguably reaches its quality zenith not in Alsace but in Italy's German-speaking ALTO ADIGE, a judgment given weight by the fact that, recently, a Pinot Bianco (Sirmian, from the co-op NALS-MARGREID) was voted Italy's best white. Here are 12 top producers of this crisp, mineral, complex yet subtle wine, all from Alto Adige. *Hors classe*: Sirmian (Nals Margreid); Vorberg (CANTINA Terlano). 5★: Eichhorn (Manincor); Helios (Kranzelhof). 4★: Klaser (Niklas); DeSilva (Peter Solva); Castel Turmhof Cuvée Anna (TIEFENBRUNNER); Haselhof (Josef Brigl); Plattenriegl (Girlan); Prunar (Erste & Neue); Schulthauser (San Michele-Appiano); Castel Juval (Unterortl).

Salice Salentino Pug DOC r ★★→★★★ 06 07 08 10 11 (13) Best-known of SALENTO's many (too many) NEGROAMARO-based DOCs, made famous by veteran firms like Leone de Castris, Candido, TAURINO, Apollonio, VALLONE. RISERVA after 2 yrs.

Salvioni Tus ★★★ Small high-quality operation of irrepressible Giulio Salvioni. BRUNELLO and ROSSO di MONTALCINO among the v. best available, worth the not-inconsiderable price.

Sandrone, Luciano Pie ★★★ Exponent of modern-style ALBA wines with deep, concentrated BAROLO Cannubi Boschis and Le Vigne. Also gd DOLCETTO, BARBERA d'Alba, NEBBIOLO d'Alba.

San Felice Tus ★★→★★★ Important historic TUS grower, owned by Gruppo Allianz. Fine CHIANTI CLASSICO and RISERVA POGGIO Rosso from estate in Castelnuovo Berardenga. Vitiarium is an experimental v'yd for obscure varieties, the excellent Pugnitello (IGT from that grape) a first result. Gd, too: IGT Vigorello (first SUPER TUSCAN, from 1968), BRUNELLO DI MONTALCINO Campogiovanni.

Gaglioppo: star Calabrian red grape. Brisk tannins, beautiful aromas. Look for it.

San Gimignano Tus Tourist-overrun TUS town famous for its towers and dry white VERNACCIA DI SAN GIMIGNANO DOCG, often overpriced, occasionally convincing as a wine if not as a *vin de terroir*. Some gd SANGIOVESE-based reds under DOC San Gimignano. Producers incl: FALCHINI, Cesani, Guicciardini Strozza, Montenidoli, Mormoraia, Il Palagione, Panizzi, Podera del Paradiso, Pietrafitta, Pietrasereno, La Rampa di Fugnano.

Sangiovese di Romagna Mar DOC r ★★→★★★ Often well-made even classy varietal red from what may be the birthplace of SANGIOVESE. Gd producers incl Cesari, Drei Donà, Paradiso, San Patrignano, Tre Monti, Trere (E-R DOC), Villa Venti (Primo Segno), ZERBINA. Seek also IGT RONCO delle Ginestre, Ronco dei Ciliegi from CASTELLUCCIO.

San Giusto a Rentennano Tus ★★★→★★★★ Top CHIANTI CLASSICO estate owned by cousins of RICASOLI. Outstanding SANGIOVESE IGT Percarlo, sublime VIN SANTO (Vin San Giusto).

San Guido, Tenuta Tus *See* SASSICAIA.

San Leonardo T-AA ★★★ Top TRENTINO estate of Marchesi Guerrieri Gonzaga, consultant Carlo Ferrini. Main wine is Bordeaux blend **San Leonardo**, "the SASSICAIA of the north". Also v. promising MERLOT Villa Gresti.

San Michele Appiano T-AA Top ALTO ADIGE co-op, esp for whites. Look for PINOT BIANCO Schulthauser and Sanct Valentin (★★★) selections: CHARD, PINOT GR, SAUV BL, CAB SAUV, PINOT N, GEWURZ.

Sannio Cam DOC r p w sp ★→★★★ (w) DYA. Wines of the Samnites of inland, upland CAM. Home of FALANGHINA, but v.gd varietals (r w) too like FIANO, GRECO and AGLIANICO.

San Patrignano E-R ★★ A drug rehab colony with 100 ha of v'yd. Winemaking is overseen by Riccardo Cotarella, tendency to international style with Bordeaux-inspired Montepirolo and Noi, though excellent SANGIOVESES too (Avi and more modest Aulente).

Santadi Sar ★★★ SAR's, and one of Italy's, best co-ops, esp for CARIGNANO-based reds Terre Brune, Grotta Rossa, Rocca Rubia (all DOC CARIGNANO DEL SULCIS). Also whites **Vermentino Villa Solais**, Villa di Chiesa (VERMENTINO/CHARD).

Santa Maddalena / St-Magdalener T-AA DOC r ★→★★ DYA. Teutonic-style red from SCHIAVA grapes from v. steep slopes behind ALTO ADIGE capital Bolzano. Gd reputation, but could (ought to be?) better. Notable producers: CS St-Magdalena (Huck am Bach), Gojer, Josephus Mayr, Hans Rottensteiner (Premstallerhof), Heinrich Rottensteiner.

Sant'Antimo Tus DOC r w sw ★★→★★★ Lovely little Romanesque abbey gives its

148

name to this catch-all DOC for (almost) everything in MONTALCINO zone that isn't BRUNELLO DOCG or ROSSO DOC.

Sardinia / Sardegna The Med's second-biggest island produces much decent and some v.gd wine, eg. Turriga from ARGIOLAS, VERMENTINO of CAPICHERA, CANNONAU RISERVAS of Jerzu and Loi, Vermentino and Cannonau from Dettori and amazing sherryish VERNACCIA from CONTINI. Best DOCS: Vermentino di Gallura (eg. Canayli from CANTINA Gallura), CARIGNANO DEL SULCIS (Terre Brune and Rocca Rubia from SANTADI).

Sassicaia Tus DOC r ★★★★ 85′ 88′ 90′ 95′ 97 98′ 99 01′ 04′ 05 06 07′ 08 09 10 (11) (12) Italy's sole single-v'yd DOC (BOLGHERI), a CAB (SAUV and FR) made on First Growth lines by Marchese Incisa della Rocchetta at TENUTA SAN GUIDO. More elegant than lush, made for age – and often bought for investment, but hugely influential in giving Italy a top-quality image.

Satta, Michele Tus ★★★ Virtually the only BOLGHERI grower to succeed with 100% SANGIOVESE (Cavaliere). Also Bolgheri DOC red blends Piastraia and SUPERIORE I Castagni.

Scavino, Paolo Pie ★★★ Modernist BAROLO producer of Castiglione Falletto, esp crus Rocche dell'Annunziata, Bric dël Fiasc, Cannubi and Carobric. Gd BARBERA LANGHE Corale.

Schiava Alto Adige T-AA DOC r ★ DYA. Traditional light red, popular in Teutonic markets, from what is still the most-grown red grape of ALTO ADIGE, locally called VERNATSCH. Other Schiava DOCs incl Lago di Caldaro, SANTA MADDALENA, Colli di Bolzano.

Schiopetto, Mario F-VG ★★★→★★★★ Legendary late COLLIO pioneer, spacious modern winery. V.gd DOC SAUV BL, *Pinot Bl*, FRIULANO, IGT blend Blanc des Rosis, etc.

Sciacchetrà Lig See CINQUE TERRE.

Sella & Mosca Sar ★★ Major SAR grower and merchant with v. pleasant white Torbato (esp Terre Bianche) and light, fruity VERMENTINO Cala Viola (DYA). Gd Alghero DOC Marchese di Villamarina (CAB SAUV) and Tanca Farrà (CANNONAU/Cab Sauv). Also interesting Port-like Anghelu Ruju.

Selvapiana Tus ★★★ With possible exception of more famous NIPOZZANO, the no I CHIANTI RÙFINA estate. Best wines: RISERVA Bucerchiale, IGT Fornace; but even *basic Chianti Rúfina is a treat*. Also fine red POMINO, Petrognano.

Settesoli, CS Si ★→★★ Co-op with some 6,000 ha, giving SI a gd name with reliable, gd-value native and international varietals (*Nero d'Avola*, SYRAH, MERLOT, CAB SAUV, CHARD, Grecanico, Grillo, VIOGNIER, blends) under various labels incl Mandrarossa.

Vineyard pests: latest is *Drosophila suzukii*, new in Veneto. Lays eggs in healthy fruit.

Sforzato / Sfursat Lom ★★★ AMARONE-like dried-grape NEBBIOLO from VALTELLINA in extreme north of Lom on Swiss border. Ages beautifully.

Sicily The Med's largest island, modern source of *exciting original wines and value*. Native grapes (r: NERO D'AVOLA, NERELLO MASCALESE, Frappato; w: INZOLIA, Catarratto, Grecanico, Grillo) as well as internationals. V'yds on flatlands in west, the hills in centre and volcanic altitudes on Mt ETNA. Gd wineries too numerous to list.

Sizzano Pie See GATTINARA.

Soave Ven DOC w (sw) ★→★★★ DYA. Famous, still underrated Veronese white. Wines from the volcanic soils of the CLASSICO zone can be intense, mineral, v. fine and quite long-lived. When labelled SUPERIORE is DOCG, but best Classico producers shun the "honour", stick to DOC. Sweet RECIOTO can be superb. Best incl CANTINA del Castello, La Cappuccina, Ca' Rugate, COFFELE, Fattori, Gini, GUERRIERI RIZZARDI, Inama, Montetondo, PIEROPAN, Portinari, PRÀ, Suavia, Tamellini, TEDESCHI.

Solaia Tus r ★★★★ 85′ 90′ 95′ 97′ 99′ 01 04 06 07 08 09 10 11 (12) Potentially

ITALY

> **Chianti Classico Gran Selezione**
> From Jan 2014 a new super CHIANTI CLASSICO has been created in
> the hopes of reviving under a more official title the ever-unofficial
> and somewhat superannuated concept of SUPER TUSCAN. The new
> category will apply to specific wines that must undergo chemical and
> organoleptic analysis, and is conceived as sitting at the top of the
> Chianti Classico quality pyramid, immediately above RISERVA and two
> places above Chianti Classico. And who are the original proponents?
> Would you believe, the usual suspects (ANTINORI, BROLIO, AMA, FONTERUTOLI,
> RUFFINO) totalling some 35 or so. Many more expected in future yrs.

magnificent if somewhat massive CAB SAUV/SANGIOVESE blend by ANTINORI, made
to the highest Bordeaux specs; needs yrs of laying down.

Sorì Pie Term for a high south-, southeast-, or southwest-oriented site in PIE.

Sovana Tus MAREMMA DOC, inland nr Etruscan town of Pitigliano. Look for CILIEGIOLO
from TENUTA Roccaccia, Pitigliano, Ripa, Sassotondo, MALBEC from ANTINORI.

Speri Ven ★★★ Quality VALPOLICELLA family estate with sites such as the outstanding
Monte Sant'Urbano. Unpretentious, traditional-style CLASSICO SUPERIORE, AMARONE,
RECIOTO. No frills, just gd wine.

Spumante Sparkling. What used to be called ASTI Spumante is now just Asti.

Südtirol T-AA The local name of German-speaking South Tyrol ALTO ADIGE.

Superiore Wine with more ageing than normal and 0.5–1% more alcohol. May
indicate a restricted production zone, eg. ROSSO PICENO Superiore.

Super Tuscan Tus Wines of high quality and price developed in the 70s/80s to
get round the silly laws then prevailing. Now increasingly irrelevant. Never was
an official designation.

Tasca d'Almerita Si ★★★ New generation of Tasca d'Almeritas runs the historic,
still prestigious estate, which kept the flag of quality flying for SI in the dark yrs.
High-altitude v'yds; balanced IGT wines under its old Regaleali label, CHARD and
CAB SAUV gd, but star, as ever, is NERO D'AVOLA-based **Rosso del Conte**.

Taurasi Cam DOCG r ★★★ 01 04 06 07 08 09 10 (11) (12) The south's answer to the
north's BAROLO and the centre's BRUNELLO, needs careful handling and long ageing.
There are friendlier versions of AGLIANICO but none so potentially complex,
demanding and ultimately rewarding. Made famous by MASTROBERARDINO, other
outstanding producers are Caggiano, Caputo, FEUDI DI SAN GREGORIO, Molettieri,
LUIGI TECCE, Terredora di Paulo.

Tedeschi, Fratelli Ven ★★ →★★★ One of the original quality growers of VALPOLICELLA
when the zone was still ruled by mediocrities. "Capitel" tends to figure in the
names of octogenarian Renzo Tedeschi's best wines: AMARONE Capitel Monte
Olmi, RECIOTO Capitel Fontana, RIPASSO Capitel San Rocco.

Tenuta An agricultural holding (*see* under name – eg. SAN GUIDO, TENUTA).

Terlano T-AA w ★★→★★★ DYA. ALTO ADIGE Terlano DOC applies to one white blend
and eight white varietals, esp PINOT BL and SAUV BL. Can be v. fresh and zesty. Best:
CS Terlano (Pinot Bl Vorberg ages remarkably), LAGEDER, Niedermayr, Niedrist.

Teroldego Rotaliano T-AA DOC r p ★★→★★★ TRENTINO's best local variety makes
seriously tasty wine on the flat Campo Rotaliano. **Foradori** is tops, also gd:
Dorigati, Endrizzi, MEZZACORONA's RISERVA Nos, Zeni.

Terre Cortesi Moncaro Mar ★★★ Marches co-op; competes with the best of the
region at v. modest prices: gd VERDICCHIO DEI CASTELLI DI JESI (Le Vele), ROSSO CONERO,
RISERVA (Nerone), ROSSO PICENO SUPERIORE (Campo delle Mura).

Terriccio, Castello del Tus ★★★ Large estate south of Livorno: excellent, v. expensive
Bordeaux-style IGT Lupicaia, v.gd IGT Tassinaia. Impressive IGT Terriccio, an
unusual blend of mainly Rhône grapes.

Tuscan coast
Recent yrs have seen a rush to plant in an area not historically noted for its fine (or indeed any) wines – the coast of TUS, ie. the provinces of Pisa, Livorno, Grosseto. First it was French grapes such as the CAB brothers, MERLOT, SYRAH, PETIT VERDOT; now Italians like SANGIOVESE, CILIEGIOLO, Alicante are in fashion. Best producers: Argentiera, Belguardo (Mazzei), CAIAROSSA, CA' MARCANDA (GAJA), CASTELLO DEL TERRICCIO, COLLE Massari, Guado al Tasso (ANTINORI), Gualdo del Re, LE MACCHIOLE, LE PUPILLE, Michele SATTA, Montepeloso, MORIS FARMS, ORNELLAIA (FRESCOBALDI), POGGIO al Tesoro (ALLEGRINI), Tenuta San Guido (SASSICAIA), TUA RITA.

Tiefenbrunner T-AA ★★→★★★ Grower-négociant in quaint Teutonic castle (Turmhof) in south ALTO ADIGE. Christof T succeeds father (winemaker since 1943), making wide range of mtn-fresh white and well-defined red varietals: French, Germanic and local, esp 1,000-metre high MÜLLER-T **Feldmarschall**, Linticlarus range CHARD/LAGREIN/PINOT N.

Tignanello Tus r ★★★★ 01' 04' 06' 07' 08 09 10 (11) (12) (13) SANGIOVESE/CAB SAUV blend, barrique-aged, the wine that put SUPER TUSCANS on the map, created by ANTINORI's great oenologist Giacomo Tachis in the early 70s.

Torcolato Ven Sweet wine from BREGANZE in Ven; Vespaiolo grapes laid on mats or hung up to dry for months, as nearby RECIOTO DI SOAVE. Best incl MACULAN and CS BEATO BARTOLOMEO.

Torgiano Umb DOC r p w (sp) ★★ and **Torgiano, Rosso Riserva** DOCG r ★★→★★★ 00' 01' 04 06 07 08 09 (10) (11) (12) Gd to excellent red from Umb, virtually an exclusivity of LUNGAROTTI. **Vigna Monticchio** Rubesco RISERVA is outstanding in vintages such as 75 79 85 97 04; keeps many yrs.

Travaglini Pie Probably the main man in the somewhat underwhelming world of northern PIE NEBBIOLO, with v.gd GATTINARA RISERVA, Gattinara Tre Vigne, and pretty gd Nebbiolo Coste della Sesia.

Trebbiano d'Abruzzo Ab DOC w ★→★★★ DYA. Generally crisp, low-flavour wine, but VALENTINI's version is widely considered one of Italy's greatest whites.

Trentino T-AA DOC r w dr sw ★→★★★ DOC for 20-odd wines, mostly varietally named. Best: CHARD, PINOT BL, MARZEMINO, TEROLDEGO. Provincial capital is Trento.

Trinoro, Tenuta di Tus ★★★ Individualist TUS red wine estate, pioneer in DOC Val d'Orcia between MONTEPULCIANO and MONTALCINO. Heavy accent on Bordeaux grapes in flagship TENUTA di Trinoro, also in Palazzi, Le Cupole and Magnacosta. Andrea Franchetti also has v'yds on Mt ETNA.

Tua Rita Tus ★★→★★★★ The first producer to est Suvereto, some 20 km down coast, as the new BOLGHERI in the 90s. Producer of possibly Italy's greatest MERLOT in Redigaffi, also outstanding Bordeaux blend **Giusto di Notri**. See VAL DI CORNIA.

Tuscany / Toscana The focal point of Italian wine's late-20th century renaissance, with experimental wines such as the SUPER TUSCANS and modernized classics, CHIANTI, VINO NOBILE, BRUNELLO.

Umani Ronchi Mar ★★→★★★ Leading Mar producer, esp for VERDICCHIO (Casal di Serra, Plenio), ROSSO CONERO Cumaro, IGTS Le Busche (w), Pelago (r).

Vajra, G D Pie ★★★ The Vajra family produce immaculate BAROLO, BARBERA, DOLCETTO, FREISA, also surprisingly gd RIES, in Barolo *frazione* of Vergne. Also now own Luigi Baudana estate in Serralunga.

Valdadige T-AA DOC r w dr s/sw ★ The name (in German: *Etschtaler*) for the simple wines of the valley of the Adige, from ALTO ADIGE through TRENTINO to northern Ven.

Val di Cornia Tus DOC r p w ★★→★★★ 04 06'07 08 09 10 11 (12) DOC south of BOLGHERI. SANGIOVESE, CAB SAUV, MERLOT, SYRAH and MONTEPULCIANO. Look out for:

ITALY

Ambrosini, Jacopo Banti, Bulichella, Gualdo del Re, Incontri, Montepeloso, Petra, Russo, San Michele, TENUTA Casa Dei, Terricciola, TUA RITA.

Valentini, Edoardo Ab ★★★→★★★★ Son Francesco continues tradition of long-macerated, non-filtered, unfined, hand-bottled MONTEPULCIANO, CERASUOLO, TREBBIANO D'ABRUZZO. Quality, availability unpredictable; potentially outstanding. *See* MONTEPULCIANO D'ABRUZZO, Trebbiano d'Abruzzo. Lost some vines in freak blizzard in Dec 2013: 50 cm snow, 160 km/hr winds.

Valle d'Aosta DOC r p w ★★ Regional DOC for some 25 Alpine wines, geographically or varietally named, incl Premetta, Fumin, Blanc de Morgex, Chambave, Nus MALVOISIE, Arnad Montjovet, Torrette, Donnas, Enfer d'Arvier. Tiny production, wines rarely seen abroad but potentially worth seeking out.

Valle Isarco T-AA DOC w ★★ DYA. ALTO ADIGE DOC for seven Germanic varietal whites made along the Isarco (Eisack) River northeast of Bolzano. Gd GEWURZ, MÜLLER-T, RIES, SILVANER. Top producers: Abbazia di Novacella, Eisacktaler, Kuenhof.

Vallone, Agricole Pug ★★→★★★ Large-scale grower on SALENTO peninsula. Excellent, gd-value BRINDISI VIGNA Flaminio (r p) and SALICE SALENTINO Vereto, both having RISERVAS. Best-known for AMARONE-like, semi-dried-grape wine Graticciaia. Vigna Castello is a classy addition to the range.

Valpolicella Ven DOC(G) r ★→★★★★ Complex denomination, incl everything from light quaffers with a certain fruity warmth through stronger SUPERIORES (which may or may not be RIPASSO) to AMARONES and RECIOTOS of ancient lineage. Bitter-cherry is the common flavour characteristic of constituent CORVINA and Corvinone (plus other) grapes. Today straight Valpol is getting hard to source, all best grapes going into trendy profitable Amarone.

Valpolicella Ripasso Ven Ven DOC r ★★→★★★ 08 09 10 11 (12) VALPOLICELLA re-fermented on RECIOTO or AMARONE grape skins to make a more age-worthy wine. Gd to excellent: BUSSOLA, CANTINA NEGRAR, Castellani, DAL FORNO, QUINTARELLI, ZENATO.

Valtellina Lom DOC/DOCG r ★→★★★ Long east-west valley (most Alpine valleys run north-south) on the Swiss border. Steep south-facing terraces have for millennia grown NEBBIOLO (here called CHIAVENNASCA) and related grapes. DOCG Valtellina SUPERIORE divides into five zones: Sassella, Grumello, Inferno, Valgella, Maroggia. Wines and scenery both worth the detour. Best today are: Fay, Mamete Prevostini, Nera, Nino Negri, Plozza, Rainoldi, Triacca. DOC Valtellina has less stringent requirements. Sforzato (Sfursat) is its AMARONE.

Vecchio Samperi Si *See* DE BARTOLI.

Vendemmia Harvest or vintage.

Venegazzù Ven ★★★→★★★★ Iconic Bordeaux blend from eastern Ven producer Loredan Gasparini. Even more prestigious is the cru Capo di Stato (created for table of Itay's president).

Valpolicella: the best

VALPOLICELLA started with the Romans on the first foothills of the Alps above the Po Valley at Verona. It has never been better than today. AMARONE DELLA VALPOLICELLA and RECIOTO DELLA VALPOLICELLA have now been elevated to DOCG status, while Valpolicella RIPASSO has at last been recognized as an historic wine in its own right. The following producers make gd to great wine: Stefano Accordini ★, Serego Alighieri ★, Begali, BERTANI, BOLLA, Boscaini, Brigaldara, BRUNELLI, BUSSOLA ★, Ca' la Bianca, Campagnola, Ca' Rugate, Castellani, Corteforte, Corte Sant'Alda, CS Valpantena, Cantina Valpolicella, Valentina Cubi, DAL FORNO ★, GUERRIERI-RIZZARDI ★, MASI, Mazzi ★, Nicolis, QUINTARELLI ★, Roccolo Grassi, Le Ragose, Le Salette, Speri ★, TEDESCHI ★, Tommasi, Venturini, VIVIANI ★, ZENATO, Zeni.

Verdicchio dei Castelli di Jesi Mar DOC w (sp) ★★ →★★★ DYA. Versatile white from nr Ancona, can be light and quaffable, or sparkling, or structured, complex, long-lived (esp RISERVA DOCG, min 2 yrs old). Also CLASSICO. Best from: Accadia, Bonci-Vallerosa, Brunori, BUCCI, Casalfarneto, Cimarelli, Colonnara, Coroncino, Fazi-Battaglia, Fonte della Luna, GAROFOLI, Laila, Lucangeli Aymerich di Laconi, Mancinelli, Montecappone, MONTE SCHIAVO, Santa Barbara, SARTARELLI, TERRE CORTESI Moncaro, UMANI RONCHI.

Verdicchio di Matelica Mar DOC w (sp) ★★ →★★★ DYA. Similar to above, smaller, more inland, higher, therefore more acidic, therefore longer-lasting though less easy-drinking in youth. RISERVA is likewise DOCG. Esp Barone Pizzini, Belisario, Bisci, LA MONACESCA, Pagliano Tre, San Biagio.

Verduno, Castello di Pie ★★★ Husband-and-wife team Franco Bianco with v'yds in Neive, and Gabriella Burlotto with v'yds in VERDUNO, make v.gd BARBARESCO Rabaja and BAROLO Monvigliero with winemaker Mario Andrion.

Verduzzo F-VG DOC (Colli Orientali del Friuli) w dr sw s/sw ★★ →★★★ Full-bodied white from local variety. Ramandolo (DOCG) is well-regarded subzone for sweet wine. Top: Dario Coos, Dorigo, Giovanni Dri, Meroi. Also gd: LIS NERIS sweet IGT Tal Luc.

Vermentino di Gallura Sar DOCG w ★★ →★★★ DYA. *Best dry white of Sar*, from the northeast of the island, stronger and more intensely flavoured than VERMENTINO DI SARDEGNA. Esp from CAPICHERA, CS di Gallura, CS del Vermentino, Depperu.

Vermentino di Sardegna Lig DOC w ★★ DYA. One of Italy's most characterful whites, whether made light/dry or *robust*, grown throughout western LIG, increasingly along TUS coast and spreading inland to Umb. In SAR, grown island-wide. Gd producers: SANTADI, SELLA & MOSCA.

Vernaccia di Oristano Sar DOC w dr ★ →★★★ Vintage less important than process. SAR *flor*-affected wine, similar to light Sherry, a touch bitter, full-bodied. SUPERIORE 15.5% alcohol, 3 yrs of age. Delicious with *bottarga* (compressed fish roe), kill to try it. Top: CONTINI.

Vernaccia di San Gimignano Tus *See* SAN GIMIGNANO.

Vesuvio *See* LACRYMA CHRISTI.

Vie di Romans F-VG ★★★ →★★★★ Gianfranco Gallo has built up his father's ISONZO estate to top F-VG status. Excellent ISONZO CHARD, PINOT GR Dessimis, SAUV BL Piere and Vieris (oaked), MALVASIA/RIES/FRIULANO blend called Flors di Uis.

Vietti Pie ★★★ Veteran grower of characterful PIE wines at Castiglione Falletto, incl BARBARESCO Masseria, BARBERA D'ALBA Scarrone, Barbera d'ASTI la Crena. Mainly *textbook Barolos*: Lazzarito, Rocche, Brunate, Villero.

Vignalta Ven ★★ Top producer in COLLI EUGANEI, nr Padua (Ven); v.gd Colli Euganei CAB SAUV RISERVA, MERLOT/Cab Sauv blend Gemola.

Vignamaggio Tus ★★ →★★★ Historic, beautiful and v.gd CHIANTI CLASSICO estate, nr Greve. Leonardo da Vinci is said to have painted the Mona Lisa here. RISERVA is called – you guessed it – Castello di Monna Lisa.

Vigna (or vigneto) A single v'yd, generally indicating superior quality.

Vinitaly

Italy's biggest and most prestigious wine fair takes place every year over four days in April in the elegant city of Verona, strategically placed between east and west, north and south. Thousands of Italian and other wine producers exhibit their vinous wares over an area of several ha, and it can take up to an hour to struggle through the crowds from one end to the other. But it's worth it for Italian wine-lovers – most top producers attend and one can taste (almost) everything one's heart desires. A must for professionals and amateurs alike.

ITALY

A motley cru
The concept of "cru" has long been honoured in France, particularly in Burgundy. No one would dare suggest that Clos de Vougeot, eg., should be more than doubled in size to accommodate the whim of a single producer. Yet that is precisely what has happened in BAROLO, where Rome's high administrative court, the Consiglio di Stato, has confirmed a judgment to increase Cannubi's size from 15 to over 30 ha on the application of a single producer, MARCHESI DI BAROLO. Other growers are furious. "The decision is wrong," said one. "It casts doubt on the credibility of all the v'yd boundaries now used in Barolo."

Villa Matilde Cam ★★★ Top CAM producer of FALERNO Rosso (Vigna Camarato), Bianco (Caracci), PASSITO Eleusi.

Villa Russiz Lom ★★★ Historic estate for DOC COLLIO. V.gd SAUV BL and MERLOT (esp "de la Tour" selections), PINOT BL, PINOT GR, FRIULANO, CHARD.

Vino Nobile di Montepulciano Tus DOCG r ★★→★★★ 04 06' 07 08 09 10 (11) (12) Historic SANGIOVESE (here called Prugnolo Gentile) from the TUS town (as distinct from Abruzzo's grape) MONTEPULCIANO, often tough with drying tannins, but complex and long-lasting from best producers: AVIGNONESI, Bindella, BOSCARELLI, La Braccesca, La Calonica, Canneto, Le Casalte, CONTUCCI, DEI, Fattoria del Cerro, Gracciano della Seta, Gracciano Svetoni, Icario, Nottola, Palazzo Vecchio, POLIZIANO, Romeo, Salcheto, Trerose, Valdipiatta, Villa Sant'Anna. RISERVA after 3 yrs.

Vin Santo / Vinsanto / Vin(o) Santo T-AA, Tus DOC w sw s/sw ★★ →★★★★ Sweet wine made from PASSITO grapes, usually TREBBIANO, MALVASIA and/or SANGIOVESE in TUS ("Vin Santo"), Nosiola in TRENTINO ("Vino Santo"). Tus versions extremely variable, anything from off-dry and Sherry-like to sweet and v. rich. May spend 3-10 unracked yrs in small barrels called *caratelli*. AVIGNONESI's is legendary; plus CAPEZZANA, Corzano & Paterno, Fattoria del Cerro, FELSINA, Frascole, ISOLE E OLENA, Rocca di Montegrossi, San Gervasio, SAN GIUSTO A RENTENNANO, SELVAPIANA, Villa Sant'Anna, Villa di Vetrice. *See also* OCCHIO DI PERNICE.

Vivaldi-Arunda T-AA ★★→★★★ Top ALTO ADIGE sparkling wines. Best: Extra Brut RISERVA, Cuvée Marianna.

Viviani Ven ★★★ Claudio Viviani shows how modern a wine VALPOLICELLA and AMARONE can be. V.gd CLASSICO SUPERIORE Campo Morar, better RECIOTO La Mandrella, outstanding Amarone Casa dei Bepi, Tulipano Nero.

Voerzio, Roberto Pie ★★★ →★★★★ BAROLO modernist. Top, v. expensive, single-v'yd Barolos: Brunate, Cerequio, Rocche dell'Annunziata-Torriglione, Sarmassa, Serra; impressive BARBERA D'ALBA.

Volpaia, Castello di Tus ★★→★★★ V.gd CHIANTI CLASSICO estate at Radda. SUPER TUSCANS Coltassala (SANGIOVESE/Mammolo), Balifico (Sangiovese/CAB SAUV).

Zenato Ven ★★ V. reliable, sometimes inspired for GARDA wines, also VALPOLICELLA, SOAVE, AMARONE, LUGANA.

Zerbina, Fattoria E-R ★★★ Leader in Romagna; best sweet ALBANA DOCG (Scacco Matto), v.gd SANGIOVESE (Pietramora); barrique-aged IGT Marzieno.

Zibibbo Si ★★ dr sw Alluring SI table wine from the MUSCAT d'Alessandria grape, most associated with PANTELLERIA and extreme western Si. Dry version well exemplified by Ottoventi of Trapani, DE BARTOLI.

Zonin ★→★★ One of Italy's biggest private-estate owners, based at Gambellara in Ven, but also big in F-VG, TUS, PUG, SI and Barboursville, Virginia, USA.

Zuani Lom ★★★ Small COLLIO estate of Patrizia Felluga, daughter of MARCO FELLUGA. Superior white blend Zuani RISERVA (oaked), Zuani Vigne (unoaked).

Germany

Abbreviations used in the text:

Bad	Baden
Frank	Franken
M-M	Mittelmosel
M Rh	Mittelrhein
Mos	Mosel
Na	Nahe
Pfz	Pfalz
Rhg	Rheingau
Rhh	Rheinhessen
Sa-Un	Saale-Unstrut
Sachs	Sachsen
Würt	Württemberg

More heavily shaded areas are the wine-growing regions.

Vintages from 1988 onwards, or at least from 1997, have been one long victory march for German wine. In that time there has been no vintage of the catastrophic sort that was common in the 1960s and 70s. Climate change has been good news for German growers, and there is reason to believe it will still be. But 2013 with its late spring and difficult harvest is a reminder that climate conditions in most parts of Germany are marginal for the grapevine. This is good. Great things can only happen where there is a risk of failure. Great wines can only be produced where conditions are challenging, and even then only in small quantities, and under the scrupulous supervision of experienced, intelligent wine-growers. These growers will in future be confronted with new questions:

how can they maintain the identity of their wines? How much organic or biodynamic viticulture can they afford, and how much do they need to maintain typicality? As climates and markets change, how rigorously should they stick to tradition? German wine at the moment reflects all these questions. Nobody should take German wine for granted, even though it's better than it's ever been. But if German wine has left you behind, it could be time to start catching up.

And as always, start with the producer and the vineyard. Don't be put off by the strings of initials and bureaucratic flim-flam. If they want to put foreigners off, they're doing well.

Recent vintages

Mosel

Mosels (including Saar and Ruwer wines) are so attractive young that their keeping qualities are not often enough explored. But well-made Kabinetts gain from at least 5 years in bottle and often much more: Spätlese from 5–20, and Auslese and Beerenauslese anything from 10–30 years. As a rule, in poor years the Saar and Ruwer make sharp, lean wines, but in good years, which are increasingly common, they surpass the whole world for elegance and thrilling, steely "breeding".

2013 An exceptionally long winter delayed vintage from the beginning, and after a decent summer, autumn drowned all hopes in rain. Top growers have only half a crop. Entry-level wines look okay, but top wines are rare. Middle Mosel better than Saar and Ruwer.

2012 Classic wines mostly from QbA to Auslese. Low quantity.

2011 A brilliant vintage, particularly successful in the Saar and Ruwer, with sensational TBAs.

2010 High acidity is the identifying feature of this vintage, some good Spätlesen and Auslesen.

2009 Plenty of magnificent Spätlesen and Auslesen with perfect acidity, and balanced dry wines. Keep the best in the cellar.

2008 Not a vintage for Auslesen, but Kabinetts and Spätlesen can be fine and elegant. Drink or keep.

2007 Good quality and good quantity too. Now increasingly mature.

2006 Lots of botrytis, not only noble; drink.

2005 Very high ripeness, but with far better acidity than, say, 2003. Exceptional, especially in the Saar. Drink or keep.

2004 A fine year to drink.

2003 A vintage of heat; considerable variation in quality. Best wines may turn out to be as good as the 1959s.

2002 Succulent, lively Kabinett and Spätlese wines, now ready to drink.

2001 The best Mosel Ries since 1990. Saar and Ruwer less exciting but still perfect balance. Lots of Spätlesen and Auslesen to drink or keep.

1999 Excellent in Saar and Ruwer, lots of Auslesen; generally only good in the Mosel. Best can age further.

Fine older vintages: 97 95 94 93 90 89 88 76 71 69 64 59 53 49 45 37 34 21.

Rheinhessen, Nahe, Pfalz, Rheingau, Ahr

Apart from Mosel, Rheingau wines tend to be longest-lived of all German regions, improving for 15 years or more, but best wines from Rheinhessen, the Nahe and Pfalz can last as long. Modern-style dry wines such as *Grosses Gewächs* are generally intended for drinking within 2 to 4 years, but the best undoubtedly have the potential to age interestingly. The same holds for Ahr Valley reds: their fruit makes them attractive young, but best wines can develop for 10 years and longer.

2013 Difficult year, much variation; best in south Rheinhessen, Franconia and the Ahr Valley. Generally low yields.

2012 Quantities below average, but very good wines, classical at every level.

2011 The wines are fruity, with harmonious acidity.

2010 Uneven quality, dry wines should be drunk now.

2009 Excellent wines, especially dry. Some acidification was needed.

2008 Uneven quality. Late-harvest wines are good, particularly in the Rheingau.

2007 Dry wines are maturing faster than expected. Drink.

2006 Lots of botrytis, top estates managed fair middle-weight wines. Drink now.

2005 High ripeness levels, with excellent acidity and extract. A superb year. Drink or keep.

2004 Ripe, healthy grapes throughout the Rhine. A big crop; some dilution, though not at top estates.

2003 Rich wines; many lack acidity. Reds fared well, if alcohol levels were under control. Drink.

2002 Few challenge the best of 2001, but very good for both classic Kabinett/ Spätlese and for dry. Excellent Pinot N. Drink.

2001 More erratic than in the Mosel, but an exciting vintage for both dry and classic styles; excellent balance. Drink or keep.

1999 Quality was average where yields were high, but for top growers this was an excellent vintage of rich, aromatic wines with lots of charm, to drink soon.

Fine older vintages: 98 97 96 93 90 83 76 71 69 67 64 59 53 49 45 37 34 21.

German vintage notation

The vintage notes after entries in the German section are given in a different form from those elsewhere in the book. Two styles of vintage are indicated:

Bold type (eg. 09) indicates classic, ripe vintages with a high proportion of SPÄTLESEN and AUSLESEN; or, in the case of red wines, gd phenolic ripeness and must weights.

Normal type (eg. 09) indicates a successful but not outstanding vintage. German white wines, esp RIES, have high acidity and keep well, and they display pure-fruit qualities because they are unoaked. Thus they can be drunk young for their intense fruitiness, or kept for a decade or two to develop more aromatic subtlety and finesse. This means there is no one ideal moment to drink them – which is why no vintages are specifically recommended for drinking now.

Achkarren Bad ★★→★★★ Village on the KAISERSTUHL; opulent GRAUBURGUNDER and powerful SPÄTBURGUNDER from black volcanic soils (GROSSE LAGE v'yd Schlossberg). Best: DR. HEGER, Michel, SCHWARZER ADLER, St Remigius, and co-op.

Adelmann, Weingut Graf Würt ★★→★★★ Young count Felix Adelmann is now in charge at idyllic Schaubeck castle in WÜRT. Subtle red blends and RIES (GROSSE LAGE Süßmund).

Ahr r ★★→★★★★ 97 99 02 05 09 11 12 13 South of Bonn. Mineral, fruit-driven (and nowadays v. powerful) SPÄTBURGUNDER, FRÜHBURGUNDER from slate soils. Best producers: Adeneuer, Deutzerhof, Heiner-Kreuzberg, KREUZBERG, MEYER-NÄKEL, Nelles, Paul Schumacher, STODDEN, co-op Mayschoss-Altenahr.

Aldinger, Gerhard Würt ★★★ One of WÜRT's leading estates: dense LEMBERGER, SPÄTBURGUNDER, complex SAUV BL. Gd RIES too.

Alte Reben Old vines. Increasingly common designation on German labels, and an obvious analogy to the French term *vieilles vignes*. The analogy is perfect – no min age.

Amtliche Prüfungsnummer (APNr) Official test number, on every label of a quality wine. Useful for discerning different lots of AUSLESE a producer has made from the same v'yd.

Wines from 2003, originally considered problematic (that heat!), now at their best.

Assmannshausen Rhg r ★★→★★★★ 93 97 99 01 02 05 08 09 10 11 12 (13) Craggy RHG village known for its cassis-scented, *age-worthy Spätburgunders* from slate soils. GROSSE LAGE v'yd: Höllenberg. Growers: BISCHÖFLICHES WEINGUT RÜDESHEIM, Chat Sauvage, KESSELER, König, Mumm, KRONE and the state domain.

Auslese Wines from selective harvest of super-ripe bunches, in many yrs affected by noble rot (*Edelfäule*) and correspondingly unctuous in flavour. Dry Auslesen are often too alcoholic and clumsy for me.

Ayl Mos ★→★★★ All Ayl v'yds are known since 1971 by the name of the region's historically best site: Kupp. Such are German wine laws. Growers: BISCHÖFLICHE WEINGÜTER TRIER, *Lauer*, Vols.

Bacharach M Rh ★→★★★ 01 02 04 05 08 09 10 11 12 (13) Small, idyllic town with timbered houses, the centre of M RH RIES. Classified GROSSE LAGE: Hahn, Posten, Wolfshöhle. Growers incl Bastian, JOST, KAUER, RATZENBERGER.

Baden r w 90 97 05 08 09 10 11 12 (13) Huge sw region, 15,000 ha, best-known for the PINOTS (both r w), and pockets of RIES, usually dry. Many co-ops. Best areas: KAISERSTUHL, ORTENAU.

Bassermann-Jordan Pfz ★★★ MITTELHAARDT estate with 49 ha of outstanding v'yds in DEIDESHEIM, FORST, RUPPERTSBERG, etc. Majestic dry RIES and lavish sweet wines too.

Becker, Friedrich Pfz ★★★ Outstanding SPÄTBURGUNDER from the southernmost part of the PFALZ; some v'yds actually lie across the border in Alsace. Increasingly gd whites (RIES, PINOT GR) too.

Becker, J B Rhg ★★→★★★ 90 92 94 97 01 02 05 08 09 10 11 12 The best estate at WALLUF, now organic, known for delightfully old-fashioned, cask-aged (and long-lived) dry RIES, SPÄTBURGUNDER. Mature vintages back to the 90s.

Beerenauslese (BA) Luscious sweet wine from exceptionally ripe, individually selected berries concentrated by noble rot. Rare, expensive.

Bercher Bad ★★★ Family estate, 25 ha, at Burkheim, specialist in barrique-aged Pinot varieties from GROSSE LAGE Feuerberg. Recent emphasis on ageing in big traditional casks, eg. excellent Jechtinger Eichert PINOT N.

Bergdolt Pfz ★★★ South of Neustadt in the PFALZ, this 24-ha estate produces v. fine WEISSBURGUNDER (from Mandelberg v'yd), gd RIES and SPÄTBURGUNDER.

Bernkastel M-M ★→★★★★ 90 94 96 97 01 02 03 05 07 08 09 10 11 12 Senior wine town of the M-M, known for its perfectly round and fruity style. GROSSE LAGE: Doctor, Lay. Top growers: Kerpen, LOOSEN, Pauly-Bergweiler, PRÜM, Studert-Prüm, THANISCH (both estates), WEGELER. Any Bernkastel (Bereich), sold under the "Kurfürstlay" GROSSLAGE name is a deception: avoid.

Bischöfliches Weingut Rüdesheim Rhg ★★★ Small but noteworthy church domain based at Hildegard von Bingen's historical monastery in Eibingen, 8 ha of best sites in RÜDESHEIM, ASSMANNSHAUSEN, JOHANNISBERG. Peter Perabo, former cellarmaster of KRONE estate, is a *Pinot N specialist*, but RIES is also v.gd.

Bischöfliche Weingüter Trier Mos ★★ 130 ha of top v'yds, uniting Trier cathedral's

New EU terminology
Germany's part in the new EU classification involves, firstly, abolishing the term *Tafelwein* in favour of plain *Wein* and secondly changing LANDWEIN to *geschützte geographische Angabe* (ggA), or Protected Geographical Indication. QUALITÄTSWEIN and QUALITÄTSWEIN MIT PRÄDIKAT will be replaced by *geschützte Ursprungsbezeichnung* (gU), or Protected Designation of Origin. The existing terms – SPÄTLESE, AUSLESE and so on (*see* box, p.163) – will be tacked on to gU where appropriate; the rules for these styles won't change.

v'yds with those of three other charities. A long time underperforming; now turning round?

Blanc de noir(s) Increasingly popular still wine – white or pale pink – from red grapes (mostly SPÄTBURGUNDER, TROLLINGER, or SCHWARZRIESLING). Often technical in style, and best drunk v. cold.

Bocksbeutel Inconvenient flask-shaped bottle used in FRANK and north BAD.

Bodensee Bad Idyllic district of south BAD, on Lake Constance. Dry RIES-like MÜLLER-T a speciality, and light but delicate SPÄTBURGUNDER. Top villages: Meersburg, Hagnau. Lovely holiday wines.

Boppard M Rh ★→★★★ The wine town of M RH with GROSSE LAGE Hamm – an amphitheatre of vines. Growers: Lorenz, M Müller, Perll, WEINGART. Unbeatable ***value*** for money.

Brauneberg M-M ★★★→★★★★ **59 71 83 90 93** 94 **95 96 97 99** 01 **02** 04 **05 06** 07 **08 09** 10 11 12 (13) Top village nr BERNKASTEL; excellent full-flavoured RIES of great raciness. GROSSE LAGE v'yds Juffer, Juffer-Sonnenuhr. Growers: F HAAG, W HAAG, KESSELSTATT, Paulinshof, RICHTER, SCHLOSS LIESER, THANISCH.

Breuer Rhg ★★★→★★★★ Family estate in RÜDESHEIM and RAUENTHAL, known for distinctly dry RIES, SEKT, SPÄTBURGUNDER. Theresa Breuer follows in her father's footsteps and maintains a classical style. Gelber Orleans, from an old local vine rediscovered in the 1990s, is a white rarity.

Buhl, Reichsrat von Pfz ★★★ Historic PFALZ estate in DEIDESHEIM, FORST, RUPPERTSBERG, owned by the Niederberger family (also BASSERMANN-JORDAN, DR. DEINHARD, VON WINNING). Since 2013 led by ex-Bollinger (*see* France) cellarmaster Mathieu Kauffmann. Obviously, promising SEKT to come.

Bürgerspital zum Heiligen Geist Frank ★★→★★★ Ancient charitable estate. Traditionally made whites (***Silvaner***, RIES) from best sites in and around WÜRZBURG. Recently, particular emphasis on Ries, with complex GROSSES GEWÄCHS Stein Hagemann at the top. Monopoly Stein-Harfe.

Bürklin-Wolf, Dr. Pfz ★★→★★★★ Historic PFALZ estate, bio farming brings about age-worthy, characterful dry and off-dry RIES from best GROSSE LAGE and ERSTE LAGE sites in the MITTELHAARDT district.

Busch, Clemens Mos ★★→★★★ Bio family estate. Clemens Busch and son Florian make powerful dry and elegant sweet RIES from steep Pündericher Marienburg, Lower MOS. Best wines named for parcels with different slate soils: Fahrlay, Falkenlay, Rothenpfad, Raffes.

Castell'sches Fürstliches Domänenamt Frank ★→★★★ Historic princely estate. SILVANER, RIES, SPÄTBURGUNDER from superb monopoly v'yd ***Casteller Schlossberg*** (a GROSSE LAGE) are traditionally crafted.

Christmann Pfz ★★★ Bio estate in Gimmeldingen making rich, ***dry Ries*** and SPÄTBURGUNDER, notably from GROSSE Lage Königsbacher Idig. Steffen Christmann is president of the VDP.

Clüsserath, Ansgar Mos ★★★ Young Eva Clüsserath (married to Philipp WITTMANN) crafts mineral RIES from TRITTENHEIMER Apotheke. KABINETTS (eg. 2012) are delicious, crystalline.

Crusius, Dr. Na ★★→★★★ Family estate at TRAISEN, NAHE. Vivid and age-worthy RIES from sun-baked Bastei and Rotenfels of Traisen and SCHLOSSBÖCKELHEIM.

Deidesheim Pfz ★★→★★★★ 90 97 01 02 04 05 08 09 10 11 12 (13) Central MITTELHAART wine village. Richly flavoured, lively wines from privileged v'yds: Grainhübel, Hohenmorgen, Kalkofen, Kieselberg, Langenmorgen. Top growers: BASSERMANN-JORDAN, Biffar, BUHL, BÜRKLIN-WOLF, CHRISTMANN, DEINHARD, MOSBACHER, VON WINNING.

Deinhard, Dr. Pfz ★★★ Since 2008, a brand of the new VON WINNING estate, but continuing to produce PFALZ RIES of classical style.

Diel, Schlossgut Na ★★★→★★★★ Exquisite *v'yd-designated Ries* (eg. Goldloch and Pittermännchen of Dorsheim). Also serious SEKT, and remarkable SPÄTBURGUNDER. Caroline Diel more and more replacing her father, Armin.

Dönnhoff Na ★★★★ 90 94 96 97 99 01 02 03 04 05 07 08 09 10 11 12 Leading NAHE estate of admirable consistency. Helmut Dönnhoff specializes in restoring abandoned v'yds, and simple natural winemaking, assisted by son Cornelius. Wines are dry RIES from Bad Kreuznach (full-bodied) and Roxheim (mineral, elegant), outstanding GROSSES GEWÄCHS from NIEDERHAUSEN (Hermannshöhle), **Norheim (Dellchen)**; SCHLOSSBÖCKELHEIM (Felsenberg); dazzling EISWEIN from Oberhauser Brücke v'yd.

Durbach Bad ★★→★★★ 08 09 11 12 (13) ORTENAU village for full-bodied RIES, locally called Klingelberger, from granite soils in steep Plauelrain v'yd. Top growers: Graf Metternich, LAIBLE, H Männle, Schloss Staufenberg.

Egon Müller zu Scharzhof Mos ★★★★ 59 71 76 83 85 88 89 90 93 94 95 96 97 98 99 01 02 03 04 05 06 07 08 09 10 11 12 (13) Legendary SAAR estate at WILTINGEN. Its racy SCHARZHOFBERGER RIES is among the world's greatest wines: sublime, vibrant, immortal. *Kabinetts* featherlight but keep 10 yrs+, SPÄTLESEN miraculously rich and slender at the same time. Watch out for the 2012s: yield a mere 16 hl/ha, but (according to Egon's father's diaries) 1953 (superb yr) showed many similarities.

The 2013 vintage is a a *neidisch* (envious) vintage – one grower has poor wines, his neighbour great ones.

Einzellage Individual v'yd site. Never to be confused with GROSSLAGE.

Eiswein Made from frozen grapes with the ice (ie. water content) discarded, thus v. concentrated – of BA ripeness or more. Alcohol content can be as low as 5.5%. Outstanding Eiswein vintages: 1998, 2002, 2004, 2008.

Ellwanger Würt ★★→★★★ Jürgen Ellwanger pioneered oak-aged reds in WÜRT; his sons Jörg and Felix turn out sappy but structured LEMBERGER, SPÄTBURGUNDER and ZWEIGELT.

Emrich-Schönleber Na ★★★→★★★★ One of Germany's most reliable producers, known for precise RIES from Monzingen's classified Halenberg and Frühlingsplätzchen. Dry and sweet equally outstanding.

Erden M-M ★★★ 90 97 01 03 05 08 09 10 11 12 (13) Village adjoining ÜRZIG: noble, full-flavoured wine, often with herbal scent. Classified as GROSSE LAGE: Prälat, Treppchen. Growers: Bremer Ratskeller, J J Christoffel, LOOSEN, Mönchhof, Schmitges, WEINS-PRÜM.

Erste Lage Classified v'yd, second from top level, according to the VDP. (Not all growers belong to the VDP, though the best usually do.) At present ambiguous: for vintages before 2012: v'yd site of exceptional quality, marked with a grape logo with a "1" next to it. Starting with 2012, most of the former *Erste Lage* v'yds are renamed GROSSE LAGE (logo: grape with "GG"), while *Erste Lage* defines a new category between the ORTSWEIN level and *Grosse Lage*, similar to Burgundy's *premier cru*. However, AHR, M RH, MOS, NA and RHH will completely give up the *Erste Lage* designation; all classified v'yds will be named *Grosse Lage*. I'll test you on this later.

Erstes Gewächs Rhg "First growth". Only for RHG v'yds, but VDP-members there change to the GROSSES GEWÄCHS designation after 2012.

Erzeugerabfüllung Bottled by producer. Incl the guarantee that only own grapes have been processed. May be used by co-ops also. GUTSABFÜLLUNG is stricter, applies only to estates.

Escherndorf Frank ★★ →★★★★ 97 01 04 05 07 08 09 10 11 12 13 Village with steep GROSSE LAGE Lump ("small piece of cloth"). The name alludes to the fact that the v'yd is split into tiny parcels – owing to the laws of inheritance. SILVANER and RIES, dry and sweet. Growers: Fröhlich, H SAUER, R SAUER, Schäffer.

Feinherb Imprecisely defined traditional term for wines with around 10–20 g of sugar/litre, not necessarily tasting sweet. Favoured by some as a more flexible alternative to HALBTROCKEN. I often choose Feinherbs.

Forst Pfz ★★ →★★★★ 90 97 01 05 08 09 10 11 12 (13) An outstanding MITTELHAARDT village. Ripe, richly fragrant and full-bodied but subtle wines. GROSSE LAGE v'yds incl Jesuitengarten, Kirchenstück, Freundstück, Pechstein, Ungeheuer. Top growers: Acham-Magin, BASSERMANN-JORDAN, VON BUHL, BÜRKLIN-WOLF, DR. DEINHARD/ VON WINNING, MOSBACHER, WOLF.

Franken 90 97 01 04 05 07 08 09 10 11 12 13 (Franconia) Region of distinctive dry wines, esp *Silvaner*, mostly bottled in round-bellied flasks (BOCKSBEUTEL). The centre is WÜRZBURG, top villages: Bürgstadt, Klingenberg, RANDERSACKER, IPHOFEN, ESCHERNDORF, Volkach.

Franzen Mos ★★→★★★ From Europe's steepest v'yd, Bremmer Calmont, and nearby Neefer Frauenberg, young Kilian Franzen produces dense, mineral RIES, mostly dry. Crisp 2012 Quarzit-Schiefer dry is excellent value for money.

Fuder Traditional German cask with sizes from 500–1,500 litres, depending on the region, traditionally used for fermentation and (formerly long) ageing.

Fürst, Weingut Frank ★★★→★★★★ 97 99 01 02 05 08 09 10 11 12 13 A family estate in Bürgstadt with v'yds there and on steep terraces of Klingenberg. Outstanding quality; with long-lived *Spätburgunder (among Germany's best)*, dense FRÜHBURGUNDER, classical SILVANER, oak-aged WEISSBURGUNDER, pure CHARD and dry RIES of distinction and to age. Paul Fürst's son Sebastian brings Burgundy experience.

Beware *Bereich* and *Grosslage* – but hurrah for *Grosse Lage*

Bereich means district within an *Anbaugebiet* (region). *Bereich* on a label should be treated as a flashing red light; the wine is a blend from arbitrary sites within that district. Do not buy. The same holds for wines with a GROSSLAGE name, though these are more difficult to identify. Who could guess if "Forster Mariengarten" is an EINZELLAGE or a *Grosslage*? But now, starting with the 2012 vintage, it's getting even more tricky. You must by no means confuse *Grosslage* with GROSSE LAGE: The latter designation refers to the best single v'yds, Germany's *grands crus* according to the classification set up by wine-grower's association VDP.

Gallais, Le Mos Second estate of EGON MÜLLER ZU SCHARZHOF with 4-ha-monopoly Braune Kupp of WILTINGEN. Soil is schist with more clay than in SCHARZHOFBERG; AUSLESEN (eg. Gold Cap 2009) can be exceptional.

Geisenheim RHG town without first-class v'yds, but home of Germany's most important university of oenology and viticulture.

Graach M-M ★★★→★★★★ 90 93 94 95 96 97 99 01 04 05 07 08 09 10 11 12 (13) Small village between BERNKASTEL and WEHLEN. GROSSE LAGE v'yds: Domprobst, Himmelreich, Josephshof. Top growers: Kees-Kieren, von KESSELSTATT, LOOSEN, M MOLITOR, J J Prüm, S A PRÜM, SCHAEFER, Selbach-Oster, Studert-Prüm, WEGELER, Weins-Prüm. Threatened by planned new Autobahn.

Grans-Fassian Mos ★★★ Fine MOS estate, known for steely, age-worthy RIES from v'yds in TRITTENHEIM, PIESPORT, Leiwen, Drohn. EISWEIN a speciality.

Groebe Rhh Family company in Westhofen: expressive RIES with a sense of place.

Grosse Lage The top level of the VDP's new classification, but only applies to VDP members. *NB* Not on any account to be confused with GROSSLAGE. Meant to replace ERSTE LAGE for v. best v'yd sites. The dry wine from a *Grosse Lage* site is called GROSSES GEWÄCHS.

Germany's main grapes are Riesling (22,800 ha), Müller-Thurgau (13,100 ha) and Spätburgunder (11,700 ha).

Grosser Ring Mos Group of top (VDP) MOS estates, whose annual Sept auction at Trier sets world-record prices.

Grosses Gewächs "Great/top growth". This is the top dry wine from a VDP-classified ERSTE LAGE (until 2012), or GROSSE LAGE (since 2012). *See also* ERSTES GEWÄCHS.

Grosslage A collection of secondary v'yds with supposedly similar character – but no indication of quality. Not on any account to be confused with GROSSE LAGE.

Gunderloch Rhh ★★★→★★★★ 90 97 01 05 07 08 09 10 11 12 (13) Nackenheim estate where Johannes Hasselbach (cellarmaster) and father Fritz (boss), make some of the finest RIES on the Rhine, esp AUSLESE and above. Elegant, fruity Kabinett Jean Baptiste is perfect with spicy food. Best v'yds: Rothenberg, Pettenthal.

Gut Hermannsberg Na ★★→★★★ Former state domain at NIEDERHAUSEN, privatized and reborn in 2010. Powerful RIES from GROSSE LAGE v'yds in NIEDERHAUSEN, SCHLOSSBÖCKELHEIM, TRAISEN.

Gutsabfüllung Estate-bottled, and made from own grapes.

Haag, Fritz Mos ★★★★ 90 94 95 96 97 99 01 02 04 05 07 08 09 10 11 12 (13) BRAUNEBERG's top estate, of impeccable reliability; Oliver Haag continues the work of father Wilhelm in a slightly more modern style. *See* also SCHLOSS LIESER.

Haag, Willi Mos ★★→★★★ BRAUNEBERG family estate, led by Marcus Haag. Old-style RIES, mainly sweet, rich but balanced, and inexpensive. Gd 2012 Juffer AUSLESE.

Haart, Julian Mos ★★→★★★ Talented nephew of Theo Haart (REINHOLD HAART). First vintage 2010, v'yds in Wintrich and PIESPORT. An estate to watch.

Haart, Reinhold M-M ★★★→★★★★ Best estate in PIESPORT. Aromatic, mild RIES, SPÄTLESEN, AUSLESEN and higher PRÄDIKAT wines are *racy, copybook Mosel Ries* – with great ageing potential.

Halbtrocken Medium-dry with 9–18g of unfermented sugar per litre, inconsistently distinguished from FEINHERB (which sounds better).

Hattenheim Rhg ★★→★★★★★ 97 01 05 08 09 11 12 Town famous for GROSSE LAGEN STEINBERG, Nussbrunnen, Wisselbrunnen. Estates incl Barth, Knyphausen, Lang, LANGWERTH VON SIMMERN, Ress, Schloss Schönborn, STAATSWEINGUT. The *Brunnen* (well) v'yds lie on solid rock that collects rain like a basin – offering gd protection against drought.

Heger, Dr. Bad ★★★→★★★★ 08 09 10 11 12 (13) KAISERSTUHL familiy estate. Serious dry wines from steep v'yds in ACHKARREN and IHRINGEN, focusing on GROSSE LAGE parcel selections: Häusleboden (SPÄTBURGUNDER), Gras im Ofen and Rappenecker (WEISSBURGUNDER, GRAUBURGUNDER). Designation Vorderer Berg for the v. best Winklerberg parcels forbidden by state authorities, who disliked the name. Oak used v. prudently. Weinhaus Joachim Heger wines are from rented v'yds.

Hessische Bergstrasse ★→★★★ 09 11 12 (13) Germany's smallest wine region, situated north of Heidelberg. Pleasant RIES from STAATSWEINGÜTER, Simon-Bürkle, Stadt Bensheim.

Heyl zu Herrnsheim Rhh ★★→★★★ Historic NIERSTEIN estate, bio, now part of the ST-ANTONY estate. GROSSES GEWÄCHS from monopoly site Brudersberg can be excellent, but overall quality is uneven.

Heymann-Löwenstein Mos ★★★ Family estate at WINNINGEN nr Koblenz, 14 ha of RIES in steep terraces. Uhlen parcel selections (Blaufüsser Lay, Rothlay, Laubach) so refined that dry/off-dry distinction loses any meaning. Reinhard Löwenstein strongly advocates spontaneous fermentations (*see* box, p.164).

Hochgewächs Designation for a MOS RIES that obeys stricter requirements than plain QbA, today rarely used. A worthy advocate is Kallfelz in Zell-Merl.

Hochheim Rhg ★★→★★★★ 90 97 01 04 05 08 09 10 11 12 (13) Town east of main RHG area. Rich, distinctly earthy RIES from GROSSE LAGE v'yds: Domdechaney, Hölle, Kirchenstück, Reichestal. Growers: Himmel, *Künstler*, STAATSWEINGUT, Werner.

Hock Traditional English term for Rhine wine, derived from HOCHHEIM.

Hoensbroech, Weingut Reichsgraf zu Bad ★★→★★★ Top KRAICHGAU estate on v. calcareous loess soils. Dry WEISSBURGUNDER Michelfelder Himmelberg is a classic.

Hövel, Weingut von Mos ★★★ Fine SAAR estate with v'yds at Oberemmel (Hütte – filigree wines – is 4.8 ha monopoly), at KANZEM (Hörecker), and in SCHARZHOFBERG. Dynamic Maximilian von Kunow is now converting the estate to bio.

Huber, Bernhard Bad ★★★ Leading estate in Breisgau, with intensely fruity SPÄTBURGUNDER (esp *Alte Reben*, Bombacher Sommerhalde) and burgundy-style CHARD (Hecklinger Schlossberg).

Ihringen Bad ★→★★★★ 08 09 10 11 12 (13) Village in KAISERSTUHL. Best-known for SPÄTBURGUNDER, GRAUBURGUNDER on steep volcanic Winklerberg. Stupidly the law permits wines from the loess plateau to be sold under the same name. Top growers: DR. HEGER, Konstanzer, Michel, Stigler.

Immich-Batterieberg M-M ★★ Comeback of an old name: New owners (since 2009) produce piquant dry and off-dry RIES from Steffensberg, Ellergrub and Batterieberg v'yds in Enkirch, but no sweet wines.

Iphofen Frank ★★→★★★ 90 97 01 04 05 08 09 10 11 12 13 Famous STEIGERWALD village. Rich, aromatic, well-ageing SILVANER. Classified v'yds: Julius-Echter-Berg, Kronsberg. Growers: Arnold, JULIUSSPITAL, RUCK, *Wirsching*, WELTNER.

Jahrgang Year – as in "vintage".

Johannisberg Rhg ★★→★★★★ 90 97 99 01 04 05 07 08 09 10 11 12 RHG village known for berry- and honey-scented RIES. GROSSE LAGE v'yds: Hölle, Klaus, SCHLOSS JOHANNISBERG. GROSSLAGE (avoid!): Erntebringer. Top growers: JOHANNISHOF (Eser), SCHLOSS JOHANNISBERG, PRINZ VON HESSEN.

Johannishof (Eser) Rhg ★★→★★★ Family estate with v'yds at JOHANNISBERG, RÜDESHEIM. Johannes Eser produces RIES in perfect balance between ripeness and steely acidity.

Josephshöfer Mos 83 90 02 03 05 08 09 10 11 12 GROSSE LAGE v'yd at GRAACH, the sole property of KESSELSTATT. Harmonious, berry-flavoured RIES, both dry and sweet. Like its neighbours, under threat from new Autobahn.

Jost, Toni M Rh ★★★ Leading estate in BACHARACH with monopoly Hahn, now led by Cecilia Jost. Aromatic RIES with nerve, and recent trials with PINOT N. Family also run a second estate at WALLUF (RHG).

Juliusspital Frank ★★★ Ancient WÜRZBURG charity with top v'yds all over FRANK. Look for *dry Silvaners* (they age well), RIES and top blend BT. House style usually emphasizes power over elegance.

Kabinett *See* "Germany's quality levels" box, opposite. Germany's unique feather-weight contribution, but with climate change ever more difficult to produce.

Kaiserstuhl Bad r w Outstanding district with notably warm climate and volcanic soil. Renowned above all for SPÄTBURGUNDER and GRAUBURGUNDER.

Germany's quality levels

The official range of qualities and styles in ascending order is:

1 Wein: formerly known as *Tafelwein*. Light wine of no specified character, mostly sweetish.

2 ggA: *geschützte geographische Angabe*, or Protected Geographical Indication, formerly known as LANDWEIN. Dryish *Wein* with some regional style. Mostly a label to avoid, but some thoughtful estates use the Landwein or ggA designation in order to bypass constraints of state authorities.

3 gU: *geschützte Ursprungsbezeichnung*, or protected Designation of Origin. Replacing QUALITÄTSWEIN

4 Qualitätswein: dry or sweetish wine with sugar added before fermentation to increase its strength, but tested for quality and with distinct local and grape character. Don't despair.

5 Kabinett: dry or dryish natural (unsugared) wine of distinct personality and distinguishing lightness. Can occasionally be sublime – esp with a few years' age.

6 Spätlese: stronger, often sweeter than KABINETT. Full-bodied. Today many top SPÄTLESEN are Trocken or completely dry.

7 Auslese: sweeter, sometimes stronger than Spätlese, and often with honey-like flavours, intense and long-lived. Occasionally dry and weighty.

8 Beerenauslese (BA): v. sweet, sometimes strong and intense. Can be superb.

9 Eiswein: from naturally frozen grapes of BA or TBA quality: concentrated, sharpish and v. sweet. Some examples are extreme and unharmonious.

10 Trockenbeerenauslese (TBA): intensely sweet and aromatic; alcohol slight. Extraordinary and everlasting.

Kanzem Mos ★★★ 90 97 99 01 04 05 07 08 09 10 11 12 (13) Saar village, neighbour of WILTINGEN. GROSSE LAGE v'yd: Altenberg. Growers: BISCHÖFLICHE WEINGÜTER, OTHEGRAVEN, *Van Volxem*.

Karlsmühle Mos ★★★ Estate with two Lorenzhöfer monopoly sites making classic RUWER RIES. Consistently excellent quality.

Karthäuserhof Mos ★★★★ 90 93 95 97 99 01 04 05 07 08 09 10 11 12 (13) Outstanding RUWER estate at Eitelsbach with monopoly v'yd Karthäuserhofberg. Easily recognized by bottles with only a neck label. Polished TROCKEN wines, magnificent AUSLESEN. Christoph Tyrell has handed the estate over to a cousin.

Kasel Mos ★★→★★★ Flowery and well-ageing RUWER Valley RIES. GROSSE LAGE v'yds: Kehrnagel, Nies'chen. Top growers: Beulwitz, BISCHÖFLICHE WEINGÜTER, KARLSMÜHLE, KESSELSTATT.

Kauer M Rh ★★→★★★ Family estate at BACHARACH. Crystalline, aromatic RIES, organically grown. Randolf Kauer is professor of organic viticulture at GEISENHEIM.

Keller, Weingut Rhh ★★★→★★★★ Superlative, powerful GROSSES GEWÄCHS RIES from Dalsheimer Hubacker and pricey Ries called G-Max from an undisclosed single v'yd. Now also Ries from NIERSTEIN (Hipping and Pettenthal).

Kesseler, August Rhg ★★★ Passionate grower making fine SPÄTBURGUNDER from ASSMANNSHAUSEN and RÜDESHEIM. Also v.gd classic-style RIES (Rüdesheim, LORCH).

Kesselstatt, Reichsgraf von Mos ★★★→★★★★ 35 ha of top v'yds on the MOS and both its tributaries, eg. at BERNKASTEL, PIESPORT, KASEL, OCKFEN and in SCHARZHOFBERG. JOSEPHSHÖFER a monopoly. Recently, quality-obsessed Annegret Reh-Gartner has raised the proportion of spontaneous fermentations in FUDER casks – the result is even more mineral definition.

Kiedrich Rhg w ★★→★★★★ A village linked inseparably to the WEIL estate; top v'yd is Gräfenberg. Other growers (eg. HESSEN and Knyphausen) own only small plots here.

Kloster Eberbach Rhg Glorious 12th-century Cistercian abbey in HATTENHEIM. It is now the label of Hessische STAATSWEINGÜTER with a string of great v'yds in ASSMANNSHAUSEN, RÜDESHEIM, RAUENTHAL, and HOCHHEIM. Quality is sound but seldom outstanding.

Knipser, Weingut Pfz ★★★→★★★★ Family estate specializing in barrique-aged SPÄTBURGUNDER, fresh SAUV BL and Cuvée X (a Bordeaux blend). Bone-dry RIES HPB is an insider's choice.

Spontaneous fermentation

Spontaneous fermentation – with no added yeast – is the latest thing in Germany. The result may be heavenly, or undrinkable. Reinhard Löwenstein (HEYMANN-LÖWENSTEIN), analysed his fermentations and found 14 different bacteria species and 19 yeast strains. In a conventional fermentation, a dose of sulphur would kill the lot and a selected yeast would be introduced.

Koehler-Ruprecht Pfz ★★→★★★★ 97 99 01 02 05 07 08 09 10 11 12 Kallstadt estate, formerly known for Bernd Philippi's traditional winemaking, delivering esp long-lived, dry RIES Saumagen. Now in new hands, under Philippi's consultancy.

Kraichgau Bad Small district southeast of Heidelberg. Top growers: Burg Ravensburg/Heitlinger, HOENSBROECH, Hummel.

Kreuzberg Ahr ★★★ Ludwig Kreuzberg has made a name for mineral, not overly alcoholic, distinctly cool-climate SPÄTBURGUNDER from the AHR Valley.

Krone, Weingut Rhg ★★→★★★ 97 99 02 05 06 07 08 09 10 Estate in ASSMANNSHAUSEN, run by WEGELER, with some of the best and oldest SPÄTBURGUNDER v'yds in the GROSSE LAGE Höllenberg. Sublime reds, but RIES and WEISSBURGUNDER are less exciting.

Kühn, Peter Jakob Rhg ★★★ Excellent estate in OESTRICH. Obsessive bio v'yd management and long macerations shape nonconformist but exciting RIES.

Kuhn, Philipp Pfz ★★★ Reliable producer in Laumersheim. Dry RIES rich and harmonious, barrel-aged SPÄTBURGUNDER succulent, complex, potent. Rich barrel-fermented VIOGNIER a novelty.

Künstler Rhg ★★★→★★★★ 90 97 01 05 08 09 10 11 12 Uncompromising Gunter Künstler makes superb dry RIES in GROSSE LAGE sites at HOCHHEIM, Kostheim, and, newly, on other side of RHEINGAU at RÜDESHEIM (Roseneck, Rottland). Also excellent AUSLESE and firm SPÄTBURGUNDER.

Laible, Alexander Bad ★★→★★★ New DURBACH estate of ANDREAS LAIBLE's (*see* next entry) younger son; aromatic dry RIES and WEISSBURGUNDER. 2012 Ries Tausend Sterne is spontaneously fermented and comes close to the style of natural wine (*see* France).

Laible, Andreas Bad ★★★ Crystalline dry RIES from DURBACH's Plauelrain v'yd and gd SCHEUREBE and GEWÜRZ. Andreas Sr has now handed over to Andreas Jr.

Landwein Now "ggA". *See* "Germany's quality levels" box on p.163.

Langwerth von Simmern Rhg ★★→★★★ Famous Eltville estate, with traditional winemaking. Top v'yds incl Baiken, Mannberg (monopoly) and MARCOBRUNN. Now back on form.

Lauer Mos ★★★ Florian Lauer works hard to correct the errors of the 1971 wine law, with parcel selections from the huge AYLER Kupp v'yd. Best: Schonfels, Stirn, Kern. Magnificent 2012 AUSLESE Fass 10.

Leitz, Josef Rhg ★★★ Growing RÜDESHEIM family estate for rich but elegant dry and sweet RIES, esp from classified v'yds in the Rüdesheimer Berg.

Leiwen M-M ★★→★★★ A village neighbouring TRITTENHEIM, which is home to GROSSE LAGE Laurentiuslay.

Liebfrauenstift-Kirchenstück Rhh A walled v'yd in city of Worms producing flowery RIES renowned for its harmony. Producers: Gutzler, Schembs. Not to be confused with Liebfrauenmilch, a cheap and tasteless imitation.

Loewen, Carl Mos ★★★ Rich RIES, both dry and sweet, from Leiwen (GROSSE LAGE Laurentiuslay), from Thörnicher Ritsch, and from Longuicher Maximin Herrenberg (v'yd planted in 1896).

Loosen, Weingut Dr. M-M ★★→★★★★ 90 97 01 02 04 05 08 09 10 11 12 (13) Charismatic Ernie Loosen produces traditionally crafted RIES from old vines in BERNKASTEL, ERDEN, GRAACH, ÜRZIG, WEHLEN. Erdener Prälat AUSLESE is cultish. Reliable Dr. L Ries is from bought-in grapes. Joint-venture Ries from Washington State with Chateau Ste Michelle. *See also* WOLF in the PFALZ.

Lorch Rhg ★→★★★ Village in extreme west of the RHG. Sharply mineral wines, now re-discovered. Best: Chat Sauvage, Fricke, Johanninger, von Kanitz, KESSELER.

Löwenstein, Fürst Frank, Rhg ★★★ After Prince Carl Friedrich Löwenstein's death in 2010, both the RHG and FRANK estates have gone through changes. Now upwards trend, esp for SILVANER and RIES from listed monument Homburger Kallmuth, a dramatic steep v'yd on the Main with 12 km of terrace walls.

Marcobrunn Rhg Historic v'yd in Erbach; potentially one of Germany's v. best. Contemporary wines scarcely match its past fame.

Markgräflerland Bad District south of Freiburg. Typical GUTEDEL wine can be refreshing when drunk v. young.

Maximin Grünhaus Mos ★★★★ 83 90 97 98 99 01 05 07 08 09 10 11 12 (13) Supreme RUWER estate at Mertesdorf, v. traditional winemaking shapes herb-scented RIES of delicacy and longevity (dr and sw).

Meyer-Näkel Ahr ★★★→★★★★ Father-daughter team make fine AHR Valley SPÄTBURGUNDER that exemplify a modern, oak-aged (but nevertheless mineral) style.

Mittelhaardt Pfz The north-central and best part of the PFZ, incl DEIDESHEIM, FORST, RUPPERTSBERG, WACHENHEIM; largely planted with RIES.

Mittelmosel The central and best part of the MOS, a RIES eldorado, incl BERNKASTEL, BRAUNEBERG, GRAACH, PIESPORT, WEHLEN, etc.

Mittelrhein Northern and dramatically scenic Rhine area popular with tourists. BACHARACH and BOPPARD are the most important villages. Delicate yet *steely Ries, underrated* and underpriced. Many gd sites lie fallow.

Molitor, Markus M-M ★★★ Outstanding v'yds throughout the M-M, and a tremendous wine list. Magisterial sweet RIES; acclaimed, well-ageing SPÄTBURGUNDER.

Mosbacher Pfz ★★★ Makes some of best GROSSES GEWÄCHS RIES of FORST. Wines are traditionally aged in big oak casks.

Riesling and roast beef is worth a try – a dry Mosel or Rheingau QbA will do.

Mosel Wine-growing area formerly known as Mosel-Saar-Ruwer. From 2007, all wines from Saarburg to Koblenz are labelled as Mosel, even though conditions on the RUWER and SAAR tributaries may be v. different from the M-M. 60% RIES.

Moselland, Winzergenossenschaft Mos A huge MOS co-op, at BERNKASTEL, formed after mergers with co-ops in the NA and PFZ. 3,290 members, 2,400 ha. Little is above average.

Müller-Catoir, Weingut Pfz ★★→★★★★ Aged AUSLESEN, BA, TBA 83 90 97 98 01 can be delicious; 2011 Schlössel RIESLANER TBA.

Nackenheim Rhh ★→★★★★ 90 97 01 05 08 09 11 12 NIERSTEIN neighbour with GROSSE LAGE Rothenberg on red shale, famous for RHEINHESSEN's richest RIES, superb TBA. Top growers: GUNDERLOCH, Kühling-Gillot.

Nahe (r) w 01 05 07 08 09 10 11 12 (13) Tributary of the Rhine and dynamic wine region. A handful of top estates, dozens of lesser-known producers, excellent value. RIES of elegance and almost MOS-like raciness. EISWEIN a speciality.

Neipperg, Graf von Würt ★★★ Noble estate in Schwaigern: reds (LEMBERGER, SPÄTBURGUNDER) of grace and purity. A scion of the family, Count Stephan von Neipperg, makes wine at Ch Canon la Gaffelière in St-Émilion, and elsewhere.

Niederhausen Na ★★→★★★★ 90 97 99 01 02 04 05 07 08 09 10 11 12 Village of the middle NA Valley. Complex RIES from steep GROSSE LAGE v'yds: Felsensteyer, Hermannsberg, Hermannshöhle, Kertz. Growers: CRUSIUS, DÖNNHOFF, GUT HERMANNSBERG, Mathern, von Racknitz.

There are just 6,000 growers in the Mosel Valley now, from 23,000+ in the early 80s: c. 5,000 ha abandoned.

Nierstein Rhh ★→★★★★ 90 97 01 04 05 07 08 09 11 12 (13) Rich but balanced RIES, both dry and sweet, that need to be aged. GROSSE LAGE v'yds: Brudersberg, Hipping, Oelberg, Orbel, Pettenthal. Growers incl Gehring, GUNDERLOCH, Guntrum, HEYL ZU HERRNSHEIM, KELLER, Kühling-Gillot, Manz, Schätzel, ST-ANTONY, Strub. *Beware grosslage Gutes Domtal*: a supermarket deception.

Ockfen Mos ★★→★★★ Village that shapes sturdy, intense SAAR RIES from GROSSE LAGE v'yd Bockstein. Growers: OTHEGRAVEN, SANKT URBANS-HOF, WAGNER, *Zilliken*.

Odinstal, Weingut Pfz ★★→★★★ The highest v'yd of PFZ, 150 metres above WACHENHEIM. Bio farming and low-tech vinification bring pure RIES, SILVANER, GEWURZ. Harvest often extends into Nov.

Oechsle Scale for sugar content of grape juice.

Oestrich Rhg ★★→★★★ Exemplary steely RIES and fine Auslesen from GROSSE LAGE v'yds: Doosberg, Lenchen, St. Nikolaus. Top growers: August Eser, KÜHN, Querbach, SPREITZER, WEGELER.

Oppenheim Rhh ★→★★★ Town south of NIERSTEIN, GROSSE LAGE Kreuz, Sackträger. Growers: Heyden, Kissinger, Kühling-Gillot, Manz. Spectacular 13th-C church.

Ortenau Bad (r) w District around and south of BAD. Mainly Klingelberger (RIES) and SPÄTBURGUNDER from granite soils. Top villages: DURBACH, Neuweier, Waldulm.

Ortswein Second rank up in VDP's pyramid of qualities: a village wine, rather than a single v'yd.

Othegraven, Weingut von Mos ★★★ Fine KANZEM estate (superb GROSSE LAGE Altenberg). Since TV star Günther Jauch took over in 2010 the wines have gained in precision. 2012 SPÄTLESE ALTE REBEN and AUSLESE raise the bar. Also parcels in OCKFEN (Bockstein) and in the forgotten Herrenberg at Wawern.

Palatinate English for PFALZ.

Pfalz r w 90 97 01 05 07 08 09 10 11 12 (13) Usually balmy region bordering Alsace in the south and RHH to the north. Its MITTELHAARDT area is the source of full-bodied, mostly dry RIES. Southerly SÜDLICHE WEINSTRASSE is better suited to PINOT varieties, esp SPÄTBURGUNDER.

Piesport M-M ★→★★★★ 90 92 97 01 02 03 04 05 07 08 09 10 11 12 Tiny village with famous vine amphitheatre of GROSSE LAGE v'yds (Domherr, Goldtröpfchen, Kreuzwingert, Schubertslay). At best glorious, rich, aromatic RIES. Avoid GROSSLAGE Michelsberg. Esp gd are GRANS-FASSIAN, Joh Haart, JULIAN HAART, R HAART, Kurt Hain, KESSELSTATT, SANKT URBANS-HOF.

Prädikat Legally defined special attributes or qualities. *See* QMP.

Prinz von Hessen Rhg ★★★→★★★★ Glorious wines of vibrancy and precision from historic JOHANNISBERG estate, esp at SPÄTLESE and above, and mature vintages.

Prüm, J J Mos ★★★★ 71 76 83 88 89 90 94 95 96 97 98 99 01 02 03 04 05 07 08 09 10 11 12 (13) Legendary WEHLEN estate; also GRAACH and BERNKASTEL. Delicate but extremely long-lived wines with astonishing finesse and distinctive character. Dr. Manfred Prüm now joined by daughter Katharina.

Prüm, S A Mos ★★→★★★ More popular and less traditional in style than WEHLEN neighbour J J PRÜM. Sound, sometimes inconsistent wines.

Qualitätswein bestimmter Anbaugebiete (QbA) Middle quality of German wine, with sugar added before fermentation (as in French *chaptalization*), but controlled as to areas, grapes, etc. Its new name: gU (*see* box p.163) is little improvement.

Qualitätswein mit Prädikat (QmP) Top category, for all wines ripe enough not to need sugaring (KABINETT to TBA).

Randersacker Frank ★★→★★★ Village south of WÜRZBURG for distinctive dry RIES and SILVANER. Classified as GROSSE LAGE: Pfülben. Top growers: BÜRGERSPITAL, JULIUSSPITAL, STAATLICHER HOFKELLER, SCHMITT'S KINDER, Störrlein & Krenig.

Ratzenberger M Rh ★★→★★★ Estate making racy dry and off-dry RIES in BACHARACH; best from GROSSE LAGE v'yds: Posten and Steeger St-Jost. Gd SEKT.

Rauenthal Rhg ★★ →★★★★ *Spicy, austere but complex Ries* from inland slopes, once the RHG'S most expensive. GROSSE LAGE v'yds: Baiken, Rothenberg. Top growers incl BREUER (with monopoly Nonnenberg), KLOSTER EBERBACH, A Eser, LANGWERTH VON SIMMERN.

Rebholz, Ökonomierat Pfz ★★★→★★★★ 97 99 00 01 02 04 05 07 08 09 11 12 (13) Top SÜDLICHE WEINSTRASSE estate known for bone-dry, minerally RIES (eg. GROSSES GEWÄCHS Kastanienbusch and Ganshorn), focussed CHARD and tight, age-worthy SPÄTBURGUNDER.

Reparaturwein Wine-grower's jargon for a simple, light and slightly acidic white suitable to "repair" the palate after an exhausting tasting. Not seen on labels.

Restsüsse Unfermented grape sugar remaining in (or in cheap wines added to) wine to give it sweetness. Can range from 1 g/litre in a TROCKEN wine to 300 g/litre in a TBA.

Rheingau (r) w 90 97 99 01 04 05 07 08 09 10 11 12 The only Rhine region with south-facing slopes bordering the river. Classic, substantial RIES, famous for steely acidity, and small amounts of delicate SPÄTBURGUNDER. Also centre of SEKT production.

Rheinhessen (r) w 05 07 08 09 10 11 12 (13) Germany's largest region, between Mainz and Worms. Much dross, but also top RIES from NACKENHEIM, NIERSTEIN, etc. Remarkable spurt in quality in formerly unknown areas, from growers such as KELLER, WITTMANN in the south, WAGNER-STEMPEL in the west.

Richter, Weingut Max Ferd M-M ★★ →★★★ Reliable M-M estate, at Mülheim. Esp gd RIES KABINETT and SPÄTLESEN: full and aromatic.

Ruck, Johann Frank ★★★ Reliable, spicy SILVANER, RIES, SCHEUREBE, TRAMINER from IPHOFEN in the STEIGERWALD district of FRANK. Traditional and bone-dry in style.

The Sankt Hildegard Abbey in Rüdesheim has a wine estate run entirely by nuns.

Rüdesheim Rhg ★★→★★★★ 90 97 01 04 05 08 09 10 11 12 (13) Rhine resort with outstanding GROSSE LAGE v'yds on slate; the four best (Roseneck, Rottland, Schlossberg, Kaisersteinfels) are called Rüdesheimer Berg. Full-bodied wines, floral-flavoured and often remarkable in off-yrs. Best growers incl BREUER, Chat Sauvage, Corvers-Kauter, JOHANNISHOF, KESSELER, KLOSTER EBERBACH, KÜNSTLER, LEITZ, Ress.

Ruppertsberg Pfz ★★→★★★ MITTELHAARDT village known for elegant RIES. Growers incl BASSERMANN-JORDAN, Biffar, BUHL, BÜRKLIN-WOLF, CHRISTMANN, DR. DEINHARD / VON WINNING.

Ruwer Mos w 90 97 99 01 02 03 04 05 07 08 09 10 11 12 A tributary of the Mosel nr Trier, renowned for delicate long-lived sweet RIES and quaffable light dry versions. Best growers incl Beulwitz, KARLSMÜHLE, KARTHÄUSERHOF, KESSELSTATT, MAXIMIN GRÜNHAUS.

Saale-Unstrut Sa-Un w 03 05 08 09 11 12 Northerly region around confluence of these two rivers at Naumburg, nr Leipzig. Terraced v'yds have Cistercian origins. Mainly white varieties, quality leaders: Böhme, Born, Gussek, Kloster Pforta, Lützkendorf, Pawis.

Saar Mos w 90 93 94 97 99 01 02 04 05 07 08 09 10 11 12 (13) Hill-lined tributary of the MOS, colder climate. The most brilliant, austere, steely RIES of all. Villages incl AYL, KANZEM, OCKFEN, Saarburg, Serrig, WILTINGEN (SCHARZHOFBERG).

Saarburg Mos A small town in the SAAR Valley. Growers incl WAGNER, ZILLIKEN. GROSSE LAGE: Rausch.

Scheurebe renaissance?
Germany is famous (notorious?) for its breeding of new vines. In the 70s Huxelrebe, Ortega, Morio Muskat, Siegerrebe, Albalonga and others had their moment in the sun, and have mostly disappeared. But a trio persisted: KERNER (TROLLINGER X RIES, 1929) has found its niche in WÜRT; RIESLANER (SILVANER X Ries, 1921) is a difficult-to-grow rarity in FRANK; SCHEUREBE (Ries x Sylvaner Musqué, 1916) the most successful crossing – some growers have really old vines now, which produce aromatic, weighty dry wines and richly flavoured, concentrated sweet ones. Try KELLER, LAIBLE (both estates), RUCK, Seehof Fauth, WELTNER, WIRSCHING, WITTMANN. The leading expert for Scheurebe is the Pfeffingen estate in Bad Dürkheim, PFZ.

Sachsen 03 05 08 09 11 12 (13) Region in the Elbe Valley around Dresden. Characterful dry whites. Best growers: Richter, *Schloss Proschwitz*, Schloss Wackerbarth, Martin Schwarz, Zimmerling.

St-Antony Rhh ★★→★★★ NIERSTEIN estate with exceptional v'yds. Improvements through new owner (same as HEYL ZU HERRNSHEIM) result in v.gd 2011s. Entry-level label Bodenschatz is a bargain.

Salm, Prinz zu Na, Rhh Owner of Schloss Wallhausen ★★→★★★ in NA and Villa Sachsen ★→★★ in RHH. RIES at Schloss Wallhausen (organic) has made gd progress recently.

Salwey Bad ★★★ Leading KAISERSTUHL estate at Oberrotweil. Konrad Salwey picks early to preserve freshness and balance. Best: Henkenberg and Eichberg GRAUBURGUNDER, Kirchberg SPÄTBURGUNDER Rappen (fermented with stems).

Sankt Urbans-Hof Mos ★★★→★★★★ Large family estate based in Leiwen, v'yds along M-M and SAAR. Limpid RIES of impeccable purity and raciness.

Sauer, Horst Frank ★★★→★★★★ The finest exponent of ESCHERNDORF's top v'yd Lump. Racy, straightforward *dry Silvaner* and RIES, sensational TBA. Glorious 2011s, 12s (both dr sw).

Sauer, Rainer Frank ★★★ Rising family estate at ESCHERNDORF. Complex dry SILVANER, from vibrant KABINETT to creamy, full-bodied SPÄTLESEN.

Schaefer, Willi Mos ★★★ The finest grower of GRAACH (but only 4 ha). MOS RIES at its best: pure, crystalline, feather-light, rewarding at all quality levels.

Schäfer-Fröhlich Na ★★★ Increasingly brilliant RIES, both dry and nobly sweet, from this estate in Bockenau, NA. Superb *Grosses Gewächs* Felseneck and breathtaking EISWEIN.

Scharzhofberg Mos ★★→★★★★★ Superlative SAAR v'yd, the result of a rare coincidence of microclimate, soil and human intelligence to bring about the perfection of RIES. Top estates: BISCHÖFLICHE WEINGÜTER, EGON MÜLLER, VON HÖVEL, KESSELSTATT, VAN VOLXEM.

Schlossböckelheim Na ★★→★★★★ 97 01 02 04 05 08 09 11 12 (13) A village with top NA v'yds, incl GROSSE LAGE Felsenberg and Kupfergrube. Firm and demanding RIES ages well. Top growers incl CRUSIUS, DÖNNHOFF, GUT HERMANNSBERG, SCHÄFER-FRÖHLICH.

Schloss Johannisberg Rhg ★★→★★★ Historic RHG estate, 100% RIES, owned by Henkell (Oetker group). Usually v.gd SPÄTLESE Grünlack ("green sealing wax"), AUSLESE Rosalack; quality of the TROCKEN and FEINHERB wines more variable.

Schloss Lieser M-M ★★★→★★★★ Thomas Haag, Wilhelm Haag's elder son (*see* FRITZ HAAG) produces pure, racy RIES from underrated Niederberg Helden v'yd (outstanding 2012 GROSSES GEWÄCHS), as well as from plots in BRAUNEBERG.

Schloss Neuweier Bad ★★★ Leading producer of dry RIES from volcanic soils nr BAD. New owner since 2012.

Schloss Proschwitz Sachs ★★ A resurrected princely estate at Meissen in SACH, leading former East Germany in quality; esp with dry WEISSBURGUNDER and GRAUBURGUNDER. A great success.

Schloss Reinhartshausen Rhg ★★ Famous estate in Erbach, originally property of Prussian royal family, changed hands in 2013, lost VDP membership.

Schloss Saarstein Mos ★→★★★ Steep but chilly v'yds in Serrig need warm yrs to succeed but can deliver steely, minerally, long-lived AUSLESEN, EISWEIN.

Schloss Vollrads Rhg ★★ One of the greatest historic RHG estates, now owned by a bank. RIES in rather commercial style.

Schmitt's Kinder Frank ★★→★★★ Family estate in RANDERSACKER known for classical dry SILVANER, barrel-aged SPÄTBURGUNDER, sweet RIESLANER. Weinberg Mendelssohn RIES exemplifies an endangered species: the dry KABINETT.

Schnaitmann Würt ★★★ Excellent barrel-aged reds from WÜRT: SPÄTBURGUNDER, LEMBERGER from the GROSSE LAGE Lämmler v'yd. In conversion to organic farming.

Schneider, Cornelia and Reinhold Bad ★★★ Family estate in Endingen, KAISERSTUHL. Age-worthy SPÄTBURGUNDERS 00 01 02 05 07 08 09 denoted by letters – R for volcanic soil, C for Loess – and old-fashioned, opulent (and bone-dry) RULÄNDER.

Schneider, Markus ★★ Shooting star in Ellerstadt, PFZ. A full range of soundly produced wines.

Schoppenwein Café (or bar) wine, ie. wine by the glass.

Schwarzer Adler Bad ★★→★★★ One-star restaurant at Oberbergen, KAISERSTUHL, and wine estate for burgundy-influenced GRAU-, WEISS-, SPÄTBURGUNDER. Spectacular new cellar in 2013.

Schwegler, Albrecht Würt ★★★ Small estate known for gd, unusual red blends, such as Granat (MERLOT, ZWEIGELT, LEMBERGER and others). Worth looking for. Fancy off-dry KERNER too.

Steep slopes need up to 2,000 work-hours/year/ha, flat land under 300.

Sekt German sparkling wine, v. variable in quality. Bottle fermentation is not mandatory. Sekt specialists incl Raumland, Schembs, Schloss Vaux, S Steinmetz, Wilhelmshof.

Selbach-Oster M-M ★★★ Scrupulous ZELTINGEN estate with excellent v'yd portfolio, best-known for sweet PRÄDIKAT wines. Barrel-fermented WEISSBURGUNDER a questionable novelty.

Sonnenuhr Mos "Sundial". Name of several v'yds, esp GROSSE LAGE sites at WEHLEN and ZELTINGEN threatened by new Autobahn.

Spätlese Late-harvest. One level riper and usually also one sweeter than KABINETT. Gd examples age at least 7 yrs. Spätlese TROCKEN designation will in future be given up by most VDP members: a shame.

Spreitzer Rhg ★★★→★★★★ Andreas and Bernd Spreitzer produce deliciously racy, harmonious RIES (both dr sw), vinified with patience in FUDER casks. V'yds in HATTENHEIM, OESTRICH, Winkel.

Staatlicher Hofkeller Frank ★★ The Bavarian state domain. 120 ha of the finest FRANK v'yds, with spectacular cellars under the great baroque Residenz at WÜRZBURG. Quality sound but rarely exciting.

Staatsweingut / Staatliche Weinbaudomäne The state wine estates or domains. Some have been privatized in recent yrs.

Steigerwald Frank (r) w District in eastern FRANK. V'yds at considerable altitude; powerful SILVANER and RIES. Best: CASTELL, Roth, RUCK, WELTNER, WIRSCHING.

Steinberg Rhg ★★★ Famous HATTENHEIM walled RIES v'yd, a German Clos de Vougeot, planted by Cistercian monks 700 yrs ago. The monopoly of KLOSTER EBERBACH.

Steinwein Frank Wine from WÜRZBURG's best v'yd, Stein. Goethe's favourite too.

Stodden Ahr ★★★ Gerhard Stodden died unexpectedly in 2013, but Alexander continues his father's work: AHR SPÄTBURGUNDER with a burgundian touch.

Südliche Weinstrasse Pfz r w The district name for south PFZ. Quality has forged ahead in past 25 yrs. Best growers incl BECKER, Leiner, Münzberg, REBHOLZ, Siegrist, WEHRHEIM.

Tauberfranken Bad (r) w Underrated cool-climate district of northeast BAD: FRANK-style SILVANER and RIES from limestone soils. Frost is a problem. Best grower is Schlör.

Thanisch, Weingut Dr. M-M ★★→★★★ BERNKASTEL estate, founded 1636, famous for its share of the Doctor v'yd. After family split-up in 1988 two homonymous estates: Erben Müller-Burggraef and Erben Thanisch. Similar in quality but the latter sometimes has the edge.

Eat more game!
Some of the worst enemies of a German wine-grower have four legs, and – undeniably – gd taste. Wild boar and deer invade the v'yds as soon as acorns or other foods become short in the forest. Even electric fences can fail to keep them out, and grape losses can be up to a third. Naturally, they go for the ripest fruit. Protect AUSLESE: eat more game! And discover how well they can go together.

Traisen Na ★★★ 90 97 01 05 07 08 09 10 11 12 Small NA village, incl GROSSE LAGE v'yds Bastei and Rotenfels. RIES of concentration and class from volcanic soils. Top growers: CRUSIUS, von Racknitz.

Trier Mos Great city of Roman origin, on MOS, between RUWER and SAAR. Big charitable estates have cellars here among awesome Roman remains.

Trittenheim M-M ★★→★★★ 97 01 02 04 05 07 08 09 10 11 12 (13) Attractive M-M light wines. However, only best plots in GROSSE LAGE v'yd Apotheke deserve that classification. Growers: A CLÜSSERATH, E Clüsserath, CLÜSSERATH-WEILER, GRANS-FASSIAN, Milz.

Trocken Dry. Used to be defined as max 9 g per litre unfermented sugar. Now, owing to new EU regulations, an additional tolerance of +2 g per litre. Generally the further south in Germany, the more Trocken wines.

Trockenbeerenauslese (TBA) Sweetest, most expensive category of German wine, extremely rare, with concentrated honey flavour. Made from selected shrivelled grapes affected by noble rot (botrytis). Half-bottles a gd idea.

Ürzig M-M ★★★★ 71 83 90 93 94 95 96 97 01 02 04 05 07 08 09 10 11 12 (13) Village on red sandstone and red slate, famous for full and spicy RIES unlike other MOSELS. GROSSE LAGE v'yd: Würzgarten. Growers: Berres, Erbes, Christoffel,

LOOSEN, Mönchhof, Pauly-Bergweiler, WEINS-PRÜM. Threatened by an unneeded Autobahn bridge 160 metres high.

Van Volxem Mos ★★→★★★ Historical SAAR estate revived by brewery heir Roman Niewodniczanski. Low yields from top sites (SCHARZHOFBERG, KANZEM Altenberg, WILTINGEN Gottesfuss), and mainly dry or off-dry wines. Recently, fewer overripe flavours than previously, lower alcohol and first trials to produce sweet and nobly sweet.

Verband Deutscher Prädikatsweingüter (VDP) Pace-making association of 200 premium growers. Look for its eagle insignia on wine labels, and for the GROSSE LAGE logo on wines from classified v'yds. A VDP wine is usually a gd bet. President: Steffen CHRISTMANN.

Vollenweider Mos ★★★ Daniel Vollenweider from Switzerland has revived the Wolfer Goldgrube v'yd nr Traben-Trarbach (since 2000). *Excellent Ries*, but v. small quantities.

Wachenheim Pfz ★★★ Celebrated village with, according to VDP, no GROSSE LAGE v'yds. Top growers: Biffar, BÜRKLIN-WOLF, ODINSTAL, Karl Schäfer, WOLF.

Wagner, Dr. Mos ★★→★★★ Estate with v'yds in OCKFEN and SAARSTEIN led by young GEISENHEIM graduate Christiane Wagner. SAAR RIES with purity, freshness, eg. 2012 Saarburger Rausch AUSLESE ★★★.

Wagner-Stempel Rhh ★★★ RHH estate nr NA border in obscure Siefersheim. Excellent RIES, both GROSSES GEWÄCHS and nobly sweet.

Walluf Rhg ★★★ Underrated village, the first with important v'yds as one leaves Hessen's capital Wiesbaden, going west. GROSSE LAGE v'yd: Walkenberg. Growers: J B BECKER, JOST.

Wegeler M-M, Rhg ★★→★★★ Important family estates in OESTRICH and BERNKASTEL plus a stake in the famous KRONE estate of ASSMANNSHAUSEN. Gd in both quantity and quality. Geheimrat J brand was dry RIES pioneer in the 70s and maintains v. high standards.

Wehlen M-M ★★★→★★★★ 90 93 94 95 96 97 98 01 02 03 04 05 07 08 09 10 11 12 13 Wine village with legendary steep SONNENUHR v'yd expressing RIES from slate soils at its v. best. Sweet wines from SPÄTLESE upwards like iron fist in velvet glove – and last for decades. Top growers: Kerpen, KESSELSTATT, LOOSEN, MOLITOR, J J PRÜM, S A PRÜM, RICHTER, Studert-Prüm, SELBACH-OSTER, WEGELER, WEINS-PRÜM. New Autobahn above v'yds will have unknown influence.

Wehrheim, Weingut Dr. Pfz ★★★ Top family estate of SÜDLICHE WEINSTRASSE. Organic; mineral, v. dry wines, eg. WEISSBURGUNDER Muschelkalk, RIES, SPÄTBURGUNDER from GROSSE LAGE Kastanienbusch.

Weil, Robert Rhg ★★★→★★★★ 17 37 49 59 75 90 97 01 02 04 05 07 08 09 10 11 12 Outstanding estate in KIEDRICH owned by Suntory of Japan. Superb EISWEIN, TBA, BA; entry-level wines more variable. Gräfenberg is best of three classified v'yds.

Weingart M Rh ★★★ Outstanding estate at Spay, v'yds in BOPPARD (esp Hamm Feuerlay). Refined, mineral RIES, low-tech in style, superb value.

Weingut Wine estate.

Weins-Prüm, Dr. M-M ★★★ A small estate; based at WEHLEN. Superb v'yds in M-M. Scrupulous winemaking from owner Bert Selbach, who favours a taut and mineral style.

Weissherbst Pale-pink wine, made from a single variety, often SPÄTBURGUNDER. V. variable quality.

Weltner, Paul Frank ★★→★★★ STEIGERWALD family estate. Densely structured, age-worthy SILVANER from underrated Rödelseer Küchenmeister v'yd and neighbouring plots at IPHOFEN.

Wiltingen Mos ★★→★★★★ 90 97 01 04 05 07 08 09 10 11 12 (13) Heartland of the SAAR. SCHARZHOFBERG crowns a series of GROSSE LAGE v'yds (Braune Kupp, Kupp,

Braunfels, Gottesfuss). Top growers: BISCHÖFLICHE WEINGÜTER, LE GALLAIS, EGON MÜLLER, KESSELSTATT, SANKT URBANS-HOF, Vols, VAN VOLXEM.

Winning, von Pfz ★★★ →★★★★ DEIDESHEIM estate, incl former DR. DEINHARD. The von Winning label is used for top wines from Dr. Deinhard v'yds. *Ries of great purity* and terroir expression, slightly influenced by fermentation in new FUDER casks.

Winningen Mos ★★ →★★★ Lower MOS town nr Koblenz; excellent dry RIES and TBA. GROSSE LAGE v'yds: Röttgen, Uhlen. Top growers: HEYMANN-LÖWENSTEIN, KNEBEL, Kröber, Richard Richter.

Wirsching, Hans Frank ★★★ Renowned estate in IPHOFEN. Dry RIES, *Silvaner*, classically structured, long-lived. GROSSE LAGE v'yds: Julius-Echter-Berg, Kronsberg.

Wittmann Rhh ★★★ Philipp Wittmann has propelled this organic estate to the top ranks. Crystal-clear, mineral, dry RIES from QBA to GROSSES GEWÄCHS and magnificent TBA.

Wöhrwag ★★ →★★★ Just outside Stuttgart, this estate produces succulent reds, but above all elegant dry RIES and brilliant EISWEIN.

Wolf J L Pfz ★★ →★★★★ WACHENHEIM estate, leased by Ernst LOOSEN of BERNKASTEL. Dry PFZ RIES (esp Forster Pechstein), sound and consistent rather than dazzling.

One *Grosses Gewächs* bottle with the "grape + GG" logo costs around 70 euro-cents – empty.

Württemberg r (w) 05 07 08 09 10 11 12 13 Red wine region around Stuttgart and Heilbronn, traditionally producing light TROLLINGER. But now ambitions are rising; LEMBERGER, SPÄTBURGUNDER can be v.gd. RIES needs altitude v'yds.

Würzburg Frank ★★ →★★★★ Great baroque city on the Main, centre of FRANK wine: dry RIES and esp SILVANER. Classified v'yds: Innere Leiste, Stein, Stein-Harfe. Growers: BÜRGERSPITAL, JULIUSSPITAL, Reiss, STAATLICHER HOFKELLER, Weingut am Stein.

Zell Mos ★ →★★ Best-known lower MOSEL village, notorious for GROSSLAGE Schwarze Katz (Black Cat). A gd v'yd is Merler Königslay-Terrassen. Top grower: Kallfelz.

Zeltingen M-M ★★ →★★★ Top but sometimes underrated MOS village nr WEHLEN. Rich though crisp RIES. GROSSE LAGE v'yd: SONNENUHR. Top growers incl M MOLITOR, J J PRÜM, SELBACH-OSTER.

Ziereisen Bad ★★★ 03 04 05 07 08 09 10 11 12 (13) Outstanding estate at Efringen-Kirchen in MARKGRÄFLERLAND, mainly GUTEDEL and PINOTS. Ex-carpenter Ziereisen is a genius; even entry-level wines show class. Best are SPÄTBURGUNDERS from small plots with dialect names: Schulen and Rhini. Jaspis is the name for old-vine selections.

Zilliken, Forstmeister Geltz Mos ★★★ →★★★★ 93 94 95 96 97 99 01 02 04 05 07 08 09 10 11 12 13 Former estate of Prussian royal forester at Saarburg and OCKFEN, SAAR. Produces intensely minerally *Ries from Saarburg Rausch* and OCKFEN Bockstein, incl superb AUSLESE and EISWEIN with excellent ageing potential.

Luxembourg

Think of Luxembourg wine as a halfway house between Germany and France. Its Rieslings seem half-German, half-French: old-school Alsace Riesling on the nose, with the lightness and the sweet-and-sour notes of an off-dry Nahe. The 1,270 ha of vines along the *Moselle Luxembourgeoise* are, however, a mix. There's more Rivaner (Müller-Thurgau, 27%), Auxerrois (14%) and Pinot Gris (14%) than Riesling (12%). Auxerrois is Luxembourg's speciality, and good examples (eg. Bechelsberg from Stronck-Pinnel, Sunnen-Hoffmann or Schumacher-Lethal) show a complex spiciness, rounder than its relative Pinot Blanc. But poor Auxerrois is just sweetish and lean. Pinot Gris usually has more extract and more depth. Wine law doesn't differentiate between dry and off-dry. Most whites have strong acidity and some sweetness. A common term on labels (but of little significance) is "Premier Grand Cru". More reliable are charter designations; Domaine et Tradition, founded 20 years ago, uniting seven producers, has the most credibility. Growers-association Privatwenzer (Private Wine-growers) set up a charter in 2007, and Charta Schengen Prestige was designed to include producers in neighbouring areas of Germany and France.

Luxembourg's growers definitely benefit from global warming. Recent vinatages as 2011 and 2009 have been particularly successful; even Pinot Noir and Riesling brought excellent results. And while 2012 and 2008 were very good and 2010 was okay, 2013 was more difficult.

Alice Hartmann ★★★ 09 10 11 12 (13) Perfectionist in Wormeldange, making complex RIES from best Ries v'yd Koeppchen, incl parcel selections La Chapelle and Les Terrasses. Delicate PINOT N (Clos du Kreutzerberg). Also owns v'yds in Burgundy (St-Aubin), Middle Mosel (Trittenheim) and leases small plot in Scharzhofberg.

Aly Duhr ★★★ 08 09 11 12 (13) Family estate at Ahn. V.gd PINOT GR from Machtum (Ongkâf v'yd), gd off-dry RIES from Ahn (Nussbaum and Palmberg), elegant Ries Vendage Tardive. Culinary barrel-aged PINOT BL.

Gales ★★ →★★★ (Comparatively) large but reliable producer at Remich uniting v'yds of Caves St Martin with family estate. Best are Crémant and whites under Domaine et Tradition label. Caves St Martin has a good series called De Nos Rochers and produces Charta Schengen. It's worth seeing the old cellar labyrinth, dug into a shell-limestone *massif*.

Sunnen-Hoffmann ★★→★★★ Family estate at Remerschen, now bio; textbook AUXERROIS from Wintrange Hammelsberg; gd RIES, Crémant too.

More producers at ★★→★★★ Château de Schengen, Cep d'Or, Clos de Rochers, Duhr Frères/Clos Mon Vieux Moulin, Ruppert, Schumacher-Knepper and Stronck-Pinnel.

Young, ambitious producers set to join the top class: Fränk Kayl, Schmit-Fohl, Château Pauqué and Paul Legill.

Other gd producers: Krier-Welbes (organic), Mathis Bastian, Charles Decker, Gloden & Fils, Domaine Mathes, Schlink-Hoffeld. Domaines Vinsmoselle are a union of co-ops. Premium label Art+Vin can be gd (eg. 2011 Schengen Markusberg Pinot Gris), but one has to be selective.

Spain & Portugal

Abbreviations used in the text:

Alel	Alella	P Vas	País Vasco
Alen	Alentejo	Pen	Penedès
Alg	Algarve	Pri	Priorat
Alic	Alicante	Rib del D	Ribera
Ara	Aragón		del Duero
Bair	Bairrada	Rio	Rioja
Bei Int	Beira Interior	R Ala	Rioja Alavesa
Bier	Bierzo	R Alt	Rioja Alta
Bul	Bullas	RB	Rioja Baja
Cád	Cádiz	Set	Setúbal
Can	Canaries	Som	Somontano
C-La M	Castilla-	Tej	Tejo
	La Mancha	U-R	Utiel-Requena
C y L	Castilla y León	V'cia	Valencia
Cat	Catalunya	Vin	Vinho Verde
Cos del S	Costers del Segre		
Dou	Douro		
Emp	Empordà		
Gal	Galicia		
La M	La Mancha		
Lis	Lisboa		
Mad	Madrid, Vinos de		
Mall	Mallorca		
Min	Minho		
Mont-M	Montilla-Moriles		
Mur	Murcia		
Nav	Navarra		

How to attract people in tough times? If you are Rioja, Spain's oldest DO, coming up to its first century, the answer is with value. Even very old Rioja – and collections of old wines exist in the region, and are sometimes made available to lucky fans – is remarkably cheap. Rioja ages tremendously well: these are elegant, delicate wines, yet still full of fruit and freshness. Value is the keyword across Spain today. The country offers originality, diversity, a sense of place and drinking pleasure in spades.

In Portugal, creativity blossoms in tough times. A crackle of energy surrounds recent collaborations like Young Winemakers of Portugal, Simplesmente Vinho (terroir-focused wine-growers), even individual projects like leading winemakers Susana Esteban's and Sandra Tavares de Silva's Crochet label, which highlights the growing prominence of women in the top echelons of winemaking. And for those with money to invest in ailing estates, the rewards can be swift: new entries Ideal Drinks and Covela are cases in point.

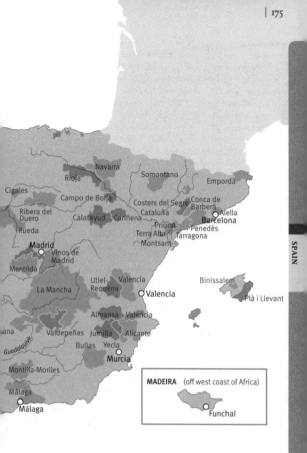

Spain

Recent Rioja vintages

2013 Late frost reduced crop. After good summer, some rain and hail around harvest. Quality will depend on severe selection. Style will be fresher, with slightly lower alcohol.

2012 Excellent quality but one of lowest yields for two decades.

2011 Lower yields, more concentrated fruit than 2010.

2010 Officially an *excelente* vintage. Top wines still to show their best.

2009 Enjoyable now, but will develop further.

2008 Best are fresh and aromatic, a little lower in alcohol.

2007 Difficult vintage; ready to drink with bright, fresh fruit.

2006 Drinking well now. Light, fragrant vintage.

2005 Another stand-out vintage on heels of 2004. Enjoy now, or keep best.

2004 Outstanding vintage. Drink now; best will keep.

2003 Very hot summer spoiled freshness of much fruit. Drink up.

Aalto Rib del D r ★★★★ Mariano García, ex-VEGA SICILIA, and the president of the CONSEJO, intends to make the best TINTO FINO. Modern, big wines, needing time. Aalto 2011 is inky with refined cedar; PS 2011 (Pagos Seleccionados, selected from 200 small plots) dense, v. spicy. Family wineries: MAURO, Maurodos (TORO).

Abadía Retuerta C y L r ★★→★★★ Next door to RIB DEL D; ripe modern style, international varieties, influential winemakers; grand hotel in former monastery. Gd-value Rívola; spicier Selección Especial; 100% TEMPRANILLO Pago Negralada; sumptuous SYRAH Pago la Garduña.

Agustí Torelló Mata Cat ★★→★★★ Family business entirely focused on CAVA, using traditional varieties. Kripta 06 and Gran Res Barrica 08 stand out.

Alicante r w sw ★→★★ Look to the Levant for great value, originality, interest. The coast provides outstanding sweet MOSCATEL from GUTIÉRREZ DE LA VEGA. Up in the hills, rich, spicy MONASTRELL thrives. Top producers: ENRIQUE MENDOZA, Bernabé Navarro (wines made in clay *tinajas*), ARTADI, Bruno Prats, Salvador Poveda. Historic curiosity reviving: sweet fortified solera-aged Fondillón from Primitivo Quiles, Gutiérrez de la Vega; more versions planned.

Alión Rib del D r ★★★★ 03 04' 05' 06 07 The more modern cousin, not the poor relation, of VEGA SICILIA. 100% TINTO FINO, Nevers oak, with dense black fruit.

Álvaro Palacios Pri r ★★★→★★★★ By charging sky-high prices, Palacios put PRI on the map. Now developing Burgundy-style village wines, offering top wine *en primeur*. Camins del Priorat is v.gd value, floral, introduction. Les Terrasses is bigger, spicier; Finca Dofí has a dark undertone of CAB SAUV, SYRAH, MERLOT, CARIÑENA. Super-pricey L'Ermita is powerful and dense from low-yielding GARNACHA. Also in BIER, RIO.

Artadi Alic, Nav, R Ala r ★★→★★★★ Outstanding modern RIO: powerful single-v'yd El Pisón needs 8–10 yrs; as does spicy, smoky Pagos Viejos. Gd-value VIÑAS de Gain. V.gd, equally modern El Sequé (r) ALIC, Artazuri (r, DYA p) NAV.

Baigorri R Ala r w ★★→★★★ Wines as glamorous as the architecture, a clear glass box; vats below. Bold modern RIO. Primary black fruits, bold tannins, fresh finish, upbeat oak. Garage wins the prizes. RES more approachable.

New from the Basque country: superbly fresh sweet wines from Chacolí grape.

Barón de Ley RB r p w ★→★★ Well-made, gd-value wines from one-time Benedictine monastery. Experiments with new varieties/blends. DYA rosado.

Báscula, La Alic, Rib del D, Rio r w sw ★★ Young brand with gd-value wines in upcoming regions, plus classics, eg. ALIC, JUMILLA, RIB DEL D, RIO, Terra Alta, YECLA. South African winemaker, British MW.

Belondrade C y L, Rue w ★★ France comes to RUEDA: Didier Belondrade arrived in 1994. Son Jean now in charge. Top is Belondrade 11, vivid, with spicy oak from barrel ferment. Second label: Apollonia 12.

Benjamin Romeo Rio r w ★★→★★★ Romeo (ex-ARTADI) is one of RIO's rock stars. Small production, *terroiriste*. Rich, *top white Que Bonito Cacareaba 12.* Flagship red Contador, "super-second" La Cueva del Contador 10. V. concentrated parcel, La VIÑA de Andrés Romeo 09.

Beronia Rio r p w ★→★★★ A transformation. Owner González Byass invested in oak, winemaking. Confidently revived RES; gd rosado. 40th anniversary bottles of '73 Beronia (first ever) v. alive.

Bierzo r w ★→★★★ Slate soils, a crunchy *Pinot-like red – Mencía* – and ethereal white GODELLO have brought young winemakers buzzing. Best: Dominio de Tares, DESCENDIENTES DE J PALACIOS, Gancedo, Luna Berberide, Peique, Pittacum. To watch: Castro Ventosa Ultreia St Jacques 08 (r).

Binissalem Mall r p w ★★ Best-known MALL DO northeast of Palma. Two-thirds red, mainly tannic Mantonegro grape. Biniagual, Binigrau, Macià Batle.

Bodega A cellar; a wine shop; a business making, blending and/or shipping wine.

Bodegas Benjamin de Rothschild & Vega Sicilia Rio, R Alt r Shiny new project, 100% TEMPRANILLO. V'yds bought secretly a decade ago. First efforts are launching as Macán Clasico 09; top wine Macán 09.

Briones R Alt Small RIO hilltop town nr Haro, peppered with underground cellars. Producers incl FINCA ALLENDE, Miguel Merino. Worth a detour to the *Dinastía Vivanco wine musuem.*

Calatayud Ara r p w ★→★★★ Rapidly improving DO rediscovering its old-vine GARNACHA. Delivers flavour and value. Best: BODEGAS Ateca (*see* JUAN GIL), Scottish El Escocés Volante (esp El Puño, La Multa); Lobban (El Gordito Garnacha by another Scot, Pamela Geddes), Virgén de la Sierra (Cruz de Piedra).

Campo de Borja Ara r p w ★→★★★ Prices creeping up but still spot-on source of gd-value DYA juicy GARNACHA and TEMPRANILLO, eg. BODEGAS Aragonesas, Borsao, Alto Moncayo.

Campo Viejo Rio r w p ★→★★ RIO's biggest brand and Spain's first carbon-neutral winery. Juicy TEMPRANILLO and GARNACHA, gd-value RES and Gran Res. Top of the range Dominio. Part of Pernod Ricard group (also Calatrava-designed Ysios winery). Makes Campo Viejo CAVA, looking at other key regions.

Canary Islands r p w ★→★★ V'yds not visited by phylloxera; original wines. No fewer than nine DOS. Best: dessert MALVASÍAS, MOSCATELS. But local dry white LISTÁN (aka PALOMINO) and Marmajuelo, black Listán Negro, Negramoll (TINTA NEGRA), Vijariego offer *enjoyable original flavours.* El Grifo fortified sweet Malvasía from DO Lanzarote is gorgeous.

Capçanes, Celler de Cat r p w sw ★→★★ One of Spain's top co-ops. Great-value, expressive wines from MONTSANT. Also a kosher specialist, esp Peraj Ha'abib 10.

Cariñena Ara r p w ★→★★ The one DO that is also the name of a grape variety. Solid, not exciting, but gd value; top pick is FINCA Aylés.

Casa Castillo Mur r ★★→★★★ Isolated estate, high up in JUMILLA. Great-value MONASTRELL 12; El Molar GARNACHA 11 has bright freshness. Also Valtosca 10 SYRAH, Las Gravas 09 single-v'yd blend, is v. mineral. Pie Franco 08, a patch of Monastrell that escaped the recent phylloxera, long, balanced.

Castaño Mur r p w sw ★→★★ The Castaño family is YECLA. Fine MONASTRELL, from value young wines to excellent Casa Cisca. Delicious sweet red DULCE 10.

Castilla y León r p w ★→★★ Spain's largest wine region. Plenty to enjoy, easy to get lost. Often great-value: famous producers and unknowns; ditto grapes. Discover DOS: Arribes (esp La Setera), BIER, CIGALES, Tierra de León, Tierra del Vino de Zamora, quality region Valles de Benavente. Red grapes incl MENCÍA, Juan Garcia, Prieto Picudo, TINTA DEL PAÍS; whites Doña Blanca. Gd, deeply coloured rosado.

Castillo Perelada Emp, Pri r p w sp ★→★★★ Glamorous estate, hotel, summer concerts; rapidly improving wines. Vivacious CAVAS esp Gran Claustro; modern reds, incl Ex Ex MONASTRELL, coastal FINCA Garbet SYRAH. Rare 12-yr-old, solera-aged GARNATXA de l'Empordà. Exceptional Casa Gran del Siurana, Gran Cruor, SYRAH blend from PRI.

Catalunya r p w sp A mere decade old, this vast DO covers the whole of Catalonia: seashore, mtn, in-between. Contains some of Spain's top names, incl TORRES and much else besides, enabling smart producers to do clever cross-DO blends.

Cava Spain's traditional-method sparkling is getting better and better. Made in PEN – in or around San Sadurní d'Anoia – but the term applies to a number of other regions, incl RIO (esp MUGA Conde de Haro). Market leaders: FREIXENET, CODORNÍU. Top names: AGUSTÍ TORELLÓ, Castell Sant Antoni, CASTILLO PERELADA, Cava de Nit, GRAMONA, Parxet, Raventós, RECAREDO (biodynamic), Sumarroca. CHARD, PINOT N were invading blends, but now much research into improving quality of traditional XAREL-LO grape. A few top producers leaving Cava DO because of historic poor image.

Chacolí / Txakoli P Vas (r) (p) w sw ★→★★ DYA The Basque wine. V'yds face chilly sea winds west of San Sebastián, hence aromatic, thrilling crunchiness of *pétillant* whites, locally poured into tumblers from a height. Top names: Ameztoi, Txomin Etxaniz. Fascinating late-harvest Urezti 10 from Itsasmendi; lusciously fresh botrytis Arima 10 from Gorka Izagirre.

Chivite Nav r p w sw ★★→★★★★ Historic NAV bodega freshening up. Popular DYA range Gran Feudo, esp Rosado, Sobre Lías (*sur lie*). Excellent *Colección 125* range, incl outstanding CHARD, one of Spain's best, delicate VENDIMIA Tardia MOSCATEL. Young PAGO wines of beautiful *Arínzano* estate, still improving. Second label **Casona** launched 2012. Long-term consultant winemaker Denis Dubourdieu. In RIO, owns VIÑA Salceda (v.gd Conde de la Salceda), in RUEDA **Baluarte** (superb DYA VERDEJO).

Cigales C y L r p (w) ★→★★★ Lying between RIB DEL D and TORO, tiny Cigales fights to make itself heard. But there is real potential beyond commercial DYA reds for serious old-vine TEMPRANILLO. Voluptuous César Príncipe; more restrained Traslanzas, Valdelosfrailes.

Clos Mogador Pri r w ★★★→★★★★ In region now filled with big names, René Barbier is a quiet godfather to younger winemakers. Clos Mogador still commands respect: 2005 was first to receive new high *Vi de Finca Qualificada* classification. Spicy, fragrant, honeyed Clos Nelin white, forerunner of a number of GARNACHA BLANCA blends.

Varying the diet

The ubiquitous TEMPRANILLO has different names according to where you are in Spain: TINTO FINO, Tinta de Toro, CENCIBEL... *see* pp.16–26. GARNACHA has fewer synonyms but is also widely spread. But Spain has been discovering a raft of other grapes. MENCÍA, Bobal, GRACIANO, Caíno, Lado, Juan García, Manto Negro, Maturana, Doña Blanca, Albillo, Samsó and more. There are around 100 different grapes being grown in Spain now, if you incl foreign invaders.

Codorníu Cos del S, Pen, Pri, Rib del D, Rio r p w sp ★→★★★★ One of the two largest CAVA firms, owned by the Raventós family, rival to FREIXENET. Gd Reina Maria Cristina, v. dry Non Plus Ultra, PINOT N. Outstanding trio of single-v'yd Cavas, **Gran Codorniu**, esp XAREL-LO bottling. Leads research into local varieties, reviving other wineries of group. Extensive v'yds of Raimat in COS DEL S improving as is Legaris in RIB DEL D; Bilbainas in RIO has juicy, popular VIÑA Pomal. *See also* SCALA DEI.

Conca de Barberà Cat r p w Small Catalan DO once purely a feeder of quality fruit to large wineries, now some excellent wineries, incl bio Escoda-Sanahuja. Top TORRES wines Grans Muralles, Milmanda both made in this DO.

Consejo Regulador Organization that controls a DO – each DO has its own. Quality as inconsistent as wines they represent: some bureaucratic, others enterprising.

Contino R Ala r p w ★★★★ Jesus Madrazo focuses on his single-v'yd (RIO's first) with consistent success. RES 07 has many yrs ahead. GRACIANO is Rio's finest expression of this difficult variety. Top: single-v'yd Viña del Olivo 08, fresh with leather, liquorice. Ripe, textured GARNACHA white blend; aromatic rosado. Serious hail in 2013.

Costers del Segre Cat r p w sp ★★→★★★★ Geographically divided DO with excellent producers, incl mountainous Castell d'Encus (run by former TORRES MD Raül

Bobet, also of FERRER-BOBET, experimenting with medieval fermenters carved out of rock): Ekam RIES, Thalarn SYRAH; also Castell del Remei, Cérvoles, Raimat.

Crianza Refers to the ageing of wine. New or unaged wine is Sin Crianza (without) or JOVEN. In general Crianzas must be at least 2 yrs old (with 6 mths–1 yr in oak) and must not be released before the third yr. *See* RES.

Cusiné, Tomás Cos del S r w ★★→★★★ One of Spain's most innovative winemakers, originally behind Castell del Remei, Cérvoles. Individual, modern wines, incl TEMPRANILLO blend Vilosell; original 10-variety white blend Auzells.

CVNE R Alt r p w ★→★★★★ Pronounced *coo-nee*, the once traditional Compañía Vinícola del Norte de España (1879), now on the up. Reliable, fruity RES; fresh, refined Imperial Gran RES 04; delicate VIÑA Real Gran Res 06. Long-ageing wines: **64** Viña Real still brilliant. CONTINO is member of group but operates independently.

Dehesa La Granja C y L r ★★★ Winery run by daughter of Alejandro Fernández (see PESQUERA) on huge family estate in Zamora, with ancient cellars. 100% TEMPRANILLO; 06 superbly dense, textured.

Denominación de Origen (DO), Denominación de Origen Protegida (DOP) The former *Denominación de Origen* (DO) and DO *Calificada* are now grouped as DOP along with the single-estate PAGO denomination. Lesser category VCPRD is becoming *Vinos de Calidad de Indicación Geografica* (VCIG). Got that?

Dinastía Vivanco R Alt r w ★★ Major family-run commercial BODEGA in BRIONES, with some interesting varietal wines. *Wine museum is worth the detour.*

Domaines Lupier Nav r ★★ Young couple making just two wines from old-vine GARNACHA: floral La Dama; dense, bold El Terroir. Bio.

Dominio de Tares Bier r w ★★ Outstanding MENCIAS; old-vine Cepas Viejas and Tares P3 particularly gd. For a taste of Prieto Picudo, try Cumal from C Y L.

Dominio de Valdepusa C-La M r w ★★→★★★ Carlos Falcó, Marqués de Griñon has been a confident rule-breaker since the 70s at family estate nr Toledo, pioneering SYRAH, PETIT VERDOT, drip irrigation, soil science, working with top consultants. Ultimately recognized as a PAGO. Wines are savoury, concentrated incl Syrah, value Caliza. Also in VINOS DE MADRID DO at El Rincón.

Dulce Sweet.

El Angosto V'cia r w ★★ A promising project run by long-est nurserymen in low-profile V'CIA DO. Look for white blend Almendros; red Angosto blend incl Marselan grape.

Empordà Cat r p w sw ★→★★ Small, fashionable DO nr French border; centre of creativity. Best wineries: CASTILLO PERELADA, Celler Marti Fabra, Pere Guardiola, Vinyes dels Aspres. Quirky, young Espelt grows 17 varieties: try GARNACHA/CARIGNAN Sauló. Sumptuous natural sweet wine from Celler Espolla: Solera Gran RES.

Enrique Mendoza Alic r w sw ★★ Pepe Mendoza is key figure in resurgence of DO and of MONASTRELL grape. Wines as expressive, individual as the man. Vibrant Tremenda 10, intense, savoury single-v'yd Las Quebradas. Honeyed, sweet MOSCATEL; plans for FONDILLÓN revival.

Espumoso Sparkling wine, but not made according to the traditional method, unlike CAVA. Therefore usually cheaper.

Ferrer-Bobet Pri r ★★→★★★ Instantly successful project from Sergi Ferrer-Salat (founder of Barcelona's Monvinic wine bar/shop) and Raül Bobet (former TORRES MD). Slate soils; old vines; culminates in Selecció Especial Vinyes Velles 10, wonderfully complex expression of PRI.

Finca Farm or estate (eg. FINCA ALLENDE).

Finca Allende R Alt r w ★★★★ Top (in all senses) RIO BODEGA at BRIONES in ancient merchant's house with splendid tower, great view of v'yds. *06' is superbly elegant, lovely now but will keep*; single-v'yd Calvario 06' is foursquare, v. youthful; Aurus

07' sumptuous with minerality. Two whites: powerful RIOJA Blanco, v. fine, oak-influenced Martires, partner to Calvario. FINCA Nueva is new range of less pricey wines. Also Finca Coronado, LA MANCHA.

Finca Sandoval C-La M r ★→★★★ Wine-writer Victor de la Serna is serious about winemaking: with Finca Sandoval (SYRAH/MONASTRELL/Bobal) he champions two indigenous varieties in an upcoming region. Second label, Salia (Syrah/GARNACHA/Bobal), simpler, half the price.

Fondillón Alic sw ★→★★★ Once-fabled sweet red from MONASTRELL, aged to survive sea voyages. Now matured in oak for min 10 yrs; some soleras (*see* Sherry) of great age. Small production by eg. GUTIÉRREZ DE LA VEGA, Primitivo Quiles.

Freixenet Pen p w sp ★→★★★ Huge CAVA firm owned by Ferrer family. Rival of similarly enormous CODORNÍU. Best-known for frosted, black-bottled Cordón Negro, standard Carta Nevada. Cava Elyssia is a real step up: refreshed by CHARD, PINOT N. Also controls Castellblanch, Conde de Caralt, Segura Viudas, Bordeaux négociant Yvon Mau.

Galicia (r) w Rainy northwestern corner of Spain; some of Spain's best whites (*see* RÍAS BAIXAS, MONTERREI, RIBEIRA SACRA, RIBEIRO, VALDEORRAS), most refreshing reds.

Gramona Pen r w sw sp ★★→★★★★ Star CAVA cellar, a leader in drive to show there is character in Cava; fifth generation makes impressive long-aged Cavas, incl Imperial Gran RES 07, *III Lustros*, Argent. Research and experimental plantings also give rise to gd XAREL-LO-dominated *Celler Batle Gran Res 01*, sweet wines, incl Icewines, impressive CHARD/SAUV BL Gra a Gra Blanco DULCE.

Gran Reserva *See* RES.

Gutiérrez de la Vega Alic r w sw ★→★★★ Small, two-centre family BODEGA of opera-loving general (retired). Produces reds but focuses on fragrant, honeyed Casta Diva range of sweet MOSCATELS. Keeps up FONDILLÓN tradition.

Hacienda Monasterio Rib del D r ★★→★★★ Cult winemaker Peter Sisseck of PINGUS ensures a high profile for TINTO FINO/CAB/MERLOT blends. Reputation is deserved with approachable RES 08; more concentrated, structured Res Especial 09.

Haro R Alt The picturesque heart of the R ALT, with the great names of RIO clustered in and around the old railway station. Visit LÓPEZ DE HEREDIA, MUGA, LA RIOJA ALTA, as well as modern RODA.

José Pariente C y L, Rue w ★★ Victoria Pariente makes crisp DYA VERDEJO of shining clarity. New Cuvée Especial 12 fermented in concrete eggs shows fascinating complexity, silky late-harvest Apasionado 12.

Joven Young, unoaked wine, becoming increasingly popular, esp as economic crisis continues. *Also see* CRIANZA.

Juan Gil Mur r ★★→★★★ Old family business relaunched in 2002 to make the best in JUMILLA. Gd young MONASTRELLS (eg. 4 Meses); dense, powerful top wines Clio and El Nido. Family group also incl modern wines in rising DOS, incl Shaya (RUEDA), Can Blau (MONTSANT).

Jumilla Mur r (p) (w) ★→★★★ Arid v'yds in mtns north of Mur; old MONASTRELL vines rediscovered by ambitious winemakers. TEMPRANILLO, MERLOT, CAB, SYRAH, PETIT VERDOT also feature. Top producer: JUAN GIL with El Nido. Also follow: Agapito Rico, Casa Castillo, CASTAÑO with Casa Cisca, Carchelo, Luzón, Valle del Carche, Valtosca.

Juvé & Camps Pen w sp ★★★ Consistently gd family firm for top-quality CAVA from free-run juice. RES de la Familia is the stalwart, with top-end Gran Res, Milesimé CHARD Gran Res.

La Calandria Nav r p ★★ One of the new wave of small producers making old-vine GARNACHA. Great-value Cientruenos.

La Mancha C-La M r p w ★→★★ Spain's least impressive wine region, south of Madrid. Best: PESQUERA'S El Vinculo, MARTÍNEZ BUJANDA'S FINCA Antigua, Volver.

SPAIN | Fin–Mas | 181

León, Jean Pen r w ★★ →★★★ Pioneer of CAB SAUV, CHARD in Spain; TORRES-owned since 1995, recovering quality under Mireia Torres. Gd, oaky Chards, expressive 3055 *Merlot*; elegant Vinya La Scala Cab Sauv.

López de Heredia R Alt r p w sw ★★ →★★★★ Remarkable "château" beside HARO station. Delicate, old-style, long-aged wines suddenly back in fashion. Cubillo is younger range with GARNACHA; darker Bosconia; delicate, ripe *Tondonia 64, 68, 70, 81, 94, 95, 96, 01, 04*. Whites have seriously extensive barrel- and bottle-age: fascinating Gravonia 00, Tondonia Gran RES *87 91 96*. Parchment-like Gran Res Rosado 00.

Loxarel Pen sp An original. Cent Nou 109 Brut Nature RES 02 is quirky treat for lovers of natural wine: traditional-method sparkling, but lees are never taken out of the bottle, so it's not CAVA. Complex, cloudy, unsulphured, v. youthful after 109 months.

Luis Cañas R Ala r w ★→★★★ Widely awarded family business; offering honest quality from JOVEN to garage-style wines. Ever-reliable Selección de la Familia RES 06, ultra-concentrated Hiru 3 Racimos 07. BODEGAS Amaren is rich, modern and concentrated.

Move to French oak from American in Rioja gives more elegance, perhaps less Rioja "typicity".

Madrid, Vinos de Madr r p w ★→★★ GARNACHA vines provide the capital's bar wines. Today old, often abandoned vines are part of a new wave of quality. Go-ahead names: Bernabeleva, with burgundian white and top Garnacha VIÑA Bonita. Also Marañones, Gosálbez-Ortí (run by former pilot), Jeromín, Divo, Viñedos de San Martín (part of Enate group), El Regajal.

Málaga Once-famous DO awakened by TELMO RODRIGUEZ who revived moribund MOSCATEL industry with subtle, sweet *Molino Real*. Exceptional No 3 Old Vines Moscatel from Jorge Ordoñez, US importer. Bentomiz, with Ariyanas wines, has an impressive portfolio of sweet and dry sweet Moscatel, also reds, incl local Romé variety.

Mallorca r w ★→★★★ Formerly tourist wines, now much improved; serious, fashionable in Barcelona, high-priced. Family cellars remain but new investment and innovation with eg. 4 Kilos. Plenty of interest in Anima Negra, tiny Sa Vinya de Can Servera, Hereus de Ribas, *Son Bordils, C'an Vidalet*. Also Biniagual. Reds blend traditional varieties (Mantonegro, Callet, Fogoneu) plus CAB, SYRAH, MERLOT. Whites (esp CHARD) improving fast. Two DOS: BINISSALEM, PLÁ I LLEVANT.

Manchuela C-La M r w Traditional region for bulk wine, now showing promise with eg. Bobal, MALBEC, PETIT VERDOT. Pioneer FINCA SANDOVAL followed by Alto Landón and Ponce, producer of *pie franco* (ungrafted vines) wine.

Marqués de Cáceres R Alt r p w ★→★★ Pioneered French winemaking techniques in RIO. Faded glory at present. Gaudium is modern style; Gran RES the classic.

Marqués de Murrieta R Alt r p w ★★★→★★★★ One of RIO's great names, famous for magnificent long-aged Castillo de Ygay Gran RES. Res Especial also outstanding. Best-value is dense, flavoursome Res. Surprisingly, also convincingly modern, if oaky, Dalmau. *Capellania* is complex, textured white, one of Rio's best.

Marqués de Riscal R Ala r (p) w ★★→★★★ Founding RIO BODEGA now better known for Frank Gehry's titanium-roofed hotel than for wine. A pity. Choose from equally modern powerful Barón de Chirel RES or pick a Gran Res. A pioneer in RUEDA (since 1972) making vibrant DYA SAUV BL, VERDEJO.

Martínez Bujanda, Familia C-La M, Rio r p w ★→★★★ Commercially astute business with a number of wineries, also makes private-label wines. Most attractive are *Finca Valpiedra*, charming single estate in RIO; FINCA Antigua in LA M.

Mas Alta Cat r ★★ Young (1999) PRI project coming to fruition with advice from

SPAIN

Rhône specialists Tardieu and Cambie. La Creu Alta is impressive blend of CARIÑENA, GARNACHA and SYRAH.

Mas Martinet Pri r ★★★→★★★★ PRI pioneer with excellent Clos Martinet. Second label: Martinet Bru 07. Now run by 2nd generation, ever-innovating, thoughtful, practising fermentation in the v'yds, and in *tinajas* (clay pots).

Mauro C y L r ★★★ No need for DO in this new-wave BODEGA in Tudela del Duero. Pedigree of Mariano Garcia of AALTO and formerly VEGA SICILIA says it all. A favourite with Spanish collectors. Mauro 09 is delicious, earthy, rich. Sister winery: Maurodos in TORO.

Méntrida C-La M r p ★→★★ Former co-op country south of Madrid, now being put on the map by Arrayan, Canopy and influential Daniel Jiménez-Landi (incl Piélago, Sotorrondero).

Gran Reservas, unlike other world classics, are released "ready to drink". But try ageing further.

Miguel Torres Cat, Pri, Rio r p w sw ★★→★★★★ Uniquely successful, consistent high-quality family firm. Miguel Torres has handed over to his son, Miguel A Torres; daughter Mireia is technical director. But he remains active and innovative, launching first Torres CAVA; also impressive focus on environment. Ever-reliable DYA CAT VIÑA Sol, grapey Viña Esmeralda, silky sweet MOSCATEL. Best reds: top PEN CAB *Mas la Plana*; CONCA DE BARBERÀ duo (Burgundian *Milmanda*, one of Spain's finest CHARDS, *Grans Muralles* blend of local varieties) is stunning. JEAN LEÓN has v.gd offerings too. In RIB DEL D Celeste 09 is improving; gd RIO Ibéricos, PRI Salmos. Not to mention some of Chile's best wines.

Monterrei Gal w ★→★★★ DYA Small but growing DO in Ourense, south-central GAL. Full-flavoured, aromatic whites from Treixadura, GODELLO, Doña Blanca. Shows more to Galicia than ALBARIÑO. Best is Gargalo.

Montsant Cat r (p) w ★→★★★ Tucked in around PRI, MONTSANT echoes its neighbour's wines at lower prices. Fine GARNACHA BLANCA, esp from Acústic. CARIÑENA, GARNACHA deliver dense, balsamic, minerally reds: Capçanes, gd-value Masroig, Can Blau, Dosterras, Étim, Joan d'Anguera, Mas Perinet, Portal del Montsant (partner to gd Portal del Priorat) all offer impressive, individual wines.

Muga R Alt r p w (sp) ★★★→★★★★ Classic family firm in HARO producing some of RIO's most aromatic, balanced reds. Gd barrel-fermented DYA VIURA reminiscent of burgundy; textbook dry rosado; reds finely crafted, delicate. Best: wonderfully fragrant Gran RES Prado Enea 05; warm, full *Torre Muga* 09; expressive, complex Aro; dense, rich, structured Selección Especial.

Mustiguillo V'cia r ★★★ Decade-old BODEGA leads renaissance of the unloved local Bobal grape with scrupulous v'yd and cellar work. Junior, juicy Mestizaje 11 is great start, while FINCA Terrerazo 11 shows refinement. Top wine is Quincha Corral 07. Experimenting with Merseguera, local white variety. Prefers to have own DO, El Terrerazo.

Navarra r p (w) ★★→★★★ Region between RIO and Pyrénées, but always in Rio's shadow. Freedom to use international varieties can work against it, confusing its real identity. Best: expressive, old-vine GARNACHA eg. Domaines Lupier. Up-and-coming names incl Pago de Larrainzar, confident, youthful Tandem, gd-value GRACIANO specialist Zorzal. Best producers: ARTADI's Artazu, CHIVITE, DOMAINES LUPIER Inurrieta, LA CALANDRIA, Nekeas, OCHOA, Otazu, Pago de Cirsus, Señorío de Sarría with gd rosado.

Nido, El Mur r ★★★★ Glamorous star in the unpromising region of JUMILLA, with hitherto unfavoured MONASTRELL grapes. From serious JUAN GIL family results are impressive. Second label, Clio, is 70% MONASTRELL, 30% CAB SAUV; dense, perfumed El Nido is in the reverse proportion. Jumilla's top wine.

Ochoa Nav r p w sw sp ★→★★ Ochoa *padre* made significant technical contribution to growth of NAV. Daughters are working to return the family BODEGA to a new glory. V.gd rosado; fine, sweet MOSCATEL; fun, sweet, Asti-like sparkling.

Pago, Vinos de Pago denotes v'yd. Roughly equivalent to French *grand cru*. But criticisms persist about lack of objective quality, differing traditions of *pagos* so far. Obvious absentees incl ALVARO PALACIOS' L'Ermita, PINGUS, Calvario (FINCA ALLENDE), CONTINO's Viña del Olivo, TORRES properties.

Pago de Carraovejas Rib del D r (RES) ★★★ V.gd TINTO CRIANZA; despite name no mere Crianza in quality. Top wine: v.gd Cuesta de las Liebres.

Palacio de Fefiñanes Gal w ★★★★ Most ethereal of ALBARIÑOS. **Standard DYA wine** one of finest. Two superior styles: creamy but light-of-touch barrel-fermented 1583 (yr winery was founded); super-fragrant, pricey, lees-aged, mandarin-scented III.

Palacios, Descendientes de J Bier r ★★★ ÁLVARO PALACIOS launched modern PRI; his nephew Ricardo Pérez is doing same for BIER, teasing out aromatic charm of MENCÍA grape. Gd-value, floral *Pétalos*. Bio, on schist soils. Villa de Corullón 12, Las Lamas 12 both superb.

Palacios Remondo RB r w ★★→★★★ Family winery: ÁLVARO PALACIOS, prince of PRI, is working to restore GARNACHA to its rightful place in RIO, as well as promoting the concept of villages or crus, as in Burgundy. Gd news for RB, though village concept is not popular in Rio: producers have always blended. Complex, oaked white Plácet originally created by brother RICARDO PALACIOS. Reds: organic, Garnacha-led, red-fruited La Montesa; big, mulberry-flavoured, old-vine 100% Garnacha Propriedad. Work in progress, but watch this space.

Pazo de Señorans Gal w ★★★ DYA Exceptionally fragrant ALBARIÑOS from a benchmark BODEGA in RÍAS BAIXAS. V. fine Selección de Añada 05, proof v. best Albariños age beautifully.

Penedès Cat r w sp ★→★★★★ Demarcated region west of Barcelona, best-known for CAVA. Identity rather confused, esp since recent arrival of extensive CAT DO. Best: Albet i Noya, Can Rafols dels Caus, Alemany i Corrio, GRAMONA, Jané Ventura, JEAN LEÓN, TORRES.

Pesquera Rib del D r ★★★★ Veteran Alejandro Fernández built global reputation of his wines and of RIB DEL D at his family v'yd opposite VEGA SICILIA. Less oak-ageing than neighbour, satisfying CRIANZA and RES, Millennium 96 (made for yr 2000); fine, mature Janus 86 for those who can afford it. Also at Condado de Haza, DEHESA LA GRANJA, El Vínculo (LA MANCHA). Visit original stone lagar in winery.

Planning a trip? Spain has 17 recognized wine routes – www.wineroutesofspain.com.

Pingus, Dominio de Rib del D r ★★★★ Consistent excellence from de luxe bio project. Pingus (Dane Peter Sisseck's childhood name) remains small. V. fine *Flor de Pingus* comes from rented v'yds, while Amelia is a single barrel named after his wife. Now growing with addition of PSI project.

Plá i Llevant Mall r w ★→★★★★ Eleven wineries comprise this tiny, lively, island DO. Aromatic whites; intense, spicy reds. Best: Toni Gelabert, Jaime Mesquida, Miguel Oliver, Vins Can Majoral. Exports small, so visit and enjoy on the island.

Priorat / Priorato Cat r w ★★→★★★★★ Gloriously isolated enclave, named after old monastery, renowned for llicorella (slate) soils, terraced v'yds, abandoned after Civil War, rescued by René Barbier of CLOS MOGADOR, ÁLVARO PALACIOS and others. Their wines remain consistently v.gd, showing characteristic mineral purity. After initial phase of heavily oaked, dense wines, elegance and more reasonable pricing appearing. Palacios has driven introduction of "village" DOs or crus within PRI. Other top names: Celler del Pont, Cims de Porrera, Clos Erasmus, Clos de l'Obac, Clos Nelin, Clos i Terrasses, Combier-Fischer-Gerin, Mas Alta,

Mas Doix, MAS MARTINET, SCALA DEI, Terroir al Limit, Val-Llach. Newer arrivals: FERRER-BOBET, TORRES.

Quinta Sardonia C y L r ★★★ One of glossy non-DO stars, based in Sardon de Duero, between ABADÍA RETUERTA and MAURO, launched by former colleague of Peter Sisseck at PINGUS. Dense, peppery, rich 09′. Member of Terras Gauda group, also incl Pittacum, BIER.

Rafael Palacios Gal w ★★★ Rafael, ÁLVARO PALACIOS' younger brother, runs this estate devoted to whites. Two styles: DYA As Sortes, intense, with citrus, white peach, v.gd acidity, a fine expression of GODELLO; textured, oak-aged Louro do Bolo.

Recaredo Pen w sp ★★★ →★★★★ Superb bio CAVA producer; also v.gd still wine. Tops is characterful, mineral *Turó d'en Mota*, from vines planted 1940, ages brilliantly.

Remelluri, La Granja Nuestra Señora R Ala r w ★★→★★★ Glorious mountainous estate. TELMO RODRIGUEZ has returned to his family property where he created intriguing DYA white from six varieties. Coming back to form.

Reserva Increasingly producers prefer to ignore the regulations. However – rare in the wine world – Res has actual meaning in Spain. Red Res must spend at least 1 yr in cask and 2 yrs in bottle; Gran Res, 2 yrs in cask and 3 yrs in bottle. With the crisis in Spain there are gd prices to be found for unsold Gran Res, and some excellent Res now goes into CRIANZAS.

Rías Baixas Gal (r) w ★★→★★★★ Atlantic DO producing DYA whites, darling of Madrid's diners, prices to match. With crisis, prices are cooling, exports increasing. Founded on ALBARIÑO grown in five subzones: Val do Salnés, O Rosal, Condado do Tea, Soutomaior, Ribera do Ulla. Best outstanding: ADEGAS Galegas, As Laxas, Castro Baroña, Castro Celta, Fillaboa, Coto de Xiabre, Gerardo Méndez, VIÑA Nora, Martín Códax, PALACIO DE FEFIÑANES, Pazo de Barrantes, PAZO DE SENORANS, QUINTA do Lobelle, Santiago Ruíz, Terras Gauda, La Val, Valdamor, *Zarate*. Growing interest in longer lees-ageing, barrel-ageing.

In Rías Baixas they add oyster shells (big local industry) to vineyard soil; it lifts the pH.

Ribeira Sacra Gal r w ★★ Source of excellent Galician whites, from terraces running dizzyingly down to river Sil. Top producers: Dominio do Bibei, Guimaro. MENCÍA v. promising, eg. perfumed La Lama 10 from Dominio do Bibei.

Ribeiro Gal (r) w ★→★★★ DYA wine in western Ourense. Whites relatively low in alcohol, acidity, made from Treixadura, TORRONTÉS, GODELLO, LOUREIRO, Lado. Top producers: Coto de Gomariz, VIÑA MEÍN, Lagar do Merens. Also speciality sweet wine style, Tostado.

Ribera del Duero r p ★→★★★★ Glamorous, pricey, but still uneven DO growing TINTO FINO. DO that incl VEGA SICILIA, HACIENDA MONASTERIO, PESQUERA, PINGUS along with AALTO has to be serious, but with 250 BODEGAS consistency is hard to find. Other top names: ALIÓN, Astrales, Cillar de Silos, Condado de Haza, Pago de los Capellanes, Pérez Pascuas. *See also* neighbours ABADÍA RETUERTA, MAURO. Others: Alonso de Yerro, Bohórquez, Dehesa de los Canónigos, Matarromera, O Fournier, Protos, Sastre,Tomás Postigo, Vallebueno.

Rioja r p w sp ★→★★★★ *See* box, opposite.

Rioja Alta, La r ★★→★★★★ One of the great old RIO BODEGAS with lovely RES, two outstanding Gran Res. Alberdi is light, pretty, cedary; Ardanza is riper, a touch spicier but still elegant, boosted by GARNACHA. Standouts are excellent, tangy, vanilla-edged Gran Res 904 (**68** 01) and fine, multilayered Gran Res 890 (98), aged 6 yrs in oak. Also owns RÍAS BAIXAS Lagar de Cervera.

Roda R Alt r ★★★ Modern BODEGA nr station in HARO. Serious RES reds from low-yield TEMPRANILLO, backed by study of clones: Roda, Roda I, Cirsión. Also outstanding Dauro olive oil.

Rioja

Rioja has it all. International fame (supported by strong marketing), beautiful countryside, TEMPRANILLO wines charming young and at 40 yrs. The region is cut three ways, and after a century or more of blending, regionality and single-v'yds are increasingly important. Alavesa (part of the Basque country) offers freshness as well as some Beaujolais-style winemaking for juicy reds. Alta is the traditional home of Rio and its great names. Warmer Rioja Baja, the traditional source of GARNACHA, is gaining recognition by the efforts of eg. ALVARO PALACIOS. Styles come in three also: a revival in quality in the Jovens, an emphasis on serious RES with gd clean oak, and ultra-modern "high-expression" producers, with shiny wineries to match, who follow their own rules. Just a few BODEGAS, notably LA RIOJA ALTA, MUGA and LÓPEZ DE HEREDIA, continue to make delicate, aromatic, old-fashioned wines. Significant new arrivals incl ROTHSCHILD & VEGA SICILIA, which launched in 2013; *garagiste* David Sampedro's Phincas. Whites are looking up, with serious Burgundy-style oak treatment and much-improved v'yd work.

SPAIN

Rueda C y L w ★★→★★★ Spain's response to SAUV BL: zesty VERDEJO. Mostly DYA whites. "Rueda Verdejo" is 100% indigenous Verdejo. "Rueda" is blended with eg. Sauv Bl, VIURA. Barrel-fermented versions remain fashionable. Cheaper versions can be feeble. Best: Alvarez y Diez, Baluarte (*see* CHIVITE), **Belondrade**, François Lurton, MARQUÉS DE RISCAL, Naia, Ossian, JOSÉ PARIENTE, Palacio de Bornos, Javier Sanz, Sitios de BODEGA, Unzu, Veracruz, Vinos de Nieva, Vinos Sanz.

Scala Dei Pri r ★★★★ V'yds of "stairway to heaven" cling to slopes that tower over old monastery. One of PRI's classics, now carefully tended by part-owner CODORNÍU. Juicy young Negre, fine, refreshing. Cartoixa is powerful CAB SAUV/GARNACHA, more supple, scented since 07. V. promising experiments with single-v'yd Garnachas.

Sierra Cantabria Rio r w ★★→★★★★ The fourth generation of family specializes in single-v'yd, minimal-intervention wines, a relatively new concept in RIO. Burgundian approach to winemaking showing intensity, elegance: Organza white blend, RES Unico, Colección Privada, Amancio. At Viñedos de Páganos estate, equally outanding: La Nieta, superb El Puntido. Other properties incl Teso la Monja in TORO.

Somontano r p w ★→★★★ Cool-climate DO in Pyrénéan foothills beginning to define itself – slowly, given so many international varieties in v'yd. Opt for MERLOT, GARNACHA, GEWURZ, CHARD. Best producers: Enate, Viñas del Vero owned by GONZÁLEZ BYASS. From its property Secastilla come Old-Vine Garnacha, GARNACHA BLANCA, glossy Clarion, Gran Vos, plus top blend Blecua.

Tares, Dominio de Bier r w ★★★ MENCÍA is a tough grape, but dark, spicy **Bembibre**, **Cepas Viejas** prove what can be achieved. Sister winery VDT Dominio dos Tares makes range from interesting black Prieto Picudo variety: simple Estay; more muscular Leione; big, spicy Cumal.

Telmo Rodríguez, Compañía de Vinos r w sw ★★→★★★ Telmo Rodríguez made his name, and many fine wines, by finding and recuperating old v'yds. Now sources and makes a wide range of excellent DO wines from all over, incl MÁLAGA (**Molino Real** MOSCATELS), RIO (Lanzaga, Matallana), RUEDA (Basa), TORO (Dehesa Gago, Gago, PAGO la Jara), **Valdeorras** (DYA Gaba do Xil GODELLO). Has returned to his family property REMELLURI in Rio – look out for rise in quality.

Toro C y L r ★→★★★★ Small DO west of Valladolid at last starting to make wines that live up to its high profile. Local Tinta de Toro was rustic, overalcoholic;

still alcoholic but today can be boldly expressive. Try Maurodos (*see* AALTO), with fresh, black-fruit-scented Prima and dense, old-vine San Román, also VEGA SICILIA-owned Pintia. Glamour comes with Numanthia Teso la Monja. Also recommended: Capo Eliseo, Estancia Piedra, Matarredonda, PAGO la Jara from TELMO RODRÍGUEZ, QUINTA de la Quietud, Sobreño.

Utiel-Requena r p (w) ★→★★ Satellite region of V'CIA forging its own identity with rustic but now improving Bobal grape. Tiny Cerrogallina shows way ahead. DO is hampered by its size (more than 40,000 ha), which makes it primarily a feeder for industrial requirements of nearby V'cia. New projects appearing, eg. Alvares Nölting, Hispano-Suizas project.

Valdeorras Gal r w ★→★★★ GALICIAN DO in northwest Ourense leaving behind its co-op-based beginnings by virtue of its DYA GODELLO. Best: Godeval, RAFAEL PALACIOS, A Tapada, TELMO RODRÍGUEZ.

Valdepeñas C-La M r (w) ★→★★ Large DO nr Andalucían border. Gd-value RIO-ish reds, made primarily from CENCIBEL grape. Fine producers: Los Llanos, Luis Megía, Félix Solís and the *Viña Albali* brand.

Valencia r p w sw ★→★★ Big exporter of table wine. Primary source of cheap, fortified, sweet MOSCATEL. Most reliable producer: Murviedro. Growing interest in inland, higher-altitude old-vines and minimal intervention in winemaking: eg. *garagiste* Rafael Cambra, EL ANGOSTO, Celler del Roure, Aranleon, new businesses all interested in old vines.

Cabernet Franc originated in the Basque Country; it used to be called Achéria.

Vega Sicilia Rib del D r ★★★★ Spain's "first growth", though surprisingly not from the prestige zone of RIO. Only Spanish wine to have real value in secondary auction market. Winemaking distinguished by meticulous care, long maturation. Wines are deep in colour, with cedarwood nose, intense and complex, finishing long; long-lived. Youthful Valbuena 05 06 08 – TINTO FINO with a little MALBEC, MERLOT – released with min 5 yrs in oak. Controlled, elegant flagship Único 98 00 02 03 is aged for 6 yrs in oak before bottling; RES Especial spends up to 10 yrs in barrel, then declared as NV. Both wines have some CAB SAUV, Merlot. Alión is more modern relative: 100% TINTO Fino aged in Nevers oak. Owns Pintia (TORO) and Oremus Tokaji (Hungary). Newest project, Rio *see* BODEGAS BENJAMIN DE ROTHSCHILD.

Vendimia Vintage.

Viña Literally, a v'yd.

Viña Meín Rib w ★★ Small estate in a gradually emerging GALICIAN DO, making two exceptional DYA whites: one steel- and one barrel-fermented; both from some seven local varieties.

Vino de la Tierra (VDT) Table wine usually of superior quality made in a demarcated region without DO. Covers immense geographical possibilities; category incl many prestigious producers, non-DO by choice to be freer of inflexible regulation and use the varieties they want.

Yecla Mur r (p) w ★→★★ Something stirs in the isolated enclave of Yecla. Only 11 producers, but a real focus on reviving MONASTRELL, esp CASTAÑO.

Portugal

Recent vintages

2013 A vintage of two halves. Great quality for (most) whites, also reds picked before the rain; mixed results after the rain.

2012 Concentrated wines, good balance, especially whites.

2011 Well-balanced year; outstanding Douro, Alentejo reds.

2010 Good quality and quantity all round. Bairrada had another excellent year.

2009 Good overall. Bairrada and Lisboa excellent. Douro, Tejo, Alentejo: big wines, high alcohol.

2008 Almost uniformly excellent; Bairrada, Alentejo particularly. Good fruit intensity, balance, aroma.

2007 Aromatic whites; well-balanced reds with round tannins.

2006 Forward reds with soft, ripe fruit; whites with less acidity than usual.

Adega A cellar or winery.

Alenquer Lis r w ★★→★★★ 09′ 10 11 12 13 Sheltered DOC gd for reds. SYRAH pioneer MONTE D'OIRO leads field with CHOCAPALHA.

Alentejo r (w) ★→★★★ 05 06 07′ 08′ 09 10 11 12 Huge, warm, southerly region divided into subregional DOCS Borba, Redondo, Reguengos, PORTALEGRE, Evora, Granja-Amareleja, Vidigueira, Moura. VIHO REGIONAL Alentejano preferred by many top estates. Rich, ripe reds, esp from Alicante Bouschet, SYRAH, TRINCADEIRA, TOURIGA NACIONAL. Whites fast improving. CARTUXA, ESPORÃO, MALHADINHA NOVA, MOUCHÃO, MOURO, PESO, JOÃO PORTUGAL RAMOS and dos Coelheiros have potency, style. Watch: Dona Maria, SÃO MIGUEL, do Rocim, Terrenus, TIAGO CABAÇO, Susana Esteban, QUINTA do Centro.

Algarve r p w sp ★→★★ Southern coast VINHO REGIONAL. Crooner Cliff Richard's ADEGA do Cantor led shift from quaffers to quality; MALHADINHA NOVA's involvement at QUINTA do Convento do Paraiso should raise the bar. Watch: Monte da Casteleja, Quinta do Frances, Quinta dos Vales.

Aliança, Caves Bair r p w sp ★★→★★★ Large firm with four BAIR estates, incl QUINTA das Baceladas; gd reds and classic-method *sparkling*. Interests in Beiras (Casa d'Aguiar), ALEN (Quinta da Terrugem), DÃO (Quinta da Garrida) and DOU (Quatro Ventos).

Alorna, Quinta de Tej ★→★★ Historic family estate; modern, gd-quality/-value wines. Winemaker Martta Reis Simões has delicate touch, esp flagship red, white Marquesa de Alorna.

Ameal, Quinta do Vin w sp sw ★★★ V.gd LOUREIRO by ANSELMO MENDES, incl age-worthy, oaked Escolha, Special Late-Harvest, ARINTO ESPUMANTE.

Aphros Vin r p w sp ★★★ Permaculture bio estate with food forest. Top LOUREIRO (Daphne, with skin contact), Vinhão (oaked Silenus) esp food-friendly.

Aveleda, Quinta da Vin r p w ★→★★ DYA Home of eponymous estate-grown wines and Casal García, born 1939 and still VIN's biggest-seller.

Bacalhoa, Quinta da Set r w ★★★ 04 05 06 07 08′ 09 10 11 Once owned by the royal family, now BACALHOA VINHOS, the focus of this National Monument estate is CAB SAUV (planted 1979). Fleshier Palácio de Bacalhoa has more MERLOT. Gd white Bordeaux blend with ALVARINHO.

Bacalhoa Vinhos Alen, Lis, Set r p w sp sw ★★→★★★ Principal brand and HQ of Madeiran billionaire José Berardo's Group (incl BACALHOA and holdings in CAVES ALIANÇA and HENRIQUES & HENRIQUES). Barrels of delectable SETÚBAL MOSCATEL, incl rare Roxo displayed alongside fine art collection. Modern, well-made Serras de Azeitão, Catarina, Cova da Ursa (PENÍNSULA DE SETÚBAL), TINTO da Anfora (ALENTEJO).

Bágeiras, Quinta das Bair r w sp ★★★→★★★★ (GARRAFEIRA r) 03 04′ 05′ 08′ 09

Stunning, traditionally crafted *garrafeira* BAGA (r), white built to age. Res (Baga with TOURIGA NACIONAL), Pai Abel (young v'yd) more forward. Wild, individual flavours. Fine, artisanal *zero dosage* sparkling, ages superbly.

Bairrada r p w sp ★ →★★★★ 03' 04 05' 06 07 08' 09' 10' 11 12 13 Atlantic-influenced DOC. Traditional strengths: age-worthy sparkling, BAGA reds. Fortified Baga (revived by FILIPA PATO) set for official (DOC) approval. Top Baga specialists: CAVES SÃO JOÃO, FILIPA PATO, LUÍS PATO, Sidónia de Sousa, QUINTA DAS BÁGEIRAS. Watch: Quintas de Baixo (now NIEPOORT in charge), Vadio, CAMPOLARGO, ALIANÇA, Colinas de S. Lourenço (IDEAL DRINKS) bring flair to recently permitted French varieties, esp CAB SAUV, PINOT N (Colinas). VINHO REGIONAL is Beira Atlântico.

Top tip: sparkling wine from Bairrada. Pink or white, great acidity, v. stylish.

Barca Velha Dou r ★★★★ 82' 83 85 91' 95' 99 00 04 Portugal's iconic red, created in 1952 by FERREIRA. Made in exceptional yrs. Intense, complex, with deep bouquet, it forged DOU's reputation for stellar wines. Aged several yrs pre-release. Second label, Casa Ferreirinha *Res Especial*, is v.gd buy.

Beira Interior ★→★★ Large DOC between DÃO and Spanish border. Huge potential from old, high (up to 700 metres) v'yds, esp for white Síria, Fonte Cal. Newcomer Beyra, QUINTAS do Cardo, dos Currais impress.

Branco White.

Brito e Cunha, João Dou r w ★★→★★★ 05 07 08' 09 10 Small riverside QUINTA with guest houses. Intense, elegant reds (now Vintage Port) from Quinta de San José, esp RES. More widely sourced Azéo also gd.

Buçaco Bei At r w ★★★ (r) 01 04 05' 06' 07 10 *Bussaco Palace Hotel's* Manueline Gothic architecture as frothy as wines are stern. Fortunately, guests can taste mature vintages (back to 40S). Reds blend BAIR BAGA/DÃO TOURIGA NACIONAL, whites DÃO Encruzado with Bair MARIA GOMES/Bical.

Bucelas Lis w ★★ DYA (unless oaked). Tiny DOC making tangy, racy ARINTO (known as "Lisbon Hock" in 19th-century England). QUINTA DA ROMEIRA excels.

Cabaço, Tiago Alen Exciting new-wave producer. Talented Susana Esteban (now with own eponymous label) skilfully blends native and international varietes, incl fruity ".beb" (from *beber* – to drink), to more food-friendly ".com" (*comer* – to eat) and pun-ful flagship "blog".

Campolargo Bair r w sp ★→★★★ Large estate; pioneer of Bordeaux varieties, PINOT N. Characterful wines from local grapes too, esp CERCEAL, ARINTO (w), Alvareloa (r).

Carcavelos Lis br sw ★★★ A local initiative to revive this almost defunct DOCS traditional toothsome apéritif and dessert wines revolves around new brand Conde de Oeiras.

Cartuxa, Adega da Alen r w sp ★★→★★★★ 17th-century cellars remain a tourist magnet but a modern winery has increased fruit and freshness from gd-value EA reds and Cartuxa RES to well-structured flagship Pêra Manca red 97 98 01 03 05' 07 08' 09 and its Hermitage-like white counterpart.

Carvalhais, Quinta dos Dão r p w sp ★★→★★★ (r) SOGRAPE's principal DÃO brand. Just-retired chief winemaker Manuel Vieira leaves a strong legacy, esp flagship TOURIGA NACIONAL Unico, v.gd Encruzado (w).

Casal Branco, Quinta de Tej r w sp ★→★★ Large family estate. Solid entry-level blends (local, international grapes). Best is Falcoaria range: old-vine CASTELÃO (r), FERNÃO PIRES (w), new Alicante Bouschet.

Castro, Alvaro Dão ★★★→★★★★ Wines of uncommon character and finesse mostly under family QUINTA names, de Saes and de Pellada. RES, Primus (w), *Pape* (r) excellent. Denser Carrocel (TOURIGA NACIONAL) needs time. Dado/Doda is DÃO/DOU blend made with NIEPOORT. New old-vine cuvées are traditional field blends from select parcels.

Chocapalha, Quinta de Lis r p w ★★→★★★ (r) Modernist using top Portuguese and international grapes. 100% TOURIGA NACIONAL flagship "CH" by Chocapalha v.gd.

Chryseia Dou r ★★→★★★ 05' 06 07 08' 09 11' Basing Bordeaux's Bruno Prats and SYMINGTON FAMILY ESTATES partnership at QUINTA de Roriz has increased the minerality of this polished red. Second label: *Post Scriptum* 07 08 09 10. Prazo de Roriz gd value.

Churchill Estates Dou r p w ★★→★★★ 05 06 07 08 09' 10 11' Fruity white, ROSADO, TOURIGA NACIONAL. Best: old-vine, mineral, grippy reds from north-facing QUINTA da Gricha, esp QUINTA da Gricha, Grande Res.

Colares Lis r w ★★ Tiny coastal DOC. Ungrafted Ramisco vines on sand produce *tannic reds*, mineral MALVASIA whites. Newcomers Fundação Oriente, Stanley Ho, Casal Santa Maria and Monte Cascas bring modern flair to ADEGA Regional de Colares' traditional style.

Conceito Dou ★★→★★★ Precocious talent Rita Ferreira Marques does style, substance. Strikingly labelled DOU Superior wines are modern in their clarity and finesse, traditional in their use of local varieties, incl an unusual PINOT N-like Bastardo. Also ALVARINHO VIN, New Zealand SAUV BL, South African red.

Covela Vin Neglected, having fallen into receivership, this estate nr the DOU has bounced back under new owners Brazilian Marcelo Lima and Brit Tony Smith. New VIN from Avesso grapes is star.

Crasto, Quinta do Dou r w ★★→★★★★ (r) 05' 06 07' 08 09' 10 11' Family-owned Cima Corgo estate. Jewel in the crown is two v. old field-blend parcels, producing Vinha da Ponte 01 03 04 07' 10', María Theresa 03' 05' 06 07 09' 11'; also (great-value) Res, v.gd varietals (TOURIGA NACIONAL, TINTA RORIZ). Crasto Superior, Flor de Crasto from young DOU Superior v'yd. Gd Port.

Dão Dão r p w sp ★★→★★★ 03' 04 05 06 07' 08' 09 10 11' Historic DOC reviving. Modern pioneers CARVALHAIS, ALVARO CASTRO, DÃO SUL, QUINTAS MAIAS, ROQUES make structured, elegant, perfumed reds, textured whites. Second wave incl Vinha Paz, da Falorca, do Mondego, JULIA KEMPER, Casa da Passarella, CASA DE MOURAZ, MOB (collaboration between winemakers from POEIRA, VALE MEÃO, WINE & SOUL). New VINHO REGIONAL: Terras do Dão.

Dão Sul Dão r w sp ★★→★★★ Changes at top have seen rationalization of modern but eclectic portfolio – das Tecedeiras (DOU) sold to COVELA and do Encontro (BAIR) range pruned. Core brands: QUINTA dos Grilos, Quinta Cabriz, organic Paco dos Cunhas de Santar and CASA DE SANTAR (DÃO), Encostas do Douro (Dou), do Encontro (Bair), do Gradil (LISB), Herdade Monte da Cal (ALEN).

Denominacão de Origem Controlada (DOC) Demarcated wine region controlled by a regional commission. *See also* VR.

Doce (vinho) Sweet (wine).

Douro soil has less than 2% organic matter versus 12% in neighbouring Minho.

Douro r p w sw ★★→★★★★ 03' 04' 05' 06 07' 08' 09' 10 11' Home of Port, but table wine, red and now white, has a firm grip. Perfume, fruit, minerals typify its best reds. Top whites textured, complex. Both can have freshness, balance. Look for BARCA VELHA, CRASTO, DUAS QUINTAS, NIEPOORT, PASSADOURO, POEIRA, VALE DONA MARIA, VALE MEÃO, VALLADO, WINE & SOUL. Watch: JOÃO BRITO E CUNHA, CONCEITO, QUINTA de Cottas (w), Maritávora (w), Muxagat, QUINTAS DO NOVAL, da Touriga. VR is Duriense.

Duas Quintas Douro Dou r w ★★★ (r) 04 05 06 07' 08 09' 10 11' Port shipper Ramos Pinto's quest for balance, finesse initially focused on blending fruit from two QUINTAS (dos Bons Ares, 600 metres; Ervamoira, 110–340 metres). New toys incl traditional varieties Tinta da Barca (r) and Folgasao (w), concrete eggs, Austrian wooden fermenters.

Duorum Dou r w ★★→★★★ Joint project of JOÃO PORTUGAL RAMOS and Jose Maria Soares Franco. New O Leucura Cota 200 and 400 reds from old vines at 200 and 400 metres showcase the DOU's diversity of terroir. Gd-value, fruity Tons entry level from new 250 ha Castelo Melhor v'yd in Dou Superior. V.gd Vintage Port.

Esporão, Herdade do Alen r w sw ★★→★★★ 07′ 08′ 09 10 11′ 12 A large estate making high-quality modern wines. Gd-value fruity, entry-level brands, esp Monte Velho. Varietal range, Esporão RES, Private Selection, GARRAFEIRA and v.-limited-edition Torre 04′, 07′ offer increasing complexity. New PORTALEGRE v'yd at 500 metres will augment freshness. Promising DOU estate too (QUINTA das Murças).

Espumante Sparkling. Best from BAIR, esp BÁGEIRAS, Kompassus, Colinas São Lourenço (see IDEAL DRINKS), DOURO (esp Vértice), Távora – Varosa and VIN.

Ferreira Dou r w ★→★★★★ SOGRAPE-owned Port shipper. Dizzying array of DOU wines under Casa Ferreirinha labels, from entry-level Esteva to BARCA VELHA. Top wines mostly from QUINTA da Leda but new top white and Vinha Grande rosé hail from Quinta do Sairrão at 650 metres.

Fonseca, José María da Lis r p w dr sw sp ★★→★★★ Historic family-owned estate. SET fortified MOSCATEL pioneer, using back catalogue to great effect in Apoteca, 20-yr-olds Alambre and Roxo. Popular volume branded wines LANCERS, PERIQUITA. Once cutting-edge brands eg. Vinya, Domini (DOU), Hexagon seem dated.

Foz de Arouce Bei At ★★→★★★ With a sheltered, southerly location and JOÃO PORTUGAL RAMOS at the helm of his parents-in-law's estate, BAGA reds (esp old-vine Vinhas Velhas Res de Santa Maria) are broad-shouldered. Characterful CERCEAL white is v.gd.

Garrafeira Label term: traditionally a merchant's "private res". Must be aged for min 2 yrs in cask and 1 yr in bottle (often aged much longer).

Horácio dos Reis Simões Set Innovative boutique producer of MOSCATEL from SET, esp late-harvest and fortified Moscatel Roxo (incl single-cask and Excellent, non-vintage blend). Thrilling fortified Bastardo.

Ideal Drinks Bair, Dão, Vin Founder, Swiss watch designer and businessman Carlos Dias brings experience marketing luxury goods to an ultra-ambitious range made by ex-DÃO SUL man Carlos Lucas with consultancy from Bordeaux's Pascal Chatonnet. Already Portugal's best CAB SAUV, still and sparkling (PINOT N) rosé (Colinas São Lourenço, BAIR). From VIN, arguably its best LOUREIRO (Paço de Palmeira) and a top-tier ALVARINHO (QUINTA da Pedra). Quinta de Bella (Dão) shows promise.

Kemper, Júlia Dão ★★★ r w Lisbon lawyer Júlia de Melo Kemper has breathed new life into QUINTA do Cruzeiro, the estate that has been in her family's ownership for 400 yrs. Organically cultivated (and certified) 15 ha of vines were planted in 2003 and the original 50s winery restored. Whites, a blend of Encruzado and MALVASIA Fina are particularly stylish. Foot-trodden reds are no slouch.

Lagoalva, Quinta da Tej r p w ★★ Young winemakers Diogo Campilho and Pedro Pinhão target a new generation with fruity, fresh blends of native grapes with CHARD, SAUV BL, SYRAH; oak can be overenthusiastic. V.gd varietal Alfrocheiro, Hobby Abafado (fortified FERNÃO PIRES).

Lancers p w sp ★ Semi-sweet (semi-sparkling) ROSADO, widely shipped to the USA by JOSÉ MARÍA DA FONSECA. Rosé Free is alcohol-free.

Lavradores de Feitoria Dou r w ★★→★★★ Collaboration of 18 producers with unusual strength in whites, esp SAUV BL, Meruge (100% Viosinho). Gd reds, incl Três Bagos Res, QUINTA da Costa das Aguaneiras, elegant Meruge (mostly TINTA RORIZ from a north-facing 400-metre v'yd).

Lisboa VR on west coast; best-known DOCS: ALENQUER, BUCELAS, CARCAVELOS, COLARES. CHOCAPALHA and MONTE D'OIRO spearhead quiet revolution of boutique producers;

international and top local grapes. Biomanz (Jampal), Casal Figueira (Vital) show a quirkier side. Watch: do Convento, Vale da Capucha, João Cabral Almeida (SAUV BL) and, for PINOT N, Casal Sta Maria, QUINTA de Sant'Ana.

Madeira r w ★→★★★★ Island world-famous for fortifieds. Modest table wines (Terras Madeirenses VR, Madeirense DOC); Primeira Paixão VERDELHO; Seiçal's BRANCO and Rosé are a cut above.

Maias, Quinta das Dão ★★→★★★ Sister of QUINTA DOS ROQUES; v'yd now certified organic. Flor das Maias 05 07 is showy TOURIGA NACIONAL-dominated blend. V.gd varietal wines, esp Jaen, MALVASIA Fina, DÃO's only VERDELHO.

Malhadinha Nova, Herdade da Alen r p w sw ★★★ 05 06 07 08' 09 10' Classy family estate with country house hotel. V.gd entry-level da Peceguina (blends and varietal), incl new VIOGNIER. Modern with a classic twist, flagship TINTO and Marias da Malhadinha are rich, spicy, muscular.

Mateus Rosé r p (w) sp ★ World's bestselling, medium-dry, lightly carbonated rosé now sports a (relatively) serious side: Fabulously Fruity ARAGONEZ, Delightfully Dry BAGA/SHIRAZ reds. New Expressions range incl MARIA GOMES/CHARD and three rosé blends (Baga/Shiraz; Baga/MUSCAT; Aragonez/ZIN).

Mendes, Anselmo Vin w sw sp ★★→★★★★ ALVARINHO-focused range incl Contacto, Muros Antigos, Muros de Melgaço and top-notch, oak-aged Curtimenta, single-v'yd Parcela Única. Gd LOUREIRO too. New: Pardusco – silky, modern red VIN.

Minho Vin River between north Portugal and Spain, also VR. Some leading VIN producers prefer VR Minho label.

Monte d'Oiro, Quinta do Lis r w p ★★→★★★ (Res) 04' 05 06' 07 08' 09 Portugal's best SYRAH, now incl Lybra rosé, thanks to initial consultancy, vine cuttings (Syrah 24 from 60-yr-old Hermitage vines) from Chapoutier (see France). V.gd VIOGNIER (Madrigal) too. Bento & Chapoutier Ex-Aequo Syrah/TOURIGA NACIONAL brand now subsumed in Monte d'Oiro range.

Moscatel do Douro Dou The elevated Favaios region produces surprisingly fresh, fortified MOSCATEL Galego (Muscat à Petit Grains) to rival those of SET. Look out for: ADEGA Cooperativa Favaios, PORTAL, Poças (see Port chapter), NIEPOORT.

> ### Roman *lagars*
> The Romans may have introduced them but Portugal is the spiritual home of *lagars*. These food-treading-friendly fermentation vats are as cherished as a Mercedes Benz and, similarly, come in a range of finishes: traditional granite, marble and wood or gleaming stainless steel. Options incl the vinous equivalent of cruise control – robotic feet.

Mouchão, Herdade de Alen r w ★★★→★★★★ 01 03' 05' 06 07 08 Leading traditional estate, focused on Alicante Bouschet, incl museum release (Colheitas Antigas), top yrs only, *Tonel 3–4*, also fortified Licoroso, grappa. Modern Ponte das Canas blend is an Alicante Bouschet blend with Portuguese grapes and SHIRAZ; Dom Rafael is value.

Mouraz, Casa de Dão ★★ Modern but characterful gd-value wines from several family-owned v'yds (140–400 metres), the DÃO's first to be organically cultivated (certified 1996). Alr label is from bought-in DOU, VIN, ALEN organic grapes.

Mouro, Quinta do Alen r ★★→★★★★ 00 04' 05' 06' 07 08' 09 Imposing, concentrated reds, mostly ALEN grapes, but also TOURIGA NACIONAL (gd varietal), CAB SAUV. Flagship Mouro Gold in top yrs 99 00 02 05 06' 07' 08. Modern, forward Vinha do Mouro gd-value.

Murganheira, Caves ★ Largest producer of ESPUMANTE. Gd vintage Bruto is PINOT N. Owns RAPOSEIRA.

Niepoort Dou r p w ★★★→★★★★ Family Port shipper and DOU wine pioneer with ever-expanding range of exceptional wines. New single- (125-yr-old field blend) v'yd Turris (r) shows move towards greater restraint and terroir expression, as do new Coche (only white with malolactic fermentation), single-v'yd Bioma (r) as well as icons Redoma (r p w, incl w RES) 06' 07' 08' 09' 10 (11); Robustus (r) 04 05 07' 08 09; Batuta (r) 05' 07 08' 09' 10' 11'; Charme (r) 05' 06 07' 08 09 10' 11'; Tiara (w). Experimental Projectos range incl Dou RIES (!), SAUV BL, PINOT N. Non-Dou wines incl Docil (VIN LOUREIRO), QUINTAS de Baixo (BAIRRADA) and da Lomba (DÃO), Ladredo (Ribeira Sacra, Spain).

Noval, Quinta do Dou r ★★→★★★ AXA-owned Port shipper, since 2004 making DOU wines (or Duriense VR with SYRAH), incl gd-value Cedro, Labrador (100% Syrah, named after winemaker's dog), v.gd varietal TOURIGA NACIONAL.

Palmela Set r w ★→★★★ CASTELÃO-focused DOC. Can be long-lived.

Passadouro, Quinta do Dou r w ★★→★★★ WINE & SOUL's Jorge Serôdio Borges makes superbly concentrated estate wines incl old-vine RES 05' 06 07' 08 09' 10 11'. TOURIGA NACIONAL comes from QUINTA do Sibio, whites from elevated granite v'yds. Entry label Passa gd value. V.gd Port.

Pato, Filipa Bair r w sp ★★★ LUÍS PATO's dynamic daughter is now focused on BAIR and BAGA for reds thanks to fruity entry-level FP Baga's super-short skin contact. Her "wines with no make-up" philosophy puts terroir centre-stage for flagship Nossa Calcario – a silky but fresh Baga and burgundian white (Bical). Espirito de Baga revives fortified tradition. Next project: amphora-aged white.

Varietal fortifieds are banned for Port but, labelled *Abadafo* or *Licoroso*, are in vogue elsewhere.

Pato, Luís Bair r w sw sp ★★→★★★★ 01' 03' 04 05' 06 07 08' 09' 10 11' Fine *seriously age-worthy, single-v'yd Baga*: Vinhas Barrio, Pan, Barrosa, Pé Franco single-v'yd cuvées from ungrafted vines: QUINTA do Ribeirinho (sandy soils), Valadas (chalky clay soils). Earlier-drinking reds incl *Vinhas Velhas*, Quinta do Ribeirinho 1st Choice (BAGA/TOURIGA NACIONAL blend), João Pato (Touriga Nacional), Baga Rebel (fermented on Bical skins), wacky red FERNÃO PIRES (fermented on Baga skins). Whites gd too, esp single-v'yd Vinha Formal. Sparkling wines, sweet Abafado range less nuanced. New: unsulphured Baga Natural, sealed under screwcap.

Pegões, Adega de Set r p w sw sp ★→★★ Dynamic co-op producing varietals and blends of natives and internationals. Stella label and low-alcohol Nico (w) offer gd clean fruit. Colheita Seleccionada (r w) exceptional value.

Península de Setúbal Set VR (formerly Terras do Sado). Established producers (eg. ADEGA DE PEGÕES, BACALHOA VINHOS, Casa Ermelinda Freitas) are on Azeitão's gentle chalky slopes or mineral-rich sandy soils of Sado and Tagus rivers. Newcomers lie further west and south. Watch: Herdades da Comporta and do Cebolal, Soberanas.

Periquita The nickname for the CASTELÃO grape, and successful brand name and trademark of JOSÉ MARÍA DA FONSECA.

Peso, Herdade do Alen ★→★★★ SOGRAPE-owned estate in Vidigueira, southern ALEN. Benefits of cooling influences (the Atlantic, 50 km away and the Serra de Portel) revealed in accomplished range, esp flagship Ícone and RES.

Poeira, Quinta do Dou r w ★★★→★★★★ 05' 06 07' 08' 09' 10' 11' QUINTA DE LA ROSA's winemaker Jorge Moreira's own label. Elegant red from cool, north-facing slopes; new white is mineral, estate-grown, oak-aged ALVARINHO (VR Duriense). Classy second label Pó de Poeira (r).

Portal, Quinta do Dou r p w sw sp ★★★ 04 05' 06 07 08 09 10 11 Best-known for oaky modern reds incl Grande RES, flagship Auru. V.gd late-harvest; fortifed MOSCATEL do DOU. New: sparkling rosé; Fémina, Dou's first DOCE (sweet wine).

Portalegre Alen r p w ★→★★★ Wine writers Richard Mayson (QUINTA do Centro) and João Afonso (Solstício/Equinócio), Lisbon chef Vitor Claro, consultant Rui Reguinga (Terrenus), former QUINTA DO CRASTO winemaker Susana Esteban have flocked to ALEN's northernmost subregion (DOC). ESPORÃO too. Elevation, granite and schist, old vines (incl field blends), gd rainfall account for fresh, structured, mineral wines. Region to watch.

Quinta Estate (*see* under name, eg. PORTAL, QUINTA DO).

Ramos, João Portugal Alen r w Leading modernist's estate. Fruity but always elegant ALEN range, esp Vila Santa, Ramos RES, QUINTA da Viçosa, Marqués de Borba incl v.gd Res 05 07 08 09 11'. New 2011 reds incl v.gd TOURIGA NACIONAL, stunning flagship Estremus (Alicante Bouschet/TRINCADEIRA).

Raposeira Dou w sp ★★ Well-known classic-method fizz using native varieties and CHARD.

Real Companhia Velha Dou r p w sw ★★→★★★ Since POEIRA's Jorge Moeira took charge in 2010, the wines have become as precise, focused as man himself, esp reds from north-facing QUINTA das Carvalhas. Delaforce ALVARINHO, QUINTA de Cidro GEWURZ and SÉM show skill with atypical varieties.

Romeira, Quinta da w ★★→★★★ Leading BUCELAS estate. Honeyed, ripe, citrus-streaked ARINTO-based whites, the best (Regia Premium, oaked Morgado Sta Catherina Res) mineral. Gd-value Prova Regia Arinto is VR LISBOA.

Roques, Quinta dos Dão r w sp ★★★ (r) 05 06 07' 08' 09 10 11 V.gd age-worthy red blends, esp RES and GARRAFEIRA 03' 08'. Pioneer of varietal Encruzado, TOURIGA NACIONAL, TINTA RORIZ, Tinta Cão, Alfrocheiro Preto. New Jaen plantings reflect upswing of interest in Spain's MENCÍA. Gd-value, entry-level Correio label.

Rosa, Quinta de la Dou r p w ★★★ 06 07' 08' 09' 10 11' Rich but elegant reds, esp RES. Expect more oomph from new single-v'yd cuvée from hot spot Val de Inferno re-planted 2007. QUINTA das Bandeiras Passagem from warmer DOU Superior is spicier. Gd whites, incl Passagem.

Rosado Rosé; despite the success of MATEUS ROSÉ, a curiously unexploited category. Colinas São Lourenço Principal Tête de Cuvée Rosém, Sparkling Brut Rosé set new standards (see IDEAL DRINKS).

Santar, Casa de Dão r w sp ★★→★★★ Under DÃO SUL leadership making poised reds and textured but mineral, fresh Encruzado whites, esp flagship Condessa de Santar.

São João, Caves Bair r w sp ★★→★★★ Traditional, family-owned firm known for v.gd, old-fashioned reds, esp *Frei João*, Poço do Lobo (BAIR), Porta dos Cavaleiros (DÃO), of which older vintages (cellared since 1963) now being released. New management, updated range incl gd ARINTO/CHARD white and sparkling blends.

São Miguel, Herdade de Alen r p w ★★→★★★ A dynamic operation making smart modern wines. Entry-level Ciconia, RES, firmer Montinho gd value. São Miguel label: serious, well-defined estate wines, esp Res, Dos Descobridores range. Private Collection is showier. Same team behind impressive new Herdade da Pimenta.

Seco Dry.

Setúbal (r) (w) br (dr) sw ★★★ Tiny DOC south of the river Tagus. Moreish fortified dessert wines, best beautifully balanced. Mainly MOSCATEL, incl rare red Moscatel Roxo. Main producers: BACALHOA VINHOS, JOSÉ MARIA DA FONSECA. Watch: António Saramago, HORÁCIO DOS REIS SIMÕES, Adriano Tiago.

Soalheiro, Quinta de Vin w sp ★★★ 06 07' 08' 09 10 11 12 Exciting, age-worthy ALVARINHO from organically cultivated Melgaço v'yd incl stunning old-vine Primeiras Vinhas, barrel-fermented Res, off-dry Dócil.

Sogrape Vin ★→★★★★ Portugal's biggest player makes both MATEUS ROSÉ, BARCA VELHA: jewels in the crown for contrasting reasons. Portfolio encompasses VIN

(Azevedo, Gazela, Morgadio da Torre), DÃO (CARVALHAIS), ALEN (HERDADE DO PESO), DOU (Barca Velha, FERREIRA, Sandeman and Offley Port). Approachable multi-regional brands incl Grão Vasco, Pena de Pato, Callabriga.

Sousa, Alves de Dou r w ★★★ 04' 05' 06 07 08' 09 Characterful terroir-focused range from seven QUINTAS incl rugged Abandonado, more polished Vinha de Lordelo reds. Old-school "bottle late and release later" philosophy, also with BRANCO da Gaivosa (skin contact) white. Expanding Port range.

Symington Family Estates Dou r w ★★→★★★★ Port shipper producing premium table wines since 2000, incl CHRYSEIA with Bruno Prats, more recently at QUINTA do Vesúvio. Bigger volume Altano brand is from three Vilariça Valley organic DOU Superior v'yds. Best: organic red and two 100% TOURIGA NACIONALS from QUINTA do Ataíde – RES (aged in American oak), Block 62 (French oak).

Tejo r w The DOC and VR of the area around the river Tagus. Steadily shifting from a quantity to quality focus as production moves from fertile riverbanks to poorer soils now planted to TOURIGA NACIONAL, TINTA RORIZ, CAB SAUV, SYRAH, PINOT N, CHARD, SAUV BL as well as local stalwarts CASTELÃO, FERNÃO PIRES. Solid performers: CASAL BRANCO, QUINTA DA ALORNA, Falua. More ambitious incl QUINTA DA LAGOALVA, Pinhal da Torre, Rui Reguinga (Tributo), Casca Wines.

Tinto Red.

Trás-os-Montes Mountainous inland DOC, just north of the DOU; (VR Transmontano). Leading light: Valle Pradinhos.

Vale Dona Maria, Quinta do Dou r w ★★★→★★★★ 04' 05' 06 07' 08' 09' 10 11' Cristiano van Zeller makes *v.gd plush yet elegant reds*, incl CV, Casa de Casal de Loivos, subtly rich white VZ. Gd-value Van Zellers range from bought-in fruit. New: two single-parcel estate wines: Vinha do Rio, Vinha da Francisca, also forward but elegant Rufo (r w).

Vale Meão, Quinta do Dou r ★★★→★★★★ 05 06 07' 08 09' 10' 11' Leading DOU Superior estate; once source of BARCA VELHA. V.gd second label: Meandro. Marked shift towards elegance tempers lead grape TOURIGA NACIONAL's excesses, while granite soils achieve same for single-parcel F Olazabal Monte Meão Granito, now joined by varietal F Olazabal Monte Meão TINTA RORIZ.

Silk purse, sow's ear? Lowly Languedoc vine Alicante Bouschet is the Alentejo's shining star.

Vallado Dou r p w ★★★ (r) 04 05' 06 07 08' 09' 10 11 Dynamic family estate at Regua, with DOU Superior v'yd too (QUINTA do Orgal). New winery, boutique hotel and bespoke wooden box for rare pre-phylloxera Adelaide Tributa Very Old Port scream luxury. Dou wines are reasonably priced, incl v.gd RES, flagship old-vine red Adelaide 05 07 08' 09' 11', varietal Sousão, TOURIGA NACIONAL, dry MOSCATEL.

Vinho Regional (VR) Same status as French Vin de Pays. More leeway for experimentation than DOC.

Vinho Verde r w sp ★→★★★ DOC between river DOU and north frontier, for fresh "green wines". Large brands (DYA) usually blends with added carbon dioxide. Best: single-QUINTA, unspritzy, age-worthy, esp ALVARINHO from Monção, Melgaço (eg. ANSELMO MENDES, QUINTAS DE SOALHEIRO, do Reguengo, de Melgaço, do Feital, da Pedra, do Regueiro) and LOUREIRO from Lima (eg. QUINTA DO AMEAL, APHROS, NIEPOORT Docil, Paço de Palmeria). Red Vinhão grape is acquired taste worth a try (eg. APHROS).

Wine & Soul Dou r w (r Pintas) 06 07' 08' 09' 10' 11' Winemaking couple Sandra Tavares and Jorge Serôdio Borges' intense wines: stunning Guru (w), elegant QUINTA da Manoella Vinhas Velhas, denser Pintas from neighbouring sites. V.gd second labels (r): Pintas Character, Manoella (r). V.gd Ports (*see* Port chapter).

Port, Sherry & Madeira

S herry is one of the world's great traditional drinks. Yet in Jerez the new ideas keep coming. Take En Rama wines, for example. They're unfiltered, which means we can taste the wine much as the cellarmaster does, straight from the butt. The demand for aged Finos – those on the edge of turning into Amontillados – has been exceptional this year, and it's another great-value category, along with those exceptional Amontillados, Palo Cortados and Olorosos bottled at 20 or 50 years old. Are we getting a bit blasé about supersweet PX? It seems not.

Port has its successes too, but the great quality of the 2011 vintage, and the growing popularity of top-end Tawnies cannot disguise the Port industry's problems. Swingeing price hikes for spirit are bringing the viability of its bread-and-butter volume wines into sharp focus and reinforcing the growing economic importance of Douro table wines. Fortunately more and more table wine producers are drawn to making premium Port, despite the unwieldy (and increasingly controversial) bureaucracy associated with its production. In Madeira, although plantings of the noble white grapes, along with rarities Terrantez and Bastardo, are on the up, small remains reassuringly beautiful – but doesn't, unfortunately, apply to the price.

Recent Port vintages

"Declared" when the wine is outstanding and meets the shippers' highest standards. In good but not quite classic years most shippers now use the names of their quintas (estates) for single-quinta wines of great character but needing less ageing in bottle. The vintages to drink now are 1966, 1970, 1977, 1980, 1983, 1985, 1987, 1992, 1994, though I drank Warre 2011 with chocolate and loved it. Don't be scared to try.

2013 Mid-harvest rain made for a difficult year, especially for Touriga Nacional.

2012 Single-quinta year. Very low-yielding, drought-afflicted.

2011 Classic year, widely declared. Inky, outstanding concentration and stucture. Stars: Noval Nacional, Taylors Quinta de Vargellas Vinha Velha, Fonseca.

2010 Single-quinta year. Hot, dry but higher yields than 2009. Stars: Vesuvio, Dow da Senhora da Ribeira.

2009 Controversial year. Declared by Fladgate, but not Symington's or Sogrape. Stars: Taylor's, Niepoort, Fonseca, Warre's.

2008 Single-quinta year. Low-yielding, powerful wines. Stars: Noval, Vesuvio, Taylor Terra Feita, Passadouro.

2007 Classic year, widely declared. Deep-coloured, rich but well-balanced wines. Taylor's and Vesuvio are stars.

2006 Difficult; few single-quintas. Stars: Vesuvio, Roriz, Barros Quinta Galeira.

2005 Single-quinta year. Stars: Niepoort, Taylor de Vargellas, Dow da Senhora da Ribeira – iron fist in velvet glove.

2004 Single-quinta year. Stars: Pintas, Taylor de Vargellas Vinha Velha, Quinta de la Rosa – balanced, elegant wines.

2003 Classic vintage year. Hot, dry summer. Powerfully ripe, concentrated wines, universally declared. Drink from 2015–20.

2001 Single-quinta year. Stars: Noval Nacional, Fonseca do Panascal, do Vale Meão – wet year; relatively forward wines.

2000 Classic year. A very fine vintage, universally declared. Rich, well-balanced wines for the long term. Drink from 2018.

Almacenista Sher Small producer, literally wholesaler, sells to Sherry shipper not to public. Often source of individual, complex Sherries. LUSTAU pioneered outstanding portfolio eg. MANZANILLA PASADA Cuevas Jurado 1/80.

Álvaro Domecq Sher ★★→★★★ Founded 1998, based on SOLERAS of Pilar Aranda, JEREZ's oldest bodega. Polished, elegant wines. Gd FINO La Janda. Excellent 1730 VORS series, incl PALO CORTADO, OLOROSO.

Alvear Mont-M ★★→★★★ Largest MONTILLA producer of v.gd FINO-like wine, esp Fino CB. V. fine exceptionally sweet, raisined PX. Silky, supple SOLERA 1927.

Andresen Por ★★→★★★ Family-owned house. V.gd wood-aged Ports, esp 20-yr-old TAWNY, *Colheitas* **1900'** and **1910'** still bottled on demand; **80' 91' 97 00**. Pioneered on-trend 10-, 20-, 40-yr-old WHITE PORTS. New: 2011 VINTAGE PORT.

Barbadillo Sher ★→★★★★ A former bishop's palace above SANLÚCAR expresses Barbadillo's ambitions. Well-known for some of Sanlúcar's finest wines, incl Solear MANZANILLA, and a pioneer of Manzanilla EN RAMA, with four seasonal SACAS. Reliquía range is top, esp AMONTILLADO and tangy, precise PALO CORTADO. To come: centenarian single-barrel Amontillado. Also Castillo San Diego, budget PALOMINO table wine.

Barbeito Mad ★★→★★★ Purity of fruit and elegance distinguish Ricardo Freitas' young no-added-caramel COLHEITAS (incl complex single-cask wines), 20-, 30-, 40-yr-old (new; named Mae Manuela after his mother) MALVASIA and the first (1992) FRASQUEIRA he made.

Barros Almeida Por ★→★★★ Focuses on wood-aged ports. V.gd 20-yr-old TAWNY, COLHEITAS **78' 80'**, Very Old Dry White and Colheita (35) WHITE PORTS. New: v.gd 2011 VINTAGE. Owned by Sogevinus (along with BURMESTER, CÁLEM, KOPKE). Most structured of the four.

Barros e Sousa Mad ★★★ Another independent family firm bites the dust. Acquired by PEREIRA D'OLIVEIRA in 2013. The upside: 100% CANTEIRO-aged range, incl rare Bastardo Old Res and 5 -yr-old Listrao blend, will reach a wider audience.

Blandy Mad ★★→★★★★ Historic family firm (CEO Chris Blandy) regained control of the MADEIRA WINE COMPANY in 2012. Initiatives incl acquiring two v'yds and a rare auction of demi-john-aged wines (1887–1954). Vast *Funchal lodges* (now with accommodation) offer visitors rich pickings, incl fine old vintages (BUAL **1920'**, **1969'**, MALMSEY **1985**, Terrantez **1976**, SERCIAL **1910'**), 20-yr-old Terrantez and younger COLHEITAS (Bual **1996**, VERDELHO and Sercial **1998**).

Borges, HM Mad ★→★★★ Improbably founded by Henrique Menezes Borges in 1877 during phylloxera scourge. Fruity 10-yr-olds and gd new 20-yr-old VERDELHO.

Bual (or Boal) Mad Classic Madeira grape: tangy, smoky, sweet wines; not as rich as MALMSEY. Perfect with cheese and lighter desserts.

En Rama Finos on sale seasonally: put your name down with your wine merchant.

Burmester Por ★→★★★ Elegance is the hallmark of this Sogevinus-owned house, esp sophisticated 20-, 40-yr-old TAWNY, COLHEITAS **55' 89**, age-dated WHITE PORTS, incl fine 40-yr-old.

Butt Sher 600-litre barrel of long-matured American oak used for Sherry. Filled 5/6 full, allows space for FLOR to grow. Popular in Scotland, post-Sherry use, for adding final polish to whisky.

Cálem Por ★→★★★ Sogevinus-owned; vibrant, fruity style. Velhotes is main brand. V.gd COLHEITAS, 40-yr-old TAWNY, 10-yr-old WHITE PORT. New: gd 2011 VINTAGE PORT.

Canteiro Mad Method of naturally ageing the finest Madeira in warm, humid lodges (warehouses). Subtler, more complex wines than ESTUFAGEM.

Chipiona Sher Zone of production of MOSCATEL grapes for Sherry. Leading producer: César Florido.

Churchill Por ★★★ A relative newcomer in an old game. V.gd VINTAGE PORT **82 85**

91 94 97 00 03 07' 11', Single-QUINTA da Gricha 00 **01 03' 04 05'** 06 07 09', LBV. Benchmark WHITE PORT, elegant 20-yr-old TAWNY.

Cockburn Por ★★→★★★ Historic shipper bought by SYMINGTON FAMILY ESTATES in 2010. Special RES RUBY now aged for longer in wood, and more vibrant LBV 1 yr less. V.gd VINTAGE PORT 63 67 70 75 83' **91 94** 97 00 03' 07' 11', single-QUINTA dos Canais 01' 05' 06 07' 08 09'.

Colheita Por, Mad Vintage-dated Port or Madeira of a single yr, cask-aged at least 7 yrs for Port and 5 yrs for Madeira. Bottling date shown on the label.

Cossart Gordon Mad MADEIRA WINE COMPANY-owned brand. Drier style than BLANDY. V.gd 5-yr-old RES, COLHEITAS (*Bual 1995, 1997*, VERDELHO 1995, MALVASIA **1996, 1998**, Harvest 1999) and old vintages (Terrantez 1977, BUAL **1908, 1961**).

Croft Por ★★→★★★ Fladgate-owned historic shipper. Return to foot-treading (2003) brings more backbone to lean, fleshy VINTAGE PORT 66 70 75 77 82 85 **91 94** 00 03' 07 09' 11'; QUINTA da Roêda is lighter. Popular styles: Indulgence, Triple Crown, Distinction and pioneering Pink, a ROSÉ PORT.

Crusted Port of RES RUBY quality, usually non-vintage, bottled young then aged so it throws a deposit, or "crust"; needs decanting. Gd examples: GRAHAM, FONSECA, DOW, CHURCHILL.

At almost 1.4% of Port production, 5x more Rosé Port is made than Crusted Port.

Delgado Zuleta Sher ★→★★ Oldest (1744) SANLÚCAR firm; crisp, penetrating wines. *La Goya* MANZANILLA PASADA EN RAMA XL is typically salty. Top: Monteagudo AMONTILLADO Viejo, v. original; powerful, piercing, 40-yr-old Quo Vadis?

Dios Baco Sher ★→★★ Family-owned JEREZ bodega (Baco=Bacchus). Baco Imperial VOS, VORS wines are stars esp VORS PALO CORTADO.

Domecq Sher One of the great names in Sherry, its SOLERAS and family members working in the business dispersed after takeovers. VORS wines now sold by OSBORNE; *La Ina, Botaina, Rio Viejo*, Viña 25 by LUSTAU.

Douro Por The river that lends its name to the region. Subregions: Baixo Corgo and, best for Port, Cima (Upper) Corgo and Douro Superior. Rises in Spain, where it is the Duero.

Dow Por ★★★→★★★★ Historic shipper owned by SYMINGTON. Drier VINTAGE PORT 66 70 72 75 77 80 83 85' **91 94** 97 00' 03 07' 11', esp single-QUINTA from Bomfim (Senhora da Ribeira is richer). Purchase of Quinta da Sabordela adds 30 ha to Bomfim, where new visitor centre underway.

Duorum Por ★★→★★★ Joint project of JOÃO PORTUGAL RAMOS and ex-FERREIRA winemaker Jose Maria Soares Franco producing v.gd dense, pure-fruited VINTAGE PORT (07 11') from centenarian vines. Second label Vinha de Castelo Melhor from mix of old and young DOURO Superior vines.

Emilio Hidalgo Sher ★★★→★★★★ Small, outstanding family bodega. All wines (except PX) start by spending time under FLOR. Excellent mature (15 yrs old) La Panesa FINO, supple Gobernador OLOROSO, intense El Tresillo AMONTILLADO, rare Amontillado Tresillo 1874 and Santa Ana PX 1861.

Equipo Navazos Sher ★★★→★★★★ A collection of finest Sherries by a team (*equipo*) working almost as négociants. Jesus Barquín and Eduardo Ojeda seek out outstanding single BUTTS from SOLERAS; also single-v'yd Sherries eg. FINO no 35 Macharnudo Alto. Their quality has attracted a new generation worldwide to treasures of Jerez. Bottlings started at number 1, eg. Bota (BUTT) no. 1. Separate MANZANILLA line "*I Think*" EN RAMA. Also making PALOMINO table wine with Dirk NIEPOORT, and sparkling wine in Penedès, using Sherry for *dosage*, with Sergi Colet.

Espiritus de Jerez Sher ★★ The boutique collection of businessman Roberto Anillo has just four exceptional wines. Presented in perfume-like bottles, taken from fine old SOLERAS.

Estufagem Mad Bulk process of slowly heating, then cooling, cheaper Madeiras to attain characteristic scorched-earth tang; less subtle than CANTEIRO process. Shift to c. 45°C (113°F) from 50°C (122°F) improves freshness.

Fernando de Castilla Sher ★★→★★★★ Small bodega brilliantly revived since 2000 by Jan Pettersen, formerly of OSBORNE. Reliable Classic collection, outstanding Antique Sherries. All qualify as VOS or VORS, though Pettersen avoids the system. Complex, 8-yr-old FINO, fortified to historically correct 17%; AMONTILLADO, PALO CORTADO, OLOROSO, PX all terrific. Also v. fine brandy, and vinegar.

Ferreira Por ★★→★★★ Historic Port house owned by SOGRAPE. Esp gd spicy RES (Don Antónia) and 10- and 20-yr-old TAWNY (QUINTA do Porto, *Duque de Bragança*). VINTAGE PORTS 66 70 75 77 78 80 82 83 85 87 90 91 94 95′ 97 00 03 07′ 11′, incl v.gd LBV on the up.

Fladgate Por Independent family-owned partnership. Owns leading Port houses TAYLOR, FONSECA, CROFT and now KROHN, whose fine stocks of TAWNY Port will consolidate Fladgate's lead in this growing category. Also owns Oporto luxury hotel The Yeatman.

Flor Sher Spanish for "flower": refers to the layer of *Saccharomyces* yeasts that develop naturally and live on top of FINO/MANZANILLA Sherry in a BUTT 5/6 full. *Flor* consumes oxygen and other compounds (process known as "biological ageing") and protects wine from browning (oxidation). Traditional AMONTILLADOS begin as Finos or Manzanillas before the *flor* dies naturally or with addition of fortifying spirit. *Flor* grows a thicker layer nearer the sea at EL PUERTO DE SANTA MARÍA and SANLÚCAR, hence lighter character of Sherry there.

Fonseca Guimaraens Por ★★★→★★★★ FLADGATE-owned Port house, founded 1815. V.gd Bin 27 and organic Terra Prima RES. Sumptuous, structured VINTAGE PORTS 66′ 70 75 77′ 80 83 85′ 92 94′ 97 00′ 03′ 07 09 11′. Single-QUINTA Panascal and blended Vintage Port Guimaraens made if no classic declaration.

Frasqueira Mad "Vintage" (single yr) Madeira bottled after at least 20 yrs in wood, usually much longer. Date of bottling compulsory; the longer in cask, the more concentrated and complex.

Sherry goes dry

Goodbye to the alluring-sounding "OLOROSO dulce" and "sweet AMONTILLADO". Now, if you want to call it Sherry, it has to be dry. If it's not dry it's either "medium" (5–115 g/litre residual sugar); or sweeter "cream" (115–140 g/litre). Look out for phrases like "a blend of Oloroso Sherries".

Garvey Sher ★→★★★ One of the great old names of JEREZ, formerly owned by RUIZ-MATEOS family (also Soto, Teresa Rivero, VALDIVIA). Known for San Patricio FINO, *Tío Guillermo* AMONTILLADO, age-dated 1780 line.

González Byass Sher ★★★→★★★★ GB (founded 1845) remains a family business, renewing itself with enthusiasm. Cellarmaster Antonio Flores inherited the job from his father; is a debonair presence. From the most famous of FINOS, *Tío Pepe*, he has developed a fascinating portfolio: EN RAMA; elegant Palmas range, 3 aged Finos (6-, 8-, 10-yrs-old); 40-yr-old AMONTILLADO. Alongside are consistently polished Viña AB Amontillado, Matúsalem OLOROSO, Noë PX. Also gd brandies; table wines, incl Beronia (Rioja), Vilarnau (Penedès), Viñas del Vero (Somontano); plus CROFT Original Pale Cream. Latest enterprise is Finca Moncloa, local red wine bodega: sweet Tintilla de Rota from eponymous grape (aka GRACIANO) revives a historic fortified wine.

Gould Campbell Por ★★★ Lesser-known SYMINGTON-owned Port shipper, not tied to specific QUINTAS so has free rein and can punch above its weight, eg. 77. Gd-value, full-bodied VINTAGE PORTS 70 77' 80 83' 85' 91 94 97 00 03' 07.

Graham Por ★★★→★★★★ SYMINGTON-owned Port house. Full range: esp gd Six Grapes RES RUBY; age-dated TAWNY range, rare COLHEITAS 52', 61' 69 82; succulent VINTAGE PORTS 63 66 70' 75 77' 80 83' 85' 91' 94' 97 00' 03' 07' 11', incl new Stone Terraces from two consistently excellent stone-terraced parcels at QUINTA dos Malvedos, home of age-worthy single-Quinta.

Guita, La Sher ★→★★★ Gd *Manzanilla*. Grupo Estévez owned (also VALDESPINO).

Gutiérrez Colosía Sher ★→★★★ Rare remaining riverside bodega in EL PUERTO DE SANTA MARÍA. Former ALMACENISTA. Excellent old PALO CORTADO.

Harvey's Sher ★→★★★ Once-great Sherry name. Famed for Bristol Cream. VORS wines show briskness of old age.

Henriques & Henriques' first harvest of Terrantez (3,000 kg) almost doubles Madeira's Terrantez production.

Henriques & Henriques Mad ★★→★★★★ Madeira shipper and long-term grower with 11ha; now the island's biggest grower of Terrantez grape. Pioneer of breezy extra-dry apéritif Monte Seco, 20-yr-old MALVASIA and Terrantez; uses seasoned whiskey and bourbon barrels. Strong on tradition too, esp 15-yr-old (NB Sercial), vintage (eg. VERDELHO 1934, Terrantez 1954, Malvasia 1954, BUAL 1957'). New: 2001 SERCIAL Single Harvest.

Herederos de Argüeso Sher, Man ★★→★★★ One of SANLÚCAR's top producers. V.gd San León, dense and salty *San León Res* and youthful Las Medallas; also impressively lively VORS AMONTILLADO Viejo.

Hidalgo-La Gitana Sher ★★→★★★★ Est (1792) family firm fronted by Javier Hidalgo. Famed for pale, light delicate MANZANILLA La Gitana. EN RAMA is much more expressive version. Intense, savoury, single-v'yd, aged *Pastrana Manzanilla Pasada*. Outstanding VORS, incl Napoleon AMONTILLADO, Wellington PALO CORTADO, Triana PX.

Jerez de la Frontera Centre of Sherry region, between Cádiz and Seville. "Sherry" is a corruption of the ancient name, pronounced *hereth*. In French, *Xérès*. Hence DO is Jerez-Xérès-Sherry.

Justino Mad ★→★★★ The largest Madeira shipper, owned by rum giant La Martiniquaise; produces the Broadbent label too. Esp known for TINTA NEGRA COLHEITA 1996' 1999, Terrantez Old RES NV. Gd FRASQUEIRA eg. SERCIAL 1940, VERDELHO 1954, BOAL 1964.

Kopke Por ★★→★★★ The oldest Port house (1638). Forte is sweet-fruited COLHEITAS 35' 41' 66 80' 87 89 91'; age-dated TAWNY and WHITE PORT – outstanding 40-yr-olds. New: 375th Anniversary Special edition 1940 Colheita.

Krohn Por ★→★★★ Exceptional stocks of aged TAWNY, COLHEITA 61' 66' 67' 76' 82' 83' 87' 91 97 dating back to 1863. Now FLADGATE-owned; some stock being diverted to TAYLOR. VINTAGE PORTS on the up 07' 09 11.

LBV (Late Bottled Vintage) Por Robust, bright-fruited Port from a single yr, kept in wood for twice as long as VINTAGE PORT (around 5 yrs). Commercial styles broachable on release without decanting. Best are age-worthy unfiltered versions eg. CHURCHILL, FERREIRA, NIEPOORT, QUINTA Nova de Nossa Senhora do Carmo, Quinta DO NOVAL, SMITH WOODHOUSE, WARRE.

Leacock Mad Long, distinguished track record for FRASQUEIRA. Since 1981 acquisition by the MADEIRA WINE COMPANY, focused on volume, esp St John brand (but 1969 SERCIAL is v.gd).

Lustau Sher ★★★→★★★★ Bodega famous for treasure trove of Sherries from own SOLERAS and ALMACENISTAS. Star *capataz* (winemaker) Manuel Lozano launched the identifying and shipping of Almacenista Sherries. Try La Ina FINO, Botaina

AMONTILLADO, East India Solera. Emilín is superb MOSCATEL, VORS PX is outstanding, carrying age and sweetness lightly. One of the few to release vintage Sherries, eg. profound OLOROSO AÑADA 97.

Madeira Vintners Mad A new start-up Madeira company (the first harvest in 2012 was processed at BARBEITO, new winery installed in 2013) takes, necessarily, a new approach. Without old wines to blend (although old stocks have recently been purchased) grapes are sourced via long-term contracts with select growers with the aim of building complexity around subregional and v'yd-specific terroir-driven wines.

Madeira Wine Company Mad An association of all 26 British Madeira companies formed in 1913. Just two firms then, it now accounts for over 50% of bottled Madeira exports. Back in Blandy family control after 20 yrs in partnership with SYMINGTON. Other principal brands: COSSART GORDON, LEACOCK, Miles retain own house style. All except basic wines CANTEIRO-aged.

Shot in the arm

Madeira, once synonymous with sedate holidays for seniors, has been given a shot in the arm by extreme sports like kite-surfing. The winds of change blow through the wine industry too. New blood incl MADEIRA WINE COMPANY's 30-something CEO Chris Blandy, who has bought the company's first v'yds, and MADEIRA VINTNERS, whose unique focus is terroir-driven Madeira.

Maestro Sierra Sher ★★★ *Small, traditional bodega*, brilliant quality, run by Carmen Borrego, following on from her mother Pilar Plá. Delicately fresh 12-yr-old AMONTILLADO; nutty, elegant Amontillado 1830 VORS.

Malmsey (Malvasia Candida) Mad The sweetest and richest of traditional Madeira grape varieties, yet with Madeira's unique sharp tang. Perfect with rich fruit, chocolate puddings.

Montilla-Moriles ★→★★★ Andalucian DO nr Córdoba. At the top end: superbly rich PX, some with long ageing in SOLERA. Once known simply for cheaper versions of FINO styles. Top producers: ALVEAR, PÉREZ BARQUERO, TORO ALBALÁ. Important source of PX for use in DO JEREZ.

Niepoort Por ★★★→★★★★★ Small family-run Port house; sensational table wines and top-notch range of VINTAGE PORTS incl classic 66 70' 75 77 78 80 82 83 87 91 92 94 97 00' 03 05' 07 09' 11', unique *garrafeira* (aged in demijohns) and single-v'yd Bioma (formerly "Pisca"). Exceptional TAWNY, COLHEITAS. VV, a 999-bottle Tawny blend (base component: 1863) celebrates 170th anniversary. Now making table wine with EQUIPO NAVAZOS.

Noval, Quinta do Por ★★★→★★★★ Elegantly structured VINTAGE PORTS 63' 66 67 70 75 78 82 85 87 91 94' 95 97 00' 03' 04 07' 08' 11', incl v. intense *Nacional* from 2.5 ha ungrafted vines. Often made outside classic declared yrs, eg. 2004, whose launch date (2014) is even less conventional. Second vintage label: Silval. V.gd age-dated TAWNY, COLHEITAS (new: 2000). Early drinking Noval Black RES; table wines from younger v'yds.

Offley Por ★→★★ Principal QUINTA (Boa Vista) sold by Sogrape in 2013 (leaving 450 ha to supply this fruit-driven brand). Gd TAWNY Ports. Aperitif/cocktail styles incl Cachuca RES WHITE PORT, ROSÉ PORT.

Osborne Sher ★★→★★★★ Historic (1772) bodega at gateway to EL PUERTO DE SANTA MARÍA. FINO QUINTA and mature Coquinero Fino classics of El Puerto. Superb v. old SOLERAS, incl AOS AMONTILLADO, P (Delta); P PALO CORTADO, OLOROSO Seco BC 200, PX Solera Vieja. Owns former DOMECQ VORS incl 51–1a Amontillado. Its black bull logo now recognized as a national icon. Also makes table wines in Rioja, Rueda, Ribera del Duero; renowned for brandies.

Palomino Neutral variety which forms the base wine for all styles of Sherry except MOSCATEL and PX. Once widely planted across Spain, still v. important in Canary Islands as Listán Blanco for table wine.

Passadouro Por Consistently gd single-QUINTA VINTAGE PORT, made by NIEPOORT 1992–2000, since by former WINE & SOUL's Jorge Serôdio Borges. Concentrated foot-trodden LBV, RES RUBY.

Paternina, Federico Sher ★→★★★ Based on the cellars of Díez Hermanos. Light, young Sherries; plus superb aged VORS. Excellent AMONTILLADO-style *Fino Imperial*, Victoria Regina OLOROSO, Vieja Solera PX. Owned by Paternina of Rioja.

Pedro Romero Sher ★→★★ Leading MANZANILLA producer, esp PASADA-style Aurora. Owns v. old SOLERAS, incl from Gaspar Florido. Oldest is piercing, concentrated, Ansar Real PALO CORTADO solera founded 1820.

Pereira d'Oliveira Vinhos Mad ★★★ Family-owned house with vast resource of rare, bottled-on-demand FRASQUEIRA, now boosted by BARROS E SOUSA purchase. Recent "new" releases: 1875 SERCIAL and MALVASIA, 1912 VERDELHO. 15-yr-old wines upwards CANTEIRO-aged.

Pérez Barquero Mont-M ★→★★★ A leader in revival of MONTILLA PX. Fine Gran Barquero FINO, AMONTILLADO, OLOROSO; v.gd La Cañada PX.

Porto Cruz Por Port's largest brand, owned by La Martiniquaise. Flashy multi-media visitor centre contrasts with neighbouring lodges, as do lighter Ports aimed at a younger, broader church.

Puerto de Santa María, El Sher One of three towns forming the "Sherry Triangle". Production now in decline; remaining bodegas incl former ALMACENISTA GUTIÉRREZ COLOSÍA, OSBORNE and TERRY. Puerto FINOS are prized as less weighty than JEREZ, not as "salty" as SANLÚCAR.

Quinta Por Portuguese for "estate". "Single-quinta" used to denote VINTAGE PORTS from shipper's quinta v'yds; declared in gd, not great yrs, now increasingly used in top yrs too. Examples: DUORUM, ALVES DE SOUSA, PASSADOURO, Romaneira, Tedo, Whytingham's Vale Meão, Vale D. Maria, WINE & SOUL's Pintas.

Ramos Pinto Por ★★★ Dynamic house owned by Champagne Roederer. Tweaks to VINTAGE PORT bringing greater structure. V.-fine single-QUINTA (Ervamoira) and repackaged RP age-dated TAWNY range, incl unusual single-v'yd QUINTA de Ervamoira (10-yr-old) and do Bom Retiro (20-yr-old).

Reserve / Reserva Por Better than basic premium Ports, bottled without a vintage date or age indication. Mostly RUBY; some TAWNY and WHITE PORT.

Rosé Port Por New (2009) growing Generation X category prompted by CROFT's pioneering "Pink," now made by most shippers. Quality variable. Serve chilled, on ice or, most likely, in a cocktail.

At the spring *Feria* in Seville they mix Fino with 7Up. Bad idea.

Royal Oporto Por ★→★★ REAL COMPANHIA VELHA's main Port brand (also owns QUINTA de Ventozelo and Delaforce). Gd TAWNY (average 5 yrs in wood), COLHEITAS and VINTAGE PORTS.

Rozès Por ★★★ Port shipper owned by Champagne house Vranken. VINTAGE PORT, incl LBV, sourced from DOURO Superior QUINTAS (Grifo, Anibal, Canameira). Terras do Grifo Vintage is blend of all three 07 09' 11; v.gd LBV from Grifo only.

Ruby Por Youngest, cheapest Port style: simple, sweet, red; best is labelled RES.

Ruiz-Mateos Sher Family business that made big investments in Jerez. Ultimate financial collapse has seriously undermined economic stability of some bodegas and brands.

Saca A withdrawal of Sherry for bottling. For EN RAMA wines the most common *sacas* are in *primavera* (spring) and *otoño* (autumn), when the FLOR is richest and most protective.

Sánchez Romate Sher ★★→★★★ Old (1781) family firm with wide, improving range. 8-yr-old *Fino Perdido*, nutty AMONTILLADO NPU, PALO CORTADO Regente, excellent VORS AMONTILLADO and OLOROSO La Sacristía de Romate, unctuous Sacristía PX. Also brandy Cardenal Mendoza.

Sandeman Sher ★→★★ More famous for its Port than its Sherry. VOS wines most interesting, incl Royal Esmeralda AMONTILLADO, Royal Corregidor Rich Old OLOROSO.

Sandeman Port Por ★★→★★★ Latterly best-known for v.gd age-dated TAWNY, esp 20-, 40-yr-old, but VINTAGE PORTS 63 66 70 75 77 94 97 00 03 07' 11' shine since 2009 when SOGRAPE invested in QUINTA do Seixo winery. LBV, densely structured 2011 Vintage. Second label: fruity Vau Vintage.

Sanlúcar de Barrameda Sher The third of the Sherry triangle towns (along with JEREZ and PUERTO de STA MARÍA), at mouth of the river Guadalquivir. Humidity in low-lying cellars encourages FLOR. Sea air is said to give wines a salty character; analytically unproven but evident. Wines aged under *flor* in Sanlúcar bodegas qualify for DO MANZANILLA-Sanlúcar de Barrameda.

Sercial Mad Both the wine and the grape: driest of all Madeiras. *Supreme apéritif,* gd with gravad lax or sushi. *See* Grapes chapter.

Silva, C da Por ★★→★★★ Port shipper. Making waves with v. sophisticated new Dalva Golden WHITE COLHEITA range 52' 63 71'; gd TAWNY too.

Smith Woodhouse Por ★★★ SYMINGTON-owned small Port firm founded in 1784. Gd unfiltered LBV; some v. fine vintages (drier style) 63 66 70 75 77' 80 83 85 91 94 97 00' 03 07. QUINTA da Madelena is single-quinta VINTAGE PORT.

Solera Sher, Mad System for blending Sherry and, less commonly now, Madeira. Consists of topping up progressively more mature BUTTS with slightly younger wines of same sort from previous stage, or *criadera*. Maintains vigour of FLOR, gives consistency and refreshes mature wines. Min age for FINO, MANZANILLA is 2 yrs in solera.

Bottle of Terrantez 1715 sold for £6,465 at Christie's (2013): £32/year of age.

Sousa, Alves de Por Domingos Alves de Sousa, ex-engineer, makes Douro wines from family's estate. Accomplished, fast expanding range of Ports: VINTAGE 09' 11', 20-yr-old TAWNY, Caldas WHITE PORT.

Tawny Por Wood-aged Port (hence tawny colour), ready to drink on release. RES and age-dated (10-, 20-, 30-, 40-yr-old) wines ratchet up in complexity. Limited release COLHEITAS and Very Old Tawny Ports (*see* TAYLOR, GRAHAM, NIEPOORT, VALLADO, WINE & SOUL) now vie with VINTAGE (and cost a gd deal more).

Taylor, Fladgate & Yeatman (Taylor's) Por ★★→★★★★ Historic port shipper, FLADGATE's jewel in the crown. Imposing VINTAGE PORTS 66 70 75 77' 80 83 85 92' 94 97 00' 03' 07' 09' 11', incl single-QUINTAS (Vargellas, Terra Feita), rare Vargellas Vinha Velha from 70-yr-old+ vines. Market leader for TAWNY incl v.gd age-dated. Acquisition of KROHN stock sees a 1863 follow-up to limited-edition Very Old Tawny Scion and a 1964 COLHEITA, the first in a series of 50-yr-old wines.

Toro Albalá Mont-M ★→★★★ PX only here, and some venerable old wines in addition to the young wines. Among them lively AMONTILLADO Viejísimo and superb, treacly Don PX Gran Res.

Tradición Sher ★★→★★★★ Small, serious bodega, founded 1998, originally focused on VOS, VORS. Now has delicate FINO, fine salty AMONTILLADO, v. balanced PX. Vintage Sherries incl superb 70 75 OLOROSOS.

Urium Sher Newest arrival in JEREZ (2009). A small bodega promising high quality.

Valdespino Sher ★★→★★★★ Famous JEREZ bodega producing Inocente FINO from the esteemed Macharnudo v'yd (EN RAMA version bottled by EQUIPO NAVAZOS).

Sherry styles

Manzanilla Fashionably pale, dry, low-strength: green-apple character; a popular, unchallenging introduction to the flavours of Sherry. Matured in the maritime conditions of SANLÚCAR DE BARRAMEDA where the FLOR grows more thickly, and the wine is said to acquire a salty tang. Drink cold from a newly opened bottle with tapas (or oysters). Do not keep. Eg. HEREDEROS DE ARGÜESO, San León RES.

Manzanilla Pasada Manzanilla aged longer than most; v. dry, complex. Eg. HIDALGO-LA GITANA's single-v'yd Manzanilla Pasada Pastrana.

Fino Dry; weightier than Manzanilla; 2 yrs age min (as Manzanilla). Eg. GONZÁLEZ BYASS Tío Pepe. Serve as Manzanilla. Don't keep. Trend for mature FINOS aged 6–12 yrs, eg. FERNANDO DE CASTILLA Antique.

Amontillado A Fino in which the layer of protective yeast *flor* has died, allowing the wine to oxidize, creating more complexity. Naturally dry. Eg. LUSTAU Los Arcos. Commercial styles may be sweetened.

Oloroso Not aged under *flor*. Heavier, less brilliant when young, matures to nutty intensity. Naturally dry. May be sweetened with PX and sold as *dulce*. Eg. EMILIO HIDALGO Gobernador (dr), Old East India (sw). Keeps well.

Palo Cortado V. fashionable. Traditionally a wine that had lost its FLOR – between Amontillado and Oloroso. Today often blended to create the style. Difficult to identify with certainty, though some suggest it has a keynote "lactic" or "bitter butter" note. Dry, rich, complex: worth looking for. Eg. BARBADILLO Reliquía, FERNANDO DE CASTILLA Antique.

Cream Blend sweetened with grape must, PX and/or MOSCATEL for an inexpensive, medium-sweet style. Unashamedly commercial. Eg. HARVEY's Bristol Cream, CROFT Pale Cream. EQUIPO NAVAZOS La Bota No. 21 is outstanding exception.

En Rama Manzanilla or Fino bottled from the BUTT with little or no filtration or cold stabilization to reveal full character of Sherry. More flavoursome but less stable, hence unpopular with some retailers. Back in fashion with trend for more natural wines. The *saca* or withdrawal is typically when *flor* is most abundant. Keep in fridge, drink up quickly.

Pedro Ximénez (PX) Raisined sweet, dark, from partly sun-dried PX grapes (grapes mainly from MONTILLA; wine matured in JEREZ DO). Concentrated, unctuous, decadent, bargain. Sip with ice-cream. Overall, world's sweetest wine. Eg. Emilio Hidalgo Santa Ana 1861, LUSTAU VORS.

Moscatel Aromatic appeal, around half sugar of PX. Eg. Lustau Emilín, VALDESPINO Toneles. Unlike PX not required to be fortified. Now permitted to be called "Jerez".

VOS / VORS Age-dated sherries: some of the treasures of the Jerez bodegas. Exceptional quality at relatively low prices. Wines assessed by carbon dating to be more than 20-yrs-old are called VOS (Very Old Sherry/Vinum Optimum Signatum); those over 30-yrs-old are VORS (Very Old Rare Sherry/Vinum Optimum Rare Signatum). Also 12-yr-old, 15-yr-old examples. Applies only to Amontillado, Oloroso, Palo Cortado, PX. Eg. VOS Hidalgo Jerez Cortado Wellington. Some VORS wines are softened with PX: sadly producers can be overgenerous with the PX.

Añada "Vintage" Sherry with a declared vintage. Runs counter to tradition of vintage-blended SOLERA. Formerly private bottlings now winning public accolades. Eg. Lustau Sweet Oloroso Añada 1997.

Sherry style terms are cross-referenced throughout this chapter

> **Sherry on the up**
> Sherry is on the up. There's an annual International Sherry Week.
> In 2014 Jerez was European Wine City. Tapas bars are finally serving
> convincing tapas. There's even a hashtag: #sherryrevolution. All that's
> left is to Smash the Schooner, and all the other tiddly Sherry glasses
> still lurking in cupboards.

Terrific dry AMONTILLADOS, Tio Diego, *Coliseo*; vibrant SOLERA 1842 OLOROSO VOS; remarkable Toneles MOSCATEL, Jerez's best. Owned by Grupo Estévez (also owns MARQUÉS DEL REAL TESORO, LA GUITA).

Valdivia Sher ★★→★★★ Former home of RUIZ-MATEOS family now with uncertain future. V.gd 15-yr-old Sacromonte AMONTILLADO, gd OLOROSO.

Vallado, Quinta da Dou Owned by descendants of 19th-century DOURO/Porto grande dame, Dona Antónia Adelaide Ferreira. Best-known for Douro wines but Adelaide Tributa, a 1,300-bottle Very Old (pre-phylloxera) TAWNY Port spearheads revived Port tradition, plus release of 100-yr box set of 10-, 20-, 30-, 40-yr-old Tawny and VINTAGE PORTS 09 11.

Verdelho Mad Style and grape of medium-dry Madeira; pungent but without the austerity of SERCIAL. Gd apéritif or pair with pâté. Increasingly popular for table wines.

Vesúvio, Quinta do Por ★★★★ With NOVAL, a single-QUINTA Port on par with the best VINTAGE PORTS 91 92 94 95' 96' 97 98' 99 00' 01 03' 04 05' 06 07' 08' 09 10 11'. The only SYMINGTON FAMILY ESTATES Port still foot-trodden by people (not robotically). Capela da QUINTA Vesuvio 07' 11' is from relatively level low-lying parcel nr river.

Vila Nova de Gaia Por Town across the river DOURO from Oporto. Traditional home to the major Port shippers' lodges, though shippers increasingly moving out of the centre for modern facilities elsewhere.

Vintage Port Por Classic vintages are the best wines declared in exceptional yrs by shippers between 1 Jan and 30 Sept in the second yr after vintage. Bottled without filtration after 2 yrs in wood, it matures v. slowly in bottle-throwing a deposit – always decant. Modern vintages broachable earlier but best will last more than 50 yrs. Single-QUINTA Vintage Ports also drinking earlier; best can last 30+ yrs.

Warre Por ★★★→★★★★ The oldest of British Port shippers (1670), now owned by SYMINGTON FAMILY ESTATES. V.gd, rich, age-worthy VINTAGE 63 66 70' 75 77' 80' 83 85 91 94 97 00' 03 07' 09' 11'. Elegant Single-QUINTA and 10-, 20-yr-old TAWNY Otima reflect Quinta da Cavadinha's cool elevation. Also v.gd Vintage Character (Warrior) and unfiltered LBV.

White Port Por Port from white grapes. Ranges from dry to sweet (*lagrima*); mostly off-dry and blend of yrs. Apéritif straight or drink long with tonic and fresh mint. Growing niche: age-dated (10-, 20-, 30-, or 40-yr-old), eg. ANDRESEN, KOPKE, QUINTA de Santa Eufemia; rare COLHEITAS eg. C DA SILVA's Dalva Golden White.

Williams & Humbert Sher ★ →★★★★ Traditional bodega, initially a famous name, then involved in private-label wines. Improving again, eg. vintage EN RAMA FINO 2006. Bestsellers incl Dry Sack and Winter's Tale AMONTILLADOS. V.gd old wines incl *Dos Cortados* PALO CORTADO, As You Like It sweet old OLOROSO 1/21.

Wine & Soul Dou Excellent table wines. Jorge Serôdio Borges' inheritance of QUINTA da Manoella's stocks mean powerful Pintas VINTAGE augmented by a 10-yr-old TAWNY and stunning 300-bottle 5G Very Old Tawny.

Switzerland

Abbreviations used in the text:

Aar	Aargau
Ber	Bern
Gris	Grisons
Neu	Neuchâtel
Schaff	Schaffhausen
Thur	Thurgau
Tic	Ticino
Val	Valais
Vd	Vaud
Zür	Zürich

Switzerland is not part of the EU, but it epitomizes the spirit of Europe at its best. For centuries the country has been mixing German, French and Italian influences into its own cultural heritage, from politics and economics to food and wine. The interaction has been especially fruitful in wine. And it is real interaction, not imitation: wine-growers in Switzerland's French-speaking cantons talk about terroir as if they were French, and cling to the Chasselas grape, hardly grown abroad but delicately reflecting the different terroirs of French-speaking Switzerland.

Italian-speaking Ticino had to overcome the habit of producing nothing more than house wine for private consumption after World War Two, just like many parts of Italy. But in doing so, the Ticinesi introduced Merlot to their home region, decades before it became fashionable to plant Bordeaux varieties everywhere. Last but not least, Switzerland's German-speaking regions share their preference for Pinot vines with Germany's neighbouring region Baden, and with Alsace. But the Alemannic Swiss growers also work in their own way, often looking for a compromise between French and German paradigms. As a result, these wines exhibit strong individuality and a sense of place. The only problem with Swiss wine is that it is hardly ever widely available internationally. The 15,000 hectares' production is tiny, and the most sought-after specialities are usually sold out weeks after bottling. Even for the Swiss it is sometimes impossible to get hold of Swiss wine – at least of the most desirable bottles.

Recent vintages

2013 Late and uneven flowering, local hail, but overall quality appears
to be very good. Low quantity: up to 50% less than usual.

2012 A winemaker's vintage. A difficult year with hail and rain.
Promising, though.

2011 Very good vintage, from a unusually long, warm autumn.

2010 A classic vintage. Very elegant; less volume than 2009.

2009 One of the best of recent years.

2008 Difficult year with lots of rain. Quality okay but not tops.

Older fine vintages: 2005 (all wines), 2000 (esp Pinot N, Valais reds),
1999 (Dézaley), 1997 (Dézaley), 1990 (all).

Aargau A wine-growing canton southeast of Basel, 400 ha, mainly PINOT N, MÜLLER-T.
Growers: Döttingen co-op, Haefliger, Hartmann, Litwan, Meier (zum Sternen).

Aigle Vd (r) w ★★ Well-known commune for CHASSELAS. BADOUX' Les Murailles is
famous, but can be v. light. Try Terroir du Crosex Grillé.

AOC The equivalent of French appellation contrôlée, but unlike in France, it is not
nationally defined and every canton has its own rules. 85 AOCs countrywide.

Bachtobel, Schlossgut Thur ★★★ The late Hans Ulrich Kesselring was one of the
country's most respected growers until his sudden death in 2008. A young
team led by his nephew continues to produce refined PINOT N from slopes
nr Weinfelden.

Badoux, Henri Vd ★★ Big producer, old-style commercial wines. His CHASSELAS AIGLE
les Murailles (classic lizard label) is the most popular Swiss brand.

Baumann, Ruedi Schaff ★★★ 00′ 03 05′ 08 09 10 11 12 A leading estate at
Oberhallau; berry-scented, age-able PINOT N, esp -R-, Ann Mee, Zwaa (collaboration
with nearby Bad Osterfingen estate).

Bern Capital and homonymous canton. Wine villages on Lake Bieler (La Neuveville,
Ligerz, Schafis, Schernelz, Twann) and Lake Thuner (Spiez). 240 ha, mainly
CHASSELAS, PINOT N. Top growers: Andrey, Johanniterkeller, Schlössli, Steiner.

Besse, Gérald et Patricia Val ★★★ Leading VAL family estate, mostly on steep sloping
terraces; range of elegant FENDANT (Les Bans), GAMAY from granite soils, powerful
old-vines Ermitage (MARSANNE).

Bovard, Louis Vd r w ★★→★★★★ DÉZALEY family business for 10 generations: Louis-
Philippe Bovard is *grand seigneur* of CHASSELAS; textbook Dézaley La Médinette
lasts 10 yrs+; v.gd EPESSES, ST-SAPHORIN, red Dézaley. Elegant, classic wines with
clear signature. Start your Chasselas study here.

Bündner Herrschaft Gris r p w ★★→★★★★ 02 05′ 09′ 10 11 12 (13) BLAUBURGUNDER
(PINOT N) with accentuated fruit and structure (mild southerly winds and cool
climate from nearby mtns). Individualistic growers and only four villages:
FLÄSCH, JENINS, MAIENFELD, MALANS.

Calamin Vd GRAND CRU of LAVAUX, nr EPESSES and neighbouring DÉZALEY; a tarter style
of CHASSELAS. Only 16 ha, growers incl Dizerens, DUBOUX, Testuz.

Chablais Vd ★★→★★★ Wine region at the upper end of Lake GENEVA, top villages:
AIGLE, YVORNE, esp known for CHASSELAS. Name is derived from Latin *caput lacis*,
head of the lake.

Wine regions

Switzerland has six major wine regions: VAL, VD, GENEVA, TIC, Trois Lacs
(NEU), Bienne / BER, Vully / FRIBOURG) and German Switzerland, which
comprises ZÜR, SCHAFF, GRIS, AAR, St Gallen, Thur and some smaller wine
cantons. And contrary to Switzerland's reputation for making white
wines, 60% of wines are red, mostly PINOT N.

Chanton, Josef-Marie and Mario Val ★★★ *Terrific Valais spécialités*; v'yds up to 800 metres altitude: HEIDA, Lafnetscha, Himbertscha, Eyholzer Roter, Plantscher, Resi, Gwäss. Also gd PINOT N.

Chappaz, Marie-Thérèse Val ★★★→★★★★ Small estate at Fully, famous for magnificent sweet wines (GRAIN NOBLE CONFIDENCIEL) of Petite ARVINE and ERMITAGE (MARSANNE). Hard to find.

Côte, la Vd r p w ★→★★★ Largest VD region and AOC (2,000 ha) west of Lausanne, mainly CHASSELAS of v. light and commercial style. Top growers (eg. CRUCHON, DOMAINE LA COLOMBE) use bio methods for more depth, character. Best-known villages: Mont-sur-Rolle, FÉCHY, Morges.

Cruchon, Henri Vd ★★→★★★ Bio producer of LA CÔTE, 36 ha, v. consistent, known for CHASSELAS and range of other varieties (Altesse, CHARD, SAUV BL, GAMAY, Gamaret, Servagnin aka PINOT N). Top growth is refined, age-worthy Pinot N Raissennaz.

Switzerland exports only 1–2% of its wine production.

Dézaley Vd (r) w ★★★→★★★★ 83' 90' 97 99 00 **03** 05' 09' 10 11 12 (13) Celebrated LAVAUX GRAND CRU on steep slopes of Lake GENEVA, 50 ha, reclaimed in the 12th century by Cistercian monks. Potent CHASSELAS develops with age. Best: *Louis Bovard*, DUBOUX, *Fonjallaz*, Monachon, Testuz, Ville de Lausanne. Try vintages back to 1976 at Georges Wenger's restaurant in Le Noirmont.

Dôle Val ★★ A traditional red blend: PINOT N plus some GAMAY. VALAIS' answer to Burgundy's Passetoutgrains, but lighter, less tannic and more fruity. Try BESSE, Gilliard, MERCIER, PROVINS. Lightly pink Dôle Blanche is pressed straight after harvest.

Domaine la Colombe Vd w ★★→★★★ Family estate of FÉCHY, LA CÔTE, 15 ha, bio. Raymond Paccot is a defender of CHASSELAS, producing top examples in a fresh, elegant, mineral style (eg. La Brez).

Duboux, Blaise Vd ★★★ 5-ha family estate in LAVAUX. Outstanding DÉZALEY *vieilles vignes* Haut de Pierre (v. rich, but still mineral style), CALAMIN Cuvée Vincent. Also Plant Robert, a local clone of GAMAY.

Epesses Vd (r) w ★→★★★ 09 10 11' 12 (13) Well-known LAVAUX AOC, 130 ha surrounding GRAND CRU CALAMIN: sturdy, full-bodied whites. Growers incl BOVARD, Luc Massy, DUBOUX, Fonjallaz.

Féchy Vd ★→★★★ Famous though unreliable AOC of LA CÔTE, mainly CHASSELAS. V.gd grower: LA COLOMBE.

Federweisser / Weissherbst German-Swiss pale rosé or even white made from BLAUBURGUNDER.

Fendant Val w ★→★★★ VAL appellation for CHASSELAS. The ideal wine for fondue or raclette. Try BESSE, Domaine Cornulus, GERMANIER, SIMON MAYE, PROVINS. Compared to Chasselas from VD FENDANT more vibrant, fruit-driven (often tropical).

Fläsch Gris ★★★→★★★★ Wine village in BÜNDNER HERRSCHAFT, remarkable for schist soils and mineral, austere PINOT N that ages v. well. Lots of recommendable family estates, esp members of Adank, Hermann, Marugg families. GANTENBEIN is outstanding.

Flétri / Mi-flétri Late-harvested grapes for sweet/slightly sweet wine.

Fribourg 115 ha on the shores of Lake Murten (Mont Vully): full-bodied CHASSELAS, elegant TRAMINER, round PINOT N. Try Château de Praz, Cru de l'Hôpital, Derron.

Fromm, Georg Gris ★★★ 02 05' **08** 09' 10 11 12 Top grower in MALANS, 4 ha, known for fragrant, subtle PINOT N. (eg. Schöpfliwingert). Georg(e) Fromm also founded the Fromm in Marlborough, NZ – sold most of his stake there in 2007.

Gantenbein, Daniel & Martha Gris ★★★★ 05 08 09' 10' 11 12 (13) Most famous growers in Switzerland, based in FLÄSCH. Top PINOT N from DRC clones (*see* France), RIES clones from Loosen (*see* Germany), exceptional CHARD in v. limited quantity.

Geneva City and wine-growing canton, 1400 ha. Dominated by unambitious GAMAY, CHASSELAS. Ambitious growers do better with international varieties and PINOT N, eg. Domaine des Balisiers, Domaine Grand'Cour (Pellegrin), Novelle, Les Hutins. Most and best v'yds on Lake Geneva belong to another canton, VD.

Germanier, Jean-René Val ★★→★★★ Important VAL estate, best-known for reliable FENDANT Les Terrasses, elegant SYRAH Cayas and seductive Mitis (sweet AMIGNE from Vétroz).

Glacier, Vin du (Gletscherwein) Val Fabled oxidized, wooded white from rare Rèze grape of Val d'Anniviers. Almost impossible to find on sale. Keep looking. If you love Sherry, this is a must.

Grain Noble ConfidenCiel Val Quality label for authentic sweet wines, grown on the vine. Try Domaine du Mont d'Or, CHAPPAZ, Philippe Darioli, Gérard Dorsaz, GERMANIER, PROVINS.

Vineyards everywhere
The Swiss plant vines almost everywhere. Even in the mtn regions of inner Switzerland and along the Jura foothills there are vines, wherever there's a plot of land, however small. Smaller cantons: Luzern (42 ha), Schwyz (39 ha), Jura (14 ha), Appenzell (both parts together 5 ha), Zug (2 ha), Glarus (2 ha), Uri, Ob- and Nidwalden (all three together 4 ha).

Grand Cru Val, Vd Inconsistent term; some VAL communes (eg. SALGESCH for PINOT N) have local regulations. In VD "Premier Grand Cru" may be used for wide range of single-estate wines. Switzerland has only two *grands crus* in the sense of a classification of v'yd sites: CALAMIN and DÉZALEY.

Grünenfelder, Irene Gris r ★★★ Weingut Eichholz, Jenins. V. limited production. Wonderful Crémant.

Grisons (Graubünden) Mtn canton, mainly German-Swiss with a smaller Italian-speaking part south of Alps (Misox, esp MERLOT). PINOT N king, CHARD v.gd, also MÜLLER-T. See BÜNDNER HERRSCHAFT. Best growers in other areas: Cicero, Manfred Meier, von Tscharner.

Jenins Village in BÜNDNER HERRSCHAFT with shallow, poor soil, producing expressive PINOT N with depth and density. Many gd growers: GRÜNENFELDER, Obrecht, Pelizzatti, Sprecher von Bernegg.

Johannisberg VAL name for SILVANER, often off-dry or sweet. Excellent: *Domaine du Mont d'Or.*

Lavaux Vd (r) w ★★→★★★★ Best region on Lake GENEVA, 30 km of steep south-facing terraces east of Lausanne, now UNESCO world heritage site. Two GRANDS CRUS: DÉZALEY, CALAMIN and several village AOCS.

Maienfeld Gris The novel *Heidi* is set in this BÜNDNER HERRSCHAFT village. But Maienfeld's delicate, fruit-driven PINOT N deserves attention too. Top growers: Lampert, Moehr-Niggli, Schloss Salenegg.

Malans Gris Village in BÜNDNER HERRSCHAFT. Top PINOT N producers incl Donatsch, FROMM, Liesch, Studach, Wegelin. Nearly extinct local grape: Completer; late ripening, idiosyncratic, acidic, often phenolic white. Monks used to drink it with their day's last prayer (Compline). Adolf Boner is keeper of the Grail.

Maye, Simon et Fils Val r w ★★★ 05' 09' 10 11' 12 (13) Perfectionist family estate at St-Pierre-de-Clages. Dense SYRAH *vieilles vignes*; spicy and powerful Païen (HEIDA); concentrated PINOT N. FENDANT, DÔLE v.gd too.

Mémoire des Vins Suisses Association uniting 50 leading growers in effort to create stock of Swiss icon wines to prove their ageing capacities. Oldest wines are from 1999. One public tasting every yr.

Mercier, Anne-Catherine & Denis Val ★★★ Growers in SIERRE, only 6 ha, producing some of the most sought-after CORNALIN 99 02 05' 09' 10 11 12 and SYRAH.

Morges Vd r p w ★→★★ DYA Large AOC with 39 communes: CHASSELAS, fruity reds. Try Château de Vufflens.

Neuchâtel 595 ha around city and lake. CHASSELAS usually v. light (10–11%) and slightly sparkling (mostly vinified *sur lie*). PINOT N from local clone (Cortaillod) can be exquisite, also gd OEIL DE PERDRIX, PINOT GR, CHARD. Best growers: Château d'Auvernier, La Maison Carrée, Domaine de Chambleau, Porret, Tatasciore, Ville de Neuchâtel.

Non Filtré Spécialité available from January from NEU: unfiltered CHASSELAS. First Swiss wine of the new vintage. Try Christian Rossel.

Oeil de Perdrix Neu PINOT N rosé, allegedly the colour of a partridge's eye. Originally from NEUCHÂTEL, now found elsewhere.

Pircher, Urs Zür ★★★→★★★★ 05' 08 09' 10 11 12 Top estate at Eglisau, steep south-facing slope overlooking Rhine. Stadtberger Barrique from old Swiss clones is one of the most complex and best-ageing PINOT N of Switzerland. Whites (GEWURZ, Räuschling, PINOT GR) stand out for purity of fruit, raciness.

Provins Valais Val ★→★★★ Huge co-op and biggest producer: 4,000+ members, 1,500 ha. Gd oak-aged Maître de Chais range, and reliable entry-level wines. Winemaker Madeleine Gay does a great job.

Rouvinez Vins Val r w ★→★★★ Well-distributed VAL producer at SIERRE. Try Château Lichten and CORNALIN from Montibeux, cuvées La Trémaille (w) and Le Tourmentin (r).

St Jodern Kellerei Val ★★→★★★★ VISPERTERMINEN co-op (founded 1978), famous for HEIDA Veritas from ungrafted old vines – a unique and superb reflection of Alpine terroir.

St-Saphorin Vd (r) w ★★→★★★ 09 10 11' 12 Famous CHASSELAS AOC in LAVAUX for lighter whites than DÉZALEY, but often with the same mineral delicacy. Try Pierre Monachon's Les Manchettes.

Salgesch Val ★★→★★★★ German-speaking village in VAL, PINOT N stronghold on calcareous soils. GRAND CRU regulations since 1988 (concerning yields and must weight). No v'yd classification. Growers incl A&D Mathier, Albert Mathier, Cave du Rhodan.

Salvagnin r ★→★★ 10 11 GAMAY and/or PINOT N appellation. Rustic, light-bodied red Spécialité from VAUD. Try Uvavins. Not popular with the young generation.

Schaffhausen ★→★★★ German-Swiss canton/town on the Rhine, with the famous Falls. BLAUBURGUNDER, also MÜLLER-T and spécialités. Best-known village is Hallau, but be v. careful. Top growers incl BAUMANN, Bad Osterfingen, Stamm. GVS is a gd co-op.

Schenk SA Vd ★→★★★ Europe-wide wine giant, based in Rolle, founded 1893. Owns firms in Burgundy and B'x, Germany, Italy, Spain. Top address for classic-style Swiss wines, often underrated. Founder of the Clos, Domaines & Châteaux (association of Swiss noble wines), strong in the Vaudois Premiers Grands Crus Movement. Affordable, excellent examples of CHASSELAS.

In Valais, more than 20,000 land-owners share 5,000 ha of vines.

Schwarzenbach, Hermann Zür r w ★★★ Leading family estate on Lake ZÜRICH. Best-known for crisp whites that go well with freshwater fish: local variety Räuschling, MÜLLER-T. Also excellent Completer, PINOT N.

Sierre Val r w ★★→★★★★ Sunny resort; rich, luscious VAL wines. Best-known names: Imesch, MERCIER, ROUVINEZ, Maurice Zufferey.

Sion Val r w ★★→★★★★ Capital/wine centre of VAL, domicile of big producers: Charles Bonvin Fils, PROVINS VALAIS, Robert Gilliard, Varone.

Stucky, Werner Tic ★★★→★★★★ Immigrant from German Switzerland to TIC (in 1981), changing Merlot del Ticino from light and fruity to dense, oak-aged. Today, three wines: Temenos (Completer/SAUV BL), Tracce di Sassi (MERLOT), Conte di Luna (Merlot/CAB SAUV). One of Stucky's best v'yds is only accessible via a funicular.

Ticino ★★→★★★★ 05' 08 09' 10 11 (12) Italian-speaking part of southern Switzerland, mainly MERLOT. Best are well-structured and far from "international" in style, eg. Gialdi, Huber, Kaufmann, Klausener, Kopp von der Crone Visini, STUCKY, Tamborini, Zanini, ZÜNDEL. Also Azienda Mondò in Sementina, specializing in old Bondola grape.

Valais (Wallis) Largest wine canton, in dry, sunny upper Rhône Valley. Many local varieties (eg. white AMIGNE, HUMAGNE Blanche, Petite ARVINE; red CORNALIN, HUMAGNE Rouge), wide spectrum of soils (granite, schist, lime); styles from dry CHASSELAS (FENDANT) to barrel-aged reds and sweet. MARSANNE and SYRAH doing v. well. Top: BESSE, CHANTON, CHAPPAZ, Darioli, Domaine Cornulus, Domaine du Mont d'Or, Didier Joris, Dorsaz, GERMANIER, SIMON MAYE, MERCIER, PROVINS VALAIS, La Rodeline, La Romaine, ROUVINEZ, ST JODERN KELLEREI, Maurice Zufferey.

Vaud (Waadt) Wine canton known for conservative spirit, incl CHABLAIS, LA CÔTE, LAVAUX, and small outposts at Lake Murten and Lake NEUCHÂTEL. Important big producers: Bolle, Hammel, Obrist, Schenk. CHASSELAS is main grape – but only gd terroirs justify growers' loyalty.

Vinattieri Ticinesi ★★→★★★★ 09' 10 11' (12) One of the leading MERLOT producers of the TIC. Luigi Zanini (junior and senior) create an amazing diversity, from light Grotto Wine (designed to be drunk in traditional taverns) to Pomerol-style red. Top wines are Castello Luigi and red Vinattieri.

Good neighbours: Valais and Aosta Valley

Mtn valleys are shut off and isolated? Not really. VAL growers found out that they share some of their local varieties with their neighbours across the Alps, in the Aosta Valley. Aosta's CORNALIN is Valais' HUMAGNE Rouge, not Valais' Cornalin. But Petite ARVINE is the same s and n of Mont Blanc. Most telling similarity, according to a Valais grower: "*Nos vâches sont les mêmes*" – same cattle breed.

Visperterminen Val w ★→★★★ Upper VAL v'yds, esp for HEIDA. One of the highest v'yds in Europe (at 1,000 metres+; called Riben). See it from the train to Zermatt or Saas Fee. Try CHANTON, ST JODERN KELLEREI.

Yvorne Vd (r) w ★★→★★★ Top CHABLAIS AOC for rich CHASSELAS. Best v'yd sites lie on the detritus of a 1584 avalanche. Try Commune d'Yvorne, Château Maison Blanche, Domaine de l'Ovaille.

Zündel, Christian Tic ★★★→★★★★ 02 05' 09 10 11 12 German-Swiss geologist in TIC. Pure and age-worthy MERLOT/CAB SAUV Orizzonte. Recent emphasis on wonderful cool climate CHARD.

Zürich Largest wine-growing canton in German Switzerland. Mainly BLAUBURGUNDER and MÜLLER-T. Räuschling a local speciality. Best growers: Gehring, Lüthi, PIRCHER, SCHWARZENBACH, Zahner

Austria

Abbreviations used in the text:

Burgen	Burgenland
Carn	Carnuntum
Kamp	Kamptal
Krems	Kremstal
Low A	Lower Austria
M Burg	Mittelburgenland
N'see	Neusiedlersee-Hügelland
S/W/SE Sty	Styria
Therm	Thermenregion
Trais	Traisental
Wach	Wachau
Wag	Wagram
Wein	Weinviertel

A ustria is an extraordinary success story. Only 25 years ago, Austrian wine stood with its back to the wall, after a scandal caused by ruthless bulk-wine companies. But hundreds of Austrian family estates answered by reinventing Austrian wine as individual, terroir-driven and expressive. Today, the country possesses dozens of top estates whose wines are globally recognized. A few are cult wines, especially some of the sweetest, but many more are good-value, brilliantly grown and made wines to drink every day; Grüner Veltliner, Austria's speciality grape, is particularly good at producing appealing wines at every level. The DAC category has also been a success; in 2012, one DAC alone (Weinviertel) sold four million bottles – all of them fulfilling high standards of production and control, and this at a moderate price point. Now red wines from Blauburgunder (Pinot Noir), St-Laurent, Blaufränkisch and its cross, Zweigelt, are finding an international audience.

Recent vintages

2013 Rollercoaster vintage. Late budburst, uneven fruit set (especially for Grüner V), hot and dry summer, then rain. Very good for sweet wines.

2012 Quantities down from 2011. Quality satisfactory or better.

2011 One of finest vintages in living memory.

2010 Hand-picking and meticulous work were imperative, yields down by as much as 55%.

2009 Uneven, with some outstanding whites (Lower Austria, Styria) and reds (Neusiedlersee, Middle Burgenland).

2008 The coolest year since 2004. Some outstanding results.

2007 Good in Styria and, in Burgenland, for Blaufränkisch, Zweigelt and Pinot N. Better for Grüner V than for Ries.

Achs, Paul N'see r (w) ★★★ 10 11 12 Fine GOLS producer obsessed with his terroir. High quality across the board, esp BLAUFRÄNKISCH Ungerberg, elegant PINOT N.

Alphart Therm ★★→★★★ Traditional, reliable estate, gd PINOT N and esp ROTGIPFLER (06' Rodauner Top Selection still incredibly fresh).

Alzinger Wach w ★★★★ 05 06 07 08 09 10 11 12 Top estate: highly expressive RIES, GRÜNER V, esp from Steinertal v'yd.

Angerhof-Tschida N'see w ★★★★ 03 05 06 08 09 11 12 Outstanding nobly sweet wines: MUSKAT Ottonel, Sämling (SCHEUREBE), WELSCHRIESLING.

Aumann Therm r w Modern, ambitious producer, interesting ST-LAURENT.

Ausbruch PRÄDIKAT wine with high sugar levels between BA and TBA (*see* box, Germany p.163). Traditionally produced in RUST.

Ausg'steckt ("Hung out") Green bush hung above the door of a HEURIGEN when open.

Beck, Judith N'see r w ★★→★★★ Rising accomplished bio winemaker. Well-crafted red blends (based on BLAUFRÄNKISCH or ZWEIGELT) and gd PINOT N, *St-Laurent*.

Brandl, Günter Kamp w ★★★ 09 10 11 12 Consistently *fine Kamptal estate*, known esp for RIES, GRÜNER V Novemberlese.

Braunstein, Birgit N'see r w ★★ Organic estate; gd BLAUFRÄNKISCH LEITHABERG and cuvée Oxhoft.

Bründlmayer, Willi Kamp r w sw sp ★★★★ 05 06 07 08 09 10 11' 12 Scrupulously working Willi Bründlmayer makes world-class RIES, GRÜNER V, esp Ries Heiligenstein Alte Reben, GV Käferberg. Also Austria's best sparkling *méthode traditionelle*.

Burgenland Province and wine region in the east bordering Hungary. Warm climate for textbook BLAUFRÄNKISCH, esp in M BURG and SÜDBURGENLAND, and ideal conditions for botrytis wines around shallow NEUSIEDLER SEE (Lake Neusiedl).

Buschenschank A wine tavern, often a HEURIGE country cousin.

Carnuntum Low A r w Dynamic region southeast of VIENNA; gd reds, often ST-LAURENT based. Best: Glatzer, Grassl, G Markowitsch, Muhr-van der Niepoort, Netzl.

Christ r w Reliable VIENNA producer; leading light in the GEMISCHTER SATZ movement.

Districtus Austriae Controllatus (DAC) The appellation system designed for the most typical and best marketed wines of an area, first introduced in 2002 and rapidly gaining acceptance. Currently nine DACs, incl EISENBERG, KAMP, KREMS, LEITHABERG, M BURG, NEUSIEDLERSEE, TRAIS, WEIN, Wiener GEMISCHTER SATZ. Most DACs define "classical" and RES wines, all of them strictly limit the range of admitted varieties.

Domäne Wachau Wach r w ★★→★★★ Excellent co-op (formerly "Freie Weingärtner"), producing a third of all WACH wines. Cellars at Dürnstein, v'yds in best sites, eg. Achleiten, Singerriedel, Kellerberg, Loibenberg.

Ehmoser Wag r w ★★★ Small individualist producer, gd GRÜNER V Aurum, terrific *juicy, crunchy Zweigelt*.

Eisenberg S Burg Small DAC (since 2009) around the Eisenberg v'yd, elegant BLAUFRÄNKISCH from slate soils.

Erste Lage First Growth according to ÖTW v'yd classification, currently around 50 v'yds along the Danube. In STY, Second Growth (*see* GROSSE LAGE).

Esterhazy Burgen r (w) ★★ Princely house at Eisenstadt (BURG) back in business with new winery.

Federspiel Wach Medium level of VINEA WACHAU categories, roughly corresponding to Kabinett (*see* box, Germany p.163). Elegant, dry wines, not quite featherweight, suited to typical Austrian cooking, eg. Tafelspitz or Wiener Schnitzel.

Feiler-Artinger N'see r w sw ★★★→★★★★ 03 04 05 06 07 08 09 10 11 12 Outstanding RUST estate with top AUSBRUCH dessert wines *often v.gd value* for money, red blends. Beautiful baroque house too.

Gemischter Satz Vienna Traditional white wine made from different grape varieties grown and fermented together. Since 2011 DAC for VIENNA. No variety may exceed

On another planet

Six growers around VIENNA have started trials to play Mozart's Symphony No. 41 in C Major 9 ("Jupiter") to their GRÜNER V musts. The protagonists of these so called "sonor wines" believe that the sound waves from loudspeakers installed inside their steel tanks have positive effects on the fermentation. Probably depends on who's playing.

50% of the blend. Historically a way of minimizing frost risk to any one variety; now fashionable again.

Gesellmann, Albert und Silvia M Burg r w (sw) ★★★ Estate famous for making BLAUFRÄNKISCH Hochberc and red cuvées Opus Eximium, G, Bela Rex. Gd CHARD Steinriegel too.

Geyerhof Krems r w ★★ Organic pioneer producing elegant RIES, GRÜNER V.

Gols N'see r w Wine commune on north shore of LAKE NEUSIEDL, known for mild climate and shallow soils. Top producers: ACHS, BECK, G HEINRICH, NITTNAUS, PITTNAUER, PREISINGER, Stiegelmar.

Graf Hardegg Wein r w ★→★★★ A large organic WEIN estate, with reputation for v.gd VIOGNIER.

Gross S Sty ★★★ Perfectionist S STY producer concentrating on regional character. Esp SAUV BL, MUSKATELLER, GEWÜRZ and his own favourite PINOT BL.

Grosse Lage Sty Highest classification level in STY, but not in use along Danube (see ERSTE LAGE). For further confusion see Germany.

Gsellmann & Hans N'see r w ★★ Bio estate in GOLS, known for red blends (esp Gabarinza), gd dry PINOT BL.

Gumpoldskirchen Therm Famous HEURIGEN village south of VIENNA, centre of THERM. Signature white varieties: ZIERFANDLER, ROTGIPFLER. Gd producers: Biegler, Spaetrot and Zierer.

Gut Oggau N'see r w ★★→★★★ Ambitious bio producer, making well-balanced, distinctly cool-climate BLAUFRÄNKISCH with just a little oak influence. Excellent dry GRÜNER V and GEWURZ.

Haider N'see sw ★★★ 13 grape varieties on 13 ha, best-known for TBA (see box, Germany p.163).

Hajszan Neumann Vienna ★★→★★★ Bio-certified estate (Demeter) producing mineral RIES Neubergen and pure GEMISCHTER SATZ Weissleiten.

Heinrich, Gernot N'see r w dr sw ★★★★ 06 07 08 09 10 11 12 Accomplished GOLS estate, member of PANNOBILE group. Outstanding single-v'yd red wines: Salzberg.

Heinrich, J M Burg r w ★★★ 05 06 08 09 11 12 Leading M BURG producer. V.gd BLAUFRÄNKISCH Goldberg RES. Succulent cuvée Cupido.

Heuriger Wine of most recent harvest. **Heurigen** are also wine taverns in which growers-cum-patrons serve their own wine with simple local food – a Viennese institution since before Beethoven.

Hiedler Kamp w sw ★★★ Consistently fine grower, concentrated wines from steep terraced v'yds. Powerful RIES Maximum.

Hirsch Kamp w ★★★ 05 06 09 11 12 Fine organic-going-bio grower. Esp fine Heiligenstein, Lamm, Gaisberg v'yds. Austria's screwcap pioneer.

Hirtzberger, Franz Wach w ★★★★ 05 06 07 08 10 11' 12 Top producer at Spitz an der Donau. *Highly expressive, mineral Ries*, GRÜNER V esp from the Honivogl, Singerriedel v'yds.

Högl Wach ★★★ Fine RIES, GRÜNER V from steeply terraced v'yds on primary rock, eg. Schön and Bruck.

Horitschon M Burg M BURG region for reds: IBY, WENINGER.

Igler M Burg r ★★→★★★ Red specialist, esp refined PINOT N Ried Fabian, BLAUFRÄNKISCH M BURG DAC, and blends Ab Ericio, Vulcano. Careful viticulture, winemaking.

Illmitz N'see sw SEEWINKEL region famous for BA, TBA (*see* box, Germany p.163). Best from ANGERHOF, HAIDER, KRACHER, Lang, Opitz.

Jamek, Josef Wach w ★★→★★★ Traditional estate with restaurant and property in some of best WACH v'yds: Klaus, Achleiten, Hochrain.

Johanneshof Reinisch Therm ★★ Family winery making some gd reds esp PINOT N, ST-LAURENT, also ZIERFANDLER and ROTGIPFLER. Top v'yd is Spiegel.

Juris (Stiegelmar) N'see ★★→★★★ Well-regarded GOLS grower. CHARD, SAUV BL and gd reds (ST-LAURENT, PINOT N).

Jurtschitsch Kamp ★★★ A large but reliable KAMP estate, best-known for entry level-brand GrüVe. Outstanding RES wines from ERSTE LAGE sites, now organically farmed.

Kamptal Low A r w Wine region along river Kamp north of WACH, broader in style. Top v'yds: Heiligenstein, Käferberg, Lamm. Best: BRANDL, BRÜNDLMAYER, Eichinger, HIEDLER, HIRSCH, JURTSCHITSCH, LOIMER, SCHLOSS GOBELSBURG. Kamp is DAC for GRÜNER V, RIES.

Kerschbaum, Paul M Burg ★★★ 05 06 07 08 09 11 12 Rapidly expanding BLAUFRÄNKISCH specialist, individual and often fascinating wines.

Klassifizierte Lage Second Growth in classification system of OTW. *See also* ERSTE LAGE.

Klosterneuburg Wag r w Main wine town of Donauland. Rich in tradition, with a wine college founded in 1860. Best: Stift Klosterneuburg, Zimmermann.

KMW Abbreviation for Klosterneuburger Mostwaage ("must level"), unit used in Austria to measure sugar content in grape juice. 1 degree KMW = 4.86 degrees Oechsle (*see* Germany).

Knoll, Emmerich Wach ★★★★ 83 86' 88 90 99' 01 03 04 05 06 07 08 09 10 11 12 Outstanding traditional estate in Loiben. *Delicate, fragrant Ries, complex Grüner V* from Loibenberg, Schütt v'yds, and legendary, long-lasting Vinothekfüllung.

Kollwentz N'see ★★★★ 05 06 07 08 09 10 11 12 An outstanding producer with a wide spectrum of wines, incl SAUV BL Steinmühle, CHARD Tatschler, BLAUFRÄNKISCH (Point, Setz), PINOT N Dürr, nobly sweet Sämling (SCHEUREBE). Plus top *red blend: Steinzeiler*.

Kracher N'see sw ★★★★ 01 02 03 04 05 06 07 08 09 10 11 12 Top-class ILLMITZ producer specializing in botrytized sweet BA and TBA (*see* box, Germany p.163), often blends.

Kremstal (r) w Wine region and DAC for GRÜNER V, RIES. Top: Buchegger, Malat, MOSER, NIGL, SALOMON-UNDHOF, WEINGUT STADT KREMS.

Krutzler S Burg r ★★★★ 06 07 08 09 11' 12 Outstanding south BURG family estate (fifth generation). Classical BLAUFRÄNKISCH that is reliable at every level. Most prestigious: Perwolff.

Lackner-Tinnacher SE Sty w sw ★★→★★★ SÜD-OSTSTEIERMARK estate known for aromatic dry MUSKATELLER, elaborated single-v'yd SAUV BL.

Laurenz V. ★★ Brand created by Laurenz Maria Moser V, aimed at popularizing GRÜNER V worldwide. Grapes from KAMP, KREM, WEIN. Five different styles: "Charming", "Singing", "Silver Bullet", etc. Better known abroad than at home.

Leithaberg N'see V'yd hill and DAC on the northern shore of LAKE NEUSIEDL. Interesting geology: limestone and mica schist. And a lively group of producers in search of terroir expression.

Loimer, Fred Kamp w ★★★→★★★★ 05 06 07 09 11 12 Thoughtful bio producer, 50% GRÜNER V (best: Spiegel), also excellent RIES (Steinmassl, Heiligenstein).

Mantlerhof Krems ★★ A grower with a well-considered, traditional approach. Gd ROTER VELTLINER.

Mittelburgenland Wine region on the Hungarian border: stuctured, age-worthy BLAUFRÄNKISCH (also DAC). Producers incl GESELLMANN, J HEINRICH, Iby, IGLER, KERSCHBAUM, Wellanschitz, WENINGER.

Moric N'see ★★★★ 05 06 09 10 11 12 Wines of elegance and depth from old BLAUFRÄNKISCH vines in Lutzmannsburg and Neckenmarkt.

Morillon Traditional designation for CHARD in south STYRIA.

Moser, Lenz Krems ★→★★ Austria's largest producer (2,700 ha), based nr Krems.

Neumayer Trais w ★★★ Top estate making powerful, focused dry GRÜNER V, RIES.

Neumeister SE Sty ★★★ 08 09 11 12 Modernist, meticulous producer, esp fine SAUV BL, CHARD.

Neusiedlersee N'see r w dr sw Wine region north and east of LAKE NEUSIEDL. Growers: ACHS, BECK, G HEINRICH, JURIS, KRACHER, NITTNAUS, PÖCKL, UMATHUM, VELICH. Eponymous DAC limited to ZWEIGELT.

The average vineyard holding in Austria is 2.3 ha for each of 20,000 growers.

Neusiedlersee-Hügelland r w dr sw Wine region west of LAKE NEUSIEDL around RUST on the lake shores, and Eisenstadt in the Leitha foothills (*see* LEITHABERG DAC). Best: BRAUNSTEIN, FEILER-ARTINGER, KOLLWENTZ, MORIC, PRIELER, SCHRÖCK, TRIEBAUMER.

Neusiedler See (Lake Neusiedl) Burgen Shallow BURGEN lake on Hungarian border, largest reed-growing area in Europe, and a nature reserve. Autumn mists encourage botrytis.

Niederösterreich (Low A) Northeastern region with 58% of Austria's v'yds, divided in three parts: areas around the Danube (KAMP, KREM, TRAISENTAL, WACH), the huge WEIN (northeast) and the south (CARN, THERM).

Nigl Krems ★★★★ Outstanding KREM estate at Senftenberg, dry whites with remarkable mineral character.

Nikolaihof Wach ★★★ 05 06 07 08 09 10 11 12 Bio pioneer producing wines with ageing potential, often v. closed when young. 1998 Steinriesler RIES stayed 13 yrs in cask, bottled in 2012. Outstanding Ries Steiner Hund.

Nittnaus, Anita and Hans N'see r w sw ★★★ Rising bio producer; age-worthy BLAUFRÄNKISCH Kalk & Schiefer, Tannenberg, LEITHABERG DAC. Also v.gd red blends (esp Comondor), TBA (*see* box, Germany p.163).

Österreichische Traditionsweingüter (ÖTW) Kamp, Krems, Trais, Wag Association engaged in the classification of ERSTE LAGE v'yds around the Danube. Currently 23 members, but no WACH estates.

Ott, Bernhard Low A ★★★ GRÜNER V specialist from WAGRAM, culinary wines both elegant (Fass 4) and powerful (Rosenberg). Tannic amphorae-fermented Qvevre needs time in a decanter.

Pannobile N'see Union of nine NEUSIEDLERSEE growers centred on GOLS, aiming to express the mild "pannonic" climate of their region. Members: ACHS, BECK, GSELLMANN, G HEINRICH, NITTNAUS, PITTNAUER, PREISINGER.

Pfaffl Wein r w ★★★ 07 08 09 11 12 Large estate, 75 ha. Top WEIN DAC RES wines.

Pichler, Franz X Wach ★★★★ 05 06 07 08 09 11 12 Great producer. Intense, *iconic* Ries (Unendlich, Loibenberg), GRÜNER V (esp Kellerberg).

Pichler, Rudi Wach w ★★★★ 05 06 09 10 11 12 Expressive RIES, GRÜNER V from top sites (Achleiten, Steinriegl, Hochrain).

Pittnauer, Gerhard N'see ★★★ Organic NEUSIEDLERSEE red wine specialist, one of Austria's finest for ST-LAURENT.

Pöckl, Josef & René N'see ★★★ 09 11' 12 Complex red blends: Admiral and Rêve de Jeunesse.

Polz, Erich & Walter S Sty ★★→★★★ 06 08 09 10 11 12 V.gd large growers, 70 ha, top v'yd: Hochgrassnitzberg: SAUV BL, CHARD.

Prager, Franz Wach ★★★★ 05 06 07 08 09 11 12 Mineral RIES, GRÜNER V from top sites, impeccable elegance: Wachstum Bodenstein, Achleiten, Klaus, Steinriegl.

Preisinger, Claus N'see r ★★★ Gifted young winemaker producing some of Austria's finest PINOT N. Cuvée Paradigma is based on BLAUFRÄNKISCH. In conversion to bio.

Prieler N'see r w ★★★ Consistently fine producer. Esp gd BLAUFRÄNKISCH Goldberg.

Proidl, A und F Krems ★★★ Individual grower; age-worthy RIES and GRÜNER V.

Reserve Attribute for DAC and other wines of origin, min 13% alcohol and prolonged (cask) ageing.

Ried Austrian term for v'yd.

Rust N'see r w dr sw Historic town on shore of LAKE NEUSIEDL, beautiful 17th-century houses testify to centuries of fine wine, esp of Ruster AUSBRUCH. Top: FEILER-ARTINGER, Giefing, SCHRÖCK, E TRIEBAUMER.

Sabathi, Hannes S Sty ★★★ Youthful, highly professional estate. Fine single-v'yd whites (esp SAUV BL Merveilleux).

Salomon-Undhof Krems w ★★★ Classical, well-structured KREM whites, v. reliable.

Sattlerhof S Sty w ★★★★ 07 08 09 10 11' 12 Crystalline, precise SAUV BL, MORILLON from v. steep v'yds.

Schiefer, Uwe S Burg ★★★ Ex-*garagiste* producing complex BLAUFRÄNKISCH of mineral elegance, esp from Szapary, Reihburg v'yds. Already 11 ha.

Grüner Veltliner, Brauner Veltliner and Roter Veltliner are unrelated to each other.

Schilcher W St Rustic, thirst-quenching rosé from indigenous Blauer Wildbacher grapes, speciality of west STY. Try: Domäne Müller, Schilcherei Jöbstl, Reiterer.

Schilfwein (Strohwein) Sweet wine made from grapes air-dried on straw matting, Vin Santo-style.

Schloss Gobelsburg Kamp r w dr sw ★★★★ 05 06 07 08 09 10 11' 12 Renowned estate in possession of the Cistercian monastery Zwettl and run by Michael Moosbrugger, a scholar of WILLI BRÜNDLMAYER. Rewarding at every level, excellent single-v'yd RIES, GRÜNER V; fine PINOT N; magnificent TBA (*see* box, Germany p.163).

Schloss Halbturn N'see r w sw ★★★ 06 09 11 12 Ambitious estate; international approach to Austrian varieties and terroir. Esp cuvée Imperial, PINOT N.

Schlumberger sp Largest sparkling winemaker in Austria. Also Loire (France).

Schmelz Wach w ★★★ Fine, underrated producer, outstanding RIES Dürnsteiner Freiheit, GRÜNER V Pichl Point.

Schröck, Heidi N'see (r) w sw ★★★ AUSBRUCH of great purity, focus from a thoughtful RUST grower.

Schuster, Rosi N'see ★★★ 09 11 12 Refined BLAUFRÄNKISCH; sappy, complex ST-LAURENT.

Seewinkel ("Lake corner") Part of NEUSIEDLERSEE around ILLMITZ, ideal for botrytis.

Smaragd Wach Highest category of VINEA WACHAU, usually richer than dry Spätlese (*see* box, Germany p.163), depending on producer sometimes botrytis-influenced.

Spätrot-Rotgipfler Therm Typical blend of THERM. Aromatic, weighty wines, often with orange-peel aromas. *See* Grapes chapter.

Steinfeder Wach VINEA WACHAU category for light, fragrant, dry wines.

Stift Göttweig ★★ Baroque Benedictine monastery nr Krems. New broom; fine single-v'yd wines.

Styria (Steiermark) Southernmost region of Austria, known for aromatic, fresh dry whites. *See* SÜDSTEIERMARK, SÜD-OSTSTEIERMARK, WESTSTEIERMARK.

Südburgenland S Burg r w Small eastern wine region. V.gd BLAUFRÄNKISCH. Best: KRUTZLER, SCHIEFER, WACHTER-WIESLER.

Süd-Oststeiermark SE Sty (r) w STY region with excellent v'yds. Best: NEUMEISTER, Ploder-Rosenberg, Winkler-Hermaden.

Südsteiermark S Sty Best STY region close to Slovenian border, cool-climate whites (SAUV BL, MUSKATELLER) from steep slopes, best growers: GROSS, LACKNER-TINNACHER, POLZ, SABATHI, SATTLERHOF, TEMENT and Wohlmuth. An insider tip is the area's MORILLON wines from shell limestone.

Tegernseerhof Wach w ★★ Rising grower of v. interesting RIES, GRÜNER V.

Tement, Manfred S Sty w ★★★★ 96 97 01 02' 03' 04 05 07 08 09' 10 11 12

Perfectionist producer: whites with immaculate fruit. Esp SAUV BL, MORILLON from Zieregg site, IZ (intra-cellular fermentation) a cult step-up.

Thermenregion Region of hot springs east of VIENNA. Indigenous grapes (eg. ZIERFANDLER, ROTGIPFLER), serious reds (ST-LAURENT, PINOT N). Producers: ALPHART, Biegler, Fischer, Reinisch, Stadlmann.

Traisental Small district south of Krems on Danube. Lighter whites than in WACH. Top producers: Huber, NEUMAYER.

Triebaumer, Ernst N'see r (w) (sw) ★★★★ 05 06 07 08 09 10 11' 12 A great RUST producer making BLAUFRÄNKISCH (incl legendary Mariental) and CAB SAUV/MERLOT blend. V.gd AUSBRUCH.

Uhudler S Burg Local south BURGEN speciality. Wine made directly from American rootstocks, with a foxy, strawberry taste. Uh.

Umathum, Josef N'see r w dr sw ★★★ Fine, thoughtful producer. Dense, powerful reds, incl PINOT N, BLAUFRÄNKISCH. Gd whites too.

Velich N'see w sw ★★★→★★★★ Cultish producer. Powerful, creamy CHARD Tiglat. Some of top sweet wines in SEEWINKEL.

Veyder-Malberg Wach ★★★→★★★★ A 2008 start-up, cultivating some of WACHAU's most labour-intensive v'yds; handmade wines of great purity and finesse.

Vienna w (r) Wine region in suburbs. Mostly simple wines, served to tourists in HEURIGEN. Quality producers: HAJSZAN NEUMANN, WIENINGER, Zahel.

Vinea Wachau Wach WACH growers association founded 1983. No v'yd classification, but strict quality charter and definition of three categories for dry wine: STEINFEDER, FEDERSPIEL, SMARAGD.

Wachau World-renowned Danube region, home to some of Austria's most mineral, long-lived RIES, GRÜNER V. Top: ALZINGER, Donabaum, DOMÄNE WACHAU, HIRTZBERGER, HÖGL, JAMEK, KNOLL, NIKOLAIHOF, F PICHLER, R PICHLER, Pichler-Krutzler, PRAGER, SCHMELZ, TEGERNSEERHOF, VEYDER-MALBERG.

Wachter-Wiesler, Weingut S Burg r ★★★ Christoph Wachter, in his mid-20s, is shooting star of EISENBERG DAC, producing fruit-driven, dense, only discreetly oak-influenced BLAUFRÄNKISCH.

Wagram (r) w Region west of VIENNA, incl KLOSTERNEUBURG. Mainly loess soils and GRÜNER V. Best: EHMOSER, Fritsch, Stift Klosterneuburg, Leth, OTT, Wimmer-Czerny, Zimmermann.

Weingut Stadt Krems Krems r w ★★ Co-op capably steered by Fritz Miesbauer, esp RIES and GRÜNER VELTLINER. Miesbauer also vinifies for STIFT GÖTTWEIG.

Weinviertel (r) w ("Wine Quarter") Largest Austrian wine region, 13,000 ha between Danube and Czech border, eponymous DAC. Largely simple whites, ambitious growers succeed in combining freshness, regional character. Try: Ebner-Ebenauer, GRAF HARDEGG, Gruber, PFAFFL, Weinrieder, Zull.

Weninger, Franz M Burg r (w) ★★★★ 05 06 07 08 09 11' 12 Top estate at Horitschon, *fine reds esp Blaufränkisch*, from clay- and iron-rich soils (Dürrau v'yd). Also in Hungary: Weninger-Gere.

Weststeiermark W St p Small wine region specializing in SCHILCHER. Best: Klug, Lukas, DOMAINE MÜLLER, Reiterer, Strohmeier.

Wien Vienna *See* VIENNA.

Wieninger, Fritz Vienna r w sp ★★★ 06 07 08 09 11 12 Leading grower with HEURIGEN: CHARD, RIES, PINOT N, gd GEMISCHTER SATZ. Best v'yds: Nussberg, Rosengartl.

Winkler-Hermaden SE Sty r w sw ★★★ Certified organic producer, mainly on volcanic soils. Excellent SAUV BL, TRAMINER, PINOT GR, MORILLON, also one of the region's few v.gd reds ZWEIGELT-based Olivin.

Winzer Krems Krems Large co-op with 1,300 growers.

England & Wales

We're concentrating on sparkling wine again this year – and after a run of good to very good vintages between 2003 and 2010, the last three have been decidedly tricky for English and Welsh winemakers. There were low yields in 2011, even lower in 2012, and a very late harvest in 2013, despite what was generally considered a good summer. Flowering didn't finish until the last week of July and the grapes never caught up. However, for sparkling wine, low sugars and high acids are just what are required and with generally large yields, growers are sounding a lot more confident than they have been for a couple of years.

Bluebell Estates E Sussex ★ Newish sparkling producer using both SEYVAL BL and traditional Champagne varieties. Hindleap Rosé **10** and **09** Blanc de Blancs best wines. Nr Bluebell Railway.

Bolney Wine Estate W Sussex ★ Est in 1972, now in second-generation hands and starting to make some impressive sparkling. CHARD-based Blanc de Blancs **08** and Rosé **09** well worth trying. Gd visitor facilities.

Breaky Bottom E Sussex ★★ One of UK's longest-lasting v'yds now approaching 40th yr with same owner/winemaker. CHARD-based Cuvée Princess Colonna **08**, 95% SEYVAL-based Cuvée Alexandre Schwatschko **08** best wines and ageing well.

Camel Valley ★★★ Cornwall's only major v'yd and one of the UK's best. Annie's Anniversary **10** made from SEYVAL BL and **09** PINOT N Rosé Brut both excellent.

Chapel Down Kent ★★★ Sparkling here gets better and better. New 73-acre Aylesford v'yd now cropping, so supplies more consistent. Entry-level NV Brut and NV Rosé Brut both gd value. **06** PINOT Res also ageing well. V.gd restaurant and shop.

Coates & Seely Hants ★★ Relatively new entrants to English sparkling wine market; v.gd quality. NV Brut Res is best wine.

Furleigh Estate ★★ Dorset Champagne-grape newcomer gets better and better. **10** Rosé and **09** Blanc de Noirs both great wines. **09** Blanc de Blancs also excellent.

Gusbourne Kent ★★ Newcomer with growing reputation; bought in 2013 and set to become a major producer with plans to challenge the top slot. Brut Res **08** and Blanc de Blancs **08** best wines.

Hambledon Vineyard England's oldest commercial v'yd now revived with big investment, big ambitions. First release of fizz in 2014.

Henners E S'x Newcomer making impact with first vintage. **09** Res and **09** Vintage both excellent wines.

Herbert Hall 2010 Brut from Kent's Marden V'yd is a delight.

Hush Heath Estate Kent ★★ Top producer; excellent wines under Balfour Brut label. Next vintage (**10**) won Gold at Decanter World Wine Awards. Also gd apple juice and range of flavoured ciders.

Jenkyn Place Hants Well-sited v'yds, some gd wines. Best are subtle, toasty Brut **09** and fruity Brut Rosé **09**.

Nyetimber W S'x ★★★ UK's best-known and largest producer. Best: Classic Cuvée **09**, Rosé **09** and single-vy'd Tillington **09**.

Plumpton College E S'x ★★ UK's only wine college now starting to make interesting wines. The Dean Blush Brut NV best wine.

Ridge View E S'x ★★★★ Great quality, consistency, gd value keep this winery at top of UK producers. Best wines: crisp, lemony Grosvenor Blanc de Blancs **10**; toasty classic cuvée Cavendish **09**. Consults to others, incl v.gd Upperton, Wyfold, Theale V'yd.

Wiston W S'x New, 16 acres on chalk downland; ex-NYETIMBER winemaker in charge. **09** South Down Cellars Bin 3, NV Blanc de Blancs best, though v. high acidity.

Central & Southeast Europe

More heavily shaded areas are the wine-growing regions.

Prague · CZECH REPUBLIC
SLOVAK REPUBLIC
Bratislava · Danube
Budapest
MOLDOVA
Ljubljana · Zagreb · HUNGARY · ROMANIA · Chişinău
SLOVENIA · CROATIA · Drava · Timişoara · Olt · Prut
BOSNIA-HERZEGOVINA · Sava · Belgrade · Bucharest · Danube
Split · Sarajevo · SERBIA · Danube
Adriatic Sea · MONTENEGRO · Varna
Dubrovnik · Podgorica · BULGARIA · Black Sea
Sofia · Plovdiv
Skopje
Tirana · MACEDONIA
ALBANIA

Abbreviations used in the text:

Bal	Balaton	N Croa	North Croatia
Cri & Mar	Crişana & Maramures	N Hun	North Hungary
Dalm	Dalmatia	N/S Pann	North/South Pannonia
Dob	Dobrogea	Pod	Podravje
Mold	Moldova	Pos	Posavje
Mun	Muntenia & Oltenia Hills	Prim	Primorje
Ist	Istria	Tok	Tokaj

HUNGARY

At long last Hungary is gaining the global recognition that her best wines and winemakers deserve. And most importantly, it's not just for sweet Tokaji, but for serious reds and dry whites too. This in turn means that foreign importers want the wines, so they're getting easier to find. At the same time, the wealth of tiny producers who will never export means that an exploratory visit to can be highly rewarding. And Budapest is a thrilling place to start.

Árvay Tok w dr sw ★★ Family winery in TOK since 2009 with 17 ha.

Aszú Tok Botrytis-affected and shrivelled grapes, and the resulting sweet wine from TOK graded in sweetness from 3 PUTTONYOS up to 6 (5 to 6 only from 2014). Only in some yrs: gd aszú in 05 06 07 08 09 (11); very promising 2013.

Aszú Essencia Tok Still seen on labels but not legal since 2010; was second-sweetest TOKAJI level (7 PUTTONYOS+). Do not confuse with ESSENCIA/ESZENCIA.

Badacsony Bal w dr sw ★★→★★★ Volcanic slopes north of Lake BALATON; full, rich whites. Look for Laposa (fine, mineral), *Szeremley* (age-worthy KÉKNYELŰ, SZÜRKEBARÁT), Villa Sandahl (esp Magic Rain, Cappucino Oil RIES) and Villa Tolnay.

Balaton Region, and Central Europe's largest freshwater lake. BADACSONY, Balatonfüred-Csopak (Béla és Bandi, Feind, Figula, Jasdi; impressive Siralomvágó OLASZRIZLING), Balatonmelléke (DR. BUSSAY), SOMLÓ to the north. BALATONBOGLÁR to the south.

Balatonboglár r w dr ★★→★★★ Wine district, also major winery of TÖRLEY, south of Lake BAL. Gd producers: Budjosó, GARAMVÁRI, Ikon, KONYÁRI, Légli Géza, Légli Otto, and Pócz.

Barta Tok w dr sw ★★★ 09 11 Highest v'yd in TOK, producing impressive dry whites (esp FURMINT Válogatás) with top winemaker Attila Hommona. Also v.gd sweet SZAMORODNI, FURMINT Késői Szüret.

Béres Tok w dr sw ★★→★★★ Gd ASZÚ 06 07 (08) and dry FURMINT 09 esp Lőcse and Diókút HÁRSLEVELŰ.

Bikavér N Hun r ★→★★★ 07 08 09' 11 Means "Bull's Blood". DHC for EGER and SZEKSZÁRD only, min three red varieties, oak-aged for min 12 mths. Local regulations encourage KÉKFRANKOS and historically KADARKA. Supérior is min four varieties and restricted yield. Best for Egri Bikavér: Bolyki, Demeter, Grof Buttler, GÁL TIBOR, ST ANDREA, Thummerer. In SZEKSZÁRD look for Eszterbauer, HEIMANN, Meszáros, Takler, Sebestyén.

Bor is wine: *vörös* is red; *fehér* is white; *édes* is sweet, *száraz* is dry, *válogatás* is selected.

Bock, József S Pann r ★→★★★ 08 09' 11 A leading family winemaker in VILLÁNY. Noted for weighty rich reds. Best incl CAB FR Selection, Bock Cuvée, Capella Cuvée, SYRAH.

Bodrogkeresztúr Village in TOK region. Gd producers: DERESZLA, Füleky (gd 07 ASZÚ), PATRICIUS, TOKAJ Nobilis (brilliant Barakonyi HÁRSLEVELŰ 09'), Puklus (try Kabar).

Bussay, Dr. Bal w ★★ 09 (11) Doctor and winemaker in Balatonmelléke. Intense TRAMINI, PINOT GR, OLASZRIZLING. Also v.gd Kerkaborum wines with HEIMANN.

Csányi S Pann r ★→★★ Large winery in VILLÁNY. Csányi Kővilla and top Teleki ranges worth a try.

Degenfeld, Gróf Tok w dr sw ★★→★★★ Large TOK estate with luxury hotel, now organic methods. Sweet wines best: 6 PUTTONYOS 08, Andante 08; also pretty semi-dry DYA MUSCAT Blanc.

Demeter Zoltán Tok w sw ★★★→★★★★ 08' 09' 11 12 Elegant dry wines, esp Veres and Lapis FURMINTS; excellent Szerelmi HÁRSLEVELŰ. Eszter late-harvest also v.gd.

Dereszla Tok w dr sw ★★★ 05 06 07' 08 09 10 11 Re-equipped since 2007 by owners, d'Aulan family from Champagne. V.gd ASZÚ and *flor*-aged dry SZAMORODNI Experience. Also try Kabar and v.gd FURMINT Lapis.

Districtus Hungaricus Controllatus (DHC) Term for Protected Designation of Origin (PDO). Symbol is a local crocus and DHC on label.

Disznókő Tok w dr sw ★★★→★★★★ 06 07' 08 Important TOK estate, owned by French insurer AXA. Fine expressive ASZÚ, Kapi the top cru. Also gd-value late-harvest 2011 and fresh, steely DYA FURMINT.

Dobogó Tok (r) w dr sw ★★★→★★★★ 06' 07' 08 09 11 Impeccable small TOK estate. Benchmark ASZÚ and late-harvest Mylitta, superb Mylitta Álma, thrilling dry FURMINT 2011, esp Betsek DŰLŐ and *pioneering Pinot N* Izabella Utca.

Dűlő Named v'yd; single site.

Duna Duna Great Plain. Districts: Hajós-Baja (try Sümegi), Csongrád (Somodi), Kunság (Frittmann: decent Kadarka, Generosa).

Eger N Hun r w dr ★★→★★★ Top red region of north. Egri BIKAVÉR is most famous. CAB FR, PINOT N, SYRAH increasingly important; DHC for Debrői HÁRSLEVELŰ. Try: Bolyki, Gróf Buttler, Demeter, *Gál Tibor*, Kaló Imre, KOVÁCS NIMRÓD, Pók Tamás, ST ANDREA, Thummerer.

Egri Csillag N Hun "Star of Eger". New dry white blend modelled on BIKAVÉR. Blend of at least four grapes; min 50% must be local Carpathian varieties.

Essencia / Eszencia Tok ★★★★ Syrupy, luscious, aromatic juice that trickles from ASZÚ grapes, produced in any top aszú yr but only rarely bottled. Alcohol 2–3%+; sugar can be up to 800 g/litre. Reputed to have miraculous medicinal properties. Do not confuse with ASZÚ-ESSENCIA – historically for 7+ PUTTONYOS wines but not used since 2010.

Etyek-Buda N Pann Dynamic region noted for expressive, crisp whites and fine sparklers, esp CHARD, **Sauv Bl**, PINOT GR and promising for PINOT N. Leading producers: Etyeki Kúria (esp Pinot N, SAUV BL), Nyakas (Budai label), György-Villa (premium wines from TÖRLEY), Haraszthy, Rókusfalvy and newcomer Kertész.

Gál Tibor N Hun r w ★★ New winery in EGER and improved wines from son of late TIBOR GÁL, famed as winemaker at Ornellaia (Tuscany, Italy). Try appealing EGRI CSILLAG 2012, PINOT N 09, BIKAVÉR Supérior 09.

Garamvári Bal r p w sp ★★ Family-owned v'yd. Gd DYA IRSAI OLIVÉR and v.gd Sinai CAB SAUV. Also owns **Chateau Vincent**, Hungary's top bottle-fermented fizz (try Evolution Rosé, Prestige Brut).

Gere Attila S Pann r (p) ★★★→★★★★ 06' 07' 08 09' Leading light in VILLÁNY making some of country's best reds, esp rich Solus MERLOT, intense Kopar Cuvée, top Attila selection. **Cab Sauv** is gd value and ages well.

Heimann S Pann r ★★→★★★ 07 08 09' 11 Family winery in SZEKSZÁRD impresses, esp superb Barbár 09, v.gd Iván-Volgyi KADARKA (winery has unique v'yd of rare Kadarka clones), selected KÉKFRANKOS.

Hétszőlő Tok w dr sw ★★ Noble first-growth TOK estate bought in 2009 by Michel Rebier, owner of Cos d'Estournel (Bordeaux). KÖVÉRSZŐLŐ 07 is appealing.

Hilltop Winery N Pann r w dr ★★ 09 11 12 In Neszmély. Meticulous, gd-value DYA varietal whites. Also v.gd: ART The Dream, Muzeális, v'yd selection Premium range. PINOT N, MALBEC also worth trying.

Homonna Tok w dr ★★★ 09' Fine, elegant FURMINT, esp Hatari v'yd.

Kikelet Tok w dr sw ★★★ Bordeaux-trained woman winemaker making inspired dry wines and excellent SZAMORODNI 08.

Királyudvar Tok w dr sw ★★★→★★★★ 06' 07' 08 11(dr) TOK winery in old royal cellars at Tarcal, owned by Anthony Hwang (*see also* Vouvray). Excellent dry and sec FURMINT, Cuvée Ilona (late-harvest), stunning Cuvée Patricia and superb 6 PUTTONYOS Lapis ASZÚ.

Konyári Bal r p w dr ★★→★★★ 09 11 (12) Father and son making high-quality estate wines at BALATONBOGLÁR: esp fruity DYA rosé; consistent Loliense (r w); excellent Szárhegy (w); Jánoshegy KÉKFRANKOS; top Páva (r).

Kovács Nimród Winery N Hun r w dr ★★ 09 11' (12) EGER producer impressing with KÉKFRANKOS 11, Grand Bleu, Rosé and Battonage CHARD.

Mád Tok Important historic town in heart of TOK region. Gd producers: Alana-TOKAJ, BARTA, OROSZ GÁBOR, Demetervin, Lenkey, Holdvölgy, KIKELET, ROYAL TOKAJI, SZEPSY, SZENT TAMÁS WINERY, Tokaj Classic.

Malatinszky S Pann r p w dr ★★★ 06' 07 08 09' 11 Certified organic from 2012. Excellent unfiltered Kúria CAB FR, CAB SAUV, Kövesföld (r), Pinot Bleu. Also tasty DYA Le Sommelier rosé and Serena (w).

Mátra N Hun (r) w ★→★★ Gd fresh whites. Better producers: Benedek, Gábor Karner (notable KÉKFRANKOS), NAG, Szöke Mátyás, Borpalota (Fríz label), NAGYRÉDE estate.

Szürkebarát means "grey monk" and is the Hungarian name for Pinot Gris.

Mézes-Mály Tok Top TOK cru in Tarcal. Try ROYAL TOKAJI and tiny but excellent Balassa.

Mór N Pann w ★→★★ Small, sleepy region, being revived almost single-handedly by Maurus winery. Try fiery Ezerjó and decent CHARD, TRAMINI, RIES.

Nagyréde Estate N Hun (r) p w ★ Gd-value, commercial DYA varietal wines under Nagyréde, MÁTRA Hill, Spice Trail labels.

Oremus Tok w dr sw ★★→★★★★ 05 06' 07 08 09 11 Site of historic TOK v'yd of founding Rákóczi family, owned by Spain's Vega Sicilia: first-rate ASZÚ; v.gd dry FURMINT **Mandolás**.

> **Kadarka comeback**
> KADARKA is reviving. Hugely important before phylloxera, it fell out of favour as more robust, productive vines took over. Today the best have a Pinot-like elegance and freshness. HEIMANN has a unique collection of clones and old cuttings, and its Ivan-Volgyi DŰLŐ is one of the best. Also in SZEKSZÁRD, look out for Eszterbauer Nagyapám ("my grandfather's") and Vesztergombi József's Remete-Bor. In EGER, Grof Buttler makes an elegant version, while down south in VILLÁNY, SAUSKA's is richer but still fresh and vibrant.

Orosz Gábor Tok w dr sw ★★→★★★ 03' 05 06 07 08 09 11 Improving producer: excellent dry single-v'yd Király HÁRSLEVELŰ 09, 6 PUTTONYOS ASZÚ. Second label is Bodvin.

Pajzos-Megyer Tok w dr sw ★★→★★★ 05 06' 07 08 09 11 Jointly managed TOK properties. Megyer in cooler north of region, esp dry FURMINT, dry and sweet MUSCAT. Pajzos makes richer, age-worthy sweet wines only.

Pannonhalma (r) (p) w dr ★★→★★★ 11 12 Northern wine region, esp the 800-yr-old Pannonhalma Abbey and its winery. Stylish, aromatic whites, esp OLASZRIZLING, TRAMINI, SAUV BL. Gd-value Tricollis, lovely top Hemina (w).

Patricius Tok w dr sw ★★ 05 06' 07 08 09 11 Substantial TOK estate since 2000. Consistent, gd-value dry FURMINT, late-harvest Katinka, 6 PUTTONYOS ASZÚ 03.

Pécs S Pann (r) w ★→★★ Wine region nr southern city of Pécs. Known for whites, incl local CIRFANDL. Ebner PINOT N impresses.

Pendits Winery Tok w dr sw ★★ 03 05 06 09 11 Only Demeter-certified bio estate in Hungary. Luscious ASZÚ, attractive sweet FURMINT, pretty dry MUSCAT.

Puttonyos (putts) Indication of sweetness in TOKAJI ASZÚ. Today sugar concentration/ litre is measured, so 3 PUTTONYOS = 60 g/litre, 4 = 90 g/litre, 5 = 120 g/litre, 6 = 150 g/litre. Historically a *puttony* was a 25-kg bucket or hod of aszú grapes. The number of puttonyos added to a 136-litre barrel of base wine or fermenting must determined the final sweetness of the wine.

Royal Tokaji Wine Co Tok dr sw 05 06 07' 08' Pioneer joint-venture at MÁD that led renaissance of TOK in 1990 (I am a co-founder). Mainly first-growth v'yds. 6-PUTTONYOS single-v'yd bottlings: esp MÉZES-MÁLY, Betsek, Szent Tamás, Nyulászó plus 5 PUTTONYOS 2008. Also from 2011 complex dry FURMINT, Furmint DŰLŐ-válogatás, luscious, gd-value Late Harvest (Mád Cuvée in the USA). Promising new consultant winemaker.

St Andrea N Hun r w dr ★★★ 06' 07 08 09' 11 Top name in EGER, leading way in modern, high-quality BIKAVÉR (Merengő, Hangács, Áldás). Excellent white blends: Napbor, Örökké, organic Boldogságos, plus v.gd PINOT N.

Sauska S Pann, Tok r p w ★★→★★★★ 07 08 09' 11' (12) Immaculate winery in VILLÁNY. Beautifully balanced KADARKA, KÉKFRANKOS, CAB FR and impressive red blends, esp Cuvée 7 and Cuvée 5. Also Sauska-Tokaj with focus on v.gd dry whites, esp Cuvée 105, FURMINT Birsalmás, Medve Furmint.

Somló Bal w ★★→★★★ 07 08 09 11 Dramatic volcanic hill famous for mineral-rich whites: *Juhfark* ("sheep's tail"), OLASZRIZLING, FURMINT, HÁRSLEVELŰ. Region of small producers making long-lived intense wines, esp Fekete Bela, Györgykovács, Hollóvár, Royal Somló, Spiegelberg, Somlói Apátsági. Bigger Tornai (esp Top Selection range, Grofi HÁRSLEVELŰ), Kreinbacher/St Ilona also v.gd.

Sopron N Pann r ★★→★★★ Recently dynamic district on Austrian border overlooking Lake Fertő. KÉKFRANKOS most important, plus CAB SAUV, SYRAH, PINOT N. Top producer is bio *Weninger*, also try v. characterful wines of Ráspi (esp Electus ZWEIGELT). To watch: Pfneiszl, Luka, Taschner.

Szamorodni Tok Literally "as it was born"; for TOK produced from whole bunches with no separate ASZÚ harvest. Dry or sweet (*édes*), depending on proportion of Aszú grapes present. Best dry versions are *flor*-aged; try *Tinon*, DERESZIA and Karádi-Berger. Gd sweet versions KIKELET, SZEPSY, Höldvolgy.

Szekszárd S Pann r ★★→★★★ Ripe, rich reds from KÉKFRANKOS, CAB SAUV, CAB FR, MERLOT. Also KADARKA being revived and BIKAVÉR. Look for: Dúzsi (noted for rosé in all styles), Domaine Gróf Zichy, Eszterbauer (esp Tüke Bikavér, Kadarka), HEIMANN, Lajver (for bright rosé), Mészáros, Sebestyén, Szent Gaál, TAKLER, Remete-Bor (Kadarka), Vida (v.gd Hidaspetre Kékfrankos).

Szent Tamás Tok w sw ★★ 11 12 New winery in MÁD with ISTVÁN SZEPSY Junior. Dry FURMINT Szent Tamás, HÁRSLEVELŰ and Late Harvest 3909. Useful restaurant.

Szepsy, István Tok w dr sw ★★★★ 03' 05 06 07 08' 09 10 11' Brilliant, standard-setting TOK producer in MÁD. Winner of 2013 Winemakers' Oscar. Superb DŰLŐ dry FURMINT, esp Urágya, SZENT TAMÁS, Betsek. Also Király HÁRSLEVELŰ, sweet SZAMORODNI 03 06 08. Shares family name with creator of ASZÚ method.

Szeremley Bal w dr sw ★★★ 09 11' 12 Pioneer in BADACSONY. Intense, mineral RIES, *Szürkebarát*, (aka PINOT GR), KÉKNYELŰ, and appealing sweet Zeus.

Takler S Pann r ★★ 07 08 09' 11' Significant family producer in SZEKSZÁRD, making super-ripe, supple reds. Best: Res selections of CAB FR, KÉKFRANKOS, SYRAH, BIKÁVER. Super-cuvée Regnum well-regarded locally and in the USA.

Tibor Gál N Hun r w dr ★→★★ Winery in EGER founded by the late Tibor Gál, famed as winemaker at Ornellaia, Tuscany. Son (also Tibor) is building new cellars; smaller range of wines is improving.

Tinon, Samuel Tok w dr sw ★★→★★★ 00 01 04 05 07 Sauternais in TOK since 1991. Distinctive and v.gd Tok ASZÚ with v. long maceration and barrel-ageing. Also superb *flor*-aged *Szamorodni*.

Tokaj Kereskedőház Tok w dr sw ★→★★ Aka Crown Estates, still state-owned, working with over 2,000 small growers. New winemaker Karoly Áts (ex-ROYAL TOKAJI) looks set to make changes and improve previously disappointing quality.

Tokaj Nobilis Tok w dr sw ★★★ A superb small producer, Sarolta Bárdos was winemaker of year in Tokaj 2012. Notable ASZÚ 07 and dry wines from Barakonyi v'yd.

Tokaj / Tokaji w dr sw ★★→★★★★ Tokaj is the town and wine region; Tokaji is the wine.

There are more than 500 extinct volcanoes in the region of Tokaj.

Tolna S Pann Antinori-owned ★★ Tűzkő is most important estate. Gd TRAMINI, CHARD, Talentum (r).

Törley r w dr sp ★→★★ Innovative large company. Well-made, international varietals (PINOT GR, CHARD, PINOT N), also local varieties IRSAI OLIVÉR, Zenit, Zefir. Major fizz producer (esp *Törley*, Gala, Hungaria Grande Cuvée labels) and v.gd classic method, esp François Rosé Brut, President Brut. Chapel Hill is well-made, gd-value brand; György-Villa for top selections (try Juhfark, SYRAH).

Villány S Pann Most southerly wine region and best red zone. Noted for serious ripe Bordeaux varieties (esp CAB FR) and blends, also try juicy examples of local *Kékfrankos* and PORTUGIESER. Recent appearance of gd SYRAH and PINOT N in cooler spots. High-quality producers: *Bock*, CSÁNYI, ATTILA GERE, Tamás Gere, Heumann, *Malatinszky*, SAUSKA, Tiffán, *Vylyan*, WENINGER-GERE, Wunderlich.

Vylyan S Pann r ★★→★★★ 06' 07 08 09' Stylish PINOT N. Also try CAB FR, SYRAH and excellent v'yd-selected MERLOT Pillangó. *Duennium Cuvée* (Cab Fr, CAB SAUV, Merlot, ZWEIGELT) is flagship red.

Weninger N Hun r ★★→★★★ 06 07 08 09 10 11 A benchmark winery in SOPRON run by Austrian Franz Weninger Jr. Bio since 2006. Single-v'yd *Spern*

Steiner Kékfrankos one of best in country. SYRAH, PINOT N and red Frettner blend also impressive.

Weninger-Gere S Pann r ★★★ 06' 07' 08 09 Joint-venture between Austrian Franz Weninger Sr and GERE ATTILA. CAB FR Selection excellent, gd-value Cuvée Phoenix and DYA fresh rosé.

BULGARIA

The current fascination with new grape varieties continues, though there's a definite trend towards blending these with indigenous grapes – mostly red – and some older, almost forgotten varieties are being revived. Cabernet Franc has transferred particularly successfully to Bulgaria and is increasingly popular, though Cabernet Sauvignon and Merlot, and the local Mavrud and Melnik, are still the pack leaders.

Assenovgrad Thrace r ★→★★ Specialist and largest producer of local grape varieties MAVRUD and RUBIN.

Bessa Valley Thrace r ★★★ Stephan von Neipperg (Canon la Gaffelière, Bordeaux) and K-H Hauptmann's winery nr Pazardjik. SYRAH by Enira 09, BV by Enira 09 and Enira Res 08. The only quality Bulgarian wine readily available in the UK.

Black Sea Gold Thrace (Pomorie) (r) w ★ New investment at this coastal winery has led to improved quality; try Villa Ponte CAB SAUV and SYRAH 09 and Arte Ante Cab Sauv 08.

Borovitsa Danube r w ★★→★★★ A rare old v'yd with distinctive terroir close to Danube. Dux 06, complex, well-balanced fruit and oak, recommended. Les Amis CHARD 08, PINOT N Cuvée Enrique 09 worth trying. Interesting blend of old variety Evmolpia and MERLOT. Sensum 10 has been voted Bulgaria's no.1 wine for the last 3 yrs. This is the place where God sends messages in bottles.

Castra Rubra Thrace r ★★ Michel Rolland from B'x advises successful young team. Award-winning Castra Rubra 09, Butterfly's Rock 09. Via Diagonalis 08 should age well.

Chateau de Val Danube r ★★ Small producer of distinctive wines: Grand Claret Res 09. Cuvée Trophy 10.

Damianitza Thrace r (w) ★★ Struma Valley MELNIK specialist. Uniqato RUBIN and Melnik 08; elegant Kometa No Man's Land MERLOT and CAB SAUV 08, tongue-twister Dzindzifkite CAB FR 10.

Domaine Boyar Thrace Big exporter, with wineries at Blueridge and Korten. Gd, consistent everyday quality. Also award-winning single-v'yd Solitaire Grands Cépages 09. In same range a smooth CAB FR 11, silky MERLOT 11. New Platinum CHARD 11, Cab Sauv 11, and established Quantum and Ars Longa ranges.

Dragomir Thrace r (w) ★★ Boutique winemakers. CAB SAUV and MERLOT Reserva 10, Pitos 09 and Karizma 09.

Ivo Varbanov Thrace r (w) ★★ Concert pianist making fine wines from organic v'yd in Sakar, incl La Puerta del Vino SYRAH 10, Ondine Syrah 09, Wandering Shadows 09.

Katarzyna Thrace r w ★★★ Southern winery to follow: Le Voyage SYRAH/CAB FR 11 is impressive. Also: Question Mark 11 (stylish CAB SAUV/MERLOT blend), Katarzyna Reserva 07.

Levent Danube (r) w ★★ Small winery in Russe, gd fresh whites, esp Levent Family Selection 10. K2 CAB SAUV and CAB FR 10, Grand Selection CHARD 11, Cab Sauv Grand Selection 11.

Logodaj Thrace r w ★→★★ Struma Valley. Hypnose Res MERLOT single-v'yd 10. Look for Nobile CHARD Barrel-Fermented 11. Stylish Artis CAB SAUV/CAB FR 10.

Midalidare Estate Thrace r w ★★ Boutique winery, impressive. Esp single-v'yd: Grand Vintage MALBEC Mogilovo 10, Grand Cuvée Mogilovo 10, RIES Mogilovo 11. Elegant SAUV BL/SÉM 12.

Minkovi Brothers Thrace r w ★★→★★★ Cycle range: well-priced varietals and blends of two grapes (bicycles) or three (tricycles). Le Photographe SYRAH 12. Oak Tree 10 is subtle, complex, balanced. Also From the Cellar MERLOT/CAB SAUV 09.

Bulgar best

Look out for these wines:

Chateau Burgozone: CAB FR 10, VIOGNIER 11.

Angelus Estates: Stallion 10, Stallion Classic 10. Equine names, French inspiration.

Villa Yustina: whites, and Monogram MAVRUD, RUBIN 09.

Medi Valley: Incanto SYRAH 10.

Miroglio, Edoardo Thrace r w ★★ Italian investor, v'yds at Elenovo. Soli Invicto 10; Elenovo CAB SAUV Res 09. Miroglio Brut Metodo Classico 07 (and rosé 08) known as *Bulgaria's best fizz*, gd in any company, dry, gently sparkling. Bouquet Nouveau 12 in style of Beaujolais Nouveau, using Bouquet grape.

Preslav Thrace (r) w ★→★★ Rubaiyat CHARD 09 recommended, also Rubaiyat CAB SAUV, MERLOT, SYRAH 08. Gd TRAMINER Golden Age 11, RIES Novi Pazar 11. SAUV BL 13 is gooseberry-fresh.

Santa Sarah Thrace r w ★★ Privat MAVRUD/CAB SAUV 08; Bin 49 CAB FR 11; Bin 41 MERLOT 11, Bin 42 RUBIN 11.

Strymon Thrace r ★→★★ Winery in the warm southwest. Smooth MERLOT 10 and Merlot Res 10, CAB SAUV Res 11. Promising Rosé from Cab Sauv and SYRAH 11.

Terra Tangra Thrace r w ★★ In highly rated Sakar Mtn. Gd full-bodied RUBIN 10; MERLOT 10; MAVRUD 10, highly recommended Roto 09, complex blend of CAB SAUV/ Merlot/CAB FR/SYRAH/Mavrud.

Varna Wine Cellar Danube (r) w ★→★★ Coastal winery, gd for moderately priced, promising SAUV BL 12 and RIES/Varnenski MISKET 12.

Yamantievi Thrace r w ★→★★ Villa Armira range: SHIRAZ and MERLOT Res, both 09; Marble Land CHARD 09.

SLOVENIA

Slovenia is the source of some beautifully balanced and intriguing whites, and its historically backward eastern zone, Štajerska, is now coming to the fore with brilliantly vibrant, crisp, aromatic whites and even the occasional elegant red. Economic pressures don't help, though.

Batič Prim w sw ★→★★ 09 11 12 Famous for "natural" wines in VIPAVA. Zaria Rosé is the top seller.

Bjana Prim sp ★★ V.gd traditional-method PENINA from BRDA, esp Cuvée Prestige and Brut Rosé.

Blažič Prim w ★★→★★★ 06 08 11 12 From BRDA. Notable REBULA, SAUVIGNONASSE and complex white blend Blaž Belo in top yrs.

Brda (Goriška) Prim Top-quality district in PRIM. Many leading wineries, incl BJANA, BLAŽIČ, EDI SIMČIČ, Dolfo (esp sparkling Spirito 10) Erzetič, JAKONČIČ, Klinec, KRISTANČIČ, MOVIA, Prinčič, ŠUREK, Simčič, VINSKA KLET GORIŠKA BRDA, ZANUT and orange wines (whites fermented with skins) from Kabaj and Klinec.

Burja Prim r w ★★→★★★ 11 Project in VIPAVA, focus on local grapes Zelen and

MALVAZIJA under Petite Burja label. Bela Burja is modern take on traditional blend. Burja Noir is one of country's best PINOT N.

Conrad Fürst Pod w ★★ 11 Newcomer making wine from restituted historic family v'yds nr Jeruzalem. V.gd FURMINT, PINOT BL so far.

Čotar Prim r w ★★ 03 04 06 08 Pioneer of long-lived "natural" wines from KRAS, esp Vitovska (w), MALVAZIJA, SAUV BL, TERAN, Terra Rossa red blend.

Cviček Pos Traditional low-alcohol, sharp, light red blend of POS, based on Žametovka grape. Try Bajnof.

> ### Slovenia's quality wines
> All wines have to pass a tasting to gain quality status. *Vrhunsko vino z zaščitenim geografskim poreklom*, or *Vrhunsko vino ZGP*, is the term for top-quality PDO wines, though not widely used because of cost of additional v'yd checks. *Kakovostno vino ZGP* is more common for quality wines. *Deželno vino PGO* is for PGI wines. For quality sweet wines, descriptions are: *Pozna Trgatev* (Spätlese), *Izbor* (Auslese), *Jagodni Izbor* (BA), *Suhi Jagodni Izbor* (TBA). (*See* box, Germany p.163 for more on quality level definitions.) *Ledeno Vino* is Icewine, *Slamno Vino* is straw wine from semi-dried grapes and PENINA is natural sparkling wine.

Dveri-Pax Pod r w sw ★★→★★★ 09 10 11 12 Benedictine-owned estate nr Maribor. Crisp, mineral, v.gd-value whites, esp SAUV BL, FURMINT, RIES. Excellent single-v'yds: Furmint Ilovci, Sauv Bl Vagyen, Ries "M". Also superb sweet wines, esp rare SIPON 09 straw wine.

Edi Simčič Prim r w ★★★→★★★★ 06 07 08 09 11 Perfectionist in BRDA; red wine superstar with Duet Lex and top blend Kolos. Whites getting fresher, purer. Excellent SIVI PINOT, REBULA, white blend Triton Lex. Superb Kozana single-v'yd CHARD.

Guerila Prim r w ★★ Bio producer in VIPAVA; benchmark local DYA PINELA and Zelen.

Heaps Good Wine Pod r w ★★ Promising newcomer. Kiwi Nick Gee and wife Marija make bright, fruit-focused PINOT N, MODRA FRANKINJA; rich PINOT GR in Štajerska.

Istenič Pos sp ★→★★ 03 06 08 Reliable long-lived PENINA. Basic is N°1, best: Gourmet Rosé and Prestige.

Istria Aka Slovenska Istra. Coastal zone extending into Croatia; REFOŠK, MALVAZIJA. Best: Bordon (E Vin rosé, Malvazija), Korenika & Moškon (PINOT GR, Kortinca red), Rojac (Renero, Stari d'Or), Pucer z Vrha (Malvazija), SANTOMAS, VINAKOPER

Jakončič Prim r w sp ★★★ 09 10 11 12 V.gd BRDA producer with elegant style, esp Bela Carolina REBULA/CHARD blend, PENINA and Rdeča (r) Carolina.

Joannes Pod r w sp ★★ 08' 09' 10 11 RIES specialist nr Maribor, wines age well. Also fresh light PINOT N, promising PENINA.

Kogl Pod r w sp ★★ 11 12 Small hilltop estate nr Ormož, dating from 1542. Main range is fine unoaked Mea Culpa wines.

Kras Prim Small, famous district on Terra Rossa soil in PRIM. Best-known for TERAN and MALVAZIJA.

Kristančič Dusan Prim r w ★★→★★★ 09 11 family winery in BRDA. Top Pavó wines are exciting, esp Bordeaux blend Rdeče 09.

Kupljen Pod r w ★★ 11 12 Consistent dry wine pioneer nr Jeruzalem. Gd RENSKI RIZLING, SIVI PINOT, FURMINT, PINOT N. Best is White Star of Stiria.

Ljutomer Ormož Pod Famous subdistrict in POD for crisp, delicate whites and top sweet wines. Best: PRA-VINO, CONRAD FÜRST, HEAPS GOOD WINE, P&F, KOGL, Krainz, KUPLJEN, VERUS.

Marof Pod r w ★★ →★★★ 11' 12 Exciting winery in Prekmurje. DYA classic range: v.gd LAŠKI RIZLING Bodonci, RENSKI RIZLING. Selected Breg wines excellent, esp CHARD and SAUV BL.

Movia Prim r w sp ★★★→★★★★ 03 05 07 08 09 11 High-profile bio winery led by charismatic Ales Kristančič. Excellent Veliko Belo (w) and Veliko Rdeče (r), plus v.gd MODRI PINOT. Sparkling Puro is a showpiece, but orange Lunar is controversial.

P&F Pod r w sp ★★ 11 12 (13) Former state winery and v'yds returned to original Puklavec family, renamed P&F (Puklavec & Friends). Now v.gd-value, *consistent crisp, aromatic whites* in P&F range. Selected Gomila gold label wines are excellent esp FURMINT, SAUV BL. Jeruzalem Ormož label for local market.

Penina Designation for quality sparkling wine (*charmat* or traditional method). Look for RADGONSKE GORICE (largest), ISTENIČ, BJANA, MOVIA, Vino Gaube (Gaudium Rosé Brut, CHARD), Dolfo (Spirito).

Podravje Region in the northeast. Noted for crisp dry whites; often better value than west. A few light reds from PINOT N and MODRA FRANKINJA.

Posavje Region in the southeast. Best wines are sweet, esp PRUS, Šturm (★★★★ Icewine and botrytis versions of MUSCAT).

PRA-VinO Pod w sw 06' 07 09 11 12 1970s pioneer of private wine production, son and grandson now in charge. World-class ★★★★ sweet wines, incl Icewine (*ledeno vino*) and botrytis wines from SIPON, LAŠKI RIZLING and RIES. Drier styles are improving.

Primorje Region in the southwest from Slovenian ISTRIA to BRDA. Aka Primorska.

Prus Pos w sw Small family producer making stunning ★★★★ 03 04 06 09 11 sweet wines, esp Icewines and botrytis wines from Rumeni MUŠKAT, RIES, SAUV BL.

Pullus Pod r w sp ★★→★★★ 11 12 13 V.gd crisp modern whites from Ptuj winery, esp Pullus SAUV BL, RIES. Excellent "G" wines (esp Sauv Bl); lovely sweet RENSKI RIZLING 08.

Radgonske Gorice Pod ★ Producer of bestselling Slovenian sparkler Srebrna (silver) PENINA, classic-method Zlata (golden) Penina, and popular demi-sec black label TRAMINEC.

Santomas Prim r w ★★★ 06 09 10 12 Istrian estate, some of the country's best *Refošk* and REFOŠK/CAB SAUV blends, esp Antonius, Grande Cuvée. Mezzoforte is v.gd-value, Casme Ré rosé tasty.

Šćurek Prim r w sw ★★ →★★★ 07 08 09 10 11 12 Gd consistent BRDA producer. DYA varieties BELI PINOT, CHARD, REBULA. Best wines focus on local grapes, esp Stara Brajda (r w), Pikolit, Up.

Simčič, Marjan Prim r w sw ★★★★ 07 08 09 10 11 12 Whites, esp SIVI PINOT, SAUVIGNONASSE, REBULA, CHARD, SAUV BL Selekcija impress. Teodor Belo (w) and Teodor Rdeče (r) are superb. MODRI PINOT is elegant. Notable Opoka single-v'yd range, esp Sauv Bl and MERLOT. Sweet Leonardo is great.

Štajerska Slovenija Pod Important wine district in east since 2006. Check out Gaube (esp CHARD Kaspar), Frešer, Kušter, Valdhuber, Miro Vino (esp SIPON).

Steyer Pod w sw sp ★★ 10 11 12 TRAMINER specialist in Štajerska: dry, sparkling, oak-aged, sweet. Decent SAUV BL, CHARD, Ranina.

Teran: a native grape variety in Croatia, but a PDO in Slovenia. Confused?

Sutor Prim r w ★★★ 09' 10 11' Excellent producer from VIPAVA. CHARD is one of country's best, ages well. V.gd SAUV BL, fine MALVAZIJA, elegant MERLOT-based red.

Tilia Prim r w ★★ 09 10 11 12 (13) Husband-and-wife team in VIPAVA. Appetizing Sunshine range esp SAUV BL and PINOT GR; premium Golden Tilia range esp fine PINOT N.

Valdhuber Pod r w ★ 12 13 Dry pioneer in POD. Refreshing straightforward whites.

SLOVENIA

Verus Pod r w ★★★ 11' 12' (13) Fine, focused, mineral whites, esp v.gd FURMINT, crisp SAUV BL, flavoursome PINOT GR, refined RIES. Pure, fine PINOT N 11 12.

Vinakoper Prim r w ★→★★ 08 09 11 12 (13) Large company with own v'yds in ISTRIA. Gd-value Capris line (DYA MALVAZIJA, REFOŠK); premium Capo d'Istria SHIRAZ and CAB SAUV.

Vinska Klet Goriška Brda Prim r w ★→★★★ 08 **09** 11 12 (13) Forward-looking major winery in BRDA. Gd consistent DYA whites, esp Quercus SIVI PINOT, PINOT BL, REBULA. Bagueri is premium oaked range, Krasno Belo is v.gd unoaked blend. Excellent A+ red and white only in best vintages.

Vipava Prim Valley noted for cool breezes in PRIM, and source of some fine wines. Also large former state winery, Vipava 1894, where new winemaker (from GUERILA) is making changes. Producers: BATIČ, BURJA, GUERILA, Štokelj (best PINELA), Mlečnik, SUTOR, TILIA.

Zanut Prim r w ★★ 06 08 11 12 Family winery in BRDA; excellent SAUVIGNONASSE, intense SAUV BL and in top yrs single-v'yd MERLOT Brjač.

Zlati Grič Pod w sp ★ New investment in this estate nr Maribor, with 75 ha. Try Konjiška Rosé PENINA.

CROATIA

Croatia is now a fully fledged member of the EU, and already standing tall with some fine original wines (and not over-modest prices). But her wine producers have some new problems to deal with. One is the potential loss of the name Prošek, used for centuries for a sweet passito wine in Croatia, because the EU has declared it is too similar to Italy's light bubbly Prosecco. The other is a dispute with Slovenia over the name Teran. Slovenia has registered this as a PDO for wine from the Refošk grape from Kras; Istrian winemakers, however, regard Teran as their native grape. Teran is a synonym for Slovenia's Refošk, which may or may not add to the confusion.

Agrokor r w ★→★★ 09 10 11 12 Group with over 30% of Croatian market, and several wineries, incl Agrolaguna selling as Vina Laguna Festigia (gd MALVAZIJA, Malvazija Riserva, rosé, Terra Rossa, Castello), Vina Belje (esp MERLOT, Goldberg GRAŠEVINA, premium CHARD).

Arman, Franc Ist r w ★★ 11 12 Sixth-generation family winery. V.gd precise whites esp CHARD, classic MALVAZIJA.

Badel 1862 Dalm r w ★★ 09 10 11 12 Four wineries. Best: Korlat SYRAH and Cuvée from Benkovac winery. Gd-value Duravar range esp SAUV BL, GRAŠEVINA. Gd PLAVAC and Ivan Dolac from PZ Svirče.

Babić: old black grape from stony sea-terraces round Šibenik, now revived. Pronounced "Babich", as in NZ.

Benvenuti Ist r w ★★ ISTRIAN family winery. Gd DYA, aged versions of MALVAZIJA, v.gd TERAN 09.

Bodren N Croa w sw ★★→★★★ 10 11 Excellent sweet wines incl CHARD, TRAMINER, RIES and Triptih blend. Superb Icewine.

Bolfan N Croa w dr ★→★★ 11 12 Nr Zagreb with 20 ha incl bio and "natural" wines. RIES, PINOT N rosé best.

Bura-Mrgudić Dalm r ★★→★★★ Complex 09 is one of country's best DINGAČ.

Capo Ist w r dr ★★ New quality-focused producer in ISTRIA. V.gd Stella range, esp SAUV BL Sagittarius, CAB FR Aries, PINOT N Gemini.

Cattunar Ist r w dr ★★ 10 11 12 Family-owned hilltop estate. MALVAZIJA, esp rich Collina, is v.gd.

Coronica Ist r w ★★ 09 11 12 Notable ISTRIAN winery, esp barrel-aged Gran MALVAZIJA and benchmark Gran TERAN.

Dalmatia Rocky coastal zone and islands to south of Zadar, with a warm Mediterranean climate.

Dingač Dalm 06 07 08 09 First quality designation in 1961, now PDO, on Pelješac Peninsula in southern DALM. Noted for robust full-bodied reds from PLAVAC MALI. Look for: BURA-MRGUDIČ, Kiridžija, Lučić, Matuško, Madirazza 09', SAINTS HILLS, Vinarija Dingač (300-ha co-op with v.gd-quality Dingač, Postup).

Galić N Croa r w ★★ 09 11 12 Promising new producer in SLAVONIJA, esp GRAŠEVINA, red blend Crno 9, fine PINOT CRNI.

Grgić Dalm r w ★★→★★★ 07 08 Legendary Napa Valley producer returned to Croatian roots to make PLAVAC MALI, rich POŠIP on Pelješac Peninsula.

Hvar Dalm Beautiful island with world's oldest continuously cultivated v'yd and UNESCO protection. Noted for PLAVAC MALI, incl Ivan Dolac designation. Gd: Carić, Plančič, ZLATAN OTOK, PZ Svirče, TOMIČ.

Iločki Podrumi N Croa r w ★★ 11 12 Family-owned since split with Agrokor. Second-oldest cellar in Europe: built to make wine in 1450. Try premium GRAŠEVINA, TRAMINAC and Principovac range.

Istria North Adriatic Peninsula. MALVAZIJA is the main grape. Gd also for CAB SAUV, MERLOT, TERAN. Look for FRANC ARMAN, BENVENUTI, CATTUNAR, Clai (orange wines esp Sveti Jakov), CAPO, CORONICA, Cossetto (Malvazija Rustica, Mozaik), Degrassi (MUSCAT, Terre Bianche), Gerzinič (Malvazija), Kabola (esp Malvazija Amfora), KOZLOVIČ, MATOŠEVIČ, MENEGHETTI, Peršurić (Croatia's best sparkling wines, esp Misal Millenium Brut) Pilato (Malvazija, PINOT BL) RADOVAN, Ritoša, ROXANICH, SAINTS HILLS, TRAPAN.

Vrhunsko vino: premium-quality wine; *Kvalitetno Vino:* quality wine; *Stolno Vino:* table wine. *Suho:* dry; *Polsuho:* semi-dry.

Korta Katarina Dalm r w ★★★ 08 09 11 12 Modern interpretations of traditional styles from Korcula. Excellent POŠIP and PLAVAC MALI, esp Reuben's Res.

Kozlović Ist w ★★→★★★ 09 11 12 MALVAZIJA grape in all its forms, esp exciting, complex Santa Lucia and Akacia (aged in acacia barrels). New Santa Lucia Crno 11 is promising.

Krauthaker, Vlado N Croa r w sw ★★★ 10 11 12 Top producer from KUTJEVO, esp CHARD Rosenberg, GRAŠEVINA Mitrovac, and sweet Graševina Izborna Berba. PINOT N Selekcija 11 shows promise.

Kutjevo N Croa Name shared by a town in SLAVONIJA, heartland of GRAŠEVINA, and ★→★★ Kutjevo Cellars.

Matošević Ist r w ★★→★★★ 10 11 12 Benchmark MALVAZIJA, esp Alba Antiqua. Also v.gd Grimalda (r w).

Meneghetti Ist r w ★★ 09 10 11 Sleek red and white blends, as well as fine and precise MALVAZIJA.

Miloš, Frano Dalm r sw ★★ 06 09 Built reputation with powerful Stagnum, but PLAVAC is more approachable.

Postup Dalm Famous v'yd designation northwest of DINGAČ. Full-bodied rich red wines from PLAVAC MALI. Donja Banda, Miličič, Mrgudič Marija and Vinarija Dingač are noted.

Croatia's natives

Croatia has 39 indigenous grapes, incl red BABIĆ (best is GRACIN), Bogdanuša (from HVAR), Debit (try Bibich Lučica), Gegič (try Boškinac), Grk (try GRGIČ), Maraština (aka MALVAZIJA; Sladić is gd), Pošip (Krajančič is notable) and Vugava (STINA).

Prošek Dalm Now controversial sweet passito wine from DALM, using dried local grapes Bogdanuša, Maraština, Prč. Look for Hectorovich from TOMIČ.

Radovan Ist r w ★★→★★★ 09 11 12 Family producer of impeccable whites and superb CAB SAUV and MERLOT.

Roxanich Ist r w ★★→★★★ 07 08 Natural producer making powerful, intriguing amber wines (MALVAZIJA Antica, Ines U Bijelom) and impressive complex reds, esp TERAN Ré, Superistrian Cuvée, MERLOT.

Saints Hills Dalm, Ist r w ★★→★★★ 08 09 10 Three v'yds plus two wineries; Michel Rolland consults. V.gd Nevina MALVAZIJA/CHARD from Istria; PLAVAC MALI St Roko has potential. Also serious DINGAČ.

Slavonija N Croa Region in north, historically for whites but gd reds now, esp PINOT N. Look out for Adzič, Bartolovič, Belje, Enjingi (esp GRAŠEVINA, Venje), GALIČ, KRAUTHAKER, KUTJEVO, Mihalj, Zdjelarevič. Also famous for its oak.

Stina Dalm r w ★★ 09 10 11 12 Brand name of Jako Vino winery on Brač island. Dramatic steep v'yds producing v.gd POŠIP, PLAVAC MALI, Crljenak and rare Vugava.

Suha Punta Dalm r w ★★→★★★ 08 09' (11) (12) Small but impressive winery nr Primošten, co-owned by Professor Leo Gracin, making country's best BABIĆ from rocky sea-facing v'yds.

Original Zin: Zinfandel's original Croatian name was *Tribidrag*, which means "early ripening". Also known as Crljenak.

Teran REFOSCO wine (REFOŠK) from the karst soils of Istria. Rustic, acidic, appetizing.

Tomac N Croa r w sp ★★ Estate nr Zagreb with 200-yr history, famous for sparkling wines and pioneering amphora wines.

Tomič Dalm r w ★★ 08 09 11 Outspoken personality on island of HVAR, campaigning for PROŠEK (produces Hectorovich). Also gd reds, esp PLAVAC Barrique.

Trapan, Bruno Ist r w ★★ 10 11 12 Young winemaker winning praise for MALVAZIJA, incl aged Uroboros and fresh Ponente. Pioneer with SYRAH in ISTRIA.

Zlatan Otok Dalm r w ★★→★★★ 09 10 Sons have recently taken over so expect changes. Previously famous for huge reds, esp Zlatan PLAVAC Grand Cru. V'yd investments now showing in better balanced wines: Zlatan Plavac Barrique, Crljenak and excellent POŠIP 12.

BOSNIA & HERZEGOVINA, MACEDONIA (FYROM), SERBIA, MONTENEGRO

Some important new investments and a growing wine and food culture are making these Balkan heartlands a good place to explore.

Bosnia & Herzegovina has indigenous plummy red Blatina and grapey white Žilavka vines (try Hercegovina Produkt for both) plus characterful, ripe Vranac (try Vinarija Vukoje and Tvrdoš Monastery). Other new names that have gained international recognition: Vilinka winery, Vinarija Škegro and Podrum Andjelic.

Macedonia (Republic of or even FYROM due to ongoing disagreements with Greece) is now showing the results of significant money coming into wine. Giant Tikveš has French consultancy for its impressive Bela Voda and Barovo single-v'yd wines, and also gd grapey Temjanika and Vranec Special Selection. Stobi has invested over €20m, impressing with exciting but refined PETIT VERDOT and SHIRAZ, plus v.gd Vranec Veritas, Žilavka, CHARD, MUSCAT Ottonel. On a smaller boutique scale, Chateau Kamnik impresses, esp Chard Barrique, 10 Barrels CAB SAUV, 10 Barrels SYRAH; Bovin's Imperator regularly wins awards but its Dissan Vranec is more drinkable and Alexandar is decent. Dalvina makes pleasant Župljanka and gd red blend Armageddon.

Serbia's nine wine regions now feature a couple of global-standard producers. Radovanovič CAB Res is classy and Aleksandrovič also impresses, esp Trijumf whites, PINOT N-based Trijumf Noir and Rodoslav. Other interesting wines incl Prokupac (local red grape with potential) from Ivanovič; excellent Kremen CAB SAUV from Matalj winery; Vino Budimir's Triada and Svb Rosa (both based on Prokupac), Spasič (Tamjanika), Vinarija Kovačevič and Zvonko Bogdan.

Montenegro's v'yds are confined to the coastal zone and around Lake Skadar: 13 Jul Plantaže is the major producer but consistent (try Procorde Vranac), also look out for first private winery Milenko Sjekloča (decent Vranac).

CZECH REPUBLIC

The Czech Republic is divided into two wine regions, the tiny Bohemia (Boh) and 20-times larger Moravia (Mor). Wine consumption as well as prices are on the increase, while wines amass medals in international competitions; virtually all production is eagerly consumed on the home market.

Baloun, Radomil Mor One of the first to go private in 1990. Now investing and stylishly modernizing two dilapidated former wine co-ops with own (not EU) money invested.

Bohemia Sekt Group Boh, Mor Biggest player and largest Sekt producer; owns Víno Mikulov, Habánské Sklepy, Château Bzenec, Pavlov.

Dobrá Vinice Mor Maverick inspired by Slovenia's Aleš Kristančič. Undoubtedly the best whites in the country.

The Ice Wine du Monde contest: held in Moravia, almost £1 million subsidy... 86 entries.

Dva Duby Mor Dedicated terroirist, cultivating just 4 ha in Dolní Kounice's Frankovka-land (BLAUFRÄNKISCH) according to Maria Thun's principles.

Lobkowicz, Bettina Boh Now going solo in Mělník, north of Prague. Outstanding PINOT N and classic-method sparkling RIES.

Sonberk Mor Impressive facility with Slovak money behind, known for much-lauded straw wine.

Stapleton & Springer Mor Joint-venture between Jaroslav Springer and ex-US ambassador Craig Stapleton. Just four varieties, all red, with emphasis on PINOT N. Arguably the finest reds around.

Vinselekt Michlovský Mor Huge operation, a multitude of ranges, varying quality. The best of the big players, always ready to innovate.

Znovín Mor Large company run by ever-enterprising Pavel Vajčner with a range to suit all pockets. Winner of 2013 Winery of the Year.

SLOVAK REPUBLIC

The six wine regions lie on the foothills of the central mountainous plateau and along the southern and eastern borders: Malokarpatská (Little Carpathians), Juhoslovenská (Southern Slovakia), Nitrianska (Nitra), Stredoslovenská (Central Slovakia), Východoslovenská (Eastern Slovakia) and the smallest, Tokajská (Tokaj), in the far east, adjacent to its more celebrated Hungarian namesake. Classic central European varieties dominate along with international favourites. As in the Czech Republic, there are few signs of any crisis here with lots of big money continuing to flow into swanky new wineries such as Elesko, a huge facility unrivalled in Central Europe, with restaurant, art gallery (Warhol originals) and money from abroad.

Kiwi Nigel Davies flies in to advise. Other notable producers incl: Château Béla (Mužla) with Egon Müller zu Scharzhof involvement, Karpatská Perla (Šenkvice), Malík & Sons (Modra), Roman Janoušek, Víno Matyšák (both Pezinok), Vinanza (Vráble), JJ Ostrožovič (Veľká Tŕňa in Tokaj). Sekt comes from JE Hubert, now the nation's biggest producer and in the hands of Germany's Dr. Oetker.

ROMANIA

Romania boasts the most developed wine culture of the Black Sea region, humiliated by the communists but at last resurgent. Recently it has reached a turning point, with more realistic pricing and a strong focus on exports. The 30,000 ha of better vineyards planted since joining the EU in 2007 are coming into production and old, poor-quality sites are disappearing. Painful economic measures have hit wine sales in the domestic market, though premium wines are still growing strongly. As one of the biggest new member states, with excellent natural conditions for the vine, Romania seems set for a better future.

Avincis Mun r w ★→★★ 11 12 Go-ahead revived family winery with bright young Alsace winemaker in DRĂGĂȘANI.

Banat Small wine region in west. *See* RECAȘ WINERY. Also location of promising new Italian estate, Petro Vaselo (try Alb 11, Ovas 09, Melgris 11).

Budureasca Mun r w ★→★★ 11 12 300-ha estate in DEALU MARE. Consistent Budureasca, Origini labels.

Cotnari Mold DOC region in MOLD, noted for centuries for its sweet wines. Now mostly medium to sweet GRASĂ, FETEASCĂ ALBĂ, TĂMÂIOASĂ and dry Frâncuşă. Also ★ Cotnari Winery, with 1,200 ha. Collection wines, esp *sweet versions, can be long-lived and impressive*.

Crama Girboiu Mold r w ★ Founded 2005; 200 ha in Vrancea. Bacanta label is best.

Crama Oprisor Mun r w ★★→★★★ 09 10 11 12 Val Duna is gd-value export label. V.gd Crama Oprisor range, esp La Cetate, Caloian, Maiastru, Smerenie.

Davino Winery Mun r w ★★★ 07′ 09′ 10 11 12 One of Romania's very best producers with 68 ha in DEALU MARE. V.gd Dom Ceptura (r w), excellent Revelatio 12 (w), Purpura Valahica 09. Flamboyant (r) 09 is superb, while Rezerva red 07 sets new quality standards for Romania.

Dealu Mare / Dealul Mare Mun Means "The Big Hill". Historic quality zone and DOC on south-facing slopes in Mun. Location of promising new boutiques: LACERTA, Rotenberg (MERLOT, esp Menestrel, Notorius), Crama Basilescu (Merlot, FETEASCĂ NEAGRĂ).

Romania has fifth-largest vineyard area in Europe and sixth-largest production (c. 5.4 million hectolitres).

Dobrogea Black Sea region. Incl DOC regions of MURFATLAR, Badabag and Sarica Niculitel. Historically famous for sweet, late-harvest CHARD and now for full-bodied reds. New organic estate Vifrana shows promise.

Domeniile Ostrov Dob r w ★ €20m investment with 1,200 ha in DOB. Commercial DYA CAB SAUV, MUSCAT Ottonel.

Domeniile Sahateni Mun r w ★→★★ 09 11 12 70-ha estate in DEALU MARE. Try Artisan (w) and Artisan TĂMÂIOASĂ ROMÂNEASCĂ). Also promising SYRAH 11.

Domeniul Coroanei Segarcea Mun r w sw ★★ 10 11 12 Historic royal estate. Best for aromatic whites, incl SAUV BL, TĂMÂIOASĂ (also rare semi-sweet rosé). Decent CHARD, CAB SAUV, PINOT N.

Drăgăşani Mun Dynamic region on river Olt. PRINCE ŞTIRBEY pioneered revival, joined by AVINCIS, Negrini (v.gd SAUV BL/FETEASCĂ REGALĂ blend), Isarescu, Via Sandu. Gd for aromatic crisp whites, esp local Crâmpoşie Selecţionată, TĂMÂIOASĂ, zesty Sauv Bl. Distinctive local reds: Novac, Negru de Drăgăşani.

Halewood Romania Mun r p w ★★ 09 10 11 12 British-owned company with new quality focus since 2009. Best wines: Hyperion FETEASCĂ NEAGRĂ, CAB SAUV, Chronos PINOT N, Theia CHARD. Single-v'yd series also v.gd: La Catina Pinot N, Feteascǎ Neagrǎ, Scurta VIOGNIER/TĂMÂIOASĂ. La Umbra is gd-value commercial brand, esp PINOT N, SHIRAZ.

Jidvei w ★→★★ Romania's largest v'yd; 2,460 ha in Jidvei subregion in TRANSYLVANIA. Variable quality; best from Owner's Choice range by consultant Marc Dworkin (also Bulgaria's BESSA VALLEY), esp FETEASCĂ ALBĂ Maria, Mysterium Traminer/ SAUV BL, CHARD Ana.

Lacerta Mun r w ★★ 10 11 12 New quality-focused estate in DEALU MARE. Try Cuvée IX red and Cuvée X white, also SHIRAZ, FETEASCĂ NEAGRĂ .

Liliac Trnsyl r w ★★ 11 12 Promising new 60-ha estate in Transylvania. Refined, fresh whites esp FETEASCĂ REGALĂ, Crepuscul (w), Private Selection SAUV BL, delicious sweet Nectar.

> ### DOC
> *Denumire de Origine Controlată* is the Romanian term for PDO.
> Sub-categories incl DOC-CMD for wines harvested at full maturity,
> DOC-CT for late-harvest and DOC-CIB for noble-harvest. *Vin cu
> indicatie geograficǎ* is term for PGI.

Moldova / Moldovia The largest wine region northeast of Carpathians. Borders Republic of Moldova. DOC areas incl Bohotin, COTNARI, Huşi, Iaşi, Odobeşti, Coteşti, Nicoreşti.

Muntenia & Oltenia Hills Major wine region in south covering DOC areas of DEALU MARE, Dealurile Olteniei, DRĂGĂŞANI, Pietroasa, Sâmbureşti, Stefaneşti, Vanju Mare.

Murfatlar DOC area in DOBROGEA nr Black Sea; subregions are Cernavoda, Megidia.

Murfatlar Winery Dob r w ★→★★ Major domestic player in region of same name. Variable quality; best are Trei Hectare (FETEASCĂ NEAGRĂ, CAB SAUV, CHARD). New boutique winery MI Crama Atelier with Nederburg (*see* South Africa) winemaker Răzvan Macici, incl Arezan, Leat 6500 and Sable Noble ranges.

Petro Vaselo Ban r w ★→★★ 11 12 Promising new Italian estate in BANAT. Try CHARD, Ovas red blend, Melgris FETEASCĂ NEAGRĂ.

Prince Ştirbey Mun r p w ★★→★★★★ 10 11 12 Pioneering estate in DRĂGĂŞANI. V.gd dry whites, esp local Crâmpoşie Selecţionată, SAUV BL, FETEASCĂ REGALĂ, TĂMÂIOASĂ ROMÂNEASCĂ. Tasty rosé and local reds (Novac, Negru de Drăgăşani); new v.gd bottle-fermented sparkling.

Recaş Winery Ban r w ★★→★★★ 11 12 Progressive British/Romanian estate in BANAT region. V.gd-value, bright varietal wines sold as Paparuda, I heart, Frunza, Castel Huniade, Terra Dacica. Excellent premium wines, esp Solo Quinta, Sole, Cuvée Uberland. Selene reds, esp FETEASCĂ NEAGRĂ 11, made with Alesso Planeta, are exciting.

Senator Mold r w ★ Sizeable winery based in Odobeşti with 900 ha. Private Collection and Monser labels, Varius SAUV BL best so far.

SERVE Mun r w dr ★★→★★★ 08 09' 10 11 12 Top DEALU MARE winery founded by the late Count Guy de Poix of Corsica. Vinul Cavalerului whites and rosé gd, excellent Terra Romana range esp CHARD, Milenium (r), Cuvée Amaury (w), notable red quality flagship ***Cuvée Charlotte***.

> **Romania's wine regions**
> MUN is the major wine region in the south, covering the DOC areas
> of DEALU MARE, Dealurile Olteniei, DRĂGĂŞANI, Pietroasa, Sâmbureşti,
> Stefaneşti, Vanju Mare. DOB lies next to the Black Sea; its most
> important DOC is MURFATLAR. CRI & MAR is in the northwest (incl much
> improved Wine Princess and Nachbil). BANAT is a small wine region
> in the west. TRANSYLVANIA is a cool mtn plateau in the centre of
> Romania (whites with gd acidity). MOLD is the largest wine region,
> lying northeast of the Carpathians. DOC areas incl Bohotin, COTNARI,
> Huşi, Iaşi, Odobeşti, Coteşti, Nicoreşti.

Transylvania Cool mtn plateau in centre of Romania. Mostly white wines with gd acidity from FETEASCĂ ALBĂ and REGALĂ, MUSCAT, TRAMINER, RIES ITALICO.

Villa Vinea r w ★★ New Italian-owned estate in TRANSYLVANIA since 2011. Gd whites, esp GEWURZ, SAUV BL, FETEASCĂ REGALĂ.

Vinarte Winery Mun r w ★★ →★★★ 07' 08 09 10 11 V.gd Italian investment with three estates: Villa Zorilor in DEALU MARE, Castel Bolovanu in DRĂGĂŞANI, Terase Danubiane in Vanju Mare. Best: Soare CAB SAUV, Prince Matei MERLOT. Also gd-value Castel Starmina range, esp TĂMÂIOASĂ ROMÂNEASCĂ, SAUV BL, Negru de Drăgăşani.

Vincon Vrancea Winery Mold r w dr sw ★ 2,150 ha in Vrancea, plus DOBROGEA and DEALU MARE.

Vinia Mold r w dr sw ★ Major producer of COTNARI wines at Iaşi.

Vitis Metamorfosis Mun r w ★★ 09 10 11 12 Founded as joint venture between Italy's Antinori family and HALEWOOD. Top: Cantus Primus CAB SAUV (09). V.gd Vitis Metamorfosis esp white blend, plus MERLOT and FETEASCĂ NEAGRĂ.

WineRo Dob r ★★ 09 11 Premium estate owned by same team as Bulgaria's Bessa Valley. Now making impact with rich reds incl Alira MERLOT, CAB SAUV and Grande Vin Cuvée.

MALTA

Malta's vineyards cannot hope to supply the island's entire consumption – the place isn't big enough, and tourism tends to take precedence when it comes to land use. Plus much of the wine on sale here is made locally from grapes imported from Italy. Real Maltese wine is subject to *Demoninazzjoni ta' Origini Kontrollata*, or DOK, rules, which are in line with EU practices. The traditional, indigenous grapes are Girgentina (w) and Gellewza (r), but many international grapes are also grown. Antinori-backed Meridiana is in the lead, producing excellent Maltese Isis and Mistral CHARDS, Astarte VERMENTINO, Melquart CAB SAUV/MERLOT, Nexus Merlot, **outstanding Bel Syrah** and premium Celsius Cab Sauv Res from island vines. Volume producers of note are Delicata, Marsovin and Camilleri.

Greece

If you still haven't discovered the quality and originality of Greek wines now is the time to start. The flavours are unlike any others, the wines terroir driven and beautifully balanced. But these days Greek consumers drink less and more cheaply, so for producers, exports are the only way out. Image, not quality, has held back exports until now, but in 2013 overseas sales were up 11% by volume, and by value 30% in the USA, 55% in Canada. That bodes well for the future: there won't always be a crisis, but there will always be Assyrtiko and Aghiorgitiko. Abbreviations: Aegean Islands (Aeg), Attica (Att), Central Greece (C Gr), Cephalonia (Ceph), Ionian Islands (Ion), Macedonia (Mac), Northern Greece (N Gr), Peloponnese (Pelop), Thessaloniki (Thess).

Aivalis Pelop ★★★ Boutique NEMEA producer of dark wines. Top (and pricey) wine "4", from 120-yr-old+ vines. Monopati, less ambitious Nemea. Interesting ASSYRTIKO.

Alpha Estate Mac ★★★→★★★★ Impressive, highly acclaimed estate in cool-climate Amindeo. Excellent MERLOT/SYRAH/XINOMAVRO blend, pungent SAUV BL, exotic Mmalagousia, unfiltered New-World-style Xinomavro from old, ungrafted vines. Top wine Alpha 1, the winemaker's pick of the harvest, demands ageing.

Amyntaion Mac (POP) The coolest appellation of Greece, XINOMAVRO-dominated. Fresh but dense reds, excellent rosés, both still and sparkling.

Antonopoulos Pelop ★★★ PATRAS-based winery, with top-class MANTINIA, crisp Adoli Ghis (w), burgundian Anax CHARD and CAB-based Nea Dris (stunning 04 06). Top wine: violet-scented Vertzami/CAB FR.

Argyros Aeg ★★★→★★★★ Top SANTORINI producer; exemplary VINSANTO aged 20 yrs in cask (★★★★). Exciting KTIMA (w) ages for a decade, oak-aged Vareli (w) and sweet Mezzo (lighter than Vinsanto). Try ageing rare MAVROTRAGANO (r) for 15 years+.

Avantis C Gr ★★★ Boutique winery in Evia with v'yds in Boetia as well. Dense SYRAH, Aghios Chronos Syrah/VIOGNIER, pungent SAUV BL and rich MALAGOUSIA, interesting Oneiropagida value range. Top wine: Rhône-like single-v'yd Collection Syrah 03 04 05 06 07.

Biblia Chora Mac ★★★ Both top quality and huge commercial success. Pungent SAUV BL/ASSYRTIKO. Ovilos CAB SAUV and Areti AGHIORGITIKO are stunning. Ovilos (w), from Assyrtiko and SÉM, could rival top white Bordeaux.

Boutari, J & Son ★→★★★ Producer with several wineries. Excellent value, esp *Grande Reserve Naoussa* to age for decades. V. popular MOSCHOFILERO. Top SANTORINI Kalisti Res (oaked), Skalani (r) from CRETE and herbal Flliria (r) from GOUMENISSA.

The whole of Greece makes 35% less wine/annum than Bordeaux.

Cair Aeg ★★ Large winery in RHODES specializing in sparkling (the 96 rosé is the *best sparkling* ever made in Greece), but Pathos still range (r w) is v.gd value.

Carras, Domaine Mac ★→★★ Pioneer estate at Sithonia, Halkidiki, with its own OPAP (Côtes de Meliton). Chateau Carras 01 02 03 04 05, ambitious SYRAH and MALAGOUSIA, but Limnio (r) might be the best value of all.

Cephalonia Ion Important island with three appellations: ROBOLA (w), MUSCAT (w sw) and MAVRODAPHNE (r sw). A must-visit for all wine-lovers.

Crete An exciting, ever-improving island region, with young producers taking a close, fresh look at tradition, while investing in local, almost extinct vine varieties, eg. Vidiano: white, recently rescued, herbal flavours.

Daskalaki, Silva ★★ Imaginative producer, flirting with bio. Try Silva sweet Liatiko or dry but exotic MALVASIA.

Dougos Thess ★★→★★★ On slopes of Olympus. Exciting range, esp Opsimo (dry late-harvest, r), RAPSANI. Exemplary Methymon 7 from seven varieties (r) 08 10.

Douloufakis Crete ★★→★★★ Excellent producer nr Heraklion. Dafnios range is a bargain. Aspros Lagos (r and w) among best of CRETE.

Driopi Pelop ★★★ Venture of TSELEPOS in NEMEA. Serious (esp single-v'yd KTIMA), high-octane style. Tavel-like Driopi rosé.

Economou Crete ★★★ One of the great artisans of Greece, with brilliant, esoteric Sitia (r). Not for everyone, nor for the faint-hearted.

Feggites Mac ★★ Winery in Drama, owned by the Tsalkos family. Interesting range, top Deka (w) and Bandol-like rosé. Younger generation makes an impact with Thyrsus, a VIOGNIER/MALAGOUSIA blend.

Malagousia with four years' age is the perfect wine to accompany artichokes.

Gaia Aeg, Pelop ★★★ Top-quality NEMEA- and SANTORINI-based producer. Fun Notios range. New-World-like AGHIORGITIKO. Thought-provoking, top-class, dry white Thalassitis SANTORINI; revolutionary *wild-ferment Assyrtiko*. Top wine: Gaia Estate 99 00 01 03 04 05 06 07 08, dazzling "S" (Aghiorgitiko with touch of SYRAH).

Gentilini Ion ★★→★★★ Exciting Cephalonia whites, incl *v.gd Robola*. Dry MAVRODAPHNE (r) v.gd, serious SYRAH. Selection ROBOLA (which redefines the variety) not appellation wine as law forbids screwcap. Eclipse (r) is rare, but worth the hunt.

Gerovassiliou Mac ★★★→★★★★ Perfectionist tiny estate nr Salonika. Benchmark ASSYRTIKO/MALAGOUSIA, smooth SYRAH/MERLOT blend, top Malagousia. Complex Avaton (r) 03 04 05 06 07 08 from rare indigenous varieties and Syrah 01 02 03 04 05 06. For many, the quality leader.

Goumenissa Mac (OPAP) ★→★★ XINOMAVRO/Negoska oaked red, lighter than NAOUSSA. Esp Aidarinis (single v'yd is ★★★), BOUTARI (esp Filiria), Tatsis.

Hatzidakis Aeg ★★★→★★★★ Low-tech but top-class producer redefining SANTORINI appellation. Stunning range, bordering on the experimental. Nihteri, Mylos and Pyrgos ASSYRTIKO bottlings could age for decades. Not your average dry whites.

Hatzimichalis C Gr ★→★★ Large estate in Atalanti. Huge range, many bottlings labelled after v'yds. Top red Kapnias CAB SAUV, top white Veriki. Interesting Prima Terra range with an increasing focus on Greek varieties.

Hatzivaritis Mac ★★ Puts POP GOUMENISSA back in fashion. Lovely XINOMAVRO blends.

Helios Pelop New umbrella name for Semeli, Nassiakos and Orinos Helios wines. Top Nassiakos MANTINIA, complex NEMEA Grande Res.

Karadimos C Gr ★★→★★★ Small estate bringing new vision. One of the best ASSYRTIKO outside SANTORINI and one of the best XINOMAVRO outside Macedonia.

Karydas Mac ★★★ Small estate and great v'yd in NAOUSSA crafting classic, compact but always refined XINOMAVRO of great breed. Age for a decade.

Katogi-Strofilia ★★→★★★★ V'yds, wineries in Attica, Peloponnese, Epirus. Katogi: first premium Greek wine. Top: KTIMA Averoff (from original Katogi CAB SAUV v'yd); Rossiu di Munte range from altitudes of 1,000 metres+. Charming Strofilia (w).

Katsaros Thess ★★★ Small winery on Mt Olympus. KTIMA red, a CAB SAUV/MERLOT, has staying power. Esoteric CHARD and broad-shouldered Merlot. Second generation, Euripides Katsaros, will provide a solid future.

Kikones ★★→★★★ Owner-winemaker Melina Tassou worked some vintages in Burgundy and it shows in her wines. Possibly the best in Thrace, and gd value.

Kir-Yanni Mac ★★→★★★★ V'yds in NAOUSSA and Amindeo. Vibrant whites Samaropetra and Tesseris Limnes are charmers; Akakis sp a joy. Reds Ramnista, Diaporos and Blue Fox are trendsetting.

Kourtakis, D ★★ Huge and reliable merchant trading as Greek Wine Cellars: excellent value reds and *mild Retsina*.

Ktima Estate, domaine.

Lazaridi, Nico Mac ★→★★★ Wineries in Drama, Kavala. Gd Château Nico Lazaridi (r w). Top: Magiko Vouno (oaky SAUV BL), CAB SAUV enjoy cult status in Greece.

Lazaridis, Kostas Att, Mac ★★★ V'yds, wineries in Drama, Attika (sold under Oenotria Land label). Popular Amethystos label. Top: amazing Cava Amethystos CAB SAUV 97 98 99 00 01 02 03 04, followed closely by Oenotria Land Cab Sauv/ AGIORGITIKO. Michel Rolland (Bordeaux) consults – try Chateau Julia MERLOT.

Limnos Aeg Island making mainly dessert wines, from delicious, lemony MUSCAT of Alexandria but also some refreshing dry whites. Best producer: Hatzigeorgiou, making a convincing MOSCATO d'Asti lookalike.

Lyrarakis Crete ★★→★★★ V.gd producer from Heraklio with delicious range. Whites from the rare Plyto and Dafni practically saved these varieties from extinction (and single-v'yd versions are extraordinary). Deep, complex SYRAH/Kotsifali.

Manoussakis Crete ★★★ Impressive estate with Rhône-inspired blends. Delectable range under Nostos brand, led by age-worthy ROUSSANNE & SYRAH.

Mantinia Pelop (POP) w High altitude, cool region. Fresh, crisp, utterly charming, sometimes sparkling *Moschofilero*. More German than Greek in style.

Matsa, Ktima Att ★★ Historic small estate, now owned by BOUTARI but still run by the legendary Roxani Matsa. Her MALAGOUSIA is a leading example of the variety.

Mediterra Crete ★★ Gd, large-volume producer from PEZA. Herbaceous Xerolithia (w), spicy Mirabelo (r). oaky Nobile (w) to age.

Mercouri Pelop ★★★ One of the most beautiful family estates in Europe. V.gd KTIMA (r), delicious RODITIS, age-worthy Cava (r). Classy REFOSCO (r), stunning sweet Belvedere MALVASIA and excellent sweet MAVRODAPHNE.

Mitravelas Pelop ★★→★★★ Outstanding producer in NEMEA, promising great things from AGHIORGITIKO.

Monemvassia-Malvasia Latest POP; Monemvassia, ASSYRTIKO, Kydonitsa grapes used to re-create legendary, sun-dried, sweet whites of Middle Ages. Definitely watch.

Mylonas Att ★★ New, rising producer; soft reds, delicious whites. Try his Savatiano.

Naoussa Mac (PDO) High-quality region for sophisticated, excellent XINOMAVRO. Best on a par with Italy's Barolo and Barbaresco, sometimes lasting even longer.

Nemea Pelop (POP) Source of dark, spicy AGHIORGITIKO wines. Huge potential for quality here. High Nemea merits its own appellation. Koutsi is frontrunner for cru status (*see* DRIOPI, GAIA, HELIOS, MITRAVELAS, NEMEION, PAPAÏOANNOU, SKOURAS).

Nemeion Pelop ★★★ A KTIMA in NEMEA, high prices (esp Igemon red), with wines to match. Owned by Vassiliou, an Attica producer.

Oenoforos Pelop ★★→★★★ V.gd producer, fantastic high v'yds. V. elegant RODITIS Asprolithi. Delicate Lagorthi (w), nutty CHARD (magnum only), delicate Mikros Vorias (r w). Ianos is prestige range – try ageing the Chard for at least 5 yrs.

Palyvos Pelop ★★→★★★ Excellent NEMEA producer known for modern, big-framed reds. Multi-vintage Noima (r) one of country's most expensive – gorgeous nevertheless.

Papagiannakos Att ★★→★★★ Determined to put the Savatiano grape back on the quality map, via modern RETSINA and Vareli: oaked, non-resinated Savatiano. Age it for a decade and serve it as a dead ringer for Burgundy.

The crisis has meant less new oak on many reds. Hooray for the crisis.

Papaïoannou Pelop ★★★ If NEMEA were Burgundy, Papaioannou would be Jayer. Classy reds (incl PETIT VERDOT); flavourful whites. A benchmark range of Nemeas: KTIMA Papaïoannou, Palea Klimata (old vines), Microklima (a micro-single v'yd) and top-end Terroir (a super-strict, 200%-new-oaked selection).

Patras Pelop White POP based on RODITIS from v. diverse terroir: some great parts, some less so. Also home of POP MAVRODAPHNE and Rio-Patras sweet MUSCAT, with widely varying results.

Pavlidis Mac ★★★ Ambitious estate at Drama. Acclaimed ASSYRTIKO/SAUV BL.

GREECE

Greek appellations
Terms are changing in line with other EU countries. The quality appellations of OPAP and OPE are now fused together into the POP (or PDO) category. Regional wines, known as TO, will now be PGE (or PGI). The base category of table wine (EO) will be phased out. The swiftness of transition from old terms to new amazed everyone, incl the Greeks.

Emphasis: varietals incl classy Assyrtiko, SYRAH and TEMPRANILLO. KTIMA (r) from AGHIORGITIKO/Syrah is dazzling. Top-ranking stuff.

Peza Crete POP nr Heraklio. Vilana (w), Mandilaria/Kotsifali (r). Underperforming.

Pyrgakis Pelop ★★→★★★ Highly experimental KTIMA capitalizing on the highest parts of NEMEA. Esp new PETIT VERDOT and 24 CHARD. Opulent style.

Rapsani Thess ★★★ Historic POP from Mt Olympus. Introduced in the 1990s by TSANTALIS, but new producers, such as DOUGOS, are showing different styles of the appellation. XINOMAVRO, Stavroto and Krasato.

Retsina Speciality white with Aleppo pine resin added. Modern, high-quality wines, eg. The Tear of the Pine from Kehris, are stunning. Damaged image a pity.

Rhodes Aeg Easternmost island and POP. Home to lemony, elegant Athiri whites and popular sparklings. Top wines: CAIR (co-op) rosé sparkling.

Samos Aeg (POP) Island nr Turkey famed for sweet golden MUSCAT. Esp (fortified) Anthemis and (sun-dried) Nectar. Rare old bottlings can be ★★★★ without the price tag, such as the hard-to-find Nectar 75.

Santo Aeg ★★→★★★ Important co-op of SANTORINI. Vibrant portfolio: dazzling Grande Res, rich yet crisp VINSANTOS. Standard ASSYRTIKO, Nyhteri great value.

Santorini Aeg ★★★★ Volcanic, dramatic island north of CRETE and POP for white (dr sw). Luscious VINSANTO and MEZZO, mineral, bone-dry white from ASSYRTIKO. Oaked examples can also be amazing. Top producers: GAIA, HATZIDAKIS, SIGALAS, SANTO, ARGYROS. Possibly cheapest ★★★★ whites around, able to age for 20 yrs.

Sigalas Aeg ★★★★ Top SANTORINI estate, makes fine oaked Vareli. Stylish VINSANTO. Also explores MOURVÈDRE-like MAVROTRAGANO (try the 08 09 10). Nyhteri and Cavalieros are simply sublime.

Skouras Pelop ★★★ Innovative estate, eg. screwcaps on CHARD Dum Vinum Sperum. Mineral, wild-yeast Salto MOSCHOFILERO. Top reds: high-altitude Grande Cuvée NEMEA, Megas Oenos and solera-aged Labyrinth. V. stylish Fleva SYRAH.

Spiropoulos Pelop ★★ Organic producer in MANTINIA, NEMEA. Oaky Porfyros (AGHIORGITIKO, CAB SAUV, MERLOT). Sparkling Odi Panos has potential. Firm single-v'yd Astala Mantinia.

Tetramythos Pelop ★★ Promising winery exploring cool v'yds. Excellent MALAGOUSIA, Mavro Kalavritino and the first natural (see French chapter) RODITIS of Greece.

Tsantalis ★→★★★ Producer in Macedonia, Thrace and other areas. Gd Metoxi (r), RAPSANI Res and Grande Res; gd-value, organic CAB SAUV. Top-range monastery wines from Mount Athos, eg. excellent Avaton, cult Kormilitsa. Major exporter.

Tselepos Pelop ★★★ Top-quality MANTINIA producer. Greece's best GEWURZ and best MERLOT (Kokkinomylos). Others: oaky CHARD, v.gd spark Amalia, astounding single-v'yd Avlotopi CAB SAUV. See also DRIOPI.

Vinsanto Aeg Sun-dried sweet ASSYRTIKO and Aidani from SANTORINI. Deserves long ageing, in oak and bottle. Best are ★★★★, practically indestructible.

Voyatzi Ktima Mac ★★ Small estate nr Kozani. Classy XINOMAVRO, startling CAB FR sold as Tsapournakos.

Zafeirakis Thess ★★→★★★ Small KTIMA in Tyrnavos, uncharted territory for quality wine. Fastidious winemaker. Limniona red, a v. promising and rare variety. MALAGOUSIA is sublime.

Zitsa Mountainous Epirus POP. Delicate Debina (w, still or sp). Best: Glinavos.

Eastern Mediterranean & North Africa

EASTERN MEDITERRANEAN

Wine culture here is very ancient. Islam apart, there is still great potential, particularly in Israel, Lebanon and Turkey. Each country has its traditional variety: Carignan in Israel, Cinsault in Lebanon, Mavro in Cyprus and a whole host of them in Turkey, but Syrah seems well suited to the whole area, and gives wines of fruit, spice and complexity. There are still many old-vine Syrah vineyards in North Africa, but it is a comparatively new arrival in the Eastern Med.

Cyprus

The Cyprus economy was hit hard by the collapse of its banking system, but tourism is already bouncing back and the wine industry, especially the more innovative small estates, is in surprisingly good shape. Investment in vineyards is pushing up quality, and so is better understanding of how to handle local grapes like tricky Maratheftiko and the dominant local white Xynisteri.

Argyrides Estate (Vasa) r w ★★ 09 10 11 (12) Immaculate pioneering estate winery. Excellent MARATHEFTIKO. V.gd CHARD and Agyrides red blend. VLASSIDES consults.

Ayia Mavri w sw Gorgeous ★★ wines from late-harvest and semi-dried MUSCAT.

Constantinou r w ★→★★ Self-taught winemaker in Lemesos region impressing with Ayioklima XYNISTERI 11 and SHIRAZ 09.

ETKO r w br ★→★★ One of the original big four producers, but now focusing on higher quality from its Olympus winery, esp SHIRAZ, rosé. Makes St Nicholas, Centurion Commandaria (*see also* box, below).

Cyprus is one of only three countries in world never affected by vine pest phylloxera.

Hadjiantonas r w ★★ 09 10 11 12 Spotless family winery owned by a pilot, making v.gd CHARD, XYNISTERI, rosé, SHIRAZ.

KEO ★ Stick to estate wines Keo Mallia. St John is ★★ Commandaria.

Kyperounda r w ★★→★★★ 10 11 12 Probably Europe's highest v'yd at 1,450 metres. White Petritis is island's best wine from XYNISTERI. V.gd CHARD, CAB SAUV, SHIRAZ; excellent value Andessitis red. Recently launched top red Epos, and new Commandaria worth trying (*see also* box, below).

Makkas r w ★→★★ 10 11 12 Boutique family winery nr Pafos, new winery due 2014. Gd MARATHEFTIKO, SHIRAZ, red blend.

SODAP r w p ★→★★ 11 12 Largest producer, grower-owned co-op with state-of-art Kamanterena winery at Stroumbi village in hills. DYA whites, lively rosé: gd value, appetizing. Look for Island Vines, Mtn Vines (esp SÉM), Kamanterena labels.

Tsiakkas r w dr ★★ Banker turned winemaker with help from VLASSIDES. Makes gd

---

Commandaria

Possibly the most ancient wine still in production, documented as far back as 800 BC. Rich, dark, sweet and made from sun-dried XYNISTERI and MAVRO, grown in the PDO region covering 14 villages in the Troodos Mtns. Traditionally only made by the big four (best: 100% XYNISTERI St Barnabas from SODAP, St John (KEO), Centurion (ETKO). Recently several new producers have brought their own interpretations to market, esp Anama project, KYPEROUNDA, TSIAKKAS.

> **Cyprus regions**
> Lemesos, Paphos, Larnaca, Lefkosia have regional wine status (PGI).
> PDOs cover Commandaria, Laona-Akamas, Pitsilia, Vouni-Panayias/
> Ambelitis, wine villages of Lemesos. Only 2% is produced as PDO.

zesty DYA whites, esp SAUV BL, XYNISTERI, lively rosé. Also red Vamvakada (aka MARATHEFTIKO), new modern Commandaria (*see also* box, p.239).

Vasilikon, K&K r w ★→★★ One of the biggest small wineries. Always reliable DYA XYNISTERI and decent reds: Ayios Onoufrios 10, Methy 09.

Vlassides r w ★★→★★★ 08 09 10 11 12 UC Davis-trained Sophocles Vlassides makes some of island's best wines. SHIRAZ is benchmark for this variety's potential on Cyprus. Also v.gd Lefkos white (XYNISTERI/SAUV BL), CAB SAUV, Private Collection (r).

Zambartas r p w ★★→★★★ 09 10 11 12 (13) Father and Australian-trained son making intense CAB FR/LEFKADA rosé, v.gd SHIRAZ/Lefkada red, excellent MARATHEFTIKO, zesty XYNISTERI. New Epicurean red blend 11 to watch for.

Israel

Vineyards are being planted now in the higher-altitude Upper Galilee, Golan and in the Judean Hills, instead of the hot coastal regions. Wines are showing more elegance and balance, and flavourful Mediterranean-style blends are becoming popular. Syrah, Carignan and Petite Sirah provide local character, though Cabernet Sauvignon is still king. Kosher wines have a world market. Abbreviations: Galilee (Gal), Golan (Gol), Judean Hills (Jud), Negev (Neg), Samson (Sam), Shomron (Shom); Upper Galilee (Up Gal).

Adir Up Gal r ★★ V.gd herbal, peppery SHIRAZ and full-bodied Plato.

Amphorae Gal r w ★→★★ Michel Rolland of Bordeaux advises. Gd MERLOT/BARBERA.

Assaf Gol r w ★→★★ Elegant, well-made CAB SAUV. Gd reds.

Barkan-Segal Gal, Sam, r w ★★ Owned by Israel's largest brewery. The two brands, Barkan and Segal, are marketed separately. V.gd PINOTAGE and Segal Argaman (Israeli vine). Assemblage Reihan is quality regional blend from the Up Gal.

Binyamina Gal, Sam r w ★→★★ The Cave is best red, and delicious GEWURZ dessert.

Bravdo Sam r w ★→★★ Big CHARD, spicy SHIRAZ and gd CAB FR-based blend Coupage.

Carmel Up Gal, Shom r w sp ★★→★★★ Founded by a (Lafite) Rothschild. Bought by international consortium recently. Strong v'yd presence in Up Gal. Elegant Limited Edition 05 07' 08' 09. Award-winning Kayoumi v'yd SHIRAZ. Characterful old-vine CARIGNAN, PETITE SIRAH. Complex Mediterranean-style blend.

Château Golan Gol r (w) ★★ Flavourful SYRAH. Eliad is a Bordeaux blend.

Clos de Gat Jud r w ★★★ Classy estate with big, blowsy wines. Powerful Sycra SYRAH 06 07' 09 and buttery CHARD are superb. Chanson (r w) gd value. Rare MUSCAT.

Dalton Up Gal r w ★★ New v. gd single-v'yd SÉM. Flagship is rich Matatia.

Domaine du Castel Jud r w ★★★ Family estate in Jerusalem mtns, owned by perfectionist and Francophile Eli Ben Zaken. Characterful, supple Grand Vin 06' 07 08' 09' 10. Second label, Petit Castel, great value. V.gd rosé.

Ella Valley Jud r w ★→★★ Gd-value Ever Red has mouthfilling flavour.

Flam Jud r (w) ★★★ Owned by sons of ex-CARMEL winemaker. Superb, elegant Noble 08' 09, a Bordeaux blend. Earthy SYRAH/CAB. Fresh white is gd value.

Galilee Quality region in north, esp higher-altitude Up Gal.

Galil Mtn Up Gal r w ★★ Gd-value Yiron and Meron blends. Owned by YARDEN.

Golan Heights Gol High-altitude plateau, with volcanic tuff and basalt soil.

Judean Hills Jud Mountainous region on the way to Jerusalem.

Kosher Means "pure". Requirements do not change winemaking procedures, so quality should not be affected. Not all Israeli wineries are kosher.

Lewinsohn Gal r w ★★★ Quality *garagiste* in a garage. Exquisite, lean CHARD. Red a chewy Mediterranean blend of SYRAH, CARIGNAN and PETITE SIRAH.

Margalit Gal r ★★★ Father and son making elegant wines, in particular Bordeaux blend Enigma 08' 09 10', characterful CAB FR and prestige *Special Res*.

Mony Jud, Sam r w ★★ Israeli-Arab owned, Canadian winemaker; producing kosher wine in a monastery. Fragrant COLOMBARD, v.gd CHARD, full-flavoured SHIRAZ.

Pelter Gol r w (sp) ★★ Trio, tight blend of CAB S, MERLOT and CAB FR.

Ramot Naftaly Up Gal r ★→★★ Cherry-fresh BARBERA and deep, complex PETIT VERDOT.

Recanati Gal r w ★★→★★★ Pioneering Mediterranean style. Award-winning Special Res 07 08' **09**', complex CARIGNAN, chewy PETITE SIRAH, excellent SHIRAZ. Yasmin (r w) great value. Prestige white from MARSANNE and ROUSSANNE promising.

Samson Sam Region incl the Judean plain and foothills, southeast of Tel Aviv.

Sea Horse Jud r (w) ★→★★ Idiosyncratic *garagiste* with exotic blends.

Shomron Shom Region with v'yds around Mt Carmel and Zichron Ya'acov.

Shvo r w ★★ Rustic red from Mediterranean varieties. Aromatic CHENIN BL.

Sphera Jud w ★★ Stylish start-up, specializing only in white. One to watch.

Tabor Gal r w sp ★★ Underrated. Quality whites, v.gd-value reds. Best Israeli SAUV BL. New ROUSSANNE. Deep, spicy CAB SAUV/PETITE SIRAH blend.

Teperberg Jud, Sam r w sp ★→★★ Israel's largest family-owned winery. Juicy MALBEC.

Tishbi Jud, Shom r w sp ★→★★ Veteran grape-growing family. New CARIGNAN.

Tzora Jud r w ★★→★★★ Terroir-led winery, talented winemaker. Neve Ilan exquisitely balanced CHARD. Prestige Misty Hills **07** 09 10' a complex CAB SAUV/SYRAH blend. Judean Hills red great value. Jean-Claude Berrouet, ex-Petrus, is the consultant.

Vitkin Jud r w ★★ Small winery specializing in rarer varieties. V.gd CARIGNAN.

Yarden Gol r w sp ★★→★★★★ Pioneering winery. Well-balanced Odem V'yd CHARD. Rare Bordeaux blend Katzrin **00'** 03 04' 07 08', Rom **06'** 07 08 flagships. Excellent El Rom v'yd CAB SAUV. New, quality sparkling rosé, peerless vintage Blanc de Blancs, luscious Heights Wine dessert. Zelma Long (California) consults.

Yatir Jud, Neg r (w) ★★★→★★★★ Desert winery with forest v'yds up to 900 metres. Rich, velvety, concentrated Yatir Forest **05'** 06 07 08' 09 10 outstanding. Edgy SYRAH, mouthfilling CAB SAUV, powerful PETIT VERDOT. Owned by CARMEL.

> **Arab springboard**
>
> Unexpectedly gd wines from unlikely places: excellent Domaine Bargylus from Syria, praise-worthy Saint George wines from Zumot Winery, Jordan, intriguing Palestinian Hamdani Jandali, made by Cremisan Monastery. Even in Egypt there are new ventures worth watching.

Lebanon

Lebanese wines used to be essentially French in character, but newer wineries are making fuller, oakier, international styles. Whites are better than in the recent past; the best reds show sun, spice and a hint of mystery. Vineyards are being planted in areas other than the Bekaa: Batroun, Mt Lebanon, Jezzine.

Cave Kouroum r w ★→★★ Vibrant SYRAH, full-bodied but well-balanced.

Chateau Belle-Vue r ★★★ Le Chateau and La Renaissance are top-notch reds.

Château Ka r ★★ Great-value CAB SAUV/MERLOT/SYRAH blend.

Château Kefraya r w ★★→★★★ Full-bodied, concentrated, spicy *Comte de M* 07 08 09' from CAB SAUV, SYRAH. Fruity Les Bretèches. Plush Vissi d'Arte (CHARD, VIOGNIER).

Chateau Ksara r w ★★ Founded 1857 by Jesuits. Excellent-value wines. Mouthfilling, fruity Res du Couvent. Silky Le Souverain of interest (CAB SAUV and Arinarnoa).

Château Marsyas r (w) ★★ Crisp CHARD, SAUV BL; deep, powerful red. Owners of complex, minerally Dom Bargylus ★★★ (Syria). Stephane Derenoncourt consults.

Chateau Musar r w ★★★★ Icon wine of the eastern Mediterranean created by Serge Hochar. Long-lasting CAB SAUV/CINSAULT/CARIGNAN 96 97 99 00' 01' 02 03 04 05' 06. Unique and original style. Hochar red matures faster. Oaky white from indigenous Obaideh and Merwah can survive, if not improve, for 40 yrs.

Clos St-Thomas r w ★★ Silky red wines. Fresh, fruity PINOT N. Les Emirs great value.

Domaine de Baal r (w) ★★ Quality red from CAB SAUV, MERLOT, SYRAH. Organic v'yd.

Domaine des Tourelles r w ★★→★★★ Upfront, fruity, meaty SYRAH. Elegant Marquis des Beys. Flowering of reborn winery.

Domaine Wardy r w ★→★★ New-World-style Private Selection. Crisp, fresh whites.

IXSIR r w ★★ Ambitious winery. Big prestige red El in New-World style. Hubert de Bouard of St-Émilion's Château Angelus is involved.

Karam r w ★→★★ Gd boutique winery in Jezzine, south Lebanon. Exotic MUSCAT.

Massaya r w ★★→★★★ Entry-level Classic wines are v.gd value. Silver Selection red is complex Rhône-style blend showing sun and spice. The prestige Gold Res is full of fruit, herbs and spice, from CAB SAUV, MOURVÈDRE and SYRAH.

Turkey

Turkish wineries have plenty to cope with, including governmental and religious opposition to alcohol (the national drink is now claimed to be ayran). But Turkey has launched itself on the world market with some success. Local grape varieties, eg. indigenous red ÖKÜZGÖZÜ, BOĞAZKERE, Kalecik Karasi and white NARINCE, Emir, are a source of real interest abroad and the wines are improving.

Büyülübag r (w) ★★ One of the new small, quality wineries. Gd CAB SAUV.

Corvus r w ★★→★★★ Boutique winery on Bozcaada island. Corpus is powerful.

Doluca r w ★→★★★ Karma CAB SAUV/ÖKÜZGÖZÜ, CHARD/NARINCE v.gd blends combining local and international varieties.

Kavaklidere r w sp ★→★★★ Leader of move to quality. Best: ÖKÜZGÖZÜ, SYRAH from Pendore estate. Gd-value, entry-level Yakut. Stephane Derenoncourt consults.

Kayra r w ★→★★ Concentrated ÖKÜZGÖZÜ for quality, Buzbag for flavourful drinking.

Pamukkale r w ★→★★ Gd-value flavourful Anfora CAB SAUV.

Sarafin r w ★→★★ Gd CAB SAUV and SAUV BL. Brand owned by DOLUCA.

Sevilen r w ★→★★ Lime-fresh FUMÉ BLANC with great acidity. Deep SYRAH.

Sulva r w ★★ New winery. Delicious ROUSSANNE/MARSANNE.

Urla r w ★ Deep, rich NERO D'AVOLA with dried-fruit character.

Vinkara r w ★ Lively Kalecik Karasi, full of spice and red fruit.

NORTH AFRICA

Castel Frères Mor r p ★ Gd-value brands like Bonassia, Sahari, Halana, Larroque.

Celliers de Meknès, Les Mor r p w ★→★★ Dominates Moroccan market. Top wine: Château Roslane. Riad Jamil CARIGNAN best value.

Domaine Neferis Tun r p w ★→★★ Calastrasi joint venture. Selian CARIGNAN best.

Les Deux Domaines Mor r ★★ Depardieu-Bernard Magrez (Bordeaux) joint venture at Meknes; SYRAH and GRENACHE sold as Kahina and Lumière.

Thalvin Mor r p w ★★ Fresh whites. Raisiny Tandem SYRAH ★★★ Morocco's best international ambassador.

Val d'Argan Mor r p ★→★★ At Essaouira on west coast. Aromatic herbal ROUSSANNE.

Vignerons de Carthage Mor r p w ★ Best from UCCV co-op: Magon Magnus red.

Volubilia Mor r p w ★★ Promising new joint venture. Excellent *vin gris*.

Asia & Old Russian Empire

ASIA

China It is still a leap of faith for the typical wine consumer to believe that China is a serious wine-producing country. Sure, it has one of the largest v'yd areas in the world, more than the USA, and produces a staggering 100 million cases of wine/year. But what is the quality like? Most is consumed inside China, but we are increasingly seeing Chinese wines on shelves in the UK, the USA and Canada. There are definitely quality wines being made, largely with help from European wine superstars like the Lurton and Rothschild families from Bordeaux and multinational wine companies like Pernod-Ricard, Torres and Rémy Cointreau. From a viticultural perspective, China has challenges. Wine regions in the south and east have high humidity, causing fungal diseases, yet wineries in Shandong and Hebei are combating this effectively. Without doubt, the leading areas are inland: Ningxia and Shanxi, in terms of climate, rival parts of Australia and California. (Mind-bogglingly grandiose Chateau Changyu Moser XV winery in Ningxia cost €70m to build and is named after Austrian consultant Lenz Moser: red, white, v.gd Icewine.) The Helan Mtn subregion is also one to watch. Best producers, with consistently gd wines over several yrs, are Grace V'yds, Catai, Domaine Helan Mtn. It is worth searching out Cabernet Gernischt (certainly of French origin) for something unique.

India Much of India is unsuited to viticulture because of long summer monsoon rains, high humidity and heat. However the high-altitude areas in Maharashtra nr Mumbai, Karnataka nr Goa, and more recently Nandi Hills nr Bangalore, have allowed serious winemaking to start, mirroring the double digit growth in wine consumption over the past 15 yrs. Now 60,000 ha are planted across India – although over half is still the inferior Sultana grape. India's first commercial winery, Chateau Indage, opened in 1988; it is still the largest, with over 800 ha throughout Maharashtra. It has inspired others: Sula (730 ha) and the much smaller, more recent Chateau d'Ori (160 ha), both in Nashik. Moët has two sparklers, Chandon Brut and Chandon Brut Rosé, from Nashik. Grover V'yds in the cooler Nandi Hills is significant, Michel Rolland consults. India's best grapes so far seem to be SYRAH and CAB SAUV, with CHARD and SAUV BL.

Japanese wine is full of contradictions, yet quality is continuing to improve. Modern winemaking goes back to 1875, but has been dominated by the practice of blending up to 95% imported grape must or even fully made wine with the local product; the result is (legally) labelled as Wine of Japan. The indigenous Koshu grape is being intensely studied and heavily hyped: it's white, delicate, pleasant and can be made dry or sweet, barrel- or lees-aged. Grace and Mercian are gd; Lumière fizz too. Since the Japanese authorities declared Yamanashi a Geographical Indication based on WTO rules, confidence in "Yamanashi Wine" has grown. With 500 ha planted, it is not just Koshu, but European varieties such as CHARD, MERLOT, CAB SAUV that are among the better wines. There are still significant plantings of hybrid varieties like Yama Sauvignon, Muscat Bailey A, and Black Queen, mostly for domestic consumption. Yamanashi, Hokkaido and Nagano make up the vast majority of v'yd plantings as most of Japan suffers from excessive humidity and significant summer rainfall. This, combined with rich but acidic soils, restricts production. The number of qualified winemakers is on the rise; look out for Ayana Misawa from Grace V'yds, who has studied in Bordeaux and Stellenbosch. These wines are sold throughout the world. Look out too for wines from Soryu, Kizan, Takahata.

OLD RUSSIAN EMPIRE

Things are moving in the right direction: bit by bit modern quality wines are replacing the dull, industrial production that was the Soviet legacy. Most vineyards are planted around the Black Sea where natural conditions are favourable, if occasionally risky. Large companies dominate, but a new wave of small local producers has emerged. Excepting Georgia, all countries give priority to international grapes, not always justified. Russia is rediscovering indigenous grapes, though these wines are still niche. Georgia is on the rise. Armenia may be the next exciting place: international consultants Michel Rolland, Alberto Antonini and Paul Hobbs have started to make wine there.

Georgian wines have been allowed back in Russia: will quality be maintained? Georgia has a unique viticultural heritage spanning more than 7,000 yrs. There are around 500 indigenous grape varieties, but red SAPERAVI (intense, tannic, with great potential but often made sweet to suit Russian taste) and white RKATSITELI (lively, refreshing) cover most of the v'yds. Traditional whites are fermented with skins, but most whites and reds are made in modern styles. Kakheti (Southeast) produces 70% of all five defined areas. Thirty leading producers have formed an association that incl GWS, Tbilvino, Telavi Wine Cellar, Teliani Valley, Askaneli Brothers, Château Mukhrani, Kindzmarauli Corporation, Mildiani, Pheasant's Tears, Badagoni, Shumi and Schuchmann.

Georgia's *kevris*, used for winemaking for 8,000 years, now have UNESCO World Heritage status.

Moldova made fine wines under the tsars, and every second bottle in the USSR came from there. Now producers are feeling more confident again. There are four geographic areas. European grapes are historically grown along with local Rara Neagră, Plavai, Galbenă, Djiharda, Bătuta Neagră and FETEASCĂ ALBĂ. Historic red blends Roşu de Purcari (CAB SAUV, MERLOT, MALBEC) and Negru de Purcari (Cab Sauv, Rara Neagră, SAPERAVI) are revived by flagship Moldovan winery Vinăria Purcari. Other quality producers incl Acorex Wine Holding, Vinăria Bostavan, Château Vartely, Dionysos Mereni, DK Intertrade, Lion Gri, Cricova (sparkling).

Russian paradox: wine is now recognized as an agricultural product, but cannot be mentioned in the press or advertised, because it is an alcoholic beverage. Anonymous stuff from imported bulk and genuine wines are both made under Russian labels, misleading consumers. Wineries still need to win trust at home by producing consistent quality and investing in promotion. Most v'yds and wineries are in the southwest; the Krasnodar region is the biggest producer. Foreign consultants lend expertise for companies of note: Château le Grand Vostock, Fanagoria, Kuban Vino, Gai-Kodzor, Tsimlianskiye Vina, Abrau-Durso (*charmat* and traditional-method sparkling), Lefkadia. Russian *garagistes* are a new phenomenon, but volumes are tiny. European varieties (r w) are widely used: indigenous red Krasnostop and Tsimliansky candidates for Russian authenticity.

Ukraine Wine is grown around the Black Sea and on the border with Hungary. Natural conditions are favourable, but most production is industrial. Odessa leads in volume, but Crimea has greater quality potential, also proved by new wines from small growers, eg. Pavel Shvets. Historically the best (often excellent) Ukrainian wines were modelled on Sherry, Port, Madeira, Champagne. While Shampanskoye remains an essential, local sales of fortified and sweet wines are sliding. Still, gd fortifieds are not to be missed from historic producers, incl Massandra, Koktebel, Magarach, Solnechnaya Dolina. In large wineries, try Novy Svet and Artyomovsk Winery for traditional-method sparkling, Inkerman and Odessavinprom for dry wines. Names to watch: Veles (Kolonist), Guliev Wines.

United States

Abbreviations used in the text
(*see also* Principal Vineyard/
Viticultural Areas p.246, p.261):

Clark	Clarksburg, CA		
Coomb	Coombsville, CA		
Mont	Monterey, CA		
Mend	Mendocino, CA		
Oak Knoll	Oak K, CA		
San LO	San Luis Obispo, CA	CT	Connecticut
Santa Cz Mts	Santa Cruz Mountains, CA	ID	Idaho
Sierra F'hills	Sierra Foothills, CA	NJ	New Jersey
Santa B	Santa Barbera, CA	Tex	Texas
Son	Sonoma, CA	VA	Virginia

CALIFORNIA

This is the source of more than 90% of US wine, and the beneficiary of an exceptional run of outstanding vintages in this century. And we aren't just talking Napa. California, from the Pacific to the Sierra Foothills, from the Mexican border to the redwood forests of the north, is (at last) focusing on terroir, finding the right grape for the right place and listening to what the vines tell them rather than getting hung up on number games played by wine critics. Growers are increasingly turning away from the super-concentrated and jammy wines that created a cult following only because they beat their chests like gorillas, and are crafting more supple and elegant wines with, in many cases, the ability to age. You can find almost any grape variety in Califonia these days – and you should look. There are exceptions: Napa producers focused on producing what are termed "luxury goods" rather than wines aren't going to change course in a hurry. But otherwise, California is on the up.

Principal vineyard areas

There are over 100 American Viticultural Areas (AVAs) in California. Below are the key players.

Alexander Valley (Alex V) Son. Warm region in upper Russian RV. Gd Sauv Bl nr river; Cab Sauv, Zin on hillsides.

Anderson Valley (And V) Mendocino. Pacific fog and winds follow Navarro River inland; gd Ries, Gewurz, Pinot N; v.gd Zin on benchlands.

Arroyo Seco Monterey. Warm AVA; gd Cab Sauv, Chard.

Calistoga (Cal) Napa. Northern end of Napa V. Red wine territory.

Carneros (Car) Napa, Son. Cool AVA at north tip of San Francisco Bay. Gd Pinot N, Chard; Merlot, Syrah, Cab Sauv on warmer sites. V.gd sparkling.

Dry Creek Valley (Dry CV) Son. Outstanding Zin, gd Sauv Bl; gd hillside Cab Sauv and Zin.

Edna Valley (Edna V) San LO. Cool Pacific winds; v.gd minerally Chard.

Howell Mtn Napa. Classic Napa Cab Sauv from steep hillside v'yds.

Livermore Valley (Liv V) Alameda. Historic district mostly swallowed by suburbs but regaining some standing with new-wave Cab Sauv and Chard.

Mt Veeder Napa. High mtn v'yds for gd Chard, Cab Sauv.

Napa Valley (Napa V) Napa. Cab Sauv, Merlot, Cab Fr. Look to sub-AVAs for meaningful terroir-based wines. Note: Napa V is an area within Napa.

Oakville (Oak) Napa. Prime Cab Sauv territory.

Paso Robles (P Rob) San LO. Excellent Zin, Rhône varietals.

Red Hills Lake County. Promising for Cab Sauv, Zin.

Redwood Valley Mendocino. Warmer inland region; gd Zin, Cab Sauv, Sauv Bl.

Russian River Valley (Russian RV) Son. Pacific fog lingers; Pinot N, Chard, gd Zin on benchland.

Rutherford (Ruth) Napa. Outstanding Cab Sauv, esp hillside v'yds.

Saint Helena Napa. Lovely balanced Cab Sauv.

Santa Lucia Highlands (Santa LH) Mont. Higher elevation with gd Pinot N, Syrah, Rhônes.

Santa Maria Valley (Santa MV) Santa B. Coastal cool; gd Pinot N, Chard, Viognier.

Sta Rita Hills (Sta RH) Santa B. Excellent Pinot N.

Santa Ynez (Santa Y) Santa B. Rhônes, Chard, Sauv Bl the best bet.

Sonoma Coast (Son Coast) Son. V. cool climate; edgy Pinot N.

Sonoma Valley (Son V) Son. Gd Chard, v.gd Zin; excellent Cab Sauv from Sonoma Mountain (Son Mtn) sub-AVA. Note: Sonoma V is an area within Son.

Spring Mtn Napa. Terrific Cab Sauv; v.gd Sauv Bl.

Stags Leap (Stags L) Napa. Classic Cab Sauv; v.gd Merlot.

Recent vintages

California is too big and too diverse for any neat summary to stack up. Keeping that in mind, the following assessments can be useful in a general way.

2013 Another large harvest with excellent quality prospects.

2012 Cab Sauv looks oustanding. Very promising for most varieties.

2011 Another difficult year, below-average crop. Those who picked later reported very good quality – Cab Sauv, Pinot N.

2010 A very difficult year, cool and wet. But some outstanding bottlings, esp Rhône varieties and Zin.

2009 Reds, whites show good balance, ageing potential. Napa Cab Sauv excellent.

2008 Uneven quality. Acid levels low; some areas' grapes may not have ripened.

2007 Rain; results mixed, especially for Cab Sauv.

2006 Cab Sauv improving with age. Overall, above-average.

2005 Cab Sauv especially good early on but fading fast.

2004 Some of the early promise has faded. Wines for short-term consumption.

2003 A difficult year all around. Overall, spotty.

Abreu Vineyards Napa V ★★★ 05 07 09 10 11 12 Supple CAB SAUV with a powerful opening, long, layered finish. Gd cellar choice for up to 15 yrs.

Acacia Car ★★★ Always gd, sometimes outstanding CHARD and PINOT N from single-v'yds in Napa Car. Also a super VIOGNIER.

Alanté Vineyard St Helena ★★★ Low-production, outstanding CAB SAUV from a single v'yd. Gd structure with layered finish; capable of ageing.

Alban Vineyards Edna V ★★→★★★ An original rider with the Rhône Rangers, still out in front of the herd. Top wines are VIOGNIER, GRENACHE.

Alma Rosa Sta RH ★★★→★★★★ Richard Sanford, a Central Coast PINOT N master, has moved on to new ground with organic v'yds and palate-pleasing **Pinot N** that is better than ever. V.gd rosé, CHARD.

Altamura Vineyards Napa V ★★★ 01 02 03 04 05 06 07 08 09 10 CAB SAUV built to last. Be patient and it will show gd depth and long, echoing flavours.

Amador Foothills Winery Sierra F'hills ★★→★★★ The ZIN is a go-to; SAUV BL has bright minerality. Rhône varieties under Katie's Côte label are crowd-pleasers.

Andrew Murray Santa B ★★→★★★ It's Rhônes around the clock here and the hits keep coming. SYRAH is a favourite but don't overlook VIOGNIER, ROUSSANNE.

Anthem Napa V ★★★ 10 11 12 Just when you thought Napa was well mapped, a newcomer turns up, producing small lots of CAB SAUV from top v'yds. Look esp for Beckstoffer Las Piedras V'yd. Superb rendering of Napa Cab Sauv.

Antica Napa V ★★★ 09 10 11 12 It took a few yrs to sort out Piero Antinori's (*see* Italy) Napa v'yds, but the wines are at last meeting expectations, with a bright and balanced CAB SAUV and a lovely, rounded CHARD.

The first *Vitis vinifera* vines in California were planted in 1770.

Araujo Napa V ★★★★ 01 02 03 04 05 06 08 09 10 11 12 Massive, long-lasting CAB SAUV from historic *Eisele v'yd*. Sold to Pinaults of Château Latour in 2013.

Artesa Car ★★→★★★ A range of wines from North Coast v'yds. Flagship wines are the estate bottling, esp PINOT N, CHARD. New ALBARIÑO is delicious. Owned by the Raventós family (Codorníu) of Catalonia.

Au Bon Climat Santa B ★★★→★★★★★ Jim Clendenen has been a leader in est the Central Coast style for toasty CHARD, rich PINOT N; light-hearted PINOT BL.

Babcock Vineyards Santa Y ★★★ Central Coast pacesetter sources outstanding PINOT N and v.gd CHARD, SAUV BL from cool-climate v'yds.

Balletto Russian RV ★★★ Outstanding estate CHARD and PINOT N. Delicious new bottling of *Pinot Gr* takes the grape seriously. Gd SYRAH from estate vines.

Beaulieu Vineyard Napa V ★★ →★★★ 07 09 10 11 12 Say "thanks for the memory" to this once-top estate, but Georges de Latour Private Res CAB SAUV can still hold its head up. Beaulieu Coastal Estate label budget wines can be acceptable.

Beckman Vineyards Santa Y ★★★ Outstanding SYRAH from Purisimia Mtn V'yd in Santa Y Valley, backed by a v.gd GRENACHE rosé. Bio.

Bella Son ★★★ 09 10 11 ZIN specialist scouts Son v'yds for superb bottlings, esp The Belle Canyon Zin featuring quintessential Dry CV brambly fruit. Lily Hill Estate from DCV a powerful counterpoint. Recently added excellent PINOT N.

Benovia Russian RV ★★★ Outstanding PINOT from Cohn V'yd; gd GRENACHE from Son Mtn; best of show is the silky Russian RV CHARD.

Benziger Family Winery Son V ★★ →★★★ A pioneer in bio farming. Look for estate bottling, esp CAB SAUV, MERLOT, SAUV BL.

Beringer Blass Napa ★ →★★★ (CAB SAUV) 01 05 07 09 10 Historic winery's single-v'yd Cab Sauv Res are massive, but age-worthy. Velvety, powerful Howell Mtn MERLOT is v.gd. Founder's Estate gd bargain line.

Bernardus Mont ★★ →★★★ 07 08 09 10 11 12 The Marinus red Bordeaux blend is superb, gd for short-term ageing but delicious as a youngster. Gd SAUV BL, CHARD.

Blair Vineyards Mont ★★★ Small lots of v'yd-designated PINOT N and a v.gd Bordeaux blend are highlights. Also unusually complex PINOT GR from Arroyo Seco.

Bogle Vineyards Central V ★ →★★★ Consistently gd and sometimes v.gd everday budget wines. Old-Vine ZIN leads the way. Current favourite is Phantom, superb blend of Zin, MOURVÈDRE, PETITE SIRAH from Lodi and Sierra F'hills.

Bokisch Lodi ★★ →★★★ A leader in California's Spanish revival, with v.gd TEMPRANILLO backed by outstanding GARNACHA and ALBARIÑO.

Bonny Doon Mont ★★★ →★★★★ 08 (Le Cigare Volant) Since *terroirist* Randall Grahm sold his mass-market budget brands to concentrate on bio single-v'yds, there has been a sharp improvement. Flagship *Le Cigare Volant* has moved into ★★★★ territory. Vin Gris de Cigare is one of California's top rosés.

Bonterra *See* FETZER.

Bouchaine Car ★★★ Carneros pioneer puts best foot forward with estate PINOT N, CHARD; recent addition of Son Coast SYRAH is excellent; v.gd RIES.

Bronco Wine Company Founded by Fred Franzia, nephew of the late Ernest GALLO. Franzia uses low-cost Central Valley grapes for his famous Charles Shaw Two-Buck Chuck. There are dozens of other labels incl Napa Creek and Napa Ridge. Quality is not the point: Franzia is selling wine as a popular beverage.

Buehler Napa ★★★ 05 07 09 10 11 12 An underrated Napa treasure, Buehler consistently delivers balanced CAB SAUV in a pleasing brambly style with gd structure. Also look for an outstanding ZIN from Napa grapes and a v.gd CHARD from Russian RV fruit.

Burgess Cellars Napa V ★★★ (CAB SAUV) 05 07 09 10 11 12 Powerful and age-worthy Cab Sauv from Howell Mtn grapes.

Cain Cellars Napa V ★★★ 05 07 09 10 11 12 Cain Five, a supple and layered blend of the five Bordeaux reds from Spring Mtn grapes, is at the head of the class. Consistent and *age-worthy*.

Cakebread Napa V ★★★ →★★★★ 03 05 06 07 09 10 11 12 CAB SAUV, structured for ageing but delicious after 4 or 5 yrs in bottle, is a gold standard. SAUV BL ranks among the best; CHARD v.gd.

Calera ★★★★ 07 08 09 10 11 Josh Jensen, who fell in love with PINOT N while at Oxford, offers an outstanding portfolio of Pinot N, esp Reed, Selleck; also intense, flowery VIOGNIER and a rare ALIGOTÉ.

Cass P Rob ★★ →★★★ They just keep coming. Yet another Central Coast specialist in Rhône varieties getting it right. SYRAH is superb with deep chocolate/coffee tones and a long finish.

> **New-look Chardonnay**
> There has been a welcome change in California CHARD over the past
> three or four vintages. Winemakers are stepping back from the in-your-
> face buttery, oaky style and opting for a more nuanced approach. These
> new-wave wines tend to have more assertive acidity and a refreshing
> minerality that encourage a second glass.

Castoro Cellars P Rob ★★★ Tasting from white to red, the ROUSSANNE is a super
starter wine. Move on to a pleasing SYRAH and a lovely ZIN blend called Zinfusion.
A trip worth taking.

Caymus Napa V ★★★→★★★★ 01 05 06 07 09 10 11 12 Special Selection CAB SAUV is
a Napa icon, consistently one of California's most formidable: strong, intense,
slow to mature. The regular Napa bottling is no slouch. V.gd CHARD under the
Mer Soleil brand from Monterey grapes. Gd-value second label Conundrum.

Chalk Hill Son ★★★ Terroir-driven, esp CHARD and Estate Red blend.

Chalone Mont ★★★ Historic Mont mtn estate; intense PINOT N, minerally CHARD.

Chamisal Vineyards Edna V ★★★ Chamisal has been making outstanding Central
Coast CHARD, PINOT N for four decades. Recent bottlings have raised the bar, esp
unoaked Chard and v.gd SYRAH.

Chappellet Napa V ★★★→★★★★ 01 05 06 07 08 09 10 11 12 Pioneer (1969) on
Pritchard Hill, St Helena. *Signature label* CAB SAUV is capable of serious ageing;
also v.gd CHARD, CAB FR, MERLOT; NB CHENIN BL. Chappellet owns Sonoma-Loeb,
specializing in Chard and PINOT N from Car and Russian RV.

Charles Krug Napa V ★★→★★★ Historically important winery enjoying a comeback
led by a supple and elegant CAB SAUV; SAUV BL is excellent.

Chateau Montelena Napa V ★★★→★★★★ (CHARD) 09 10 11 (CAB SAUV) 01 03 05 06 07
09 10 11 Balanced and supple Cab Sauv for drinking young or putting away for
at least a decade. Chard is also a keeper.

Chateau St Jean Son ★★→★★★ Cinq Cépages, a blend of five Bordeaux red varieties,
is top card here; gd SAUV BL, CHARD.

Chimney Rock Stags L ★★★ 03 05 07 09 10 11 An often underrated producer of
balanced, age-worthy CAB SAUV.

Christopher Creek Dry CV ★★→★★★ PETITE SIRAH specialist recently changed owners
but appears to be in gd hands. Look esp for Dry CV ZIN and v.gd VIOGNIER. Of
course, don't go home without the Petty Sir.

Claiborne & Churchill Edna V ★★→★★★ Alsace style; several bottlings of RIES, other
aromatic whites. Look esp for estate Ries, dry GEWURZ. PINOT N also worth a try.

Clark-Clauden Napa V ★★★→★★★★ 05 07 09 10 11 12 Outstanding CAB SAUV: focused
fruit, lasting wraparound flavours. Also v.gd SAUV BL. Much *underrated* producer.

Clayhouse P Rob ★★→★★★ Old-vine PETITE SIRAH restores faith in that variety. It has
it all: lovely black-cherry, chocolate, black pepper and a long finish. Also look for
Adobe, a delicious white blend.

Clos du Bois Son ★★→★★★ Briarcrest CAB SAUV and Calcaire CHARD can be v.gd. Rest
of line-up are quaffable everyday wines. No problem there.

Clos du Val Napa V ★★★ 05 07 09 10 11 Consistently outstanding CAB SAUVS, never
overstated in style, and much underrated. Chard *is a delight* and a SÉM/SAUV BL
blend called Ariadne is a charmer.

Conn Creek Napa V ★★★ 03 05 06 07 09 10 11 12 Structured CAB SAUV, from
several Napa V v'yds. Gd candidate for cellar, esp Ruth bottling.

Constellation ★→★★★ Owns wineries in California, NY, Washington State, Canada,
Chile, Australia, NZ. Produces 90+ million cases/yr, the world's biggest wine
company. Once a bottom-feeder, now going for the top, incl ROBERT MONDAVI,
FRANCISCAN V'YD, Estancia, Mt Veeder, RAVENSWOOD, Simi, among others.

CALIFORNIA

Continuum Napa V ★★★ Tim Mondavi is most likely doing what he always wanted to do make a single wine from Bordeaux varieties – and early results are more than promising. The 2011 in particular is supple and pleasing. Built for keeping.

Corison Napa V ★★★★ 95 96 97 99 00 01 02 05 06 07 09 10 11 12 Cathy Corison is a national treasure. While many in Napa V follow the $iren call of powerhouse wines for big scores and little pleasure, Corison continues to make flavoursome, *age-worthy Cab Sauv*. Top choice is the luscious and velvety Kronos V'yd.

Cornerstone Cellars Howell Mtn ★★★ 01 02 03 05 07 09 10 11 Impressive Howell Mtn CAB SAUV with focus on harmony, balance; v.gd Cab Sauv from valley floor.

Cuvaison Napa V ★★★ 01 03 05 07 08 09 10 11 CAB SAUV from Mt Veeder is superb; v.gd CHARD, SYRAH.

Dancing Coyote Clark ★★★ GRÜNER V is not normally in the same sentence as "California"; this fancifully named winery pulls off a stunning example, grown in the Clark region of the Sacramento Delta. Watch this coyote.

Dashe Cellars Dry CV ★★→★★★ A happy obsession with Dry CV ZIN, with single-v'yd bottlings capturing the classic Dry CV brambly style.

David Bruce Santa Cz Mts ★★★ 09 10 11 (CHARD) Legendary mtn estate still on top of the game with powerful, long-lasting Chard and superb PINOT N.

Davis Bynum Son ★★★ V.gd Russian RV single-v'yd PINOT N; lean yet silky CHARD.

Dehlinger Russian RV ★★★★ Tom Dehlinger maintains standing as a ZIN master; consistently ★★★★ wines from estate Russian RV v'yd. Also v.gd CHARD, SYRAH.

Delicato Vineyards ★→★★ Long-time (eight generations) wine family has moved beyond jug wines to more upscale bottlings from v'yds in Napa, Mont and Lodi. Popular innovations are the Bota wines, premium varieties in 3-litre boxes.

Diamond Creek Napa V ★★★★ 99 00 01 03 06 07 09 10 11 Austere CAB SAUV from hillside v'yds on Diamond Mtn – Gravelly Meadow, Volcanic Hill, Red Block Terrace. Wines age beautifully. One of Napa's jewels, overshadowed in recent yrs by some of Napa's more glitzy cult Cabs.

Domaine Carneros Car ★★★→★★★ Vintage Blanc de Blancs La Rêve consistently rates as one of the best sparklers in the state; also a v.gd NV bubbly rosé. An outstanding range of PINOT N and CHARD led by The Famous Gate Pinot.

Domaine Chandon Napa V ★★→★★★ Top bubbly is the NV Res Étoile; also v.gd rosé sparkler. Still wines incl gd Car PINOT N.

Dominus Estate Napa V ★★★★ 97 99 01 02 05 06 07 08 09 10 11 12 Elegantly austere winery and wine of Christian Moueix of Pomerol. One of Napa's great treasures. Don't rush it; the wine amply repays cellar time with supple layers of intense flavours; long wraparound finish.

Donum Estate N Coast ★★★ PINOT N, CHARD specialist with estate v'yds in Car, Russian RV, And V. Wines are silky and elegant with Car bottling the flagship.

Dry Creek Vineyard Dry CV ★★→★★★ Has been a leader in the Heritage ZIN movement: v. impressive line-up of single-v'yd bottlings. V.gd SAUV BL, CHENIN BL.

Duckhorn Vineyards Napa V ★★★→★★★★ Known for dark, tannic, plummy-ripe single-v'yd MERLOTS (esp Three Palms), CAB SAUV-based Howell Mtn bottling. Also Golden Eye PINOT N, made in a robust style at an Anderson V winery. An excellent Russian RV CHARD and Pinot N have been added to Duckhorn's Migration label.

Dunn Vineyards Howell Mtn ★★★★ 91 95 97 99 01 03 06 07 09 10 11 Randy Dunn makes superb and *intense Cab Sauv* from Howell Mtn estate. They age magnificently; more restrained bottlings from valley floor for short-term drinking. One of few Napa V winemakers to resist the stampede to jammy, lush wines to curry critics' favour.

Dutton-Goldfield Son Coast ★★★→★★★★ Exceptional terroir-based PINOT N, CHARD from Son Coast and Russian RV v'yds. Wines are modern California classics.

Edmunds St John ★★★ Steve Edmunds has scanned California v'yds for decades, sourcing at times offbeat varieties to make v.gd wines. Recent eg.: delicious El Dorado Bone-Jolly GAMAY Noir Rosé. Another is Basseti V'yd SYRAH from San LO.

Edna Valley Vineyard Edna V ★★★ Lovely and true-to-variety SAUV BL for openers, then crisp CHARD with generous tropical fruit. Finish with impressive SYRAH.

Elizabeth Spencer Napa V ★★★ Outstanding Ruth CAB SAUV, gd ageing potential. V.gd CHARD from Russian RV, delightful CHENIN BL from Mend anchor the portfolio.

Elyse Vineyards Napa V ★★★ 05 08 09 10 11 All bases covered here, starting with small lots of single-v'yd CAB SAUV; bright fruit, layered flavours, excellent ageing potential. V.gd old-vine ZIN.

Fetzer Vineyards Mend ★★→★★★ Leads in organic/sustainable viticulture. Consistent-value from least expensive range (Sundial, Valley Oaks) to brilliant Res. Also owns BONTERRA v'yds (all organic grapes) where *Roussanne and Marsanne are stars*.

Field Family Lodi ★★→★★★ Lodi-based producer sources Napa grapes for v.gd CAB SAUV from Dr. Konrad v'yd on Mt Veeder. Also gd estate SYRAH.

Flora Springs Wine Co Napa V ★★★ 05 06 07 09 10 11 12 (CAB SAUV) Sometimes-overlooked Napa gem, esp Signature series incl Trilogy (amazing Cab Sauv-based jewel from hillside v'yds); Soliloquy, a v.gd SAUV BL from Oak AVA; fine CHARD.

Flowers Vineyard & Winery Son ★★★ Son Coast pioneer; first CHARD planted 1991. Flowers now farms organically; won praise for intense coastal PINOT N and Chard.

Foley Johnson Napa V ★★★ Producer of small lots from select v'yds, nice touch with MERLOT, esp a velvety Ruth bottling. CAB SAUV from Coomb AVA a winner.

Foppiano Son ★★→★★★ One of California's grand old wine families, est 1896. Outstanding ZIN yr in, yr out. Leads in rich, firmly structured PETITE SIRAH, known as "petty sir" among rearguard. Appealing CAB SAUV, lively SAUV BL, gd estate rosé.

Woodzee turns old Mondavi barrels into sunglasses. Too much oak on the nose?

Forman Vineyard Napa V ★★★★ 00 01 03 05 07 09 10 11 12 Ric Forman, a dedicated, some might say fanatic *terroirist*, makes elegant, age-worthy CAB SAUV-based wines from hillside v'yds. Also v.gd CHARD.

Foxen Canyon Santa B ★★★ Prolific producer of a wide variety from Central Coast, but the heart of the line-up is several v.gd v'yd bottlings of PINOT N.

Franciscan Vineyard Napa V ★★→★★★ Magnificent, red Bordeaux blend consistently excellent; Cuvée Sauvage CHARD also quite gd.

Frank Family Vineyards Ruth ★★★ Gorgeous CAB SAUV hitting on all keys. Gd for early drinking but will repay a decade+ in the cellar, esp Res bottling. Winton Hill Cab Sauv, dark and brooding, is splendid. Also brilliant SANGIOVESE.

Freemark Abbey Napa V ★★★→★★★★ 01 03 05 07 09 10 11 12 *Stylish Cab Sauv worthy of cellar time* from often-underrated classic producer. Esp single-v'yd Sycamore, Bosche bottlings.

Freestone Son Coast ★★★→★★★★ Intense but balanced OLD CHARD, PINOT N from vines only a few miles from the Pacific show gd structure, long finish, esp Chard.

Frog's Leap Ruth ★★★→★★★★ 01 02 03 05 07 09 10 11 (CAB SAUV) John Williams, a leader in organic, bio movement, says all starts in v'yd. Supple Cab Sauv, capable of ageing; toasty CHARD, zesty ZIN and lean, *minerally Sauv Bl* are all excellent.

Gallo Sonoma Son ★→★★★ Coastal outpost of Central Valley giant sources grapes from several Son v'yds. CAB SAUV can be v.gd, also the single-v'yd CHARD. New line of Gina Gallo signature wines are consistently ★★★.

Gallo Winery, E & J ★→★★★ California's biggest winery is an easy target for wine snobs, but Gallo has done more to open up the American palate to wine than any other company. Its 1960s Hearty Burgundy was groundbreaking. Continues basic commodity wines, but has created a line of regional varieties: Anapauma, Marcellina, Turning Leaf and more, all wines of modest quality perhaps but predictable and affordable.

> **Grenache Blanc – the word is out**
> California winemakers are learning to embrace the joys of GRENACHE
> BLANC, something their colleagues in France and Spain have been on
> to for centuries. At its best, the wine offers a delicious combination of
> fruit and a spicy, herbal quality that is v. pleasing. There are fewer than
> 300 acres planted across the state, but wherever it grows – from the
> Sierra F'hills to the coast, even in cooler parts of the Central Valley like
> Lodi – the wine offers a zesty freshness and charm.

Gary Farrell Son ★★★ V.gd to excellent PINOT N and CHARD from cool-climate v'yds. The Rocholi v'yd Chard from Russian RV is superb. Gd ZIN and a splendid SYRAH.

Geyser Peak Son ★★ →★★★ Reliable producer of CAB SAUV and CHARD now featuring wines under the River Ranches collection, with SAUV BL top of the line.

Gloria Ferrer Car ★★→★★★ Built by Spain's Freixenet for sparkling wine, now producing spicy CHARD and bright, silky PINOT N plus other varietals, all from Car fruit. Bubbly has developed a sweet tooth with the addition of Va de Vi, a blend of Pinot N, Chard, MOSCATO.

Grace Family Vineyard Napa V ★★★★ 01 03 05 06 07 09 10 11 Stunning CAB SAUV for long ageing. One of the few cult wines that might actually be worth the price.

Grgich Hills Cellars Napa V ★★★ →★★★★ 05 07 08 09 10 11 12 CAB SAUV, now bio, outstanding; supple, age-worthy CHARD. SAUV (FUMÉ) BL, rustic ZIN worth a look.

Groth Vineyards Oak ★★★★ 99 00 01 05 06 07 09 10 11 Estate CAB SAUV offers supple, wraparound flavours, structured for ageing. Res Cab Sauv more tightly wound. Excellent CHARD, SAUV BL.

Hahn Mont ★★ →★★★ Mont mainstay offers bewildering variety of brands, eg. Cycles Gladiator, Smith & Hook. Under Hahn label go for Santa LH PINOT N, CHARD.

Hall Napa V ★★★★ 07 08 09 10 11 Napa CAB SAUV is v. fine, with full-palate layers of flavour. A stunning Diamond Mtn Cab Sauv and a v.gd St Helena Bergfeld Cab Sauv are offered in the small-lot Artisan series. Minerally SAUV BL is delicious.

Halter Ranch P Rob ★★ →★★★ Ancestor, red Bordeaux blend, outstanding. Cote du Paso (r w) v.gd. Gd ZIN. Super SYRAH blended with GRENACHE, TANNAT.

Hanna Winery Son ★★★ Son classic with outstanding SAUV BL, PINOT N from Russian RV. CAB SAUV, MERLOT from Alex V v'yds superb. New rosé a treat.

Hanzell Son V ★★★★ Historic artisan producer of outstanding and terroir-driven CHARD *and Pinot N* from estate vines. Both repay a few yrs' cellar time. Deserves to be ranked with the best of California.

Harlan Estate Napa V ★★★★ 06 07 09 10 11 Concentrated, sleek cult CAB SAUV from perfectionist estate with luxury prices. Bill Harlan owns Meadowood Club.

Harmony Cellars Santa B ★★ →★★★ New boutique winery featuring wines from Central Coast. Look esp for BARBERA. Also excellent ZIN, PETITE SIRAH.

Harney Lane Lodi ★★ →★★★ Open with a v.gd glass of ALBARIÑO or a lovely TEMPRANILLO rosé. Move on to Lizzy's Old-Vine ZIN. You are in your comfort zone here.

HdV Wines Car ★★★★ Fine, complex *Chard* with a mineral edge from grower Larry Hyde's v'yd in conjunction with Aubert de Villaine of DRC (*see* France). Also a v.gd CAB SAUV and SYRAH from Hyde's v'yd.

Heitz Cellar Napa V ★★★ 01 03 05 07 09 10 11 Napa history, incl iconic Martha's V'yd CAB SAUV; recent bottlings of Trailside V'yd Cab Sauv, with uplifted, balanced fruit, are a match for Martha. Don't overlook the restrained, elegant CHARD.

Heller Estate Mont ★★★ Layered and supple *Cab Sauv* is v.gd as is the charming CHENIN BL and PINOT N. Rosé too.

Hess Collection, The Napa V ★★★ CAB SAUV from Mt Veeder estate v'yd hits a new quality level, esp the exceptional 19 Block Cuvée, a blockbuster with gd manners; Lake County SAUV BL is v.gd; CHARD crisp and bright. See the art gallery.

Honig Napa V ★★★ Steadily improving quality, esp the CAB SAUV, rich and deeply flavoured, which should age well. SAUV BL is delicious.

Hoyt Cellars P Rob ★★★ Artisan producer of gd CAB SAUV, TEMPRANILLO. Also a pleasing CHARD with bright fruit and a gulpable PINOT GRIGIO.

Husch Mend ★★→★★★ Exceptional value CAB SAUV, CHARD, SAUV BL. Recent release of an estate-bottled Res Cab Sauv shows promise of better things to come.

Inglenook Oak ★★★ When Francis Ford Coppola said he was going to restore Inglenook to its former glory he didn't mean a new paint job. Rubicon, now under the Inglenook label, marks a return to classic Napa CAB SAUV – balanced, elegant and true to the great Inglenook tradition. Blancaneaux is a complex, rich blend of ROUSSANNE, MARSANNE, VIOGNIER. As for the museum winery....

Iron Horse Vineyards Son ★★★→★★★★ Joy, new top-of-line NV bubbly, is amazing. Bottled in magnum with 10–15 yrs on lees, combines elegance, power. Wedding Cuvée also a winning sparkler. Recent release of a 2004 LD Brut is superb. V.gd CHARD, PINOT N; look for Corral V'yd Chard and refreshing unoaked Chard.

Ironstone Sierra F'hills ★★→★★★ This Sierra F'hills destination winery is more than just a pretty face. Old-Vine ZIN is among state's best; CAB FR is v.gd, as is charming Christine Andrew SAUV BL.

Jade Mountain N Coast ★★★ Best offering is La Provençale, a blend of red Rhône varieties; v.gd CAB SAUV from North Coast; fine CHARD.

Jordan Alex V ★★★★ (CAB SAUV) 98 99 00 01 02 05 07 09 10 11 12 Consistently balanced, elegant wines from showcase Alex V estate. The Cab Sauv is a homage to Bordeaux – and it lasts. Minerally, delicious CHARD ditto to Burgundy.

Jorian Hill Santa Y ★★★ Superb Rhône-inspired wines from organic v'yds. Brilliant VIOGNIER, outstanding BEEspoke, a Rhône red blend; gd rosé.

Joseph Phelps Napa V ★★★★ (Insignia) 99 00 01 03 05 06 07 08 09 10 11 12 A true Napa "first growth". Phelps CAB SAUV, esp Insignia and Backus, are always nr the top, capable of long ageing. Ovation CHARD is v.gd.

Joseph Swan Son ★★★ Long-time Russian RV producer of intense old-vine ZIN and single-v'yd PINOT N. Often overlooked Rhône varieties also v.gd, esp ROUSSANNE/MARSANNE blend from Saralee's v'yd.

J Vineyards Son ★★★ Outstanding bubbly, esp a creamy brut, a zesty brut rosé and a luscious late-disgorged vintage. Also gd PINOT N, CHARD, refreshing VIOGNIER.

Kathryn Kennedy Santa Cz Mts ★★★ CAB SAUV specialist in the cool Santa Cz Mts. Consistent, age-worthy, restrained wines have been compared to Left Bank Bordeaux. Decant younger wines, or put away for a decade.

Kendall-Jackson ★★→★★★ Legendary market-driven CHARD, CAB SAUV. Even more noteworthy for developing a diversity of wineries under the umbrella of Artisans & Estates.

Ruby Cabernet is a wine grape, not a transvestite entertainer.

Kent Rasmussen Winery Car ★★★→★★★★ Outstanding Car wines for more than a quarter-century. Look esp for minerally CHARD and full-palate lushness of PINOT N. Ramsay is an alternative label for limited bottlings.

Kenwood Vineyards Son ★★→★★★ (Jack London CAB SAUV) 03 05 07 08 09 10 11 Consistently gd quality at fair prices. Jack London Cab Sauv is high point. V.gd Artist Series Cab Sauv. Several v.gd bottlings of ZIN; gulpable, delicious SAUV BL.

Kistler Vineyards Russian RV ★★★ Specialist in cool-climate Son County CHARD, PINOT N; over 12 v'yd-designated wines in any given yr. Wines much in demand.

Konsgaard Napa ★★★→★★★★ An amazing CHARD from Judge V'yd that could be from the heart of Burgundy. Outstanding CAB SAUV, delicious ALBARIÑO.

Korbel ★★ Largest US producer of classic-method fizz, with focus on fruit flavours. Recently added an organic bottling and a gd Brut Rosé. For your next picnic.

Kosta Browne Son ★★★ PINOT N specialist with a Burgundian touch and wide range. Current favourite is a Son Coast bottling with intense black-cherry fruit. Also v.gd Russian RV bottlng and flinty, intriguing PINOT N from Santa LH.

Kunde Estate Son V ★★★ Now in second century of winemaking, firmly anchored by historic Son V v'yd. Several tiers of wines but best in class is Family Estate selection, esp CHARD and v.gd CAB SAUV.

La Follette Russian RV ★★★ A Russian RV newcomer specializing in single-v'yd PINOT N and CHARD. DuNah V'yd Pinot from hillside v'yd is outstanding, as is Sangiacomo Chard.

La Jota Howell Mtn ★★★→★★★★ 01 03 04 05 07 09 10 11 Supple and age-worthy CAB SAUV, MERLOT; CAB FR is one of state's best. All wines from mtn v'yds.

Lamborn Family Vineyards Howell Mtn ★★★→★★★★ Superstar winemaker Heidi Barrett makes age-worthy CAB SAUV, full-flavoured ZIN from estate v'yd.

Lange Twins Lodi ★★ A pleasing SAUV BL calls for another glass. Caricature, a CAB SAUV/ZIN blend, is a delicious elbow-bender.

Larkmead Napa V ★★★→★★★★ 10 11 Historic Cal estate being revived. Balanced, *outstanding Cab Sauv*; delicious SAUV BL. New release Tocai FRIULANO, a delight.

La Rochelle Santa LH ★★→★★★ Mission here is small lots of PINOT N headed by excellent McIntyre V'yd estate bottling. V.gd Soborantes V'yd, zesty Pinot N rosé.

Laurel Glen Son V ★★★★ 01 03 05 06 09 10 11 Supple, age-worthy CAB SAUV from hillside v'yd on Son Mtn has rated nr the top for three decades. Founder Patrick Campbell sold the winery in 2011, but don't despair. Every indication is that new owners are determined to maintain the standard.

Lava Cap Sierra F'hills ★★→★★★ This Sierra F'hills pioneer offers a solid line-up, incl excellent ZIN, v.gd SYRAH, appealing GRENACHE.

Lohr, J ★★→★★★ One of California's underrated treasures. Wines better every yr. Excellent CAB SAUV, series of MERITAGE reds are first-rate, made chiefly from P Rob fruit. PINOT N picture is also looking bright with excellent version from Arroyo Seco. Cypress is gd budget line.

Long Meadow Napa V ★★★→★★★★ Destination winery in Napa with restaurant and a working farm. It hasn't hurt the wines. Supple, age-worthy CAB SAUV has reached ★★★★ status; lively Graves-style SAUV BL. Ranch House Red is true elbow-bender. V'yd organically farmed.

Louis M Martini Napa ★★★ 05 06 07 09 10 11 12 Napa treasure; brilliant comeback since 2002 GALLO buy-out. Gallo took hands-off approach, giving Mike Martini the tools and letting him work with the great CAB SAUV and ZIN v'yds the family had owned for decades. Look esp for Cab Sauv from *Monte Rosso* and Alex V. Son County bottling of Cab Sauv is everyday pleasure.

L'Uvaggio Lodi ★★★ Italian specialist offering excellent BARBERA; also VERMENTINO and splendid rosé reminiscent of northern Spain. New bottling of PRIMITIVO is tops. Can't go wrong here.

McIntire Vineyards Santa LH ★★→★★★ McIntire family, long-time growers, now make their own wines and do a fine job. PINOT N offers rich cherry fruit backed by gd acidity. Brilliant CHARD with deep minerality and long finish. Now MERLOT too.

MacPhail Son ★★★ Intense, tightly wound PINOT N, gd CHARD, refreshing Pinot N rosé from Son Coast.

Malk Family Vineyards Stags L ★★★ Elegant, supple CAB SAUV is outstanding example of Stags L typicity. Will age so get it by the case. Also v.gd SAUV BL.

Marimar Torres Estate Russian RV ★★★★ Several bottlings of CHARD, PINOT N from Don Miguel estate in Green Valley. Chard is complex, ages 5 yrs. Acero Chard is unoaked, *a lovely expression of Chard fruit*. Pinot N from Doña Margarita v'yd nr the ocean is intense and rich. Gd SYRAH/TEMPRANILLO blend, zesty ALBARIÑO/Chard blend. V'yds now all bio.

Markham Napa V ★★★ Outstanding CAB SAUV, MERLOT made with restraint, balance. Enjoy when young or keep for a decade.

Martinelli Russian RV ★★→★★★ Jackass Hill old-vine ZIN has cult status; several single-v'yd bottlings of intense PINOT N.

Mayacamas Vineyards Mt Veeder ★★★ Bob Travers and his wife, Elionor, made outstanding *Cab Sauv* to age decades from their Mt Veeder v'yd for more than 40 yrs. Fans hold their breath since Charles Banks, a former partner in the cult SCREAMING EAGLE, bought Mayacamas in 2013.

Meritage Basically a Bordeaux blend, red or white. The term was invented for California but has spread. It's a trademark, and users have to belong to The Meritage Alliance. It's supposed to rhyme with heritage but often doesn't.

Merry Edwards Russian RV ★★★★ Salute to Burgundy with California attitude. PINOT N rounded, layered with flavour and edged with dark spice. As a bonus there is a lovely SAUV BL. Merry Edwards, who was voted into the Vintners Hall of Fame in 2012, is a national treasure.

Merryvale Napa V ★★★ Profile is a balanced, luscious CAB SAUV, backed by Silhouette, a rich CHARD; gd MERLOT and v.gd PINOT N. Fruit-forward line under Starmont label.

There is more variation in soils in Napa County than in all of Bordeaux.

Mettler Family Wines Lodi ★★★ The Mettler family have made wine for five generations. They make only ZIN, CAB SAUV, PETITE SIRAH and they do it right: supple, balanced wines, a treat to drink.

Michael David Lodi ★★→★★★ One of the best of the new-wave Lodi producers. Look esp for 7 Deadly ZINS, a light-hearted picnic-plus entry. Appealing CHARD and Petite-Petit, an unusual blend of PETITE SIRAH and PETIT VERDOT.

Miner Family Vineyards Oak ★★★ Powerful CAB SAUV-based reds with gd ageing potential. Look esp for the Icon bottling, a blend of Bordeaux varieties.

Morgan Santa LH ★★★ Top-end single-v'yd PINOT N, CHARD. Esp fine, unoaked Chard Metallico. Estate Double L v'yd farmed organically. Cotes du Crows is charming.

Mt. Brave Mt Veeder ★★★ CAB SAUV is splendid, with soft tannins but gd balance in rounded finish. Also gd MALBEC, MERLOT.

Mumm Napa Valley Napa V ★★★ Stylish bubbly, esp *delicious Blanc de Noirs* and rich, complex DVX single-v'yd fizz to age a few yrs in bottle; also a v.gd Brut Rosé. CHARD, PINOT N worth a glass or three.

Nalle Son ★★★★ Doug Nalle makes balanced, delicious ZINS, a pleasure to drink young, better to age. He's been doing it for decades and always gets it right. CHARD, PINOT N also excellent.

Navarro Vineyards And V ★★★ V.gd RIES, GEWURZ from cool-climate pioneer. Star turn is PINOT N, in two styles: estate-bottled homage to Burgundy from And V grapes; brisk, juicy bottling from bought-in grapes.

Newton Vineyards Spring Mtn ★★★→★★★★ 03 05 06 07 09 10 11 12 The Puzzle, elegant blend of Bordeaux varieties, merits ★★★★. Gd ageing potential. V.gd CAB SAUV, MERLOT, CHARD. Red Label bottlings are fruit-forward, fun to hang out with.

Niebaum-Coppola Estate *See* Inglenook.

Oakville Ranch Oak ★★★ Sometimes overlooked jewel, this estate on Silverado Trail makes consistently gd CAB SAUV and creamy CHARD. Robert's CAB FR is superb.

Ojai Santa B ★★★ Extensive list of v.gd PINOT N, CHARD, Rhônes offered by former AU BON CLIMAT partner Adam Tolmach. Esp Presidio V'yd Pinot N, SYRAH. Rosé based on Syrah is delicious.

Opus One Oak ★★★★ 05 07 09 10 11 Mondavi-Rothschild creation in the heart of Napa has made glorious wines, though not always. *Excellent current form*, esp 2009 – drinkable now but leave it alone for a few yrs.

Ovid Oak ★★★→★★★★ 05 07 An exciting new estate in the hills above Oak. Bright

Bordeaux blends are the star turn but Syrah is also outstanding. Wines are organically farmed.

Pahlmeyer Napa V ★★★ CAB SAUV-based Pièce de Résistance is superb. Right Bank is a v.gd blend of MERLOT, CAB FR. Supple Merlots are a treat. CHARD, PINOT N from Son Coast are excellent.

Paloma Vineyard Spring Mtn ★★★ →★★★★ Intense, massive MERLOT with a dash of CAB SAUV, from v'yd nr summit of Spring Mtn; California's best? Will age 10+ yrs. Palomita is v.gd SYRAH-based blend.

Parducci Mend ★★ →★★★ Reliable, gd-value wines from historic winery. True Grit PETITE SIRAH is brilliant.

Patianna Vineyards Russian RV ★★★ →★★★★ Patty Fetzer makes maybe best SAUV BL in state from bio v'yds in Son County. SYRAH also v.gd, with ageing potential.

Patz & Hall N Coast ★★★ →★★★★ Excellent series of single-v'yd PINOT N, CHARD. Pisoni V'yd Pinot N from Santa LH is top of the line. Pinot N and Chard from Hudson V'yd in Car esp gd.

Paul Hobbs ★★★ Carries the single-v'yd banner to extreme lengths, with eight different CHARDS, five PINOT NS, six CAB SAUVS and a single lonely SYRAH. They have in common depth, intensity, sometimes a lushness not light-years from jammy. All worth a look.

Pedroncelli Son ★★ Old hand in Dry CV producing bright, elbow-bending ZIN, CAB SAUV and solid CHARD.

Peju Napa V ★★★ Something of a showcase winery, but the quality is in the bottle. The Ruth Res CAB SAUV has gd ageing potential.

Periano Lodi ★★ →★★★ Outstanding old-vine ZIN from new-wave Lodi producer; v.gd VIOGNIER, CHARD; gd TEMPRANILLO.

Peter Michael Winery Mont ★★★★ The single-v'yd concept is the driving force of this Englishman's winery, with a dozen bottlngs of excellent CHARD, PINOT N. Les Pavots, a blend of red Bordeaux varieties, is flagship.

Philip Togni Vineyards Spring Mtn ★★★★ 00 01 03 05 07 09 10 11 12 Veteran winemaker makes v. *fine long-lasting Cab Sauv* from Spring Mtn. Tanbark Hill CAB SAUV is less expensive for earlier drinking.

Pine Ridge Napa V ★★★ All about CAB SAUV made from several Napa v'yds. Can be tannic and concentrated, esp Fortis. The Stags L bottling is silky, graceful. Epitome, made only in best yrs, can be superb.

Quintessa Napa V ★★★★ Supple red blend from this bio Ruth estate shows balanced fruit in a homage to Bordeaux. Can age.

Quivira Dry CV ★★★ A v.gd range of Rhône varieties, esp GRENACHE from a bio estate. ZIN is excellent. Gd rosé.

Qupé Santa B ★★★★ Focus is remarkable range of Rhônes, esp brilliant *Marsanne*. Glass or two of PINOT BL or SYRAH would also be welcome. Don't forget the PINOT N.

Rafanelli, A Son ★★★ The Rafanellis have made ZIN for four generations and they do it right: classic intense Zin with bright, brambly fruit will age, but it's so delightful young, why bother? Also gd CAB SAUV.

Ravenswood *See* CONSTELLATION.

Raymond Vineyards and Cellar Napa V ★★★ 01 03 05 07 09 10 11 12 CAB SAUV is the story here and it is well-told. The wines are balanced, understated but apt for long ageing, esp the flagship Generations blend. Also gd CHARD.

Ridge Santa Cz Mts ★★★★ (CAB SAUV) 99 00 01 03 05 07 08 09 10 11 12 Ridge founder Paul Draper is one of the key figures in modern California wine. Supple, harmonious estate *Montebello Cab Sauv* is superb. Also outstanding single-v'yd ZIN from Son, Napa V, Sierra F'hills, P Rob. And don't overlook *outstanding Chard* from wild-yeast fermentation. *Chapeau*, Paul.

Robert Keenan Wines Napa V ★★★ →★★★★ Often overlooked producer of supple

CAB SAUV, MERLOT, CHARD from estate vines on Spring Mtn as well as from valley floor. Res Cab Sauv is consistent ★★★★ quality.

Robert Mondavi ★★ Spotty performance of this Napa icon under CONSTELLATION ownership. Basic Napa CAB SAUV is a look back at Napa classics.

Rochioli Vineyards & Winery Son ★★★ Excellent estate PINOT N, brilliant CHARD and v.gd SAUV BL.

Roederer Estate And V ★★★★ One of the top three sparklers in California and hands-down *the best rosé*. Owned by Champagne Roederer. The house style tends to restraint and supple elegance, esp in luxury cuvée L'Ermitage.

Roger Craig Wines Napa V ★★★ →★★★★ 01 03 05 07 09 10 11 12 CAB SAUV specialist focusing on power and complexity with bottlings from Mt Veeder, Howell Mtn and Spring Mtn. Affinity is supple, elegant homage to Bordeaux. ZIN from Howell Mtn is v.gd.

Round Pond Estate Ruth ★★★ Bovet range of Res CAB SAUV explores Napa terroir. Estate Cab Sauv from Ruth grapes is v.gd, with rounded flavours and bright fruit; v.gd SAUV BL too.

Rusack Santa MV ★★★ Small production winery with outstanding Res CHARD; v.gd single v'yd PINOT N from Santa MV; gd rosé.

Saddleback Cellars Napa V ★★★ 01 05 06 07 08 10 11 12 Owner-winemaker Nils Venge is a legend in Napa V. Lush ZIN, long-lived CAB SAUV. Gd SAUV BL.

St Clement Napa V ★★★ 99 00 01 03 05 06 07 09 10 11 Several bottlings of single-v'yd CAB SAUV, esp Armstrong V'yds Diamond Mtn and multi-v'yd blend Oroppas, show supple power, deep flavours; also v.gd MERLOT, SAUV BL, CHARD.

St Francis Son ★★★ Fruit-friendly wines mostly from Son County grapes; esp gd VIOGNIER, CAB SAUV, excellent old-vine ZIN.

Saintsbury Car ★★★ V.gd terroiristic PINOT N, CHARD from Car vyds. Wines are intense but balanced and engaging. Vincent Vin Gris is a tasty pink.

St-Supéry Napa ★★→★★★ SAUV BL one of best in state; powerful, silky MERLOT; outstanding CAB SAUV, CHARD from Dollarhide Estate V'yd.

Santa Cruz Mountain Vineyard Mend ★★★ Intense estate PINOT N, capable of ageing. GRENACHE from century-old Mend vines is remarkable; gd CAB SAUV in rustic style.

Sbragia Family Wines N Coast ★★★ Ed Sbragia, former winemaker at BERINGER, now on his own finding gd v'yds in Napa and Son to make outstanding CHARD, ZIN, CAB SAUV. Expect a fourth star soon.

Scharffenberger Mend ★★★ The NV Brut Rosé is flat out the best California bubbly buy going. Complex wine with a rich finish balancing the open fruit. Tex Sawyer has been making fizz in Mend for decades. He's got it down.

Schramsberg Napa V ★★★★ J Schram, the creamy and utterly delicious luxury cuvée, has been called California's Krug. Blanc de Noirs is outstanding, as is Brut, while Res is rich, intense. Second label Mirabelle is v. agreeable. V.gd CAB SAUV, J Davies, from mtn estate vines. Schramsberg stands the test of time.

Screaming Eagle Napa V Small lots of cult CAB SAUV at luxury prices for those who like and can afford that kind of thing.

Seghesio Son ★★★ Several v'yd bottlings of superb ZINS, drinkable when young,

---

Turn on the taps

Step up to the bar and order a glass of wine and you may be surprised to see it coming from a tap, v. much like beer. Yes, wine on tap is the coming thing. The wine is stored in kegs and hooked into an inert gas system that pushes the wine out into the glass. The keg system works best with fruit-forward wines. The wines are not only fresher but the keg system offers cost savings as well.

taking on depth with age. Omaggio, CAB SAUV/SANGIOVESE blend, is worth a look. V.gd BARBERA, Sangiovese and lovely ARNEIS, rare in California.

Selene Napa V ★★★★ Mia Klein makes small lots of Bordeaux varietals, and they are superb. Dead Fred V'yd CAB SAUV is top dog, sometimes facing a challenge from Hyde V'yd SAUV BL. There's even a rosé, hurrah.

Sequoia Grove Napa V ★★★ Several bottlings of single-v'yd CAB SAUV, all excellent, intense, concentrated but balanced and built to last. CHARD is also v.gd.

Shafer Vineyards Napa V ★★★→★★★★ (CAB SAUV) 01 02 03 05 07 09 10 11 12 Third-generation family makes potent prize-winners at Stags L. Rich, intense Cab Sauv, esp Hillside Select, plus one of state's best MERLOTS.

Sierra Vista Sierra F'hills ★★★ There's a whole lot of Rhône in the Sierra F'hills, incl outstanding MOURVÈDRE, GRENACHE. Also Old-Vine Own-Root unoaked CHARD.

Silverado Vineyards Stags L ★★★ Solo CAB SAUV shows off Stags L AVA terroir and is excellent; fine CHARD, SAUV BL.

Silver Oak ★★★ Separate wineries in Napa V and Alex V make CAB SAUV only. Napa bottling is classic Cab Sauv, Alex V a bit more supple. Both have loyal following.

Sinskey Vineyards Car ★★★ Outstanding Car MERLOT; single-v'yd CAB SAUV, CHARD; esp bright, charming PINOT N.

Smith-Madrone Spring Mtn ★★★ Superb RIES in off-dry style: brilliant floral minerality. Also v.gd powerful CAB SAUV from high-elevation v'yd. Vines not irrigated.

Sodaro Estate Napa V ★★★ Veterans Bill and Dawnine Dyer are consultants at this newish family winery, so don't look for cult-wine knockoffs here. Wines are elegant, balanced, esp CAB SAUV-based Felicity; v.gd MALBEC.

Sonoma-Cutrer Vineyards Son ★★★ Excellent CHARD, PINOT N from cool-climate v'yds in Russian RV and Son Coast. Chard, made in a flinty style, capable of ageing.

Spottswoode St Helena ★★★★ 97 00 01 03 05 06 07 09 10 11 12 Add to the shortlist of California "first growths". The **outstanding Cab Sauv** is irresistible, will age. Brilliant SAUV BL is a bonus.

Spring Mountain Vineyard Spring Mtn ★★★ Signature Elivette CAB SAUV blend is concentrated with layers of flavour, will age. Estate Cab Sauv v.gd, as is SAUV BL.

Staglin Family Vineyard Ruth ★★★ 03 05 07 09 10 11 12 An elegant CAB SAUV from Rutherford Bench v'yd has gd ageing potential. Estate CHARD is complex, mineral; gd SANGIOVESE.

Stag's Leap Wine Cellars Stags L ★★★★ 00 01 03 05 07 09 10 11 12 Celebrated for silky, seductive CAB SAUVS (SLV, Fay, top-of-line Cask 23), MERLOTS. Gd CHARD is often overlooked. Quality is still gold standard since founder Warren Winiarski sold to Chateau Ste Michelle and Marchese Antinori.

Stags' Leap Winery Napa *See* BERINGER BLASS.

Steele Wines ★★★ Jed Steele is legendary in California. For 40+ yrs he has been finding the right v'yd for the right wine; from A–Z, ALIGOTÉ to ZIN; supple, balanced wines, a pleasure to drink.

Stephen Ross Edna V ★★★ A rising star for PINOT N and CHARD. Burgundian approach adds complexity to single-v'yd bottlings from mostly Edna V grapes. Don't miss the ZIN.

Sterling Napa V ★★→★★★ Showplace 1970s winery, early leader in serious MERLOT; gd CHARD, CAB SAUV.

Stony Hill Napa V ★★★★ (CHARD) 97 99 00 01 03 05 06 07 09 10 11 Legendary pioneer of incredibly long-lived Chard, graceful and supple, and now a CAB SAUV, restrained and balanced, a new Napa classic.

Sutter Home *See* TRINCHERO FAMILY ESTATES.

Swanson Oak ★★★ Alexis CAB SAUV is lean, supple with excellent fruit and balanced finish. Also v.gd MERLOT. Gd SANGIOVESE, Rosato under the Salon label.

Tablas Creek P Rob ★★★ Holy ground for Rhônistas. V'yd based on cuttings from

Châteauneuf, a joint venture between Beaucastel (*see* France) and importer Robert Haas. Côtes de Tablas Red and White are amazingly gd, as is the Tablas Creek Esprit.

Talbott, R Mont ★★★ Supple, engaging CHARD, PINOT N from single v'yds in Mont, with a nod to Burgundy. Look esp for Sleepy Hollow Chard from Santa LH.

Talisman N Coast ★★★ PINOT N is the whole story for Talisman, with half a dozen entries from North Coast v'yds. Red Dog V'yd from Son Mtn is the plot leader with Weir V'yd from Yorkville Highlands in Mend a close second.

Thomas Fogarty Santa Cz Mts ★★★ Spicy, intense GEWURZ here is about as gd as it gets in California. Estate CHARD is layered, complex with some ageing potential; gd PINOT N.

Tor Wines Napa V ★★★ 07 09 10 11 Napa veteran Tor Kenward on his own with several bottlings of CAB SAUV; best is from famed To Kalon v'yd. Rich, intense, to age. Also a fine CHARD from Hudson V'yd. Also look for Kenward's homage to the Rhône under Rock label. GRENACHE is a jewel.

Transcendence Santa B ★★→★★★ Outstanding GRENACHE-anchored Rhône blend Parea; Zotovich v'yd CHARD is excellent as well. V.gd PINOT N from Sta RH.

Treana (Hope Family Wines) P Rob ★★ Only two wines, Treana Red, based on CAB SAUV; Treana White, a VIOGNIER/MARSANNE blend. You can't go wrong with either.

Trefethen Family Vineyards Oak ★★★ 03 04 05 07 08 10 11 12 Historic family winery in Napa. RIES is splendid and will age. CAB SAUV on upward curve in recent vintages. CHARD can be excellent, also ages. Excellent VIOGNIER.

Trinchero Family Estates Napa V ★→★★★ Long-time Napa producer (remember SUTTER HOME White ZIN?) moving upmarket with a series of CAB SAUVs. Esp Chicken Ranch V'yd bottling; Cab Sauv under Napa Wine Company label.

Urban wineries: over 100 in California now, from San Francisco Bay to Brooklyn.

Trione Son ★★★ Top grower now making superb wines from estate v'yds. The velvety Block 21 CAB SAUV from Alex V is a future ★★★★ candidate with ageing potential; v.gd PINOT N, SYRAH from Russian RV. CHARD from Russian RV superb.

Truchard Car ★★★ A Car veteran now offering brilliant bottlings of TEMPRANILLO, ROUSSANNE. Also tangy, lemony CHARD; flavourful MERLOT. CAB SAUV, SYRAH v.gd too.

Tudal St Helena ★★★ Marvellous balanced, elegant CAB SAUV. Could age well beyond a decade. Russian RV CHARD worth a look. Flat Bed Red goes in the picnic basket.

Turnbull Napa V ★★★ 05 06 07 09 10 11 Understated CAB SAUV is Napa classic, powerful yet supple, balanced. The Res bottling should be cellared for 10+ yrs. Fortuna MERLOT is outstanding; v.gd Napa PETITE SIRAH.

Valley of the Moon Son ★→★★ Reliable quaff; PINOT BL and ZIN can reach ★★ level.

Van Ruiten Lodi ★★→★★★ Old-vine ZIN is the go-to wine here. Lovely CARIGNAN.

Viader Estate Napa V ★★★★ 00 01 03 05 06 07 08 09 10 11 12 Long-lived, powerful CAB SAUV-based blends from Howell Mtn estate; V Black Label is new estate MALBEC. Look for small-lot bottlings, incl SYRAH, TEMPRANILLO under the Dare label.

Villa Ragazzi Napa V ★★★ Why can't other California wineries make gd SANGIOVESE? This is flat-out best in state. Gd CAB SAUV/SANGIOVESE blend.

Volker Eisele Family Estate Napa V ★★★→★★★★ 00 01 03 05 07 09 10 11 12 Lusciously balanced CAB SAUV-based blends, esp Terzetto bottling; new offering is Alexander, 100% Cab Sauv. Gemini is lovely, lively SAUV BL/SÉM blend. All from organic grapes.

Wente Vineyards Mont ★★→★★★ There is an obvious effort to raise the quality standard at this historic winery. New CHARD bottlings in particular are more complex. Also v.gd *Livermore Sauv Bl* and SÉM.

Whitehall Lane Ruth ★★★★ Powerful yet elegant CAB SAUV edged into ★★★★ territory with the 2009 vintage. V.gd SAUV BL.

Williams Selyem Son ★★★ Intense, smoky Russian RV PINOT N, esp Rochioli V'yds,
Allen V'yd. V.gd CHARD and ZIN.

Windward P Rob ★★★ Promising new producer, with balanced, burgundian PINOT N.

Wine Group, The Central V ★ Third-largest producer of wine in world by volume,
offering a range of everyday wines, eg. Glen Ellen, also Franzia bag-in-box.

Woodenhead Son ★★★ Brilliant new producer of single-v'yd PINOT N, ZIN. Esp Cinder
Cone Pinot N, Martinelli Road Old-Vine Zin, both from Russian RV. Quirky but
v. tasty exercise in COLOMBARD – still and bubbly – also Russian RV.

Zaca Mesa Santa B ★★★ Focus on estate Rhône varieties showing gd results. Black
Bear Block SYRAH is one of best in state; also Z Three, delicious Syrah/GRENACHE
blend and check out ROUSSANNE.

THE PACIFIC NORTHWEST

California gets all the publicity, and 90% of the sales. Part of the attraction
of the two states further north is their sense of otherness, of needing to
be in the know. Those who find California's wines a bit – shall we say – heavy,
look for refreshment up here. When they look, though, they find much more
than that: clear-etched varietal characters, distinctive regional styles, and
winemakers with we-try-harder outlooks. Now a sudden spate of new outside
investment in Northwest wine country is sparking broader interest in the
wines. Noting Washington's success with Cabernet Sauvignon and Merlot,
California's E & J Gallo Winery and Duckhorn Vineyards, for example, have
made head-turning investments in the state. Similarly, Oregon's reputation for
Pinot Noir has attracted Burgundy's Louis Jadot (Drouhin has been here for
years) and California's Jackson Family Wines to buy vineyards and wineries
there. So will this outside attention spoil Northwest wine's charm? Not likely.
These companies have learned what local wine-lovers have long known: that
the Northwest reliably produces high quality in the face of highly variable
vintages, and consistently delivers value at nearly every price point. All this
new investment should only boost the region's appeal.

Principal viticultural areas

Columbia Valley (Col V) Huge AVA in central and eastern Washington
with a touch in Oregon. Quality Cab Sauv, Merlot, Ries, Chard, Syrah.
Key sub-divisions incl Yakima Valley (Yak V), Red Mountain, Walla AVAs.

Snake River Valley (Snake RV) Idaho's only AVA; partially in Oregon.

Southern Oregon (S Or) Warm-climate region incl AVAs Rogue,
Applegate (App V) and Umpqua Valleys (Um V). Tempranillo, Syrah,
Viognier are v.gd; lots of experimentation.

Willamette Valley (Will V) Oregon's home for cool-climate Pinot N and
Pinot Gr, plus v.gd Chard and dry Ries. Important child AVAs incl Dundee
Hills, Chehalem Mts, Yamhill-Carlton (Y-Car), Eola-Amity Hills.

Walla Walla Valley (Walla) Child AVA of Col V with own identity and vines
in Washington and Oregon. Home of important boutique brands and prestige
labels focusing on quality Cab Sauv, Merlot, Syrah.

The new urban

Urban wineries are taking over Seattle and Portland. Portland has
Southeast Wine Collective, Bow and Arrow Wines and Boedecker
Cellars; Seattle has Falling Rain, Cloudlift and Omnivore Cellars. Lower
costs and proximity to large markets are the attraction. In 2014 there
were over 40 wineries in Portland and Seattle.

Recent vintages

2013 Warm summer, then unusual September coolness and rain. Crisp
   Washington whites and well-balanced reds; Oregon Pinot N will be
   good, but very producer- and site-specific.

2012 Balanced Washington and well-focused, richly fruity Oregon wines.

2011 Classic Oregon Pinot N. In Washington a cool, late harvest produced
   higher-acid, age-worthy wines.

2010 Very cool everywhere, so lower alcohol, higher-acid wines with fresh
   varietal character.

2009 Washington produced concentrated wines. Challenging in Oregon, but
   wines are ripe and pleasing.

2008 Lush, crowd-pleasing Oregon wines; Washington made leaner, complex
   reds and crisp whites.

Oregon

Abacela Vineyards S Or ★★★ Spanish varieties specialist; consistent leader in
   TEMPRANILLO and ALBARIÑO, also v.gd SYRAH, VIOGNIER. Paramour is excellent Rioja-
   style blend.

Adelsheim Vineyard Will V ★★★ →★★★★ 08 09' 10' 11 12' Leading pioneer producer
   with top-notch single-v'yd PINOT N, v.gd Res CHARD, Pinot N and fun AUXERROIS.

Amalie Robert Estate Will V ★★★ 08' 09 10 Family winery making multiple
   excellent estate PINOT N. Also v.gd CHARD and interesting cool-climate Will V
   VIOGNIER and SYRAH.

Anam Cara Cellars Will V ★★★ 08 09 10' Family winery crafting PINOT N with grace
   and depth, esp Nicholas Estate; Dry RIES is also superb; new CHARD is promising.

Antica Terra Will V ★★★ 08 09 10 11' Maggie Harrison left California's Sine Qua
   Non to make Will V PINOT N that now has a cult-like following. Recently added
   highly touted small-batch CHARD.

Archery Summit Will V ★★★ 08 09' 10 11 Impressive PINOT N from estate v'yds in
   Dundee Hills and Ribbon Ridge AVAs. New whites incl a concrete-fermented
   PINOT GR.

Argyle Will V ★★ →★★★ Versatile crafter of reliably excellent PINOT N, CHARD, dry and
   sweet RIES, plus multiple styles of *v.gd bubbly*. Brian Croser involved.

Beaux Frères Will V ★★★ →★★★★ 08 09' 10' 11' Prestige bio estate makes
   increasingly refined, collectible PINOT N. Part-owned by critic Robert M Parker, Jr.

Bergström Wines Will V ★★★ 08 09' 10' 11 12' Josh Bergström's popular, punchy
   PINOT N from bio estate are a treat; he's also a dab hand at CHARD, esp small-lot
   Sigrid bottling.

Average retail price of California wine is $6.13/bottle. For Oregon, it's $15.32.

Bethel Heights Will V ★★ →★★★ 09 10 11 Second-generation family winery; an
   Oregon legend. Spicy and sophisticated PINOT N, *v.gd Chard*, PINOTS GR and BL.

Brandborg Vineyard & Winery S Or ★★ →★★★ Um V PINOT N specialist (Ferris Wheel
   Estate has great complexity) also makes supple PINOT GR, v.gd GEWURZ, SYRAH.

Brick House Will V ★★★ 08 09' 10 Bio leader producing earthy, powerful PINOT N
   (esp Cuvée du Tonnelier), stylish CHARD. The true GAMAY is a fun find.

Broadley Vineyards Will V ★★★ 08 09' 10' 11' 12 Family winery, making characterful
   PINOT N from older estate vines and selected v'yds. Basic Will V release is a steal,
   Claudia's Choice is top-end winner.

Brooks Winery Will V ★★★ 09' 10 11 Leading bio producer. Zesty dry and balanced
   sweet RIES among Northwest's best. Also excellent PINOT N, esp estate Rasteban.

Chehalem Will V ★★★ 08 09' 10' 11 Powerhouse PINOT N producer, equally strong RIES,
   CHARD, PINOT GR. Age-worthy Ridgecrest Pinot N; unoaked *INOX Chard great value.*

Cowhorn S Or ★★★ App V AVA bio purist makes knock-your-socks-off SYRAH; Spiral 36 white blend is sensational. Cult winery in the making.

Cristom Will V ★★★ 08′ 09′ 10 11′ Steve Doerner consistently makes among the best PINOT N in Oregon. Jessie V'yd has a fresh savouriness and Sommers Res boasts truffle overtones.

Dobbes Family Estate Will V ★★→★★★ 08 09 10′ 11′ Eminent winemaker Joe Dobbes; prestige Will V PINOT N (Meyer V'yd tops); plus SYRAH, GRENACHE BL from S Or. Second label Wine by Joe: great bargain Pinot N, PINOT GR.

Domaine Drouhin Oregon Will V ★★★→★★★★ 07 08 09′ 10′ 11 New World branch of Burgundy's Domaine Drouhin. Consistently outstanding PINOT N, minerally CHARD. Barrel-select Laurène Pinot N is amazing. Purchase of Roseneck estate in Eola-Amity Hills brings another 122 acres of Pinot N and Chard.

Saccharomyces cerevisiae (that's wine yeast) is the official state microbe of Oregon.

Domaine Serene Will V ★★★ 08′ 09 10 11 Premium PINOT N consistently wins critical raves. Small-production CHARD is particularly tasty.

Elk Cove Vineyards Will V ★★→★★★ Excellent-value wines from second-generation winemaker. PINOT GR, RIES perennially tops; seven estate-v'yd PINOT N deliver delectable array of Will V terroirs.

Erath Vineyards Will V ★★→★★★ A founding Oregon winery now owned by Washington's Chateau Ste Michelle. Reliable value-priced PINOT-family wines; but rare single-v'd Pinot N are fabulous.

Evening Land Will V ★★★→★★★★ 09′ 10 Seven Springs Summum PINOT N and CHARD are spectacular but expensive. Silver and Gold labels are v.gd estate wines, Blue Label wines are affordable versions.

Eyrie Vineyards Will V ★★★→★★★★ 09′ 10 11 The prophet David Lett planted the first Will V PINOT N. Today son Jason extends the legacy with terrific Pinot N in graceful, classically Oregon, age-worthy style. Also v.gd CHARD and PINOT GR.

Hyland Estates Will V ★★★ 09 10 Oregon veteran Laurent Montalieu uses some of the oldest PINOT N vines in the Will V for succulent, polished wines. Also top-notch RIES, CHARD, GEWURZ,

Ken Wright Cellars Will V ★★★ 08 09′ 10 11′ Perennially popular maker of great single-v'yd PINOT N showing the range of Will V terroirs. Canary Hill is pretty, forward; Freedom Hill dense, firm.

King Estate ★★→★★★ One of state's largest wineries, offering a strong PINOT GR (a speciality) and PINOT N. Value at multiple price points.

Lange Estate Winery Will V ★★★ 09′ 10′ 11 Venerable brand on second-generation roll: mouthwatering PINOT N (Lange Estate), barrel-aged Res PINOT GR, v.gd CHARD.

Matello Will V ★★★ Artisan winery growing in importance. Lazarus and Souris PINOT N are superb, as well as strong PINOT GR, CHARD. Rising star.

Phelps Creek Vineyards ★★ →★★★ Quality-leading Columbia Gorge producer of v.gd CHARD (oaked, unoaked); pretty PINOT N releases showing Gorge fruit character.

Red, white & green

Wine geeks like to argue about the definition and possible merits of so-called "natural" wines (minimal or no artificial inputs to growing or making), but in Oregon the virtues of green viticulture are uncontroversial. Nearly 47% of the state's v'yds merit some manner of sustainable certification. They incl LIVE (Low Input Viticulture and Enology), Oregon Tilth (organic), Demeter Biodynamic®. Preserving the viability of their v'yds and surrounding environment for future generations is the aim; it's not a marketing ploy.

Ponzi Vineyards Will V ★★★→★★★★ 08 09' 10' 11 Legendary PINOT N specialist now in second generation making excellent wines. Aurora PINOT N a knockout; Res CHARD a standout. Don't miss brilliant ARNEIS.

Quady North S Or ★★→★★★ Herb Quady crafts delicious CAB FR from cooler Rogue Valley AVA sites, also intriguing styles of VIOGNIER, concentrated SYRAHS.

Rex Hill Will V ★★★ Bio farming and hand-crafting makes superb estate PINOT N, notable CHARD. Same owner as the more popularly priced A to Z Wineworks.

Scott Paul Wines Will V ★★★ 08 09' 10 PINOT N-only producer emphasizes elegance and grace with sophisticated burgundy character. Le Paulée approachable on release, Audrey gd for cellaring.

Sokol Blosser Will V ★★★ A second-generation maker of lovely PINOT N, PINOT GR from Dundee Hills, also inexpensive fun white blend called Evolution.

Soter Vineyard Will V ★★★→★★★★ 09' 10 11 California legend Tony Soter moved to Oregon to make PINOT N. Estate *Mineral Springs Ranch Pinot N* is sublime, but don't miss the tremendous sparklers: perhaps the Northwest's best.

New from Oregon: Pinot Noir in a can, to encourage "beerification" of wine. Lovely.

Spangler Vineyards S Or ★★★ V.gd warm-climate reds, esp Res CAB SAUV, PETITE SYRAH; VIOGNIER always top-notch.

Stoller Family Estate Will V ★★★ 09' 10 11 Beautifully balanced PINOT N exemplify Dundee Hills elegance; Cathy's Res is exceptional. Also v.gd Res CHARD.

Teutonic Wine Company ★★★ Barnaby and Olga Tuttle are iconoclastic Oregonians making delicious Mosel-inspired RIES, crisp white blends and Germanic-styled PINOT N. Brilliant up-and-comer.

Willamette Valley Vineyards Will V ★★→★★★ Popular publicly owned winery makes excellent estate PINOT N, CHARD; v.gd inexpensive RIES.

Washington & Idaho

Andrew Will Wash ★★★→★★★★ 07' 08 09' 10 Chris Camarda makes stunning red blends from outstanding Col V v'yds. Sorella has big fruit, Ciel du Cheval more structured.

Betz Family Winery Wash ★★★→★★★★ 06 07' 08 09' 10 11 Master of Wine Bob Betz makes Rhône styles from top Col V v'yds. La Serenne SYRAH is extraordinary; powerhouse La Côte Patriarche comes from state's oldest Syrah vines.

Brian Carter Cellars Wash ★★→★★★ Blends only, all masterful. Try unconventional PETIT VERDOT-driven Trentenaire, Byzance Rhône blend, or aromatic white Oriana.

Cadence Wash ★★★ Compelling Bordeaux-style blends incl powerful Coda from Red Mtn fruit and spicy CAB FR-dominant Bel Canto.

Cayuse Walla, Wash ★★★→★★★★ 06' 07 08' 09' 10 11 Cult bio winery delivering *spellbinding Syrah* (esp Cailloux) and amazing GRENACHE, but you have to be on mailing list to get any.

Charles Smith Wines Walla, Wash ★★→★★★ Marketeer/winemaker Charles Smith commands high prices with powerful (too much so?) reds. Royal City SYRAH is a favourite; also inexpensive Kung Fu Girl RIES.

Chateau Ste Michelle Wash ★★→★★★★ Flagship brand of Northwest's largest wine company offers wines in all prices/styles, from v.gd quaffers (excellent Col V Dry RIES) to TBA-style rarities (Eroica Single Berry Select). Gd-value Col V-labelled, premium Ethos Res.

Chinook Wines Col V, Wash ★★★ 08 09' 10 11 Husband (vines) and wife (wines) have a history of fine, value CAB FR (the rosé is delightful), MERLOT, CHARD, SAUV BL.

Cinder Wines Snake RV, ID ★★★ Breakout ID winery making small amounts of marvellous VIOGNIER, a unique MOURVÈDRE/TEMPRANILLO blend, and v.gd SYRAH.

Col Solare Col V, Wash ★★★ 05 06' 07 08 09' CHATEAU STE MICHELLE and Tuscany's

Antinori partner to make a single Col Solare red blend each vintage, invariably complex, long-lasting. Less-expensive Shining Hill blend more approachable.

Columbia Crest Col V, Wash ★★→★★★ Washington's largest winery makes masses of gd, affordable wines under Grand Estates and Two Vines labels. Dandy Res wines esp Walter Clore (r); H3 wines are all from Horse Heaven Hills AVA.

Cote Bonneville Yak V, Wash ★★★ 06 07 08 09' Kerry Shiels uses estate DuBrul V'yd fruit from steep basalt ground and wins medals for deep, sleek CAB blends, esp *Carriage House*. Don't overlook RIES.

DeLille Cellars Wash ★★★→★★★★ 06 07' 08 09 10' Sophisticated producer of age-worthy reds. Harrison Hill CAB SAUV from state's second-oldest v'yd is penetrating; Chaleur Estate blends consistently superb; Grand Ciel is signature wine.

Doubleback Walla, Wash ★★★ 07 08 09 10' Created by football star Drew Bledsoe, the signature CAB SAUV blend (made by Chris Figgins) is a beautiful expression of Walla flavours.

Dusted Valley Vintners Walla, Wash ★★★ Fast-rising star; impressive wines. Popular for Stained Tooth SYRAH; beautiful Old-Vine CHARD or any single-variety release.

Efeste Wash ★★★ Brilliant newcomer for zesty RIES, racy CHARD from cool Evergreen V'yd, also v.gd SYRAHS.

Almost all of Washington's vines are ungrafted; phylloxera is nearly non-existent.

Fidélitas Col V, Wash ★★★ 07 08' 09 10 Charlie Hoppes makes superior Bordeaux-style wines. Luscious Optu red blend; Ciel du Cheval V'yd CAB SAUV shows power of Red Mtn AVA fruit.

FIGGINS (Or), Walla, Wash ★★★ Chris Figgins grew up with his father's LEONETTI CELLAR, but he has est his own identity with Figgins Estate red blend and RIES. New Toil PINOT N from Oregon is a portent of things to come.

Gramercy Cellars Walla, Wash ★★★ 09' 10 11 Master sommelier-turned-winemaker, Greg Harrington, makes voluptuous SYRAHS. Recently added earthy TEMPRANILLO, herby CAB SAUV winners too.

Hedges Family Estate Red Mtn, Wash ★★★ Venerable family winery produces polished and reliable wines, esp estate red blend and DLD SYRAH.

Hogue Cellars, The Col V, Wash ★★→★★★ Stylish value single-variety wines under the Hogue brand. Genesis- and Res-labelled wines are more focused and in smaller production.

Januik Wash ★★★ Artisan wines from a veteran winemaker. Cold Creek CHARD is superb; Champoux V'yd CAB SAUV is edgy and winning.

Koenig Winery Snake RV, ID ★★→★★★ Reliable SYRAH, MERLOT, CHARD. The CSPV is an unusual CAB SAUV/PETIT VERDOT blend.

L'Ecole No 41 Walla, Wash ★★★→★★★★ Everything is gd here. Grab Apogee or Perigee (each from a different v'yd) red blend for a treat, or the cultish SÉM for a remarkably bright, aromatic white.

Leonetti Cellar Walla, Wash ★★★→★★★★ 04' 05 06 07' 08 09 10 Legendary, cult-status winery for elegant, refined, collectable CAB SAUV, MERLOT, SANGIOVESE.

Long Shadows Walla, Wash ★★★→★★★★ Allen Shoup's unique venture brings seven globally famous winemakers to Washington to make their signature variety with Col V fruit. Pedestal MERLOT by France's Michel Rolland is luscious, Feather CAB SAUV by California's Randy Dunn is refined. And all the others are equally impressive.

McCrea Wash ★★★ Rhône-in-the-Northwest pioneer makes first-class wines. The Sirocco blend has layers of complexity. Don't miss exotic Counoise or multiple styles of SYRAH.

Maison Bleue Col V, Wash ★★★ Newish boutique turning heads, esp Upland V'yd GRENACHE and pinpoint-correct MARSANNE, VIOGNIER.

> **Northern light**
> Washington vines get about two hours more sunlight for ripening during the growing season than Napa (Oregon vines get one more hour). Night temperatures are also cooler so grapes naturally retain more acidity for bright flavours. Almost all Northwest v'yds have cold winters so vines are dormant. V'yds west of the Cascades are cool-climate, thanks to sea air. East of the Cascades it's a different matter: dry as dust, with irrigation essential.

Maryhill Winery Wash ★★→★★★ Popular Columbia Gorge AVA producer; huge range. Res ZIN and Res CAB FR are always v.gd, also RIES.

Millbrandt Vineyards Col V, Wash ★★ Well-made value varietal wines; consistent quality from the Wahluke Slope and Ancient Lakes AVAs.

Nefarious Cellars Col V, Wash ★★★ Wife-and-husband craft producer in the Lake Chelan AVA making v.gd SYRAH, VIOGNIER, RIES.

Northstar Walla, Wash ★★★→★★★★ 06 07' 08 Winemaker "Merf" Merfeld is a MERLOT maven. Recent Premier Merlot is drop-dead gorgeous, Walla Walla Merlot is sultry.

Pacific Rim Wash ★★→★★★ RIES specialist making oodles of tasty, inexpensive yet eloquent Dry and Organic. For profoundly, *single-v'yd releases*, incl bio-farmed, are unbeatable.

Pepper Bridge Walla, Wash ★★★ 06' 07 08 09 10' Estate Pepper Bridge and Seven Hills V'yds are among Washington's best. CAB SAUV sensuous and rich, MERLOT spicy and aromatic.

Quilceda Creek Wash ★★★★ 01 02' 03' 04' 05'' 06 07 09 Extraordinary, often 100-point-scoring *Cab Sauv* from one of the most lauded producers in North America: dense, intense, tremendously long-lasting. Find it if you can.

Ste Chapelle Snake RV, ID ★→★★ ID's first and largest winery makes quaffable RIES, inexpensive bubbly and Icewines.

Seven Hills Winery Walla, Wash ★★★ Respected esp for silky CAB SAUV (Klipsun V'yds is massive and beautiful), though VIOGNIER is a delight too.

Snoqualmie Vineyards Col V, Wash ★★ Innovative producer of v.gd CAB SAUV, MERLOT. Naked Wines (no oak) from organic v'yds are v. popular. Look esp for luscious Naked RIES.

Spring Valley Vineyard Walla, Wash ★★★ 06' 07 08 09 10' Nina Lee SYRAH is lip-smacking gd; Uriah MERLOT is blend deep and refined; Frederick red blend is suave and polished.

Syncline Wash ★★★ James Mantone makes excellent wines from Columbia Gorge and Col V fruit. Subduction Red is hedonistic, GRENACHE BLANC is great.

Waterbrook Walla, Wash ★→★★ Large producer of diverse, gd-value wines in multiple styles at many price points.

Woodward Canyon Walla, Wash ★★★→★★★★ (CAB SAUV) 02 03 04' 06 07 09 Impeccable wines. *Old Vines Cab Sauv* is refined, complex; Charbonneau MERLOT scrumptious, ageable; estate BARBERA a silky surprise.

NORTHEAST, SOUTHEAST & CENTRAL

From winter's icy grip on Lake Erie to Georgia's blisteringly hot summers, the eastern United States is a vast and diverse area. It's still in its infancy compared to the rest of the wine world, but progress in wine quality and quantity is swift and impressive. Good Rieslings from upstate New York, savoury Cabernet Francs from Long Island and complex Bordeaux red blends from Virginia all represent today's remarkable outpouring from the East.

Recent vintages

In such a broad region there are many isolated exceptions, but overall the 2013 harvest yielded good quantity, quality and flavour, though perhaps it was not quite as outstanding as 2010 and 2012 in much of the East. Summer was a little rainier and cooler in many regions, but warmer, dry weather at harvest time promised well. In general, harvest began at the normal time, unlike in 2012, when it started three weeks earlier than usual.

21 Brix NY ★★★ 12 13 Young winery (founded 2011) in NY appellation of Lake Erie has already garnered kudos for astonishingly gd wines incl CHARD, RIES and GEWURZ.

Alba NJ ★ Unique microclimate for gd PINOT N and CAB FR, and excellent RIES.

Anthony Road Finger L, NY ★★★★ 10 12 13 Talented German winemaker crafts some of the best dry and semi-dry RIES in the US, as well as fine GEWURZ, PINOT GR and late-harvest Vignoles and CAB FR.

Barboursville VA ★★★★ 09 10 11 12' 13 Historic VA estate founded 1976 by Italy's Zonin family on site once frequented by Thomas Jefferson. Consistent leader in the East, with succulent Bordeaux-style blend and excellent CAB FR, plus outstanding Italian varieties, incl BARBERA and NEBBIOLO. NB the rich ***Malvaxia***. Elegant inn and Tuscan-style restaurant.

Bedell Long I, NY ★★★★ 09 10 11 12' 13 Stylish LONG ISLAND estate, one of the East's premier producers. Influential winemaker turns out notable CHARD, GEWURZ and MERLOT; superb SYRAH and CABS plus dynamite blends. Knowledgeable tasting-room staff, handsome gardens.

Boxwood VA ★★★★ 10 12 13 Classy small estate specializing in high-end Bordeaux-style red blends.

Breaux VA ★ 10 12 13 va hilltop v'yd an hour from Washington DC. Gd SAUV BL, VIOGNIER, MERLOT, NEBBIOLO.

Casa Larga ★★ 10 11 12 Fine FINGER LAKES family-run estate with notable RIES, GEWURZ, PINOT N and VIDAL Icewine.

Channing Daughters Long I, NY ★★★ 10 (11) 12 13 South Fork estate with v.gd Tocai FRIULANO, PINOT GRIGIO and a variety of savoury rosés; also MERLOT, CABS FR and SAUV and v. creative blends.

Chateau O'Brien VA Est 2005; promising MALBEC, PETIT MANSENG, PETIT VERDOT, CAB FR and TANNAT.

Chester Gap VA ★★ 11 12 13 High-altitude v'yds yield excellent wines, incl exceptional PETIT MANSENG and gd VIOGNIER, MERLOT, CAB FR and a dynamic red blend.

Chrysalis VA ★★ 10 12 13 Benchmark VIOGNIER and Norton; v.gd PETIT MANSENG, ALBARIÑO, TANNAT and PETIT VERDOT.

Delaplane VA ★★★ 10 12 13 Spectacular vistas of Blue Ridge Mtns; complex wines, incl CHARD, VIOGNIER, TANNAT, CAB FR and toothsome Bordeaux-style red blends.

Finger Lakes NY Bucolic region in upstate NY with deep glacial lakes whose mass of water helps protect vines in harsh winters. Most of the 342 wineries cluster around the four major lakes. Top wineries incl ANTHONY ROAD, DR. KONSTANTIN FRANK, FOX RUN, HEART & HANDS, HERMANN J WIEMER, KEUKA SPRING, LAMOREAUX LANDING, Ravines, MCGREGOR, Red Tail Ridge, KING FERRY, Silver Thread, STANDING STONE and Swedish Hill. Up-and-coming: Kemmeter Wines.

Fox Run Finger L, NY ★★ 10 12 13 FINGER LAKES producer of quality RIES, CHARD, GEWURZ, rosé, PINOT N. Café overlooking Lake Seneca features local cheese etc.

Frank, Dr. Konstantin (Vinifera Wine Cellars) Finger L, NY ★★★★ 08 09 10 11 12 13 Est more than 50 yrs ago and first FINGER L estate to plant *vinifera*. Produces some of the best ***Ries*** in the US, plus excellent GEWURZ; gd CHARD, RKATSITELI and PINOT N. Fine Château Frank sparkling.

Georgia With more than 15 wineries, look for Wolf Mtn, Frogtown, Three Sisters,

Habersham V'yds, Tiger Mtn. In Atlanta, Château Élan, a conference centre, resort and winery, produces wines based on native Muscadine grapes.

Glen Manor Vineyards VA ★★ 10 11 12 13 Gd SAUV BL and impressive red Bordeaux-style blend.

Hamptons, The (aka South Fork) Long I, NY Coastal LONG I region with three wineries: CHANNING DAUGHTERS, Duckwalk and WÖLFFER ESTATE.

Heart & Hands Finger L, NY ★★★ 09 10 11 12 13 Small operation (2,000 cases) producing much-admired RIES and PINOT N.

Hermann J Wiemer Finger L, NY ★→★★ 08 11 12 13 One of the East's most esteemed wineries, est by German winemaker in 1976. Dazzling RIES, excellent CHARD and GEWURZ, also exceptional sparkling wine.

Hillsborough VA ★★ 11 12 13 VA winery with gd CAB S and PETIT MANSENG, plus interesting blends such as PETIT VERDOT/TANNAT/FER SERVADOU.

Horton 11 12 13 Early VA visionary (first vintage 91). Signature VIOGNIER, Norton.

Hudson River Region NY Borders the scenic Hudson River 90 minutes' drive north of Manhattan. America's oldest winemaking and grape-growing region, now has 42 wineries.

Hardscrabble: not a word game, but poor vineyard soils of steep Blue Ridge Mountains.

Keswick VA ★★ 10 12 13 V.gd VIOGNIER, TOURIGA, CAB SAUV plus unique and ageable late-harvest Norton.

Keuka Spring Finger L, NY ★★ 11 12 For 25 yrs one of FINGER LAKES' most reliable producers of RIES and Vignoles. Gd CAB FR, PINOT N and MERLOT.

King Family Vineyards VA ★★ 10 12 13 Gd Meritage, CHARD, VIOGNIER, CAB FR, succulent *vin de paille*-style Viognier/PETIT MANSENG dessert wine.

King Ferry / Treleaven Wines Finger L, NY ★★ 12 13 V. fine RIES, CHARD, rosé, MERITAGE. Exceptional dessert wines, incl late-harvest Vignoles and Ries.

Lake Erie NY, Oh, Penn Tri-state AVA that incl portions of NY, PENNSYLVANIA and OHIO. Standout producers: 21 Brix and Mazza Chautauqua Cellars. Look for RIES, PINOT GR, CHARD, Icewine and high-quality eau de vie.

Lamoreaux Landing Finger L, NY ★★★ 08 10 11 12 13 Handsome winery with superb lake views. Excellent *Chard*, RIES, GEWURZ, MERLOT and Icewine.

Linden VA ★★★ 10 12' 13 An hour's drive west of Washington DC. One of VA's best and most influential estates; notable high-altitude wines, incl zesty SAUV BL, also CAB FR, PETIT VERDOT, lean, energetic Bordeaux-style red blends, excellent late-harvest PETIT MANSENG.

Long Island NY Easy access from NYC. One of earliest wine regions in the East (first winery est 1973); 53 commercial wineries, two AVAs: Long I/NORTH FORK and Long I/THE HAMPTONS, aka The South Fork), with most estates on NORTH FORK. Leaders incl BEDELL, CHANNING DAUGHTERS, MACARI, PAUMANOK, SHINN ESTATE, SPARKLING POINTE and WÖLFFER.

Macari Long I, NY ★★★ 07 09 10 11 12 Handsome estate with savoury CHARD, MERLOT, Bordeaux-style reds.

McCall Long I, NY ★★★★ 10 11 12 One of LONG ISLAND's finest young estates (first vintage 07) already wowing with excellent PINOT N, CHARD, MERLOT and Bordeaux-inspired red blends.

McGregor ★★ 10 11 12 Venerable FINGER L winery est 1980. Gd CAB FR, CAB SAUV, PINOT N, RIES.

Maryland 64 wineries are producing surprisingly fine wines, from PINOT GR to Bordeaux-style reds. Black Ankle, Knob Hall, Slack, Sugarloaf and Big Cork have risen to impressive heights. Elk Run's CAB FR and other reds continue to please.

Michael Shaps / Virginia Wineworks VA ★★★ 09 10 12 13 Superb VIOGNIER, one of the VA's best, plus complex CHARD, notable PETIT VERDOT, CAB FR, MERLOT and fine

> **Frozen north**
> How do you grow grapes in places that are just too cold? Join the
> Northern Grapes Project: 12 universities, 19 producer groups, 3,000+
> acres of cold-hardy grapes from the upper Midwest to New England.
> Grapes incl Prairie Star, Petit Amie and Edelweiss.

MERITAGE. Succulent Raisin d'Etre dessert-style made with dried Petit Verdot and
Cab Fr grapes.

Michigan 102 wineries now, with Bel Lago, Black Star, Boathouse, Bowers
Harbor, Brys, Chateau Fontaine, Chateau Grand Traverse, Fenn Valley, Tabor
Hill, L Mawby and St Julian leading the pack and turning out impressive RIES,
GEWURZ and PINOT GR; v.gd CAB FR and blends. Also notable: Chateau Chantal, 45
North, Lawton Ridge, Left Foot Charley, 2 Lads and Verterra. Up-and-coming:
Hawthorne V'yds, Laurentide.

Millbrook NY ★★ 12 13 Hudson Valley estate with decent CHARD, FRIULANO, CAB FR.

Missouri The University of Missouri has a new experimental winery to test
techniques and grape varieties in local conditions. Best so far: SEYVAL BL, VIDAL,
Vignoles (sweet and dry versions) and Chambourcin. Stone Hill in Hermann
produces v.gd Chardonel (a frost-hardy hybrid of Seyval Bl and CHARD), Norton
and gd Seyval Bl and Vidal Blanc. Hermannhof is also drawing notice for
Vignoles, Chardonel and Norton. Also notable: St James for Vignoles, Seyval,
Norton; Mount Pleasant in Augusta for rich fortified and Norton; Adam
Puchta for fortifieds and Norton, Vignoles, Vidal Blanc; Augusta Winery
for Chambourcin, Chardonel, Icewine; Les Bourgeois: gd SYRAH, Norton,
Chardonel, Montelle, v.gd Cynthiana and Chambourcin.

New Jersey Leading wineries in this small state incl Cape May (CHARD, CABS SAUV /
FR and PINOT GRIGIO), Unionville (Chard, Pinot Grigio and PINOT N) and ALBA
(outstanding dry GEWURZ, RIES, Chard, plus the largest planting of Pinot N on
the East Coast).

New York (NY) New York state has advanced at an astounding pace in wine quality,
v'yd acreage and number of wineries. With 342 producers today NY has gained
108 wineries in the past five yrs. Significant regions: FINGER L, LONG I, HUDSON R
and Catskills, Central NY, LAKE ERIE, Niagara Escarpment, Greater Adirondacks,
Lake Ontario, Lake Champlain, Thousand Islands, NY City.

North Carolina This southern state now has 120 wineries, incl Biltmore, Childress,
Duplin (for Muscadine), Hanover Park, Iron Gate, Laurel Gray, McRitchie,
Old North State, Ragapple Lassie, RayLen, Raffaldini, Shelton, Westbend. Top
varieties: CHARD, VIOGNIER, CAB FR and native Muscadine.

North Fork Long I, NY Ritzy summer playground for Manhattanites. Its potato-
fields became the first Long I v'yds. Top estates incl BEDELL, CHANNING DAUGHTERS,
MACARI, PAUMANOK, SHINN ESTATE, SPARKLING POINTE, WÖLFFER.

Ohio 188 wineries, five AVAs. Some exceptional PINOT GR, RIES, PINOT N, Icewine.
In Southern Ohio CAB FR. Top producers: Breitenbach, Debonné, Ferrante,
Firelands, Harpersfield, Henke, Kinkead Ridge, Markko, Paper Moon, St Joseph
and Valley V'yds.

Paumanok Long I, NY ★★★ 08 10 12 13 Family-run NORTH FORK (LONG I) founded
1982. Quality RIES, CHARD, Bordeaux-inspired red blends. Exceptional CHENIN BL.

Pennsylvania 170 wineries. Top estates: Blair (PINOT N, CHARD), Briar Valley (RIES, CAB
FR), Allegro (red Bordeaux blend), Galen Glen (GRÜNER VELTLINER and ZWEIGELT),
Galer (Bordeaux reds), Karamoor (Cab Fr, red blends), Manatawny Creek (CHARD,
GEWURZ, PINOT GRIGIO, Cab Fr, MERITAGE), Nimble Hill (Ries, Gewurz), Penns Wood
(Chard, Pinot Grigio, MERLOT, CABS), Pinnacle Ridge (Bordeaux blend, Chard),
Waltz (Chard, Cabs), Va La (Italian varieties).

Pollak VA ★★ 10 12 13 Top VA producer of CHARD, PINOT GR, rosé, CAB FR, MERLOT, MERITAGE, VIOGNIER.

Ravines Finger L, NY ★★★ 10 11 12' 13 FINGER L estate owned by French-raised oenologist producing exceptional v'yd-designate and other gd dry *Ries*.

RdV VA ★★★ 12 13' Young estate (opened 2011) producing serious, intensely flavourful and complex blends inspired by Bordeaux, plus California brio.

Red Tail Ridge Finger L, NY ★★★ 12 13 Stunningly gd wines from new estate (founded 2004) incl RIES, CHARD, DORNFELDER, PINOT N.

Shinn Estate Long I, NY ★★★★ 09 10, 11, 12, 13 Superior CHARD, SAUV BL, MERLOT, MALBEC. Lovely little inn.

Sparkling Pointe Long I, NY ★★→★★★ Estate specializing in sparkling wines made by French winemaker Gilles Martin, some with bottle-age, others youthful and vivacious.

Swedish Hill Finger L, NY ★★★ 12 13 Pioneering winery (since 1969); consistently gd CHARD, RIES, sparkling, Vignoles late-harvest and CAB FR.

Unionville Vineyards NJ ★ 12 13 Notable CHARD, RIES, PINOT GR; fine Bordeaux-style red.

Veritas VA ★★ 10 12 13 Gd producer with fine sparkling, CHARD, VIOGNIER, CAB FR, MERLOT, PETIT VERDOT and Bordeaux-inspired red blend. Elegant little inn.

Villa Appalaccia VA ★ 10 12 13 On the scenic Blue Ridge Parkway, Italian-inspired estate produces PRIMITIVO, SANGIOVESE, PINOT GR, VERMENTINO and MALVASIA Bianca.

Middleburg Virginia is America's 198th AVA, and the state's seventh.

Virginia One of the fastest-growing wine-producing states in the East, with 248 wineries. Overall quality has skyrocketed, with wines of real style and elegance now; esp gd VIOGNIER, PETIT MANSENG, PETIT VERDOT, CAB FR, TANNAT.

Wisconsin Best is Wollersheim Winery, specializing in variations of Maréchel Foch. Prairie Fumé (SEYVAL BL) is a commercial success.

Wölffer Estate Long I, NY ★★ 10 12' 13 Lovely Tuscan-inspired estate with fine CHARD, praiseworthy CAB SAUV and gd MERLOT from talented German-born winemaker.

THE SOUTHWEST

Wine is booming here. The region now has 616 wineries – a 23% increase in two years – and the competition has triggered a dramatic increase in quality at the best wineries. It's a fragile boom, though. The last few vintages have been hot and dry with large swathes of damaging hail. This has reduced crops, which has placed a great deal of pressure both on wineries to find viable grapes and on vineyard owners to raise prices. The combination of higher-priced grapes and lower yields has forced many winemakers to seek grapes from less problematic areas on the West Coast. Customers want reasonably priced wine made from local fruit and there's just not enough to go around. So, *caveat emptor*. You can tell a lot about a winery from how truthfully it labels its wines.

Arizona Arizona Stronghold: ★★ excellent white blend Tazi, v.gd CHARD and red blend called Nachise. Caduceus Cellars: ★★ owned by Tool lead singer Maynard James Keenan; top reds Sancha, Anubis and Nagual del la Naga and v.gd rosé Lei Li Rose. Callaghan V'yds: ★★★ one of Arizona's best wineries, esp red blends Padres and Caitlin's. Cimarron: label of Dick Erath of Oregon producing red blend Rojo del Sol. Dos Cabezas: ★ look for rosé called Pink Wine, red blends Campo and Aguileon. Keeling Schaefer V'yds: ★★ Best Friends VIOGNIER and Three Sisters SYRAH. Lawrence Dunham V'yds: ★ gd Viognier and v.gd PETITE SIRAH. Lightning Ridge: v.gd PRIMITIVO. Page Springs: ★ Rhône-style (r w), plus excellent Colibri Syrah and v.gd Petite Sirah and La Flor Rosa rosé. Pillsbury

Wine Company: ★→★★ filmmaker Sam Pillsbury makes excellent WildChild White and Roan Red. Sand-Reckoner V'yds: gd red blend "7".

Becker Vineyards Tex ★★★→★★★★ Superb collection of interesting wines. Esp CAB SAUV Res Canada Family, Newsom Cab Sauv, VIOGNIER, Res MALBEC, Clementine.

Bending Branch Tex ★★→★★★ Young winery already producing a number of excellent wines, incl PICPOUL Blanc, PETITE SIRAH and Newsom V'yds CAB SAUV.

Brennan Vineyards Tex ★→★★★ Excellent VIOGNIER and white Rhône blend called Lily, v.gd TEMPRANILLO, CAB SAUV and SYRAH.

Brushy Creek Tex Owned by a nuclear physicist who likes to experiment. Wines change on an annual basis, but Rhône varietals always gd.

Cap Rock Tex Much-medalled High Plains winery with remarkable ***Roussanne***.

Colorado Bookcliff: ★★ excellent CAB FR, Bordeaux blend called Ensemble, v.gd PETITE SIRAH and SYRAH. Boulder Creek: ★ excellent MERLOT, plus v.gd Cab Fr and rosé called Dry Rose. Canyon Wind: excellent PETIT VERDOT, Merlot and Bordeaux blend IV. Creekside: ★ award-winning Cab Fr and Syrah, excellent red blend Robusto. Graystone: specializes in three Port-styles, all v.gd. Grande River: MERITAGE White, VIOGNIER, Cab Fr, Petit Verdot, MALBEC. Guy Drew: ★★★ excellent Viognier, GEWURZ, unoaked CHARD, Syrah, Metate. Infinite Monkey Theorem: ★★ excellent red blend called 100th Monkey, v.gd Petit Verdot and VIOGNIER/ROUSSANNE blend Blind Watchmaker White, and gd line of canned wines. Jack Rabbit Hill: bio and organic, PINOT GR, M&N. Ruby Trust Cellars: ★★ new and heavily touted winery with three v.gd to excellent red blends. Two Rivers: ★ excellent RIES, v.gd Merlot, Syrah. Winery at Holy Cross: ★ excellent Cab Fr, v.gd Syrah, Merlot.

Dotson Cervantes Tex ★ Outstanding dessert wine Gotas de Oro.

Duchman ★★★ One of Tex's best; nr-perfect VERMENTINO, DOLCETTO; excellent TREBBIANO.

Fall Creek V'yds Tex ★★★ One of Tex's oldest wineries. Gorgeous Salt Lick TEMPRANILLO, consistent, top Bordeaux blend Meritus, v.gd Res CHARD, delicious off-dry CHENIN BL.

Haak Winery Tex ★ Gd MALBEC, dry Blanc du Bois; one of US best "Madeira" copies.

Inwood Estates Tex ★★★ Exceptional TEMPRANILLO and v.gd PALOMINO/CHARD blend. Small but outstanding producer.

Llano Estacado Tex ★★ One of Texas's earliest and largest wineries. V.gd Viviana (w) and Viviano (r), Port-style.

Lost Oak Tex ★ V.gd VIOGNIER, TEMPRANILLO, gd MERLOT.

McPherson Cellars Tex ★★★ The first big award-winner in Texas; some of the best Rhône-varietal wines in the state. Delicious Rosé of SYRAH, excellent ROUSSANNE.

Messina Hof Wine Cellars Tex ★ Excellent RIES, esp late-harvest. V.gd Papa Paolo Port-style wines.

Nevada Churchill V'yds: gd SÉM/CHARD. Pahrump Valley: v.gd PRIMITIVO, TEMPRANILLO.

New Mexico Black Mesa: ★★ Coyote, PINOT N, Woodnymph RIES. Gruet: ★★★★ ***excellent sparkling wines***, esp Blanc de Noirs, also excellent CHARD, Pinot N. Heart of the Desert: v.gd SYRAH, GEWURZ. Luna Rossa: ★★ v.gd SHIRAZ, TEMPRANILLO. Noisy Water: esp Chard and Shiraz. Ponderosa Valley: ★ v.gd Chard and off-dry Jemez Red. Southwest Wines: ★★★ esp St Clair MALVASIA Bianca and sparkling wines DH Lescombes Brut and St Clair Bellissimo.

Oklahoma Chapel Creek: ★ v.gd MUSCAT, RIES, TEMPRANILLO, Norton. Ponderosa Valley: ★ esp RIES and Jemez Red. Summerside V'yd: ★★ esp v.gd Cream "Sherry". The Range V'yd: gd white blend called Jackwagon. Whispering Meadows: v.gd CAB.

Pedernales Cellars Tex ★★★ Award-winning VIOGNIER Res, excellent TEMPRANILLO, Viognier and GARNACHA Dry Rosé. MERLOT is the bargain of the list.

Spicewood Vineyards Tex ★★ Exceptional Sancerre-like SAUV BL and v.gd SÉM.

Val Verde Tex A fifth-generation tradition. V.gd Port-style.

William Chris Wines Tex ★ In tiny Hye, this winery is widely considered one of Texas's finest. Best buys are red blends Emotion and Enchanté.

Mexico

There are about 55,000 hectares of wine grapes planted in Mexico. Wine has been made there since the Spanish conquest and the first winery, Hacienda San Lorenzo, was established in 1597. It's now called Casa Madero and is still in production in the Parras Valley of central Mexico. Most of the wine grapes in the nation's centre go for brandy production. Quality wine production is in the coastal valleys of northern Baja, especially the Guadalupe Valley southeast of Tijuana. Although the temperature can reach 38°C (100°F), cooling Pacific winds can drop the temperature by up to 16°C (29°F) after sunset. In the past decades, there has been an explosion of boutique wineries, some showing good quality.

Bibayoff Vinos ★★→★★★ V'yds were first planted in the 19th century by Russian immigrants. Hillside vines are dry-farmed. Outstanding ZIN and a v.gd Zin/CAB SAUV blend. Zesty CHENIN BL.

Bodegas Santo Tomás ★★→★★★ Oldest winery in Baja, founded in 1888, has a respectable portfolio of wines. Best offerings: TEMPRANILLO, CAB SAUV, SAUV BL.

Casa de Piedra ★★★ Artisan producer making Vino de Piedra, v.gd blend of CAB SAUV/TEMPRANILLO and Piedra del Sol, CHARD, and three sparklers.

Château Camou ★★→★★★ Top marks to Gran Vino Tinto, a velvety, balanced CAB SAUV-based blend, with a supple, elegant finish. Gran Vino Tinto ZIN is powerful statement of the variety.

LA Cetto ★→★★★ Baja's largest winery, est 1928, offers a range of wines from simple quaffs to more complex CAB SAUV, ZIN from specific v'yds. Don Luis is top of line with v.gd Cab Sauv blend and floral VIOGNIER.

LA Cetto not only offers picnic facilities but its own bull-ring.

Monte Xanic ★★→★★★ Est 1987, Monte Xanic quickly built a reputation for top quality; CAB SAUV is excellent, deeply flavoured with long finish; also v.gd MERLOT. CHENIN BL, with a dash of COLOMBARD, is a delightful apéritif.

Rognato ★★→★★★ Small new winery making excellent CAB SAUV and super red blend, Tramonte, with layers of flavour and lasting finish. Gd future prospects.

Tres Mujeres ★★→★★★ Gd example of the new wave of artisan producers in Baja. Excellent TEMPRANILLO; v.gd GRENACHE/CAB SAUV and La Mezcla del Rancho.

Viñas de Garza ★★ Viñas de Garza is a newcomer making v.gd reds. Top of the list is Tres Valles, an engaging blend of CAB SAUV and GRENACHE.

Vinisterra ★★ New producer has taken the Rhône route, with the best offering Pedregal, a deeply flavoured blend of SYRAH and MOURVÈDRE.

MEXICO

Canada

Canada now has some 600 wineries from coast to coast. Vineyard land is becoming scarce in the pioneering Niagara Peninsula and the Okanagan Valley of British Columbia, so entrepreneurs are expanding to new sites on Vancouver Island, Ontario's Prince Edward County, Quebec's Eastern Townships and further east into Atlantic Canada. The best wines are mostly dry and reflect a fresh, cool-climate style. Across the country a new energy from young vintners, with broader international experience, is contributing to a steady rise in production and quality standards. In Ontario Chardonnay, Riesling, Pinot Noir and Cabernet Franc stand out while in British Columbia the stars are Pinot Gris, Chardonnay, Pinot Noir, red blends and Syrah. On the Atlantic coast, Nova Scotia makes some good sparkling wine and small amounts of aromatic whites.

Ontario

Four appellations of origin, all adjacent to Lakes Ontario and Erie: Niagara Peninsula (Niag), Lake Erie North Shore, Pelee Island, Prince Edward County (P Ed). Niagara Peninsula boasts ten growing areas.

13th Street Niag r w sp ★★ 07 10' 11 12 (13) Winemaker Jean-Pierre Colas uses estate and purchased fruit in his GAMAY, CHARD, RIES, SAUV BL, SYRAH and sparkling; the best are tagged Old Vines, Res and Essence.

Cave Spring Niag r w sw sp ★★★ 10' 11 12 (13) Limestone, shale and clay soils are key to producing top RIES, esp CSV (old vines) and Estate labels, elegant, old-vines CHARD, exceptional late-harvest.

Château des Charmes Niag r w sw ★★ 09 10' 11 12 (13) The 114-ha Bosc family farm is a charter member of Sustainable Winegrowing Ontario; RIES from bone-dry to Icewine. Equuleus is flagship Bordeaux-style red.

Le Clos Jordanne Niag r w ★★★ 09 10' 11 12 (13) Thriving under winemaker Sebastien Jacquey's elegant, organic burgundian-style CHARD and PINOT N in three tiers: Village Res, Single V'yd and Grand Clos.

Creekside Niag r w ★★★ 09 10 11 (12) Gd buzz for Broken Press and Res SHIRAZ, red blends, CHARD and excellent SAUV BL. NB organic, single-barrel Undercurrent lots.

Flat Rock Niag r w ★★ 10' 11 12 (13) 80 acres on Jordan Bench yield modern cool-climate style RIES, PINOT N, CHARD. Single-block Nadja's Ries is usually best.

Henry of Pelham Niag r w sw sp ★★ 10' 11 12 (13) Family-run, Niagara-centric; CHARD and RIES; unique Baco Noir and Ries Icewine. Exceptional Cuvée Catherine Brut fizz and Speck Family Reserve (SFR).

Hidden Bench Niag r w ★★★★ 09 10' 11 (12) Less is more; 40-ha artisanal Beamsville Bench winery. Outstanding RIES, PINOT N, CHARD and Nuit Blanche white blend.

Inniskillin Niag r w sw ★★ 10' 11 12 (13) The pioneer Icewine house is evolving under winemaker Bruce Nicholson. Look for delicious RIES, PINOT GR, PINOT N, super CAB FR, speciality Ries, VIDAL Icewine.

Peller Estates Ice Cuvée sparkling uses Icewine as *liqueur de dosage*. Why not?

Jackson-Triggs Niag r w ★★ 10' 11 12 (13) State-of-art winery. Top labels incl Grand Res Entourage sparkler and Gold Series Delaine V'yd CHARD, PINOT N, SHIRAZ.

Malivoire Niag r w ★★★ 09 10' 11 12 (13) Martin Malivoire leads an eco-friendly operation making excellent Tête de Cuvée GAMAY and CHARD; tasty PINOT N, GEWURZ.

Norman Hardie P Ed r w ★★★★ 09 10' 11 (12) Iconic P Ed pioneer hand-crafting burgundian-style CHARD, PINOT N; v.gd RIES. Cuvée L series made in finest yrs.

Pearl Morissette Niag r w ★★ 10 11 (12) François Morissette (winemaker/partner) trained under Frédéric Mugnier makes original RIES aged in *foudre*, CHARD, CAB FR, PINOT N with concrete eggs and *foudres*.

Ravine Vineyard Niag r w ★★★ 10' 11 12 (13) The 14-ha St David's Bench v'yd lies over an ancient Niagara River watercourse. V.gd Res CHARD and CAB FR; Sand and Gravel range are the drink-now labels.

Stratus Niag r w ★★★ 07 08 09 10 11 (12) Iconoclast JL Groux guides LEEDS-certified (ie. green) winery; Stratus blends (r w) are king; plus v.gd RIES, SYRAH.

Tawse Niag r w ★★★★ 09 10' 11 12 (13) The gold standard in eco-friendly wine production making outstanding CHARD, RIES, high-quality PINOT N, CAB FR, MERLOT; v'yds certified organic and bio.

Vineland Niag r w sw ★★★ 09 10' 11 12 (13) Niagara Escarpment country estate with first-class restaurant. Fine RIES, Icewine, SAUV BL and CAB FR.

British Columbia

BC has identified five appellations of origin: Okanagan Valley (Ok V), Similkameen Valley, Fraser Valley, Vancouver Island and the Gulf Islands.

Blue Mountain Ok V r w sp ★★★ 09 10 11 12 (13) Next generation Matt and Christy Mavety bring new energy to a great sparkling wine programme; age-worthy PINOT N, CHARD, PINOT GR. Outstanding Res Pinot N.

Burrowing Owl Ok V r w ★★ 09 11 12 (13) Pioneer South Okanagan estate. Excellent CAB FR; v.gd PINOT GR, SYRAH. Acclaimed boutique hotel and restaurant.

CedarCreek Ok V r w ★★★ 09 11 12 (13) Terrific low-alcohol aromatic line-up: RIES, GEWURZ, Ehrenfelser. Solid MERLOT; top-end Platinum VIOGNIER, CHARD, SYRAH, PINOT N.

Church & State Wines Ok V r w ★★ 09 10 11 12 (13) Stylish Coyote Bowl winery in South Okanagan making Tre Bella (white Rhône blend) CHARD, VIOGNIER, SYRAH; signature red Bordeaux blend is Quintessential.

Hester Creek Ok V r w ★★ 09 10 11 12 (13) Electric TREBBIANO off 40-yr-old vines; flagship red blend The Judge. Aromatic PINOT GR, PINOT BL, CAB FR. Guest villa and restaurant.

Jackson-Triggs Okanagan Ok V r w sw ★★ 09 11 12 (13) Popular, easy-drinking style: excellent SHIRAZ, Meritage (*see* California), outstanding RIES Icewine. Impressive Rhône-style SunRock Shiraz.

Mission Hill Ok V r w ★★★ 08 09 11 12 (13) Okanagan leader making v.gd Res varietal series, Legacy series: Perpetua, Oculus, Quatrain, Compendium.

Nk'Mip Ok V r w 09 11 12 (13) Part of $25m Aboriginal resort and spa. Fine PINOT BL, RIES, PINOT N; top: Qwam Qwmt PINOT N, SYRAH. Desert Cultural Centre must-see.

Osoyoos Larose Ok V r ★★★ 07 08 09 10 11 12 (13) A benchmark, single-v'yd, age-worthy Bordeaux-style blend with a new French winemaker Mathieu Mercier and new owner Groupe Taillan.

Painted Rock Ok V r w ★★★ 10 11 12 (13) Steep-sloped 24-ha Skaha Bench site under guidance of Bordelais consultant Alain Sutre: v.gd SYRAH, CHARD, red blend.

Pentâge Winery Ok V r w ★★ 10 11 12 (13) 5,000-case Skaha Bench producer making fine VIOGNIER, PINOT GR, GEWURZ, Rhône-style blends (r w).

Quails' Gate Ok V r w ★★ 10 11 12 (13) Family-owned estate; terroir-based PINOT N, excellent Res. CHARD, aromatic RIES, CHENIN BL, cult-like following for Old-Vines Foch.

Red Rooster Ok V r w ★★ 10 11 12 (13) Fresh, friendly, aromatic wines are signature of this Naramata Bench producer. Top picks: CHARD, PINOT GR, RIES, MERLOT.

Road 13 Ok V r w ★★★ 10 11 12 (13) Winemaker JM Bouchard all about site-specific wines. Premium tier under Jackpot designation: CHENIN BL, VIOGNIER, SYRAH, PINOT N.

Tantalus Ok V r w ★★★ 10 11 12' (13) Site-obsessed, self-proclaimed "New Pioneers" cultivating the oldest (1927) continuously producing v'yds. PINOT N, RIES are the story. Res Ries is outstanding.

South America

Abbreviations
used in the text:

Aco	Aconcagua
Bío	Bío-Bío
Cach	Cachapoal
Casa	Casablanca
Cata	Catamarca
Cho	Choapa
Col	Colchagua
Coq	Coquimbo
Cur	Curicó
Elq	Elqui
Ita	Itata
La R	La Rioja
Ley	Leyda
Lim	Limarí
Mai	Maipo
Mall	Malleco
Mau	Maule
Men	Mendoza
Neu	Neuquén
Pat	Patagonia
Rap	Rapel
Río N	Río Negro
Sal	Salta
San A	San Antonio
San J	San Juan

Recent vintages

Vintages differ more than they used to, certainly in the newer areas. But the differences are small compared with those of classic European regions. The appeal of South America is that of youth, vigour, vibrancy. Current vintages (especially 2013) are best for most, but top reds need ageing: up to 5–6 years.

CHILE

The wine clock runs faster in South America, and Chile is a reflection of that. Merlot is already looking like a part of history. Carmenère is still ticking over, and the main varieties are still Cabernet Sauvignon and Sauvignon Blanc. But there are two themes now: one is diversity and the other is risk – which means risking acidity and cool climates, not risking oak and overripeness; those are so last decade. Wines are fresh now, and balanced. The most fashionable regions include Lo Abarca, Aconcagua Costa, Elqui and Malleco, where the wines have a sense of place; where Syrah has aroma and Pinot Noir lightness and freshness. Diversity means that new varieties have burst noisily onto the scene. Carignan, Grenache and Muscat rub shoulders with the old favourites, often from very remote vineyards. Chile has never looked so exciting.

Aconcagua The river moderates the climate of this warm region, traditionally a source of sturdy reds. New coastal v'yds look interesting. SYRAH has star quality.

Almaviva Mai ★★★★ Expensive but classy Bordeaux-style red, mainly CAB SAUV. CONCHA Y TORO/Baron Philippe de Rothschild joint venture. V.gd Epu Cab Sauv, CARMENÈRE.

Altaïr Wines Rap ★★★ Complex, precise CAB SAUV/SYRAH/CAB FR/PETIT VERDOT blend; Pascal Chatonnet consults (Bordeaux). Second label: Sideral, earlier drinking.

Alto Las Gredas S Regions ★★★ Owner-winemaker María Victoria Petermann makes only this top CHARD from 2 ha in Araucania. Tense, mineral, tasty.

Antiyal Mai ★★→★★★ Bio specialist Alvaro Espinoza; complex red blends with CAB SAUV, CARMENÈRE, SYRAH, PETIT VERDOT. Pure Carmenère bio from Escorial single-v'yd.

Apaltagua Rap ★★→★★★ CARMENÈRE specialist drawing on old-vine fruit from Apalta (Col). Grial is rich, herbal flagship wine (Res also gd).

Aquitania, Viña Mai ★★★ Chilean/French joint venture, making excellent Sol de Sol CHARD; now also v.gd SAUV BL from Mall Valley, v.gd aged Lazuli CAB SAUV from Quebrada de Macul.

Arboleda, Viña Aco, Casa, Ley ★★→★★★ Part of the ERRÁZURIZ/CALITERRA stable, with whites from Ley and CASA. Best for youngest SAUV BL, reds (CAB SAUV, SYRAH, MERLOT) from ACO, incl excellent CARMENÈRE.

Aristos Cach, Mai ★★→★★★ Terroir specialist Pedro Parra and two French winemakers making a must-try Duquesa CHARD, classy CAB from highest v'yd (Duque), Baron blend of Cab/MERLOT/SYRAH. Fast-growing, fast-moving project.

Bío-Bío Southern region, cool enough for interesting RIES, GEWURZ, PINOT N. Promising for fizz too.

Botalcura Cur ★★ French winemaker Philippe Debrus makes big reds, incl NEBBIOLO. Try young, cheap Porfía G Res MALBEC.

Caliboro Mau ★★★ Francesco Marone Cinzano is the soul of Erasmo, a refined CAB SAUV, CAB FR, MERLOT blend, and a rare Torontel Late Harvest.

Caliterra Casa, Col, Cur, Ley ★→★★ Sister winery of ERRÁZURIZ. CHARD, SAUV BL improving, reds becoming less one-dimensional, esp Tributo range and flagship red Cenit. Bio-Sur is organic range.

Standard price of País grapes? €0.08/kg. In Champagne, grape price is c.€6/kg.

Calyptra Cach ★★★ Frenchman François Massoc makes excellent Zahir CAB SAUV and Gran Res CHARD. Now improving with v.gd SAUV BL (look for Gran Res). Among best of Cach.

Carmen, Viña Casa, Col, Elq, Mai ★★→★★★ Organic pioneer; keen on CARMENÈRE. Ripe, fresh CASA CHARD Special Res; v.gd reds like PETITE SYRAH, MERLOT, top Chilean CAB SAUV Gold Res.

Casablanca Casa This was as cool as Chile got 10 yrs ago; now other, newer regions cooler, Casa practically traditional. Gd CHARD, SAUV BL; promising MERLOT, PINOT N.

Casa Marín San A ★★★ Cutting-edge white specialist producing v.gd RIES, GEWURZ, PINOT GR. Cipreses v'yd just 4 km from the sea: brilliant SAUV BL. New late-harvest, nobly rotten RIES.

Casas del Bosque Cach, Casa ★★→★★★ Since 2010 vintage NZ Grant Phelps (ex-VIU MANENT) is winemaker. Elegant range, incl SYRAH Res, SAUV BL.

Casa Silva Col ★★★ Wines from Col estate (Altura blend), and now from v'yds in coastal zone of Paredones (v.gd SAUV BL). Cool Coast and Gran Terroir ranges do exactly what they say. Look out for SAUVIGNON GRIS, VIOGNIER, new Lake Ranco wines (from chilly far south) and delicate new Fervor fizz.

Clos des Fous Cach, Casa, S Regions ★★ Specialist in extreme southern terroirs; natural (see France), minimal intervention. Try Locura 1 CHARD.

Clos Ouvert Mau ★★ New winery; natural winemaking (see France). Interesting wines: Huaso (PAÍS), red blend Otono, Louis Antoine Luyt CARMENÈRE (MAU).

> **Hooray for history**
>
> As Santiago expands, v'yds get bulldozed. Santa Carolina and US
> ampelographer Dr. Andy Walker have started a Heritage Foundation
> Block: 40 selections of 17 varieties, all from v. old vines and all v.
> different from laboratory clones. It's also trying to revive old winemaking
> techniques: picking earlier for freshness and lower alcohol, using less
> oak and wild yeasts. Initial results look v.gd. Back to the future.

Concha y Toro ★ →★★★★ Still the leader: winemaker Ignacio Recabarren still ahead of the game. Don't miss Terrunyo range: outstanding SAUV BL, plus RIES, CAB SAUV, CARMENÈRE, SYRAH; classic Cab Sauv Marques de Casa Concha (Puente Alto) and **Don Melchor** (MAI). Aslo Icon Carmenère Carmín (Peumo), subtle CHARD Amelia (CASA), remarkable Maycas Chard and PINOT N (LIM), new Series Riberas MALBEC (Col). Plus varietals and blends Trio and Casillero del Diablo. *See also* ALMAVIVA, TRIVENTO (Argentina).

Cono Sur Casa, Col, Bio ★★ →★★★ PINOT N, headed by Ocio, still gd but looking a little heavy compared to newer releases elsewhere. Others: 20 Barrels Selection (MERLOT, CAB SAUV); new innovations called Visión (Bío RIES Single V'yd Block 23 is superb). Also in Res Especial look for *dense, fruity Cab Sauv*, delicious VIOGNIER, rose-petal GEWURZ, impressive SYRAH. Second label: Isla Negra, owned by CONCHA Y TORO.

Cousiño Macul Mai ★★ →★★★ Historic Santiago winery. Reliable Antiguas Res MERLOT; zesty SAUVIGNON Gris; top-of-the-range Lota is still one of Chile's top blends.

De Martino Cach, Elq, Mai, Mau, Ita ★★ →★★★ Subtle winemaking (top reds now see no new oak), best-known for single-v'yd, old-vine CARMENÈRE (speciality), CAB SAUV, MALBEC, CHARD, but also impressing with Legado range, Vigno CARIGNAN. Alto Los Toros v'yd is 2,000 metres high. MUSCAT is hottest grape today, esp Viejas Tinajas made the old way in *tinajas*, big clay jars.

Elqui Bone-dry northern region cooled by sea breezes; v'yd altitudes range from 350–2,200 metres (Chile's highest); brilliant SYRAH, top PINOT N, SAUV BL. Look for Falernia, superb Mayu. Big cacti too.

Emiliana Casa, Rap, Bio ★ →★★★ Organic/bio specialist involving Alvaro Espinoza (*see* ANTIYAL). Complex, SYRAH-heavy "G" and Coyam show almost Mediterranean-style wildness; cheaper Adobe and Novas ranges v.gd for affordable complexity.

Errázuriz Aco, Casa ★ →★★★ Besides the top Don Maximiano, and fragrant KAI CARMENÈRE, pick the new wild-ferment wines from Coastal ACO (PINOT N, SAUV BL, SYRAH). Also The Blend: GRENACHE/MOURVÈDRE/Syrah/ROUSSANNE. *See also* ARBOLEDA, CALITERRA, SEÑA, VIÑEDO CHADWICK.

Fournier, Bodegas O Ley, Mau ★★ →★★★ Sister venture of same-name Argentine winery; v'gd Ley SAUV BL, MAU red blends Centauri and Alfa Centauri.

Garcés Silva, Viña San A ★★ →★★★ The brand at this no-expense-spared operation is Amayna; rich, ripe styles with a bit of alcohol removed for gd balance. Best of both worlds. SAUV BL is particularly gd.

Hacienda Araucano Casa, Rap ★★ →★★★ Bordeaux winemaker François Lurton's makes a top CAB SAUV, plus complex Gran Araucano SAUV BL (CASA), refined CARMENÈRE/Cab Sauv blend Clos de Lolol and Alka Carmenère.

Haras de Pirque Mai ★★ →★★★ Estate in Pirque. Character SYRAH is top, also smoky SAUV BL, stylish CHARD, dense CAB SAUV/MERLOT. Solid red Albis (Cab Sauv/ CARMENÈRE) made with Antinori (*see* Italy).

Lapostolle Cach, Casa, Col ★★ →★★★★ Impressive French-owned estate; bio-farmed v'yds. SÉM is the best of increasingly elegant whites; Cuvée Alexandre MERLOT, SYRAH and CARMENÈRE-based Clos Apalta pick of fine reds. Lush style challenged by new Collection label: single-v'yd Syrah, Carmenère from around the country.

Leyda, Viña San A ★★ →★★★ Pioneer in coastal Leyda. Elegant *Chard (Lot 5* Wild

Yeasts is the pick); lush PINOT N (esp Lot 21 cuvée, lively rosé); firm, spicy Canelo SYRAH. Garuma SAUV BL is restrained but concentrated. Also Kadun Sauvignon Gris, sparkling Blanc de Blancs.

Limarí One of new cool areas that are actually deserts; what's not a vine is probably a cactus. Gd for SYRAH, SAUV BL, esp CHARD, thanks to limestone in many v'yds.

Loma Larga Casa ★★→★★★ Top Chilean MALBEC, v. different from Argentine versions because of oceanic influence. Impressive CAB FR (also rosé), SYRAH.

Maipo A famous wine region close to Santiago. Chile's best CAB SAUVs often come from higher, eastern subregions such as Pirque and Puente Alto. There are many big names.

Matetic San A ★★★ Dynamic producer, stars are: fragrant, **zesty Sauv Bl** (for ageing); spicy, berry EQ SYRAH. Gd PINOT N, CHARD. Corralillo label v. consistent.

Maule Southernmost region in Central Valley. Claro, Loncomilla, Tutuven Valleys. CARIGNAN from Cauquenes currently in vogue.

Maycas del Limarí Lim →→★★★ CONCHA Y TORO offshoot; SAUV BL, CHARD, PINOT N, SYRAH full-flavoured and elegant. Quebrada Seca CHARD taut, minerally flagship.

Montes Casa, Col, Cur, Ley ★★→★★★★ Highlights of a wide first-class range from a feng-shui winery: Alpha CAB SAUV; Bordeaux-blend Montes Alpha M; *Folly Syrah from Apalta*; intense Purple Angel CARMENÈRE (founder likes angels). Also v.gd SAUV BL, PINOT N from both Ley and new, cool Zapallar. Look for Outer Limits range esp Sauv Bl, CINSAULT.

Montsecano ★★★ Cool, high-altitude, small-scale, bio PINOT N made by five Chileans and Frenchman, André Ostertag. Top stuff.

Morandé Casa, Mai, Mau ★★→★★★ Brut Nature NV (CHARD, PINOT N) is top sparkling. Take a look at Edición Limitada CARIGNAN (Loncomilla), spicy SYRAH/CAB SAUV; top wine is Cab Sauv-based House of Morandé. Res Pinot N is sappy, v.gd. Don´t miss Vigno (Carignan/Syrah/Chard).

Elqui has 300 days of sun each year, 60 days of cloud, five days of rain.

Neyen Rap ★★★ Apalta project for Patrick Valette of Bordeaux; intense old-vine CARMENÈRE/CAB SAUV blend. Now owned by VERAMONTE.

Odfjell Mai, Mau ★→★★★ Red specialist with v.gd CARMENÈRE, CARIGNAN (from MAU); pick young Orzada Carignan, Aliara (SYRAH/MALBEC/Carignan).

Pérez Cruz, Viña Mai ★★★ Interesting Chaski PETIT VERDOT; Edición Limitada COT; balanced, classic Waiki CAB SAUV.

Polkura Col ★★ Independent and focused on Marchigue SYRAH; also rich MALBEC.

Quebrada de Macul, Viña Mai ★★→★★★ Ambitious winery making gd CHARD, plus excellent Domus Aurea, one of most elegant, classic CAB SAUVs from Chile.

Rapel Quality region divided into Col and Cach valleys. Best for hearty reds, esp CARMENÈRE, SYRAH, but watch for cooler coastal subregions Marchihue, Paradones.

RE Mai ★★★ Pablo MORANDÉ´s innovative new project: unusual blends Cabergnan (CAB SAUV/CARIGNAN), Pinotel (PINOT N/MOSCATEL). Unorthodox flavours new to Chile.

Ribera del Lago Mau Amazing SAUV BL from clay soil, and Laberinto PINOT N.

San Antonio San A Coastal region west of Santiago benefiting from sea breezes; best for whites, SYRAH, PINOT N. Lo Abarca is notable site. Ley is subregion.

San Pedro Cur ★→★★★ Massive Cur-based producer. 35 South (35 Sur) for affordable varietals; Castillo de Molina a step up. Best are 1865 Limited Edition reds, Kankana del ELQUI SYRAH, elegant Cabo de Hornos. Under same ownership as ALTAÏR, Viña Mar, Missiones de Rengo, Santa Helena, TARAPACÁ.

Santa Alicia Mai ★→★★★ Red specialist. Best: firm but juicy Millantu CAB SAUV-based flagship wine, and lithe but structured Anke Blend 1 (CAB FR/PETIT VERDOT).

Santa Carolina, Viña ★★→★★★ Extensive range from several regions, highlights are the Specialties range (SAN A SAUV BL, LIM CHARD, MAI SYRAH); pick Cauquenes

CARIGNAN, Cach MOUVÈDRE or Rap PETIT VERDOT. VSC blends at all levels. New Herencia (CARMENÈRE) from Peumo excellent but pricey.

Santa Rita Mai ★★→★★★★ Long-est MAI winery working with Aussie Brian Croser. Best: *Casa Real Cab Sauv*, but Pehuén and Casa Real (CARMENÈRE), Triple C (CAB SAUV/CAB FR/Carmenère), Floresta range (esp Cab Fr, MERLOT, SAUV BL) nearly as gd. Medalla Real CHARD superb value.

Seña Aco ★★★★ Est with ROBERT MONDAVI, but now wholly owned by the Chadwick family of ERRÁZURIZ, this blend of Bordeaux grapes from hillside v'yd in ACO holds its own against world's best in comparative tastings.

Tabalí ★★→★★★ Source of refined cooler-climate wines, often influenced by limestone soils. New v'yds 1,800 metres up: bought for walnuts, now growing grapes. Single-v'yd, terroir-driven Talinay CHARD, SAUV BL, PINOT N; new VIOGNIER.

By law, Chilean vineyard workers must be supplied with factor-30 sun cream.

Tarapacá, Viña Casa, Ley, Mai ★★ Steadily improving historic winery, part of VSPT group. Top: Tara-Pakay (CAB SAUV/SYRAH), Etiqueta Negra Gran Res (Cab Sauv).

Torres, Miguel Cur ★★→★★★★ Fresh whites incl Nectaría RIES and gd reds, esp sturdy *Manso de Velasco* single-v'yd CAB SAUV (ages superbly), CARIGNAN-based Cordillera. Conde de Superunda is top cuvée, also organic range Tormenta, pretty-but-simple sparkling Estelado Rosé NV País (best use of País so far). Pioneering plantings in Empedrado zone of MAU.

Undurraga Casa, Ley, Lim, Mai ★★ TH (Terroir Hunter) range changed this MAI producer from dowdy to vanguard. Best: Altazor (CAB SAUV-based), LIM SYRAH, SAUV BL from Ley, CASA; also MAU CARIGNAN. Try lively Brut Royal CHARD/PINOT N, Titillum sparklings, peachy Late Harvest SÉM.

Valdivieso Cur, San A ★→★★★ Major producer impressing with Res and Single V'yd range (esp CAB FR, MALBEC) from top terroirs around Chile (*Ley Chard* esp gd). V.gd sparkling NV red blend Caballo Loco, wonderful CARIGNAN-based Éclat.

Vascos, Los Rap ★→★★★ Lafite-Rothschild venture now improving its Bordeaux wannabe reds. Top: Le Dix, Grande Res.

Ventisquero, Viña Casa, Col, Mai ★→★★★ Ambitious winery named after a hanging glacier; labels incl Chilano and Yali; top wines are two Apalta reds: rich but fragrant Pangea SYRAH; CARMENÈRE/Syrah blend Vertice. Promising Herú CASA PINOT N. Grey range incl Pinot N, Carmenère, MERLOT, esp juicy Mediterranean-blend GCM (GRENACHE/CARIGNAN/MATARÓ). Try Enclave CAB SAUV (MAI).

Veramonte Casa, Col ★★ Ripe but elegant reds from Col (Primus blend is pick); fresher styles from CASA, where Ritual PINOT N, Res SAUV BL stand out.

Villard Casa, Mai ★★ Sophisticated wines made by French-born Thierry Villard. Gd MAI reds, esp PINOT N, MERLOT, Equis CAB SAUV, CASA whites.

Viñedo Chadwick Mai ★★★→★★★★ Stylish CAB SAUV improving with each vintage from v'yd owned by Eduardo Chadwick, President of ERRÁZURIZ.

Viu Manent Col ★★ Emerging Col winery. Focused on MALBEC range: fragrant Viu 1, Gran Res, Secreto. Also CARMENÈRE-based El Incidente; v.gd late-harvest SÉM.

Costa del Chile

Chile has a new appellation system (yes, just when you'd finally got to grips with the old), which divides the country into Costa (Coastal), Entre Valles (Central Valley) and Andes. The existing appellations will be used as well, but the point is that the coastal area and the Andes are mostly cooler than the Central Valley. So if you want a cool-climate wine, the label might give you more help than before.

ARGENTINA

Flavours in Argentina are as bold as they ever were, and the wines are as punchy. But the global trend to better balance is kicking in here, as well. The way Argentina balances its wines is by planting higher, for lower temperatures and, especially, cooler nights to preserve acidity. From "bigger is better" Argentina is moving towards "higher is better" – 1,600 metres, as in the Uco Valley, is almost the new normal (okay, a slight exaggeration); in the Valles Calchaquies vines are planted at 2,600 metres. But height isn't the only solution; there are 3,000 hectares along the Río Negro in Patagonia. If you can't go up, go south.

Achaval Ferrer Men ★★★ Super-concentrated but elegant Altamira, Bella Vista, Mirador old single-v'yd MALBECS.

Aleanna Men ★★★ Alejandro Vigil (CATENA winemaker) and Adrianna Catena make innovative Enemigo and Gran Enemigo blend.

Alpamanta Men ★★ Organic (becoming bio) winery with Chilean Alvaro Espinoza (*see* ANTIYAL) as consultant. V.gd top MALBEC, also gd entry-level range Natal.

Alta Vista Men ★→★★★ The French d'Aulan family produces top *Alto* (MALBEC/CAB SAUV) and trio of pioneering single-v'yd Malbecs – Alizarine, Serenade (Luján de Cuyo), Themis (Uco Valley).

Altocedro Men ★★→★★★ Owner and winemaker Karim Mussi Saffie's trump cards are MALBEC, TEMPRANILLO, blended together for top wine Desnudos.

Altos las Hormigas Men ★★★→★★★★ Top single-v'yd MALBEC based on old Uco Valley vines. Also impressive basic Malbec, BONARDA. Italian influences from Attilio Pagli, Alberto Antonini. Now more focus on soils, led by Pedro Parra. Brilliant Appellation range.

Antucura Men ★★→★★★ The owners set out to create an super-ultra-premium wine, with advice from Michel Rolland (*see* Bordeaux). Besides Antucura blend, look for new Barrandica range.

Atamisque Men ★→★★★ Impressive reds, esp MALBEC/MERLOT/CAB SAUV Assemblage. Also CHARD, PINOT N. Catalpa, Serbal (esp VIOGNIER) range also v.gd value. Some 80-yr-old Malbec vines.

Benegas Men ★★→★★★★ Top-notch CAB FR and Meritage Benegas Lynch label. Using old vines from Libertad v'yd (Maipú), Uco Valley; new MALBEC from Gualtallary.

Bressia Men ★★→★★★★ Family winery; classic MALBEC-dominated blends Profundo, Conjuro. Plus Monteagrelo range, excellent Lágrima Canela (CHARD/SÉM).

Callia San J ★★ Gd-value wines based on SYRAH. Top Grand Callia blend.

Canale, Bodegas Humberto Rio N ★→★★★ Most traditional winery in Pat, advised by Susana Balbo (wines), Pedro Marchevski (v'yds).

Carmelo Patti Men ★★ Independent winery making classic CAB SAUV, MALBEC.

Caro Men ★★★ CATENA's joint venture with the Rothschilds of Lafite (France): seriously classy Caro and younger Amancaya.

Casa Bianchi Men ★→★★★ V. traditional. V.gd sparkling, well-balanced Famiglia range, esp CAB SAUV/CHARD. Top Enzo (red blend), María Carmen (Chard). Look for Leo brand, joint venture with Lionel Messi´s Foundation.

Casarena Men ★★→★★★ V.gd *entry-level Malbec*, CAB SAUV, plus new single-v'yd MALBECS from Agrelo y Perdriel; outstanding CAB FR.

Catena Zapata, Bodega Men ★★→★★★★ MALBEC pioneer. Consistently gd range from Alamos, Catena, Catena Alta to flagship Nicolas Catena Zapata and Malbec Argentino, plus Adrianna and Nicasia single-v'yd Malbecs. Best local CHARD from Gualtallary, White Stones, White Bonnes. Working hard with CAB SAUV.

Chacra Rio N ★★★ *Superb terroir-driven Pinot N* from tiny bodega owned by Piero Incisa della Rocchetta of Sassicaia (*see* Italy), top Treinta y Dos from 1932 v´yd; also lush but light Mainqué MERLOT. Don´t miss 2012 vintage.

Chakana Men ★★→★★★ Winery to watch for v.gd varietals, top MALBEC Ayni.

Clos de los Siete Men ★★ Consistent Vistaflores (Uco Valley) blend of MALBEC, MERLOT, SYRAH, CAB SAUV, winemaking overseen by Michel Rolland (*see* DIAMANDES, MONTEVIEJO, Cuvelier los Andes, Mariflor). New white release planned for 2014.

Cobos, Viña Men ★★★ Ultra-rich but elegant MALBECS from Californian Paul Hobbs, best from Marchiori v'yd. Bramare, Felino are second, third tiers, esp CAB SAUV. Also look for Marchiori & Barraud wines from Cobos winemakers.

Colomé, Bodega Sal ★★→★★★ Bodega in remote Calchaquí Valley owned by California's Hess Collection. Pure, intense, bio, MALBEC-based reds, lively TORRONTÉS, smoky TANNAT. Malbec Auténtico honours tradition. Latest challenge: Altura Máxima Malbec planted at 3,100-metre altitude.

DiamAndes Men One of CLOS DE LOS SIETE wineries, owned by Bonnie family of Château Malartic-Lagravière (Bordeaux), making solid, meaty Gran Res (MALBEC/CAB SAUV); lively VIOGNIER, CHARD; young Malbec.

Alcohol in Malbec risen 1.5% in last 20 years: hence need for high-altitude vineyards.

Dominio del Plata Men ★★→★★★ Susana Balbo makes v.gd wines under Susana Balbo, BenMarco, Zohar, Anubis labels. Nosotros is bold MALBEC/CAB SAUV flagship. Signature is top CAB SAUV. Also v.gd BenMarco Expresivo, gd-value Crios range (incl excellent TORRONTÉS).

Doña Paula Men ★→★★★ Estate owned by SANTA RITA (*see* Chile). Best: Selección MALBEC, CHARD; consistent DP Estate, Los Cardos range. Top new Malbecs Single Parcels from Gualtallary, Altamira (Uco Valley) v'yds. Vibrant 2012 RIES.

Etchart Sal ★★→★★★ Traditional, high-altitude producer. Top TORRONTÉS, gd Arnaldo B red blend. New Gran Linaje range (Torrontés/MALBEC/CAB SAUV).

Fabre Montmayou Men, Rio N ★★→★★★ French-owned, started in 1990s, bought old v'yds in Luján de Cuyo, RÍO N (Infinitus); gd second label Phebus; also gd-value Viñalba, top MALBEC, CAB SAUV, Grand Vin.

Finca Decero Men ★★→★★★ Wines from Remolinos v'yd in Agrelo, lush but modern. Go for PETIT VERDOT, blended Amano.

Fin del Mundo, Bodega Del Neuq ★→★★ More focus on entry-level wines. Special Blend is MALBEC/CAB SAUV/MERLOT; also single-v'yd Fin. Michel Rolland consults.

Flichman, Finca Men ★★→★★★ Owned by Sogrape (*see* Portugal), impressing with SYRAH. Dedicado blend (mostly CAB SAUV) best. Paisaje de Tupungato (Bordeaux blend), Paisaje de Barrancas (SYRAH-based); top MALBEC Parcela 26 (Uco Valley).

Fournier, O Men ★→★★★ Spanish-owned. Urban Uco v.gd entry-level range; B Crux (TEMPRANILLO/MERLOT/MALBEC blend, SAUV BL), Alfa Crux (Malbec and blend). Top site to visit in Uco Valley, v.gd restaurant. *See* Chile.

Kaikén Men ★★→★★★ Owned by Montes (*see* Chile); top Mai MALBEC, also Ultra CAB SAUV and Malbec, Corte blend, with grapes from different regions.

Krontiras Men ★★→★★★ Greek-owned MALBEC specialist converting to bio.

La Anita, Finca Men ★★→★★★ High-class reds, esp CAB SAUV, MALBEC, MERLOT. Also SYRAH, intriguing whites, attractive rosé PETIT VERDOT. New young winemaker promises more elegance.

La Riojana La R ★→★★ Big Fairtrade producer. *Raza Ltd Edition Malbec* is top wine, but quality, value at all levels, esp TORRONTÉS.

Las Moras, Finca San J ★→★★ Leader in SAN J with solid Gran SHIRAZ plus TANNAT, MALBEC, VIOGNIER. Intense Malbec/BONARDA blend Mora Negra.

Luca / Tikal / Tahuan / Alma Negra Men ★★→★★★ Classy boutique wineries owned by Nicolas Catena's children Laura (Luca) and Ernesto (Tikal/Tahuan/Alma Negra). Plus v.gd sparkling, excellent La Posta del Viñatero range, but PINOT N is key.

Luigi Bosca Men ★★→★★★★ Wide range topped by stylish Icono (MALBEC/CAB SAUV), classic Finca Los Nobles Malbec/PETIT VERDOT. Cab Sauv/Bouchet (aka CAB FR).

also v.gd, as are Gala blends, esp white (VIOGNIER /CHARD/RIES). Plus gd entry-level Finca La Linda. But hot picks today are Unique Terroir Malbec, PINOT N, Ries.

Manos Negras ★★→★★★ Two ex-CATENA staff making wines in several parts of Argentina. Altamira MALBEC top wine. TeHo, ZaHa are related labels, also v.gd Res, plus fruity PINOT N, TORRONTÉS.

Masi Tupungato Men ★★→★★★ Owned by Masi of Valpolicella (*see* Italy). Passo Doble is fine *ripasso*-style MALBEC/CORVINA/MERLOT blend; Corbec is even better Amarone lookalike (Corvina/Malbec).

Mendel Men ★★★ High-end MALBEC, incl Finca Remota from Altamira, delicate Unus blend. SÉM from 70-yr-old vines; CAB SAUV. V.gd Lunta range, new TORRONTÉS.

Mendoza Most important wine province (over 70% of plantings). Best subregions: Agrelo, Uco Valley (incl Gualtallary, Altamira), Luján de Cuyo, Maipú.

Michel Torino Sal ★★ Big Cafayate enterprise making gd to v.gd wines in all ranges, incl Don David, esp MALBEC, CAB SAUV. Altimus is rather oaky flagship.

Moët-Hennessy Argentina Men ★→★★ Top sparkling makers under Moët et Chandon supervision; esp Baron B and the innovative Delice. Plus gd varietals range. *See* TERRAZAS DE LOS ANDES.

Monteviejo Men ★★→★★★★ Part of CLOS DE LOS SIETE, founded by late Catherine Péré-Vergé of Pomerol. Marcelo Pelleriti makes the wines in France and Argentina. From MEN: superb, tiny La Violeta; Lindaflor MALBEC; v.gd CHARD. Also Monteviejo blend, Petite Fleur, Festivo range.

Nieto Senetiner, Bodegas Men ★★→★★★ MALBEC at all levels, esp from Res to top-of-range Cadus; plus new single-v´yds, blends. Also BONARDA.

Noemia ★★★→★★★★ Outstanding Patagonian old-vine, terroir-driven MALBEC made by Hans Vinding-Diers. Also J Alberto, A Lisa (incl rosé), stylish Bordeaux blend "2" (CAB SAUV/MERLOT).

Norton, Bodega Men ★→★★★ Historic bodega with v.gd reds, esp MALBEC, CAB SAUV, blends Privada and icon Gernot Langes, lots of v.gd sparkling. New single-v´yd MALBEC Lote Único. All come from Luján de Cuyo.

Passionate Wine Men ★★→★★★ Montesco Parral (MALBEC/BONARDA/CAB SAUV), Agua de Roca SAUV BL, vibrant PINOT N. Young Bonarda, top Malbon (Malbec/Bonarda). Matías Michelini is young consultant making wine with his family.

Peñaflor Men ★→★★★ Argentina's biggest wine group, incl FINCA LAS MORAS, ANDEAN V´YDS (SAN J), MICHEL TORINO (SAL), SANTA ANA, finer TRAPICHE (MEN).

Chardonnay in Patagonia can ripen two weeks later than in (high) Uco Valley, and can have 2% less alcohol.

Piatelli Sal ★→★★★ Wineries in Cafayate, Luján de Cuyo. TORRONTÉS, modern reds esp CAB SAUV, MALBEC.

Piedra Negra Men ★→★★★ Top is Piedra Negra MALBEC. Also Chacayes (Malbec-based blend), earthy CAB SAUV Gran Lurton, fragant white Corte FRIULANO. Many entry-level wines esp PINOT GRIGIO.

Poesia Men ★★→★★★ Same owner as Clos l'Église, Bordeaux; dedicated to reds. Stylish, mouthfilling Poesia blend (CAB SAUV/MALBEC); fine Clos des Andes (Malbec); juicy Pasodoble Malbec /SYRAH/Cab Sauv.

Portillo, Finca El Men ★★ V.gd, value varietals from Uco Valley, esp MALBEC, SAUV BL.

Porvenir de Cafayate, El Sal ★★→★★★ Young Cafayate estate with juicy, oaky Laborum varietals, incl fine, firm TANNAT. Amauta blends also gd, elegant TORRONTÉS. Advised by flying winemaker Paul Hobbs.

Pulenta Estate Men ★★→★★★ Owned by third generation. V.gd entry-level La Flor. Best: Pulenta Gran Corte (CAB SAUV/MALBEC/MERLOT/PETIT VERDOT), CAB FR.

Renacer Men ★★→★★★ Flagship Renacer (mostly MALBEC); v.gd Punto Final Malbec, CAB SAUV. Interesting Enamore: Amarone-style red made with Allegrini (*see* Italy).

Riglos Men ★★★ Vines in Finca Las Divas, in Gualtallary, Tupungato. Try new releases 2011 Gran Corte (MALBEC/CAB SAUV/CAB FR), Cab Fr, Cab Sauv, Malbec. V.gd Quinto SAUV BL.

Río Negro Pat's oldest wine region. Gd PINOT N, MALBEC; also SAUV BL, SÉM.

Ruca Malen Men ★★→★★★ Promising red specialist with v'yds in Luján de Cuyo and Uco Valley. Top range Kinien MALBEC, CAB SAUV; rich PETIT VERDOT, SYRAH (Ruca Malen label); v.gd sparkling. Winery restaurant has tourism award.

Salentein, Bodegas Men ★★→★★★ Winemaker José Galante is changing style here. Primus MALBEC, CHARD, PINOT N are top, elegant. New single-v'yd more vibrant. Try Numina, Saletien Res range, sparkling wines.

Salta Northerly province with some of the world's highest v'yds, esp in Calchaquí Valley. Subregion Cafayate renowned for TORRONTÉS.

San Juan Second-largest wine region, focused on SYRAH, BONARDA, PINOT GRIGIO, TANNAT.

San Pedro de Yacochuya Sal ★★★ Cafayate collaboration between Michel Rolland (*see* France) and Etchart family. Ripe but fragrant TORRONTÉS, dense MALBEC SPY, powerful Yacochuya (unique Malbec from oldest vines).

Schroeder, Familia Neuq ★★ V.gd Saurus Select range, esp PINOT N, fragrant MALBEC. Top Familia Schroeder Pinot N/Malbec. Interesting CAB SAUV, sparkling.

Sophenia, Finca Men ★★→★★★ Pioneer in Tupungato; harvests at dawn to retain freshness. Gd Altosur entry-level, v.gd Res MALBEC, CAB SAUV, Rhône-style SYRAH; highlights are Synthesis Blend, SAUV BL.

Tapiz Men ★★ Punchy SAUV BL (from La R), v.gd red range topped by serious Black Tears MALBEC, Res Selección de Barricas (CAB SAUV/Malbec/MERLOT), Merlot.

Terrazas de los Andes Men ★★★ Premium varietal specialist, esp MALBEC, CAB SAUV. Single-v'yds in Perdriel, Las Compuertas, Altamira. Perfumed TORRONTÉS (SALTA). Joint venture with Cheval Blanc (Bordeaux): superb *Cheval des Andes* blend.

Toso, Pascual Men ★★→★★★ Californian Paul Hobbs heads a team making gd-value, tasty range, incl ripe but finely structured Magdalena Toso (mostly MALBEC), Malbec/CAB SAUV single-v'yd Finca Pedregal.

Trapiche Men ★★→★★★ Leader in all ranges, esp for MALBEC. Trio of single-v'yd Malbecs, Las Palmas CAB SAUV shines out; Iscay blends, esp SYRAH-based. Better value under Oak Cask, Fond de Cave, Broquel (gd CAB FR), Medalla labels.

Trivento Men ★→★★★ Owned by CONCHA Y TORO of Chile. Eolo MALBEC is pricey flagship, but Golden Malbec, SYRAH, CHARD top value.

Val de Flores Men ★★★ Michel Rolland owns this old (and bio) MALBEC v'yd in Vistaflores. Deep, elegant, earthy, with firm tannins. For ageing.

Viña Alicia ★★★★ Stylish, pricey range incl NEBBIOLO, PETIT VERDOT (Cuarzo), Tiara white blend (RIES/ALBARIÑO/SAVAGNIN). Also MALBEC Brote Negro, SYRAH.

ViñaVida Men ★★★ Amazing v'yds in Vistaflores, including a circular parcel dedicated to search for the perfect MALBEC. Wines under Luxury Small Lots concept, with Roberto de la Mota as consultant. Top values: Malbec, a blend, PETIT VERDOT 2011, others coming soon.

Zuccardi Men ★→★★★ Dynamic estate producing gd-value Santa Julia range, better Q label (impressive MALBEC, CAB SAUV, TEMPRANILLO), spicy Emma Zuccardi BONARDA, deep yet elegant blend Zeta. Also gd fortified Malamado (r w). Best of all new terroir wines Aluvional from Uco Valley.

Choosing Malbec

Styles vary. SAL and Cata give structure and power; RÍO N and NEU give more elegance, with often a touch of PINOT N in the blend. MEN is still the main region, but the higher-altitude Uco Valley gives more freshness than Luján de Cuyo or other parts of MEN. Often entry-level MALBECS show the cheerful style better than oaked-up premium ones.

BRAZIL

B razil is a massive producer of wine, but most vines are not *Vitis vinifera*.
Most decent wines come from the Italian-influenced Serra Gaûcha region
(with DO Vale dos Vinhedos and IGP Pinto Bandeira). Other spots include
Campanha, next to Uruguay, Serra do Sudeste, Planalto Catarinense, Vale do
São Francisco (two crops a year). Grapes include Bordeaux varieties, Tannat, Pinot
Noir, Touriga Nacional, Tempranillo, Alicante Bouschet, Barbera, Malbec, Syrah,
Chardonnay, Viognier, Riesling, Sauvignon Blanc, Pinot Gris, Gewurztraminer,
Malvasia. It's all a bit experimental at the moment, but the will is there.

Alto de la Ballena ★→★★ Nr Punta del Este; young, crisp, ocean-influenced wines.
Cave Geisse ★★ Sparkling specialist Chilean Mario Geisse; Brut Nature, Blanc de Noirs.
Miolo ★→★★★ Pioneer and major producer, big on Portuguese grapes such as
TINTA RORIZ, TOURIGA NACIONAL. Try Castas Portuguesas. Michel Rolland consults.
Elegant sparkling.
Pizzato Vinhas ★★ V.gd DNA 99 single-v'yd MERLOT from Vale dos Vinhedos. Fausto
label for fresh varietals; Pizzato label for more depth, esp Concentus.
Quinta da Neve ★★ PINOT N from from coolest region of Santa Catarina, v. aromatic.
Salton A massive producer of fizz and still wines. Quality varies. Intense label incl
gd CAB FR and TEROLDEGO.
Valmarino Vinicola ★★ Surprisingly gd CAB FR. Try Valmarino from Serra Gaucha.

Other good names to look for in Brazil: Casa Valduga, Dunamis, Lidio Carraro.

URUGUAY

S plendid Tannat for those not afraid of structure and acidity: expect rich
blackberry fruit, violet aromas and a very firm chassis. It goes a treat with
a local barbecue. To drink without food you might prefer Sauvignon Blanc or
Albariño, or some softer Merlot. A maritime climate means freshness and
brightness is the national style.

Bouza ★→★★★ Old cars, gd food, v.gd wines from boutique winery. Top: Parcela
Unica TANNAT (A6, B6), rich blend Monte Vide Eu (Tannat/MERLOT/TEMPRANILLO).
Garzon ★★ Alberto Antonini consults. Don´t miss TANNAT, SAUV Bl, crisp ALBARIÑO.
Look too for delicate olive oil.
Juanico Establecimiento ★→★★★ Country's largest producer, with gd to v.gd wines
at all prices. Top red is Preludio Familia Deicas, delicious, complex TANNAT/CAB
SAUV /CAB FR/MERLOT/PETIT VERDOT/Marselan blend.
Pisano ★→★★ Traditional winery, v.gd reds and whites. Try Río de los Pájaros range.

OTHER SOUTH AMERICAN WINES

Bolivia The Tarija Valley is the heart of Bolivia's tiny wine industry. With the heat
tempered by altitude, SYRAH, CAB, MALBEC produced with some success. Kohlberg,
Aranjuez, Campos de Solana, La Conception, Casa Grande, Magnus, Uvairenda are
working to position their wines as an experience of height.
Peru Pisco was, is, and will continue to be the king of Peruvian drinks. Wine
evolves slowly but steadily. Enjoy with Peruvian cuisine: Tacama Blanco de
Blancos, Don Manuel, Gran Blanco Fina Res, Intipalka young MALBEC/MERLOT.

ARGENTINA/BRAZIL/URUGUAY

Australia

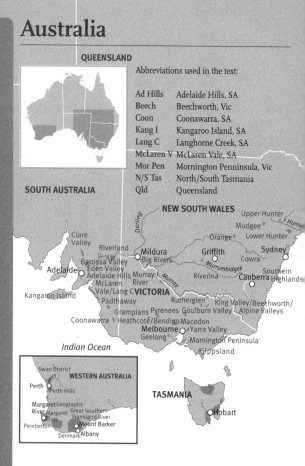

QUEENSLAND

Abbreviations used in the text:

Ad Hills   Adelaide Hills, SA
Beech   Beechworth, Vic
Coon   Coonawarra, SA
Kang I   Kangaroo Island, SA
Lang C   Langhorne Creek, SA
McLaren V   McLaren Vale, SA
Mor Pen   Mornington Penninsula, Vic
N/S Tas   North/South Tasmania
Qld   Queensland

SOUTH AUSTRALIA

NEW SOUTH WALES

Upper Hunter
Mudgee
Lower Hunter
Orange
Sydney
Clare Valley
Riverland
Mildura
Big Rivers
Griffith
Cowra
Barossa Valley
Adelaide
Eden Valley
Adelaide Hills
Murrumbidgee
Murray
Riverina
Canberra
Southern Highlands
McLaren Vale/Lang C
VICTORIA
Kangaroo Island
Padthaway
Rutherglen
King Valley/Beechworth
Coonawarra
Grampians Pyrenees Goulburn Valley
Alpine Valleys
Heathcote/Bendigo Macedon
Melbourne
Yarra Valley
Indian Ocean
Geelong
Mornington Peninsula
Gippsland

Swan District
WESTERN AUSTRALIA
Perth
Perth Hills
TASMANIA
Margaret River
Geographe
Great Southern
Frankland River
Hobart
Pemberton
Mount Barker
Denmark Albany

The downfall was televised but the revolution took place off-camera. Overeager planting of new vineyards and a resultant oversupply of grapes has characterized Australian wine over the past 15–20 years. There's been too much to go around. This has gone hand-in-hand with an obvious creep north in alcohol levels; these two trends are not directly linked but not entirely disconnected, either. Both eras, though, have now had their marching orders served. The macho, hairy-chested world of Australian wine has acceded to metrosexual spruce. Elegance is no longer a dirty word. Chardonnay, once the pom-pom rah-rah variety of the great southern land, has generally gone from fat to slim in style – too slim at times, but increasingly the mantra is to err on the elegant side. Pinot Noir, once consumed at the expense of having your chromosomes questioned, is now ascendant. All those young plantings in the second half of the 90s? They're now mature. It's a different cloth from which Australian wine is being cut. It's not unexciting.

Recent vintages

New South Wales (NSW)

2013 Short, sharp season. Hot and cold. Rich reds and whites. Hunter Sem and Canberra Ries especially good.

2012 A wet, cold year. Sem could pull a rabbit out and perhaps Cab Sauv too, but generally disappointing.

2011 The Hunter Valley escaped the floods of further south, but it was still a cold, damp year.

2010 Regular heavy rain made for a tricky year in most districts. Lighter reds, good whites.

2009 Excellent vintage all over although reds better than whites. Generally a successful year.

2008 Good whites; torrential rain then destroyed virtually all Hunter reds. Canberra reds outstanding.

Victoria (Vic)

2013 Wet winter followed by a warm, dry summer. Good season all round and all over.

2012 Turning out better than first expected. Reds and whites of very good to exceptional quality.

2011 Wet; disease pressure in vineyards. Generally better for whites than reds.

2010 Temperate vintage with no great alarms or surprises. Whites and reds should be good from most districts.

2009 Bush fire (and resultant smoke taint). Extreme heat and drought. Yarra Valley worst affected. Some surprises to be found.

2008 Reds excellent in Grampians, Mornington Peninsula, Yarra Valley.

South Australia (SA)

2013 Water was a problem so yields were generally well down. Will be streaky.

2012 Yields were down but a brilliant year. Confirmed as a great Ries year; Cab Sauv should be a particular stand-out.

2011 Horribly cool and wet. Lean whites, herbal/spicy reds. But some interesting results.

2010 Excellent year. Clare, Eden Valley Ries both very good. Shiraz from all major districts best since 2005. Coonawarra Cab Sauv on song.

2009 Hot. Adelaide Hills good whites, reds. Coonawarra reds excellent. McLaren Vale, Barossa Valley generally good for Shiraz.

2008 Excellent wines picked prior to March heatwave, non-fortified "Ports" for those picked after. Coonawarra reds best.

Western Australia (WA)

2013 Both Cab Sauv and Chard had particularly strong years. Some rain pressure late but, again, the gods were kind.

2012 The drought continued, so too the run of beautiful, warm/hot vintages.

2011 Warm, dry, early vintage. Particularly good Cab. Delicate whites less successful. WA's great run of vintages continued.

2010 Reds generally better than whites. Some caught by late rains but mostly very good.

2009 Especially good for Margaret River (r w), Pemberton (w). Margaret River often experiences polar-opposite conditions to the regions of the eastern states: here so again.

2008 The best for many years across all regions and all varieties.

AUSTRALIA

Accolade Wines Name for all wines/wineries previously under HARDYS, CONSTELLATION groups. Prolonged slumber shows minor signs of rousing. Wakey wakey.

Adelaide Hills SA Best SAUV BL region: cool 450-metre sites in Mt Lofty ranges. CHARD, SHIRAZ best performers now. SHAW & SMITH, ASHTON HILLS, MIKE PRESS firing away.

Alkoomi Mt Barker, WA r w (RIES) 02' 04' 05' 07' 10' 11' 12' 13 (CAB SAUV) 01' 02' 05' 07' 08' Veteran maker of fine RIES; rustic, long-lived reds. Needs a rev.

All Saints Estate Rutherglen, Vic r w br ★★ Producer with a history of great fortifieds. Wooded MARSANNE, CHARD, Pierre CAB blend. Gd table wines.

Alpine Valleys Vic Geographically and varietally similar to KING VALLEY. Best: MAYFORD, Feathertop, Ringer Reef. Aromatic whites, but TEMPRANILLO is region's comet.

Andrew Thomas Hunter V, NSW r w ★★★ Fine producer: old-vine SEM; silken, lavishly oaked SHIRAZ.

Angove's SA r w (br) ★ MURRAY VALLEY family recently celebrated 125 yrs in wine business. Some organic offerings. Cheapies (r w) usually outstrip try-too-hard super-premiums.

Annie's Lane Clare V, SA r w ★ Part of TWE. Consistently gd, boldly flavoured wines. Flagship Copper Trail (can be) excellent, esp RIES, SHIRAZ. Sauntering along.

Arrivo Adelaide Hills, SA r ★★ Long-maceration, tannic, minty NEBBIOLO. Dry, complex, sexy rosé. Minute quantities.

Ashton Hills Adelaide Hills, SA r w (sp) ★★★ (PINOT N) 97' 04' 05' 08' 09' 10' 12 Long-lived RIES, compelling Pinot N made by seminal winemaker Stephen George from 30-yr-old v'yds.

Bailey's of Glenrowan NE Vic r w br ★★★ Rich SHIRAZ, magnificent dessert MUSCAT (★★★★) and TOPAQUE. Part of TWE. V'yds now grown organically. PETIT VERDOT a gd addition. Up and about. New Rutherglen Durif.

Balgownie Estate Vic r w ★★ Old name for medium-bodied, well-balanced, minty CAB, BENDIGO. Now with separate YARRA V arm. Hits and misses.

Balnaves of Coonawarra SA r w ★★★ Grape-grower since 1975; winery since 1996. Lusty CHARD; v.gd spicy, medium-bodied SHIRAZ. Full Tally CAB SAUV flagship.

Bannockburn Vic r w (CHARD) 05' 06' 08' 10' 11 (PINOT N) 02' 04' 05' 06' 07' 08' 10' 11 Intense, complex Chard and Pinot N. Funkified SAUV BL. Winemaker Michael "Gloverboy" Glover – ex-cyclist – in yellow jersey form.

Banrock Station Riverland, SA r w ★ 1,600-ha property on Murray River, massive 243 ha v'yd, owned by ACCOLADE. Gd budget wines, but waning.

Barossa is so-called because of spelling error. Named after Spain's Barrosa Ridge, site of the Peninsular War.

Barossa Valley SA Spiritual home of blood-and-thunder Aussie red wine. Local specialties: v.old-vine SHIRAZ, MOURVÈDRE, CAB SAUV, GRENACHE. Remains lively, prominent, responsive to changing tastes.

Bass Phillip Gippsland, Vic r ★★★ (PINOT N) 02' 04' 10' 11 Tiny amounts of variable but at times exceptional Pinot N in three quality grades. CHARD improving (09 Premium v.gd). There's Oz Pinot N, then there's Bass Phillip. World within itself.

Bay of Fires N Tas r w sp ★★→★★★ Pipers River outpost of ACCOLADE empire. Stylish table wines, Arras super-cuvée sparkler. Complex PINOT N. Accolade determined to keep it a secret.

Beechworth Vic Continental region in the lee of the Victorian Alps. Rugged high country. CHARD, SHIRAZ best-performing varieties, with Italian varietal reds (NEBBIOLO, SANGIOVESE) in minute quantity. CASTAGNA, GIACONDA, Sorrenberg, SAVATERRE flagbearers. A. Rodda Wines one to watch.

Bendigo Vic Warm-to-hot central Victorian region with dozens of small v'yds. BALGOWNIE ESTATE, Sutton Grange, Bress, HARCOURT VALLEY V'YDS, Turner's Crossing, Water Wheel best performers. Traction slipping.

Best's Grampians, Vic r w ★★★ (SHIRAZ) 97' 04' 05' 09' 10' 11' 12 Conservative family winery; *v.gd mid-weight reds*. Thomson Family Shiraz from 120-yr-old vines superb. Shiraz across range in career-best form. Excellent Old-Vine PINOT MEUNIER.

Bindi Macedon, Vic r w ★★★→★★★★ (PINOT N) 04' 06' 08' 10' 12 Ultra-fastidious, terroir-driven maker of outstanding, long-lived Pinot N, CHARD.

Blue Pyrenees Pyrenees, Vic r w sp ★ 180 ha of mature v'yds. CAB SAUV quality mildly resurgent. Reds with strong gum-leaf flavours/aromas.

Boireann Granite Belt QLD r ★★→★★★ Consistently best producer of red wines in Qld (in tiny quantities). SHIRAZ/VIOGNIER the stand-out. Hard to find.

Brand's of Coonawarra Coon, SA r w ★★ 96' 98' 05' 09' 10 Owned by MCWILLIAM'S. Custodian of 100-yr-old vines. Quality struggles at the top end but the main fighting range (CAB SAUV, SHIRAZ, CHARD) delivers gd fruit-and-oak flavour.

Bremerton Lang C, SA r w ★★ Red wines with silky-soft mouthfeel and mounds of flavour. Thrived since Willson sisters took over family winery. Full-bodied CAB, SHIRAZ. No prisoners taken.

Brokenwood Hunter V, NSW r w ★★★ (ILR Res SEM) 02' 03' 05' 06' (Graveyard SHIRAZ) 98' 00' 05' 06' 07' 09' 11 and Cricket Pitch Sem/SAUV BL fuel sales. Figurehead of the Hunter region.

Brookland Valley Margaret R, WA r w ★★ Volume producer of v.gd SAUV BL, CHARD, CAB SAUV. Budget Verse 1 SEM/Sauv Bl and Cab/MERLOT gd value. ACCOLADE owned.

Brown Brothers King V, Vic w br dr sw sp ★★ (Noble RIES) 02' 04' 05' 08 Old family firm. Wide range of crowd-pleasing styles, varieties. General emphasis on sweetness. MONDEUSE/CAB SAUV blend is best red. Extensive GLERA (as in Prosecco) plantings. Recently bought extensive Tasmanian PINOT N (and other) v'yds, released now under TAMAR RIDGE/Devil's Corner range.

By Farr / Farr Rising Vic r w ★★★★ 08' 09' 10' 11' 12 Gary Farr and son Nick's own labels/winery, after departure from BANNOCKBURN. CHARD, PINOT N can be minor masterpieces. Nick mostly in charge now. Quality soaring. Wines to get the heart racing.

Campbells Rutherglen, Vic r (w) br ★★ Smooth, ripe reds (esp Bobbie Burns SHIRAZ); extraordinary Merchant Prince Rare MUSCAT, Isabella Rare TOPAQUE (★★★★).

Canberra District NSW Both quality and quantity on increase; site selection important; cool climate. CLONAKILLA best-known. COLLECTOR, CAPITAL, Ravensworth, EDEN ROAD the new guns.

Capel Vale WA r w ★★ 165-ha estate with v'yds across four regions. Wide range varieties, prices. Variable quality, but when they're gd....

Cape Mentelle Margaret R, WA r w ★★★★ (CAB SAUV) 01' 07' 08' 10' 11 In outstanding form. Robust Cab has become a more elegant (and lower alcohol) style, CHARD v.gd; also ZIN, v. popular SAUV BL/SEM. SHIRAZ on rise. Owned by LVMH Veuve Clicquot (*see* France).

Capital Wines Canberra, NSW r w ★★ Estate's Kyeema v'yd has history of growing some of region's best. SHIRAZ (table and sparkling), RIES stand-outs. V.gd MERLOT.

Carlei Estate Yarra V, Vic r w ★ Winemaker Sergio Carlei sources PINOT N, CHARD from cool regions to make characterful wines. Organic/bio.

Casella Riverina, NSW r w ★ The [YELLOW TAIL] phenomenon incl multimillion-case sales in the USA. Like Fanta at times: soft and sweet. But both 2013 CAB SAUV, SEM/SAUV BL v.gd value.

Castagna Beechworth, Vic r ★★★★ (SYRAH) 02' 04' 05' 06' 08' 10 Filmmaker/ cook/vigneron Julian Castagna leads the Oz bio brigade. Estate-grown SHIRAZ/ VIOGNIER, SANGIOVESE/Shiraz excellent. Rosé and Sparkling Shiraz often Oz's best. Non-estate range named Adam's Rib.

Chalkers Crossing Hilltops, NSW r w ★ Coolish climate wines by French-trained Celine Rousseau; esp SHIRAZ. Alcohol levels worryingly high but quality maintained.

Chambers Rosewood NE Vic (r) (w) br ★★★ Viewed with MORRIS as greatest maker of sticky TOPAQUE, *Muscat*. Far less successful table wines.

Chapel Hill McLaren V, SA r (w) ★★ →★★★ Leading MCLAREN V producer. SHIRAZ, CAB lead way, but TEMPRANILLO and esp GRENACHE both v.gd. Il Vescovo white blend promising. Range has ballooned in recent yrs.

Charles Melton Barossa V, SA r w (sp) ★★★ Tiny winery with bold, luscious reds, esp Nine Popes, an old-vine GRENACHE/SHIRAZ blend. Shiraz continues to shine. Steady as she blows.

Clarendon Hills McLaren V, SA r ★★ Full-monty reds (high alcohol, intense fruit) made with grapes grown on hills above MCLAREN V. Prominent past but jury's out on current era.

Clare Valley SA Small, pretty, high-quality area 145-km north of Adelaide. Best toured by bike. Australia's most prominent RIES region. Gumleaf-scented SHIRAZ; earthen, tannic CAB SAUV. WENDOUREE, TIM ADAMS, GROSSET, MOUNT HORROCKS lead way.

Clonakilla Canberra, NSW r w ★★★★ (SHIRAZ) 01' 03' 05' 06' 07' 08 09' 10' 12 *Deserved leader of the Shiraz/Viognier brigade.* RIES, VIOGNIER excellent.

Coldstream Hills Yarra V, Vic r w (sp) ★★★ (CHARD) 02' 03' 04' 05' 06' 07' 08' 10' 11' 12 (PINOT N) 96' 02' 04' 06' 10' 12 Est 1985 by critic James Halliday. Delicious Pinot N to drink young, *Res to age*. V.gd Chard (esp Res). Recent single-v'yd releases added much sparkle. Part of TWE.

Collector Wines Canberra, NSW r ★★★ (Res SHIRAZ) 06' 07' 08' 09' 12 Collector Wines turned out to be collectable. Layered, spicy, perfumed complex Res Shiraz.

Constellation Wines Australia (CWA) *See* ACCOLADE WINES.

Coonawarra SA Southernmost v'yds of state: home to some of Australia's best (value and quality) CAB SAUV; successful CHARD, SHIRAZ. WYNNS the region's beating heart. BALNAVES, MAJELLA, KATNOOK, BRAND'S all key. Striking red soil on a thick bed of limestone.

Coriole McLaren V, SA r w ★★ (Lloyd Res SHIRAZ) 98' 02' 04' 06' 09 To watch, esp for SANGIOVESE and old-vine Shiraz Lloyd Res. Interesting FIANO.

Craiglee Macedon, Vic r w ★★★ (SHIRAZ) 97' 00' 02' 06' 08' 10 Salt-of-the-earth producer. Northern Rhône inspired. Fragrant, peppery Shiraz, age-worthy CHARD. Shiraz/VIOGNIER new addition.

Crawford River Heathcote, Vic w ★★★ Consistently one of Australia's best RIES from this ultra-cool region.

Cullen Wines Margaret R, WA r w ★★★★ (CHARD) 04' 05' 08' 09' 10' 11 (CAB SAUV / MERLOT) 98' 04' 05' 07' 09' 11 Vanya Cullen makes substantial but subtle SEM / SAUV BL, outstanding Chard, elegant, sinewy Cab/Merlot. Bio.

Cumulus Orange, NSW r w ★ By far the largest v'yd owner and producer in Orange. Variable quality.

Curly Flat Macedon, Vic r w ★★★ (PINOT N) 05' 06' 07' 10' 11 Robust but perfumed Pinot N (esp impressive) on two price/quality levels. Full-flavoured CHARD. Both are age-worthy.

Dalwhinnie Pyrenees, Vic r w ★★★ (CHARD) 05' 06' 07' 10' (SHIRAZ) 04' 05' 06' 07' 08' 10' Rich Chard, CAB SAUV, Shiraz. Best PYRENEES producer.

d'Arenberg McLaren V, SA r w (br) (sw) (sp) ★★★ Sumptuous SHIRAZ and GRENACHE. Many varieties and wacky labels (incl The Cenosilicaphobic Cat SAGRANTINO). Regional leader.

Deakin Estate Vic r w ★ High-volume, high-value varietal table wines. V. low-alcohol MOSCATO. Spicy SHIRAZ. Remarkable consistency.

De Bortoli Griffith, NSW, Yarra V, Vic r w (br) dr sw ★★★★ (Noble SEM) Both irrigation-area winery and leading YARRA V producer. Excellent, cool-climate PINOT N, SHIRAZ, CHARD, SAUV BL and v.gd sweet, botrytized, Sauternes-style Noble Sem. Yarra V arm is where all the action is now.

Devil's Lair Margaret R, WA r w ★★★ Opulent CHARD, CAB SAUV/MERLOT. Fifth Leg popular second label. New 9th Chamber Chard raises the quality bar. Part of TWE.

Domaine A S Tas r w ★★★ Swiss owner-winemakers Peter and Ruth Althaus are perfectionists, making v.gd oak-matured SAUV BL and polarizing cool-climate CAB SAUV. Charismatic.

Domaine Chandon Yarra V, Vic (r) (w) sp ★★ Gd cool-climate sparkling and table wine. Owned by Moët & Chandon (*see* France). Known in UK as Green Point. Hand has hovered over the excitement button for a long time.

> **High woes**
> The Aussie dollar has been high for a number of yrs now. It's put enormous pressure on the local wine industry. Australia has long thought of itself as the world's "best-value wine producer" but even in its own backyard the high dollar has made imports cheap (and put the clamps on exports). How long can Australian producers hold their breath?

Eden Road r w ★★★ Energetic producer making wines from Hilltops, TUMBARUMBA, CANBERRA DISTRICT regions. V.gd SHIRAZ, CHARD, CAB SAUV. Keeps raising bar.

Eden Valley SA Hilly, rock-strewn region home to HENSCHKE, TORZI MATTHEWS, Radford, PEWSEY VALE and others; cutting RIES, (perfumed, bright) SHIRAZ of excellent quality.

Elderton Barossa V, SA r w (br) (sp) ★★ Old vines; rich, oaked CAB SAUV, SHIRAZ. All bases covered. Some organics/bio.

Eldridge Estate Mor Pen, Vic r w ★★★ Winemaker David Lloyd is a fastidious experimenter. PINOT N, GAMAY, CHARD worth the fuss.

Epis Macedon, Vic r w ★★★ (PINOT N) Can an ex-footballer grow delicate Pinot N? Alec Epis proves it's possible. Long-lived Pinot N; elegant CHARD. Cold climate.

Evans & Tate Margaret R, WA r w ★★ Owned by MCWILLIAM's since 2007. Quality has taken sudden jolt north in past yr. SHIRAZ, CAB SAUV, CHARD ones to watch. Value.

Faber Vineyards Swan V, WA r ★★★ (Res SHIRAZ) 03' 07' 08' 09' 10 John Griffiths is guru of WA winemaking. His home estate grows quality, concentrated SHIRAZ. Redefines what's possible in the hot Swan V.

Ferngrove Vineyards Gt Southern, WA r w ★ Cattle farmer Murray Burton's 223-ha wine venture. Gd RIES, MALBEC, CAB SAUV.

Flametree Margaret R, WA r w ★★★ Exceptional CAB SAUV; spicy, seductive SHIRAZ; occasionally compelling CHARD.

Fletcher Pyrenees, Vic r Tiny production (less than 100 dozen per wine). NEBBIOLO focused. Subsequent releases have yet to frank a promising debut.

Fraser Gallop Estate Margaret R, WA r w ★★★ New breed of MARGARET RIVER; concentrated CAB SAUV, CHARD, (wooded) SEM/SAUV BL. Flying.

Freycinet Tas r w (sp) ★★★ (PINOT N) 00' 05' 07' 08' 09' 10' 11 East-coast winery producing dense Pinot N, gd CHARD, excellent Radenti sparkling.

Frogmore Creek Tas r w ★★ Off-dry RIES, age-worthy CHARD, undergrowthy PINOT N. Epitome of cool-climate Australian wine.

Geelong Vic Region w of Melbourne. Excellent performer to follow since re-establishment in mid-1960s. Cool, dry climate. Best names: BANNOCKBURN, BY FARR, PARADISE IV, LETHBRIDGE, Bellarine Estate.

Gemtree Vineyards McLaren V, SA r (w) ★★ Warm-hearted SHIRAZ alongside TEMPRANILLO and other exotica, linked by quality. Largely bio.

Geoff Merrill McLaren V, SA r w ★★ Ebullient maker of Geoff Merrill and Mt Hurtle brands. Ticking along.

Giaconda Beechworth, Vic r w ★★★★ (CHARD) 99' 02' 05' 06' 08' 10' 11 (SHIRAZ) 04' o6' o8' 10' In the mid-1980s Rick Kinzbrunner walked up a steep, dry, rocky hill and came down a winemaking (living) legend. Arguably Australia's best Chard producer. Excellent Shiraz. NEBBIOLO of promise.

Giant Steps / Innocent Bystander Yarra V, Vic ★★★ Buoyant zeitgeist producer. Fun, funky but serious, excellent-quality, single-v'yd CHARD, PINOT N. 2012 vintage a high point.

Glaetzer-Dixon Tas r w ★★★ GLAETZER clan famous in Australia for cuddly warm-climate SHIRAZ. Then Nick Glaetzer turned all this on its head by setting up shop in cool TAS. Euro-style RIES, Rhôney Shiraz, meaty PINOT N. Exciting.

Glaetzer Wines Barossa V, SA r ★★ Hyper-rich, unfiltered, v. ripe old-vine SHIRAZ led by iconic Amon-Ra. V.gd examples of high-octane style.

Goulburn Valley Vic Old region in temperate mid-Vic. Full-bodied, savoury table wines. MARSANNE, CAB SAUV, SHIRAZ the pick, TAHBILK, MITCHELTON mainstays. Also referred to as Nagambie Lakes.

Grampians Vic Region previously known as Great Western. Temperate region in Vic's northwest. High-quality spicy SHIRAZ, sparkling Shiraz. Home to SEPPELT, BEST'S, MOUNT LANGI GHIRAN.

They said it would never make it: Granite Belt in sunny Queensland is starting to turn heads.

Granite Belt Qld High-altitude, (relatively) cool, improbable region just north of Qld/NSW border. Spicy SHIRAZ, rich SEM.

Grant Burge Barossa V, SA r w (br) (sw) (sp) ★★ Smooth reds and whites from best grapes of Burge's large v'yd holdings. Beginning to stir.

Great Southern WA Remote cool area; Albany, Denmark, Frankland River, Mount Barker, Porongurup are official subregions. First-class RIES, SHIRAZ.

Greenstone Vineyard Heathcote, Vic r ★★→★★★ Partnership between David Gleave MW (London), Alberto Antonini (Italy), Australian viticulturist Mark Walpole; v.gd SHIRAZ, gd SANGIOVESE.

Grosset Clare V, SA r w ★★★ (RIES) oo' o2' o5' 10' 12' 13 (Gaia) 98' 99' o2' o4' o5' Fastidious winemaker. Foremost Australian Ries, lovely CHARD, v.gd *Gaia* CAB SAUV/MERLOT. Variable PINOT N.

Hanging Rock Macedon, Vic r w sp ★★ (HEATHCOTE SHIRAZ) oo' o1' o2' o4' o6' o8' Successfully moved upmarket with sparkling Macedon and Heathcote Shiraz, but quiet of late.

Harcourt Valley Vineyards Bendigo, Vic r ★★ This estate has sprung thoroughly to life in recent yrs. Dense, syrupy, seductive SHIRAZ, MALBEC, CAB SAUV, with help from American oak.

Hardys r w (sw) sp ★★★ (Eileen CHARD) o2' o4' o6' o8' o9' 10' 12 (Eileen SHIRAZ) o2' o4' o6' Historic company now part of ACCOLADE. Chard excellent. Shiraz wobbly. New Eileen PINOT N promising.

Heathcote Vic The 500-million-yr-old Cambrian soil here has great potential for high-quality reds, esp SHIRAZ. Been more hype than substance, but runs now being added to the board.

Heggies Eden V, SA r w dr (sw) ★★ V'yd at 500 metres owned by S Smith & Sons; v.gd RIES, VIOGNIER. *Chard is still the in-the-know tip.*

Henschke Eden V, SA r w ★★★★ (SHIRAZ) 86' 90' 91' 96' o2' o4' o6' o9 (CAB SAUV) 86' 88 90' 96' o2' o4' o6' Pre-eminent 140-yr-old family business known for delectable Hill of Grace (Shiraz), v.gd Cab Sauv, red blends, gd whites and scary prices.

Hewitson SE Aus r (w) ★★★ (*Old Garden Mourvèdre*) 98' 99' o2' o5' o9' 10 Dean Hewitson sources parcels off v. old vines. SHIRAZ and varietal release from "oldest MOURVÈDRE vines on the planet".

Hollick Coon, SA r w (sp) ★ Gd CAB SAUV, SHIRAZ. Lively restaurant with v'yd views.

Houghton Swan V, WA r w ★★ Famous old winery of Western Australia. Part of ACCOLADE. Soft, ripe Supreme is top-selling, age-worthy white; *a national classic*. V.gd CAB SAUV, SHIRAZ, etc. sourced from MARGARET RIVER, GREAT SOUTHERN.

Howard Park WA r w ★★★ (RIES) 02' 04' 07' 08' 11' 12' (CAB SAUV) 94' 99' 01' 05' 07' 09' 10 (CHARD) 04 05' 07' 08' 10' 11 Scented Ries, Chard; earthy Cab. Second label *MadFish v.gd value.* Huge range now; increasing emphasis on PINOT N.

Hunter Valley NSW Great name in NSW, subtropical coal-mining area 100 miles n of Sydney. Mid-weight, earthy SHIRAZ, gentle SEM can live for 30 yrs. Classic terroir-driven styles. TYRRELL'S, MOUNT PLEASANT, BROKENWOOD the pillars.

Jacob's Creek (Orlando) Barossa V, SA r w (br) (sw) sp ★★ Pioneering company, owned by Pernod Ricard. Almost totally focused on various tiers of Jacob's Creek wines, covering all varieties and prices. St Hugo CAB, brand's best red, celebrated 30th release in 2013.

Jamsheed Pyrenees and Yarra V, Vic ★★★ Exciting producer, esp SHIRAZ from YARRA V, GRAMPIANS, PYRENEES, BEECH. Complex, savoury expressions.

Jasper Hill Heathcote, Vic r w ★★★ (SHIRAZ) 99' 02' 04' 06' 08' 09' 10' Emily's Paddock Shiraz/CAB FR blend, Georgia's Paddock Shiraz from dry-land estate are intense, long-lived. Bio.

Jim Barry Clare V, SA r w ★★★ Great v'yds provide v.gd RIES, McCrae Wood SHIRAZ, richly robed, oaked, pricey The Armagh Shiraz.

John Duval Wines Barossa V, SA r ★★★ John Duval – former chief red winemaker for PENFOLDS (and Grange) – makes *delicious Rhôney reds* that are supple and smooth, yet amply structured.

Kaesler Barossa V, SA r (w) ★★ Gd (in heroic, full-on style) but variable; alcohol levels often tip balance. Old vines.

Katnook Estate Coon, SA r w (sw) (sp) ★★★ (Odyssey CAB SAUV) 91' 96' 98' 99' 04' 08' 09 Pricey icons *Odyssey*, Prodigy SHIRAZ. Concentrated fruit, oak.

Kilikanoon Clare V, SA r w ★★★ RIES, SHIRAZ excellent performers in recent yrs. Luscious, beautifully made. Big end of town style-wise.

Kingston Estate SE Aus r w ★ Kaleidoscopic array of varietal wines. Big volume, big value (mostly).

King Valley Vic Altitude between 155–860 metres has massive impact on varieties, styles. Around 30 brands headed by BROWN BROTHERS, Dal Zotto, Chrismont, PIZZINI.

Knappstein Wines Clare V, SA r w ★★ Reliable RIES, CAB SAUV/MERLOT, SHIRAZ, CAB SAUV. Owned by LION NATHAN. New medium-bodied, perfumed Shiraz/MALBEC adds charm to range.

Kooyong Mor Pen, Vic r w ★★★ PINOT N, CHARD of power, structure, PINOT GR of charm. Single-v'yd wines. Now among Australia's finest.

Lake Breeze Lang C, SA r (w) ★★ Succulently smooth, gutsy, value SHIRAZ, CAB SAUV. Struggles to produce top-end wine but in mid-range consistently impresses.

Lake's Folly Hunter V, NSW r w ★★★ (CHARD) 97' 99' 00' 01' 04' 05' 07' (CAB SAUV) 00' 01' 05' Founded by Max Lake, pioneer of HUNTER V Cab Sauv. Chard often better than for Cab Sauv blend. As individual as ever.

Langmeil Barossa V, SA r w ★★ Owns world's oldest block of SHIRAZ (planted in 1843) plus other old v'yds, often producing opulent full-kitchen-sink Shiraz.

Larry Cherubino Wines Frankland R, WA r w ★★★ Intense SAUV BL, RIES, *spicy Shiraz*, curranty CAB SAUV. Ambitious label with multiple ranges. Making great strides.

Lazy Ballerina McLaren V, SA r ★ Young viticulturist James Hook makes robust, polished reds, mostly with SHIRAZ.

Leasingham Clare V, SA r w ★★ Once-important brand with v.gd RIES, SHIRAZ, CAB SAUV, Cab Sauv/MALBEC blend. Husk of former self. Brand owned by ACCOLADE; v'yds, winery sold off.

Leeuwin Estate Margaret R, WA r w ★★★★ (CHARD) 99' 02' 04' 05' 06' 07' 08' 10' Leading West Australia estate. Superb, age-worthy Art Series *Chard*. SAUV BL, RIES less brilliant. *Cab Sauv* now v.gd.

Leo Buring Barossa V, SA w ★★★ 02' 04' 05' 06' 08' 13' Part of TWE. Exclusively RIES; Leonay top label, *ages superbly*.

Lethbridge Vic r w ★★★ Stylish, small-run producer of CHARD, SHIRAZ, PINOT N, RIES. Outside the square.

Limestone Coast Zone SA Important zone, incl Bordertown, COON, Mt Benson, Mt Gambier, PADTHAWAY, Robe, WRATTONBULLY.

Lindemans r w ★★ Owned by TWE. Low-price Bin range now its main focus, far cry from former glory. Lindeman's COON Trio reds v.gd but unexciting.

Lion Nathan NZ brewery; owns KNAPPSTEIN, PETALUMA, ST HALLETT, STONIER, TATACHILLA.

Macedon and Sunbury Vic Adjacent regions: Macedon higher elevation, Sunbury nr Melbourne airport. Quality from CRAIGLEE, Granite Hills, HANGING ROCK, BINDI, CURLY FLAT and EPIS.

Mac Forbes Yarra V, Vic ★★★ Contemplative single-v'yd releases, mainly PINOT N, RIES. Slowly building enviable reputation.

McLaren Vale SA Historic, maritime region on southern outskirts of Adelaide. Big-flavoured reds have great appeal in the USA, but CORIOLE, CHAPEL HILL, WIRRA WIRRA, GEMTREE, Inkwell, Brash Higgins, SC PANNELL and growing number of others show elegance as well as flavour.

McWilliam's SE Aus r w (br) (sw) ★★★ Family owned. Hanwood, EVANS & TATE, BRAND'S, MOUNT PLEASANT its key pillars, but with an assortment of other labels. Active again following a slumber. Making keen use of TUMBARUMBA CHARD.

Main Ridge Estate Mor Pen, Vic r w ★★★ Rich, age-worthy CHARD, PINOT N. Doyen of MOR PEN wine. Minuscule estate.

Majella Coon, SA r (w) ★★★ Opulent, crowd-pleasing, quality SHIRAZ, CAB SAUV. Super-reliable.

Margaret River WA Temperate coastal area s of Perth. Powerful CHARD, structured CAB SAUV, spicy SHIRAZ. CULLEN, LEEUWIN, MOSS WOOD, VOYAGER ESTATE, FRASER GALLOP, DEVIL'S LAIR, FLAMETREE and many others. Great touring (and surfing) region.

Mayford NE Vic, Vic r w ★★ Tiny v'yd in a private, hidden valley. Put Alpine Valleys on the map. SHIRAZ, CHARD, developing TEMPRANILLO.

New trendy grape: Tempranillo. Plantings exceed all expectations.

Meerea Park Hunter V, NSW r w ★★ Brothers Garth and Rhys Eather have taken 20 yrs to be an overnight success. Age-worthy SEM, SHIRAZ.

Mike Press Wines Adelaide Hills, SA r w ★ Tiny production, tiny pricing. SHIRAZ, CAB SAUV, CHARD, SAUV BL. Fast become the crowd favourite of bargain-hunters.

Mitchelton Goulburn V, Vic r w (sw) ★★ Stalwart producer of RIES, SHIRAZ, CAB SAUV, plus speciality of *Marsanne*, ROUSSANNE. Serious refurbishment underway.

Mitolo r ★★ High-quality SHIRAZ, CAB SAUV. Heroic but (often) irresistible wines.

Moorilla Estate Tas r w (sp) ★★ Nr Hobart on Derwent River. Gd RIES, CHARD; PINOT N. Superb restaurant, extraordinary art gallery. Folks (rightly) flock from far and wide.

Moorooduc Estate Mor Pen, Vic r w ★★★ Stylish, sophisticated producer of CHARD, PINOT N. Influential.

Moppity Vineyards Hilltops, NSW r w ★★ Making a name for its Res SHIRAZ/VIOGNIER (Hilltops), CHARD (TUMBARUMBA). Excellent show record in recent yrs.

Mornington Peninsula Vic Exciting cool coastal area 40 km se of Melbourne. Many quality boutique wineries to explore. Wine/surf/beach/food playground.

Morris NE Vic (r) (w) br ★★★★ RUTHERGLEN producer of Australia's greatest dessert MUSCATS, Tokays/TOPAQUES.

Moss Wood Margaret R, WA r w ★★★ (CAB SAUV) 90' 91' 01' 04' 05' 10 Makes

MARGARET RIVER's most opulent wines from its 11.7 ha. SEM, CHARD, super-smooth *Cab Sauv*. Oak-rich.

Mount Horrocks Clare V, SA r w ★★★ Fine dry RIES, sweet Cordon Cut Ries; *Chard best in region*. SHIRAZ, CAB SAUV getting better.

Mount Langi Ghiran Grampians, Vic r w ★★★★ (SHIRAZ) 96' 04' 05' 08' 09' 10 Rich, peppery, *Rhône-like Shiraz*. V.gd sparkling Shiraz. Excellent Cliff Edge Shiraz. Cool climate star. Great site.

Mount Mary Yarra V, Vic r w ★★★ (PINOT N) 00' 02' 05' 10' (Quintet) 84' 88' 90' 92' 96' 98' 04' 10' The late Dr John Middleton made tiny amounts of suave CHARD, vivid Pinot N and an elegant CAB SAUV blend. All age impeccably. Jury is out on modern era.

Wine the world has missed? Aussie Pinot Noir. Quality (and interest) gone through the roof.

Mudgee NSW Longest region northwest of Sydney. Sizeable reds, fine SEM, full CHARD. Struggling now to gain traction.

Murray Valley SA Vast irrigated v'yds. Now at centre of climate-change firestorm.

Ngeringa Adelaide Hills, SA r w ★★ Perfumed, bio-grown PINOT N. Rhôney SHIRAZ. Savoury rosé. Complexity reigns.

Ninth Island Tas *See* PIPERS BROOK (Kreglinger).

Ochota Barrels Barossa V, SA r w ★★★ Quixotic producer making hay with (mostly) old-vine GRENACHE, SHIRAZ from MCLAREN V, BAROSSA. Hero of Oz's "new guard".

O'Leary Walker Wines Clare V, SA r w ★★★ Low profile but excellent quality. CLARE V RIES standout. MCLAREN V SHIRAZ oak-heavy but gd.

Orange NSW Cool-climate, high-elevation region. Lively SHIRAZ (when ripe). Excellent (intense) SAUV BL, CHARD.

Padthaway SA Large area developed as overspill of COON. V.gd SHIRAZ, CAB SAUV. Salinity an issue. Less prominent than it was a decade back.

Pannell, SC McLaren V, SA r ★★★ Excellent SHIRAZ and (esp) GRENACHE-based wines. NEBBIOLO to watch. Reputation rising (fast).

Paringa Estate Mor Pen, Vic r w ★★★★ Maker of spectacular PINOT N, SHIRAZ. Fleshy, fruity, flashy styles. Irresistible.

Paxton McLaren V, SA r ★★ Significant v'yd holder. Largely organic/bio. Ripe but elegant SHIRAZ and GRENACHE. Hugely influential – by its deeds – in Australia's bio movement.

Pemberton WA Region between MARGARET RIVER and GREAT SOUTHERN; initial enthusiasm for PINOT N replaced by RIES, CHARD, MERLOT, SHIRAZ.

Penfolds r w (br) (sp) ★★★★ (Grange) 52' 53' 55' 60' 62' 63' 66' 71' 76' 78' 83' 86' 90' 96' 98' 99' 02' 04' 05' 06' 08' 09 (CAB SAUV Bin 707) 90' 91' 96' 98' 02' 04' 06' 08' Originally Adelaide, now everywhere. Consistently Australia's best warm-climate red wine company. Yattarna CHARD, Bin Chard now of comparable quality to reds. St Henri SHIRAZ much loved.

Penley Estate Coon, SA r w ★ Rich, textured, fruit-and-oak CAB SAUV; SHIRAZ/Cab Sauv blend; CHARD. Reds now routinely high in alcohol.

Perth Hills WA Fledgling area 30-km east of Perth, with large number of growers on mild hillside sites.

Petaluma Adelaide Hills, SA r w sp ★★★ (RIES) 02' 07' 11' 12' 13 (CHARD) 05' 06' 07' 12' (CAB SAUV COON) 90' 91' 98' 99' 04' 05' 07' '08 Seems to miss ex-owner/ creator Brian Croser. Bought by LION NATHAN in 2002. Reds richer from 1988. Gd but low-key now.

Peter Lehmann Wines Barossa V, SA r w (br) (sw) (sp) ★★★ Defender of BAROSSA V faith. Well-priced wines, often in substantial quantities. Luxurious, sexy Stonewell SHIRAZ among many others (r w). Peter died 2013; company continues.

Pewsey Vale Adelaide Hills, SA w ★★★ Glorious RIES, standard and (aged-release) The Contours, grown on lovely tiered v'yd.

Piano Piano Beechworth, Vic r w New producer working a v'yd in next paddock on from GIACONDA. Powerful CHARD.

Pierro Margaret R, WA r w ★★ (CHARD) 96' 01' 02' 06' 07' 08' 09' 11' Producer of expensive, tangy SEM/SAUV BL and ballsy Chard.

Pipers Brook Tas r w sp ★★★ (RIES) 02' 04' 06' 07' 09' (CHARD) 00' 02' 05' 07' 08' Cool-area pioneer; gd Ries, *restrained Chard and sparkling* from Tamar V. Second label: Ninth Island. Owned by Belgian Kreglinger family.

Pirramimma McLaren V, SA r w ★ Century-old family business with large v'yds moving with the times; snappy packaging.

Pizzini King V, Vic r ★★ (NEBBIOLO) 98' 02' 05' 10 Leads the charge towards Italian varieties in Australia. Nebbiolo, SANGIOVESE, blends. Heartbeat of the King V.

Plantagenet Mt Barker, WA r w (sp) ★★★ Wide range of varieties, esp rich CHARD, SHIRAZ, vibrant, potent, age-worthy CAB SAUV. 40 yrs young.

Primo Estate SA r w dr (sw) ★★★ Joe Grilli's many successes incl v.gd MCLAREN V spicy SHIRAZ/SANGIOVESE, rich Shiraz, tangy COLOMBARD and potent Joseph CAB SAUV/MERLOT.

Punch Yarra V, Vic r w ★★★★ Lance family ran Diamond Valley for decades. When they sold, they retained the close-planted PINOT N v'yd. It grows detailed, decisive, age-worthy wines. Rebounding strongly from 2009 fires.

Pyrenees Vic Central Vic region producing rich, often minty reds. DALWHINNIE, TALTARNI, BLUE PYRENEES, Mount Avoca, FLETCHER, Dog Rock wineries all ascendant.

Richmond Grove Barossa V, SA w ★ Gd RIES at bargain prices; not much else. Owned by JACOB'S CREEK.

Riverina NSW Large-volume irrigated zone centred on Griffith.

Robert Oatley Wines Mudgee, NSW r w ★★→★★★ Robert Oatley created ROSEMOUNT ESTATE. Ambition burns anew. New Finisterre range v.gd.

Rockford Barossa V, SA r w sp ★→★★★ Small producer from old, low-yielding v'yds; reds best, also iconic sparkling Black SHIRAZ.

> **Backflip with a double twist**
>
> Organized wine (judging) shows have been a major part of the Australian wine scene for the past 50 yrs. In general they've tended to foster bigger, bolder styles of wine – so much so that high-fruit, high-oak wines are often called "show styles". In a dramatic shift in taste, though, the opposite is now true. Lean, (often) stalky, elegant, low-oak wines are pulling all the major gongs. Needless to say, Australia's warm-climate producers don't like it one little bit.

Rosemount Estate r w ★★ Major volumes. In doldrums for nearly a decade but on the hop of a sudden. Creaming them on Australian wine show circuit. GRENACHE, SHIRAZ esp.

Ruggabellus Barossa V, SA r ★★★ Causing a stir. Funkier, more savoury version of the BAROSSA. Old oak, minimal sulphur, wild yeast, whole bunches/stems. Blends of GRENACHE, SHIRAZ, MATARO, CINSAULT.

Rutherglen and Glenrowan Vic Two of four regions in the northeast Vic zone, justly famous for sturdy reds and magnificent fortified dessert wines.

St Hallett Barossa V, SA r w ★★★ (Old Block) 90' 91' 98 99' 02' 04' 06' 08' 10' Old Block SHIRAZ the star; rest of range is smooth, stylish. LION NATHAN-owned.

Saltram Barossa V, SA r w ★★★ Excellent-value Mamre Brook (SHIRAZ, CAB SAUV), prestige No 1 Shiraz are leaders. Underestimated. TWE owned.

Samuel's Gorge McLaren V, SA r ★★★ Justin McNamee makes SHIRAZ, TEMPRANILLO of character and place.

Savaterre Beechworth, Vic r w ★★★ (PINOT N) 02' 04' 06' 08' 10' 12 Tough run of seasons but excellent producer of CHARD, PINOT N; now close-planted SHIRAZ. 12 Pinot N best of line.

Seppelt Grampians, Vic r w br (sw) sp ★★★ (St Peter's SHIRAZ) 85' 86' 96' 97' 02' 04' 06 08' 09' Historic name owned by TWE. Impressive array of region-specific RIES, CHARD, SHIRAZ.

Seppeltsfield Barossa V, SA r br ★★ National Trust Heritage Winery bought by KILIKANOON in 2007. Fortified wine stocks back to 1878. Table wines released in 2012 promising.

Setanta Wines Adelaide Hills, SA r w ★★ The Sullivan family from Ireland can turn out wonderful RIES, GRENACHE, SHIRAZ, CAB SAUV.

Sevenhill Clare V, SA r w (br) ★ Owned by the Jesuitical Manresa Society since 1851. Consistently gd SHIRAZ; RIES.

Seville Estate Yarra V, Vic r w ★★★ (SHIRAZ) 97' 99' 04' 05' 06' 10' Excellent CHARD, Shiraz, PINOT N. Reds esp spicy, (white) peppery.

Shadowfax Vic r w ★★ Stylish winery, part of historic Werribee Park. V.gd CHARD, PINOT N, SHIRAZ. Never a bad wine.

Shaw & Smith Adelaide Hills, SA (r) w ★★★ Founded by Martin Shaw and Australia's first MW, Michael Hill-Smith. Crisp *harmonious* Sauv Bl, complex barrel-fermented M3 CHARD and, surpassing them both, SHIRAZ. Daylight to PINOT N but it's improving. Addition of winemaker Adam Wadewitz another plus.

Shelmerdine Vineyards Heathcote, Vic r w ★★ Elegant wines from estate in the YARRA V, HEATHCOTE. PINOT N, SAUV BL, SHIRAZ, CHARD can all be v.gd.

Southern NSW Zone NSW Incl CANBERRA, Gundagai, Hilltops, TUMBARUMBA.

Spinifex Barossa V, SA r w ★★★ Small, high-quality producer of complex SHIRAZ, GRENACHE blends. Nothing over-the-top. Wonderful BAROSSA producer.

Stanton & Killeen Rutherglen, Vic r br ★★ The untimely death of Chris Killeen in 2007 was a major blow but his children carry on in gd style. Fortified vintage is the star.

Stefano Lubiana S Tas r w sp ★★★ Beautiful v'yds on the banks of the Derwent River, 20 minutes from Hobart. Excellent PINOT N, sparkling, MERLOT, CHARD.

Stella Bella Margaret R, WA r w ★★★ Humdinger wines. CAB SAUV, SEM/SAUV BL, CHARD, SHIRAZ, SANGIOVESE/Cab Sauv. Highly individual. Sturdy, characterful.

Stoney Rise Tas r w ★★★ Joe Holyman was wicket-keeper for TAS; holds first-class record for highest no. of catches on debut; now looks after all winemaking tasks for his outstanding PINOT N, CHARD.

Stonier Wines Mor Pen, Vic r w ★★ (CHARD) 02' 06' 07' 08' 12 (PINOT N) 00' 02' 04' 06' 08' 09' 12 Consistently gd, with Res notable for elegance. LION NATHAN-owned.

Sunbury Vic *See* MACEDON AND SUNBURY.

Swan Valley WA Located 20 mins n of Perth. Birthplace of wine in the west. Hot climate makes strong, low-acid wines. FABER V'YDS leading quality way.

Tahbilk Goulburn V, Vic r w ★★★ (MARSANNE) 93' 01' 06' 08' 13 (SHIRAZ) 76' 02' 04' 06' 10 Historic family estate: long-ageing reds, also RIES and some of Australia's best old-vine *Marsanne*. Res CAB SAUV can be outstanding; value for money ditto. Rare 1860 Vines Shiraz. Stirring.

Taltarni Pyrenees, Vic r w sp ★★ SHIRAZ, CAB SAUV in best shape in yrs. Long-haul wines but jack-hammer no longer required to remove tannin from your gums.

Tamar Ridge N Tas r w (sp) 230 ha+ of vines make this a major player in TAS. Acquired in 2010 by BROWN BROTHERS. Releases under new ownership so far have failed to excite.

Tapanappa SA r ★★★ WRATTONBULLY collaboration between Brian Croser, Bollinger,

AUSTRALIA

J-M Cazes of Pauillac. Splendid CAB SAUV blend, SHIRAZ, MERLOT. Surprising *Pinot N* from Fleurieu Peninsula.

TarraWarra Yarra V, Vic r w ★★★ (Res CHARD) 02' 04' 05' 06' 08' 10' 11 (Res PINOT N) 00' 04' 05' 06' 10' Has moved from hefty and idiosyncratic to elegant and long. Res far better than standard. Beautiful estate.

Tasmania Cold island region with hot reputation. Outstanding sparkling, PINOT N, RIES. CHARD, SAUV BL, PINOT GR v.gd.

Busiest hive of small-batch winemaking in Oz is Yarra Valley. Sleepy Hollow days over.

Tatachilla McLaren V, SA r w ★ Significant production of whites and gd reds. Acquired by LION NATHAN in 2002. Off the boil.

Taylors Wines Clare V, SA r w ★★ Large-scale production led by RIES, SHIRAZ, CAB SAUV. Exports under Wakefield Wines brand with success.

Ten Minutes by Tractor Mor Pen, Vic r w ★★★ Wacky name, smart packaging, even better wines. *Chard, Pinot N both excellent* and will age.

Teusner Barossa V, SA r ★★★ Old vines, clever winemaking, pure fruit flavours. Leads a BAROSSA V trend towards "more wood, no good". All about grapes.

Tim Adams Clare V, SA ★★ Ever-reliable RIES, CAB SAUV/MALBEC blend, SHIRAZ and now TEMPRANILLO.

Topaque Vic Iconic Rutherglen sticky Tokay gains a clumsy new name, thanks to the EU.

Torbreck Barossa V, SA r (w) ★★★ The most stylish of the cult wineries beloved of the US. Focus on old-vine Rhône varieties led by SHIRAZ. Rich, sweet, high alcohol. Acrimonious split lead to founder Dave Powell's departure in 2013.

Torzi Matthews Eden V, SA r ★★ Aromatic, stylish SHIRAZ. Excellent value. Torzi Schist Rock Shiraz difficult to say politely after a glass or two: but worth the effort.

Treasury Wine Estates (TWE) Aussie wine behemoth. Merger of Beringer Blass and Southcorp wine groups. Dozens of well-known brands, LINDEMANS, PENFOLDS, WYNNS, DEVIL'S LAIR, COLDSTREAM HILLS, SALTRAM, BAILEYS OF GLENROWAN among them.

Trentham Estate Vic (r) w ★ 60,000 cases of family grown and made, sensibly priced wines from "boutique" winery on Murray River.

Tumbarumba NSW Cool-climate NSW region nestled in the Australian Alps. Sites 500–800 metres. CHARD the star.

Turkey Flat Barossa V, SA r p ★★★ Top producer of bright-coloured rosé, GRENACHE, and SHIRAZ from core of 150-yr-old v'yd. Controlled alcohol and oak. New single-v'yd wines.

Two Hands Barossa V, SA r ★★ Brash SHIRAZ from PADTHAWAY, MCLAREN V, Lang C, BAROSSA V, HEATHCOTE. The whole box and dice.

Tyrrell's Hunter V, NSW r w ★★★★ (SEM) 01' 05' 08' 09' 10' 11' 13 (Vat 47 CHARD) 00' 02' 04' 07' 09' 10' 12 Australia's greatest maker of Sem, Vat 1 now joined with series of individual v'yd or subregional wines. *Vat 47*, Australia's first Chard, continues to defy the climatic odds. Outstanding old-vine 4 Acres SHIRAZ and Vat 9 Shiraz.

Vasse Felix Margaret R, WA r w ★★★★ (CAB SAUV) 98' 99' 01 04' 07' 08' 09' 10 With CULLEN, pioneer of MARGARET RIVER. Elegant Cab Sauv for mid-weight balance. Generally resurgent. Complex CHARD on rapid rise.

Voyager Estate Margaret R, WA r w ★★★ Sizeable volume of (mostly) estate-grown, rich, powerful SEM, SAUV BL, CHARD, CAB SAUV/MERLOT. Terrific quality.

Wantirna Estate Yarra V, Vic ★★★★ Regional pioneer showing no sign of slowing down. CHARD, PINOT N, Bordeaux blend all v.gd.

Wendouree Clare V, SA r ★★★★ Treasured maker (tiny quantities) of powerful, tannic and concentrated reds, based on SHIRAZ, CAB SAUV, MOURVÈDRE, MALBEC. Recently moved to screwcap. Buy for next generation.

West Cape Howe Denmark, WA r w ★★ The minnow that swallowed the whale in 2009 when it purchased 7,700-tonne Goundrey winery and 237 ha of estate v'yds. V.gd SHIRAZ, CAB SAUV blends.

Westend Estate Riverina, NSW r w ★★ Thriving family producer of tasty bargains, esp Private Bin SHIRAZ/Durif. Creative, charismatic Bill Calabria is in charge. Recent cool-climate additions v.gd value.

Willow Creek Mor Pen, Vic r w ★★ Gd gear. Impressive producer of CHARD, PINOT N in particular. Ex-STONIER winemaker Geraldine McFaul in charge.

Wirra Wirra McLaren V, SA r w (sw) (sp) ★★★ (RSW SHIRAZ) 02' 04' 05' 06' 07' 09' 10' (CAB SAUV) 02' 04' 05' 06' 09' 10' High-quality wines in flashy new livery. RSW Shiraz has edged in front of Cab Sauv. The Angelus Cab Sauv named Dead Ringer in export markets.

Wolf Blass Barossa V, SA r w (br) (sw) (sp) ★★→★★★ (Black Label CAB SAUV blend) 90' 91' 96' 02' 04' 05 06' 08' Owned by TWE. Not the noisy player it once was but still a volume name. Top-end wines showing less (though still lots of) oak.

Woodlands Margaret R, WA r (w) ★★★ 7 ha of 35-yr-old+ CAB SAUV among region's top v'yds; younger, still v.gd plantings of other Bordeaux reds. Reds of brooding impact.

Wrattonbully SA Important grape-growing region in LIMESTONE COAST ZONE for 30 yrs; profile lifted by activity of TAPANAPPA, Peppertree.

Wynns Coon, SA r w ★★★★ (SHIRAZ) 55' 86' 90' 91' 96' 98' 99' 04' 05' 06' 09' 10' 12 (CAB SAUV) 57' 60' 82' 85' 86' 90' 91' 94' 96' 98' 00' 02' 04' 05' 06' 09' 10' 12 TWE-owned COON classic. RIES, CHARD, Shiraz, *Cab Sauv* all v.gd, esp Black Label Cab Sauv, *John Riddoch Cab Sauv*. Recent single-v'yd releases add lustre.

Yabby Lake Mor Pen, Vic r w ★★★★ Joint venture between movie magnate Robert Kirby, Larry McKenna, Tod Dexter. Quality rose sharply with winemaker Tom Carson. Single-site CHARD, PINOT N excellent. Major show trophy winner in 2013.

Yalumba Barossa V, SA, SA r w sp ★★★ 163 yrs young, family owned. *Full spectrum of high-quality wines*, from budget to elite single-v'yd. In excellent form. Entry-level Y Series v.gd value.

Yarra Valley Vic Historic area just northeast of Melbourne. Growing emphasis on v. successful PINOT N, CHARD, SHIRAZ, sparkling. Deceptively gd CAB SAUV.

"Natural wines" have caught the eye of Aussie hipsters as elsewhere. The land of fair-dinkum straight-shooters isn't the place it once was.

Yarra Yarra Yarra V, Vic r w ★★ Increased to 7 ha, giving greater access to fine SEM/ SAUV BL, CAB SAUV, each in classic Bordeaux style.

Yarra Yering Yarra V, Vic r w ★★★★ (Dry Reds) 90' 91' 93' 94 97' 99' 00' 01' 02' 04' 05' 06' 08' 09' 10 Best-known Lilydale boutique winery. Powerful PINOT N; deep, herby CAB SAUV (Dry Red No 1); SHIRAZ (Dry Red No 2). Luscious, daring flavours (r w). Much-admired founder Bailey Carrodus died in 2008. Acquired 2009 by KAESLER.

Yellow Tail NSW *See* CASELLA.

Yeringberg Yarra V, Vic r w ★★★ (MARSANNE/ROUSSANNE) 00' 02' 04 05 06' 09' 12 (CAB SAUV) 84' 88' 90 97' 98 00' 04 05' 06' 08' 10' Dreamlike historic estate still in the hands of founding family. Small quantities of v.-high-quality Marsanne, Roussanne, CHARD, Cab Sauv, PINOT N.

Yering Station / Yarrabank Yarra V, Vic r w sp ★★★ On site of Vic's first v'yd; replanted after 80-yr gap. Excellent Yering Station table wines (Res CHARD, PINOT N, SHIRAZ, VIOGNIER); Yarrabank (v.gd sparkling wines in joint venture with Champagne Devaux).

Zema Estate Coon, SA r ★ One of the last bastions of hand-pruning in COON. Powerful, straightforward reds. Looking for a spark.

New Zealand

Abbreviations used in the text:

Auck	Auckland
B of P	Bay of Plenty
Cant	Canterbury
N/C Ot	North/Central Otago
Gis	Gisborne
Hawk	Hawke's Bay
Hend	Henderson
Marl	Marlborough
Mart	Martinborough
Nel	Nelson
Waih	Waiheke Island
Waip	Waipara
Wair	Wairarapa

Northland

Auckland
Auckland · Waiheke Island
Auckland
Waikato · Bay of Plenty
Gisborne
Hawke's Bay
Wairarapa
Nelson (incl Martinborough)
Nelson · Wellington
Marlborough · Blenheim
Waipara
Canterbury · Christchurch
North Otago (incl Waitaki Valley)
Central Otago
Dunedin

Tasman Sea

Pacific Ocean

New Zealand's 700 wine producers are a much happier bunch than a few years ago, when a "savalanche" of Sauvignon Blanc drove prices down and numerous wineries out of business. The balance of supply and demand has been restored and export prices are climbing. No region on earth grows more Sauvignon Blanc than Marlborough. In the UK, Marlborough Sauvignon Blanc is losing ground to cheaper bottlings from Chile and South Africa, but aromatic, appetizingly crisp Kiwi Sauvignon Blanc is wildly popular in Australia's heat. The USA – where NZ's profile has been boosted by hobbit movies and the America's Cup – is likely to emerge shortly as the biggest market for NZ wine; already Kim Crawford Marlborough Sauvignon Blanc sells a million cases a year. But NZ is not a one-trick pony. Its scented, supple Pinot Noirs are among the finest in the New World; its aromatic whites from Pinot Gris, Riesling and Gewurztraminer are carving out export niches, and there are still regions short of their due recognition. And of course markets, China among them, as yet unconquered.

Recent vintages

2013 Record but overall high-quality crop, reflecting warm days and clear, cool nights. Ripe, disease-free grapes, retaining freshness and acidity. Especially good in the North Island and Marlborough.

2012 Very racy Marlborough Sauv Bl. Best for whites in Hawke's Bay. Central Otago fine all round.

2011 Regions in the middle of the country – including Marlborough – fared best; elsewhere, a stiff test of grape-growing and winemaking skills.

2010 Aromatic, strongly flavoured Marlborough Sauv Bl with firm acid spine. Hawke's Bay had outstanding Chard.

Akarua C Ot r (p) (w) (sp) ★★★ Well-respected producer at Bannockburn. Powerful Res PINOT N, impressive mid-tier Pinot N; v.gd, drink-young style, Rua. Intense RIES; scented, full-bodied PINOT GR. Vivacious sparklings: NV, Rosé.

Allan Scott Marl w (r) (sp) ★★ Medium-sized family producer. Gd RIES (some vines 30+ yrs old); tropical-fruit-flavoured SAUV BL. Recent focus on organic and sparkling.

Alpha Domus Hawk r w ★★ V.gd CHARD and VIOGNIER. Concentrated Bordeaux-style reds, esp savoury MERLOT-based The Navigator 10', and notably dark, rich CAB SAUV The Aviator 10'. Top wines labelled AD (superb Noble Selection from SEM). Everyday range The Pilot.

Amisfield C Ot r (p) (w) ★★ Fleshy, smooth PINOT GR; tense, minerally RIES (dr sw); lively, ripe SAUV BL; classy Pinot Rosé and dark, rich PINOT N (RKV Res is Rolls-Royce model). Lake Hayes is lower tier label.

Ara Marl r w ★★ Huge v'yd in Waihopai Valley. Quality advances since 2011 under winemaker Jeff Clarke (ex-Montana.) Dry, ripe SAUV BL; floral, fruity PINOT N. Top tier: Resolute, followed by Select Blocks, then Single Estate, then Pathway. Value.

Astrolabe Marl (r) w ★★ Label part-owned by winemaker Simon Waghorn. Rich, harmonious Voyage SAUV BL (oak-aged Taihoa Sauv Bl generous, complex). Also gd PINOT GR, RIES, CHARD, PINOT N.

Ata Rangi Mart r (p) (w) ★★★ Small, highly respected. Seductively fragrant, powerful, long-lived *Pinot N* 09' 10 11, is one of NZ's greatest (oldest vines planted 1980). Delicious younger-vine Crimson PINOT N. Rich, complex Craighall CHARD and off-dry Lismore PINOT GR.

Auckland Largest city (northern, warm, cloudy) in NZ with 1% of v'yd area. Nearby wine districts: Hend, Kumeu/Huapai/Waimauku (both long est); newer (since 1980s): Matakana, Clevedon, Waih. Stylish, ripe, savoury, MERLOT/CAB blends in dry seasons (10' 13'), bold, peppery SYRAH; rich, underrated CHARD.

Auntsfield Marl r w ★★ Excellent wines from site of the region's first v'yd, planted in 1873, uprooted in 1931 and replanted 1999. Strong, tropical-fruity SAUV BL, fleshy, rich PINOT N (Heritage is esp lush, powerful).

Awatere Valley Marl Key subregion, with few wineries but huge v'yd area (more than HAWK), pioneered in 1986 by VAVASOUR. Slightly cooler and drier than the WAIRAU VALLEY, with racy, herbaceous ("tomato stalk") SAUV BL; tight, vibrant RIES, PINOT GR; scented, often slightly herbal PINOT N.

Babich Hend r w ★★→★★★ Sizeable family firm (1916). HAWK, MARL v'yds and new winery in Marl for 2014 vintage. Refined, age-worthy, single-v'yd Irongate CHARD 10' 11, v. elegant Irongate CAB/MERLOT/CAB FR 10'09'. Ripe, dry Marl SAUV BL is big seller. Mid-tier Winemakers Res (oak-aged Sauv Bl esp gd).

Bald Hills C Ot r (p) (w) ★★ Bannockburn v'yd with full-bodied, slightly sweet RIES and generous, savoury, complex PINOT N 12; 3 Acres is drink-young style.

Bell Hill Cant r w ★★★ Tiny, elevated v'yd on limestone. Rare but strikingly rich, finely textured CHARD and gorgeously scented, powerful, velvety PINOT N 10'. Second label: Old Weka Pass.

Bilancia Hawk r (w) ★★★ Small producer of classy SYRAH (incl v. powerful, nutty, spicy, hill-grown La Collina 10' 09' 08 07, floral, peppery Syrah (v.gd value); and fleshy, soft PINOT GR.

Blackenbrook Nel r w ★★ Small winery with outstanding aromatic whites, esp highly perfumed, rich, Alsace-style GEWURZ, PINOT GR and (rarer) MUSCAT. Punchy SAUV BL; v. promising MONTEPULCIANO. Second label: St Jacques.

Borthwick Wair r w ★★ V'yd at Gladstone with lively, tropical-fruit SAUV BL; rich, dryish ries; peachy, toasty CHARD; fleshy, dry PINOT GR; perfumed, supple PINOT N.

Brancott Estate Marl r w ★→★★★ Brand of PERNOD RICARD NZ that replaced Montana worldwide. Top wines: Letter Series (eg. "B" Brancott SAUV BL). Huge-selling, lively, herbaceous MARL Sauv Bl; floral, easy-drinking South Island PINOT N. New, mid-tier Special Res range (rich Sauv Bl, PINOT GR). Living Land: organic. Flight: low-alcohol. Chosen Rows: v. classy, tight, long-lived Sauv Bl 10'.

Brightwater Nel (r) w ★★ Impressive whites, esp crisp, flavour-packed SAUV BL; fresh, med-dry RIES; lively, citrus, gently oaked CHARD, and rich, gently sweet PINOT GR. PINOT N fast improving and gd value. Top wines: Lord Rutherford.

Brookfields Hawk r w ★★ Long-est winery; solid line-up. Powerful, long-lived, "gold label" CAB SAUV/MERLOT; gd CHARD, PINOT GR, GEWURZ, VIOGNIER, SYRAH (esp spicy Hillside Syrah 09). Satisfying, mid-priced Burnfoot Merlot and Ohiti Cab Sauv.

Cable Bay Waih r (p) w ★★ Mid-sized Waih producer with v. refined CHARD; sturdy, complex VIOGNIER; bold yet stylish SYRAH. Subtle, fine-textured MARL SAUV BL. Second label: Selection.

Canterbury NZ's fifth-largest wine region; most v'yds are in relatively warm, sheltered, northern Waip district. Greatest success with RIES (since mid-80s) and later PINOT N. Emerging strength in PINOT GR. SAUV BL also widely planted.

Carrick C Ot r w ★★★ Bannockburn winery: intense RIES (dry, medium C OT; sweetish Josephine); tight, elegant CHARD; densely packed PINOT N 11, built to last.

Central Otago (r) 10' 12 (w) 10' 12 13 Cool, low-rainfall, high-altitude inland region (NZ's third-largest) in south of South Island. Centre is Queenstown. Scented, crisp RIES, PINOT GR; PINOT N (75% v'yd area) is perfumed, vibrant, with drink-young charm; top wines mature 5 yrs+. Promising Champagne-style sparkling.

Chard Farm C Ot r w ★★ Pioneer winery with fleshy, oily PINOT GR; typically perfumed, mid-weight, supple PINOT N (River Run: floral, charming; Mata-Au more complex). Light, smooth Rabbit Ranch Pinot N.

Church Road Hawk r w ★★→★★★ PERNOD RICARD NZ winery with deep HAWK roots. Rich style of CHARD; ripe, partly oak-aged SAUV BL; Alsace-style PINOT GR; dark, full-flavoured MERLOT/CAB SAUV (value). Impressive Grand Res wines; superb claret-style red TOM 07' 09'. McDonald Series, between the standard and Grand Res ranges, offers eye-catching quality and value.

Churton Marl r w ★★ Elevated Waihopai Valley site with subtle, bone-dry SAUV BL; sturdy, creamy VIOGNIER; fragrant, harmonious PINOT N 10' 11 (esp The Abyss: oldest vines, greater depth). NZ's first PETIT MANSENG 12.

Clearview Hawk r (p) w ★★→★★★ Coastal v'yd (also drawing grapes from inland) with bold, savoury Res CHARD; impressive oak-fermented Res SAUV BL; dark, rich Res CAB FR, Enigma (MERLOT-based), Old Olive Block (CABS SAUV/Fr blend). Second tier: Beachhead, Cape Kidnappers.

Clifford Bay Marl r w ★★ Gd, affordable range from Foley Family Wines. Fresh, racy gooseberry, lime SAUV BL is best; scented PINOT GR; floral, charming PINOT N.

Clos Henri Marl r w ★★→★★★ Est by Henri Bourgeois of Sancerre. Weighty, well-rounded SAUV BL (stony soils) one of NZ's best; sturdy, ripe, firm PINOT N (clay). Second label: Bel Echo. Third label Petit Clos, from young vines, is value.

Cloudy Bay Marl r w sp ★★★ Large-volume SAUV BL (weighty, dry, finely textured, some barrel ageing since 2010); NZ's most famous wine (13'). CHARD (robust, complex, crisp 11), PINOT N (rich, supple 10' 11) both classy. Pelorus vintage sparkling (toasty, rich), elegant, Chard-led NV. Rarer GEWURZ; Late Harvest RIES; barrel-aged, medium-dry Ries; Te Koko (oak-aged Sauv Bl) – all full of personality. Powerful, vigorous, youthful C OT Pinot N (Te Wahi) since 2010. LVMH-owned.

Constellation New Zealand Auck r (p) w ★→★★ NZ's largest wine company, previously Nobilo Wine Group, now owned by US-based Constellation Brands. Strength in solid, mid-priced wines. Nobilo MARL SAUV BL (fresh, tropical) big seller in the USA. Superior varietals labelled Nobilo Icon (punchy, herbaceous Sauv Bl); v.gd, sweet-fruited Drylands Sauv Bl. *See* KIM CRAWFORD, MONKEY BAY, SELAKS.

Cooper's Creek Auck r w ★★→★★★ An innovative medium-sized producer with well-made, gd-value wines from four regions. Excellent Swamp Res CHARD;

> **Top dog**
> Which is NZ's largest wine producer? For decades it was Montana, which in 2000 purchased its biggest rival, Corbans, and is now called PERNOD RICARD NZ. The right answer is CONSTELLATION NEW ZEALAND, based in New York; leading brands incl NOBILO, KIM CRAWFORD, MONKEY BAY, SELAKS, Drylands. DELEGAT'S/OYSTER BAY sits in second place. The largest family-owned producer is VILLA MARIA; brands incl ESK VALLEY, VIDAL, TE AWA, Thornbury.

gd SAUV BL, RIES; MERLOT; top-value VIOGNIER. SV (Select V'yd) range is mid-tier. NZ's first: ARNEIS 06, GRÜNER V 08, ALBARIÑO 11.

Craggy Range Hawk r w (p) ★★★ High-flying winery with large v'yds in HAWK and MART. V. stylish CHARD, PINOT N; excellent, rich, mid-range MERLOT and SYRAH from GIMBLETT GRAVELS; strikingly dense, ripe Sophia (Merlot), The Quarry (CAB SAUV), show-stopping SYRAH Le Sol 09' 10' 11. Latest reds more supple, refined.

Delegat's Auck r w ★★ V. large company (two million cases a yr), controlled by brother-and-sister team Jim and Rose Delegat. V'yds in HAWK and MARL. Hugely successful OYSTER BAY brand. Delegat range revamped from 2012: tight, crisp, citrus CHARD; full-flavoured, herbaceous SAUV BL; vibrantly fruity, supple MERLOT.

Destiny Bay Waih r ★★→★★★ Expatriate Americans produce Bordeaux-style reds: brambly and silky. Flagship is substantial, deep, savoury Magna Praemia (08' mostly CAB SAUV). Mid-tier: Mystae 09. Classy but v. pricey.

Deutz Auck sp ★★★ Champagne house gives name to refined sparklings from MARL by PERNOD RICARD NZ. Popular NV is lively, toasty (min 2 yrs on lees). Vintage Blanc de Blancs is finely scented, vivacious, piercing. Rosé is crisp, toasty, strawberryish. Prestige, from 2005, is classy, mostly CHARD.

Distant Land Auck r w ★★ Newish brand from old family winery (Lincoln). Crisp, strong MARL SAUV BL; well-spiced GEWURZ; scented, rich Marl PINOT N.

Dog Point Marl r w ★★★ Grower Ivan Sutherland and winemaker James Healy (both ex-CLOUDY BAY) make complex, tight, oak-aged SAUV BL (Section 94); CHARD (elegant, citrus, age-worthy); rich, finely textured PINOT N 10' 11, one of region's best. Also weighty, dry, unoaked Sauv Bl 12'.

Dry River Mart r w ★★★ Small pioneer winery, now US-owned. Reputation for elegant, long-lived CHARD, RIES, PINOT GR (NZ's first outstanding Pinot Gr), GEWURZ; late-harvest whites; floral, sweet-fruited, slowly evolving PINOT N 09' 10, 11; dense, elegant SYRAH 11.

Elephant Hill Hawk r (p) w ★★ German-owned v'yd, stylish winery at Te Awanga on coast, also draws grapes from inland. Sophisticated, pure VIOGNIER; rich CHARD; scented PINOT GR; floral, concentrated SYRAH.

Eradus Marl ★★ AWATERE VALLEY producer of freshly herbaceous, strong-flavoured SAUV BL, v.gd PINOT GR and charming PINOT N.

Escarpment Mart r (w) ★★★ Fleshy barrel-fermented PINOT GR and robust CHARD; best-known for complex, concentrated PINOT N from Larry McKenna, ex-MARTINBOROUGH V'YD. Top label: Kupe 10' 11. Single-v'yd, old-vine reds launched from 2006. Mart Pinot N is regional blend 10' 11.

Esk Valley Hawk r p w ★★→★★★ Owned by VILLA MARIA. Top MERLOT-based reds (esp Winemakers Res blend 11 10' 09'); excellent Rosé; full-bodied, peachy, buttery CHARD; crisp, dryish CHENIN BL, VERDELHO. Flagship red: The Terraces (powerful, spicy, single-v'yd blend, MALBEC/Merlot/CAB FR 09' 06').

Fairhall Downs Marl r w ★★ Single-v'yd wines from high Brancott Valley site. Weighty, dry PINOT GR; peachy, nutty, full-flavoured CHARD; rich, sweet-fruited SAUV BL; perfumed, smooth PINOT N. Second label: Torea (value).

Felton Road C Ot r w ★★★★ Star winery at Bannockburn. Bold yet graceful PINOT N Block 3 and 5 10' 11 12' from The Elms v'yd; light, intense RIES (dr s/sw) top; rich, citrus, long-lived CHARD (esp Block 2); key label is perfumed, poised Bannockburn Pinot N **12'**. Other v. fine single-v'yd Pinot N: Cornish Point, Calvert.

Forrest Marl r (p) w ★★ Mid-size winery; wide range. Reliable SAUV BL and RIES; gorgeous botrytized Ries; v. tasty HAWK Newton/Forrest Cornerstone (Bordeaux red blend). Distinguished flagship range, John Forrest Collection. Popular low-alcohol (9%) Ries and Sauv Bl: The Doctors'.

Framingham Marl (r) w ★★ Owned by Sogrape (*see* Portugal). Strength in aromatic whites: intense, zesty RIES (esp rich Classic) from 30-yr-old vines. Perfumed, lush PINOT GR, GEWURZ. Subtle SAUV BL. Scented, silky PINOT N.

In the hot UK summer of 2013, one way to keep cool was enjoying popsicles of Kim Crawford wine.

Fromm Marl r w ★★★ Distinguished PINOT N, esp valley-floor Fromm V'yd **10' 09'** and hill-grown *Clayvin* V'yd (more perfumed, supple **10'**). Also stylish, citrus Clayvin CHARD and RIES Dry. Earlier-drinking La Strada range also v.gd. Clayvin V'yd leased to GIESEN, but Fromm will still draw grapes.

Gibbston Valley C Ot r (p) w ★★→★★★ Pioneer winery with popular restaurant at Gibbston. Most but not all v'yds at Bendigo. Strong reputation for PINOT N, esp rich C OT blend and exuberantly fruity Res **12' 09'**. Racy, medium-dry RIES and scented, full-bodied PINOT GR. Gold River Pinot N: drink-young charm.

Giesen Cant (r) w ★→★★ Large family winery. Most is tangy MARL SAUV BL. Generous, gently sweet RIES (value). Also punchy The Brothers Sauv Bl and weighty, rich, barrel-fermented The August Sauv Bl. Fast-improving PINOT N (esp The Brothers).

Gimblett Gravels Hawk Defined area (800 ha planted), with free-draining, low-fertility soils noted for rich Bordeaux-style reds (typically MERLOT-predominant, but stony soils suit CAB SAUV) and floral, vibrant SYRAH. Best of both are world-class. Also powerful, age-worthy CHARD, VIOGNIER.

Gisborne (r) **10' 13'** (w) **13' 10'** NZ's fourth-largest region, on east coast of North Island; shrunk in past 5 yrs. Abundant sunshine but often rainy; v. fertile soils. Key is CHARD (deliciously fragrant in youth, best mature well.) Excellent GEWURZ, VIOGNIER; MERLOT, PINOT GR more variable. Interest in ALBARIÑO. Star winery: MILLTON.

Gladstone Vineyard Wair r w ★★ Tropical SAUV BL; weighty, smooth PINOT GR; gd dry RIES; classy VIOGNIER; v. graceful PINOT N under top label, Gladstone; 12,000 Miles is lower-priced brand.

Grasshopper Rock C Ot r ★★→★★★ Estate-grown at Alexandra. Subregion's finest red **10' 11 12'**: graceful, harmonious, cherry and dried-herb flavours. Great value.

Greenhough Nel r w ★★→★★★ One of region's top small producers; immaculate RIES, SAUV BL, CHARD, PINOT N. Top label: Hope V'yd (complex, organic Chard; fleshy, old-vine PINOT BL; mushroomy Pinot N **08' 10.**)

Greystone Waip (r) w ★★★ Star producer with notably full-bloomed and rich aromatic whites (RIES, GEWURZ, PINOT GR); fast-improving CHARD, SAUV BL, PINOT N. Bought MUDDY WATER in 2011.

Greywacke Marl r w ★★→★★★ Impressive wines from Kevin Judd, ex-CLOUDY BAY. Pure, penetrating SAUV BL; weighty, complex CHARD; fleshy PINOT GR; gently sweet RIES; silky, savoury PINOT N. Barrel-fermented Wild Sauv is full of personality.

Grove Mill Marl r w ★★ Attractive whites, esp punchy SAUV BL, slightly sweet RIES; reds less exciting. Value, lower-tier Sanctuary brand. Owned by Foley Family Wines.

Haha Hawk ★★ Flavour-packed MARL SAUV BL, creamy-smooth Marl CHARD, fragrant, moderately complex Marl PINOT N. All bargain-priced.

Hans Herzog Marl r w ★★★ Warm, stony v'yd at Rapaura with powerful, long-lived MERLOT/CAB SAUV (region's greatest); MONTEPULCIANO; PINOT N; sturdy, dry VIOGNIER, PINOT GR; fleshy, oak-aged SAUV BL. Sold under Hans brand in Europe, the USA.

Hawke's Bay (r) **09' 10' 13'** (w) **10' 13'** NZ's second-largest region. Long history of winemaking in sunny, warm climate. Rich, classy MERLOT and CAB SAUV-based reds in gd vintages; SYRAH (floral, vibrant plum and black pepper flavours) a fast-rising star; powerful, peachy CHARD; ripe, rounded SAUV BL (suits oak); NZ's best VIOGNIER. Central Hawk (elevated, cooler) suits PINOT N.

Highfield Marl r w sp ★★ Stunning views from Tuscan-style tower. Light, intense RIES, citrus, mealy CHARD; immaculate, racy SAUV BL and generous, savoury PINOT N. Elstree sparkling variable lately. Second label: Paua.

Huia Marl (r) w (sp) ★★ Satisfying, organic SAUV BL; bold, savoury PINOT N 10'. Complex Brut 06. Lower-priced range: Hunky Dory.

Hunter's Marl (r) (p) w (sp) ★★ →★★★ Pioneer, medium-sized winery with classic, dry, tropical-fruit SAUV BL. Vibrant, gently oaked CHARD. Excellent sparkling (*MiruMiru*). RIES, GEWURZ, PINOT GR all rewarding and value. PINOT N easy-drinking.

Invivo Auck r w ★★ Energetic company with intense, nettley, mineral MARL SAUV BL, full-bodied, dry Marl PINOT GR and sound, moderately complex C OT PINOT N.

Isabel Estate Marl r w ★→★★ Family estate; formerly outstanding PINOT N, SAUV BL, CHARD; lately variable quality; signs of return to form in 2013. Crisp PINOT GR.

Jackson Estate Marl r w ★★ Rich, ripe Stich SAUV BL is consistently excellent; v. attractive, gently oaked CHARD and rich, sweet-fruited PINOT N 10'. Usually value.

Johanneshof Marl (r) w sp ★★ Small winery acclaimed for perfumed, gently sweet, soft GEWURZ (one of NZ's finest). Crisp, dry, lively sparkling; v.gd RIES and PINOT GR. PINOT N from cool, wet site is less exciting.

Jules Taylor Marl r p w ★★ Impressive range, incl rich, citrus, creamy CHARD; sturdy, dry PINOT GR; classy, intense SAUV BL; fragrant, dense PINOT N 11'. Value.

Julicher Mart r w ★★ Small producer with gd whites (esp vibrant, citrus, slightly biscuity CHARD); distinguished, savoury PINOT N 10' 11. 99 Rows is second-tier Pinot N and v.gd value.

Kim Crawford Hawk ★→★★ Brand owned by CONSTELLATION NEW ZEALAND. Easy-drinking wines, incl scented, tasty MARL SAUV BL (gd-quality, one million cases a yr). Top range SP (Small Parcel), incl weighty, ripe, tropical-fruit Spitfire Sauv Bl.

Kumeu River Auck (r) w ★★★ Rich, complex Estate CHARD 10' 11 is multisite blend. Single-v'yd Mate's V'yd Chard (planted 1990) is more opulent 10' 11; single-v'yd Hunting Hill Chard 10' 11 is rising star, notably refined, tight-knit. Weighty, floral PINOT GR; sturdy, earthy PINOT N.

Lake Chalice Marl (r) w ★★ Medium-sized producer with vibrant, creamy CHARD and incisive, slightly sweet RIES; gd SAUV BL (esp intense, zingy The Raptor). Solid PINOT N. Platinum is premium range. Lower tier: The Nest.

Lawson's Dry Hills Marl (r) (p) w ★★→★★★ Gd-value wines. Incisive, faintly oaked SAUV BL and exotically perfumed, sturdy GEWURZ. Dry, toasty, bottle-aged RIES, CHARD. Fast-improving PINOT N. Top-end range: The Pioneer.

Lindauer Auck ★★ Hugely popular sparkling brand, esp bottle-fermented Lindauer Brut, sold in 2010 by PERNOD RICARD NZ to LION NATHAN. Latest releases show maturity, complexity, value.

Lowburn Ferry C Ot r ★★ PINOT N specialist. Flagship is The Ferryman (elegant, feminine 10'). Also Home Block (fleshy, rich, silky 10' 12); Skeleton Creek (not always estate-grown, but concentrated, complex.)

> **Méthode Marlborough**
> Sparkling wine is MARL's latest favourite: nine producers have joined forces to promote it. It must be grown in Marl and based on PINOT N, CHARD or PINOT MEUNIER, bottle-fermented and lees-aged for at least 18 months. CLOUDY BAY Pelorus, Daniel Le Brun (from LION NATHAN), NAUTILUS are main brands. Sparkling SAUV BL more of an acquired taste....

Mahi Marl r w ★★ Stylish, complex wines from Brian Bicknell, ex-SERESIN. Sweet-fruited, finely textured SAUV BL (part oak-aged); weighty, vibrant, gently oaked CHARD; savoury, mushroomy PINOT N.

Man O' War Auck r w ★★★ Largest v'yd on Waih. Crisp whites from CHARD, SAUV BL; impressive PINOT GR (grown on adjacent Ponui Island). Dense Bordeaux-style reds (esp Ironclad **10**'); powerful, spicy, firm Dreadnought SYRAH **10**'.

Margrain Mart r w sp ★★ Small winery with tight, age-worthy CHARD, RIES, PINOT GR, GEWURZ, CHENIN BL. Rich, complex PINOT N. River's Edge is early-drinking. Lean, lively sparkling: La Michelle.

Marisco Marl r w ★★ Owned by Brent Marris, ex-WITHER HILLS. Fast-growing Waihopai Valley producer with two brands, The Ned and (latterly) Marisco the King's Series. Well-regarded SAUV BL, CHARD, PINOT GR, PINOT N.

The town centre of Martinborough is laid out on the pattern of the Union flag.

Marlborough (r) **10' 12 13**' (w) **13**' NZ's largest region by far (two-thirds of all plantings) at top of South Island. Warm, sunny days and cold nights give aromatic, crisp whites. Intense SAUV BL, from sharp, green capsicum to ripe tropical fruit. Fresh, medium-dry RIES (recent wave of sweet, low-alcohol wines); some of NZ's best PINOT GR and GEWURZ; CHARD is leaner than HAWK but can mature well. High-quality sparkling and botrytized Ries. PINOT N underrated, top examples (from north-facing clay hillsides) among NZ's finest. Interest stirring in GRÜNER V.

Martinborough Wair (r) **09 10 13**' (w) **10' 13**' Small, prestigious district in south WAIR (foot of North Island). Warm summers, dry autumns, gravelly soils. Success with several white grapes (SAUV BL, PINOT GR widely planted), but acclaimed since mid-late 1980s for sturdy, rich, long-lived PINOT N.

Martinborough Vineyard Mart r (p) (w) ★★★ Distinguished small winery; famous PINOT N **07' 10**', cherryish, spicy, nutty, complex. Rich, biscuity CHARD; intense RIES (dr s/sw); rich, medium-dry PINOT GR. Also single-v'yd Burnt Spur and drink-young Te Tera ranges (top-value Pinot N).

Matahiwi Wair r w ★→★★ One of region's larger wineries. Top range, Holly, incl rich, peachy, toasty CHARD; barrel-fermented, passion fruit/lime SAUV BL; generous, savoury PINOT N. Second label: Mt Hector.

Matawhero Gis r (p) w ★★ Former star GEWURZ producer of the 1980s, now with new owner and gd, fruit-driven CHARD, Gewurz (fleshy, soft), ALBARIÑO, ARNEIS, GRÜNER V. Top range: Church House.

Matua Valley Auck r w ★→★★ Producer of NZ's first SAUV BL in 1974 (AUCK grapes). Now owned by TWE, with v'yds in four regions. GIS (esp Judd CHARD), HAWK and MARL wines; most are pleasant, easy-drinking. Shingle Peak Sauv Bl (crisp, lively, flavoursome) is value. Luxury range of Single V'yd wines, incl striking, impressively complex Marl Chard **11**' and bold MERLOT, SYRAH **10**'.

Mills Reef B of P r w ★★→★★★ Impressive wines from estate v'yds in the GIMBLETT GRAVELS and other HAWK grapes. Top Elspeth range incl rich CHARD, powerful Bordeaux-style reds and SYRAH (latest vintages more refined, supple). Res range reds also concentrated, fine value.

Millton Gis r (p) w ★★→★★★★ Region's top winery; wines certified organic. Hill-grown single-v'yd Clos de Ste Anne range (CHARD, CHENIN BL, VIOGNIER, SYRAH, PINOT N) is concentrated, complex, characterful. Long-lived *Chenin Bl* (distinctly honeyed in wetter vintages), is NZ's finest. Riverpoint V'yd Viognier classy and value. Lower-tier range: Crazy by Nature.

Misha's C Ot r w ★★ Large v'yd at Bendigo. Consistently classy GEWURZ, PINOT GR, RIES (dry Lyric and slightly sweet Limelight); vibrant, tangy SAUV BL; savoury, complex PINOT N (Verismo is oak-aged longer).

Mission Hawk r (p) w ★★ NZ's oldest wine producer; first vines 1851; still run by

Catholic Society of Mary. Solid varietals: fruit-driven SYRAH and PINOT N (from MART) are top value. Res range incl gd Bordeaux-style reds, Syrah, oak-aged SAUV BL, CHARD. Top label: Jewelstone (v. classy Chard and CAB/MERLOT 09'). Purchased large AWATERE VALLEY v'yd in 2012 (crisp, incisive MARL SAUV BL).

Mondillo C Ot r w ★★ Rising star at Bendigo with scented, citrus, slightly sweet RIES and enticingly floral, weighty, tasty PINOT N **10** 09' 12.

Monkey Bay r w ★ CONSTELLATION NEW ZEALAND brand, modestly priced, popular in US. Easy-drinking CHARD; gently sweet SAUV BL; light PINOT GR; fresh, fruity MERLOT.

Morton Estate B of P r w sp ★→★★ Mid-size producer with v'yds in HAWK, MARL. Powerful Black Label CHARD, outstanding Coniglio Chard 10'. White Label Chard, Premium Brut gd, top value; ditto VIOGNIER, PINOT GR. Reds less exciting.

Mountford Waip r w ★★→★★★ Small, top-class producer on limestone slopes. Fleshy, v. savoury PINOT N (esp The Gradient, The Rise 09'). Powerful, complex CHARD.

Mount Riley Marl r w ★★ Medium-sized family firm. Punchy, gd value SAUV BL; finely textured PINOT GR; gd drink-young CHARD, easy-drinking PINOT N. Top range is Seventeen Valley (elegant, complex CHARD 11).

Mt Difficulty C Ot r (p) w ★★→★★★ Quality producer in warm Bannockburn. Powerful, concentrated PINOT N: Roaring Meg for early consumption; single-v'yd Pipeclay Terrace dense, lasting 09'. Classy whites (RIES, PINOT GR), satisfying rosé.

Muddy Water Waip r w ★★→★★★ Small, high-quality producer, now owned by GREYSTONE. Intense, lively RIES (among NZ's best); mineral CHARD; savoury, notably complex PINOT N (esp Slowhand 10' based on oldest, low-yielding vines).

Mud House Cant r w ★★ Large MARL-based producer of South Island wines (incl WAIP, C OT), bought in 2013 by Australia-based Accolade Wines. Brands: Mud House, WAIPARA HILLS, Hay Maker (lower tier). Regional blends: punchy Marl SAUV BL (classy, value). Top Estate selection (single-v'yds); Single V'yd range (from growers).

Nautilus Marl r w sp ★★ Medium-sized, v. reliable range of distributors Négociants (NZ), owned by S Smith & Sons (see Yalumba, Australia). Top wines incl tight, dry SAUV BL (released with bottle-age), classy CHARD (complex, subtle); savoury PINOT N, Alsace-style PINOT GR; and intense, yeasty sparkler. Mid-tier: Opawa (fruit-driven). Lower tier: Twin Islands.

Nelson (r) 09 10 13 (w) 10' 13 Smallish region west of MARL; climate wetter but equally sunny. Clay soils of Upper Moutere hills (full-bodied wines) and silty WAIMEA plains (more aromatic). Strengths in aromatic whites, esp RIES, SAUV BL, PINOT GR, GEWURZ; also gd (sometimes outstanding) CHARD, PINOT N.

Neudorf Nel r (p) w ★★★→★★★★ Top small winery. Powerful, mineral *Moutere Chard* 10' 11 12 one of NZ's greatest; superb, savoury Moutere PINOT N (esp Home V'yd 10'). SAUV BL, PINOT GR and RIES also top-flight. Delightful dry Pinot Rosé.

Ngatarawa Hawk r w ★★ Mid-sized producer, Corban family-owned. Top Alwyn range: powerful CHARD; generous MERLOT/CAB 09'. Mid-range: Glazebrook, Stables Res.

No. 1 Family Estate Marl sp ★★ Family-owned company of Daniel Le Brun, ex-Champagne. No longer owns DANIEL LE BRUN brand. Specialist in often v.gd sparkling wine, esp refined, tight-knit, NV Blanc de Blancs, Cuvée No 1.

Nobilo Marl See CONSTELLATION NEW ZEALAND.

Obsidian Waih r (p) w ★★→★★★ V. stylish Bordeaux blend (The Obsidian 08' 10'), VIOGNIER, CHARD, SYRAH, TEMPRANILLO under top brand Obsidian Res (was Obsidian). Gd-value Waih reds (incl MERLOT, Syrah, MONTEPULCIANO, Tempranillo) under second-tier Obsidian label (was Weeping Sands).

Oyster Bay Marl r w ★★ From DELEGAT'S, this is a marketing triumph, with sales exceeding 1.5 million cases; top white wine in Australia. Vibrant fruit-driven wines with a touch of class, from MARL and HAWK. SAUV BL (punchy, passion fruit/lime, huge seller), citrus, gently oaked CHARD (v. popular in the USA), PINOT GR; PINOT N, MERLOT, easy-drinking sparklers.

One-offs

Hunting in NZ for BARBERA, MARSANNE, Marzemino, NEBBIOLO, PETIT MANSENG, PETIT VERDOT, ROUSSANNE, TOURIGA, Wurzer, ZINFANDEL? Quite a short hunt: the country (at the time of writing) boasts just one example of each.

Palliser Mart r w ★★ →★★★ One of the district's largest and best. Excellent tropical-fruit SAUV BL, CHARD, RIES, PINOT GR, bubbly (best in MART) and perfumed, rich, harmonious PINOT N 09' 10. Top wines: Palliser Estate. Lower tier: Pencarrow (great value, rising share of output).

Pask Hawk r w ★★ Mid-size winery (was C J Pask). Extensive v'yds in GIMBLETT GRAVELS. SYRAH, CAB SAUV, MERLOT-based reds under mid-tier Gimblett Road label value in gd vintages; CHARD, VIOGNIER too. Top Declaration range less convincing.

Passage Rock Waih r w ★★ Opulent SYRAH, esp Res (Waih's most awarded wine 10' 12); non-Res fine-value 10'. Gd Bordeaux-style reds, whites solid (esp VIOGNIER).

Pegasus Bay Waip r w ★★★ Pioneer family firm with superb range: taut, slow-evolving, *complex Chard*, SAUV BL/SEM; rich, zingy, medium RIES (big seller); lush, silky PINOT N 10' 11, esp mature-vine Prima Donna 10' 11. Second label: Main Divide, v.gd value, esp PINOT GR.

Peregrine C Ot r w ★★ Crisp, concentrated whites (esp RIES, dry, slightly sweet Rastaburn), highly attractive CHARD 12'. Finely scented, rich, silky PINOT N 09' 11. Saddleback Pinot N esp gd value.

Pernod Ricard NZ Auck r (p) w sp ★ →★★★★ NZ's third-largest producer, formerly MONTANA. Changes since 2010 incl sale of many brands (esp Corbans, LINDAUER); axing of Montana brand in favour of BRANCOTT ESTATE; disposal of large GIS and HAWK wineries. Wineries in AUCK, Hawk and MARL. Extensive co-owned v'yds for Marl whites, incl huge-selling Brancott Estate SAUV BL. Strength in sparkling, esp DEUTZ Marl Cuvée. Classy, rich, gd-value CHURCH ROAD reds and quality CHARD. Other key brands incl STONELEIGH (tropical-fruit-flavoured Sauv Bl).

Pisa Range C Ot r (w) ★★→★★★ Small v'yd with powerful, arrestingly rich Black Poplar PINOT N 10', crisp, dryish PINOT GR and rich, slightly sweet RIES.

Puriri Hills Auck r (p) ★★→★★★ Classy, silky, seductive MERLOT-based reds from Clevedon 08' 10'. Res is esp rich and plump, with more new oak.

Pyramid Valley Cant r w ★★→★★★ Tiny elevated v'yd at Waikari. Estate-grown, floral, increasingly generous PINOT N (Angel Flower, Earth Smoke 10'); arrestingly full-bodied CHARD 10'. Classy Growers Collection wines from other regions. Not universally admired, but strong personality.

Quartz Reef C Ot r w sp ★★→★★★ Small, quality, bio producer with crisp, dry PINOT GR; sturdy, spicy PINOT N 10' 11 12', Bendigo Estate esp concentrated 10' 11; intense, yeasty, *racy sparkling* (vintage esp gd).

Rippon Vineyard C Ot r w ★★→★★★ Stunning pioneer v'yd on shores of Lake Wanaka. Scented, feminine Mature Vine PINOT N 10'. Jeunesse Pinot N from younger vines; powerful, complex Tinker's Field Pinot N (from oldest vines 10'). Slowly evolving whites, esp outstanding, steely, minerally RIES 10' 11'.

Rockburn C Ot r (p) w ★★ Crisp, racy PINOT GR (slightly sweet), GEWURZ, RIES (medium-sweet), SAUV BL. Fragrant, rich PINOT N 10' 12, blended from Cromwell Basin (mostly) and Gibbston grapes, is best.

Sacred Hill Hawk r w ★★→★★★ Mid-size, partly Chinese-owned. Acclaimed Riflemans CHARD 10' 13', powerful but refined, from inland, elevated site. Dark, long-lived Brokenstone MERLOT 09' 10', Helmsman CAB/Merlot 09' 10', Deer Stalkers SYRAH from GIMBLETT GRAVELS 09' 10'. Punchy MARL SAUV BL. Halo: mid-tier. Other brands: Gunn Estate, Wild South (gd-value Marl range).

Saint Clair Marl r (p) w ★★ →★★★ Largest family-owned producer in the region with extensive v'yds. Highly acclaimed for pungent SAUV BL from lower Wairau Valley

– esp great-value regional blend and strikingly rich Wairau Res. Easy-drinking RIES, PINOT GR, CHARD, MERLOT, PINOT N. Res is top range; then a huge array of classy, second-tier Pioneer Block wines (incl v.gd GRÜNER V); then gd-value regional blends; fourth tier is Vicar's Choice.

Seifried Estate Nel (r) w ★★ Region's biggest winery. Long respected for gd, medium-dry RIES, GEWURZ; now gd-value, often excellent SAUV BL, CHARD. Peachy, spicy GRÜNER V. Best: Winemakers Collection. Old Coach Road is third tier. Whites better than reds.

Selaks Marl r w ★→★★ Old producer of Croatian origin, now brand of CONSTELLATION NEW ZEALAND. Solid, easy-drinking Premium Selection range. Res range: tangy, herbaceous MARL SAUV BL. Winemaker's Favourite range often excellent value, esp rich, creamy HAWK CHARD.

Seresin Marl r w ★★→★★★★ Medium-sized winery. Subtle, sophisticated SAUV BL (partly barrel-fermented; certified organic), is one of NZ's finest; v. tight, rich Res Sauv Bl from oldest vines (11') Excellent CHARD, PINOTS N and GR, RIES; second-tier Momo (gd-quality/value). Overall, complex, finely textured wines.

Sileni Hawk r (p) w ★★ Large producer, known for CHARD, MERLOT and MARL SAUV BL. Top wines: EV (Exceptional Vintage Chard 10'). Mid-range incl lush The Lodge Chard, rich Triangle Merlot 10'), then Cellar Selection (gd, easy-drinking Merlot, dry PINOT GR). Rich, smooth Marl Sauv Bl (esp The Straits).

Spy Valley Marl r (p) w ★★→★★★ High-achieving company with extensive v'yds. Richly flavoured aromatic whites (RIES, GEWURZ, PINOT GR) offer superb value; also v. impressive SAUV BL, CHARD and PINOT N. Satisfying, dry Pinot N Rosé. Classy top selection: Envoy (incl rich, subtle Chard, Alsace-style Pinot Gr and Mosel-like Ries). Second label: Satellite.

Staete Landt Marl r w ★★ V'yd at Rapaura (Wairau Valley): refined CHARD (biscuity, rounded); top-flight Annabel SAUV BL (fleshy, rich, tropical); creamy, complex, dry PINOT GR; graceful PINOT N. Promising VIOGNIER, SYRAH. Second label: Map Maker.

Stonecroft Hawk r w ★★ Small winery. NZ's first serious SYRAH (since 1989), more Rhône than Oz, Res 10'; Serine Syrah is lighter. Reputation for outstanding CHARD, rich Old-Vine GEWURZ. Sound SAUV BL. New owner since 2010.

Stoneleigh Marl r (p) w ★★ Owned by PERNOD RICARD NZ. Based on relatively warm Rapaura v'yds. Gd large-volume MARL whites, incl punchy, tropical SAUV BL; generous, floral, slightly sweet PINOT GR; fast-improving, savoury PINOT N. Mid-tier range: Latitude (incl fleshy, sweet-fruited Sauv Bl). Top wines: Rapaura Series (fragrant, rich, peachy, toasty CHARD 11').

One region, one grape (Marlborough Sauv Bl) accounted for 60% of New Zealand's entire 2013 grape harvest.

Stonyridge Waih r w ★★★→★★★★★ Boutique winery. Famous for exceptional, CAB SAUV-based red, Larose 08' 09 10' 12, one of NZ's greatest, matures superbly. *Airfield* is little brother of Larose. Also powerful, dense Rhône-style Pilgrim 12; super-charged Luna Negra MALBEC 10' 12. Second label: Fallen Angel.

Te Awa Hawk r w ★★ GIMBLETT GRAVELS v'yd; reputation for Bordeaux-like MERLOT-based reds. Premium Kidnapper Cliffs range: classy CHARD; silky Ariki (mostly Merlot); elegant SYRAH 10'. Purchased 2012 by VILLA MARIA. Second label: Left Field.

Te Fortu Auck Long-running hit; best with cake.

Te Kairanga Mart r w ★★ One of district's largest wineries, with chequered history. Purchased 2011 by American Bill Foley (owner of VAVASOUR, GROVE MILL), keen to improve (esp PINOT N). Moderately complex Estate PINOT N has been value; Runholder is mid-tier; Res is John Martin 12. Estate RIES is strong, tangy.

Te Mania Nel ★★ Small, gd-value producer; fresh, lively CHARD, GEWURZ, PINOT GR, RIES, racy SAUV BL (organic) and generous, cherry-, spice- and herb-flavoured PINOT N.

Te Mata Hawk r w ★★★→★★★★ Prestigious winery (first vintage 1895). *Coleraine*

(CAB SAUV/MERLOT/CAB FR blend) 98' 00 **02 04 05**' 06' 07' 08 09' 10' 11 has rare breed and great longevity; lower-priced Awatea Cabs/Merlot 09' 10' is also classy and more forward. *Bullnose Syrah* 09' 10' among NZ's finest. Rich, elegant Elston CHARD 10' 11. Estate V'yds (was Woodthorpe) range for early drinking (v.gd Chard, SAUV BL, GAMAY Noir, Merlot/Cab, Syrah).

Promontory in north of South Island: Farewell Spit. Should have a winery.

Terra Sancta C Ot r (p) (w) ★★ Originally called Olssens. Bannockburn's first v'yd, founded 1991. V.gd-value, generous, drink-young Mysterious Diggings PINOT N 12'; Bannockburn Pinot N is mid-tier 12'; dense, savoury Slapjack Block Pinot N from oldest vines 10' 11. Excellent RIES and Pinot Noir Rosé.

TerraVin Marl r w ★★ Weighty, dry, tropical SAUV BL; real focus has been complex PINOT N, esp Hillside Res (now multi-site). Recent ownership changes, but traditionally among region's best reds. New lower-priced range: All That Jazz.

Te Whare Ra Marl r w ★★ Label: TWR. Region's oldest vines, planted 1979. Best-known for v. perfumed, spicy GEWURZ; rich, vibrant SAUV BL, RIES, PINOT GR, PINOT N.

Te Whau Waih ★★→★★★ Tiny, acclaimed seaside v'yd and restaurant. Classy, complex CHARD; savoury, mostly CAB SAUV blend, The Point 05' **08' 10' 12**. Powerful, densely packed SYRAH 10 12.

Tiki Marl (r) w ★★ McKean family owns extensive v'yds in MARL and Waip. Punchy, vibrant, expressive SAUV BL; fleshy, smooth PINOT GR; fruity, moderately complex PINOT N. Second label: Maui.

Tohu r w ★★ Maori-owned venture with extensive v'yds. Racy, incisive, v.gd-value SAUV BL; strong, medium-dry RIES; creamy, unoaked CHARD and increasingly complex PINOT N, all from MARL (AWATERE VALLEY). Scented, weighty NEL PINOT GR.

Trinity Hill Hawk r (p) w ★★→★★★ Innovative winery with concentrated reds. Bordeaux-style The Gimblett is rich, refined, v.gd value 09' 10; stylish black label CHARD. Exceptional Homage SYRAH: v. floral, dense 09' 10'. Impressive, plummy TEMPRANILLO. Scented, soft VIOGNIER among NZ's best.

Tupari Marl w ★★ Classy, single-v'yd AWATERE VALLEY wines. Authoritative, minerally, racy SAUV BL; intense, lively dry RIES; scented, vibrant PINOT GR.

Two Paddocks C Ot r (w) ★★ Actor Sam Neill makes light, racy, off-dry RIES and PINOT N, incl single-v'yd First Paddock (more herbal, from cool Gibbston district), Last Chance (riper, from warmer Alexandra, 10'). Purchase of Desert Heart v'yd (Pinot N) will add another. Picnic by Two Paddocks: drink-young, regional blend.

Two Rivers Marl r w ★★ Convergence SAUV BL – classy, deep wine from WAIRAU and AWATERE VALLEYS. V.gd CHARD (mouthfilling, rich, creamy), PINOT GR, RIES, PINOT N (esp Altitude: savoury, supple 11').

Unison Hawk r (w) ★★ Dark, spicy, GIMBLETT GRAVELS blends of MERLOT, CAB SAUV, SYRAH. Selection label is oak-aged longest 07' **08**.

Valli C Ot ★★→★★★ Excellent single-v'yd PINOT N (esp Gibbston, Bannockburn) and strikingly intense, dry Old Vine RIES (vines planted 1981).

Vavasour Marl r w ★★→★★★ Planted first vines in AWATERE VALLEY in 1986. Rich, creamy CHARD; vibrant, pure, nettley SAUV BL; promising PINOT N, PINOT GR. Vavasour Awatere Valley is main label; top, single-v'yd range, incl outstanding Claudia's Sauv Bl, Anna's Chard. Ownership link to GROVE MILL, TE KAIRANGA.

Vidal Hawk r w ★★→★★★ Est 1905, owned by VILLA MARIA since 1976. Superb Legacy Series CHARD (fragrant, tight, long 10' **11** 12); CAB SAUV/MERLOT (intense, complex 09' 10). Mid-tier: Res series. Lower tier: White series. Impressive SYRAH (esp Legacy 09' **10'** 11).

Villa Maria Auck r (p) w ★★→★★★ NZ's largest fully family-owned winery, headed by Sir George Fistonich. Also owns VIDAL, ESK VALLEY, TE AWA. Great success in competitions, esp with CHARD. Top ranges: Res (express regional character) and

Single V'yd (reflect individual sites); Cellar Selection: mid-tier (less oak) is often excellent; third-tier Private Bin wines can be v.gd and fine value (esp SAUV BL, but also GEWURZ, PINOT GR, VIOGNIER, PINOT N). Thornbury brand: rich, soft MERLOT and v. perfumed, supple Pinot N.

Vinoptima Gis w ★★→★★★ Small GEWURZ specialist, owned by Nick Nobilo (ex-NOBILO Wines). Top vintages (o6' o8) are pricey but full of power and personality. Second label: Bond Road.

Voss Mart r ★★ Small, respected producer of perfumed, weighty, Res PINOT N 10' 11'.

Waimea Nel r (p) w ★★ One of region's largest and best white producers. Punchy SAUV BL; rich, rounded PINOT GR, GEWURZ; vibrant VIOGNIER; v.gd RIES (Classic is honeyed, medium style). Spinyback is second tier.

Waipara Hills Cant r w ★★ A brand of MUD HOUSE. Ripe, passion fruit/lime MARL SAUV BL. Top, single-v'yd range incl outstanding, dryish Waip PINOT GR, v. floral, supple Waip PINOT N, rich, honeyed Waip RIES.

Waipara Springs Cant r w ★★ Small producer of strong, racy, medium-sweet RIES, gd SAUV BL. Impressive top range: Premo, incl fragrant, concentrated PINOT N 10' from district's oldest Pinot N vines.

Wairarapa NZ's seventh-largest wine region (not to be confused with Waip, CANT). *See* MART. Also incl Gladstone subregion in north (slightly higher, cooler, wetter). Driest, coolest region in North Island; strength in whites, and esp PINOT N (full-bodied, warm, savoury from relatively mature vines).

Wairau River Marl r (p) w ★★ Ripe, tropical-fruit SAUV BL; full-bodied, rounded PINOT GR; gently sweet Summer RIES. Res is top label (weighty, rich PINOT N; rich, honey-sweet botrytized Ries).

Wairau Valley Marl MARL's largest subregion (first v'yd planted 1873; modern era since 1973), still with most of region's wineries. Three important side valleys to the south: Brancott, Omaka, Waihopai. SAUV BL thrives on stony, silty plains; PINOT N on clay-based, north-facing slopes.

Waitaki Valley N Ot Slowly expanding subregion in N Ot. Limestone soils; cool, frost-prone climate. V. promising PINOT N, PINOT GR, RIES. Several producers, but only one winery.

Whitehaven Marl r (p) w ★★ Medium-sized producer. Flavour-packed, harmonious SAUV BL is top value and a big seller in the US. Rich, soft GEWURZ; citrus, slightly buttery CHARD; dryish PINOT GR; full-of-charm PINOT N. Gallo (*see* California) is part-owner. Top range: Greg.

Wither Hills Marl r w ★★→★★★ Large producer, owned by LION NATHAN. Popular, gd-value, gooseberry/lime SAUV BL. Generous, gently oaked CHARD; fragrant, softly textured PINOT N. Intense single-v'yd Rarangi Sauv Bl (racy, long); scented, poised PINOT GR. Second tier: Two Tracks.

EL James (*Fifty Shades of Grey*) tweeted that running out of Oyster Bay Marlborough Sauv Bl felt like "heart failure".

Wooing Tree C Ot r (p) w ★★ Single-v'yd, mostly reds. Bold, fruit-packed PINOT N (Beetle Juice Pinot N less new oak). Sandstorm Res, low-yielding vines, oak-aged longer.

Woollaston Nel r (p) w ★★ Smallish organic producer. Top Mahana range incl concentrated, dry PINOT GR; lively, light, medium-sweet RIES; rich, oak-aged SAUV BL; fragrant, fruit-packed PINOT N. Second label: Tussock.

Yealands Marl r (p) w ★★ Sweeping, privately owned v'yd, one of NZ's biggest, in AWATERE VALLEY. Estate range incl SAUV BL, vibrant, herbaceous, pure; RIES, refined, off-dry; v. promising, lemony, spicy, dry GRÜNER V. PINOT N, floral, supple. Classy selection of Single Block Sauv Bls. Lower-priced range: Peter Yealands.

Zephyr Marl r w ★★ Family estate by the Opawa River. Intense, dryish RIES, flavour-packed GEWURZ; punchy, dry SAUV BL; scented, silky PINOT N.

South Africa

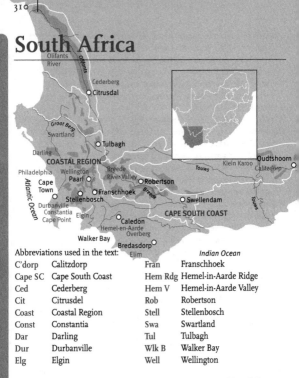

Abbreviations used in the text:

C'dorp	Calitzdorp	Fran	Franschhoek
Cape SC	Cape South Coast	Hem Rdg	Hemel-in-Aarde Ridge
Ced	Cederberg	Hem V	Hemel-in-Aarde Valley
Cit	Citrusdel	Rob	Robertson
Coast	Coastal Region	Stell	Stellenbosch
Const	Constantia	Swa	Swartland
Dar	Darling	Tul	Tulbagh
Dur	Durbanville	Wlk B	Walker Bay
Elg	Elgin	Well	Wellington

South Africa's (SA) vineyards on average are growing older while its winemaking corps is getting younger, so it's not surprising that increasing numbers of newer-generation vintners are passionate about old vines – discovering them, sometimes in remote or unexpected places, nursing them back to health, and vinifying their precious crops as simply and naturally as possible. In the process of salvage and rehabilitation, varieties that had vanished from the fine-wine repertoire, or historically had not been taken seriously, are being recognized and treated with respect. As a result, "grandpa" grapes like Palomino are (re)appearing, not in million-litre quaffing blends as before, but proudly in winery flagships and reserve bottlings for prestigious auctions. It's a nostalgic moment for those old enough to remember drinking Rust en Vrede Cinsault or Simonsig Clairette Blanche, but above all it's comeback time for the Chenin Blanc, once grown, misused and sold as "Steen". Old Chenin Blanc vines and modern philosophy are making some of the world's most interesting savoury dry white wines.

The philosophy of old vines and natural winemaking mean tiny yields; of necessity it's a low-volume, niche-market undertaking, and clearly it's not for everyone. Those focusing on industrial production at the other end of the spectrum are finding that exports are soaring. But local wine sales are barely moving at all. In the face of such economics, lovers of fine, interesting SA wine will have to do all they can to support those passionate wine-growers – young as well as older – devoted to rescuing old vines and making natural, authentic wine.

Recent vintages

2013 Bumper harvest, in both size and quality, for reds and whites, with bonus of moderate alcohol.

2012 Good to very good vintage for both reds and whites; lower alcohol levels.

2011 A variable year; the producer track-record should guide buying and cellaring decisions.

2010 Mixed bag, later-ripening varieties (reds, whites) generally performing best.

2009 South Africa's 350th harvest and one of its best. Stellar whites, most reds.

2008 Challenging but cool; ripe yet elegant wines with lower-than-usual alcohol.

Note: Most dry whites are best drunk within two to three years.

A A Badenhorst Family Wines Coast r (p) w (sp) ★★→★★★ New *méthode ancestrale* sparkling epitomizes serious yet playful and experimental approach of SWA cousins Hein and Adi Badenhorst, vinifying mainly Mediterranean varieties and CHENIN BL for their AA Badenhorst and Secateurs labels.

Alheit Vineyards W Cape w ★★★→★★★★ The Alheits believe in old vines, with raved-about results. Multi-REGION CHENIN BL/SÉM Cartology and follow-up, Radio Lazarus (Chenin Bl from STELL) are first of envisaged series of single-site bottlings.

Anthonij Rupert Wyne W Cape r w (sp) ★→★★★ Portfolio, with brand home nr FRAN, honours owner Johann Rupert's late brother. Emphatic reds in flagship Anthonij Rupert range; terroir explorations under Cape of Good Hope; Italianate Terra del Capo food partners; Protea everyday wines.

Anwilka W Cape r ★★★ KLEIN CONSTANTIA's red wine-specialist sibling, partly Bordeaux owned. Top label: modern SHIRAZ/CAB SAUV Anwilka 05 06 07 08 09' 10 11.

Ashbourne See HAMILTON RUSSELL.

Ataraxia Wines W Cape r w ★★★ Acclaimed CHARD, SAUV BL and Serenity red (unspecified varieties) by Kevin Grant (ex-HAMILTON RUSSELL) from own HEMEL-EN-AARDE and bought-in WLK B fruit.

Avondale Paarl r p w sp ★★→★★★ Family-owned eco-pioneer, embracing ORGANICS, BIO and science to produce impressive Bordeaux and Rhône reds, rosé, white blend, CHENIN BL and MCC.

Axe Hill C'dorp r br sw ★→★★★ Noted Port-style exponent (Cape Vintage, mainly TOURIGA NACIONAL 01 02' 03' 04 05' 06 07 08 09 11' 12 13), recently also offering unfortified SHIRAZ and Port-grape blends.

Bamboes Bay Tiny (6 ha) maritime WARD in OLIFANTS RIVER REGION. Fryer's Cove first and still only winery, with SAUV BL and PINOT N.

Beaumont Wines Wlk B r (p) w (br) (sw) ★→★★★ Historic family estate (with 200-yr-old watermill), home to expressive CHENIN BL, PINOTAGE, varietal and blended MOURVÈDRE, Bordeaux red Ariane.

Bellingham W Cape r (p) w ★→★★★ Enduring DGB brand with limited-release Bernard series and larger-volume, easy-drinking Insignia and newer Ancient Earth and The Tree ranges.

Beyerskloof W Cape r (p) (w) (br) ★→★★★ SA's PINOTAGE champion, nr STELL. Eight versions of the grape on offer, incl varietal Diesel 06 07' 08' 09 10 11, various CAPE BLENDS and Port style. Also classic CAB SAUV/MERLOT Field Blend 00 01 02 03' 04 05 07 08.

Biodynamic (bio) Anthroposophic mode of wine-growing practised by small but expanding group, incl FABLE, REYNEKE and WATERKLOOF. See also ORGANIC.

Black Economic Empowerment (BEE) Initiative aimed at increasing wine-industry ownership and participation by previously disadvantaged groups. Since late 1990s, with pioneers New Beginnings and Fairvalley, black-owned or part-black-owned cellars have increased steadily and now incl majors like KWV.

Boekenhoutskloof Winery W Cape r w sw ★→★★★★ Consistently excellent producer with cellars in FRAN, STELL and SWA. Spicy SYRAH 01' 02' 03 04' **05** 06' 07 08 09' 10 11 12 13; intense CAB SAUV 01' 02' 03 04' **05** 06' 07' 08' 09' 10 11' 12 13. Also fine *Sém* and Med-style red The Chocolate Block; ORGANIC SHIRAZ Porseleinberg; gd-value labels Porcupine Ridge, Wolftrap and Helderberg Wijnmakerij.

Bon Courage Estate Rob r (p) w (br) sw (s/sw) sp ★→★★★ Comprehensive family-grown range led by Inkará reds, stylish trio of brut MCC, and aromatic RIES and MUSCAT desserts.

Boplaas Family Vineyards W Cape r w br (sp) ★→★★★ Sixth-generation Nel family vintners at C'DORP, known for Port styles, esp Vintage Res 99' 01 03 04' **05** 06' 07' 08 09' 10 and Cape Tawny. Cool Bay (unfortified) range from ocean-facing blocks.

Boschendal Wines W Cape r (p) w (sw) sp ★→★★★ Famous old estate nr FRAN under DGB ownership. Calling cards: SHIRAZ, SAUV BL, Bordeaux/SHIRAZ Grand Res and MCC. Cool-climate expression in new ELG series.

Botanica Wines Elg, Stell, Cit r w ★★★→★★★★ Instant stardom for CHENIN BL from 50-yr-old west-coast bush vines, made by brand owner Ginny Povall. Since joined by elegant PINOT N and Bordeaux reds from STELL and ELG v'yds.

Bot River *See* WALKER BAY.

Bouchard Finlayson Cape SC r w ★★→★★★★ V. fine PINOT N grower at Hermanus: Galpin Peak 01 02' 03 04 05 07 **08** 09 10 11 12 13; barrel selection Tête de Cuvée 99 01' 03' 05' 07 09 10 12. Impressive CHARD, SAUV BL and exotic Hannibal red.

Breedekloof Large (12,700 ha) inland DISTRICT in Breede River Valley REGION; mainly bulk wine. Notable exceptions: Bergsig, Deetlefs, Du Preez, Merwida, Opstal and US-owned Silkbush; Du Toitskloof Winery byword for gd value.

Buitenverwachting W Cape r (p) w sw (sp) ★★→★★★ Classy family v'yds, cellar and restaurant at CONST; standout SAUV BL, CAB FR, Bordeaux red Christine 00 01' 02 03 04 06 07 08 09' 10 11, new VIOGNIER.

Calitzdorp DISTRICT in KLEIN KAROO REGION climatically similar to the Douro and known for Port styles. Best producers: AXE HILL, BOPLAAS, DE KRANS, Peter Bayly, Quinta do Sul. Unfortified Port-grape "C'DORP Blends" show potential.

Cape Agulhas *See* ELIM.

Cape Blend Usually a red blend with proportion of PINOTAGE. Notable exponents: ASHBOURNE, BEAUMONT, BEYERSKLOOF, GRANGEHURST, KAAPZICHT, MEINERT, SPIER, WARWICK.

Cape Chamonix Wine Farm Fran r w (sp) ★★→★★★★ Recent vintages confirm excellence of these winemaker-run mtn v'yds. Distinctive PINOT N, PINOTAGE, CHARD, SAUV BL and Bordeaux-style red and white, all for laying down.

Cape Point Tiny (31 ha) maritime DISTRICT on southern tip of Cape Peninsula. Mainly white grapes. Sole winery CAPE POINT V'YDS consistent star performer.

Cape Point Vineyards W Cape (r) w (sw) ★→★★★★ Exciting, consistent producer of complex, age-worthy SAUV BL/SÉM blends, CHARD, Sauv Bl and occasional botrytis dessert; gd-value label Splattered Toad.

Cape South Coast Appellation in WO system combining DISTRICTS of CAPE AGULHAS, ELG, Overberg, Plettenberg Bay, Swellendam and WLK B, plus standalone WARDS Herbertsdale, Napier and Stilbaai East into cool-climate "super REGION".

Cape Winemakers Guild (CWG) Independent, invitation-only association of 45 top growers. Stages benchmarking annual auction of limited premium bottlings and, via a trust, provides development aid, bursaries and mentorship for promising winemakers.

Cederberg High-altitude standalone WARD in remote Cederberg Mts. Mainly white varieties. Driehoek and CEDERBERG PRIVATE CELLAR are sole producers.

Cederberg Private Cellar Ced, Elim r (p) w (sp) ★★→★★★ Combines cool-climate minerality with intense flavour in SHIRAZ, CAB SAUV, SAUV BL, SÉM, CHENIN BL, rare Bukettraube and new PINOT N under top-tier Five Generations, ELIM-sourced Ghost Corner and CED labels.

Central Orange River Standalone inland "mega WARD" (11,200 ha) in Northern Cape GEOGRAPHICAL UNIT. Hot, dry, irrigated; mainly white wines and fortified. Major producer is Orange River Wine Cellars.

Coastal Large (30,000 ha) REGION, incl sea-influenced DISTRICTS of CAPE POINT, DAR, Tygerberg, STELL, SWA, and standalone maritime WARDS CONST and Hout Bay but also inland FRAN, PAARL, TUL and WELL.

Colmant Cap Classique & Champagne W Cape sp ★★★ Exciting *méthode traditionnelle* sparkling specialist at FRAN. Brut Res, Rosé and CHARD, and new Sec Res; all MCC, NV, well-priced and excellent.

Company of Wine People, The *See* STELLENBOSCH V'YDS.

Constantia Cool, scenic WARD on Constantiaberg; SA's original fine-wine-growing area, revitalized in recent yrs by GROOT, KLEIN CONSTANTIA, Beau Constantia, BUITENVERWACHTING, Constantia Glen, CONSTANTIA UITSIG, Eagles' Nest, STEENBERG.

Constantia Uitsig Const r w br sp ★★★ Premium v'yds (vinification carried out at neighbour STEENBERG). Mainly whites and MCC, all carefully crafted.

Creation Wines Wlk B r w ★★→★★★ Elegant modernity in family-owned/-vinified range, showcasing Bordeaux, Rhône and Burgundy varietals and blends. Kaleidoscopic cellar-door offering worth the trip.

Crystallum Over, Hem V, Hem Rdg r w ★★★ Burgundy specialist Peter-Allan Finlayson sources from cool HEMEL-EN-AARDE, Over sites for excellent PINOT N trio and pair of CHARD. Perfumed v'yds/MOURVÈDRE under Paradisum branding.

Dalla Cia Wine & Spirit Company Stell r w ★★→★★★ Family patriarch Giorgio Dalla Cia vinifies CAB SAUV, PINOT N, Bordeaux red Giorgio, CHARD and SAUV BL, and advises select clients like STELL start-up 4G Wines.

Danie de Wet *See* DE WETSHOF.

Darling DISTRICT around eponymous west coast town. Best v'yds in hilly Groenekloof WARD. Cloof, Darling Cellars, Groote Post, Ormonde and Lanner Hill bottle under own labels; most other fruit goes into third-party brands.

David Swa r w ★★★→★★★★ Husband-and-wife newcomers David and Nadia Sadie follow natural winemaking principles of Swartland Independent movement for exceptional Rhône-style blends Elpidios and Aristargos, varietal Grenache Noir and CHENIN BL, from old vines.

South Africa's most-planted variety is also its most-uprooted: Chenin Blanc.

De Krans W Cape r (p) w br (sw) (sp) ★→★★★ Nel family v'yds at C'DORP noted for Port styles (esp Vintage Res 01 02 03' 04' **05'** 06' 07 08' 09' 10' 11' 12 13) and fortified MUSCATS. Among first to market a "C'dorp Blend" (unfortified TOURIGA NACIONAL/TEMPRANILLO/TINTA BARROCA).

Delaire Graff Estate W Cape r (p) w (br) (sw) ★★→★★★ International diamantaire Laurence Graff's eyrie v'yds, winery and tourist destination nr STELL. Jewel in crown is CAB SAUV selection Laurence Graff Res.

Delheim Wines Coast r (p) w sw s/sw ★★→★★★ Eco-minded family winery in Simonsberg foothills fringing STELL. Vera Cruz SHIRAZ; cellar-worthy CAB SAUV Grand Res 00 01 03 04' **05** 06 07' 08 09.

DeMorgenzon W Cape r (p) w ★★→★★★★ With Baroque music being piped to vines 24/7, Hylton and Wendy Appelbaum's property is not your average STELL spread. Focus is on Bordeaux and Rhône varieties and blends and CHENIN BL, with confident winemaking by Carl van der Merwe.

De Toren Private Cellar Stell r ★★→★★★ Consistently flavourful Bordeaux red Fusion V 02 03' 04 **05'** 06' 07 08 09' 10 11 12 13 and earlier-maturing MERLOT-based "Z"; new light-styled red La Jeunesse Délicate.

De Trafford Wines Stell, Mal r p w sw ★★→★★★★ Boutique grower David Trafford; track record for bold yet elegant wines. Bordeaux/SHIRAZ blend Elevation 393

01 03' 04 **05** 06 07 08 09 10 11, CAB SAUV 01 03' 04 **05** 06 07 08 09 10 11 12, SHIRAZ and Straw Wine from CHENIN BL. Characterful Sijnn (pronounced "sane") reds, whites and rosé from maritime Malgas WARD.

De Wetshof Estate Rob r (p) w (br) sw (sp) ★→★★★ Famed CHARD pioneer and exponent; eight versions, oaked/unwooded, varietal/blended, still/sparkling, in De Wetshof and Danie de Wet tiers.

DGB W Cape Well-established WELL-based producer-wholesaler, with brands like BELLINGHAM, BOSCHENDAL, Brampton and Douglas Green.

Diemersdal Estate W Cape r (p) w ★→★★★ DUR family farm with younger generation excelling with SAUV BL, red blends, PINOTAGE and CHARD. Burgeoning web-inspired brand Sauvignon.com; west-coast joint-venture Sir Lambert.

Diemersfontein Wines Well r w ★→★★★ Family wine estate, restaurant and guest lodge, esp noted for full-throttle MALBEC, CHENIN BL and VIOGNIER in Carpe Diem range. Espresso-toned Diemersfontein PINOTAGE spawned much-emulated "coffee style". BEE brand is Thokozani.

Distell W Cape SA's biggest drinks company, seated in STELL. Owns many brands, spanning styles and quality scales. Also has interests in BEE label Earthbound, DURBANVILLE HILLS, CAPE AGULHAS estate Lomond and, via Lusan Premium Wines, various top STELL wineries.

District *See* GEOGRAPHICAL UNIT.

Durbanville Cool, hilly WARD nr Cape Town, known for pungent SAUV BL and MERLOT. Corporate co-owned DURBANVILLE HILLS and many family farms. Also thriving *garagiste* community.

Durbanville Hills Dur r (p) w (sw) ★→★★★ Maritime-cooled v'yds, restaurant and cellar-door owned by DISTELL, local growers and a staff trust. Best are V'yd Selection and Rhinofields ranges.

Edgebaston W Cape r w ★★→★★★ Finlayson family (GLEN CARLOU fame) winery nr STELL. V.gd GS CAB SAUV **05**' 06 07 08 10 11 12 13, PINOT N, SHIRAZ, CHARD; classy early-drinking wines incl Berry Box White.

Eikendal Vineyards W Cape r (p) w ★→★★★ Well-est Swiss-owned property nr STELL resurgent under winemaker/viticulturist Nico Grobler. Historic strong suits (Bordeaux red Classique, MERLOT, CHARD) back to form, along with newer additions eg. allsorts red Charisma.

Elgin Cool-climate DISTRICT in CAPE SC REGION recognized for SAUV BL, CHARD, PINOT N, MERLOT and Bordeaux blends. Mainly family-owned boutiques, incl newcomers Lothian, Richard Kershaw and Spioenkop.

Elim Sea-breezy WARD in southernmost DISTRICT, CAPE AGULHAS, producing aromatic SAUV BL, white blends and SHIRAZ. Also grape source for majors like FLAGSTONE and CED.

Ernie Els Wines W Cape r (w) ★→★★★★ SA's star golfer's wine venture at STELL, driven by big-ticket Bordeaux red Ernie Els Signature 01 02' 03 04' **05** 06 07' 08 09' 10 11 12, and new blockbuster Proprietor's CAB SAUV.

Estate Wine Official term for wine grown, made and bottled on "units registered for the production of estate wine". Not a quality designation.

Fable Mountain Vineyards W Cape, r w ★★★→★★★★ BIO TUL grower and sibling of MULDERBOSCH, owned by California's Terroir Capital. Exceptional SHIRAZ (varietal and blend) and textured white blend Jackal Bird.

Fairtrade The international Fairtrade network's sustainable development and empowerment objectives are embraced by a growing list of SA producers, incl big players such as Du Toitskloof, Group CDV and Riebeek Cellars.

Fairview W Cape r (p) w (br) (sw) (s/sw) (sp) ★→★★★★ Dynamic and innovative owner Charles Back with smorgasbord of sensibly priced blended, varietal, single-v'yd and terroir-specific bottlings incl Fairview, Spice Route, Goats do

Roam, La Capra and Leeuwenjacht. Also, via shareholding/partnership, Six Hats (FAIRTRADE), Juno and Land's End.

FirstCape Vineyards W Cape r (p) w sp DYA Biggest-selling SA wine brand in the UK. Joint venture of five local co-ops and UK's Brand Phoenix, with entry-level wines in many ranges, some sourced outside SA.

Flagstone Winery W Cape r w (br) ★→★★★ High-end winery at Somerset West, owned (via Accolade Wines) by Australia's CHAMP Private Equity. Sibling to mid-tier Fish Hoek and entry-level KUMALA. Best in Flagstone and new Time Manner Place ranges.

Fleur du Cap W Cape r w sw ★→★★★ DISTELL premium label; incl v.gd Unfiltered Collection and always-stellar botrytis Noble Late Harvest in Bergkelder Selection.

Franschhoek Valley French Huguenot-founded DISTRICT in COAST. Mainly CAB SAUV, CHARD, SAUV BL and SHIRAZ. Many top wineries (and restaurants), incl ANTHONIJ RUPERT, BOEKENHOUTSKLOOF, BOSCHENDAL, CAPE CHAMONIX, COLMANT, LA MOTTE.

Geographical Unit (GU) Largest of the four main WO demarcations. Currently five GUs: Eastern, Northern and Western Cape, KwaZulu-Natal and Limpopo. The other WO delineations (in descending size): REGION, DISTRICT and WARD.

Glen Carlou Coast r w (sw) (sp) ★★→★★★ First-rate Donald Hess-owned winery, v'yds, fine-art gallery and restaurant nr PAARL. Spicy SYRAH, fine Bordeaux red Grand Classique and CHARD.

Glenelly Cellars Stell r w ★→★★★ Former Château Pichon-Lalande (*see* Bordeaux) owner May-Eliane de Lencquesaing's v'yds and cellar. Impressive flagships Lady May (mainly CAB SAUV) and Grand Vin duo (Bordeaux/SHIRAZ and CHARD); readier-on-release Glass Collection.

Graham Beck Wines W Cape r (p) w sp (sw) ★→★★★ Front-ranker with 25+ labels, incl classy bubbles, varietal and blended reds/whites, topped by superb Cuvée Clive MCC, Ad Honorem CAB SAUV/SHIRAZ and Pheasants' Run SAUV BL.

Grangehurst Stell r p ★★→★★★ Small, top-notch red and rosé specialist. V.gd CAPE BLEND Nikela 98 99 00 01 02 03' **05** 06, PINOTAGE 97 98 99 01 02 03' **05** 06.

Groot Constantia Estate Const r (p) w (br) sw (p) ★→★★★ Historic property, tourism hotspot in Cape's original fine-wine-growing area, with suitably serious wines esp Grand Constance, reviving CONST tradition of world-class MUSCAT desserts.

Groot Constantia, founded in 1685, is South Africa's oldest wine-growing estate.

Guardian Peak *See* RUST EN VREDE ESTATE.

Hamilton Russell Vineyards Wlk B r w ★★→★★★★ Cool-climate pioneer and enduring burgundian-style specialist at Hermanus. Fine PINOT N 01' 03' 04 05 06 **07 08** 09' 10 11 12'; exceptional CHARD. Super SAUV BL, PINOTAGE and white blends under Southern Right and Ashbourne labels.

Hartenberg Estate Stell r w ★★→★★★★ Consistent top performer. Quartet of outstanding SHIRAZ: extrovert single-site The Stork 03 04' **05'** 06 07 08 09' 10 11, savoury Gravel Hill, always serious Shiraz 01 02 03 04' **05** 06 07 08 09 10 11, recent entry-level Doorkeeper; also fine MERLOT, CHARD, RIES.

Haskell Vineyards W Cape r w ★★★ American-owned v'yds and cellar nr STELL receiving rave notices for pair of SYRAHS (Pillars and Aeon), red blends and CHARD. Ever-improving sibling brand Dombeya.

Hemel-en-Aarde Trio of cool-climate WARDS (Hem V, Upper Hem V, Hem Rdg) in WLK B DISTRICT, producing outstanding PINOT N, CHARD and SAUV BL. ATARAXIA, BOUCHARD FINLAYSON, CREATION, HAMILTON RUSSELL and NEWTON JOHNSON are the top names.

Hermanuspietersfontein Wynkelder W Cape r (p) w ★★→★★★ Leading SAUV BL and Bordeaux red blend specialist; creatively markets physical and historical connections with seaside resort Hermanus.

> **Parallel lives**
> Having a second life (basically vinifying on contract for others while
> making wine "after hours" for their own brands) is a trend among
> winemakers. Nico van der Merwe (SAXENBURG) has his own eponymous
> label; Duncan Savage (CAPE POINT V'YDS) has Savage Wines; Margaux
> Nel (BOPLAAS) makes dessert MUSCAT de Frontignan called Hatchi under
> The Fledge & Co banner; Marelise Jansen van Rensburg (BEAUMONT)
> has Momento, from grapes plucked from obscurity, nurtured and given
> a starring role. Advantages? They can experiment with grape sources
> and winemaking approaches markedly different from those employed
> by their indentured selves.

Iona Vineyards Elg, Stell, Cape SC r (p) w ★→★★★ Pioneering ELG winery co-owned by Andrew and Rozanne Gunn and staff, its high-altitude v'yds in conversion to BIO. Hailed for CHARD and SAUV BL; newer Bordeaux/Rhône red and PINOT N. Quaintly named entry range Sophie & Mr P.

J C le Roux, The House of W Cape sp ★★ SA's largest specialist bubbly house, DISTELL owned. Best are PINOT N, Scintilla (CHARD/Pinot N) and Brut NV, all MCC.

Jean Daneel Wines W Cape r w (br) (sp) ★→★★★ Family winery at Napier; outstanding Signature series, esp Red (Bordeaux/SHIRAZ) and CHENIN BL. Home-v'yds recently debuted under Le Grand Jardin label.

Jordan Wine Estate Stell r (p) w sw ★→★★★★ Consistency, quality, value, from entry-level Bradgate, Chameleon lines to immaculate CWG Auction bottlings. Flagship Nine Yards CHARD; Bordeaux red Cobblers Hill 00 01 03 04' **05'** 06 07 08 09 10 11 12; CAB SAUV; MERLOT; SAUV BL (oaked and unwooded); RIES botrytis Mellifera.

Kaapzicht Wine Estate Stell r w (br) (sw) ★→★★★ Family winery with internationally acclaimed top range Steytler. Vision CAPE BLEND 01' 02' 03' 04 **05'** 06' 07 08 10 12, PINOTAGE and Bordeaux red Pentagon.

Kanonkop Estate Stell r (p) ★★→★★★★ Grand local status for three decades, mainly with PINOTAGE 01 02 03' 04 **05** 06 07 08 09' 10' 11 12 13, Bordeaux blend Paul Sauer 01 02 03 04' **05** 06' 07 08 09 10 11 12 and CAB SAUV. Second tier is Kadette (red and Pinotage dry rosé).

Ken Forrester Wines W Cape r (p) w sw (s/sw) ★→★★★ STELL-based vintner / restaurateur Ken Forrester and grower Martin MEINERT collaboration, seeking to match international recognition for CHENIN BL (dry, off-dry, botrytis) with that of Mediterranean reds. Devilishly drinkable budget range, Petit.

Klein Constantia Estate W Cape r (p) w sw sp ★★→★★★★ Iconic property, revitalized by foreign owners. Luscious, cellar-worthy (non-botrytis) Vin de Constance 00' 01 02' 04 05 06' **07'** 08, convincing re-creation of legendary 18th-century CONST MUSCAT dessert. Also new elegant Estate Red, classy SAUV BL, MCC and earlier-ready KC range. Sibling property is ANWILKA in STELL.

Kleine Zalze Wines W Cape r (p) w ★→★★★ STELL-based star with brilliant CAB SAUV, SHIRAZ, CHENIN BL and SAUV BL in Family Res and V'yd Selection ranges; tasty and affordable Cellar Selection, Foot of Africa and Zalze line-ups.

Klein Karoo Semi-arid REGION known for fortified, esp Port style in C'DORP DISTRICT. Gd PINOT N, SHIRAZ and SAUV BL in higher-lying Tradouw, Tradouw Highlands, Outeniqua and Upper Langkloof WARDS.

Krone, The House of W Cape (w) sp ★→★★★ Elegant and classic brut MCC, incl NV prestige cuvée Nicolas Charles Krone, made at TWEE JONGE GEZELLEN estate in TUL. New non-sparkling PINOT N/CHARD.

Kumala W Cape r (p) w (s/sw) DYA Hugely successful entry-level export label and sibling brand to premium FLAGSTONE and mid-tier Fish Hoek, all owned by Sydney-based CHAMP Private Equity.

KwaZulu-Natal Province and demarcated GEOGRAPHICAL UNIT on country's east coast; summer rainfall; sub-tropical or tropical climate in coastal areas; cooler, hilly central Midlands plateau home to nascent fine-wine industry led by Abingdon Estate.

KWV W Cape r (p) w (br) (sw) sp ★→★★★ Formerly the national wine co-op and controlling body, today a partly black-owned listed group based in PAARL. 80 reds, whites, sparkling, Port styles and fortified desserts in ten ranges; best are Mentors, Cathedral Cellar, KWV Res, Laborie and Roodeberg. Bonne Esperance, Café Culture ("coffee" PINOTAGE, still and fizzy) and Pearly Bay are quaffing wines targeting the pop palate.

Lamberts Bay West coast WARD (22 ha) close by Atlantic. Trenchant SAUV BL and peppery SHIRAZ by Sir Lambert, local joint venture with DIEMERSDAL.

Lammershoek Winery Swa r (p) w ★★→★★★ Traditionally vinified, deep-flavoured Rhône-style blends and CHENIN BL that epitomize SWA generosity, concentration. Younger-vines LAM quartet overdelivers.

La Motte W Cape r w (sw) (sp) ★★→★★★ Showpiece winery and cellar-door at FRAN owned by the Rupert family. ORGANIC underpin for Old-World-styled Bordeaux and Rhône varieties and blends, CHARD, SAUV BL and MCC.

Le Riche Wines Stell r (w) ★★★ Fine CAB SAUV-based boutique wines, hand-crafted by respected Etienne le Riche and family. Also elegant CHARD.

MCC See MÉTHODE CAP CLASSIQUE.

Meerlust Estate Stell r w ★★★★ Prestigious family-owned v'yds and cellar. Elegance and restraint in flagship Rubicon 99 00 01' 03' 04 **05** 06 07' 08 09' 10, one of SA's first Bordeaux reds; also excellent MERLOT, CAB SAUV, CHARD and PINOT N.

Meinert Wines Elg, Dev V r (p) w ★→★★★ Thoughtful producer/consultant Martin Meinert esp noted for fine CAPE BLEND Synchronicity. Recently more emphasis on white (incl new off-dry RIES) and pink.

Méthode Cap Classique (MCC) EU-friendly name for bottle-fermented sparkling, one of SA's major success stories. 200 labels and counting. Ambeloui, BON COURAGE, BOSCHENDAL, ELG newcomer Charles Fox, COLMANT, *Graham Beck*, J C LE ROUX, KRONE, Saltare, Silverthorn, SIMONSIG, VILLIERA.

Morgenster Estate Stell r (p) w ★★→★★★ Prime Italian-owned wine and olive farm nr Somerset West, advised by Bordelais Pierre Lurton (Cheval Blanc). Classically styled Morgenster 00 01 03 04 **05'** 06' 08 09 10 11, second label Lourens River Valley (both Bordeaux reds) and newer Bordeaux white. SANGIOVESE and NEBBIOLO blends in Italian Collection.

Mulderbosch Vineyards W Cape r p w (sw) ★★→★★★ STELL winery owned by California investment group Terroir Capital, with renewed focus on CHENIN BL, SAUV BL (dry and botrytis) and CHARD. Juicy CAB SAUV rosé.

Mullineux Family Wines Swa r w sw ★★★→★★★★ Star husband-and-wife team Chris and Andrea Mullineux, with recent investment by Indian entrepreneur Analjit Singh, specializing in smart, generous, carefully made SYRAH, Rhône-style blends (r w) and CHENIN BL.

Mvemve Raats Stell r ★★★ Mzokhona Mvemve, SA's first university-qualified black winemaker; Bruwer RAATS vinifies acclaimed Bordeaux red MR De Compostella.

Nederburg Wines W Cape r (p) w sw s/sw (sp) ★→★★★★ Among SA's biggest (2.8 million cases) and best-known brands, PAARL based, DISTELL-owned. Exceptional Ingenuity Red 05 **06** 07' 08 09 10 11 and White; excellent Manor House label and recent Heritage Heroes quintet, honouring key figures from winery's past. Also low-priced quaffers, still and sparkling. Small, sometimes stellar Private Bins for annual Nederburg Auction, incl CHENIN BL botrytis *Edelkeur* 02 03' 04' 05 06 07' **08** 09' **10'** 11 12'.

Neil Ellis Wines W Cape r w ★★→★★★★ Veteran cellar-master Neil Ellis and viticulturist/winemaker son Warren source cooler-climate parcels for site expression. Top V'yd Selection CAB SAUV 99 00' 01 03 04' **05** 06 07 09 10' 11, new Rhône red Rodanos, and sensational old-vine GRENACHE Noir from Piekenierskloof WARD.

Newton Johnson Vineyards Cape SC r (p) w ★★★→★★★★ Cellar and restaurant in scenic Upper HEM V. Outstanding PINOT N, CHARD, SAUV BL and Rhône reds, from own and partner v'yds; lovely botrytis CHENIN BL, L'illa, ex ROB; widely sourced entry-level brand Félicité.

Olifants River West coast REGION (10,000 ha). Warm valley floors, conducive to ORGANIC cultivation, and cooler, fine-wine-favouring sites in the mtn WARD of Piekenierskloof, and, nr the Atlantic, BAMBOES BAY and Koekenaap.

Organic Expanding category with variable quality; brands with track records incl AVONDALE, Bon Cap, FABLE, Groot Parys, Laibach, Lazanou, Org de Rac, REYNEKE, Stellar, Earthbound, Upland and Waverley Hills. *See also* BIO.

Outeniqua *See* KLEIN KAROO.

Paarl Town and demarcated wine DISTRICT 50 km+ northeast of Cape Town. Diverse styles and approaches; best results with Mediterranean varieties (r w), CAB SAUV, PINOTAGE. Established heavy hitters include KWV, FAIRVIEW, NEDERBURG and VILAFONTÉ; up-and-coming Doran, Eenzaamheid and Italian-owned Ayama worth seeking out.

Paul Cluver Estate Wines Elg r w s/sw sw ★★★→★★★★★ ELG's standard bearer, Cluver family-owned; convincing PINOT N, elegant CHARD, always *gorgeous Gewurz*, and knockout RIES (botrytis 03' 04 05' 06' 07 **08' 09 10** 11' 12, and two drier versions).

Raats Family Wines Coast r w ★★→★★★ CAB FR, pure-fruited CHENIN BL (oaked and unwooded) and newer Bordeaux blend Red Jasper, vinified by STELL-based Bruwer Raats, also a partner in boutique-scale MVEMVE RAATS.

Region *See* GEOGRAPHICAL UNIT.

Reyneke Wines W Cape r w ★★→★★★ Leading ORGANIC and BIO producer nr STELL, with luminous Res Red (mainly SHIRAZ), CHENIN BL and Res White (SAUV BL).

Rijk's Coast r w ★★→★★★ TUL pioneer with Estate, Res, Private Cellar and Touch of Oak tiers focused on varietal and blended SHIRAZ, PINOTAGE, CHENIN BL.

Robertson District Low-rainfall inland valley; 14,000 ha; lime soils; conducive climate for ORGANIC production. Historically gd CHARD, dessert styles (notably MUSCAT); more recently SAUV BL, SHIRAZ, CAB SAUV. Major cellars: BON COURAGE, DE WETSHOF, GRAHAM BECK, ROBERTSON WINERY, Rooiberg, SPRINGFIELD; also many family wineries.

Robertson Winery Rob r (p) w (br) sw s/sw (sp) ★→★★ Consistency, value throughout extended portfolio. Best: No 1 Constitution Rd SHIRAZ; also v.gd V'yd Selection.

Rupert & Rothschild Vignerons W Cape r w ★★★ Top v'yds and cellar nr PAARL owned by the Rupert family and Baron Benjamin de Rothschild. Always-impressive Bordeaux red Baron Edmond 98 00 01 03' 04 **05 07 08** 09 10' 11 12 and graceful CHARD Baroness Nadine.

Rustenberg Wines W Cape r w (sw) ★→★★★★ Prestigious family winery nr STELL. Flagship is CAB SAUV Peter Barlow 99' 01' 03 04 **05** 06 07 08 09 10. Outstanding Bordeaux red blend John X Merriman; savoury SYRAH; single-v'yd Five Soldiers CHARD; one of handful of varietal ROUSSANNES.

Rust en Vrede Estate Stell r w ★★→★★★ Owner Jean Engelbrecht's powerful, pricey offering incl Rust en Vrede SYRAH and new CAB SAUV (both single-v'yd); Cirrus Syrah joint venture with California's Silver Oaks; Stellenbosch Ridge tribute to STELL town and its people; Donkiesbaai CHENIN BL (dry and new *vin de paille*); v.gd Guardian Peak wines.

Sadie Family Wines Stell, Swa, Oli R r w ★★★→★★★★ Organically grown and traditionally made Columella (SHIRAZ/MOURVÈDRE) 01 02' 03 04 **05'** 06 07' 08 09' 10' 11 12 13, a Cape benchmark; complex, intriguing multivariety white

Palladius; groundbreaking Old Vines series, celebrating SA wine heritage. Revered winemaker Eben Sadie also grows Sequillo (r w) with Cape Wine Master Cornel Spies.

Saronsberg Coast r (p) w (sw) (sp) ★→★★★ Art-adorned TUL showpiece with awarded Bordeaux reds, Rhône (r w) varieties and blends, and newer MCC in eponymous and Provenance ranges.

Saxenburg Wine Farm Stell r (p) w (sp) ★★→★★★ Swiss-owned v'yds, winery and restaurant. Roundly oaked reds, SAUV BL and CHARD in high-end Private Collection; premium-priced flagship SHIRAZ Select 00 01 02 03' **05'** 06' 07' 09.

Secateurs *See* A A BADENHORST FAMILY.

Sequillo *See* SADIE FAMILY.

Shannon Vineyards Elg r w (sw) ★★★ Exemplary MERLOT, PINOT N, SAUV BL, new SÉM and rare botrytis Pinot N, grown by brothers James and Stuart Downes, and vinified at NEWTON JOHNSON.

Vineyard pests: baboons test electric fences by throwing their babies at them.

Sijnn *See* DE TRAFFORD WINES.

Simonsig Landgoed W Cape r w (br) (sw) (s/sw) sp ★→★★★ Malan family estate nr STELL admired for consistency, value and lofty standards throughout wide range. Merindol SYRAH 01 02' 03 04 **05** 06 07 08 10' 11 12, Red Hill PINOTAGE 01 02 03' 04 05 06 07' 08 09 10 11 12. First 40+ yrs ago with bottle-fermented bubbly (Kaapse Vonkel) and still a leader.

Solms-Delta W Cape r (p) w (br) (sp) ★→★★★ Delightfully different wines from historic FRAN estate, partly staff-owned; Amarone-style SHIRAZ, elegant dry rosé, musky white blend, *pétillant* SHIRAZ.

Southern Right *See* HAMILTON RUSSELL.

Spice Route Winery *See* FAIRVIEW.

Spier W Cape r w (sp) ★→★★★ Large, multi-awarded winery and tourist mecca nr STELL. Flagship is brooding CAPE BLEND Frans K Smit 04 **05'** 06' 07 08 09; Spier and Savanha brands, each with tiers of quality, show meticulous wine-growing. Expressive 21 Gables and *Creative Block series* worth a taste.

Springfield Estate Rob r w ★★→★★★ Cult winemaker Abrie Bruwer traditionally vinifies pairs of CAB SAUV (Méthode Ancienne and Whole Berry), CHARD (Méthode Ancienne and Wild Yeast) and SAUV BL (Special Cuvée and Life from Stone), all oozing class, personality.

Stark-Condé Wines Elg, Stell r w ★★→★★★★ Meticulous boutique winemaker José Conde in STELL's alpine Jonkershoek. Superb CAB SAUV and SYRAH in Three Pines and eponymous ranges; improving Pepin Condé PINOT N and CHENIN BL.

Steenberg Vineyards W Cape r (p) w sp ★→★★★★ Top CONST winery, v'yds and chic cellar-door, known for SAUV BL, Sauv Bl/SÉM blends and MCC. Fine reds incl rare varietal NEBBIOLO.

Stellenbosch University town and demarcated wine DISTRICT (13,600 ha). Heart of the wine industry: the Napa of SA. Many top estates, esp for reds, tucked into mtn valleys and foothills; extensive wine tasting, accommodation and fine-dining options.

Stellenbosch Vineyards W Cape r (p) w (sw) (sp) ★→★★ Big-volume winery previously known as The Company of Wine People, with top brand Credo and easy-drinkers Arniston Bay, Versus, Welmoed and new Four Secrets.

Swartland Acclaimed warm-climate DISTRICT in COAST; 11,000 ha of mainly shy-bearing, unirrigated bush vines producing concentrated, hearty but fresh wines. A A BADENHORST, LAMMERSHOEK, MULLINEUX, SADIE FAMILY, SPICE ROUTE, Porseleinberg; gd-value Riebeek Cellars and Swartland Winery.

Thelema Mountain Vineyards W Cape r (p) w (s/sw) ★→★★★★ Pioneer of SA's modern wine revival, still top of game with **Cab Sauv** 00' 03 04 **05** 06 07 08 09 10, The Mint CAB SAUV **05** 06' 07 08 09 10 11, *et al*. Sutherland (ELG) v'yds broaden the repertoire (eg. new SHIRAZ/GRENACHE rosé).

Tokara W Cape r (p) w (sw) ★→★★★★ Wine, food and art showcase nr STELL. V'yds also in ELG, WLK B. Gorgeous and distinctive Director's Res blends (r w); bold new SYRAH; pure, elegant CHARD and SAUV BL.

Tulbagh Inland DISTRICT historically associated with white wine and bubbly, recently also with beefy reds, some sweeter styles and ORGANIC. 1,200 ha. KRONE, resurgent Lemberg, RIJK'S, SARONSBERG, FABLE, Waverley Hills.

Twee Jonge Gezellen *See* KRONE.

Vergelegen Wines W Cape r w (sw) (sp) ★★★→★★★★ Historic mansion, immaculate v'yds and wines, and stylish cellar-door at Somerset West; owned by Anglo American plc. Powerful CAB SAUV "V" 01' 03 04 **05** 06 07 08 09' 11, sumptuous Bordeaux GVB Red, mineral *Sauv Bl/Sém* White, new SÉM *vin de paille*.

Vilafonté Paarl r ★★★ California's acclaimed Zelma Long (ex-Simi winemaker) and Phil Freese (ex-Mondavi viticulturist) partnering WARWICK's Mike Ratcliffe. Two superb Bordeaux blends: firmly structured Series C, fleshier Series M.

Villiera Wines W Cape r w (br) (sw) sp ★→★★★ Grier family v'yds and winery nr STELL with excellent quality/value range. Cream of crop: Bordeaux red Monro; Bush Vine SAUV BL; Traditional CHENIN BL; brut five MCC bubblies (incl new low-alcohol Starlight). Also boutique-scale Domaine Grier nr Perpignan, France.

Walker Bay Small (970 ha), highly reputed maritime DISTRICT, with sub-appellations HEMEL-EN-AARDE, Bot River, Sunday's Glen and new Stanford Foothills. PINOT N, SHIRAZ, CHARD and SAUV BL are standouts. Top: ATARAXIA, BEAUMONT, BOUCHARD FINLAYSON, CREATION, Gabriëlskloof, HAMILTON RUSSELL, HERMANUSPIETERSFONTEIN, NEWTON JOHNSON, Luddite, Raka.

Ward The smallest of the wo demarcations. *See* GEOGRAPHICAL UNITS.

Warwick Estate W Cape r w ★★★ Tourist-cordial Ratcliffe family farm on STELL outskirts. V.-fine Bordeaux red Trilogy, new best-barrels CAB SAUV Blue Lady, perfumed CAB FR, opulent CHARD (wooded and recent unoaked).

South African appellation with smallest vine footprint is Stilbaai East: 0.15 ha.

Waterford Estate W Cape r w (sw) ★→★★★ Classy family winery nr STELL, with awarded cellar-door. Savoury Kevin Arnold SHIRAZ 01 02' 03 04 **05** 06 07 08 09, mineral CAB SAUV 01 02 03' 04 **05** 06 07 08 09 and pricey Cab Sauv-based flagship The Jem.

Waterkloof Stell r (p) w ★→★★★ British wine importer Paul Boutinot's BIO v'yds, winery, cantilevered cellar-door nr Somerset West. Top tiers: Waterkloof, Circle of Life and Circumstance; also gd-value False Bay and Peacock Ridge lines.

Wellington Warm-climate DISTRICT abutting PAARL; growing reputation for PINOTAGE, SHIRAZ, chunky red blends and CHENIN BL. Bosman/De Bos, DIEMERSFONTEIN, Doolhof, Jacaranda, organic Lazanou, Mont du Toit, Nabygelegen, Napier, Val du Charron, Welbedacht.

Wine of Origin (WO) SA's "AC" but without French crop yield, etc. restrictions. Certifies vintage, variety, area of origin. Opt-in sustainability certification additionally guarantees eco-sensitive production from grape to glass. *See also* GEOGRAPHICAL UNIT.

Winery of Good Hope, The W Cape r w (sw) ★→★★★ Polished STELL producer as eclectic as its Australian-French-SA-UK ownership. Creative, compatible blend of styles, influences, varieties and terroirs in eponymous, Radford Dale, Vinum and Land of Hope line-ups.

Worcester DISTRICT with mostly co-ops producing bulk wine; exceptions incl New Cape/Eagle's Cliff, Alvi's Drift and recently revived Leipzig.

Why doesn't wine taste of grapes?

Well, in a sense it does – though not in the direct way that apple pie tastes of apples. Grape juice alone contains sugars, including glucose and fructose (which taste different); tartaric, malic and citric acids (they taste different too); colour compounds and tannins; amino acids, peptides and proteins; aroma compounds like the green-pepper note of Cabernet Sauvignon or Sauvignon Blanc, or the terpenes that characterize Muscat and Riesling; minerals, including potassium; pectins – and water. The skins have more tannins, and the pips have different tannins. The skins also collect wild yeasts and these are so complex and varied that it might prove possible to identify individual vineyards from the families of yeasts that live there. Yeasts, wild and cultured, have their own, and varied, effects on wine flavour. And then there's the vineyard: the same grape, in different vineyards, will taste different.

I hope you're still reading. Grape juice is fermented into wine, but if that's all there was to it, buying wine would be no more complex or interesting than buying apples. Instead there are some 10,000 wine grapes in the world, all suited to different climates and soils.

Wine reflects its vineyard: dull vineyard, dull wine; great vineyard, potentially great wine. This encourages wine-lovers to admire not the closeness of flavour to that of the grape, but its distance from it. Burgundy growers want their Pinot Noir to taste not of the grape but of a particular patch of a particular slope: its clay, its stones, its chalk, its sunshine and rain. We splash out on Pauillac because we want the haunting complexity that comes only from those gentle gravel hills; otherwise cheap branded Cabernet Sauvignon would do the job just as well.

And yet it all starts with grapes. In the pages that follow I want to explore the why, how and where of grapes. The more we discover about them, the more fascinating they become. I hope you think so too.

In the beginning
The origins of the vine

The story of human cultivation of the vine is the story of the spread of civilization and the movement of populations. All cultivated vines – all 10,000 or so varieties of grapevine – are the descendants of wild vines. And while there doesn't (so far) seem to be an Eve-vine theory to parallel the way that the study of mitochondrial DNA has hypothesized a single female ancestor for humanity, DNA studies seem to have pinpointed where the vine was first cultivated.

Or at least, they have pinpointed the two most likely places, both in the Middle East. Southeast Anatolia is one; Transcaucasia the other. The upper reaches of the Tigris and Euphrates rivers, in the Taurus Mountains, are the favourite candidates. It's partly the enormous range of cultivated vines native to these regions that give the clue, and partly the close relationships between the DNA of local wild vines (that still proliferate here) and that of the local cultivated varieties. When did it happen? Presumably some while after humans discovered that wine – which will occur naturally, provided that ripe grapes are left in warm conditions for a few days – had an agreeable flavour and could cheer you up after a hard day. Wild grapes would have been plentiful, and would have been a useful part of the diet. From grapes to wine is a very small step.

The step from wild vines to cultivated ones is bigger. Wild vines come in male and female versions; cultivated ones are hermaphrodites. The difference in the shape of the seeds is a useful clue for archeologists trying to determine if the inhabitants of a particular early settlement were cultivating the vine or not; but why should vines make this jump?

A tiny percentage, maybe two or three per cent, of wild vines are hermaphrodite. Hermaphrodite vines would be easier to cultivate and would produce a more certain crop, giving them an obvious advantage. And since the only way to propagate vines identical to their parents is by taking cuttings, every time a berry from an early vine fell to the ground and the seed germinated and took root, a new variety of vine was born. Some would have found favour with early farmers for their sweetness and flavour and the attractiveness of their wine; others would have been dismissed. Already we are on the way to today's 10,000 or so known varieties.

Surely humans in different parts of the globe would have discovered the same sort of thing independently? Quite possibly, but at the moment it looks as if other centres of early vine cultivation – the Iberian Peninsula was one, as was Sardinia – were not starting from scratch, because there doesn't seem to be any DNA relationship between early cultivated vines and wild ones here.

Putting a date on the first cultivation of the vine, or the first wine, is a matter of guesswork at the moment – or romance.

Gold drinking vessel from Achaemenid Iran, 6th–5th century BC

There is evidence of both wild and cultivated vines in Neolithic (8500–4000 BC) and later sites in southeast Anatolia and Transcaucasia. The remains of liquid containing tartaric acid, identified by infrared spectrometry, has been found in Neolithic settlements from the sixth millenium BC in northern Iran; the presence of tartaric acid is a certain pointer to grapes. The liquid had been in stoppered jars, laid on their sides, and terebinth tree resin had been added as a preservative.

It really shouldn't come as a surprise that the grapevine was first cultivated around the headwaters of the Tigris and Euphrates. The Fertile Crescent was where many "founder crops", those from which agriculture throughout the world is derived, were first cultivated: chickpeas, lentils, rye, peas, emmer and einkorn wheat come from here. As do languages: all the Indo-European tongues have been shown to have originated here. To say that wine and the vine are part of the warp and weft of human civilization is not an exaggeration.

International grapes
The travellers

Some grapes have swept across the world, carrying all before them, and put down roots in every winemaking corner of every continent. Others have hardly shifted from their native soil – and some have edged so close to extinction that the rediscovery of forgotten grapes is the current fixation.

When the wine pendulum swings, it swings surprisingly fast. In the 1980s the world went wild for Cabernet Sauvignon and Chardonnay. Why those two? There was a combination of reasons. Red Bordeaux and white burgundy were the classic table wine styles that every drinker knew; they'd been exported, especially the former, across the globe. (Historically, which wines became internationally famous was an accident of trade routes, often of politics, access to river and sea transport, and a wine robust enough to survive shipping.) They were the styles at which winemakers in the New World, importing cuttings for table wine, decided to aim. And as luck would have it, they are possibly the two most obliging grape varieties in the world. They'll grow pretty much anywhere and produce something recognizable. International wine styles were born.

And we loved them. They were lush, juicy, buttery, toasty, ripe and bursting with fruit. They became the new ideal. Growers in Italy, Spain, France, Bulgaria, Chile and a host of other countries wanted to follow suit. Sometimes, as in France or Italy, AC laws forbade them; it was then considered extremely modern to ignore the AC and sell your Cabernet as Vin de Pays or the equivalent, sometimes at a pretty eye-watering price. Where Cabernet led, Merlot and, to a lesser extent, Cabernet Franc followed; Chardonnay had little competition in the white stakes until Sauvignon Blanc took over NZ.

Which other grapes travelled? Some had crossed oceans and continents well before the 1980s, and well before "international" became a style descriptor. The oldest vines of Shiraz (alias Syrah) are in Australia's Barossa Valley; Chile has some 200-year-old

Shiraz grapes in the Barossa Valley, Australia

Carignan, California some ancient Zinfandel. Syrah is now showing its international potential in NZ (wonderful Gimblett Gravels), Chile (Elqui and Limarí) and many other places: choose your soil and climate and Syrah can be more interesting than most Cabernet Sauvignon. Pinot Noir, as we saw in last year's supplement, is being mastered in more and more countries. Among white grapes, Riesling, Pinot Blanc, Gewurztraminer and Viognier are all successful far from home.

But how do you define "home"? Every grape had an origin somewhere, and usually the area with the greatest genetic diversity of that vine is where it has lived longest, and probably where it began. Syrah thus belongs to the Rhône, Garnacha probably to Spain though possibly to Sardinia; but it's been in France since the 18th century and certainly isn't regarded as an import there. Riesling probably originated in Germany's Rheingau and spread all over central and eastern Europe from Alsace to Turkey – and also with real success to Australia. Local names vary (Renski Rizling in Slovenia, Riesling Renano in Italy) but usually nod at its origin. Likewise with Blaufränkisch: perhaps originally from Franconia, it went to other parts of Germany from Lemberg in Styria and Limberg in Lower Austria, and is known in Germany as Lemberger or Limberger.

Other vines have travelled without passports and been renamed wherever they have settled. The Ugni Blanc of France is the Trebbiano of Italy. There are at least six different varieties in northern Italy called Bonarda. The Fernão Pires of Portugal's Bairrada region is also the Maria Gomes of Bairrada. The aliases of Negroamaro include Abruzzese, Albese, Jonico, Lacrima, Purcinara and Uva Olivella: not bad for a vine that's only recently moved outside Puglia. More recently, Valpolicella producer Rizzardi couldn't identify a vine in its vineyards – so simply named it Marcobono after the vineyard manager. It's a long tradition.

Indigenous grapes
The stay-at-homes

You can travel the world to find fame – or you can stay at home and wait until it comes to you.

Indigenous grapes are now known, more smartly, as autochthonous grapes. It's a good word for a dinner party, but don't leave it too late. It covers all those grapes, which, for one reason or another, were never planted far from the spot where they first took root. All European countries have them, simply because every vine seedling, as we've seen, is different from both its parents. Over the thousands of years that vines have been cultivated, there've been a good few stray seedlings.

It would be tempting to think that it was the best vines that were taken elsewhere, and the lesser ones that stayed behind. But it's not as simple as that. Roads, rivers, political treaties and population movements determined what went where in the past. Barolo would have been much more famous much earlier had it had better links with the outside world. Conversely, the Hunter Valley was selected for planting not because of its perfect climate or soil, but because it was conveniently close to Sydney and had prosperous coalmines. Why did the wonderful Petit Manseng of southwest France never travel further than Spain's Basque Country, while Côt, from nearby Cahors, was taken to Argentina, where it has flourished as Malbec? Simple. Côt had been planted in Bordeaux, and it was cuttings from Bordeaux (probably in a mixed bag) that established it in Argentina. The reason we don't associate it with Bordeaux now is that it wasn't replanted there after the 1956 frosts: it always ripened dangerously late. To travel successfully, vines have to be adaptable. Argentina, as it turned out, suited Malbec better than Bordeaux had done. But Nebbiolo and Sangiovese, those two red stars of Italy, have proved extremely fickle abroad. Some vines like such particular conditions that they're extremely difficult to move.

Vines that are difficult to grow – because they yield poorly, or get diseases, or ripen too late for the local climate – have seldom been favoured by growers. (The exception is Pinot Noir, and here the number of edicts telling Burgundians not to grow Gamay on the Côte d'Or suggests that they might have preferred to do so.) It's the winning vines that get propagated. It's impossible to know how many varieties have become extinct over the centuries; but it's astonishing to see how many are being rescued now. Partly it's the desire of winemakers for something different, now that they've been through international varieties and come out the other side; partly it's the belief that a point of difference in your wine can attract attention from a sated market. In Champagne there is Arbane, in Italy a whole raft: black Casetta, black Ciliegiolo, white Cococciola, black Foglia Tonda; in Hungary black Csókaszőlő; in Switzerland white Himbertscha; in

Le Nombre d'Or uses Arbane, Pinot Meslier and Fromenteau (Pinot Gris) in the blend

Greece black Limniona; in Catalonia Torres is identifying and using forgotten grapes to excellent effect. The list could go on – and on and on. Turkey and Georgia have umpteen native grapes that are hardly explored. Trade tastings reveal more rediscoveries, and visits to vineyards disclose more experimental plots of cuttings taken here, there and everywhere. Often careful viticulture can reduce problems of disease susceptibility; planting in a better spot may speed ripening.

It may be that few of these rediscovered vines will become mainstream, but some of them, certainly, are extremely good. At the very least, this fascination with autochthonous varieties is a corrective to too much internationalism. The Cabernet and Chardonnay pendulum stopped in the nick of time.

Champagne

LE NOMBRE D'OR

CAMPANIAE VETERES VITES

BRUT

L. AUBRY FILS

à Jouy-lès-Reims

Alc.12,5% by Vol.   750 ml

ÉLABORÉ PAR SCEV L. AUBRY FILS PROPRIÉTAIRES JOUY-LÈS-REIMS FRANCE
RM-20098-04 LCVV   CONTIENT DES SULFITES   JB

On the vine
What is perfect ripeness?

The answer is that perfect ripeness is what winemakers eat, sleep and breathe; it's what all their work is focused on achieving. Picking at perfect ripeness – which may exist for as little as a single day – is the culmination of a winemaker's year, and the foundation for everything that happens in the winery. In the best establishments, that is. Many a wine factory makes do with a great deal less or more than perfection, and relies on technical wizardry to take up the slack.

Your definition of perfect ripeness depends on what you want to do: perfect ripeness in Champagne would be considered underripe in California's Napa Valley. Ideally the grapeseeds are brown, not green, and the stalk is lignified to the first joint of the cluster. (This latter doesn't happen in Champagne.) When you chew a perfectly ripe black grape, the skin tannins should be soft, not bitter. Sugar and acidity should be in balance. And getting all those things to happen at once is not easy. Really not easy.

There is sugar ripeness and there is physiological ripeness. Sugar ripeness is a doddle, providing it's warm: heat makes sugar shoot up. Physiological ripeness, however, only comes with time, and you want the two to happen together; you don't want to have to wait for physiological ripeness while the sugar rises and rises and rises – unless you're happy with 15% alcohol. Some are. And some consider that physiological ripeness is only there when the grapes are raisined and the tannins are like melted chocolate. Waiting that long will almost certainly give you extreme alcohol. But as I say, some like it.

You will have guessed by now that warm climates tend to produce sugar ripeness before physiological ripeness. This is why,

Picking by hand enables growers to select each bunch at perfect ripeness

in warmer spots, winemakers seek out cooler slopes rather than hot valley floors to try to slow sugar ripeness. There's also a certain amount you can do with pruning and training – more leaves to shade the grapes, for example. Our ideas of what constitutes physiological ripeness have changed over the years too: the tannins found in most red Bordeaux of the 70s would now be considered green. We've all become accustomed to riper tannins, and we have California and Australia to thank for that.

There is also the question of acidity. Acidity goes down as sugar goes up. Extreme ripeness means very low acidity, and wines that are not only tiring to drink, but that won't keep well. Acidity can be added in the winery (provided it's legal in that region), as can sugar to unripe grapes; both disguise the fact that for whatever reason, the winemaker has not managed to get sugar ripeness and physiological ripeness at the same time.

The reason may of course be that the grape variety and the terroir are just not suited. In Bordeaux, for example, Cabernet Sauvignon is little grown in St-Émilion because it doesn't ripen there, whereas earlier-ripening Merlot does. But put Merlot in a hot climate and you can get some very soupy wine indeed.

Overripeness nowadays is more common than underripeness: warmer summers help here. But there is one classic wine style that is based on unripe grapes, and that is NZ Sauvignon Blanc. Those shrill green-bean flavours have many followers; and if nothing else, they have broadened the spectrum of what winemakers consider perfect ripeness.

The barrel question
Why do some grapes like oak?

Actually, it would be better to ask why some grapes like new oak and others don't. Old oak is a very different kettle of fish. Use a barrel of five or six years old or more, and it will impart no vanilla notes, no toast, no coffee – none of the comforting breakfast or teatime flavours that you'll get from a brand-new barrel. What it will do is allow gentle, minute oxidation through the pores of the wood. This is how all German Riesling used to be aged in the past – in big oak barrels often decades old, that gave some roundness to what could, in cool years, be extremely acidic wine. New oak doesn't go with Riesling – in fact if I were in charge I would impose severe penalties for using it – but old oak does.

Aromatic white grapes tend to lose their aroma in new oak – or have it overtaken by the vanilla and what-have-you. If the aroma is what you want, you probably won't like the result. Sauvignon Blanc in new oak, unless it's done with great subtlety so that it adds weight without staging a takeover (and oak a couple of years old is probably better for that, giving some flavour but not too much), is a problem. It works in Bordeaux, but the Sauvignon there tends to be less stridently aromatic than in NZ or the Loire (and be blended with Sémillon). And a lot of Bordeaux "Sauvignons", if they're intended for ageing, can taste overoaked in youth – but develop beautifully over an improbable number of years. Oak-aged Viognier is having a bit of a moment, but again, the oak is not usually brand new, and again, it needs to be done with a light hand.

Oak is not the only wood, though. Cherry wood used to be traditional in Valpolicella, mostly because they have a lot of cherry trees there, but it tends to leak and most growers prefer oak. You always used to find a bit of acacia in the Chenin Blanc regions of the Loire, where it was said to give extra aroma, but suddenly it has become fashionable elsewhere. Sauvignon Blanc with a touch of acacia can become deliciously scented with quince, providing it's picked ripe in the first place; it's magic with Malvasia Istriana in Croatia, and it seems to work with Chardonnay too.

But then everything works with Chardonnay. It's the most oak-friendly white grape of all; a friendliness which has been much abused over the years. Now, mercifully, heavily oaked Chardonnays have mostly vanished in a puff of (wood)smoke; restraint is what we want. Subtle oaking sits well with the non-aromatic nuttiness or leafiness of Chardonnay, its peach notes. Even in Chablis, where Chardonnay is steely and mineral, some oak (but not too much and not too new) adds balancing weight and substance to the grander wines.

Oak on reds is taken more for granted, but overoaking exists here too, particularly in the more rustic reds of Spain and Portugal – and in California. New oak is a quick way of taming rustic tannins, which is

Small oak barrels in Castilla y Léon, Spain

why growers in places such as Toro like it, but the result can be a bit galumphing. With reds, tannins are the key. Young, fresh reds, low in tannin and intended to be drunk within a couple of years, are better without oak: think of juicy young Malbec or Tempranillo. Oak tannins are not the same as grape tannins, but if well-balanced they act in unison to support the wine and give it more ageing potential. (To overoak Pinot Noir is a terrible crime.)

But oak is not one thing, any more than grapes are. Some coopers are known for making great barrels for reds; others, using ostensibly the same oaks, are preferred for whites. To add to the possibilities and choices, coopers offer a choice of "toasts", from just-warmed-up to caramel-brown. You'll know when a caramel barrel has been used. And of course different sizes of barrels have different effects – but that's another subject.

Grapes with shoulders
Tannins, & what to expect of them

Sometimes one would be forgiven for wondering if tannins are such a great thing. "Hard" and "bitter" are the adjectives that often go with them. You could get the impression that they're regarded with anything from wariness to downright fear, as though they were a teenage gang, or an unexpected letter from the taxman. At best, winemakers seem to regard them as something to be kept under strict control.

That's partly because they're not yet thoroughly understood. There are many different sorts of tannins – some are pigmented, and give red wine its colour – and skin tannins, seed tannins and stalk tannins all taste different. Or rather, feel different, because tannins are a sensation more than a flavour. Much research at the moment is into how to measure different tannins, so winemakers can at least see what they're working with. Seed tannins are leaner and meaner, with a bitter feel, compared to the softer skin tannins – which is why seeds must be handled very gently during winemaking so that they keep their bitter tannins to themselves. Stalks, likewise, don't have to be included in the fermentation vat, and are generally only allowed in if they're very, very ripe.

But tannins have a function, and wine – red, anyway – would be a poor thing without them. Well, it wouldn't be red, for one thing.

Obviously, they give the wine structure. So does acidity, but tannins give more. If red wine is to age, it needs tannins. They're a great antioxidant, and help to keep the wine fresh. Over time their molecular chains lengthen, and longer-chain tannins feel softer in the mouth. Larger molecules also gradually drop out of the wine to form a deposit at the bottom: the main, and sometimes the only reason, why aged red wine needs to be decanted.

Tannins interact with proteins, which is why they give that dry sensation on the inside of the mouth, and unripe tannins, hard and "green", can feel very dry indeed. But it's also why tannic red is so good with meat, and the more unadorned the meat – rare beef, for example – the more it can handle quite brisk tannins.

Yet brisk tannins are not fashionable in all parts of the world. In California, as we've mentioned, the ideal is the sort of soft, velvety tannins that come with super-ripe grapes that are on their way to becoming raisins, and there's a price to pay here in terms of high alcohol and low acidity. In Italy, where there's more of a taste for acidity, tannins can be brighter and grippier, but they still mustn't, these days, be green. We're back here to the question of how to define perfect ripeness – and as we've seen, there's no single definition.

Can white grapes have tannins? Yes, they can, and long skin contact before fermentation, or fermentation on white skins, can produce quite grippy white wines. Amphora-fermented white

Succulent rare beef: perfectly suited to brisk tannins

wines, Georgia-style, can be like this – not to everyone's taste, but a fascinating alternative.

But tannin is fundamental in reds. Different grapes have different levels of tannin: Cabernet Sauvignon has lots, as do Syrah, Nebbiolo, Tannat and Portugal's Baga. Pinot Noir has much less – which doesn't make it better or worse, just different.

Grapes with a lift
Why acidity is good

Acidity isn't just good, it's essential. A glass of wine with no acidity would be undrinkable; the lower the acidity the more wine risks being cloying, fatiguing and not refreshing. That goes for red as well as white: Coca-Cola is a perfectly nice drink, but it's not a good model for wine.

Different grapes have different levels of acidity, and are handled in different ways. The piercing acidity of Furmint might be balanced by more sweetness (as in Tokaji); the acidity of Riesling might be balanced by more residual sugar, as sometimes in the Mosel, or by more weight and extract, as in the dry wines of the Rheingau. The lower acidity of Muscat might be balanced by intense fruit flavours and aromas.

There are national tendencies too. Italian whites, where acidity is often not that high, need firm backbones to keep them upright: the Italian preference has long been for white wines with a structure not far off that of reds. Italian red wines, however, usually have high acidity: it's a trait noticeable throughout the peninsula and it makes them work with heavy food. Conversely, much of Spain struggles for acidity in its wines and finds it in Graciano and Mencía, or, in whites, in the Albariño of the damper northwest; Bordeaux, cooler and more maritime and with no need to hunt for acidity in its Cabernets, finds softness in Merlot.

Why should Italy have over the centuries selected red grapes with high acidity, while Spain has mostly not? One has to remember that climates and fashions have changed in the past too, and that the grape mix we see now is the result of what grafted well after phylloxera, and what produced a reliable crop in the hungry decades of the first half of the 20th century, tempered by consumer demand

Riesling vines overlooking the Mosel, Germany

since. Seventeenth-, 18th- and 19th-century grape mixes were not the same, and were planted for different reasons. In the Douro Valley, for example, British growers in the 19th century introduced low-acidity *tintorera* (red-fleshed) varieties to their vineyards – Alicante Bouschet and Grand Noir – to replace the colour which could by law no longer be contributed by elderberries. Portuguese producers preferred Rufete: much less colour but very high acidity. All these now have almost vanished.

The choice of grape varieties in the New World was equally a balance of expediency and choice. Cuttings had to thrive in untested places. Fortified wines were the basis of Australia's early wine industry because they lasted better in a hot climate where acidity was low. When the New World planted Cabernet and Chardonnay it changed the shape of world wine. The consensus was that Europe had been supplying the world with high acidity for centuries, and we'd had enough of it; we wanted lushness and fruit.

That has only recently changed. Now there's a new emphasis on balance and freshness, and Chardonnay has rediscovered levels of acidity its adherents had forgotten. The new grapes that are being planted in the USA, Australia, NZ, Chile, Argentina and everywhere else are being selected less for expediency than because the winemaker has a passion for them and will seek out spots where they will flourish. The acid balance is still crucial in deciding what wines are made – but winemakers now can have whole countries as their playgrounds. And many of them can adjust acid levels, either up or down, in a way that northern Europeans may not. Acidity is still the key to wine, but it's no longer the slave-driver that it was.

A little learning...

A few technical words

The jargon of laboratory analysis is often seen on back-labels. It creeps menacingly into newspapers and magazines. What does it mean? This hard-edged wine-talk, unsympathetic as it is to most lovers of wine, is very briefly explained below.

Alcohol content (mainly ethyl alcohol) is expressed in per cent by volume of the total liquid. (Also known as "degrees".) Table wines are usually between 12.5° and 14.5°, though up to 16° is increasingly seen.

Acidity is both fixed and volatile. Fixed acidity consists principally of tartaric, malic and citric acids, all found in the grape, and lactic and succinic acids, produced during fermentation. Volatile acidity consists mainly of acetic acid, which is rapidly formed by bacteria in the presence of oxygen. A small amount of volatile acidity is inevitable and even attractive. With a larger amount the wine becomes "pricked"– to use the Shakespearian term. It turns to vinegar. Acidity may be natural, in warm regions it may also be added.

Total acidity is fixed and volatile acidity combined. As a rule of thumb, for a well-balanced wine it should be in the region of one gram per thousand for each 10° Oechsle (see above).

Barriques Vital to modern wine, either in ageing and/or for fermenting in barrels (the newer the barrel the stronger the influence) or from the addition of oak chips or – at worst – oak essence. Newcomers to wine can easily be beguiled by the vanilla-like scent and flavour into thinking they have bought something luxurious rather than something cosmetically flavoured. But barrels are expensive; real ones are only used for wines with the inherent quality to benefit long-term. French oak is classic and most expensive. American oak has a strong vanilla flavour.

Malolactic fermentation is often referred to as a secondary fermentation, and can occur naturally or be induced. The process involves converting tart malic acid into softer lactic acid. Unrelated to alcoholic fermentation, the "malo" can add complexity and flavour to both red and white wines. In hotter climates where natural acidity may be low canny operators avoid it.

Micro-oxygenation is a widely used technique that allows the wine controlled contact with oxygen during maturation. This mimics the effect of barrel-ageing, reduces the need for racking, and helps to stabilize the wine.

pH is a measure of the strength of the acidity: the lower the figure the more acid. Wine usually ranges from pH 2.8 to 3.8. High pH can be a problem in hot climates. Lower pH gives better colour, helps stop bacterial spoilage and allows more of the SO_2 to be free and active as a preservative.

Residual sugar is that left after fermentation has finished or been stopped, measured in grams per litre. A dry wine has virtually none.

Sulphur dioxide (SO_2) is added to prevent oxidation and other accidents in winemaking. Some of it combines with sugars etc and is "bound". Only the "free" SO_2 is effective as a preservative. Total SO_2 is controlled by law according to the level of residual sugar: the more sugar, the more SO_2 is needed.

Tannins are the focus of attention for red-winemakers intent on producing softer, more approachable wines. Later picking, and picking by tannin ripeness rather than sugar levels gives riper, silkier tannins.

Toast refers to the burning of the inside of the barrel. "High toast" gives the wine caramel-like flavours.